SECOND EDITION

Understanding Research

A Consumer's Guide

Vicki L. Plano Clark
University of Cincinnati

John W. Creswell
University of Nebraska–Lincoln

PEARSON

Boston   Columbus   Indianapolis   New York   San Francisco   Upper Saddle River
Amsterdam   Cape Town   Dubai   London   Madrid   Milan   Munich   Paris   Montreal   Toronto
Delhi   Mexico City   São Paulo   Sydney   Hong Kong   Seoul   Singapore   Taipei   Tokyo

Vice President and Editorial Director: Jeffery W. Johnston
Vice President and Publisher: Kevin M. Davis
Development Editor: Gail Gottfried
Editorial Assistant: Caitlin Griscom
Executive Field Marketing Manager: Krista Clark
Senior Product Marketing Manager: Christopher Barry
Project Manager: Lauren Carlson
Procurement Specialist: Michelle Klein
Senior Art Director: Diane Lorenzo
Cover Designer: Jennifer Hart
Cover Art: Shutterstock
Media Project Manager: Caroline Fenton
Full-Service Project Management: Mansi Negi/Aptara®, Inc.
Composition: Aptara®, Inc.
Printer/Binder: Courier-Kendallville
Cover Printer: Moore Langen
Text Font: Meridien LT Std

Credits and acknowledgments borrowed from other sources and reproduced, with permission, in this textbook appear on appropriate page within text.

Every effort has been made to provide accurate and current Internet information in this book. However, the Internet and information posted on it are constantly changing, so it is inevitable that some of the Internet addresses listed in this textbook will change.

Library of Congress Cataloging-in-Publication Data

Plano Clark, Vicki L.
   Understanding research : a consumer's guide / Vicki L. Plano Clark,
John W. Creswell.—Second edition.
      pages cm
   ISBN-13: 978-0-13-290223-6
   ISBN-10:   0-13-290223-0
1. Research—Methodology.   I. Title.
   Q180.55.M4P58   2014
   001.4—dc23

                              2013045256

10 9 8 7 6 5 4 3 2 1

PEARSON

ISBN 13: 978-0-13-290223-6
ISBN 10:   0-13-290223-0

To my parents, Jack C. and Ellen L. Plano, for all their support and encouragement and in recognition of their many scholarly accomplishments that showed me such a gratifying path to follow.

—Vicki

This text is dedicated to all of the students in my educational research classes at the University of Nebraska–Lincoln, and to all of the staff and graduate students who have devoted hours of time to projects in the research Office of Qualitative and Mixed Methods Research at the University of Nebraska–Lincoln.

—John

About The Authors

Vicki L. Plano Clark (Ph.D., University of Nebraska–Lincoln) is an Assistant Professor in Educational Studies in the College of Education, Criminal Justice, and Human Services at the University of Cincinnati. She teaches research methods courses, including foundations of research, qualitative research, and mixed methods research in the Quantitative and Mixed Methods Research Methodologies program. As an applied methodologist, Dr. Plano Clark studies how other researchers conduct their studies, and her scholarship focuses on the foundations, designs, and contexts for mixed methods research. In addition, she actively applies a variety of research approaches in research and evaluation studies in the areas of education, family research, counseling psychology, nursing, and family medicine. Prior to joining the University of Cincinnati, she spent 19 years at the University of Nebraska–Lincoln (UNL), where she initially focused on physics education as Laboratory Manager in UNL's Department of Physics and Astronomy and then switched to a focus on research methodology, which culminated with her serving as the Director of UNL's Office of Qualitative and Mixed Methods Research. In her spare time, she pursues quilt making and the game of golf, and she and her husband, Mark, take many walks with their scruffy mutt, Peet.

John W. Creswell (Ph.D., University of Iowa) is a Professor of Educational Psychology at the University of Nebraska–Lincoln. In addition to teaching at the University, he has authored numerous articles on mixed methods research, qualitative methodology, and general research design and 21 books (including new editions), many of which focus on types of research designs, comparisons of different qualitative methodologies, and the nature and use of mixed methods research. His books are translated into many languages and used around the world. He held the Clifton Institute Endowed Professor Chair for five years at the University of Nebraska–Lincoln. For the last five years, Dr. Creswell served as a co-director at the Office of Qualitative and Mixed Methods Research at the University of Nebraska–Lincoln, which provided support for scholars incorporating qualitative and mixed methods research into projects for extramural funding. He served as the founding Co-Editor for the *Journal of Mixed Methods Research* (SAGE Publications) and as an Adjunct Professor of Family Medicine at the University of Michigan, where he assisted investigators in the health sciences and education with research methodology for National Institutes of Health and National Science Foundation projects. He also served extensively as a consultant in the health services research area for the Veterans Administration. Dr. Creswell was a Senior Fulbright Scholar to South Africa and in 2008 lectured to faculty at five universities on education and the health sciences. In 2012, he again was a Senior Fulbright Scholar to Thailand. In 2011 he served as a co-leader of a national working group at NIH developing "best practices" for mixed methods research in the health sciences. In spring 2013, Dr. Creswell has been a Visiting Professor at Harvard's School of Public Health. In the summer of 2013, he conducted mixed methods training at Cambridge University in the United Kingdom. In 2014, he will be awarded an honorary doctorate from the University of Pretoria in South Africa.

Preface

New to the Second Edition

You will find several important changes in this edition that were based on user feedback and the careful review of the first edition by anonymous external reviewers. Taken together, these changes aim to make the book more focused, applicable, and practical to developing critical consumers of up-to-date research across disciplinary topic areas. The key changes include the following:

- *Enhanced focus on **reading** research.* This edition has more clearly placed the focus on reading research in all aspects of the book's content, from the introduction to each chapter's topic to how consumers can evaluate research reports. This focus helps students through the process of reading, understanding, and evaluating the key elements of research articles.
- *Advanced considerations for evaluating research.* This edition has significantly expanded its treatment of how students can learn to evaluate the research studies that they read. To facilitate this development, Chapters 3–14 include tables that introduce criteria useful for evaluating research articles and provide indicators of higher and lower quality for each of the criteria. Each chapter also includes a rating scale form that students can use to apply the criteria to study reports.
- *New full-text articles that apply the book's content.* This edition includes a total of eight new full-text articles to assist students with applying the content they are learning. The articles represent current research on diverse topics and using diverse research approaches. They are "typical" examples of the kinds of articles that students might read, meaning that they demonstrate the limitations and messiness often found in published reports of real research studies. Two of the articles include annotations to help students locate key ideas, but students are expected to provide their own annotations for the remaining articles to better develop their skills for reading research.
- *More coverage of higher-level research approaches.* Additional information has been included to provide students with resources to understand the more sophisticated methods found in published research. Examples of this additional information are tables that summarize a wider array of common quantitative and qualitative research designs (Chapters 6 and 9), the inclusion of more higher-level statistical approaches in summary tables (Chapter 8), and more consideration to the kind of claims that can be made at the conclusion of different types of research studies throughout this edition.
- *Inclusion of more examples that are up-to-date and represent diverse disciplines.* More examples from published studies have been included throughout this edition. Furthermore, the references have been extensively updated to include more current examples of published research and expanded to better represent a variety of content areas in addition to education.
- *Improved pedagogical features in the presentation of the content.* Steps have been taken to better align the pedagogical features in this edition. For example, each chapter's learning objectives focus on what the students will be able to do as critical consumers of research and are aligned with the major headings throughout the chapter. In addition, each chapter concludes with a *Reviewing What You've Learned To Do* feature that helps students to synthesize the content addressed for each specific learning objective.
- *Additional activities to practice and apply the chapter content.* The number of activities embedded within the chapters has been increased to give students more

opportunities to engage with the content and check their own understanding as they read. End-of-chapter exercises have also been expanded to include *Reading Research Articles* activities that ask students to identify features within published articles, *Understanding Research Articles* activities that ask students to apply concepts and vocabulary introduced in the chapter, and *Evaluating Research Articles* activities that ask students to critically assess published articles using the chapter content.

- **Additional scaffolding for use of the APA Style.** All information about the American Psychological Association (APA) style has been updated to the 6th edition manual (APA, 2010) in this edition. Information about recording references for different types of publications has been included in Chapter 1 and more information about the use of references and headings is included in Chapter 4. In addition, a paper that illustrates the major elements of the APA style has been included as an Appendix to provide students with a concrete example of how the style elements can look when applied in their own writing.

- **New embedded etext features to enhance students' engagement.** The etext version of the book includes several new features embedded into the chapters that facilitate students active engagement with the chapter's content. The *Reviewing What You've Learned To Do* pop-up feature provides students with 10–15 questions similar to the text bank questions and instant feedback to help them self-assess their comprehension of the chapter content. The *Reading Research Articles* activities ask students to create APA-style references for the assigned articles and provide them with feedback. In addition, they are asked to locate and annotate statements within the articles that demonstrate the chapter's content. The *Understanding Research Articles* activities ask students to complete short-answer questions about the articles and provide them with the corresponding answers to check their understanding. The *Evaluating Research Articles* activities ask students to complete their own assessment of the quality of research studies using the provided rating scales and include a small number of hints to help work through these challenging considerations.

Philosophy and Purpose for this Book

Welcome to *Understanding Research: A Consumer's Guide*! This title captures the four perspectives that guided the development of this book.

First, this is a book about **research**. We view research as a process of interconnected activities that individuals use to gain new knowledge that addresses important concerns or issues in fields such as education, social work, counseling, nutrition, and nursing. Individuals practicing research follow a general set of steps from the initial identification of a research problem to ultimately disseminating their conclusions, and knowing about the research process provides a useful framework for understanding and evaluating the information that researchers include in the reports of their studies. We also recognize that researchers today have a large toolbox of approaches for conducting their studies, including quantitative, qualitative, mixed methods, and action research. Each of these approaches is legitimate and appropriate for addressing certain types of research situations, and researchers are making extensive use of the different approaches across all major disciplines. Therefore, this book examines the application of diverse research tools to meet the needs of today's students who should become familiar with all the prominent approaches used to develop new knowledge through research studies.

Second, this book is written specifically for **consumers**. Consumers use research in their jobs. Consumers include anyone who uses the results and implications of research studies to enhance their knowledge and improve their practice. Practitioners such as teachers, school administrators, counselors, social workers, nurses, dieticians, and therapists can all benefit from becoming critical consumers of research. To effectively use the results of research, consumers need to know how to read, understand, and evaluate the quality of research. This book's content and approach have been conceptualized specifically to meet the needs of this important consumer audience.

Third, fitting the needs of a consumer audience, the focus of this book is on **understanding** research; it is not about how to conduct research. Specifically, this book addresses the skills, knowledge, and strategies needed to read and interpret research reports and to evaluate the quality of such reports. This focus is reflected in the overarching organization of the content, which is based on the major sections of a research article. After an introduction to research in Part I, Parts II–VI present chapters related to understanding the Introduction, Method, Results, and Conclusion sections of research articles that report studies using the different research approaches.

Finally, this book has been written as a *guide* that offers readers practical advice and strategies for learning to understand research reports. Throughout this book, we relate the process of research to the process of taking a journey. When travelers take journeys, they use travel guides to navigate new places, to identify special attractions and sights, and to develop an appreciation for local customs. Likewise, this guide to understanding research aims to help consumers navigate the major sections and content of research reports by identifying key elements when reading each section and developing an appreciation for how different types of research are conducted and ultimately reported.

Keep in mind that this is not an advanced text, and it does not discuss all of the approaches to research that are available. In addition, this book does not provide an exhaustive treatment of the research process, as it does not present details that are necessary for research producers, such as how to conduct statistical calculations. This is an introductory book focused on helping students who plan to be research consumers learn to read, understand, and evaluate research reports so they can better apply the results of research to their knowledge base and professional practices.

Key Features

This book is a comprehensive introduction to help students learn how to understand research articles. In developing the content and writing style, we have attempted to consider the concerns and experiences of a consumer audience by developing a book that is engaging to read, includes up-to-date content, and has a strong applied focus. The following key features highlight the approach of this book:

- It focuses on helping students learn to read and evaluate research articles.
- It provides a balanced coverage of diverse approaches to research: quantitative, qualitative, and combined approaches.
- It includes extensive examples and practice activities to engage students with the content.

Let's examine these in detail to see how each can help instructors and students achieve their course objectives.

Helps Students Learn to Read and Evaluate Research Articles

This book emphasizes helping students become competent and critical readers of research articles. To this end, we offer guides throughout the text for reading and evaluating research articles. The book also provides many features to further help students become more skilled at interpreting and evaluating research reports, including what follows:

- The organization is built around the major sections one typically finds when reading research articles and reports: Introduction, Method, Results, and Conclusions.
- Each chapter begins with a section that discusses how to locate and identify the chapter's focus when reading a research article.
- Eight full-text research articles are included. The first two articles are annotated to help readers recognize the characteristics of the different research approaches. For the remaining six articles, students are prompted to read for and identify key elements of the research report that apply the content covered in the chapters to further develop their own skills for interpreting the information presented in research articles. The articles also serve as the context for applying each chapter's content in the *Reading Research Articles* and *Understanding Research Articles* exercises found at the end of each chapter.

- The *Here's a Tip!* feature offers practical advice for applying the chapter concepts when students read actual studies.
- Criteria for evaluating published studies, including indicators of higher and lower quality, are provided. In addition, the chapters include a rating scale that students can use to apply the stated criteria to evaluate a study of their choice or as assigned by the instructor. The *Evaluating Research Articles* exercises found at the end of the chapters ask students to apply the rating scales to articles included in the book.

Balances Coverage of Diverse Approaches to Research

This book provides balanced coverage of all types of research design. This provides readers with a complete picture of educational, social science, and health science research, as it is currently practiced. The book begins with an overview of the process of research and then guides the reader through understanding how this process is presented within the major sections of a research report. The content describes and compares four major approaches to research: quantitative, qualitative, mixed methods, and action research. Keeping with the balanced coverage, the full-text articles represent three quantitative, three qualitative, one mixed methods, and one action research study.

The book also encourages readers to go beyond the general approach to recognizing and evaluating specific designs commonly used to implement each of the major approaches. The research designs are introduced as important considerations for understanding the methods and results of research reports. The highlighted research designs include:

- experimental (i.e., true experiments, quasi-experiments, and single-subject research) and nonexperimental (i.e., correlational and survey) quantitative research designs;
- narrative, grounded theory, case study, and ethnographic qualitative research designs;
- convergent parallel, sequential explanatory, sequential exploratory, and embedded mixed methods research designs; and
- practical and participatory action research designs.

Includes Extensive Examples and Practice Activities to Engage Students with the Content

Learning to understand research reports is not easy. For most students, research reports represent new vocabulary, new concepts, and new ways of thinking critically about unfamiliar information. This book incorporates many features to help students engage directly with the content so that they can better develop their understanding and skills. Examples of these features include what follows:

- Consumer-focused learning objectives that indicate concrete goals for what students will be able to do after learning the chapter content. *Reviewing What You've Learned To Do* summaries and etext quizzes at the end of the chapters help students review and self-assess their mastery of the learning objectives.
- Topics that are focused on the needs of consumers new to learning about research, such as how to identify examples of research in the literature and why reading research is relevant for practitioners.
- Practical examples from students' own real-world experiences to help explain research concepts.
- Extensive in-text examples from recently published research articles to illustrate the topics discussed. Note that citations included within example excerpts are not included in the book's reference list.
- Key terms are boldface within the text and defined in the glossary to provide easy reference.

- *What Do You Think?* exercises with *Check Your Understanding* feedback help students engage with the new content as they are reading.
- *Here's a Tip!* notes that offer students advice for applying chapter content to their own situations.
- *Reading, Understanding, and Evaluating Research Articles* application activities, short-answer questions, and evaluation activities help students apply chapter content to published research reports. Suggested answers for the short-answer questions help students assess their own progress in understanding the content, while application and evaluation activities provide opportunities to meaningfully apply the content.

SUPPLEMENTARY MATERIALS

Online Instructor's Manual with Test Bank

This supplement developed by Dr. Michelle Howell Smith provides instructors with opportunities to support, enrich, expand upon, and assess chapter material. For each chapter in the book, this manual provides lecture notes that summarize important concepts requiring review and reinforcement, strategies for teaching chapter content, and suggestions for when and how to use the supplements with the text. The test bank contains various types of items—multiple-choice, matching, short essay, and fill-in-the-blank—for each chapter. Questions ask students to identify and describe research processes and design characteristics they have learned about and to classify and evaluate quantitative, qualitative, and combined study reports.

Online PowerPoint® Slides

PowerPoint slides are available to instructors for download on www.pearsonhighered.com/educator. These slides include key concept summarizations and other graphic aids to help students understand, organize, and remember core concepts and ideas.

TestGen

This computerized test bank software allows instructors to create and customize exams. TestGen is available in both Macintosh and PC/Windows versions.

Acknowledgments

This book is a culmination of our collective experiences in the classroom, working with colleagues and students, and writing about research methods. We could not have written it without the assistance of and support from many individuals. Our thinking about teaching and writing about research methods, including many ideas that helped to shape this book, has benefited from colleagues in the Office of Qualitative and Mixed Methods Research (University of Nebraska–Lincoln) and from faculty and students in the Quantitative, Qualitative, and Psychometric Methods graduate program (University of Nebraska–Lincoln) and Quantitative and Mixed Methods Research Methodologies graduate program (University of Cincinnati). In particular, we thank Dr. Ronald J. Shope, Dr. Denise Green, Amanda Garrett, Dr. Kimberly Galt, Sherry Wang, Alex Morales, Courtney Haines, Timothy Gaskill, Theresa McKinney, Nancy Anderson, Debbie Miller, Michelle Howell Smith, and Yuchun Zhou. We also appreciate the support, expertise, and feedback that we have received during the process of preparing the second edition. We specifically thank Robert C. Hilborn of the American Association of Physics Teachers; Amanda Garrett and Doug Abbott at the University of

Nebraska–Lincoln; and Dr. Christopher Swoboda, Dr. Maria Palmieri, Jessica Wertz, Rachael Clark, Boris Yanovsky, and Laura Saylor at the University of Cincinnati for their thoughtful comments about the second edition.

In addition, VPC personally thanks John W. Creswell and Robert G. Fuller who, through their mentoring and collaboration, have profoundly shaped her professional writings and educational practices. VPC also acknowledges the amazing support and encouragement she has received throughout this project from family and friends. She is deeply grateful to Mark W. Plano Clark, Ellen L. Plano, Diandra Leslie-Pelecky, and Karen Schumacher.

We are indebted to Kevin Davis at Pearson for initiating this book and providing the vision to develop a comprehensive text for the research consumer audience. His vision and insights have influenced our thinking in writing this text in important ways. We have had the good fortune to work with two fantastic development editors at Pearson. We thank Christina Robb for her professional and personal support and insightful reactions to early revision drafts and Gail Gottfried for her patience, encouragement, and careful attention to the substantive and procedural details during the revision process. We also thank our production team, including project managers Lauren Carlson and Mansi Negi, and copy editor Evelyn Perricone, for their detailed work. Finally, we thank the reviewers who helped shape this book with their feedback and attention to detail: Carol Friesen, Ball State University; Nicole O'Grady, Northern Arizona University; Jeff Piquette, Colorado State University–Pueblo; Candyce Reynolds, Portland State University; Colleen Swain, University of Florida; and Tracy Walker, Virginia State University.

Brief Contents

Contents

**PART FOUR   Understanding the Method Sections and Results Sections
of Qualitative Research Reports   283**

**9   Qualitative Research Designs: Recognizing the Overall Plan for a
Study   285**

**An Example of Qualitative Research: The Adoption-of-Pedagogical-Tools
Study   305**

**10   Participants and Data Collection: Identifying How Qualitative Information Is
Gathered   329**

AN INTRODUCTION TO UNDERSTANDING RESEARCH

Discussions of research are all around you in your day-to-day life. You see research reported in the local news, hear about recent findings from your physician, and may even consider it when deciding which new cell phone to buy. You may even have participated in research by responding to a survey conducted over the phone about an upcoming election or answering questions about your opinions of a new product at a store. Research also plays an important role for us as professionals. Whatever our professional area is, research is often used to justify new policies and form the basis for new materials and practice guidelines.

The importance of research in our personal and professional lives is clear, but learning to understand research is not always easy. Researchers have developed a specialized process and language for conducting and reporting their studies, and you need to learn how to interpret the relevant steps and vocabulary as you read research reports. By developing your skills for understanding research, you will open up resources and knowledge that can help you become better informed about topics important to you personally and professionally. By understanding research, you will also become a critical consumer of research who is better able to evaluate the basis of new information reported from research studies.

Your first step to becoming a critical consumer of research is to develop a big picture of what research is to help you decipher the information included in research reports. Let's consider an analogy to help us think about how researchers conduct and report their research studies. When a researcher conducts a study and writes up a report, it is a lot like a traveler taking a journey to a destination and putting together a scrapbook of the trip. Travelers use road maps to find their way along unfamiliar territory and researchers use the process of research to guide their research "journeys." In Chapter 1, you will be introduced to the steps in the process of research that researchers use to plan and conduct the activities in their research studies. Knowing about this process will provide you with a general research "road map" for navigating the information you read in research reports. Travelers also take different types of journeys to reach their destinations—some use specific routes planned from the start and others allow the routes to unfold as they go in order to explore unexpected places along the way. Likewise, researchers conduct different types of studies to cover the "terrain" of interest. In Chapter 2, we will focus on two major types of research—quantitative and qualitative—that researchers use when conducting different studies. We will consider how to understand research articles that report these different types of research "journeys" using the same general "map" of the research process.

Let's get started on your own journey to becoming a critical consumer of research!

THE PROCESS OF RESEARCH: LEARNING HOW RESEARCH IS CONDUCTED AND REPORTED

The goal of this book is to help you learn how to read and make sense of research reports. To understand research reports, however, you first need to know a little about what research is and how researchers conduct and report it. By learning how research is done, you can better recognize and evaluate the information that researchers include in their reports. This chapter begins by first considering the question: What is research? Armed with a definition, you will next consider reasons for reading research studies and where you can find research studies reported. In this chapter, you will also learn the steps researchers use to conduct studies and how you find these steps discussed within the major sections of research reports.

BY THE END OF THIS CHAPTER, YOU SHOULD BE ABLE TO:

- State a definition of research and use it to recognize reports of research studies.
- Identify your reasons for needing to read research reports.
- Name different formats where you can find reports of research studies.
- Name the steps in the process of research that researchers undertake when they conduct research studies.
- Identify the major sections of a research report, and know which steps of the research process are reported within each section.
- Read a research report and recognize the information included about a study's research process.

Let's begin by taking a moment to welcome you to this endeavor of learning to read and understand research reports. Whether you are a student just starting your career or an experienced professional enhancing your knowledge, we hope you will find learning about research a rewarding experience. Whatever your profession—teacher, principal, counselor, social worker, child care provider, nurse, nutritionist, or other practitioner— reading research studies can provide you with information useful for your practice. For example, perhaps you work with children in a community of professionals that is concerned about the children getting enough physical activity to maintain healthy weights and support appropriate development. Some personnel think that a new program should be started to encourage physical activity within the schools to help children be more active. Other personnel are not convinced that such a program would be the best use of resources. In addition, no one knows what types of programs are possible, what benefits the programs can have, or which type will work best within the community.

This example is a perfect illustration of how you could benefit from reading research on an important issue such as physical activity in schools. Although you may have personal experience with this issue, you may not be familiar with how to identify and read reports of research. However, reading research on the issues that matter to you can provide you with new ideas and insights that can make a difference in your practice. Developing your skills for reading and understanding research reports starts by obtaining a good understanding of what research is and why you should want to read it. Therefore, let's start by considering how you identify research, why you should read research, and where you might find research reports.

How Do You Identify Reports of Research?

Before going any further, we need to answer the question: What is research? Simply stated, **research** is a process of steps used to collect and analyze information in order to increase our knowledge about a topic or issue. At a general level, this process of research consists of three steps:

1. Posing a question.
2. Collecting data about the question.
3. Analyzing the data to answer the question.

These steps should be a familiar process as we all have engaged in informal research many times. Toddlers use this process when they wonder how their parents will react if they knock a bowl of spaghetti on to the floor (and then try it!). Students use it when engaging in inquiry-based learning activities in science class. Sports fans use it when they gather information to decide which players to include on their fantasy teams. And you likely use it regularly when solving problems at home or at work when you start with a question, collect some information, and then form an answer. Engaging in *informal* research gives you a useful process for learning about and solving problems that you face. It also provides you with experiences that will be helpful for understanding formal research. In *formal* research, researchers have developed a more rigorous approach to the research process for studying topics than what we all use in our daily lives for solving problems. It is this more *formal* process of research that is the focus of this book.

Recognize That Formal Research Includes the Collection and Analysis of Data

When researchers conduct formal research studies, they include a few more steps in the research process than the three listed above. For example, researchers actually complete multiple steps when "posing the question" of interest in a research study. We will learn much more about these steps later in this chapter and throughout this book. For now, the key idea for identifying research is that researchers use a process of research to *collect and analyze data* in order to increase our knowledge about a topic or issue. The collection and analysis of data is what differentiates research from all other types of activities. Data are pieces of information (numbers, words, facts, attitudes, actions, and so on) that researchers systematically gather from entities, such as individuals, families, organizations, or communities. Researchers analyze or make sense of this data in some way to produce results that answer their question. Therefore, the defining feature of research is that researchers go out and gather data to answer their question as opposed to answering it based on their own opinions, experience, logic, hunches, or creativity.

When you are reading a document such as an article on a topic that interests you, you can use the definition of research to determine whether it is describing a research study. Examine the checklist for identifying a document as an example of *research* provided in Figure 1.1. We use this rating scale whenever confronted with a new article about a topic of interest. First, we examine the article's title for clues as to whether it reports a research study. Words such as *research, study, empirical, investigation,* or *inquiry* are often good clues. Next we turn to the abstract to look for evidence that the author collected and analyzed data. An **abstract** is a brief summary of an article's content written by the article's author and placed at the beginning of the article. Because abstracts are so short (often 150 words or less), authors may not include good details about their studies in them. If the abstract does not satisfy the checklist in Figure 1.1, then we examine the full text of the article to see whether the author reports the collection and analysis of data. Using this rating scale will help you distinguish reports of completed research studies from other types of scholarly writing.

Distinguish Reports of Research From Other Types of Scholarly Writing

A common pitfall for those new to research is to assume that all scholarly writings that they read represent research studies. In fact, there are *many* different types of scholarly writing about different topics that are published and available. Table 1.1 lists several

**FIGURE 1.1
A Rating Scale
for Determining
Whether an
Article Reports
a Research
Study**

- Examine the article's title, abstract, and Method section.
- For each criteria in the following rating scale, assign a rating of no (0) or yes (1) and record your evidence and/or reasoning behind the rating.
- Add up the ratings. A total of 3 should indicate that the article is a report of a research study. A total of 0–2 likely indicates that the article does not report a full research study and instead reports another type of article such as a literature review.

Criteria	Rating 0 = No 1 = Yes		Your Evidence and/or Reasoning
1. Terms are present that identify the report as research, such as *study*, *investigation*, *empirical research*, or *original research*.			
2. The authors describe gathering data.			
3. The authors describe analyzing the gathered data and report results of the analysis.			
Overall Determination 0–2 = Likely not research 3 = Likely research	**Total Score =**		**My Overall Determination =**

types of writings that you may be familiar with and may encounter as you read about topics that interest you, such as literature reviews; opinion papers; and creative writing, such as fictional stories. In addition, the table provides an example of how each type of writing might be applied to the topic of children's physical activities. In most of the forms of scholarly writing listed in Table 1.1, the authors start by posing a question in some way, but only in research studies will the authors report the systematic collection

TABLE 1.1   Different Types of Writings About Topics

Type of Writing	Typical Use	Example
Research	To collect and analyze data in order to increase our knowledge about a topic or issue	The author collected and analyzed data about daily time spent being physically active for children in first through seventh grades
Literature Review	To summarize and critique a collection of different writings about a topic	The author summarized 18 writings available in the literature about children's physical activity
Theoretical Discussion	To synthesize ideas about a topic into a framework or model that identifies key concepts and how they are related to each other	The author developed a model of the factors believed to encourage and discourage children to be physically active
Opinion Paper	To provide one individual's opinions on a topic based on his/her experiences and perspectives	The author provides her opinions on promoting children's physical activity levels based on 25 years as an elementary school physical education teacher
Program Description	To provide a description of the features involved in the implementation of a particular program from the individuals who are running the program	The author describes a special "Get Active!" program used at one middle school
Fiction Writing	To tell a story about a topic that engages the reader to think about that topic	The author tells a story of three girls growing up and playing together on a volleyball team
Poetry	To bring forth an emotional response on a topic through creative uses of language	The author creatively uses words to convey one man's memories of running through the fields by his house as a child to convey the meaning of physical activity for one person

and analysis of data to answer the question. Therefore, when you want to identify whether a written document is an example of research, focus on the collection and analysis of data as the key indication that the document reports a research study.

With these ideas in mind, let's apply the definition of research and the rating scale in Figure 1.1 to two example abstracts taken from articles found in the literature.

Example 1—Identifying an article that is a research study

An abstract written by Carrington, Templeton, and Papinczak (2003, p. 211):
This qualitative study investigated the perceptions of friendship faced by teenagers diagnosed with Asperger syndrome. This research aimed to provide teachers with an insight into the social world of Asperger syndrome from a student perspective. A multiple–case study approach was used to collect data from 5 secondary school students in Australia. Data were collected through the use of semistructured interviews. An inductive approach to data analysis resulted in a number of broad themes in the data: (a) understanding of concepts or language regarding friendships, (b) description of what is a friend, (c) description of what is not a friend, (d) description of an acquaintance, and (e) using masquerading to cope with social deficits. The insights provided by the participants in this study are valuable for teachers, parents, and anyone else involved in inclusive education.

Using the rating scale in Figure 1.1, we can conclude that this article is describing a research study. Notice how the authors used key words in the first few sentences, including *study, investigated,* and *research,* when referring to their work. This abstract also clearly satisfies items 2 and 3 on the rating scale because the authors indicate that they collected data ("data were collected through the use of semistructured interviews") and analyzed the data (using "an inductive approach to data analysis").

Example 2—Identifying an article that is NOT a research study

An abstract written by Amatea, Smith-Adcock, and Villares (2006, p. 177):
This article presents an overview of a research-informed family resilience framework, developed as a conceptual map to guide school counselors' preventive and interventive efforts with students and their families. Key processes that characterize children's and families' resilience are outlined along with recommendations for how school counselors might apply this family resilience framework in their work.

This article presents an interesting and scholarly discussion of issues and theories related to family resiliency and the implications for school counselors. Although the abstract refers to research conducted by others ("a research-informed family resilience framework"), it does not satisfy the criteria in the rating scale. Notice that the authors used terms such as *overview, developed,* and *outlined* when referring to their work. There is also no indication that the authors collected or analyzed any data based on the information provided in the abstract. Therefore, this article is *not* an example of research, but instead is an example of a theoretical discussion.

What Do You Think?

Consider the following abstract from an article about a vocabulary instruction program. Does this article report a research study? Why or why not?

An abstract written by Apthorp (2006, p. 67): The author examined the effectiveness of a vocabulary intervention that employed structured, supplemental story read-alouds and related oral-language activities. Within each of 7 Title I schools across 2 sites, 15 third-grade teachers were randomly assigned to either use the intervention (treatment condition) or continue their usual practice (control condition). Trained test examiners administered oral and sight vocabulary pre- and posttests and reading achievement posttests. At 1 site, students in treatment, compared with control, classrooms performed significantly higher in vocabulary and reading achievement. In the other site, the intervention was not more effective. Contextual factors and student characteristics appeared to affect the results.

Check Your Understanding

From this abstract, we can conclude that this article does report a research study. The author did not use the word *study*, but she notes that she "examined" an issue. We also have direct evidence that the author collected data ("oral and sight vocabulary pre- and posttests and reading achievement posttests"). Clues that these data were also analyzed are found by noting that the two groups of students were compared and different types of results from the analysis are reported (e.g., students in the treatment classrooms performed significantly higher).

Why Do You Need to Read Research Reports?

Now that you are able to identify reports of research, it is important to next consider *why* you might want to read research reports that you identify. It turns out that the reason to read research is actually suggested by its definition. Recall that research is defined as a process of steps used to collect and analyze information to increase our knowledge about a topic or issue. So far we have focused on the first half of the definition that emphasizes the collection and analysis of data, but the second half of the definition is just as important. The reason that researchers conduct and report research studies is to add to the overall knowledge base that exists about a topic. In fact, the primary way that new knowledge is gained about important issues is by scholars conducting research. Researchers are much like bricklayers who build a wall brick by brick with each study. They continually add to the wall by conducting studies about an issue and, in the process, create a stronger structure or understanding.

Whether you are a teacher, counselor, administrator, nurse, special educator, social worker, or other practitioner, the knowledge base of your profession is continually advancing because of the research that is being conducted and reported. When researchers create a strong understanding from many research studies, this understanding also can provide a strong knowledge base for practitioners. Therefore, you need to read research in order to take advantage of the new knowledge that is generated for your own knowledge base, position in policy debates, and practices.

Read Research to Add to Your Professional Knowledge

No matter how experienced you are in your practices, new problems continue to arise. For example, today we face problems such as increased violence in our schools, the increased use of technology by individuals, and rising rates of childhood obesity. You can be better equipped to develop potential solutions for problems such as these if you remain up to date in your field and continue to add to your knowledge base. Research can play a vital role in our understanding of problems because researchers study questions to which the answers are previously unknown. For example, you can better understand the problem of school violence if you read research studies that provide knowledge about the extent of violence in schools, the factors that encourage and discourage violence, and the meaning that school violence has for individuals. By reading what researchers have learned, you add to your own knowledge about a topic.

Read Research to Inform Your Position in Policy Debates

Research also creates conversations about important policy issues. We are all aware of pressing issues being debated today, such as policies regarding immigrants and their children, policies about access to health care, and policies that mandate the use of high-stakes testing. Policy makers range from federal government employees and state workers to local school board members, council members, and organization administrators. These individuals take positions and make decisions on issues important to constituencies. For these individuals, research offers results that can help them weigh various perspectives. By reading research on issues related to policies, you become informed about current debates and stances taken by other public officials as well as form your own opinions. For example, research useful to policy makers might examine the alternatives to welfare and the effect on children's schooling among lower income families, or it might examine the arguments proposed by the opponents and proponents of school choice.

Read Research to Improve Your Practice

The third reason that it is important to read research is to improve your practice—that is, to improve your ability to do your job effectively. Armed with results based on rigorous research, practitioners become professionals who are more effective, and this effectiveness translates into better outcomes, such as better learning for children or improved mental health for individuals. Today there is a push for practitioners across disciplines to use evidence-based practices. **Evidence-based practices** are personal and professional practices that have been shown to be effective through research. This means that individuals are encouraged to use practices for which there is support from research (the evidence) and not to rely solely on practices that have been done in the past. Here are three ways that research can influence your practices:

> ***Here's a Tip!***
>
> When reading a research study, look for recommendations for how the results apply to practice. These suggestions are usually listed near the end of the report and may be found under a heading such as *Implications for Practice*.

- ■ *Reading research can suggest improvements for your practice.* When researchers conduct studies to add to our knowledge about a topic, this new knowledge may result in specific suggestions for how your practice can be improved. You can learn about these suggestions by reading research reports and looking for statements at the end of the report where the authors explain the implications of the results that might pertain to your practice. For example, in a study about youth literacy habits, Nippold, Duthie, and Larsen (2005) concluded their research report with suggestions for numerous programs that could be initiated by speech-language pathologists to promote youth reading habits for all students, including those with language disorders.
- ■ *Reading research can help you improve practice by offering new ideas to consider.* You can learn about new practices that have been found to be effective in other settings or situations by reading research. For example, a high school counselor concerned about the smoking rates of students placed at risk in her school may read about a peer-counseling program reported from a different location that was found to help adolescent smokers successfully quit smoking. She could use the results of the research that she read to consider the idea of starting a peer-counseling program at her own school.
- ■ *Reading research can help you learn about and evaluate alternative approaches to use.* In many situations, there are multiple approaches that could be used in our practices. We may learn about these approaches from reading research or because they are suggested by other practitioners or policy makers within our professional settings. When faced with multiple alternatives in your practice, reading research can help you not only identify alternative approaches, but also choose the best approach from among the alternatives. When you read several research studies that have been conducted for different approaches, you can evaluate and compare the evidence that is available for the effectiveness of the different approaches. Connelly and Dukacz (1980) provided a useful process that you can use to sift through available research studies to learn about different approaches and determine which will be most useful for your situation. The process is demonstrated in Figure 1.2, which focuses on three steps that practitioners might use to select a new strategy to implement in their practice.

As shown in the figure, a reading teacher decides to incorporate more information about cultural perspectives into the classroom and wants to find the best strategy that will increase students' understanding of multiculturalism. By reading research on the topic, this teacher learns about four lines of research that suggest alternative strategies. Research suggests that incorporating diverse cultural perspectives may be done with classroom interactions by inviting speakers to the room (line A) or by having the children consider and think (cognitively) about different cultural perspectives by talking with individuals at a local cultural center (line B). It may also be accomplished by having the children inquire into cultural

**FIGURE 1.2
Using Lines of
Research to
Evaluate
Alternative
Approaches to
Practice**

Source: Adapted from
Connelly and Dukacz,
(1980), p. 29.

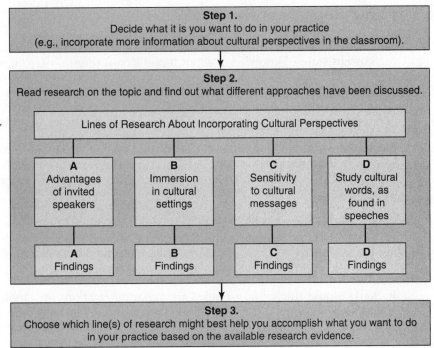

messages embedded within advertisements (line C) or by having them identify the cultural subject matter of speeches of famous Americans (line D). By critically reading the available research and the findings for each approach, the reading teacher can use the available information to weigh the different strategies and select the one to implement that has research-based evidence for its effectiveness at improving students' multicultural perspectives.

What Do You Think?

Consider the scenario introduced at the start of this chapter in which professionals are thinking about starting a program to encourage children to be more physically active at school. What are three reasons why you should read research about children's physical activity if you worked at this school?

Check Your Understanding

There are many possible reasons why you would want to read research about children's physical activity. Recall that researchers conduct and report research studies to add to the knowledge about a topic. Therefore, you can read research about children's physical activity to learn what the overall state of knowledge is about this topic. You should also read research studies to inform your position in the school's debate about whether to initiate a policy for a new physical activity program. Finally, you could read research to inform your practices. By reading and evaluating different lines of research about children's physical activity, you could learn about approaches for getting children to be more physically active at school, such as increasing time for recess and physical education class each week, incorporating a morning workout program at the start of the school day, or having students set daily activity goals.

Did you come up with similar reasons? Now consider some reasons why you need to read research on a topic related to your own professional practice.

Where Do You Find Reports of Research?

We hope you are convinced that it is important for you to read research to learn about the current state of knowledge about topics that interest you, to understand different sides of policy issues, and to improve your practices. If so, your next question might be: Where do I find reports of research to read? It turns out that you can find research discussed in a variety of published formats. Because the goal of research is to add to knowledge about various topics, researchers report their studies in formats where many different audiences, including other researchers and practitioners, can read and learn from them. In Chapter 4, we will discuss strategies you can use to find good research studies in the literature on specific topics that interest you. For now, it is helpful to simply start with an introduction to the different formats where you might read reports of research studies.

Figure 1.3 illustrates several different types of documents where you can find reports of research. Modified from a classification originally developed by Libutti and Blandy (1995), the figure is a guide to types of available published documents, including books, journal articles, and early stage materials. Let's examine these formats by considering a brief description and examples of each.

- *Books.* Books (including e-books) are major publications on a topic that are typically hundreds of pages in length and screened for quality by editors and/or book publishers. There are several types of books where you can find reports of research discussed. Reference summary books such as encyclopedias and handbooks provide overviews of available research written by a group of leading specialists in the field. These books discuss many research studies that have been conducted within a topic area. For example, the following handbook for nurses provides an overview of an extensive amount of research available about patient safety and quality:
    - Hughes, R. G. (Ed.) (2008). *Patient safety and quality: An evidence-based handbook for nurses*. Rockville, MD: Agency for Healthcare Research and Quality.
  You can also find books that report on the results from single research studies. For example, the following book describes Winkle-Wagner's (2009) research study about Black women's experiences in college:
    - Winkle-Wagner, R. (2009). *The unchosen me: Race, gender, and identity among Black women in college*. Baltimore, MD: The Johns Hopkins University Press.
  When reading about research on a topic, books can be advantageous to read because they are a format that is familiar to you, can provide you with a good introduction to the topic, and typically include an extensive amount of information. You should

FIGURE 1.3 Different Types of Documents Where Research Reports Are Found

Source: Adapted from Libutti and Blandy (1995) and Creswell (2008).

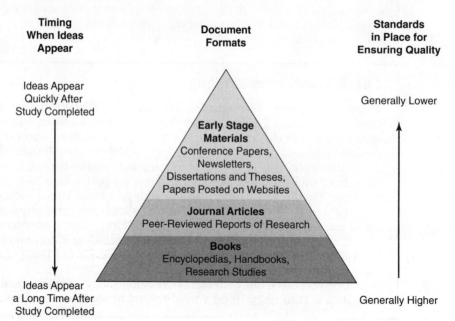

Timing When Ideas Appear	Document Formats	Standards in Place for Ensuring Quality
Ideas Appear Quickly After Study Completed	**Early Stage Materials** Conference Papers, Newsletters, Dissertations and Theses, Papers Posted on Websites	Generally Lower
	Journal Articles Peer-Reviewed Reports of Research	
Ideas Appear a Long Time After Study Completed	**Books** Encyclopedias, Handbooks, Research Studies	Generally Higher

also keep in mind that because books represent major publications, they take time to be produced and usually will not include the most recent research findings. Also, they tend to be expensive (especially handbooks and other reference books) and therefore can be difficult to obtain unless available in a local library.

■ *Journal articles.* Journals are periodical publications that publish collections of scholarly papers that relate to specific topics and are screened for quality by the editors and reviewers associated with the journal. You find scholarly journals published on printed paper and/or as documents available online. There are thousands of different scholarly journals that focus on publishing reports of research across all the different disciplines. A few examples of journals that represent this diversity include

  ■ *Journal of Educational Research*
  ■ *Journal of Counseling and Development*
  ■ *Early Childhood Research Quarterly*
  ■ *Journal of Marriage and Family*
  ■ *Journal of Professional Nursing*
  ■ *Research Quarterly for Exercise and Sport*

Scholarly journals such as these are published in "volumes" and "issues." Typically, each volume covers one 12-month period and, within each 12 months, a journal publishes a set number of issues on a regular schedule such as monthly or quarterly (similar to popular magazines that you may read). That is, if a journal is published on a monthly basis, then one volume includes 12 issues. Within each issue of a journal, you find several individual articles written by different authors. Journal articles that report research studies are typically on the order of 5–25 pages in length and are written by the individuals who actually conducted the research. For example, here are two separate articles that appeared in the fourth issue of volume number 45 of the *Journal of Nutrition Education and Behavior*:

  ■ Munoz-Plaza, C. E., Morland, K. B., Pierre, J. A., Spark, A., Filomena, S. E., & Noyes, P. (2013). Navigating the urban food environment: Challenges and resilience of community-dwelling older adults. *Journal of Nutrition Education and Behavior, 45*(4), 322–331.
  ■ Bellows, L., Spaeth, A., Lee, V., & Anderson, J. (2013). Exploring the use of storybooks to reach mothers of preschoolers with nutrition and physical activity messages. *Journal of Nutrition Education and Behavior, 45*(4), 362–367.

When reading about research on a specific topic, journal articles are generally the best source because they provide the details of the research from the viewpoint of the researchers who actually conducted the study. Research journal articles represent formal research publications that provide more details about the process of the original research than book sources (which tend to focus mostly on the results and provide little detail about the research process). Journal articles can also be more challenging to read because they report many details about the process of research in a concise way without much explanation. Although the content of this book applies to reading about research in all three of the highlighted formats, we specifically focus on how to understand research reported as journal articles so that you will develop the knowledge and skills you need to read and evaluate research studies that have been reported in this important format.

Here's a Tip!

Although you may be more accustomed to reading books about problems that concern you, focus on reading recent research studies published as journal articles to learn the most up-to-date information in your profession.

■ *Early stage material.* The final major category of literature highlighted in Figure 1.3 comprises materials at an early stage of development. Such early stage material consists of study reports posted to websites, papers presented at conferences, professional-association newsletters, drafts of study reports available from authors, and student theses and dissertations. For example, the National Art Education Association website includes a page dedicated to resources that includes relevant research:

  ■ National Art Education Association. (2013). *Research and knowledge resources.* Retrieved from http://www.arteducators.org/research/research

Early stage materials are typically formats that are more informal than books or articles and may or may not go through a formal publication process. Sometimes early stage materials are referred to as "grey literature" to indicate the lack of formality in the publication process. Despite the informality, there is no doubt that information about research studies posted to websites and available online represent a growing source of research that you may choose to read. This type of literature can be interesting because it is where new ideas and results may first appear. Unfortunately, because this work is typically early in its development, it also means that reviewers (e.g., journal editors or book publishers) have likely not monitored them to ensure their quality. Therefore, although early stage research materials are easily accessible, you must be cautious of the conclusions until the results appear in more rigorous outlets, such as scholarly journals.

In summary, when you read research to add to your knowledge, inform your position on policies, and improve your practice, we recommend that you focus on journal articles, but you may find research reported in the other discussed formats of interest too. Before we move forward to consider how you actually read the information provided in a research report, this is a good place to pause for a brief commentary about how we presented source information for the different examples above.

You may have noticed in the examples that the way we presented source information for a book looked a little different from a journal article, which looked a little different from a website. Because of the importance of being able to accurately and precisely present source information for a given document, researchers and practitioners have developed style manuals to guide how individuals identify different types of research reports. **Style manuals** provide a structure for identifying references, as well as other aspects of writing such as the format of headings. (You will learn more about headings in Chapter 4.) Numerous style guides are available that discuss formats for writing a research report. The choice of a style guide is usually determined by someone else, such as your teacher, your graduate program, or your professional association. The *Publication Manual of the American Psychological Association*, 6th edition (APA, 2010) is the most popular style guide in educational and social research. We follow the APA style guidelines throughout this book, and you can find an example of a paper written using APA style in the Appendix. For now, examine the models provided in Table 1.2 to learn how to present source information for different types of research documents using APA style.

What Do You Think?

Note the following source information about a research study published as an article in the *Journal of Autism and Developmental Disorders*. Using the model in Table 1.2 and information below, write a reference for this article using APA style. Pay careful attention to the use of uppercase letters and italics in your response.

Article Title: Use of Songs to Promote Independence in Morning Greeting Routines for Young Children with Autism

Author Names: Petra Kern, Mark Wolery, and David Aldridge

Volume Number: 37

Issue Number: 7

Year of Publication: 2007

Pages of the Article: 1264–1271

Check Your Understanding

A reference for this research report in APA style is:

Kern, P., Wolery, M., & Aldridge, D. (2007). Use of songs to promote independence in morning greeting routines for young children with autism. *Journal of Autism and Developmental Disorders, 37*(7), 1264–1271.

TABLE 1.2 **Models for How to Document Different Formats of Research Reports Using the APA (2010) Style**

Format	Document Type	Model in APA Style*	Example of the Model
Books	Summary reference book prepared by editors	Editor1, E. E., & Editor2, E. E. (Eds.). (Year). *Title of edited book*. City, ST: Publisher Name.	Damico, J. S., Muller, N., & Ball, M. J. (Eds.). (2010). *The handbook of language and speech disorders*. Oxford, UK: Blackwell Publishers.
	Book about a research study prepared by the researcher	Author, A. A. (Year). *Title of book*. City, ST: Publisher Name.	Pipher, M. (2002). *The middle of everywhere: Helping refugees enter the American community*. Orlando, FL: Harcourt.
Journal articles	Article from journal published in print	Author1, A. A., Author2, A. A., & Author3, A. A. (Year). Title of the article. *Name of the Journal, Volume#*(Issue#), page#–page#.	Harr, N., Dunn, L., & Price, P. (2011). Case study on effect of household task participation on home, community, and work opportunities for a youth with multiple disabilities. *Work, 39*, 445–453.
	Article from journal published online	Author1, A. A., & Author2, A. A. (Year). Title of the article. *Name of the Online Journal, Volume#*(issue#). Retrieved from http://www.website	Schnepper, L. C., & McCoy, L. P. (2013). Analysis of misconceptions in high school mathematics. *Networks: An Online Journal for Teacher Research, 15*(1). Retrieved from http://journals.library.wisc.edu/index.php/networks/issue/view/52
Early-stage materials	Website	Author, A. A. (Year, Month day of posting). *Title of webpage*. Retrieved from http://www.website	U.S. Department of Education (2013, June 7). *Race to the Top fund performance*. Retrieved from http://www2.ed.gov/programs/racetothetop/performance.html
	Conference paper	Author, A. A. (Year, Month). *Title of paper*. Unpublished paper presented at Conference Name, Location.	McKinney, T. R. F., Plano Clark, V. L., Garrett, A. L., Badiee, M., & Leslie-Pelecky, D. (2012, April). *Professional identity development through a nontraditional program for STEM graduate students: A grounded theory study*. Unpublished paper presented at the American Educational Research Association 2012 Annual Meeting, Vancouver, BC, Canada.
	Dissertation	Author, A. A. (Year). *Title of the dissertation* (Unpublished doctoral dissertation). Name of Institution, Location.	Morales, A. (2008). *Language brokering in Mexican immigrant families living in the Midwest: A multiple case study* (Unpublished doctoral dissertation). University of Nebraska—Lincoln, Lincoln, NE.

*When using the APA style, list the authors' names in the order they appear in the report and provide the full last names and initials for the first and middle names. Also, pay particular attention to (a) the use of italics because book titles and journal names are italicized, but article titles are not and (b) the use of capital letters because all major words in journal names are capitalized, but those in book titles or article titles are not.

What Steps Do Researchers Take When Conducting Their Studies?

Now that you know how to identify research, know why you would want to read research, and know the formats where research is reported, you are ready to consider how to read and interpret the information that researchers include in their study reports. Reading research can be challenging, particularly when you are new to it. This is because the process of conducting research is a specialized activity, and researchers use a specialized style of writing when they report their research studies in a format such as journal articles. This means that to be a critical consumer of research articles, you need to develop both an understanding of the process that researchers use when they conduct their studies and an understanding of the way that researchers describe this process in their reports. Therefore, before we turn our attention to how to read the information in research reports, we need to first introduce the steps that researchers take in their research studies.

As already indicated in the general definition of research provided at the start of this chapter, researchers complete several steps when they conduct a research study, including posing a question, collecting data, and analyzing the data. In formal research, the steps of research were historically identified as the "scientific method" based on the procedures used to conduct research in the physical sciences such as chemistry and physics. Using a "scientific method," scientists pose a question, make a prediction, gather relevant data, analyze the data to test the prediction, and interpret the result to see whether it resolves the question that initiated the research.

The steps of the scientific method provide the foundation for how researchers conduct educational and social research today. Although not all studies include predictions, researchers do use a process of steps whenever they undertake a research study. As shown in Figure 1.4, the **process of research** that researchers use in educational and social research consists of several key steps:

- identifying a research problem,
- reviewing the literature,
- specifying a purpose,
- choosing a research design,

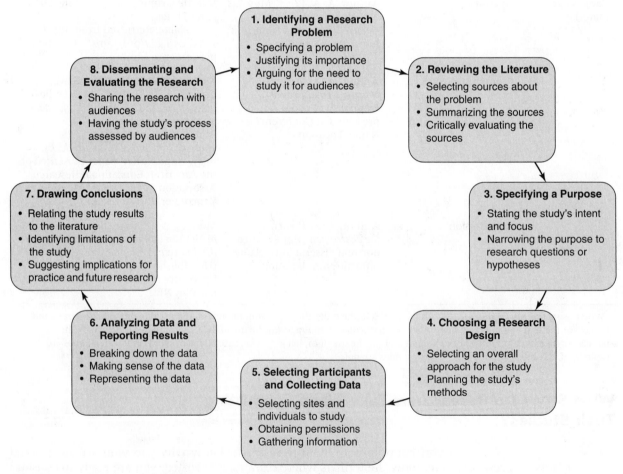

FIGURE 1.4   The Steps of the Process of Research

- selecting participants and collecting data,
- analyzing data and reporting results,
- drawing conclusions, and
- disseminating and evaluating the research.

These eight steps provide a useful framework that describes what researchers do when they conduct their studies and the information they ultimately include in their reports. To understand how this process unfolds in a study, let's examine these steps one by one in a little more detail.

Step 1—Identifying a Research Problem

Researchers begin conducting a study in their topic area by identifying a problem to study—typically an issue, concern, or problem in society that needs to be resolved. **Identifying a research problem** consists of the researcher specifying an issue that needs to be studied, developing a justification for studying it, and suggesting the importance of the study for audiences that will read the report. By specifying a problem in a research study, the researcher limits the subject matter and focuses attention on an important aspect of the topic. Some examples of research problems include the increasing violence in high schools, the distractions caused by middle school students' cell phone use, and the difficulty of finding adequate foster parents. Researchers study these problems when there is a need to add to the knowledge available about them.

Step 2—Reviewing the Literature

Once researchers have specified a research problem, it is important that they learn what knowledge has already been found by other researchers who have studied the same problem. Researchers plan their studies so that they build on and add to the accumulated knowledge about the topic, and so they do not repeat a study that has already been done. Because of these concerns, reviewing the literature is an important step in the research process. **Reviewing the literature** means that researchers locate books and journal articles on a topic, choose the literature to include in their review, and then summarize and critically evaluate the included literature. Researchers write a literature review passage that conveys what is and is not known about the topic of the research study, and they use this background information to plan their studies and to interpret the results at the end of the study.

Step 3—Specifying a Purpose

After identifying a broad research problem and reviewing the literature related to the problem, researchers next focus this problem to a specific intent for their study. **Specifying the purpose for research** consists of identifying the major intent or objective for a study and narrowing it into specific research questions to be answered or hypotheses to be tested. Researchers write a purpose statement that indicates the major focus of the study, what they want to learn, the participants that they will study, and the location or site where the study will take place. Researchers narrow their purpose statements to research questions or predictions that the researcher plans to address in the research study. This important step sets the direction and goals for a research study.

Step 4—Choosing a Research Design

Once researchers have specified a purpose for their study, they need to choose the approach that they will use to accomplish this purpose. **Choosing a research design** involves the researcher designing an overall plan for the study's methods—that is, an overall plan for selecting participants, collecting data, analyzing data, and reporting the results. Researchers first choose a research approach, such as a "quantitative" approach that emphasizes collecting and analyzing numbers, a "qualitative" approach that emphasizes collecting and analyzing words and images, or a "combined" approach that emphasizes collecting both numbers and words or images. Within the overall approach, researchers choose a particular design, or plan, that is best suited for addressing their study's purpose and answering their questions.

Step 5—Selecting Participants and Collecting Data

An essential aspect of any research study is the collection of data from participants to serve as the basis for answering the research questions and hypotheses. With a research design planned, the researcher turns to this critical step. **Selecting participants and collecting data** means that researchers select settings and individuals for a study, obtain necessary permissions to study them, and gather information by asking people questions or observing their behaviors. Of paramount concern in this process is the need to obtain accurate data from individuals in an ethical manner. This step produces a collection of numbers (e.g., test scores or frequency of behaviors) or words (e.g., responses, opinions, or quotes), depending on the study's research design. The researcher collects these data to answer the research questions of the study.

Step 6—Analyzing the Data and Reporting Results

Once researchers collect data, they next have to make sense of the information supplied by the participants in the study. While **analyzing the data**, researchers take the data apart to determine individual responses and then put the data together to summarize the information. When **reporting results**, researchers summarize the patterns they found from the analysis of the gathered data and represent these patterns in tables, figures, and discussions. This step produces the results and findings of a research study.

Step 7—Drawing Conclusions

Researchers end their studies by drawing conclusions about what they have learned. **Drawing conclusions about the research** means that researchers interpret the results that they obtained and explain how the results provide answers to the research questions. When researchers make interpretations and draw their conclusions, they often summarize the major results, compare the results to predictions or to other research studies, and suggest implications of the results for audiences. Researchers also consider the limitations of their studies and suggest implications of the results for practice and future research studies. This interpretation provides the conclusion to a research study.

Step 8—Disseminating and Evaluating the Research

As a final step to research, researchers are expected to share their work publicly. Research can only add to the knowledge of specific subject matter if people in the field can read and learn about the research! The step of sharing a research study is called **disseminating research**. After conducting a research study, researchers develop a written report and distribute it to audiences (such as practitioners or other researchers) who can use the information. It is by researchers disseminating reports of their research that studies can make a difference for the problems in society.

Researchers also share their research studies so other researchers and practitioners can evaluate the studies' procedures and results. **Evaluating research** involves individuals assessing the quality of a research study. For example, most research journals use a process called "peer review," in which experts in the field independently evaluate each study report to determine whether it is worthy of being published in the journal. This process is so important in research that research journals are often referred to as "peer-reviewed journals." Different audiences use different standards for judging the quality and utility of a research study. Researchers evaluate a study based on the quality of its literature, data collection and analysis procedures, and results. Practitioners consider the procedures, but often focus on how useful they find the implications of the study's results. Disseminating and evaluating research are an essential part of

Here's a Tip!

By reading and assessing the quality of published research reports, you actively participate in the research process by assisting with the dissemination and evaluation of research studies.

the research process so that studies and new knowledge are continually examined and critiqued by the larger community of researchers and practitioners interested in the study's topic.

By knowing about these eight steps, you now have a better idea about the process that researchers undertake when conducting their studies. Notice that the steps of the research process are illustrated as a cycle in Figure 1.4, which indicates how the conclusions, dissemination, and evaluation of one study often lead to the identification of a new problem, which starts the cycle for another research study. Consequently, researchers tend to keep cycling through these steps as they complete study after study. Most commonly, however, a research article reports what happens in only one cycle of the research process. In other words, most research articles disseminate information about the first seven steps of the process as implemented for one study.

Although Figure 1.4 and this discussion suggest that these steps occur in a neat and orderly way during a research study, that is rarely the case in practice. In many studies, the researchers implement two or more steps at the same time or go back and forth between two or more steps in an iterative (or repeating) fashion as the study unfolds. For example, as a researcher specifies the purpose for a study, he may realize that he needs to return to reviewing the literature to learn more about the problem so he can specify good research questions as part of the purpose. Another researcher may find that as she analyzes her collected data, she realizes she needs to go back and collect more data to fully answer her research question, which then requires that she complete more data analysis. Therefore, as you read research, it is important to keep in mind that the process of research is a dynamic, complicated process for researchers to complete and report. Despite the complexities inherent in a study's research process, these eight steps represent the major activities involved in all research studies, and they provide you with a useful framework for understanding the information that is included in research reports. Now that you have been introduced to the steps that researchers use in a formal research process, let's turn our attention to how you *read* the reports disseminated from formal research studies.

How Do You Identify the Steps of the Research Process Within the Major Sections of a Research Article?

Learning to read and understand written texts is actually a challenging process that most of us continue to develop throughout our educational and professional development. You may think, "No big deal, I know how to read," but knowing how to read is not the same thing as knowing how to read and understand a particular type of text. Our ability to understand and critically evaluate the information in a text document is enhanced if we already possess knowledge about the content of the text *and* if we are familiar with the underlying structure of how the information is presented. For example, you are probably very good at reading and understanding narrative stories because you have life experiences that may be similar to the story; you also know that stories are typically told with a familiar structure that includes a plot with a beginning, middle, and end, conveying events that unfold for characters over time. The goal of this book is to give you both the necessary knowledge about the process of research and the knowledge about the structure and language used to describe that process so that you can understand and evaluate the information in research reports.

Before applying these ideas to understanding the structure in research reports, let's first consider how they apply to another common type of text document used to convey a complicated process—namely, recipes. The process of cooking and developing recipes is most definitely a complicated and dynamic process. As summarized in Figure 1.5, we can think of this process as including several key steps. Cooks begin with an idea and type of dish that they want to make. From there they locate and prepare the necessary ingredients, figure out how best to combine them, and how to cook the combination so that it is safe, tasty, and a pleasure to eat. Along the way they may taste the dish and determine whether they need to go back and adjust or add to the included ingredients. Once the dish is cooked, they consider how best to serve it and store any leftovers. In the end, they evaluate how well the recipe worked and whether people enjoyed eating it.

They make notes about any changes to try in the future. When cooks share the recipes they have developed, they use a standard structure to report the information about this complicated process. They also have developed a common set of vocabulary to describe important elements of the process (e.g., chop, sauté, bake, and tsp.). This recipe structure and vocabulary has developed over the years, and today just about any cookbook you read uses the same overall structure. An example of this recipe text structure is also provided in Figure 1.5 for a recipe for Mom's famous baked beans. As you look at this structure, notice how it incorporates the steps of the process of cooking within the major sections of the recipe text.

If you are familiar with how to cook, then reading the example of the recipe in Figure 1.5 may seem trivial to you; however, that is actually the point. When you know the structure of the text, the information is much easier to understand. As with learning to read recipes, you can also learn to more easily read and understand research articles by developing your knowledge of the structure that researchers use to describe the information in their reports. Although the process of research is complex and includes many steps for a single study, over the years researchers have developed a general structure and specialized vocabulary for how they report their research studies. By learning to recognize this structure and key vocabulary, you will be well positioned to be a critical consumer of research reports that interest you!

The first step to effectively reading research reports is to recognize the overall organizational structure used in the reports. When researchers write about their studies, they organize the information into several major sections. As shown in the center of Figure 1.6, research articles are typically divided into the following six major sections:

- Front matter
- Introduction
- Method
- Results
- Conclusion
- Back matter

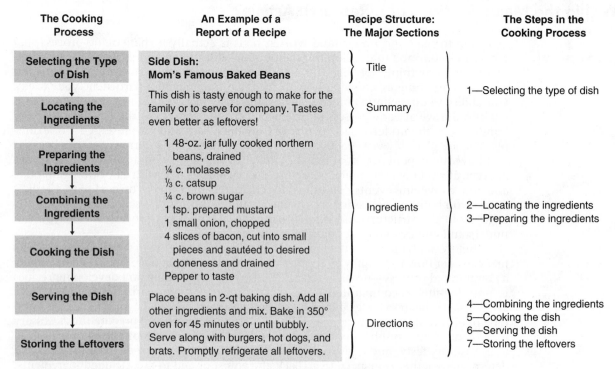

FIGURE 1.5   The Process of Cooking and the Structure of the Text Used for Recipes

Source: Recipe reprinted with permission of Ellen L. Plano.

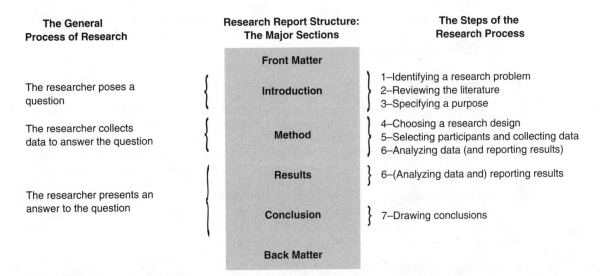

The General Process of Research	Research Report Structure: The Major Sections	The Steps of the Research Process
	Front Matter	
The researcher poses a question	Introduction	1–Identifying a research problem 2–Reviewing the literature 3–Specifying a purpose
The researcher collects data to answer the question	Method	4–Choosing a research design 5–Selecting participants and collecting data 6–Analyzing data (and reporting results)
	Results	6–(Analyzing data and) reporting results
The researcher presents an answer to the question	Conclusion	7–Drawing conclusions
	Back Matter	

FIGURE 1.6   The Major Sections of a Research Article and the Steps in the Process of Research

Note: The final step of "disseminating and evaluating research" is represented by the entire published research article.

> **Here's a Tip!**
>
> Researchers include headings in their reports to indicate the major sections and subsections. Use these headings to understand the overall structure of the report and the information that is presented.

The major sections provide an overall structure to the research articles that you read. With practice, you will learn to use these sections as landmarks to help you navigate through the information reported in articles. As you read a research study, you find information about the steps of the research process within the major sections of the report. Figure 1.6 indicates where each of the steps of the research process is typically discussed within the major sections. We do not list the final step, "disseminating and evaluating research," in the figure because the whole report represents this step. Each of the major sections and details about the corresponding steps in the research process will be discussed in Chapters 3 through 14. We introduce them here so that you can begin to recognize the overall structure as you read a research report.

Front Matter

All research reports begin with basic identifying information. The **front matter** of a research report includes the title, information about the authors, and a short abstract about the study. You find the front matter at the very start of the report document. Reading this information tells you what study is being reported and who conducted it.

- *The front matter includes the identifying information for the study report.* No matter the format used for a research report, you find that it begins with the researchers providing a short title for the reported study. Often the title identifies the topic, participants, setting, and/or approach to the research study. The title also provides a unique identification for the specific report. For a journal article, the name of the journal and the appropriate volume number and issue number will usually be identified near the article title.
- *The front matter identifies the authors of the study report.* Reports also identify the individuals who conducted the study and prepared the written report. The information about the authors in the front matter is typically limited to their names and the names of the institutions where they are each employed. The order of the authors' names also often indicates their roles, with the person listed first most often being the researcher who led the writing of the report.
- *The front matter provides an abstract of the study report.* Recall that an abstract is a short summary of a research report prepared by the authors. It is a stand-alone paragraph that briefly highlights key steps in the study's research process in a few words. Because abstracts are so short, they do not include all of the important details about the study, but they do provide a useful overview of the information that is

included in the report. You should read a study's abstract before reading the full report to obtain a quick overview of the content, which should help you understand the detailed information included in the full report.

The Introduction Section

The main text of a research report begins with the Introduction section. Researchers generally begin their research articles with one or two introductory sections that introduce the study and provide background for the study being reported. You can identify these sections by looking for headings such as *Introduction, Problem Statement, Background for the Study, Conceptual Framework,* or *Literature Review.* In many studies, however, the main text begins right after the front matter with no specific heading provided for the Introduction section.

When you read an **Introduction section**, you can expect the researcher to report information about the first three steps of the research process: identifying a research problem, reviewing the literature, and specifying a purpose.

- *The Introduction section begins by identifying the study's research problem.* Researchers begin the text of their reports by identifying a research problem, which provides a rationale for the need for the study. In an opening passage that we call the "statement of the problem," researchers describe the topic and the problem and justify the importance of studying the problem for specific audiences such as practitioners and researchers. You will learn how to read a statement of the problem passage in Chapter 3, "Statements of the Problem."
- *The Introduction section reports the review of the literature.* Researchers include their literature review in their study reports either as part of the statement of the problem or as its own separate introductory section. In either case, researchers report what they learned from reviewing articles and books to document what is already known about the problem being studied. You will gain an understanding of how researchers use the literature review in their studies along with an understanding of the steps involved in writing a formal summary of the literature about a topic in Chapter 4, "Literature Reviews."
- *The Introduction section ends with the specification of the study's purpose.* Researchers include a statement of purpose at the end of the Introduction section. The statement of a study's purpose is the most important statement in a research study report. It specifies the focus of the study and what the researchers want to learn about this focus. Researchers also state research questions and hypotheses that narrow the study's purpose to the specific questions that will be answered. Chapter 5, "Purpose Statements, Research Questions, and Hypotheses," provides information about identifying and understanding the purpose of a research study.

The Method Section

After the Introduction section(s) sets the context of the study, the researcher then reports the procedures used to conduct the study in the Method section. You can readily identify this important section because it is almost always designated with a clear heading such as *Method, Methods, Methodology,* or *Procedures.*

When you read a **Method section**, you can expect the researcher to describe the procedures used to implement the next three steps of the research process: choosing a research design, selecting participants and collecting data, and analyzing data and reporting results.

- *The Method section begins by identifying the study's research design.* When researchers conduct their studies, they choose an overall approach and research design for the study's procedures based on the specified purpose. The overall approach and research design guide the researchers' decisions about participant selection, data collection, and data analysis—that is, their decisions about their methods. Therefore, researchers identify the approach and research design as part of the description of their study's methods. You will be introduced to two overall approaches to research in Chapter 2, "Quantitative and Qualitative Research." In addition, Chapter 6,

"Quantitative Research Designs," Chapter 9, "Qualitative Research Designs," and Part Five, "Understanding Reports That Combine Quantitative and Qualitative Research," describe different research designs that researchers use within the different approaches.

- **The Method section describes the procedures used to select participants and collect data.** The focus of a report's Method section is to provide a detailed, technical discussion about the procedures that the researchers used for selecting the study participants and collecting data. Describing these procedures means the researchers discuss the setting for the research and who participated in the study, how permission to study these individuals was obtained, what data were collected, and how these data were gathered. Researchers collect many different types of data, such as asking participants to fill out forms or talking with them directly. Researchers provide detailed descriptions of the procedures they used in their reports. We discuss the procedures found in quantitative research studies in Chapter 7, "Participants and Data Collection," and the procedures found in qualitative research studies in Chapter 10, "Participants and Data Collection."
- **The Method section describes the procedures used to analyze the data.** After describing how the data were collected in the Method section, researchers often briefly describe the procedures they used to analyze that data. However, the details of the analysis and the results found from the data analysis are typically fully discussed in the report's Results section.

The Results Section

The **Results section** of an article represents the heart of the research study report. In fact, we have heard many students confess at the start of a course that in the past they have typically only read the Results section when reading research articles. Although the study results likely will remain of most interest to you, in this book you will learn how to understand and interpret them within the context of the whole study and article. The Results section is usually easy to locate in a research article because researchers usually title this section with the heading *Results* or *Findings*.

When you read a Results section, you can expect the researcher to describe one step in the research process: analyzing data and reporting results.

- **The Results section reports the details of and findings from the data analysis.** When researchers analyze the data they gathered, they prepare the responses for analysis, implement procedures to analyze the data, and summarize the results of the analysis in paragraphs, tables, and figures. They present the details of the study's findings in the Results section, which is where you learn what the researchers found from their study. You will examine how quantitative types of data are analyzed and the results reported in Chapter 8, "Data Analysis and Results," and how qualitative types of data are analyzed and the results reported in the similarly titled Chapter 11, "Data Analysis and Findings."

The Conclusion Section

Once the study results have been obtained, the next step occurs when researchers make interpretations about the procedures and results of the study. These interpretations appear within the **Conclusion section** of a report, which is often identified as the *Conclusion* or *Discussion* of the article.

When you read a Conclusion section, you can expect the researchers to describe the interpretations they made when implementing one step of the research process: drawing conclusions.

- **The Conclusion section reports the interpretations of the study.** Researchers end their study reports by summarizing the major results of the study and interpreting how the results answer the research questions stated earlier in the article. These interpretations include the researchers' determination of whether the results confirm or disconfirm expected trends or predictions or examination of the meaning of the findings for study participants. They may also include comparisons of the study's results with those found in other published studies. In addition, researchers discuss the implications and limitations of the study as part of their interpretations. You will learn how to locate and understand these discussions in Chapter 14, "Conclusions."

Back Matter

All research reports end with important information that supports the content of the study report. The **back matter** of a research report includes information such as a list of references and extra materials such as appendices. The start of the back matter immediately follows the end of the Conclusion section(s).

- *The back matter includes a list of references cited within the study report.* When researchers write their study reports, they include citations to other related scholarly information. The citations are usually brief (such as the name of the authors and the year of the publication) within the main text, and the detailed information about each source is provided in the back matter. These reference lists are generally formatted in a consistent way, such as in the APA style introduced in Table 1.2.
- *The back matter includes extra supporting materials.* Researchers may include supporting information at the end of their reports such as end notes, appendices, and biographical information about the authors. These extra materials supplement the information about the research study discussed in the main body of the report.

When you read any research report, a good strategy is to start by identifying the major sections: front matter, Introduction, Method, Results, Conclusion, and back matter. When researchers use clear headings, these can be very easy to identify. However, in some studies the authors use different words and/or include multiple sections that fall within one of these major categories. For example, some study reports have one clear Introduction section, but many reports include two or more sections at the start of the report to convey the introductory information. Therefore, it is helpful if you start by identifying where each of the major sections begins and marking them in some way in the article using a marking pen if reading on paper or a comment box if reading in an electronic format. Once you locate the major sections of a report, you can use Figure 1.6 to recall which steps of the research process you expect to be described within each of the identified sections.

How Should You Examine Research Articles That Interest You?

You have already learned a great deal about what research is, how researchers conduct it, and how it is reported. In addition, you now know why it is important for you to read, understand, and evaluate reports of research studies so that you can increase your knowledge about topics and improve your practices based on the results of good-quality research studies. You are likely eager to apply this new knowledge to actual reports of research studies, and you might be wondering how best to go about examining research reports. In this book, we will typically include three activities that will help you practice reading and evaluating research articles that interest you. By completing these activities, you will:

- *First, read and annotate the research article.* Reading a research article involves recognizing the basic content information about the study presented in the article. Start by noting what source you are examining and then write a complete, APA-style reference for the article. From there, identify the major sections and the basic information included within each section. Highlight key elements of the article and record notes in the margins that identify the elements you chose to highlight. You can use the highlighting tool and the notetaking tool in the Pearson etext as you read.
- *Second, answer questions about the research article to guide your understanding.* Understanding a research article involves making sense of the information about the study presented in the article. These activities will help you focus on key elements of

the articles, encouraging you to consider how these elements relate to the overall research approach. Eventually you will begin to ask yourself similar questions each time you read a research article.

■ *Third, evaluate the research article.* Evaluating a research article involves making judgments about the quality of the research study—how it was conducted by the authors and also how it was presented in the article. The activities guide you through evaluating the methods the researchers used and the conclusions and implications the authors presented. We will include this activity as we discuss criteria to use when evaluating the key elements of any research study, beginning in Chapter 2.

To help you develop your skills for reading, understanding, and evaluating research articles, we have included eight complete research reports, published in quality journals, for you to apply these practice activities. The activities based on these articles give you the opportunity to apply the content covered throughout this book as you read, understand, and evaluate real research reports.

Reviewing What You've Learned To Do

- ■ *State a definition of research and use it to recognize reports of research studies.*
  - ❑ Research is a process of steps used to pose a question, collect data, and analyze the data to increase our knowledge about a topic or issue.
  - ❑ Reports of research can be identified when the authors refer to their work as a research study and report that they collected and analyzed data in the study.
- ■ *Identify your reasons for needing to read research reports.*
  - ❑ Researchers, practitioners, and policy makers need to read research to learn new knowledge about specific topics, to become informed on policy debates, and to improve practice.
  - ❑ Reading research can improve practice by suggesting possible improvements, offering new ideas, and identifying and evaluating alternative approaches for practice.
- ■ *Name different formats where you can find reports of research studies.*
  - ❑ Reports of research studies are found in books, journal articles, and early stage materials. These different formats often vary in length and in the extent to which they are reviewed for quality. In addition, APA style requires the use of a different reference model when presenting source information for a study report written as a book, journal article, or early stage material.
- ■ *Name the steps in the process of research that researchers undertake when they conduct research studies.*
  - ❑ Researchers use an eight-step process of identifying a problem, reviewing the literature, specifying a purpose, choosing a research design, selecting participants and collecting data, analyzing data and reporting results, drawing conclusions, and disseminating and evaluating the study when they conduct formal research.
- ■ *Identify the major sections of a research report, and know which steps of the research process are reported within each section.*
  - ❑ Research reports have six major sections: front matter, Introduction, Method, Results, Conclusion, and back matter. Researchers report information about seven steps in the research process within the major sections of a research article.
  - ❑ The Introduction section includes information about three steps of the research process: identifying a problem, reviewing the literature, and specifying a purpose.
  - ❑ The Method section includes information about two steps of the research process: choosing a research design and selecting participants and collecting data. This section may also include information about data analysis from the step of analyzing data and reporting results.
  - ❑ The Results section includes information about the step of analyzing data and reporting results.
  - ❑ The Conclusion section includes information about the step of drawing conclusions.

■ *Read a research report and recognize the information included about a study's research process.*

❑ When reading a research report, first note the source by writing an APA-style reference and recognize the overall organizational structure of the report by identifying where each major section appears. Then, use the research process to guide your understanding of the information within each section of the report. Finally, evaluate the research study based on the quality of the authors' implementation of the research process.

✓ **To assess what you've learned to do, click here to answer questions and receive instant feedback.**

Reading Research Articles

At the end of this chapter, you will find two research articles to help you start practicing your new skills. The first article was written by Furong Xu, Jepkorir Chepyator-Thomson, Wenhao Liu, and Robert Schmidlein and was published in 2010 in a journal called *European Physical Education Review*. We will refer to this article as the "quantitative physical-activity-in-middle-schools" study. The second article was written by Patricia Tucker, Melissa M. van Zandvoort, Shauna M. Burke, and Jennifer D. Irwin and was published in 2011 in the *Journal of Early Childhood Research*. We will refer to this article as the "qualitative physical-activity-at-daycare" study.

As you read these two studies, pay special attention to the marginal annotations that we have included with the articles. These annotations signal the major characteristics of quantitative and qualitative research, which will be discussed in Chapter 2. In Chapter 2 we will reflect back on these two articles frequently to demonstrate the authors' use of those characteristics. In addition, please bear in mind that these articles may seem difficult to understand. Reading research studies will become easier in time as you learn to recognize the basic features and structure of good research. For now, here are a few tips that will facilitate your reading:

■ Look for cues for the major ideas by examining the headings and recalling the general structure of a research report, summarized in Figure 1.6.

■ Keep in mind that research is a process consisting of several steps. As you read, look for indications of the major steps of the research process: problem, literature review, study purpose, participant selection and data collection, data analysis and results, and conclusions.

■ Look for the most important statement in the study—the purpose statement—which typically begins with a phrase such as "The purpose of this study is," "This study intends to," or "The objective of this study is." This statement will help you understand what the study is trying to accomplish.

With these tips in mind, carefully read the quantitative physical-activity-in-middle-schools study by Xu et al. (2010) starting on p. 27 and the qualitative physical-activity-at-daycare study by Tucker et al. (2011) starting on p. 40. First, write a complete, APA-style reference for each article.

As you read each article, pay attention to the major sections that the authors used to organize the information. Use the highlighting tool in the Pearson etext to indicate where each major section begins within the article, and use the notetaking tool to add marginal notes that name each section you highlighted and note what information it presents about the study's research process. Among the sections you will want to find are:

1. Front matter
2. Introduction section
3. Method section
4. Results section
5. Conclusion section
6. Back matter

Note that sometimes authors will use two or more headings within one major section of their report—for example, they may introduce their study with the two headings of *Introduction* and *Literature Review*. If two or more headings in the article contribute to one of the major sections, indicate that in your marginal notes.

Click here to go to the quantitative physical-activity-in-middle-schools study by Xu et al. (2010) so that you can write a complete APA-style reference for the article and identify the major sections of the article.

Click here to go to the qualitative physical-activity-at-daycare study by Tucker et al. (2011) so that you can write a complete APA-style reference for the article and identify the major sections of the article.

Understanding Research Articles

Apply your knowledge of the content of this chapter to the quantitative physical-activity-in-middle-schools study by Xu et al. (2010) starting on p. 27 and the qualitative physical-activity-at-daycare study by Tucker et al. (2011) starting on p. 40.

1. Use the rating scale in Figure 1.1 to determine whether the quantitative physical-activity-in-middle-schools article reports a research study. What is your evidence that the article is a research study?

2. Here is a list of the major headings that appear in the physical-activity-in-middle-schools article. Which steps of the research process do you expect to find in each section?
   - Introduction
   - Methods
   - Results
   - Discussion
   - Conclusion and recommendations

3. Use the rating scale in Figure 1.1 to determine whether the qualitative physical-activity-at-daycare article reports a research study. What is your evidence that the article is a research study?

4. Here is a list of the major headings that appear in the physical-activity-at-daycare article. Which steps of the research process do you expect to find in each section?
   - Introduction
   - Methods
   - Results
   - Discussion
   - Future directions
   - Conclusion

5. Assume that you are a professional (such as an educator, administrator, nurse, or counselor) who is interested in learning about children's physical activity. Why might it be important for you to read these two research studies?

6. Think about your own professional and educational interests. Write a paragraph that describes the kinds of information that you would like to learn by reading research and the reasons why it might be useful for you to read research.

✓ **Click here to answer the questions and receive instant feedback.**

An Example of Quantitative Research: The Physical-Activity-in-Middle-Schools Study

Let's examine a published research study to apply the ideas we are learning. Throughout this book, we will refer to this study as the "quantitative physical-activity-in-middle-schools" study. This journal article reports a research study conducted and reported by Xu et al. (2010). Their study is about the opportunities for physical activity that are available for children attending middle schools. The article begins by describing the importance of physical activity and promoting physical activity in schools. The researchers decide to conduct a study to learn about the opportunities available in middle schools, along with the various factors that predict the different levels of opportunities available in schools. The researchers conduct their study by collecting data from a large number of middle school physical education teachers. They analyze the gathered data to determine the prevalence of physical activity opportunities and the factors that are related to the level of opportunities at schools. They conclude their study by interpreting the different factors that they found to be associated with physical activity opportunities.

As you read this article, pay careful attention to the marginal annotations that signal the major characteristics of quantitative research, which will be discussed in Chapter 2.

 Click here to write a complete APA-style reference for this article and receive instant feedback.

European Physical Education Review
16(2) 183–194
© The Author(s) 2010
Reprints and permissions:
sagepub.co.uk/journalsPermissions.nav
DOI: 10.1177/1356336X10381308
epe.sagepub.com

$SAGE

The front matter identifies the title of the article.

Association between social and environmental factors and physical activity opportunities in middle schools

The front matter includes information about the journal and this specific article.

The front matter identifies the article authors.

Furong Xu
University of Rhode Island, USA

Jepkorir Chepyator-Thomson
University of Georgia, USA

Wenhao Liu
Slippery Rock University, USA

and

Robert Schmidlein
Manhattanville College, USA

Abstract

The front matter includes a brief abstract that summarizes the content of the article.

School-based physical activity (PA) interventions impact children's PA involvement and thus opportunities and associated factors for the promotion of physical activity in children need to be examined. The purpose of this study was to examine physical education teachers' perceptions of PA opportunities available to students at the middle school level and indicate associated factors that might influence these opportunities. A questionnaire survey was administered to 292 public middle school teachers in 181 schools located in the southeastern region of the United States. The results of the study indicate the need for more PA opportunities for middle school children in order for them meeting the recommended daily PA involvement of 60 minutes. In addition, there were statistically significant associations between PA opportunities and facilities availability, school location, and family support, indicating that some social and environmental factors tend to impact students' PA opportunities.

Keywords

middle school, physical activity opportunity, physical education teacher, social and environmental factors

Corresponding author:
email: fxu2007@mail.uri.edu

Introduction

(01) Low levels of physical activity (PA) are a major contributor to current overweight and obesity problems in children and adolescent (Fairclough and Stratton, 2005; Lobstein et al., 2004). Even though Centers for Disease Control and Prevention (CDC, 2010) recommends 60 minutes of daily PA for children and adolescents, there only 8 percent of children and adolescent meet the recommendation (Troiano et al., 2008). The issue becomes more serious with the prediction that obese or overweight children and adolescents are expected to maintain their childhood or adolescent physiques as adults (Anderson and Butcher, 2006; USDHHS, 2001). Obesity is associated with chronic diseases such as heart disease, type 2 diabetes, stroke, some forms of cancer, and osteoarthritis, premature death or discounted quality of life (USDHHS, 2001), and high healthcare costs (Wang et al., 2003). There is clearly a need to reduce the impact of this problem and the school setting appears as a viable intervention venue to promote PA involvement, e.g. tailor an effective exercise intervention program (Edmunds et al., 2001; Wechsler and Devereaux, 2001).

(02) School is considered to be an ideal early intervention institution for PA promotion because it can reach most children and adolescents and has a strong potential effect on children's and adolescents' behaviours (Edmunds et al., 2001; Wechsler and Devereaux, 2001). However, successful school-based PA intervention at the middle school level, grades 6–8, has seldom been reported in comparison to those targeting elementary schoolchildren (Sallis et al., 2002). Middle school years are recognized to be an important time in the development of adolescents' knowledge, attitudes, beliefs, and behaviours as related to physical activity participation (Malina, 1996; Mohnsen, 2008; Sallis and Patrick, 1994), and this developmental period may impact their PA behaviours far beyond middle school years (Malina, 1996). School-based PA intervention tailored for middle school age children and adolescents therefore might be essential for PA promotion. A two-year school-based PA intervention ($n = 1295$) was piloted in an effort to reach middle school age children and adolescents but this intervention was found not effective in PA behaviours nor in changing body fat in boys (Gortmaker et al., 1999). There was another attempt to pilot school-based PA intervention, which was designed to increase the aerobic component of the school's PA program and educate children about weight control and blood pressure (McMurray et al., 2002). However, 'best practices' were difficult to determine due to the effect being small and body mass index (BMI) not changing significantly (McMurray et al., 2002). One school-based PA program was shown to be feasible in promoting PA (Sallis et al., 2002). It used a randomized, controlled, school-based trial of 26,616 middle school students in 48 middle schools over two years. It evaluated the effect of school policy and environment on student eating and PA behaviours. The approach was found to be effective in increasing PA but no changes in food choices behaviours were discovered (Sallis et al., 2002). These prior studies provided useful guidance; however, there has been no 'best practice' to promote PA in middle school age children and adolescents. Therefore, it seems that, in order to identify effective intervention strategies for this specific population, there is a need to further examine and better understand available school-based PA opportunities and factors that may influence these PA opportunities because it could be thought of as a key in promoting PA among middle school age children and adolescents.

> The literature is used to prescribe the direction of the study in quantitative research

> The research problem calls for explanation in quantitative research

(03) Accordingly, the present study was designed to explore school-based PA opportunities in public middle schools and to examine factors that may be associated with these opportunities from physical education (PE) teachers' perspectives. This study was grounded in the Social Ecological Model – a theory that deals with how multiple facets of physical and social environments may influence behaviours of middle school students (Stokols, 1996). With the use of the social

The purpose statement and research questions are narrow and specific in quantitative research. The intent is to describe trends, relationships, or differences for variables

ecological approach, it will be possible for professionals in public health and PE to extend traditional motivational and behavioral theory by examining correlates of social and environmental factors that influence students' PA opportunities and, as a result, provide better understanding how to promote PA in middle school students. Specific aims of this study were to investigate the status of PA opportunities afforded to public middle school students, and to examine interactions between existing factors and PA opportunities in the middle school setting.

Methods

Study design

(04) This study was conducted following a quantitative study design. A cross-sectional online survey was used to research PA opportunities afforded to students in middle school and to identify factors related to students' PA opportunities. Use of online survey to reduce the data collection time and cost was deemed justified because all of the potential respondents had access to the internet and there had been virtually no differences among schools in access to the internet (National Center for Education Statistics, 2006).

Participants

The researcher chooses an experimental or non-experimental research design in quantitative research.

(05) Potential study respondents were the 660 middle school PE teachers from the 421 middle schools located in the southeastern region of the United States. Of the 660 potential participants, 292 from 181 public middle schools responded to the online survey, resulting in a response rate of 44 percent, which was comparable to the average response rate of 37 percent among other published online surveys (Sheehan, 2001). Of the 292 respondents, 243 provided valid responses for this study. On average, there were 1.34 PE teachers per school responding to this survey from a total of 181 schools in 75 different counties. There was an equal representation of female ($n = 123$) and male ($n = 120$) respondents, they ranged in age from 22 to 60, had between 1 and 35 years of work experience as PE teachers, and 93 percent of them had a university degree with specialization in PE. Overall, the sample represented a group of experienced respondents who were able to provide credible information.

The researcher selects a large number of participants that are representative of a group in quantitative research.

Procedure

(06) Following approval by the University Institutional Review Board, data from participants were gathered between 20 August and 24 November 2006. The study involved two phases. In the initial phase, a piloted study was conducted to test the level of internal consistency reliability (Cronbach's alpha of 0.78) and appropriateness of the instrument, which was adapted and modified from a previous study (Barnett et al., 2006). Based on the feedback from the pilot study, the final version of questionnaire was generated including 53 questions that took approximately 30 minutes to complete. In the second phase, a convenience sample of 660 middle school PE teachers' email addresses was obtained from 421 middle schools' websites or through phone calls. A promotion email with a web link to the password-protected online survey and a generic cover letter that informed respondents about the purpose of the study, filling instructions, and privacy concerns was delivered to those email addresses. The website remained accessible for data collection for a full two months during which four reminder emails were issued to those people who had not yet responded to our survey. A prize draw after the conclusion of data collection was used as an incentive to stimulate the response rate; in total 43 prizes were given out in the form of gift cards (two $100, six $50, fifteen $20, and twenty $10 gift cards).

Instrumentation

(07)

> The researcher gathers numeric data using instruments in quantitative research.

The survey instrument used in this study was modified from the questionnaire instrument that Barnett and colleagues (2006) used to determine the PA opportunities and its association with social and environmental factors in elementary schools in Canada (Barnett et al., 2006). Permission was obtained from authors to use the questionnaire for this study and to modify some items to make the questionnaire appropriate for the target population in this study. The final version of the questionnaire contained 53 questions seeking for available PA opportunities and social environmental factors that were considered potential correlates of available PA opportunities and were consistent with the social ecological model for the study. Number of PA opportunities was calculated from questions about a frequency and duration of specific schools' PE, extra-curricular PA and participation rate, and number of special PA events that school organized per year, e.g. field trips, jump rope for heart. Social and environmental factors were assessed from school policy related to PE, physical environment, cost of human resources, availability of the transportation for after-school programs, family support, and PE teachers' personal beliefs about the benefits of PA in general and PA benefits specifically for their students (Table 1) (Barnett et al., 2006). All of the questions relating to social and environmental factors were written as statements and could be answered on a four-point scale with a minimum and a maximum score of 1 and 4 respectively. Demographic inventory was used to collect the participants' information regarding gender, age, total years of teaching, current assignment, and location of school (urban, suburban, or rural).

Data analysis

(08)

> The researcher uses statistical analyses to describe trends, relate variables, and compare groups in quantitative research.

The SPSS Version 13.0 for Windows software package and SAS Version 9.1 were used for statistical analysis. Descriptive statistical analysis was conducted to describe the characteristics of participants such as gender, age, degree, years of teaching experience, and to provide information about available PA opportunities, and school demographics. Exploratory factor analysis was used to reduce 40 originally conceived social and physical environment categories to fewer dimensions for further analysis. Principal component analysis with Varimax rotation and Kaiser Normalization was used in this analysis. The selection of each factor was based on the rotated component matrix greater than 0.50 and less than -0.50 (Darlington, 2002). Labels were allocated according to the most significant items associated with the components with reference to Barnett et al. (2006). Further, ordinal logistic regression model was used in this data analysis for prediction of PA opportunities (dependent variables) in school by using social and environmental factors (independent variables) as Barnett and colleagues (2006) suggested that social and environmental factors were essentials determinants of PA opportunities in school (a number of special physical activity events, hours of extracurricular PA offered per week, and duration of PE class). The odds ratio (OR) was used as the primary measure of strength and direction of the relationship between each independent variable and the PA opportunities that were categorized to levels (4, 3, 2, 1) with quartile range. In this analysis, odds ratios less than 1 indicated a negative relationship.

(09)

Following these analyses, multiple ordinal logistic regression analysis was run among the independent variables and dependent variables. The overall test running a full model included all variables that were highly significant with *p* values less than 0.05, which were independent variables effectively predicting PE teachers' perception of PA opportunities.

Table 1. Questionnaire overview

PA Opportunities
1. Type of physical education class schedule
2. Number of physical education classes per week
3. The duration (length) of physical education class
4. Average physical education class size
5. Types of extracurricular PA organized for students
6. Hours of extracurricular PA organized each week for students
7. Number of students participated in extracurricular PA weekly
8. Events organized for students each year

Social and Environmental Factors
1. School policies
    a. School board policy for physical education, extracurricular PA
    b. Time spent on health issues in physical education class
    c. Frequency of student exemptions from physical education class
    d. Academic load
2. PA limited by cost and resources
3. Family support
    a. Parents involvement in school activities
    b. Family interest in school activities
4. School staff support
    a. Physical education teacher involvement in school PA
    b. School has physical education supervisor/coordinator
5. Role modeling of PA
    a. Physical education teacher activity level
6. Physical environment
    a. Sports equipment
    b. Sports facilities
    c. Availability of space for storing specific student equipment
7. Organizational environment
    a. Total number of students in the school
    b. Proportion of students bussed to school
    c. Transport and scheduling
8. Sociocultural environment
    a. School location (urban, suburban and rural)
9. Physical education teacher' beliefs
    a. Benefits of PA to student
    b. Benefits of PA in general
    c. Importance of selected lifestyle factors to maintain good health
10. Physical education teacher' characteristics: age, gender, teaching experience

Source: Barnett et al., 2006: 219.

Results

PE Teachers' Perceptions of Physical Activity Opportunities

(10) Three main PA opportunities on middle school campus were categorized as: PE, extracurricular PA, and special events. As presented in Table 2, the average amount of time allocated to a PE class was 185 minutes per week (range 0–450). With regards to special events, the average for schools

188　　　　　　　　　　　　　　　　　　　　　　　　*European Physical Education Review 16(2)*

Table 2. School-based physical activity (PA) opportunities in middle school

PA opportunities	Median	Mean	SD	Range
PE class (minutes per week)	195	185	98.6	0-450
Extracurricular PA (minutes per week)	346	347	224	0-1200
Number of special PA events per year	7	6.3	2.3	0-10
Participation in extracurricular PA per week (numbers of students per week)	40	50	49	0-200
Overall PA opportunities except annual PA events and extracurricular PA (minutes per day)	39	37	19.7	0-90

Table 3. School demographic data (*n* = 181)

School physical education	Frequency	%
Schools provides PE	170	94
PE class size 30 or larger	127	70
Maximum allowable teacher to students ratio	134	74
Policy for exempting student from class	16	9
Follow National Association for PE standard	65	35.9
Adaptive PE material and equipment	41	22.6

was 6.3 special events per year. The average length of the extracurricular PA time offered by individual schools was 347 minutes per week, but the average participation rate in each school was 50 students per week, which was low given the mean enrolled number of 911 students per school. Therefore, taking into account the reported participation in extracurricular PA, duration of PE class and average school enrollment, the average time offered by those schools for daily physical opportunities was 37 minutes.

(11)　　Furthermore, as shown in Table 3, PE was rather available across the surveyed schools as 94 percent of them (*n* = 181) offer PE more than once a week, but this positive fact is counterbalanced by a large class size, given that 70 percent of classes were between 30 and 39. Furthermore, 74 percent did not have maximum allowable teacher student ratio of 1:30 required for PE teaching (NASPE, 2006). Nine percent of schools had a policy for exempting some students from enrolling in PE class; for example, student athletes were exempt from taking PE classes. With respect to curriculum materials, only 35.9 percent of schools followed the National Association for Sport and Physical Education (NASPE) standards in their school PE class. NASPE standards is a guide for K-12 grade level in the United States including key points of emphasis on specific content area (e.g. performance-related fitness), benchmarks of performance for each grade level, and appropriate assessment techniques for achievement in each specified content area (NASPE, 2006). In addition, only 22.6 percent of schools had adaptive PE material and exercise equipment that could be used by student with disabilities (e.g. adjustable basketball hoops, foam-rubber scooters for students with special needs), and 56 percent of schools had a PE supervisor/coordinator.

The researcher reports results about participants' characteristics, the instruments' performance, and the study's research questions in quantitative research.

The relationship between physical activity opportunities and associated factors

(12)　　As discussed in data analysis, factor analysis was used to synthesize and reduce questionnaire items into scales that measured PE teachers' perceptions of social and environmental factors that

Table 4. Scales resulting from exploratory factor analysis (*n* = 40)

Scale	No. of items	Reliability (Coefficient alpha)
Teachers' belief on PA benefits in general (PABG)	7	.891
Physical environment (PE)	6	.829
School policies (SP)	4	.808
Students' family support (FS)	4	.790
Teachers' beliefs on PA benefits to students (PABS)	3	.894
Cost of human resource (CHR)	3	.737
Organizational environment (OE)	2	.700

Loading items with reliability coefficients below the cutoff value for social science research ($\alpha = 0.70$) were deleted (Nunnaly, 1978)

Table 5. Unadjusted odds ratios (OR) and 95% confidence intervals (CI) for potential correlates of physical activity opportunity and associated factors

	HPA			DPEC			NSE		
Potential Correlate	OR	95% CI	P	OR	95% CI	P	OR	95% CI	P
PABG	1.55	1.03-2.32*	0.034	1.51	1.01-2.25*	0.045	0.90	0.60-1.34	0.605
Physical Environment	1.78	0.50-1.11	0.436	1.97	1.71-2.32	0.048*	0.92	0.67-1.02	0.300
School policies	1.11	0.83-1.48	0.484	0.96	0.72-1.28	0.766	0.78	0.59-1.05	0.104
Family support	1.81	1.22-2.69*	0.003	1.33	0.90-1.95	0.152	1.09	0.74-1.60	0.658
PABS	1.24	0.81-1.89	0.318	0.69	0.45-1.06	0.090	0.80	0.53-1.22	0.301
CHR	1.39	1.10-1.71*	0.003	1.08	0.82-1.43	0.591	0.81	0.61-1.07	0.141
OE	1.40	1.12-1.74*	0.003	1.09	0.88-1.35	0.421	0.85	0.68-1.06	0.140

HPA = hours of extracurricular PA; DPEC = duration of PE class; NSE = no. of special events; PABG = teachers' belief on PA benefits; PABS = teachers' beliefs on PA benefits to students; CHR = cost and human resources; OE = organization environment

were used in further analysis; the factor-loading matrix is given in Table 4, and explains 62 percent of the variation in social and environmental questions. Loading items with reliability coefficients below the cutoff value for social science research ($\alpha = 0.70$) were deleted (Nunnaly, 1978). Then, ordinal logistic regression models were used to evaluate the relationships between social and environmental factors loaded through factor analysis and PA opportunities. Results from univariate (unadjusting) and multivariable (adjusting) ordinal regression models are shown in Tables 5, 6, and 7.

(13)   The unadjusting ordinal logistic analysis (the univariate analysis) results, shown in Tables 5 and Table 6, depicted teachers' personal beliefs about the benefits of PA in general (OR = 1.55, 95 percent CI: 1.03–2.32), physical environment (OR = 1.97, 95 percent CI: 1.71–2.32), family support (OR = 1.81, 95 percent CI: 1.22–2.69), cost and human resource (OR = 1.39, 95 percent CI: 1.10–1.71), and organizational environment (OR = 1.40, 95 percent CI: 1.12–1.74). Those factors were significantly associated with students' PA opportunities in school (Table 5). As expected, school location (OR = 1.59, 95 percent CI: 1.20–3.12), teaching experience (OR = 1.03, 95 percent CI: 1.00–1.06) and teacher's educational degree (OR = 2.70, 95 percent CI: 1.02–7.14) were also significantly correlated with students' PA opportunities (Table 6). However, PE

Table 6. Unadjusted odds ratios (OR) and 95% confidence intervals (CI) for potential correlates of physical activity opportunity and school locations and respondent characteristics

Potential correlate	HPA			DPEC			NSE		
	OR	95% CI	P	OR	95% CI	P	OR	95% CI	P
Suburban	0.93	0.48-1.81	0.827	1.59	1.20-3.12	0.042*	1.12	0.57-2.19	0.745
Gender	0.94	0.60-1.48	0.792	0.90	0.57-1.42	0.652	1.10	0.70-1.73	0.681
Age	1.00	0.98-1.03	0.885	1.01	0.98-1.03	0.700	0.99	0.96-1.01	0.258
Teachers' teaching experience	1.00	0.98-1.03	0.887	0.99	0.97-1.02	0.672	1.03	1.00-1.06*	0.028
Degree	1.08	0.42-2.78	0.870	0.48	0.19-1.25	0.134	2.70	1.02-7.14*	0.045

HPA = hours of extracurricular PA; DPEC = duration of PE class; NSE = no. of special events.

Table 7. Adjusted odd ratios (OR) and 95% confidence intervals (CI) for independent correlates of physical activity opportunity in middle school

Correlate	HPA			DPEC			NSE		
	OR	95% CI	P	OR	95% CI	P	OR	95% CI	P
Family support	1.55	1.02-2.35*	0.003						
Facilities				1.43	1.02–1.99*	0.036			
Suburban				0.80	0.68–0.94*	0.007			
School policies							1.16	1.05–1.28*	0.003

HPA = hours of extracurricular PA; DPEC = duration of PE class; NSE = no. of special events.

teachers' gender and age were not correlated with students' PA opportunities. Multivariable analysis showed that family support (OR = 1.55, 95 percent CI: 1.02–2.35), school policies (OR = 1.16, 95 percent CI: 1.05–1.28), facilities (OR = 1.43, 95 percent CI: 1.02–1.99) and suburban location of the school (OR = 0.80, 95 percent CI: 0.68–0.94) were independent predictors of the availability of PA opportunities after adjusting for the effects of the other **(14)** factors (covariates) (Table 7).

Discussion

Social and environmental factors are important determinants of children's and adolescents' PA opportunities and they will eventually influence their PA behaviours (Sallis et al., 1998, 2002). Thus, it is important to target middle school level in order to promote PA for future healthy behavior. However, research is lacking with regards to examining the social and environmental factors' relationship with PA opportunities in middle school campus and studies with focus on PA opportunities are limited as well. Existing documented studies only focused on some PA opportunities, such as leisure-time (McKenzie et al., 2000), or extracurricular PA (Powers et al., 2002), or without combining data to determine opportunities at the school level (Tompkins et al., 2004). Our results extend existing knowledge by identifying school-based PA opportunities and factors associated with these opportunities at the middle school level.

PE teachers' perceptions of physical activity opportunities in middle school

(15) With regard to PA opportunities in school, our findings clearly indicated that PE continues to be an issue in middle schools. Time allocated for PE varied considerably from school to school, but the average time allocated was 185 minutes per week, which is far below the recommended 225 minutes (NASPE, 2006). Further, approximately 40 percent of schools in our study did not reach the recommended time and it is likely that the actual PE time students received weekly was even lower for the schools on block scheduling. With typical block scheduling in the United States, a PE class meets for 85–120 minutes a day, but only for 90 days a year instead of traditional 40 minutes a day and 180 days a year (Claxton and Bryant, 1996). This means, if a school was on block scheduling, the average weekly PE time counted was actually lower as students will not have PE for another half year. The result is in line with other studies reporting the erosion of the PE requirement in school (Burgeson et al., 2001; School Health Policies and Programs Study, 2000; Tompkins et al., 2004). In addition to PE, results obtained from this study also confirm findings of Powers et al. (2002) that students' lower participation rate in extracurricular physical activity is a considerable concern, given that on average only 50 students participated per school with the mean enrollment of 911 students per school.

> The researcher compares results to predictions and past studies in quantitative research.

(16) ### Association between factors and physical activity opportunities

Collectively, this cross-sectional study suggests that family support, facilities, school policies, and location have multivariate association with students' PA opportunities in school. Considering the factors impacting PE-related PA opportunities, our study revealed that large class size, facilities and school location were univariately associated with students' PA opportunities in PE. These results support the argument that large class size and limited facilities inhibit student potential PA opportunity in PE (Burgeson et al., 2001; Darst and Pangrazi, 2006; Hastie and Saunder, 1991; McKenzie et al., 2000; Young et al., 2007). However, after controlling social and physical environmental variables, only facilities and school location were multivariately associated with students' PA opportunity in PE. It might be that the actual need for facilities is directly linked to quality of PE and that an enriched environment increases students' PA opportunities (Mohnsen, 2008). Suburban schools tend to have better facilities (Wang et al., 2003) and thus offer more PA opportunities. It is encouraging to see that improvement of middle school facilities might potentially increase students' PA opportunity in PE. Some inner-city middle schools suffer from limited space, i.e. no or very small school yard, and overcrowding happens as a consequence of this space limitation during recess/lunch break. Thus, it is really challenging for students to use those opportunities to participate in informal PA. Enhanced availability of facilities is likely to be particularly important in schools with a large portion of economically disadvantaged students because PE class might be the only PA opportunity available to them during the day.

(17)   With regards to the factors associated with students' extracurricular PA opportunities in middle school, our results suggest PE teachers' personal beliefs, family support, cost of human resources, and organizational environment are such factors. However, only family support remained significantly associated with students' extracurricular PA opportunity after controlling for social and physical environmental variables. Parental encouragement and support influence their children's PA involvement (Sallis et al., 2000). Furthermore, the results suggest that overall differences in transportation among different middle schools do not seem to have a strong impact on students' extracurricular PA opportunities. However, the data of transportation obtained in this study might have been underestimated due to self-reporting.

Limitations of study

(18)   There are limitations associated with the study. First, the participants in this study were conveniently selected from easily available sources such as school websites and emails and the schools were located in the southeastern region of United States, which might decrease the extent to which the results could be generalized to all middle schools in United States. Secondly, the measures (e.g. PA opportunities) were based on perception of PE teachers, thus exposing questions related to respondents' subjectivity. Lastly, the questionnaire did not assess students' PA participation; the absence of these data hinders our understanding of the association between PA opportunities and student PA participation. To minimize the limitations of this study, future research should attempt to replicate these findings using a randomly selected nationwide sample. Furthermore, researchers should continue to refine survey instrument and other data collection methods to be used in this line of research. Objective measures of PA opportunities and student PA participation on campus are necessary to strengthen the association between PA opportunities and students' level of PA.

> The researcher interprets the limitations and implications of the results in quantitative research.

Conclusion and recommendations

(19)   Examining the association between factors and students' PA opportunities in middle school provided complementary information, which helped to identify modifiable factors and provide direction for future school-based intervention programs. Those modifiable factors such as supportive school policies, better facilities, and family support do influence availability of PA opportunities, which in turn influence students' PA behaviour choices, in line with the Social Ecological Model, and thus help to promote PA at middle school.

(20)   While this study added new information to the current knowledge, there is a need for further research at the middle school level. The factors that are correlated with students' PA opportunities should be subjected to a detailed study. Intervention programs should be developed to target modifiable factors identified in this study and PA opportunities offered in different schools ought to be further examined to more accurately assess associations. Recommendations for future research include testing the extent to which PA opportunities are proportional to the quality and quantity of children's and adolescents' PA involvement. Other research studies that can be conducted could concern educational interventions aimed at discovering effective educational components that promote children's and adolescents' involvement in PA. With collective and continuous efforts, children and adolescents can take advantage of different PA opportunities in school, which in the long run will help them to shape up and maintain a healthy lifestyle.

References

Anderson PM, Butcher KF (2006) Childhood obesity: trends and potential factors. *The Future of Children* 16(10): 19–45.

Barnett TA, O'Loughlin J, Gauvin L, Paradis G, and Hanley J (2006) Opportunities for student physical activity in elementary schools: a cross-sectional survey of frequency and correlates. *Health Education Behavior* 33: 215–32.

Burgeson CR, Wechsler H, Brener ND, Young JC, and Spain CG (2001) Physical education and activity: results from the School Health Policies and Programs Study 2000. *Journal of School Health* 71: 279–93.

> The back matter includes a list of references and information about the authors.

Center for Disease Control and Prevention (2010) *Prevalence of Obesity among Children and Adolescents: United States, Trends 1963–1965 through 2007–2008.* URL (consulted June 2010): http://www.cdc.gov/nchs/data/hestat/obesity_child_07_08/obesity_child_07_08.htm

Centers for Disease Control and Prevention, National Center for Chronic Disease Prevention and Health Promotion (2003) *Youth Risk Behavior Surveillance System (YRBSS).* URL (consulted April 2006): http://health.state.ga.us/epi/cdiee/student

Claxton D, Bryant J (1996) Block scheduling: what does it mean for physical education? *Journal of Physical Education, Recreation and Dance* 57(3): 48–50.

Darlington RB (2002) *Factor analysis.* URL (consulted Feb. 2006): http://comp9.psych.cornell.edu/Darlington /factor.htm.

Darst PW, Pangrazi R (2006) *Dynamic Physical Education for Secondary School Students* (5th edn). San Francisco, CA: Benjamin Cummings.

Edmunds L, Water E, and Elliott EJ (2001) Evidence based management of childhood *obesity. British Medical Journal* 323: 916–19.

Fairclough S, Stratton G (2005) Physical activity levels in middle and high school physical education: a review. *Pediatric Exercise Science* 17: 217–36.

Gortmaker SL, Peterson K, Wiecha J, Sobol AM, Dixit S, Fox MK, et al. (1999) Reducing obesity via a school-based interdisciplinary intervention among youth: planet health. *Archives of Pediatrics and Adolescent Medicine* 153: 409–18.

Hastie PA, Saunder JE (1991) Effects of class size and equipment availability on student involvement in physical education. *Journal of Experimental Education* 59: 212–24.

Lobstein T, Baur L, and Uauy R (2004) Obesity in children and young people: a crisis in public health. *Obesity Reviews* 5: 4–85.

McKenzie TL, Marshall SJ, Sallis JF, and Conway TL (2000) Leisure-time physical activity in school environment: an observational study using SOPLAY. *Preventive Medicine* 30: 70–7.

McMurray RG, Harrell JS, Bangdiwala SI, Bradley CB, Deng S, and Levine A (2002) A school-based intervention can reduce body fat and blood pressure in young adolescents. *Journal of Adolescent Health* 31: 125–32.

Malina RM (1996) Tracking of physical activity and physical fitness across the lifespan. *Research Quarterly for Exercise and Sport* 57: 48–57.

Mohnsen BS (2008) *Teaching Middle School Physical Education* (2nd edn). Champaign, IL: Human Kinetics.

National Association for Sport and Physical Education (2006) *2006 Shape of the Nation Report: Status of Physical Education in the USA.* Reston, VA: NASPE.

National Center for Education Statistics (2006) Internet access in U.S. public schools and classrooms: 1994–2005. URL (consulted Feb. 2007): http://nces.ed.gov/ pubsearch/pubsinfo.asp?pubid=2007020.

Nunnaly J (1978) *Psychometric Theory.* New York: McGraw-Hill.

Powers HS, Conway TL, McKenzie TL, Sallis JF, and Marshall SJ (2002) Participation in extracurricular physical activity programs at middle schools. *Research Quarterly for Exercise and Sport* 73: 187–92.

Sallis JF, Patrick K (1994) Physical activity guidelines for adolescents: consensus statement. *Pediatric Exercise Science* 6: 302–14.

Sallis JF, Bauman A, and Pratt M (1998) Environmental and policy interventions to promote physical activity. *American Journal of Preventive Medicine* 15(4): 379–97.

Sallis JF, Prochaska JJ, and Taylor WC (2000) A review of correlates of physical activity of children and adolescents. *Medicine and Science in Sports and Exercise* 32: 963–75.

Sallis JF, Kraft K, and Linton LS (2002) How the environment shapes physical activity: a transdisciplinary research agenda. *American Journal of Preventive Medicine* 22(3): 208.

School Health Policies and Programs Study (2000) Fact sheet physical education and activity. *Journal of School Health* 71. URL (consulted April 2006): http://www.cdc.gov/ HealthyYouth/shpps.

Sheehan K (2001) E-mail survey response rates: a review. *Journal of Computer-Mediated Communication* 6(2). URL (consulted April 2006): http://www.ascusc.org/jcmc/vol6/

194   *European Physical Education Review 16(2)*

Stokols D (1996) Translating social ecological theory into guidelines for community health promotion. *American Journal of Health Promotion* 10: 282–98.

Tompkins N, Zizzi S, Zedosky L, Wright J, and Vitullo E (2004) School-based opportunities for physical activity in West Virginia public schools. *Preventive Medicine* 39: 834–40.

Troiano R, Berrigan D, Dodd K, et al.(2008) Physical activity in the United States measured by accelerometer. *Medicine and Science in Sports and Exercise* 40(1): 181–8.

US Department of Health and Human Services (2001) *The Surgeon General's Call to Action to Prevent and Decrease Overweight and Obesity*. Rockville, MD: US Department of Health and Human Services, Public Health Service, Office of the Surgeon General.

Wang L, Yang Q, Lowry R, and Wechsler H (2003) Economic analysis of a school-based obesity prevention program. *Obesity Research* 11: 1313–24.

Wechsler H, Devereaux R (2001) Using the school environment to promote healthy eating and physical activity. *Preventive Medicine* 31(suppl.): S121–S137.

Young DR, Felton GM, Grieser M, Elder JP, Johnson C, Lee J, et al. (2007) Policies and opportunities for physical activity in middle school environments. *Journal of School Health* 77: 41–7.

Biographical details

Furong Xu is assistant professor of physical education in the department of kinesiology at the University of Rhode Island, Rhode Island, USA.

Jepkorir Rose Chepyator-Thomson is professor of physical education in the department of kinesiology at the University of Georgia, Georgia, USA.

Wenhao Liu is associate professor in the department of physical education at the Slippery Rock University, Slippery Rock, USA.

Robert Schmidlein is visiting assistant professor of physical education and sport pedagogy at Manhattanville College, New York, USA.

Source: This article is reprinted from *European Physical Education Review*, Vol. 16, Issue 2, pp. 183–194, 2010. Reprinted with permission of Sage Publications, Inc.

An Example of Qualitative Research: The Physical-Activity-at-Daycare Study

Let's examine another published research study to apply the ideas we are learning. Throughout this book, we will refer to this study as the "qualitative physical-activity-at-daycare" study. This journal article reports a research study conducted and reported by Tucker et al. (2011). Their study is about children's physical activity while attending daycare. The article begins by describing the importance of physical activity for young children and the need for physical activity in daycares. The researchers decide to conduct a study to learn about children's physical activity at daycare and how it might be improved. They conduct their study by collecting data from a small number of groups of daycare providers. The researchers analyze the data to describe the perspectives that providers hold about physical activity for children at daycare. They conclude by interpreting the meaning of the participants' perspectives and experiences about physical activity in daycare.

As you read this article, pay careful attention to the marginal annotations that signal the major characteristics of qualitative research, which will be discussed in Chapter 2.

 Click here to write a complete APA-style reference for this article and receive instant feedback.

Article

Journal of Early Childhood Research
9(3) 207–219
© The Author(s) 2011
Reprints and permission:
sagepub.co.uk/journalsPermissions.nav
DOI: 10.1177/1476718X10389144
ecr.sagepub.com
⑤SAGE

The front matter includes information about the journal and this specific article.

The front matter identifies the title of the article.

Physical activity at daycare: Childcare providers' perspectives for improvements

The front matter identifies the article authors.

Patricia Tucker
University of Western Ontario, Canada

Melissa M van Zandvoort
Middlesex-London Health Unit, Canada

Shauna M Burke
University of Western Ontario, Canada

Jennifer D Irwin
University of Western Ontario, Canada

The front matter includes a brief abstract that summarizes the content of the article.

Abstract

In London, Ontario, approximately 45 percent of preschoolers are insufficiently active. With the large number of preschoolers who attend childcare (54%), and the low levels of physical activity among preschool-aged children, daycare centers may be an appropriate avenue to intervene. This study sought to collect childcare providers' suggestions for improving physical activity during daycare hours and their perspectives regarding the feasibility of meeting the physical activity guidelines currently set out for preschoolers. This qualitative study targeted a heterogeneous sample of childcare providers (n = 54) working at YMCA daycare centers in London, Ontario. Eight focus groups were conducted. Saturation was reached by the fifth focus group; however, three additional focus groups were completed to confirm that the researchers continued hearing the same responses. Focus groups were audio-recorded and transcribed verbatim. Inductive content analysis was used to code and categorize emerging themes. Strategies were incorporated to ensure data trustworthiness. Childcare providers believed the children in their care were quite active and when asked what would be required to increase the physical activity participation among the preschoolers in their care, participants discussed: staff training/workshops; guest physical activity instructors; additional equipment and resources; and increased funds for physical activity. The majority of focus group participants also felt it was feasible for the preschoolers in their care to meet or exceed the preschooler physical activity guidelines. Developing programs and resources that are informed by childcare providers may be an effective way to target sedentary behaviors among the preschool-aged population. Accordingly, childcare providers' suggestions of how to maximize the opportunities for physical activity during daycare hours should be considered when developing and revising childcare curriculum, resources and policies.

Keywords

childcare, physical activity, physical activity guidelines, preschoolers, staff training

Corresponding author:
Patricia Tucker, School of Occupational Therapy, Elborn College, University of Western Ontario, London, Ontario, Canada N6G 1H1
Email: ttucker2@uwo.ca

208 *Journal of Early Childhood Research 9(3)*

Introduction

(01) The rate of childhood obesity among young children is disturbing. In Canada, researchers have found that between 26 percent and 30 percent of preschool-aged children (aged 2.5–5 years) are overweight or obese (Canning et al., 2004). High incidences of childhood overweight and obesity are also present worldwide. For example, 25 percent of American preschool-aged children have a body mass index greater than the 85th percentile for their age and sex (Ogden et al., 2006). The high rate of childhood obesity is concerning as obesity has been linked to type-2 diabetes, hypertension, hyperlipidemia, sleep apnea, and psychological issues (Daniels, 2006). Moreover, individuals who are overweight during childhood are more likely to be obese during adulthood (Whitaker et al., 1997). Clearly, obesity prevention efforts are necessary during early childhood, especially because the preschool years have been identified as a critical time for growth, development, and impacting one's risk of being obese later in life (Dietz, 1997, 2000; Whitaker et al., 1998).

(02) Physical activity, which can be defined as 'any bodily movement resulting in energy expenditure' (Sirard and Pate, 2001) has been identified as a key behavior for preventing obesity (Prentice and Jebb, 1995); yet, a recent systematic review identified that approximately 45 percent of preschool children remain insufficiently active to gain health benefits (Tucker, 2008). While many parents and teachers believe that young children are very active throughout the day, some recent studies have identified that preschool-aged children are not as active as adults perceive them to be (Fisher et al., 2005; Pate et al., 2004, 2008; Reilly et al., 2004). This misconception is cause for concern considering the high occurrence of childhood obesity in Canada and internationally. It seems Tucker's finding may be a conservative estimate of physical inactivity levels among preschoolers (Tucker, 2008), as Pate and colleagues recently noted that moderate to vigorous physical activity (MVPA) was only observed during 3.4 percent of the preschool day, translating into one hour of MVPA in a 30-hour week of daycare supervision (Pate et al., 2008). This finding is well below the National Association for Sport and Physical Education (NASPE) physical activity guidelines which suggests that preschoolers should engage in 60 minutes of structured and at least 60 minutes (and up to several hours) of unstructured physical activity per day (National Association for Sport and Physical Education, 2002).

(03) The very low rates of physical activity documented among preschool-aged children are disconcerting. Furthermore, researchers have consistently identified that girls are significantly less active than boys (Finn et al., 2002; Grontved et al., 2009; Hinkley et al., 2008; Pfeiffer et al., 2009; Tucker, 2008). Specifically, Grontved et al. reported recently that in a seven-hour preschool day, male preschoolers engaged in approximately 18 more minutes of MVPA than their female counterparts (Grontved et al., 2009). Clearly, interventions to increase physical activity among preschoolers, with a particular emphasis on female children, are necessary.

(04) Fifty-four percent of Canadian children attend daycare (Bushnik, 2006). There are approximately 867,194 spaces in regulated childcare centers across the country, 65 percent of which are for those children not yet enrolled in school (Childcare Resource and Research Unit, 2008). In Ontario, nearly 20 percent of children aged zero to five years attend regulated childcare, and this does not capture the children who are cared for at unregulated centers (Childcare Resource and Research Unit, 2008). On average, these children spend roughly 27.5 hours each week at childcare (Bushnik, 2006). Given the large number of Canadian preschoolers who attend childcare and the significant number of hours these children spend in non-parental care every week, childcare facilities may be an appropriate place to intervene to support physical activity among a large number of preschoolers. Moreover, parents of preschoolers have reported that they rely on the daycare facility to ensure that their children engage in sufficient physical activity (Tucker et al.,

> The literature is used to inform the direction of the study in qualitative research

2006). Despite this, the daycare environment has been largely overlooked in the discussion of avenues for preventing childhood obesity (Kaphingst and Story, 2009). In fact, little research exists on physical activity programs in childcare facilities (Chau, 2007) and the need to identify strategies to improve physical activity opportunities for preschool-aged children in these settings has been highlighted (Riethmuller et al., 2009). The childcare setting offers a unique opportunity to facilitate healthy active lifestyles among our youngest members of the population. In fact, the childcare center itself has been identified as a stronger predictor of physical activity than any demographic factor, such as race, gender, or age (Pate et al., 2008); it has been noted to account for between 43 percent and 50 percent of the variation in physical activity levels among preschoolers attending daycare (Finn et al., 2002; Pate et al., 2004). Interestingly, daycare staff themselves have acknowledged the critical role they play in the prevention of childhood overweight (Pagnini et al., 2007). Specifically, daycare staff believed they should encourage healthy food habits and active play at childcare in service of building a foundation for developing healthy and active behaviors that can be continued later in life (Pagnini et al., 2007). Therefore, it is important that daycare facilities offer the appropriate conditions and resources (e.g., space, time, and equipment) for young children to be active. Before interventions aimed at improving physical activity levels of children in daycare can be developed, it is important to understand the current physical activity practices occurring in daycares. Also, because daycare providers are the ones who work with groups of preschoolers on a regular basis, and can be argued to have a unique vantage point about what would work best for increasing their physical activity, childcare providers' suggestions for improving physical activity practices need to be collected. Therefore, the primary purpose of this study was two-fold: 1) to gain insight into the current physical activity levels of preschoolers, with regard to the feasibility of meeting the NASPE physical activity guidelines; and 2) to identify daycare providers' suggestions for improving these preschooler's physical activity levels. Specifically, daycare providers were asked to identify the supports they need to better engage preschoolers in active behaviors during daycare. This study was part of a larger study which sought to identify childcare providers' perspectives of: the barriers and facilitators to physical activity at daycare; current physical activity curriculum, resources and policies; as well as their suggestions for improving physical activity among preschoolers who attend daycare. Please see van Zandvoort et al. (2010) for additional findings.

| The research problem calls for exploration in qualitative research |

| The purpose statement and research questions are broad and general in qualitative research. The intent is to explore a central phenomenon. |

Methods

(05) Eight semi-structured focus groups were conducted with childcare providers (mean age = 32 years; mean years of experience = 8 years; 100% female) from London, Ontario YMCA daycare centers (mean attendance at daycares = 76 children/facility; for a full description of the study participants, please refer to Table 1). Nine daycare directors, of a possible 17, agreed to participate in the current study. In total, 54 childcare providers (of a possible 116 providers across the 17 YMCA locations) that provide services to a diverse (e.g., in terms of ethnicity, socio-economic status) group of preschoolers participated in one of eight focus groups, for a response rate of 47 percent. Each focus group had between six and eight participants. Participants also completed a short questionnaire to report the quality and availability of the space and infrastructure at the daycare facilities, as well as demographic information. Ethical approval was obtained from the University of Western Ontario Research Ethics Board and the Research Advisory Committee at the Middlesex-London Health Unit.

| The researcher chooses a qualitative approach in response to the study's exploratory purpose. |

| The researcher intentionally selects a small number of participants in qualitative research. |

All focus groups took place at YMCA daycare centers and lasted between 1.0 and 1.5 hours. **(06)** Seven focus groups were conducted in the evening when the daycares were closed, and one focus

Table 1. Demographic information ($n = 54$)

	N	%
Gender		
Male	0	0
Female	54	100
Age		
≤ 25 years	15	29.4
26–29 years	9	17.6
30–34 years	8	15.7
35–39 years	8	15.7
40–44 years	3	6.0
45 + years	8	15.8
Ethnicity		
White	46	85.2
Latin American	1	1.9
Asian	1	1.9
Arab	2	3.7
Other	3	5.6
Education		
High school	2	3.7
College	45	83.3
University	6	11.1
Graduate school	1	1.9
Employment status		
Full-time	47	87.0
Part-time	7	13.0
Years of experience		
< 5 years	23	43.4
5–9 years	13	24.5
10–14 years	7	13.2
15–19 years	5	9.5
20+ years	5	9.5

> The researcher gathers text and image data in qualitative research.

(07)

> The researcher uses thematic analysis to develop description and themes in qualitative research.

group was completed during daycare hours. An experienced moderator and assistant moderator facilitated all focus group meetings. Saturation, or the retrieval of no new information, was reached by the fifth focus group; however, an additional three focus groups were conducted to confirm that the researchers continued to hear the same responses.

All focus groups were audio-recorded and transcribed verbatim. Strategies, as outlined by Guba and Lincoln, were utilized to ensure the trustworthiness of the focus group findings (Guba and Lincoln, 1989). For example, member-checking was conducted between each question and at the end of each focus group to ensure that the moderator correctly understood the participants' responses and to confirm the assistant moderator's identification of the main points. After the focus groups, researchers meet to debrief and voice and record any potential personal biases to ensure that the analyses would not be affected by researcher bias. Inductive content analysis (using QSR NVivo 7.0) was performed independently by two researchers, who met after completing their independent analysis of the focus group transcripts to determine the common themes that emerged (Miller and Crabtree, 1999). For a full description of study methods, please see van Zandvoort et al. (2010).

Table 2. Daycare providers' reports of preschoolers' physical activity behaviors and infrastructure, space, and condition of the daycare

Activity level of preschoolers		
Inactive	1	1.9
Somewhat active	19	35.2
Very active	34	63.0
Sufficient indoor space at daycare for physical activity		
Yes	27	50.0
No	25	46.3
Somewhat	2	3.7
Sufficient outdoor space at daycare for physical activity		
Yes	45	83.3
No	6	11.3
Somewhat	2	3.8
Sufficient infrastructure and facilities for PA		
Yes	25	46.3
No	28	51.9
Condition of daycare facility		
Excellent	6	11.1
Good	30	55.6
Fair	15	27.8
Poor	3	5.6

Results

(08) Daycare providers cared for children from a variety of ethnic backgrounds (i.e., white, black, Aboriginal, Latin American, Asian, and Arab). Ninety-six percent of daycare providers reported that it is very important that preschoolers are physically active; however, despite the importance of physical activity among preschoolers, as identified by childcare providers, a large number of participants reported that their daycare lacked sufficient space and infrastructure. Table 2 provides an overview of participants' satisfaction with the indoor and outdoor space and facilities (e.g. playground equipment, sports equipment, etc.) at their daycare, in addition to the condition of their venue.

(09)   Prior to asking participants about suggestions for improving the physical activity levels of preschoolers in their care, childcare providers were asked about the current activity level of these children. Some providers believed the children were quite active, mentioning that they were busy running around during the majority of the day. One participant said the children in her care are active '. . . all day long, unless they are sleeping. They run, they play, they do a lot of action songs. Sometimes we actually have to ask them not to run. They are outside for approximately an hour in the morning and an hour in the afternoon if time permits, so really they are quite active.' Another confirmed her charges '. . . are always running around; they are always active.' Other participants provided more specific reports of activity levels when she revealed that her attendees are active for '. . . at least two and a half hours on a typical day . . .' An additional respondent reported that children in her care are active for '. . . [a]n hour in the morning and an hour in the afternoon plus we have a 10 to 15 minute large group activity'. The majority of participants were quick to report that preschoolers were engaging in approximately two to three hours of physical activity per day. Some daycare providers qualified their responses, indicating that activity levels were dependent on the individual child. For example, one respondent said, 'I would say because every child is different . . . I would say an hour and a half to two hours . . . It depends on the child and the day.' Another mentioned that 'there are some [preschoolers] that are constantly moving

> The researcher reports findings organized into themes and supported with participants' quotes in qualitative research.

outside . . .' while a separate provider noted '. . . so when we go outside, some of these children will choose just to stand, to sit by themselves, or to do quiet activities . . .' Many daycare providers expressed the noticeable variation in children's activity levels. In essence, daycare providers all noted that, overall, children were quite active during childcare hours; however, variations in activity levels were dependent upon the child and his or her personality, preferences, etc.

(10)   Only a few participants underscored that the preschoolers were not as active as they believed they should be. For example, one daycare provider said, '. . . even the time that they spend in gross motor things is very short.' One respondent expressed her disappointment by saying, '[i]t is amazing to know how unfit this generation is . . .' While, as a whole, daycare providers believed their charges were 'very active' (see Table 2), it appears as though some providers were concerned with the level of inactivity among some preschoolers.

(11)   When asked what would be required to enhance the physical activity levels of the preschoolers in their care, participants suggested: enhanced staff training/workshops; guest physical activity instructors; additional equipment and resources; and increased funds for physical activity. Each theme is discussed more thoroughly below.

Enhanced staff training/workshops

(12) Participants were interested in additional physical activity-related staff training or workshops. For example, one participant said, '[but] I guess we ourselves need some more education, I know I myself do enjoy going to workshops, I need more education.' Others confirmed, '. . . someone coming in to train one of us or a few of us on how to teach children's aerobics or children's yoga . . .' and another participant confirmed, '. . . [I want] more workshops, more about physical activity and new and different ways to provide it . . . I'd like to hear it from colleagues, like from other, you know, people that have been in the field and know what it's like.' Another provider said, 'I'd be even interested in sitting down, even if we couldn't get it through the whole [YMCA], having our center come together on a Monday night . . . and have somebody in here. Even if we used the hallway and they showed us what we could do with the hallway.' The daycare staff were clearly passionate about their jobs and were eager for workshops to improve their practice. Participants suggested incorporating physical activity workshops and training into their staff meetings or city-wide YMCA workshops. One participant even suggested having a physical activity specialist or expert at each daycare. She recommended having '. . . someone trained to be able to do those things [aerobics or yoga] . . . It would be neat if one of us was able to do that.' Regardless of the venue for the training and workshops, participants felt it was important that they receive more instruction about diverse and creative types of physical activity so that they could better instruct and engage preschoolers in such activities.

Guest physical activity instructors

(13) Daycare providers expressed their desire of having qualified people from the community come to the daycare and lead their children in physical activities. For example, one respondent noted:

> . . . we had an excellent girl down at the Y. She was absolutely amazing. And she would come over to the center and she would do . . . exercise. Oh my gosh, they loved it. First of all, it's someone new . . . For months . . . they were doing all the exercises and all the activities . . .

An additional participant noted the ability of daycare classes to teach other classes the activities and exercises they have learned. Specifically, this participant suggested:

[it] would be neat if we could have someone come to the center and say, 'this week, Barb is coming and she is going to do Yoga with Preschool 4,' and then once she showed preschool 4, then preschool 4 could show preschool 3 and then the next week, have somebody else that comes in and shows them how to do something else . . .

Participants thought it would be effective to have guest physical activity instructors come to the daycare because the children enjoy learning from someone new, and it often allows the daycare providers to learn new activities to incorporate into their daily physical activity curriculum. The only concern the focus group respondents had with the idea of guest instructors was, as one participant pointed out, '. . . it always falls back, unfortunately, on the front-line staff, so we're the ones making the hour phone call on the lunch looking for a yoga instructor to come in to [teach] the kids.' On the one hand, focus group participants were excited about the idea of having guest physical activity instructors come into their classroom, and they thought it would be an exciting opportunity for the children. However, they suggested that the logistics of arranging these guest teachers need to be streamlined to reduce the additional time required by daycare providers.

Additional equipment and resources

(14) Participants listed enthusiastically many pieces of equipment and additional resources that would help them facilitate increased physical activity among the preschoolers in their care. Respondents indicated a need for 'exercise balls,' 'hula hoops,' 'gym-type equipment (i.e., gym mats and apparatus),' and 'a climber.' Another participant said, '[we] need more bikes, more like actual equipment.'

(15) Daycare providers also spoke of their desire for additional resources that would provide ideas for engaging the children in physical activities. For example, one participant spoke of a resource she uses frequently:

> . . . a little flip calendar with an activity on one side and a recipe on the other. I don't know how many times I have gone to that and just flipped through it and 'oh, that one looks good' because I mean, like I said, we just sometimes forget about the stuff that we used to know.

(16) Daycare providers did suggest, however, that if a resource manual was to be created that it needs to be easy to use and quickly accessible. One participant stated:

> I don't have time to read a manual this [very] big. If it was short tidbits even once a week that you could stick in the communication book . . . If it's a paragraph, I have a minute to read a paragraph about a fresh new idea or fresh new resource or somebody willing to do that. Short and sweet . . .

(17) Participants had some creative ideas about different ways to facilitate resource development and sharing. Specifically, one participant mentioned:

> . . . why don't we network in a newsletter or some sort of form or at a staff meeting and say every center . . . takes turns, one center every staff meeting comes up with a new activity and sends it to everybody and shares it.

(18) Participants were clear that any extra equipment and resources that could be provided to them would help facilitate physical activity in the daycare. One participant summed up the sentiments of most daycare providers when she said, '[free] resources would be fabulous.'

Increased funds for physical activity

(19) Daycare providers spoke many times of the funding limitations experienced at their respective centers. One participant indicated that because they are required to provide gross motor activities to the children in their care, funds should be set aside to facilitate these activities. Specifically, this participant believed, '. . . they want us to do that [gross motor activity] with their children, so [we need] some kind of specific fund for gross motor.' Another stated, '. . . if there was some kind of physical activity grant that every daycare got and then with that you could go buy a bunch of new balls.' Another respondent spoke of the challenge of being provided with suggestions for physical activities, but not having the finances to put the activities into practice. She stated, '. . . it isn't just the ideas. We can come up with some fabulous ideas, but then we don't have the money to put the materials into effect.' Participants were clearly challenged by the lack of funds when implementing physical activities at their daycares.

(20) Participants also spoke of their need for gross motor space (i.e., a gym) at their daycares; for example, 'a big padded room would be fabulous.' However, the majority of the daycare facilities were unable to provide a room devoted to physical activity due to funding limitations. One participant said:

> [the] reason why we had a new center open . . . and the reason why they didn't put in one [a physical activity room] is because of money, they can't feasibly put one in because they can't make money with an empty room so it comes down to money.

(21) Respondents were also concerned by the lack of government (financial) support they receive. For example, one participant expressed, '[when] you look at the school board, the teachers get so much . . . we need government support like the teachers get.' Another echoed this sentiment when she said:

> . . . you have to replace these balls that don't last. Well it costs money, you know, and those are resources that we don't have, that we should have, that the school would have but we don't get that. The government gives us nothing.

(22) Another exclaimed, '[they] say zero to six [years] is an essential part of a child's learning and that's [when] we are working with them . . . but we have so much less resources, money . . . support, support, there's that word. Yes. It's frustrating.' Participants emphasized that they did their best to incorporate physical activity into the daycare hours and facility, but they were challenged by the lack of funds and government support they received to increase these behaviors effectively.

NASPE physical activity guidelines

(23) At the conclusion of the focus groups, the moderator described the NASPE physical activity guidelines for preschoolers and asked the daycare providers how feasible it was for the children in their care to achieve these guidelines (i.e., that preschoolers accumulate 60 minutes daily of structured physical activity, and at least 60 minutes [and up to several hours] of daily, unstructured physical activity; National Association for Sport and Physical Education, 2002). The majority of participants felt that the children in their care were already reaching the NASPE guidelines, as reflected by one participant who said simply, '[i]t's easy. We do [it] all the time. We spend more than two hours.' Another confirmed, 'I think that's very achievable here.' Other participants felt the weather was a determining factor in whether these children were 'sufficiently' physically active. For example, one individual said, '[in] good weather it would be fine . . .,' while another agreed, '[g]ood weather, yes. Crummy weather, wet weather would be a lot more of a challenge.' Overall, the majority of participants were confident that the preschoolers in their care were engaging in the recommended amount of physical activity per day (i.e., at least 120 minutes); however, a few daycare providers were concerned that the children were not achieving 60 minutes of structured physical activity per day. For example, some participants explained:

> P(3): Definitely [they engage in] the 120 minutes of physical activity, yes.

> P(5): That's a definite, but not structured.

> P(3): But not sixty minutes of structured physical activity, no.

Discussion

(24)   The primary purpose of this study was two-fold: 1) to gain insight into the current physical activity levels of preschoolers, with regard to the feasibility of meeting the NASPE physical activity guidelines; and 2) to identify providers' suggestions for improving these preschooler's physical activity levels. Considering these objectives, a number of findings warrant discussion. First, the NASPE physical activity guidelines state that 'individuals responsible for the well-being of preschoolers should be aware of the importance of physical activity and facilitate the child's movement skills' (National Association for Sport and Physical Education, 2002). Based on the results of the present study, it is clear that the vast majority of daycare providers interviewed possess an understanding of the value of physical activity among preschoolers, and do their best to facilitate these behaviors where and when possible. This coincides with the findings of an Australian study by O'Connor and Temple (2005), who noted a general agreement among family daycare stakeholders (i.e., parents, staff, and caregivers) that physical activity is an integral part of young children's lives, and consequently, of the daycare setting. The fact that 96 percent of the daycare providers in our study felt that it was 'very important' for preschoolers to be physically active may represent our most significant finding, as a discussion related to resources would be irrelevant if staff members did not acknowledge the value of physical activity.

(25)   A second finding that warrants discussion pertains to the fact that the majority of daycare providers believed that the children in their care were 'very active.' This notion was further supported by participants who indicated that they felt confident that the preschoolers were able to meet or exceed the NASPE guidelines for physical activity. While these results offer support for the conclusion that individuals who directly oversee children of preschool age (e.g., parents and caregivers) perceive that preschoolers engage in sufficient and high quality physical activity behaviors during childcare (Benjamin et al., 2008; O'Connor and Temple, 2005; Tucker and Irwin, 2009), it does not correspond with the growing literature which suggests that preschool-aged children are insufficiently active (Cardon and De Bourdeaudhuij, 2007; Pate et al., 2008; Tucker, 2008). The disconnect between daycare reports of physical activity and the actual levels of physical activity among preschools has been noted in a similar study in London Ontario (Tucker and Irwin, 2009).

(26)   It should also be noted that a number of daycare providers in the current study qualified their responses, pointing out that weather and individual differences among children influenced the physical activity levels of the preschoolers in their care. Interestingly, the caregivers and parents in O'Connor and Temple's (2005) study on physical activity levels in family daycare partially support this finding; they noted that the weather, individual caregivers, and 'diversity of children in care'

> The researcher relates the meaning of the findings with past studies in qualitative research.

influenced physical activity levels. In Canada, the weather poses a barrier for physical activity in that the climate is diverse, with seasonal temperatures ranging from extremely hot to extremely cold. This is consistent with other literature that has noted seasonal variations in physical activity due to weather (Poest et al., 1989; Tucker and Gilliland, 2007; US Department of Health and Human Services, 1984).

(27)   Given this seasonal variation in physical activity levels, a consideration of the availability of sufficient and 'quality' indoor and outdoor space is essential. This is emphasized in the NASPE guidelines, which state that 'preschoolers should have indoor and outdoor areas that meet or exceed recommended safety standards for performing large muscle activities' (National Association for Sport and Physical Education, 2002). Similarly, Timmons and colleagues have suggested that whenever possible, preschool-aged children should be given access to sufficient space and resources outdoors (Timmons et al., 2007). Interestingly, while most focus group participants in the present study felt that there was sufficient *outdoor* space for children's physical activity, only half of all respondents believed that their *indoor* space was adequate. For a variety of reasons including the weather-related issues discussed above, this perceived lack of sufficient indoor space is problematic.

(28)   The third set of findings that warrants discussion relates to the issue of structured versus unstructured physical activity. In the present study, most participants indicated that they felt that the preschoolers in their care were engaging in appropriate levels of *unstructured* physical activity per day; however, some noted lower levels of *structured* physical activity. Researchers have suggested that including regular structured physical activity into the daycare schedule might facilitate increased physical activity among preschoolers, more so than unstructured free-time for play (Cardon et al., 2009). The perceived lack of structured physical activity among preschoolers in the present study is disconcerting in that this form of activity could represent one means of ensuring that children engage in physical activity at the frequency, intensity, and duration necessary to achieve the NASPE guidelines.

(29)   Finally, it is important to highlight the needs outlined by daycare providers as it has been suggested that 'strengthening the supports and resources to the early childhood education sector during this critical period of child development should be seen as an important intervention in the attempt to reduce the incidence of childhood overweight and obesity' (Pagnini et al., 2007). Despite the fact that most daycare providers in the present study felt that the children in their care were sufficiently active, participants also outlined a number of tools and resources that would assist in enhancing the physical activity levels of these children. These included the implementation of staff training/workshops, guest physical activity instructors, additional equipment and resources, and increased funds for physical activity. These suggestions coincide with the findings of other researchers who have documented that daycare providers feel that improved resources, training, and professional development would better equip them to implement physical activity for preschool-aged children (O'Connor and Temple, 2005; Pagnini et al., 2007; Poest et al., 1989). Interestingly, in a recent study using an objective measure of physical activity, children were found to engage in more moderate to vigorous activity if their preschool had: a) higher quality scores (as rated on the Early Childhood Environment Rating Scale-Revised, including space, furnishings, personal care routines, activities, program structure); b) less fixed and more portable playground equipment; c) lower use of electronic media; and d) larger playgrounds (Dowda et al., 2009). Thus, it was concluded that daycare providers and health professionals 'can modify the preschool environment in ways that help children spend more time in physical activity and less time in sedentary pursuits.' In other words, it is not necessarily the provision of additional funds or resources that is essential, but instead, how effectively new – and existing – funds and resources

> The researcher interprets the limitations and implications of the findings as well as personal reflections about the study in qualitative research.

can be allocated and/or utilized. The training of existing staff (through workshops and guest presenters) may represent one means of effectively and efficiently enhancing physical activity behaviors in the daycare setting. It should also be noted that the majority of the daycare providers in our study were extremely eager and welcomed the idea of giving up their evenings to attend workshops and learn new skills in service of the health of preschoolers.

Future directions

(30) Due to the apparent discrepancy between what daycare providers perceive regarding preschoolers' physical activity levels (i.e., that they are sufficient and meet the NASPE guidelines for physical activity) and the literature which suggests that the majority of preschoolers' time is spent in inactivity (Oliver et al., 2007), additional research in the area is needed. Specifically, investigations that utilize objective measures to quantify physical activity (i.e., accelerometers and/or pedometers) are necessary to accurately and reliably establish physical activity levels among preschoolers (Cardon and De Bourdeaudhuij, 2007; Oliver et al., 2007).

(31)   The development and evaluation of interventions to promote physical activity among preschoolers is also imperative. While childcare centers serve as appropriate – and relatively untapped – settings for physical activity interventions, van Sluijs and colleagues noted that intervention studies in preschoolers are rare (van Sluijs et al., 2008). Additionally, Oliver and colleagues suggested that objective quantifications of preschoolers' physical activity are essential to establish the effectiveness of physical activity interventions (Oliver et al., 2007). Thus, once accurate physical activity prevalence data are available, a logical next step for researchers is to design and implement evidence-based and age appropriate intervention studies to promote physical activity among preschoolers.

Conclusion

(32) While the daycare setting represents an instrumental setting for the modification of children's physical activity and lifestyle behaviors, research suggests that physical activity levels among preschoolers are inadequate. The childcare setting has been found to be a strong predictor of physical activity (Finn et al., 2002); thus, developing and utilizing programs, strategies, and resources that are informed by daycare providers may be an effective way to target sedentary behaviors among this population. Accordingly, childcare providers' suggestions of how to maximize opportunities for physical activity during daycare hours should be considered when developing and implementing daycare interventions, curriculum, and policies.

Acknowledgements

We would like to thank Michele Brown and Alex Wilkins for their assistance with data collection and Danielle Amey for her assistance with data collection and analysis. We are also grateful to Leigh Vanderloo for her help in preparing this article. We would also like to acknowledge the support of the YMCA of Western Ontario. Special thanks are extended to the daycare providers for participating in this study.

> The back matter includes a list of references and information about the authors.

References

Benjamin SE, Haines J, Ball SC and Ward DS (2008) Improving nutrition and physical activity in child care: What parents recommend. *American Dietetic Association* 108: 1907–1911.

Bushnik T (2006) Child care in Canada. Children and Youth Research Paper Series. [89-599-MIE-No. 003], 1-99, Statistics Canada.

Canning PM, Courage ML and Frizzell LM (2004) Prevalence of overweight and obesity in a provincial population of Canadian preschool children. *Canadian Medical Association Journal* 171(3): 240–242.

Cardon G and De Bourdeaudhuij I (2007) Comparison of pedometer and accelerometer measures of physical activity in preschool children. *Pediatric Exercise Science* 19: 205–214.

Cardon G, Labarque V, Smits D and De Bourdeaudhuij I (2009) Promoting physical activity at the pre-school playground: The effects of providing markings and play equipment. *Preventive Medicine* 48: 335–340.

Chau J (2007) A review of physical activity interventions for children from 2 to 5 years of age. Available at: http://www.cpah.health.usyd.edu.au/pdfs/2007_pa_interventions.pdf (accessed 8 July 2009).

Childcare Resource and Research Unit (2008) Early childhood education and care in Canada 2008.

Daniels SR (2006) The consequences of childhood overweight and obesity. *The Future of Children* 16(1): 47–67.

Dietz WH (1997) Periods of risk in childhood for the development of adult obesity – what do we need to learn? *The Journal of Nutrition* 127(9): 1884s–1886s.

Dietz WH (2000) Adiposity rebound: Reality or epiphenomenon? *Lancet* 356(9247): 2027–2028.

Dowda M, Brown WH, McIver KL, Pfeiffer KA, O'Neill JR, Addy CL and Pate RR (2009) Policies and characteristics of the preschool environment and physical activity of young children. *Pediatrics* 123(2): e261–e266.

Finn K, Johannsen N and Specker B (2002) Factors associated with physical activity in preschool children. *Journal of Pediatrics* 140(1): 81–85.

Fisher A, Reilly JJ, Kelly L, Montgomery C, Williamson A, Paton JY and Grant S (2005) Fundamental movement skills and habitual physical activity in young children. *Medicine and Science in Sports and Exercise* 37: 684–688.

Grontved A, Pedersen GS, Andersen LB, Kristensen PL, Moller NC and Froberg K (2009) Personal characteristics and demographic factors associated with objectively measured physical activity in children attending preschool. *Pediatric Exercise Science* 21: 209–219.

Guba EG and Lincoln YS (1989) *Fourth Generation Evaluation.* London: SAGE.

Hinkley T, Crawford D, Salmon J, Okely AD and Hesketh K (2008) Preschool children and physical activity: A review of correlates. *American Journal of Preventive Medicine* 34(5): 435–441.

Kaphingst KM and Story M (2009) Child care as an untapped setting for obesity prevention: State child care licensing regulations related to nutrition, physical activity, and media use for preschool-age children in the United States. *Preventing Chronic Disease* 6(1): 1–13.

Miller WL and Crabtree BF (1999) Clinical research: A multimethod typology and qualitative roadmap. In Crabtree BF and Miller WL (eds) *Doing Qualitative Research.* Thousand Oaks, CA: SAGE, 3–30.

National Association for Sport and Physical Education (2002) *Active Start: A Statement of Physical Activity Guidelines for Children Birth to Five Years.* Reston: NASPE.

O'Connor JP and Temple VA (2005) Constraints and facilitators for physical activity in family day care. *Australian Journal of Early Childhood* 30(4): 1–9.

Ogden CL, Carroll MD and Flegal KM (2006) High body mass index for age among US children and adolescents, 2003–2006. *Journal of American Medical Association* 229(20): 2401–2405.

Oliver M, Schofield GM and Kolt GS (2007) Physical activity in preschoolers: Understanding prevalence and measurement issues. *Sports Medicine* 37(12): 1045–1070.

Pagnini D, Wilkenfield R, King L, Booth M and Booth S (2007) Early childhood sector staff perceptions of child overweight and obesity: The Weight of Opinion Study. *Health Promotion Journal of Australia* 18(2): 149–154.

Pate RR, McIver KL, Dowda M, Brown WH and Addy C (2008) Directly observed physical activity levels in preschool children. *Journal of School Health* 78(8): 438–444.

Pate RR, Pfeiffer KA, Trost SG, Ziegler P and Dowda M (2004) Physical activity among children attending preschools. *Pediatrics* 114(5): 1258–1263.

Pfeiffer KA, Dowda M, McIver KL and Pate RR (2009) Factors related to objectively measured physical activity in preschool children. *Pediatric Exercise Science* 21: 196–208.

Poest CA, Williams JR, Witt DD and Atwood ME (1989) Physical activity patterns of preschool children. *Early Childhood Research Quarterly* 4: 367–376.

Prentice AM and Jebb SA (1995) Obesity in Britain: Gluttony or sloth? *British Medical Journal* 311(7002): 437–439.

Reilly JJ, Jackson DM, Montgomery C, Kelly LA, Slater C, Grant S and Paton JY (2004) Total energy expenditure and physical activity in young Scottish children: Mixed longitudinal study. *Lancet* 363: 211–212.

Riethmuller A, McKeen K, Okely AD, Bell C and de Silva Sanigorski A (2009) Developing an active play resource for a range of Australian early childhood settings: Formative findings and recommendations. *Australian Journal of Early Childhood* 34(1): 43–53.

Sirard JR and Pate RR (2001) Physical activity assessment in children and adolescents. *Sports Medicine* 31(6): 439–454.

Timmons BW, Naylor PJ and Pfeiffer KA (2007) Physical activity for preschool children – how much and how? *Applied Physiology of Nutrition and Metabolism* 32: s122–s134.

Tucker P (2008) The physical activity levels of preschool-aged children: A systematic review. *Early Childhood Research Quarterly* 23: 547–558.

Tucker P and Gilliland J (2007) The effect of season and weather on physical activity: A systematic review. *Public Health* 121(12): 909–922.

Tucker P and Irwin JD (2009) Physical activity behaviours during the preschool years. *Child Health and Education* 1(3): 134–145.

Tucker P, Irwin JD, Sangster Bouck LM, He M and Pollett GL (2006) Preventing pediatric obesity: Recommendations from a community-based qualitative investigation. *Obesity Reviews* 7: 251–260.

US Department of Health and Human Services (1984) *Summary of Findings from National Children and Youth Fitness Study*. Washington, DC: US Government Printing Office.

van Sluijs E, McMinn A and Griffin S (2008) Effectiveness of interventions to promote physical activity in children and adolescents: A systematic review of clinical trials. *British Journal of Sports Medicine* 42(8): 653–667.

van Zandvoort, M.M., Tucker, P., Irwin, J.D., Burke, S.M. (2010). Physical Activity at Daycare: Issues, Challenges and Perspectives. Early Years: An International Journal of Research and Development, 30(2), 175–188.

Whitaker RC, Pepe MS, Wright J, Seidel KD and Dietz WH (1998) Early adiposity rebound and the risk of adult obesity. *Pediatrics* 101(3): e5.

Whitaker RC, Wright JA, Pepe MS, Seidel KD and Dietz WH (1997) Predicting obesity in young adulthood from childhood and parental obesity. *New England Journal of Medicine* 337: 869–873.

Source: This article is reprinted from *Journal of Early Childhood Research*, Vol. 9, Issue 3, pp. 207–219, 2011. Reprinted with permission of Sage Publications, Inc.

QUANTITATIVE AND QUALITATIVE RESEARCH: UNDERSTANDING DIFFERENT TYPES OF STUDY REPORTS

CHAPTER

2

*Y*ou now know that research is a process that researchers use to add to our knowledge base about various topics and that researchers report the steps of this process in their written study reports. Let's add a second idea to understanding research: Researchers conduct their studies in two ways— using a quantitative approach or a qualitative approach. The approach used in a study influences how the researcher implements the steps in the research process and the information described in a study report. In this chapter, you will learn how to identify whether a study used a quantitative or qualitative approach and the reasons why you should read both types of research. In addition, you will be introduced to the key characteristics of quantitative and qualitative research and criteria you can use to evaluate the quality of research studies using these different approaches.

BY THE END OF THIS CHAPTER, YOU SHOULD BE ABLE TO:

- Identify the overall approach used in a research report as quantitative, qualitative, or combined.
- Identify reasons why you should read research that used quantitative approaches and research that used qualitative approaches.
- Recognize the key differences in the steps of the research process as reported in quantitative and qualitative research studies.
- Evaluate the quality of quantitative and qualitative research reports.

You have just read two research studies related to children and their levels of physical activity. (*Note:* If you have not yet read the physical-activity-in-middle-schools and physical-activity-at-daycare studies at the end of Chapter 1, go back and read them before continuing with this chapter.) As you were reading about these two studies, perhaps you noticed some similarities between the articles. One similarity is that both articles were about the same general topic: youth's physical activity. The researchers in both studies also collected and analyzed data to study this topic. The organization of the two articles was also similar. Both articles included four major sections where the researchers provided an introduction to the study, a description of the methods, a presentation of results, and a discussion of conclusions about the study. You may also have noticed differences between these two examples of research. Most notably, the physical-activity-in-middle-schools study by Xu et al. (2010) focused on numbers and reporting statistics about physical activity. In contrast, the physical-activity-at-daycare study by Tucker et al. (2011) focused on words and reporting detailed descriptions of different perspectives.

At a basic level, this difference (numbers vs. words) forms the basis of the two different approaches for conducting research: quantitative and qualitative. Today, researchers actively use these two approaches to study most every topic of interest across all disciplines and professional areas. The differences, however, go beyond simply the collection of numbers or words. The differences permeate throughout the steps of the research process and ultimately lead to different criteria for assessing the quality of research studies. Therefore, to be able to understand current research you need to be able to read, understand, and evaluate research studies using these two different approaches. Let's start by considering how you can identify reports of studies that used each of the approaches.

How Do You Identify Quantitative and Qualitative Research Studies?

Recall from Chapter 1 that research is a process of steps that researchers use to collect and analyze information to increase our knowledge about a topic or issue. Although all types of research studies that you read can fit this definition, different approaches for conducting research studies have developed over time. These different approaches tend to include different types of procedures for collecting and analyzing data because they aim to generate different types of knowledge. You will learn about several different specific types of research in later chapters of this book, but for now it is helpful to consider three overall approaches to research that you may find as you read reports: quantitative research, qualitative research, and combined research.

Quantitative Research Studies Emphasize Numeric Data and Statistical Analyses to Explain Variables

In many research reports that you read, you will notice that the researchers wanted to learn about several specific concepts (often called variables or factors), gathered data in the form of numbers, and analyzed those numbers using mathematical procedures such as statistics. In this situation, you are reading a report of a quantitative research study. **Quantitative research** is a type of research in which the researcher studies a problem that calls for an explanation about variables; decides what to study; asks specific, narrow questions; collects quantifiable data from participants; analyzes these numbers using statistics and graphs; and conducts the inquiry in an unbiased, objective manner.

When you read a report of a quantitative research study, you may find that the researchers referred to the study as *quantitative*, but often they will not use that specific word. In Chapter 6, you will learn about several specific quantitative approaches that use words such as *experiment, correlation,* and *survey.* Other good signal words frequently found in quantitative reports include words that indicate numeric data, such as *variables, factors, measures,* and *survey instruments,* and words that indicate mathematical analysis, such as *statistics, differences, comparisons,* and *associations.* You will learn more about the meaning of these words and the details of quantitative research in this chapter and throughout this book.

Reread the abstract from the start of the physical-activity-in-middle-schools study found in the upper half of Figure 2.1. As you read it again, pay close attention to words and ideas that convey the researchers' use of a quantitative approach. Several of the signal words are underlined in the figure. These signal words include *factors, questionnaire survey, statistically significant,* and *associations.* Taken together, these words convey that Xu and her colleagues conducted a quantitative research study because they were focused on explaining whether several factors (or variables) were related to each other, gathered numeric data using a questionnaire survey, and analyzed the data using statistics to determine significant associations among the measured factors.

Qualitative Research Studies Emphasize Text Data and Thematic Analyses to Explore a Phenomenon

Not all research studies focus on explaining variables, gathering numeric data, or using statistics. In many research reports, you find that the researchers wanted to explore individuals' experiences and perspectives for a single concept (often called a phenomenon), gathered data in the form of words, and analyzed those words using text analysis procedures such as thematic analysis to uncover themes found in the data. In this situation, you are reading a report of a qualitative research study. **Qualitative research** is a type of research in which the researcher studies a problem that calls for an exploration of a phenomenon; relies on the views of participants; asks broad, general questions; collects data consisting largely of words (or text) from participants; describes and analyzes these words for themes; and conducts the inquiry in a subjective and reflexive manner.

Research Study Abstract

Words signaling the use of a quantitative approach

School-based physical activity (PA) interventions impact children's PA involvement and thus opportunities and associated <u>factors</u> for the promotion of physical activity in children need to be examined. The purpose of this study was to examine physical education teachers' perceptions of PA opportunities available to students at the middle school level and indicate associated <u>factors</u> that might influence these opportunities. A <u>questionnaire survey</u> was administered to 292 public middle school teachers in 181 schools located in the southeastern region of the United States. The results of the study indicate the need for more PA opportunities for middle school children in order for them meeting the recommended daily PA involvement of 60 minutes. In addition, there were <u>statistically significant associations</u> between PA opportunities and facilities availability, school location, and family support, indicating that some social and environmental factors tend to impact students' PA opportunities. (Xu et al., 2010, p. 183)

Words signaling the use of a qualitative approach

In London, Ontario, approximately 45 percent of preschoolers are insufficiently active. With the large number of preschoolers who attend childcare (54%), and the low levels of physical activity among preschool-aged children, daycare centers may be an appropriate avenue to intervene. This study sought to collect childcare providers' suggestions for improving physical activity during daycare hours and their <u>perspectives</u> regarding the feasibility of meeting the physical activity guidelines currently set out for preschoolers. This <u>qualitative study</u> targeted a heterogeneous sample of childcare providers (n = 54) working at YMCA daycare centers in London, Ontario. Eight <u>focus groups</u> were conducted. Saturation was reached by the fifth focus group; however, three additional focus groups were completed to confirm that the researchers continued hearing the same responses. Focus groups were audio-recorded and transcribed verbatim. <u>Inductive content analysis</u> was used to code and categorize emerging <u>themes</u>. Strategies were incorporated to ensure data trustworthiness. Childcare providers believed the children in their care were quite active and when asked what would be required to increase the physical activity participation among the preschoolers in their care, participants discussed: staff training/workshops; guest physical activity instructors; additional equipment and resources; and increased funds for physical activity. The majority of focus group participants also felt it was feasible for the preschoolers in their care to meet or exceed the preschooler physical activity guidelines. Developing programs and resources that are informed by childcare providers may be an effective way to target sedentary behaviors among the preschool-aged population. Accordingly, childcare providers' suggestions of how to maximize the opportunities for physical activity during daycare hours should be considered when developing and revising childcare curriculum, resources and policies. (Tucker et al., 2011, p. 207)

FIGURE 2.1 **Examples of Abstracts from a Quantitative Research Study and a Qualitative Research Study**

When you read a report of a qualitative research study, you often find that the researchers referred to their study and/or data as *qualitative*. Several other words also indicate the use of a qualitative research approach. In Chapter 9, you will learn about several specific qualitative approaches that use words such as *narrative, case study, ethnography,* and *grounded theory.* Other good signal words frequently found in qualitative reports include words that indicate narrative (or text-based) data, such as *one-on-one interview, focus group interview, transcription,* and *observation field notes,* and words that indicate textual analysis, such as *themes, content analysis,* and *description.* You will learn more about the meaning of these words and the details of qualitative research in this chapter and throughout this book.

Reread the abstract from the start of the physical-activity-at-daycare study found in the lower half of Figure 2.1. As you read it again, pay close attention to words and ideas that convey the researchers' use of a qualitative approach. Several of the signal words are underlined in the figure. These signal words include *perspectives, qualitative study, focus groups, content analysis,* and *themes.* Taken together, these words indicate that Tucker and her colleagues conducted a qualitative research study because they were focused on exploring childcare providers' perspectives, gathered text data using focus group interviews, and analyzed the data using content analysis to develop themes about the perspectives.

Combined Research Studies Include Both Quantitative and Qualitative Research to Understand a Topic

Although most published research can be usefully classified as either quantitative or qualitative, you will find reports of studies where the researchers chose to combine these two approaches in a single study. In these combined studies, the researchers are interested in both explaining variables *and* exploring a phenomenon. To do this, they use both quantitative and qualitative research to gather data in the form of numbers and words and use statistical and thematic analyses. **Combined research** is a type of research in which the researcher studies a problem that calls for explanation and exploration; asks narrow, specific questions and broad, general questions; collects data consisting of numbers and words; analyzes these data for statistical trends and themes; and combines the two sets of results into an overall understanding of the topic.

When you read a report of a combined research study, you often find that the researchers use the terms *quantitative* and *qualitative* in combination. In Chapters 12 and 13, we will learn about two approaches that combine quantitative and qualitative research called *mixed methods research* and *action research*. Other good signal words frequently found in combined research reports include *integration, combination,* and *multiple methods*. In this chapter, we will focus on understanding the two different approaches—quantitative and qualitative. You will learn more about how researchers combine these approaches in the later chapters.

Why Should You Read Both Quantitative and Qualitative Research Studies?

It is common for researchers and consumers of research to have a personal preference for one type of research over the other. On the one hand, you might be a person who is drawn to reports with "hard numbers" and "objective statistical results," and therefore have a preference for reading quantitative research studies. On the other hand, you might be a person who is drawn to reports with "individuals' stories" and "personal interpretations and description," and therefore have a preference for reading qualitative research studies. There are also some individuals who are most drawn to reports that combine both of these perspectives. Although you may prefer to read reports of one particular approach, as a consumer of research who needs to learn all about important topics, you need to become willing and able to read and understand study reports that use quantitative research *and* those that use qualitative research. This is because each type of study approach can contribute new knowledge about a topic; they just go about it in different ways and develop different types of knowledge.

> **Here's a Tip!**
>
> A useful rule of thumb to determine a study's approach is to examine how the researchers analyzed the data and reported the results. If the researcher used statistics and reported the results as numbers, then the study is probably quantitative. If the researcher analyzed the meaning of text data and reported the results as themes or categories using words, then the study is probably qualitative.

You should read reports of quantitative research to learn new knowledge about specific concepts (or variables) as measured within large groups of individuals or organizations. For example, quantitative research reports contribute new knowledge about the prevalence of a specific event, such as how often children go hungry in a community, or about what is typical, such as the average level of support for a new law being considered in an election. Quantitative research reports are also able to provide evidence about how specific concepts relate to each other, such as determining whether there is a relationship between the level of poverty in a district and the performance of the district's schools in one state, or determining whether men and women differ in terms of their beliefs about the value of preventive medicine in one clinic. When researchers use specialized procedures in their quantitative research studies, they may be able to go beyond simply finding that concepts are related. For example, some quantitative studies are able to claim that one particular variable causes an effect in other variables, such as being able to claim that a new intervention program for preschoolers causes improved outcomes in terms of school readiness. Other quantitative studies are able to claim that the studies' results apply to a larger group such as all parents or all patients. Therefore, you should read quantitative research reports to learn new knowledge about what is prevalent, what is typical, what concepts are related, and whether an intervention causes desired outcomes. In the quantitative physical-activity-in-middle-schools study by Xu et al. (2010), for example, you learned about the typical prevalence of physical activities in middle schools and the factors that are related to the level of physical activity opportunities available at a large number of middle schools.

Although it is very useful to have knowledge about overall trends, typical responses, and how specific concepts are related, that often is not sufficient for addressing the complex problems of interest to all of us as professionals. We also need knowledge about individual experiences in addition to overall trends, unique or unusual responses in addition to the typical, and why concepts are related, not just that they are related. Researchers conduct qualitative research studies in order to explore important topics to learn about the perspectives and experiences of a few individuals. You should read reports of qualitative research to learn new knowledge about the complexity and meaning of phenomena as experienced by individuals. Qualitative research reports contribute new knowledge about the meaning of a phenomenon, such as what it means to be bullied as a teenage girl or what it means to survive a violent event. Qualitative research reports are able to provide in-depth, detailed descriptions of phenomena, such as what happens in a program for new teenage mothers or how a process of caring for a spouse with Alzheimer's disease unfolds. Qualitative research reports can also uncover the unexpected, such as reasons why patients do not complete an effective program or contexts that influence how parents engage with their assigned caseworker. Although qualitative studies typically do not apply to a large number of participants, they do provide useful insights into the multiple perspectives, experiences, and contexts that occur in individuals' lives. Therefore, you should read qualitative research reports to learn new knowledge about the meaning, complexity, and uniqueness of phenomena. In the qualitative physical-activity-at-daycare study by Tucker et al. (2011), for example, you learned the different perspectives about, contexts for, and suggestions of improvements for physical activity in daycares as experienced by daycare providers.

Throughout this book, you will learn how to understand and evaluate the key elements of research studies that used quantitative and qualitative research approaches. To start developing this knowledge, let's begin by considering the major differences you can expect to find as you read about how researchers implemented each of the steps of the research process within quantitative and qualitative research reports.

What are the Key Differences in the Steps of the Research Process in Quantitative and Qualitative Studies?

To understand the important differences found in quantitative and qualitative research reports, it is necessary to first learn how researchers go about conducting their studies when they use these two approaches. Using Figure 2.2 as a guide, we will examine how researchers implement the steps of the research process when conducting quantitative studies and qualitative studies. This is one of the most important figures in this book because it summarizes the key ideas that you will be learning across the chapters. This figure relates the quantitative and qualitative approaches to the eight steps of the research process. We will revisit this figure at several points throughout the book so do not worry if you do not understand all the details from this first introduction. This figure provides you with a summary of the key differences between quantitative and qualitative studies. Notice, however, that Figure 2.2 displays a *continuum* for each step. The end points for each continuum denote the "typical" characteristics found when researchers use a quantitative or qualitative approach in their study. Many studies you read will demonstrate characteristics that consistently fall at the same end point of each continuum, but in some studies you will find that the characteristics fall somewhere along the line between the end points. Although a study may not include all of the "typical" characteristics, quantitative studies are usually characterized by the elements on the left side of the figure and qualitative studies by elements on the right side. Let's examine these characteristics in detail for each step.

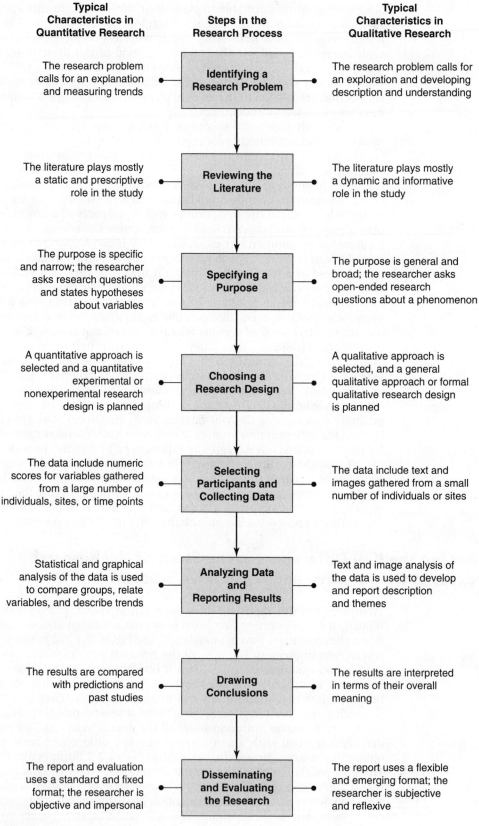

Typical Characteristics in Quantitative Research	Steps in the Research Process	Typical Characteristics in Qualitative Research
The research problem calls for an explanation and measuring trends	**Identifying a Research Problem**	The research problem calls for an exploration and developing description and understanding
The literature plays mostly a static and prescriptive role in the study	**Reviewing the Literature**	The literature plays mostly a dynamic and informative role in the study
The purpose is specific and narrow; the researcher asks research questions and states hypotheses about variables	**Specifying a Purpose**	The purpose is general and broad; the researcher asks open-ended research questions about a phenomenon
A quantitative approach is selected and a quantitative experimental or nonexperimental research design is planned	**Choosing a Research Design**	A qualitative approach is selected, and a general qualitative approach or formal qualitative research design is planned
The data include numeric scores for variables gathered from a large number of individuals, sites, or time points	**Selecting Participants and Collecting Data**	The data include text and images gathered from a small number of individuals or sites
Statistical and graphical analysis of the data is used to compare groups, relate variables, and describe trends	**Analyzing Data and Reporting Results**	Text and image analysis of the data is used to develop and report description and themes
The results are compared with predictions and past studies	**Drawing Conclusions**	The results are interpreted in terms of their overall meaning
The report and evaluation uses a standard and fixed format; the researcher is objective and impersonal	**Disseminating and Evaluating the Research**	The report uses a flexible and emerging format; the researcher is subjective and reflexive

FIGURE 2.2
Characteristics That Are Typical of Quantitative and Qualitative Research for Each Step in the Research Process

Step 1—Researchers Identify a Research Problem

Researchers identify a research problem to limit the subject matter of their study and to argue for the importance of the topic and need for the study. You find information about a study's research problem in the Introduction section of the report.

In **quantitative research,** the research problem tends to call for:

- an explanation of the relationships that exist among variables,
- a measurement of trends in a population.

In **qualitative research,** the research problem tends to call for:

- an exploration because little is known about the problem,
- a detailed description and understanding of a phenomenon.

Identifying a Research Problem in Quantitative Research.   In quantitative research, researchers identify research problems that call for an explanation of the relationships among variables. A research problem might be that schools are not able to get voters to successfully pass bond issues in their local communities and there is a need to explain the variables that predict when bond issues are successful. This problem calls for examining variables such as gender and attitude toward the quality of the schools to identify influences related to how individuals vote on bond issues. Quantitative researchers also identify research problems that call for the researcher to explain the trends in a population. For example, a research problem might be that middle school boys have underdeveloped word knowledge because they do not spend enough time reading and teachers do not know what kind of reading materials will appeal to them. This problem calls for describing the trends in middle school boys' reading preferences, which would help with the development of successful reading programs.

In the quantitative physical-activity-in-middle-schools study, Xu et al. (2010) are concerned about the problem of low levels of physical activity contributing to obesity problems for children and adolescents (see paragraph 01). They argue that schools can be useful settings for promoting the levels of physical activity for youth, but they note that there is a need to know the current trends in physical activity opportunities and a need to know what factors influence the physical activity opportunities that are available (see paragraph 02). That is, the problem in this study calls for measuring trends and for an explanation of the relationships among variables (i.e., "the school-based physical activity opportunities" and the "factors" that may influence those opportunities).

Identifying a Research Problem in Qualitative Research.   Qualitative research is best suited for research problems that call for the need to explore and learn from participants because important variables are unknown or insufficient for describing a phenomenon. For example, a researcher may be interested in the problem of the difficulty in teaching children who are deaf in distance education courses. Perhaps the literature does not adequately address the use of sign language in such courses. A qualitative research study is needed in order to explore this phenomenon from the perspective of distance education students. Unquestionably, using sign language in such courses is complex. Thus, the research problem requires both an exploration (because we do not know how to teach these children), as well as a description and understanding (because of its complexity) of the process of teaching and learning.

In the qualitative physical-activity-at-daycare study, you see the need for both exploration and understanding. In this qualitative study, Tucker et al. (2011) are concerned with the problem of childhood obesity that occurs because of inadequate levels of physical activity (see paragraph 01). They note in paragraph 04 that little is known about promoting the physical activity of young children in the daycare environment, and that we do not understand the current practices occurring in daycares or daycare providers' perspectives about activities that promote physical activity levels. Therefore, the problem in this study calls for an exploration and developing understanding.

Step 2—Researchers Review the Literature

Researchers review literature (e.g., journal articles and books) to ensure that their studies build on what is already known about a topic and will add to this understanding. You find information about a study's literature review as part of the Introduction section or in its own stand-alone introductory section.

In **quantitative research,** the literature review tends to:

- remain static, being reviewed mostly at the start of the study's research process,
- be used to prescribe the direction (i.e., the purpose statement, research questions, hypotheses) of the study.

In **qualitative research,** the literature review tends to:

- be dynamic, being reviewed at the start of the study and as new ideas emerge throughout the study's research process,
- inform the researcher's perspective, but not prescribe the direction of and the study.

Reviewing the Literature in Quantitative Research.   In quantitative research, you typically find that the researchers include a substantial literature review that they examined early in the research process. This literature plays an important role in quantitative studies in two ways: Researchers use it to justify the importance for the research problem and to suggest the specific direction for the purpose and research questions for the study. Justifying the research problem means that researchers use the literature to document the importance of the issue examined and the need for a study about it. The literature also directs the purpose statement, research questions, and hypotheses. Researchers identify key variables and the relationships expected among them from the literature, and use these variables and expected relationships to provide direction for their studies. A literature review on college students, for example, may show that we know little about the problem of "binge drinking." Existing literature, however, may identify the importance of peer groups and styles of interacting among student peer groups. Thus, a researcher might use this literature to direct a study's research questions about how peers and their interaction styles influence binge drinking on college campuses. In this way, the literature in a quantitative study both documents the need to study the problem and prescribes the direction for the research questions.

In the quantitative physical-activity-in-middle-schools study, Xu et al. (2010) cite literature at the beginning of the article in the section titled "Introduction." These authors use the literature in the first paragraph to document the problem of childhood obesity and the link between levels of physical activity and obesity. With this problem justified, they then provide a brief literature review in paragraph 02 where they discuss what is and is not known about intervention programs that promote youth physical activity within schools. In paragraph 03, they use the literature to identify a theory—the Social Ecological Model—that they used to provide direction for the social and environmental factors that they planned to measure to determine whether they are related to physical activity opportunities in middle schools. In this way, Xu et al. establish the research that has been reported in the literature on promoting physical activity in schools and foreshadow the research questions that will be addressed in the study.

Reviewing the Literature in Qualitative Research.   In qualitative research, the literature review included in the beginning of the study varies from substantial to minimal. Researchers using qualitative research usually review the literature to justify the need to study the research problem. In addition, their approach may be informed by what they have learned, but they do not use the literature to direct the research questions. This is because qualitative research relies more on the views of participants in the study and less on the direction identified in the literature. Thus, for a researcher to use the literature to prescribe a specific direction for the study is inconsistent with the qualitative approach of learning from participants. For example, one qualitative researcher who studied bullying in schools cited several studies at the beginning of the research to provide evidence for the problem, but did not use the literature to specify variables or narrow research questions.

Instead, this researcher set out to learn how students constructed their view of this experience. Although researchers often do not include extensive literature at the start of their qualitative study, they often return to the literature during the study as new ideas emerge from the data collection and analysis. For example, in a qualitative study of bullying, a finding of students feeling isolated may emerge, which causes the researchers to return to the literature to learn about past studies on youth isolation. In this way, the use of literature in qualitative studies is often more dynamic than in quantitative studies.

The literature plays more of an informative and dynamic role in the qualitative physical-activity-at-daycare study. As done by Xu et al. (2010), Tucker et al. (2011) incorporate their literature review within the report's "Introduction." Unlike the quantitative physical-activity-in-middle-schools study, however, this literature does not direct specific research questions. Instead, these sections inform the researchers about the problem of inadequate physical activity for children attending daycare and highlight the importance of learning the perspectives of daycare providers (see paragraphs 02–04). Turning to the end of the study, you find that the authors included additional literature on topics that emerged from the findings of the study (such as the role of the weather and differences among children discussed in paragraph 26). Therefore, although this study includes literature, it is used to justify the research problem and does not lead to the specific questions asked in the study. Thus, the literature is playing more of an informative and dynamic role in this study.

Step 3—Researchers Specify a Purpose

Researchers specify a purpose for their research by identifying the major intent and focus of the study, and narrowing the intent into specific questions or hypotheses. You can usually find a study's purpose statement, research questions, and hypotheses at the end of the Introduction section.

In **quantitative research,** the purpose statement, research questions, and hypotheses tend to:	In **qualitative research,** the purpose statement and research questions tend to:
<ul><li>be specific and narrow,</li><li>focus on measurable, observable variables.</li></ul>	<ul><li>be general and broad,</li><li>focus on participants' perspectives about a phenomenon.</li></ul>

Specifying a Purpose in Quantitative Research. In quantitative research, researchers specify a specific, narrow purpose to learn about several variables that can be measured or observed. The major statements that provide the direction for a quantitative study—the purpose statement, research questions, and hypotheses—are specific and narrow because quantitative researchers identify a set of predetermined variables as the focus for the study. In addition to identifying the variables when specifying a study's purpose, researchers also indicate their overall intent, such as to describe trends for or measure relationships among these variables. For example, in a study of marriage satisfaction, the researcher might narrow the study to a set of specific variables such as number of years married, number of children, employment status, and time spent together during the week, and state an intent to learn how these variables are related to individuals' reports of their marriage satisfaction.

In the quantitative physical-activity-in-middle-schools study, Xu et al. (2010) narrow their focus by selecting a few factors that they predict might be related to the physical activity opportunities available in middle schools. They state their purpose of the study at the start of paragraph 03 and focus on their specific research aims at the end of that paragraph. They say that they will examine social and environmental factors that might interact with the available physical activity opportunities. Thus, their research questions are specific to certain variables, and later in the Method section, they explain how they will measure the different variables (paragraph 07).

Specifying a Purpose in Qualitative Research. In qualitative research, researchers specify a purpose that is much more open ended than in quantitative research. Qualitative researchers state general, broad questions so that they can explore a topic and learn from participants' perspectives and experiences. The focus of a qualitative study is usually a single phenomenon of interest (as opposed to several variables in quantitative research). Researchers state this phenomenon and their intent to explore it in a purpose statement. A qualitative study that examines the "professionalism" of nurses, for example, will seek to learn from nurses, "What does it mean to be a professional?" This research question focuses on understanding a single idea—being a professional—and calls for talking to nurses to learn about their experiences and perspectives. To explore one phenomenon is at a different end of the research continuum from measuring the trends or relationships for a set of variables (see Figure 2.2).

In the qualitative physical-activity-at-daycare study, Tucker et al. (2011) end the Introduction section of their study by stating their intention to explore daycare providers' perspectives about physical activity practices for preschoolers (see paragraph 04). They narrowed this purpose to two questions focused on daycare providers' insights and suggestions about preschoolers' physical activity levels within daycare settings. That is, they wanted to learn from the perspectives of the participants and not be limited to a specific set of variables.

What Do You Think?

The following excerpts are from two studies' abstracts. Read each excerpt while considering the differences between quantitative and qualitative research for the steps of identifying a research problem, reviewing the literature, and specifying a purpose. For each excerpt, determine whether it appears to be from a quantitative study or a qualitative study and provide your evidence for your determination.

a. "Divorce is a personal experience, often negative, and each couple experiences it differently. However, the divorce experience may provide opportunities for personal growth. The purpose of [this study] was to understand the challenges and growth opportunities women who have divorced experience from their own perspective" (Thomas & Ryan, 2008, p. 210).

b. "School violence and weapons at school are a major concern for community members, school administrators, and policy makers. This research examines both student-level and school-level variables that predict middle school students' willingness to report a weapon at school under several reporting conditions" (Wylie et al., 2010, p. 351).

Check Your Understanding

a. From the information provided in excerpt (a), we can conclude that Thomas and Ryan's (2008) study about the experiences of women who have divorced is an example of qualitative research. The problem calls for the need to understand the complexity of women's experience of divorce, and the purpose is to explore these experiences from the perspectives of individuals. The intent to explore individuals' experiences with a phenomenon is typical in qualitative research.

b. From the information provided in excerpt (b), we can conclude that Wylie et al.'s (2010) study about violence and weapons at schools is an example of quantitative research. The problem calls for explaining and measuring variables, and the purpose is to examine which school-level and student-level variables predict (or are related to) students' willingness to report a weapon at school. The intent to explain how several variables are related is typical in quantitative research.

Step 4—Researchers Choose a Research Design

Once researchers have stated their study's purpose, they select an overall approach and research design that is suited to address the purpose. The research design provides a blueprint or plan for how researchers collect, analyze, and report their data in a study. You can expect to find information about the overall approach and research design for a study in the Method section of an article.

In **quantitative research,** the overall approach tends to consist of:

- choosing an experimental or nonexperimental quantitative research design.

In **qualitative research,** the overall approach tends to consist of:

- choosing a general qualitative approach or a formal qualitative research design.

Choosing a Research Design in Quantitative Research.   Researchers choose to use a quantitative approach for their research study when their problem calls for explanation, the literature provides a specific direction, and the purpose requires measurable data for several variables. Researchers select a specific quantitative research design for their quantitative approach based on the intent of their study. We will learn more about these designs in Chapter 6, but the two major types of quantitative research designs are experimental designs and nonexperimental designs. Researchers choose a type of experimental design when they want to explain the impact of an intervention (like a new curriculum) and test whether it causes an outcome (such as better reading performance). Researchers choose a type of nonexperimental design when they want to describe something about variables without applying an intervention. For example, researchers plan a correlational design to explain how variables are related to each other or a survey design to describe the trends in attitudes or behaviors of a group.

In the quantitative physical-activity-in-middle-schools study, Xu et al. (2010) wanted to examine whether the specified social and environmental factors predict (or are related to) physical activity opportunities available at schools. Therefore, they designed their study using a quantitative correlational design. This quantitative design is so common that the authors did not state the name in the study, but in Chapter 6 you will learn that words such as *related to, prediction,* and *regression analyses* (see paragraphs 04 and 08) are hallmarks of this quantitative design.

Choosing a Research Design in Qualitative Research.   As in quantitative research, qualitative researchers generally select an overall approach and research design to plan how they will conduct their study. You will learn more about these qualitative designs in Chapter 9. In many studies, researchers use what we call a general qualitative approach to gather data from participants and analyze the data for themes. In other qualitative studies, the researchers choose a more formal qualitative design such as a narrative, ethnographic, case study, or grounded theory design. An example of a qualitative research design is an ethnographic design, which a researcher chooses to understand the shared culture of a group. Researchers could also choose a grounded theory design if they want to explore individuals' experiences to develop a theory.

In the qualitative physical-activity-at-daycare study, Tucker et al. (2011) identify the general approach of their study as "a qualitative study" in the abstract. In the Method section they emphasize the use of focus group interviews and thematic analysis. The use of a general qualitative approach with focus groups is well suited for studies interested in describing the multiple perspectives that individuals' hold about a topic, such as physical activity practices in daycares.

Step 5—Researchers Select Participants and Collect Data

Researchers select participants and gather data in order to address their study's purpose and research questions. Although the selected approach and research design provide an overall plan for the study, the researchers still have to implement specific procedures, including identifying participants, obtaining their permission to study them, and collecting information from them that will be useful for answering the research questions. These procedures are reported in the Method section of an article.

In **quantitative research,** the participant selection and data collection tends to consist of:	In **qualitative research,** the participant selection and data collection tends to consist of:
■ collecting information from a large number of individuals, sites, or time points,	■ collecting information from a small number of individuals or sites,
■ collecting data using instruments with preset questions and responses,	■ collecting data using forms with general, emerging questions to permit the participant to generate responses,
■ gathering quantifiable (numeric) data.	■ gathering word (text) or image (picture) data.

Selecting Participants and Collecting Data in Quantitative Research.   In quantitative research, the intent is often to answer questions about what is typical for a large group or across time. Therefore, researchers often select a large number of individuals (or organizations) to participate in the study so the results will be more likely to represent the larger group. The more individuals studied, the stronger is the case for applying the results to a large number of people (called *generalizing* the results). Quantitative studies often include dozens, hundreds, or even thousands of participants, depending on the study's purpose. Researchers use instruments to measure the variables of interest from all of these participants. An instrument is a tool for recording data in the form of quantitative numbers or scores. It contains specific questions and response possibilities that the researcher establishes in advance of the study so all participants use the same response options. Examples of instruments are survey questionnaires (such as a survey about people's attitudes toward food stamp policies), checklists that can be used to observe an individual's behaviors (such as a checklist for recording a student's time on task in a classroom), and standardized tests (such as a license exam for counselors). In quantitative research, researchers administer instruments such as these to participants in order to collect data in the form of numbers for each variable of interest.

Participant selection and data collection is an integral part of the quantitative physical-activity-in-middle-schools study. As discussed in paragraph 05, Xu et al. (2010) studied a large number of physical education teachers (i.e., 292 teachers who participated by responding to the survey) from a region of the United States. They surveyed these teachers using an adaptation of a questionnaire instrument developed and used previously by other researchers (paragraph 07). The survey included 53 items that measured physical activity opportunities and social environmental factors (paragraph 07 and Table 1). The authors also discuss how the responses to the items are scored from a minimum of 1 to a maximum of 4.

Selecting Participants and Collecting Data in Qualitative Research.   In qualitative research, researchers focus on gathering data from a few participants to develop an in-depth exploration of the study's topic. The participants in a qualitative study are usually selected intentionally because they are individuals who can best help the researchers learn about the phenomenon of interest in the study. Researchers generally focus on a small number of participants (from 1 to several to maybe dozens) in qualitative research in order to thoroughly learn about their experiences and perspectives. Qualitative researchers do not begin data collection with a preestablished instrument to measure scores for distinct variables. Instead, qualitative researchers gather text (word) or image (picture) data. Researchers develop forms, called protocols, for recording data as the study unfolds. These forms pose a few open-ended questions so that the participants can provide their own answers to the questions. Often questions on these forms will change and emerge during data collection as the researchers learn from participants. Examples of these forms include an interview protocol, which consists of four or five questions, and an observational protocol, in which the researcher records notes describing the behavior of participants. The qualitative data gathered from these protocols might include a typed transcription of the audio recordings from interviews or notes that a researcher recorded while observing participants in their work setting.

In the qualitative physical-activity-at-daycare study, Tucker et al. (2011) collect data from 54 individuals who work as childcare providers (paragraph 05). This number is larger than found in many qualitative studies because the researchers chose to gather data using focus group interviews. In focus group interviews, several participants are interviewed at the same time so the researchers can learn from the conversations that occur among participants in addition to the conversation between the researcher and the participants. Tucker and colleagues gathered a total of eight of these group interviews, each of which lasted one hour or longer. Although the researchers did not describe the development of the interview protocol used during the focus group interviews, they note in paragraph 06 that an experienced moderator conducted the interviews and asked the participants follow-up questions to ensure that he/she correctly understood the participants' perspectives.

What Do You Think?

The following excerpts are from two studies' abstracts. Read each excerpt while considering the differences between quantitative and qualitative research for the steps of choosing a research design and selecting participants and collecting data. For each excerpt, determine whether it appears to be from a quantitative study or a qualitative study, and provide your evidence for your determination.

a. "This research investigated the effect of a three-week school based nutrition education program on the nutrition knowledge and healthy food choices of 187 fifth graders who were randomly divided into a control ($n = 97$) or an experimental ($n = 90$) group. The control group received no nutrition education while the experimental group received 45 minutes of nutrition education, 4 days a week for 3 weeks. Nutrition knowledge scores and 3-day food records were collected at the beginning of the study and after 3 weeks" (Kandiah & Jones, 2002, p. 269).

b. "A [multiple case] study is described which explored the experiences of four families each of which contained a young person who had suffered with anorexia nervosa. . . . Individual interviews were conducted with the young person with anorexia, a key sibling, both parents, and a joint family interview was also conducted" (Dallos & Denford, 2008, p. 305).

Check Your Understanding

a. From the information provided in excerpt (a), we can conclude that Kandiah and Jones' (2002) study about children's nutrition knowledge base is an example of quantitative research. The researchers used a quantitative experimental design where they gave a special nutrition education program to children in an "experimental" group and no program to children in a "control" group. They included a large number of participants (97 + 90 = 187) and gathered data in the form of scores for the variables of interest (e.g., nutrition knowledge).

b. From the information provided in excerpt (b), we can conclude that Dallos and Denford's (2008) study about families with an eating disorder is an example of qualitative research. The researchers used a qualitative case study design where they described what was happening within each participating family. They included a small number of participants (4 families) and gathered data in the form of individual and joint family interviews.

Step 6—Researchers Analyze Data and Report Results

Researchers analyze the data that they collect and report the results of the analysis. These results summarize what the researchers found and provide answers to the study's research questions. Although the data analysis procedures may be discussed in the Method section, you will find a study's results described in the Results section of the article.

In **quantitative research,** data analysis and results tend to:

- consist of statistical and graphical analysis procedures,
- compare groups, relate variables, and describe trends.

In **qualitative research,** data analysis and results tend to:

- consist of text and image analysis procedures,
- develop description and themes.

Analyzing Data and Reporting Results in Quantitative Research. In quantitative research, researchers analyze the data using mathematical procedures, including calculating statistics and plotting graphs. These analyses consist of breaking down the data into parts to answer the research questions. All quantitative studies describe trends in the data, such as the average response to an item across all participants or a graph of how the scores for a variable change over time. In addition, most quantitative studies also include statistical procedures, such as comparing scores between groups or relating scores for individuals. These procedures produce statistical results that provide information that addresses the study's research questions and hypotheses. Researchers often report their statistical results in the form of tables and figures that summarize the results of many statistical calculations.

In the quantitative physical-activity-in-middle-schools study, Xu et al. (2010) provide an overview of their analysis procedures in the Method section (see paragraphs 08–09). As discussed in paragraph 08, they use a statistical procedure called principal component analysis to help them group the questions from the survey questionnaire into useful scales (or factors) for the analysis. They also use the statistical procedure of regression analysis to determine which of the social and environmental factors best explain the variation in scores for teachers' perceptions of physical activity opportunities. The results of these different analyses are reported in the Results section of the report (paragraphs 10–13). In Tables 2 and 3, we find descriptive information about the major variables (physical activity opportunities) and the participating teachers' schools. From Tables 4–7, we see which variables best explain the variation for the measures of physical activity opportunities (e.g., hours of extracurricular physical activity, duration of physical education class). For example, in Table 7, the results indicate that *family support* is the factor that is most associated with the *hours of extracurricular physical activity (HPA).* In short, the authors report results from three phases of statistical analysis—analysis of the instrument, descriptive analysis of the variables and participants, and regression analysis. The ultimate goal was to determine which of the predictors (the social and environmental factors) best explain physical activity opportunities available in the schools.

Analyzing Data and Reporting Results in Qualitative Research. Qualitative researchers use a different approach for data analysis because the data in qualitative studies consist of words and pictures, not numbers. Rather than using statistics, the researchers analyze the gathered words and pictures to describe the central phenomenon under study. When analyzing a qualitative database, the researchers divide the text (or pictures) into segments (e.g., groups of sentences) and interpret the meaning of each segment. From the many segments, they describe the phenomenon and identify patterns in the data that highlight different perspectives about the phenomenon. The findings may be a detailed description of individual people or places. The findings may also include themes or broad categories that represent the major ideas that the researchers found in the data. In qualitative studies in which researchers both describe individuals and identify themes, a rich, complex picture emerges of the phenomenon being explored.

Tucker et al. (2011) use text analysis procedures to analyze the collected data in the qualitative physical-activity-at-daycare study. The collected data consist of the words spoken during the focus group interviews turned into typed transcripts (see paragraph 07). From these data, the authors use a text analysis procedure called "inductive content analysis" to identify themes and patterns in the data (see paragraph 07). They then report the findings from this thematic analysis in the Results section (paragraphs 08–23). They start the Results section with a description of the current activity levels occurring in the daycares as described by the participating daycare providers (including some counting of the participants' perspectives in Table 2). After the description, the authors report five themes that emerged from the conversations about the participants' suggestions for improving these activity levels. These themes included enhanced staff training/workshops (paragraph 12) and guest physical activity instructors (paragraph 13). Within each theme, the authors included actual participant words in quotes to convey how participants think and talk about the topic.

Step 7—Researchers Draw Conclusions

After reporting the results of the data analysis, researchers draw conclusions about the results and the overall study. These conclusions and implications are discussed within the Conclusion section of an article.

In **quantitative research,** the conclusions tend to emphasize:

- comparisons of results with prior predictions and past studies.

In **qualitative research,** the conclusions tend to emphasize:

- statements about the larger meaning of the findings and personal reflections about the findings.

Drawing Conclusions in Quantitative Research. In quantitative research, researchers interpret the results of the statistical analyses in light of initial predictions and prior studies on the topic. This interpretation offers the researchers' explanation as to why the results turned out the way they did, and researchers discuss how the results either support or refute the expected predictions. Researchers also consider how well the study's research process worked and discuss any limitations that occurred in their data collection and analysis procedures. Examples of common limitations discussed in the conclusions of quantitative studies include the researcher not selecting a large enough sample, instruments not producing the most accurate scores for measuring a variable of interest, or events that could not be controlled by the researcher introducing some bias into the study.

In the quantitative physical-activity-in-middle-schools study, Xu et al. (2010) conclude their study with two sections: "Discussion" and "Conclusion and Recommendations." In these sections, they discuss the main results of the study and compare their results with those found in other studies in the literature (paragraphs 14–17). They then offer their evaluation of the study in a subsection titled, "Limitations of Study" (paragraph 18). They describe three ways that their study was limited, such as by selecting participants who were convenient. They end their Conclusion section by suggesting the implications of the results for individuals who want to develop intervention programs and for other researchers who may want to conduct further research on this topic (paragraphs 19–20).

Drawing Conclusions in Qualitative Research. After developing a complex picture of the phenomenon under study through a text analysis, qualitative researchers make an interpretation of the meaning of the findings in their Conclusion sections. They may reflect on how the findings relate to existing research or draw out larger, more abstract meanings from the findings. Researchers may also state a personal reflection about the significance of the lessons learned during the study or discuss how their experiences and cultural backgrounds affect the interpretations and conclusions drawn. This is an example of qualitative researchers discussing their own role or position in a research study, called being reflexive (*reflexivity* means that the researchers reflect on their own biases, values, and assumptions, and actively write them into their research). This reflexivity may also involve discussing personal experiences and identifying how researchers collaborated with participants during phases of the project.

In the qualitative physical-activity-at-daycare study, Tucker et al. (2011) interpret and discuss the findings that they believe are most important from the study's results (paragraphs 24–29), and suggest the larger meaning of the findings for providing physical activity in daycare settings. Unlike many qualitative studies, these authors do not explicitly describe their personal reflections about the study's findings, but by selecting the results to discuss and noting what they feel is important to highlight, we get a sense of how their personal interpretations were involved. The authors conclude the article by suggesting implications of the research for practice and future research (paragraphs 30–32).

Step 8—Researchers Disseminate and Evaluate the Research

The entire research process culminates in a report that is disseminated to audiences who may benefit from what the researchers learned during the study. Different audiences also evaluate the research process as described within the research report.

In **quantitative research,** the research reports tend to:

- use standard, fixed structures and evaluative criteria,
- be written with an objective and impersonal approach.

In **qualitative research,** the research reports tend to:

- use flexible, emerging structures and evaluative criteria,
- be written with a subjective and reflexive approach.

Disseminating and Evaluating the Research in Quantitative Research.   Quantitative researchers typically report their research studies without referring to themselves or their personal reactions. The overall format for a report of a quantitative study follows a predictable pattern: introduction, review of the literature, methods, results, and conclusions. This form creates a standardized structure for quantitative studies. When audiences evaluate research, there are some basic standards that are applied to all forms of research. For example, audiences judge whether the researchers used ethical procedures when conducting the study. By using ethical procedures, researchers treat participants with respect, such as by obtaining their permissions to study them and take all steps possible to minimize the risk of harm to study participants. Audiences also judge whether the prepared article fully and honestly reports complete information about what was done in the study so that readers can make their own assessments about the quality of the study. In addition, audiences use criteria that fit the process of quantitative research when judging the quality of a quantitative research report. For example, researchers examine a quantitative study to see whether it has an extensive literature review; tests good research questions and hypotheses; uses rigorous, impartial data collection procedures; applies appropriate statistical procedures; and forms interpretations that logically follow from the results.

Looking at the quantitative physical-activity-in-middle-schools study as a whole, Xu et al. (2010) subdivide the report into standard sections typically found in quantitative studies. The study introduces the problem, literature review, and purpose statement and research questions (see paragraphs 01–03); describes the methods (see paragraphs 04–09); reports the results (see paragraphs 10–13); and offers conclusions (see paragraphs 14–20). The entire study conveys an impersonal, objective tone. The authors do not bring either their biases or their personal opinions into the study. They use proven instruments to measure variables (see paragraph 07), and they employ multiple statistical procedures (see paragraphs 08–09) to build objectivity into the study.

Disseminating and Evaluating the Research in Qualitative Research.   Qualitative researchers employ a wide range of formats to report their qualitative studies. Although the overall general form follows the standard steps in the process of research, the sequence of these "parts" of research tends to vary from one qualitative report to another. A study may begin with a long, personal narrative told in story form or with a more objective, scientific report that resembles the format found in most quantitative research. With such variability, it is not surprising that the standards for evaluating qualitative research are also flexible. Like quantitative research, audiences judge qualitative research to ensure that the researchers used ethical procedures and fully and honestly reported the details of the study. In addition, good qualitative reports need to be realistic and persuasive in order to convince the reader that the study is an accurate and credible account of individuals' experiences and perspectives. Qualitative reports typically contain extensive data collection to convey the complexity of the phenomenon or process under study. The data analysis procedures incorporate the development of description and themes as well as the interrelation of themes in order to fully capture the complexity of the phenomenon.

Looking at the organization of Tucker et al.'s (2011) qualitative physical-activity-at-daycare study as a whole, we find that it follows a structure and uses headings similar to that of a typical quantitative study. Therefore, this is an example of a qualitative study using a more objective, scientific report structure. Keeping with a more objective style, the authors do not use a personal pronoun of "we" to discuss their role in the study, which is unfortunate because we do not learn about their personal reflections about the study and its results. We do note, however, that it is through the researchers' personal interpretations that themes were identified during the analysis, individual participant quotes were included in the findings, and interpretations were made at the end of the study.

What Do You Think?

The following excerpts are from two studies' abstracts. Read each excerpt while considering the differences between quantitative and qualitative research for the steps of analyzing data and reporting results, drawing conclusions, and disseminating and evaluating the research. For each excerpt, determine whether it appears to be from a quantitative study or a qualitative study, and provide your evidence for your determination.

a. "Consistent with the authors' hypotheses, victimization history was associated with both increased stress and an increased use of avoidant coping strategies. In addition, avoidant coping partially mediated the link between victimization and stress. These findings suggest that avoidant coping may develop as an adaptive response to uncontrollable stress but that, in the long term, these strategies are a maladaptive approach to coping that acts to prolong stress" (Newman, Holden, & Delville, 2011, p. 205).

b. "Thematic analysis revealed three prominent themes: (a) *the free and busy me* highlights the increased freedom in later life enabling choices regarding activities the women would like to engage in; (b) *the secret is being positive and pragmatic* emphasizes the importance of adopting a pragmatic acceptance of growing older; and (c) *narratives of growth and stagnation* highlights the pursuit of growth among older women in order to enhance the current self. Findings emphasize the construction of later life as one of liberation, resilience and growth" (Terrill & Gullifer, 2010, p. 707).

Check Your Understanding

a. From the information provided in excerpt (a), we can conclude that Newman et al.'s (2011) study about coping strategies used when being bullied is an example of quantitative research. The authors objectively describe which variables were found to be associated with each other (e.g., victimization history is associated with increased use of avoidant coping strategies). The authors also draw conclusions about how the results compare to their predictions made in the form of hypotheses.

b. From the information provided in excerpt (b), we can conclude that Terrill and Gullifer's (2010) study about older rural women is an example of qualitative research. The authors note their use of "thematic analysis" and identify three themes that emerged from the analyzed data. The authors also draw conclusions about the larger meaning of the findings as applied to the experiences of older rural women.

How Do You Evaluate Quantitative and Qualitative Studies?

You have now read and examined two studies that were conducted and that reported on the general topic of youth's physical activity within educational settings. Both of these studies illustrated some of the key characteristics of their respective quantitative or qualitative research approach and contributed new knowledge about this important topic. In that sense, you can say that they are both "good" studies that were also relatively straightforward to read. However, both of these studies also used procedures that limit the extent to which you might want to use the results in your own context.

How do a study's procedures limit the conclusions that you should make from a study? For example, the quantitative physical-activity-in-middle-schools study was limited to one particular region of the United States, which may have very different considerations from other areas of the country when it comes to physical activity in middle schools, so we cannot know that the results will be similar elsewhere. This quantitative study also did not include any control procedures to allow the researchers to make causal claims. An example of what this means is that although the study found a relationship between the two variables of *family support* and *hours of extracurricular physical activity,* in the end we do not know if family support causes students to participate in more hours of extracurricular physical activity or if having more hours of extracurricular physical activity causes higher levels of family support. Likewise, there are notable shortcomings in the procedures used in the qualitative physical-activity-at-daycare study that limit the extent to which the study provides an in-depth exploration. For example, by including so many participants in the study, the researchers were unable to obtain detailed information about any one person's perspectives. This qualitative study also did not include an extensive qualitative database, being limited to only focus group interviews and not including additional data forms such as individual interviews or observations of what happens in daycares. Therefore, while the study provided some information into daycare providers' perspectives, in the end we do not fully learn the complexity of these perspectives or the contexts that help to shape them.

As these comments about the two studies demonstrate, learning to understand the information reported in research reports is an important skill to develop for reading research reports; however, simply understanding the information is not sufficient. You also need to *evaluate* the quality of the research you read in order to become a critical consumer of this information. Becoming a critical consumer means that you learn to judge both the strengths *and* the shortcomings of individual studies, and consider these issues when determining the extent to which the results and conclusions of particular studies warrant your attention. As this chapter has emphasized, quantitative research and qualitative research are two different approaches for conducting studies that impact every step in the process of research (refer back to Figure 2.2). These differences mean that you will need to learn to use different standards and criteria when evaluating the quality of research reports, depending on the approach that the researchers used in the study.

The remainder of this book will focus on how you read *and* evaluate each of the steps of the research process as reported in the major sections of research reports, taking into account the different approaches to research. To start you thinking about being a critical consumer of research and not just a reader of research, we provide criteria that are useful for evaluating the major sections of quantitative and qualitative research reports in Tables 2.1 and 2.2. As you read these criteria, keep in mind that they reflect the "end points" of the continua portrayed for the steps in Figure 2.2. This means that many (probably most) of the studies you read will not satisfy all of the criteria's indicators for high quality whether the study used a quantitative or a qualitative approach. This does not mean that all the research you read is "bad," but it does mean that you have to critically consider the limitations of the results that were found in the studies you read. The task ahead of you now is to learn how to understand and evaluate research in this way as discussed throughout the rest of this book.

TABLE 2.1   Criteria for Evaluating the Study in a Quantitative Research Report

	Quality Criteria	Indicators of Higher Quality in Quantitative Research
The Major Sections		
Front Matter	1. The study's authors and journal are reputable.	■ The report is written by scholars from high-quality institutions and published in a high-quality journal so you can have confidence that the study report was evaluated using rigorous standards before it was published. 　■ *Note! You will learn to recognize reputable scholars and journals in your field as you gain more experience reading research. In addition, you will learn more about indicators of quality for journals in Chapter 4.*
Introduction	2. There is a strong argument that the study is needed, is based on existing knowledge, and has an appropriate purpose.	■ The statement of the problem argues that there is a clear need for an explanation about variables and trends. ■ The literature justifies the problem and provides a solid foundation for the specific variables to be examined. ■ The study's purpose is narrow and intends to examine the impact of, relationships among, differences between, or trends for specific variables. 　■ *Note! You will learn more about evaluating a quantitative study's research problem in Chapter 3, literature review in Chapter 4, and purpose in Chapter 5.*
Method	3. The overall design, selection of participants, data collection, and data analysis procedures are rigorous and fit the study's purpose.	■ To address the study's purpose, an experimental or nonexperimental quantitative approach is chosen. ■ Accurate numeric data are gathered for the study's variables from a large number of participants or time points and the data are analyzed using appropriate statistical procedures. ■ The procedures are ethical so that participants are treated with respect and not harmed by the research. 　■ *Note! You will learn more about evaluating a quantitative study's research design in Chapter 6, participants and data collection in Chapter 7, and data analysis in Chapter 8.*
Results	4. Detailed results obtained from the appropriate analysis of the data provide answers to the study's research questions.	■ The results present objective, statistical information about the impact of, relationships among, differences between, and trends for the measured variables. 　■ *Note! You will learn more about evaluating a quantitative study's results in Chapter 8.*
Conclusion	5. Thoughtful interpretations are provided about how the results extend existing knowledge and their limitations and implications.	■ The concluding comments compare the results with predictions and past studies, interpret the limitations in the quantitative procedures, and suggest implications for audiences that clearly follow from the results. 　■ *Note! You will learn more about evaluating a quantitative study's conclusions in Chapter 14.*
Back Matter	6. The supplemental information is complete and supports specific points in the report.	■ The report includes detailed references and information about the study's context. 　■ *Note! You will learn more about evaluating a study's back matter in Chapter 14.*
Overall Evaluation		
The Whole Report	7. The research process is high quality.	■ The steps of the study's research process are logical, coherent, and consistent with the characteristics of a rigorous quantitative approach.

TABLE 2.2   Criteria for Evaluating the Study in a Qualitative Research Report

	Quality Criteria	Indicators of Higher Quality in Qualitative Research
The Major Sections		
Front Matter	1. The study's authors and journal are reputable.	▪ The report is written by scholars from high-quality institutions and published in a high-quality journal so you can have confidence that the study report was evaluated using rigorous standards before it was published. ▪ *Note! You will learn to recognize reputable scholars and journals in your field as you gain more experience reading research. In addition, you will learn more about indicators of quality for journals in Chapter 4.*
Introduction	2. There is a strong argument that the study is needed, is based on existing knowledge, and has an appropriate purpose.	▪ The statement of the problem argues that there is a clear need for an exploration of a phenomenon to develop description and understanding. ▪ The literature justifies the problem and provides a solid foundation that informs the study's approach. ▪ The study's purpose is broad and intends to explore a single phenomenon in its complexity. ▪ *Note! You will learn more about evaluating a qualitative study's research problem in Chapter 3, literature review in Chapter 4, and purpose in Chapter 5.*
Method	3. The overall design, selection of participants, data collection, and data analysis procedures are rigorous and fit the study's purpose.	▪ To address the study's purpose, a general or formal qualitative approach is chosen. ▪ Extensive text or image data are gathered about the study's phenomenon from a small number of participants and the data are analyzed using appropriate text analysis procedures. ▪ The procedures are ethical so that participants are treated with respect and not harmed by the research. ▪ *Note! You will learn more about evaluating a qualitative study's research design in Chapter 9, participants and data collection in Chapter 10, and data analysis in Chapter 11.*
Results	4. Detailed results obtained from the appropriate analysis of the data provide answers to the study's research questions.	▪ The findings present interpretive information in the form of description and themes that convey the multiple perspectives and complexity of the phenomenon. ▪ *Note! You will learn more about evaluating a qualitative study's findings in Chapter 11.*
Conclusion	5. Thoughtful interpretations are provided about how the results extend existing knowledge and their limitations and implications.	▪ The concluding comments interpret the meaning of the findings in terms of past studies and personal experience, interpret the limitations in the qualitative procedures, and suggest implications for audiences that clearly follow from the findings. ▪ *Note! You will learn more about evaluating a qualitative study's conclusions in Chapter 14.*
Back Matter	6. The supplemental information is complete and supports specific points in the report.	▪ The report includes detailed references and information about the study's context. ▪ *Note! You will learn more about evaluating a study's back matter in Chapter 14.*
Overall Evaluation		
The Whole Report	7. The research process is high quality.	▪ The steps of the study's research process are logical, coherent, and consistent with the characteristics of a rigorous qualitative approach.

Here's a Tip!

If you read a study that combines quantitative and qualitative research, then apply both sets of criteria to the study. We will learn about additional criteria that are specific for combined approaches in Chapters 12 and 13.

In Figure 2.3, we provide a rating scale to assist you in applying the quality criteria to the major sections in any quantitative and qualitative research report. Be sure to use the indicators for higher quality for quantitative research when evaluating a quantitative report and the indicators for higher quality for qualitative research when evaluating a qualitative report. For each of the criteria you locate, assign a quality rating from *fair* (1) to *excellent* (3), and document your evidence and/or reasoning behind the rating. If one of the criteria is missing or very poorly stated, then indicate *poor* (0) as your rating. Keep in mind that all research studies have limitations and potential shortcomings, and they vary in the extent of information provided in the report. Nonetheless, you should be able to understand the general flow of a good report and have it score well on most of the items listed in Figure 2.3. By adding up the rating scores for each of the criteria and using the suggested cutoff values provided at the bottom of the figure, you have a quantitative measure to help you determine your overall assessment of a research report.

Quality Criteria	Quality Rating				Your Evidence and/or Reasoning
	0 = Poor	1 = Fair	2 = Good	3 = Excellent	
The Major Sections					
1. **Front Matter:** The study's authors and journal are reputable.					
2. **Introduction:** There is a strong argument that the study is needed, is based on existing knowledge, and has an appropriate purpose.					
3. **Method:** The overall design, selection of participants, data collection, and data analysis are rigorous and fit the study's purpose.					
4. **Results:** Detailed results obtained from the appropriate analysis of the data provide answers to the study's research questions.					
5. **Conclusion:** Thoughtful interpretations are provided about how the results extend existing knowledge and their limitations and implications.					
6. **Back Matter:** The supplemental information is complete and supports specific points in the report.					
Overall Evaluation					
7. The research process is high quality.					
Overall Quality 0–10 = Low quality 11–16 = Adequate quality 17–21 = High quality	**Total Score =**				**My Overall Assessment =**

FIGURE 2.3   A Rating Scale for Evaluating the Study in a Research Report

Reviewing What You've Learned To Do

- *Identify the overall approach used in a research report as quantitative, qualitative, or combined.*
  - Quantitative research is a type of research in which the researcher studies a problem that calls for an explanation about variables; decides what to study; asks specific, narrow questions; collects quantifiable data from participants; analyzes these numbers using statistics and graphs; and conducts the inquiry in an unbiased, objective manner.
  - Qualitative research is a type of research in which the researcher studies a problem that calls for an exploration of a phenomenon; relies on the views of participants; asks broad, general questions; collects data consisting largely of words (or text) from participants; describes and analyzes these words for themes; and conducts the inquiry in a subjective and reflexive manner.
  - Combined research is a type of research in which the researcher combines quantitative and qualitative research; studies a problem that calls for explanation and exploration; asks narrow, specific questions and broad, general questions; collects data consisting of numbers and words; analyzes these data for statistical trends and themes; and combines the two sets of results into an overall understanding of the topic.
- *Identify reasons why you should read research that used quantitative approaches and research that used qualitative approaches.*
  - Reading quantitative research is useful to learn new knowledge that explains typical trends, relationships among specific variables, differences among groups, and the outcomes of interventions as measured within large groups of individuals or organizations.
  - Reading qualitative research is useful to learn new knowledge that explores the complexity and meaning of phenomena as experienced in individuals' lives.
- *Recognize the key differences in the steps of the research process as reported in quantitative and qualitative research studies.*
  - Research problems tend to call for explanation in quantitative research and for exploration in qualitative research.
  - The literature review tends to be used in more of a static, prescriptive way in quantitative research and more of a dynamic, informative way in qualitative research.
  - The purpose tends to focus on narrow questions about explaining several variables in quantitative research and on broad questions about exploring a single phenomenon in qualitative research.
  - The overall approach to conducting the study tends to use experimental and nonexperimental designs in quantitative research and a general or formal qualitative design in qualitative research.
  - Data collection tends to be in the form of numbers from a large number of individuals in quantitative research and in the form of words and pictures from a small number of individuals in qualitative research.
  - Data analysis and results tend to be in the form of statistical procedures and statistics and graphs in quantitative research and in the form of text analysis and description and themes in qualitative research.
  - Conclusions tend to emphasize comparing results with predictions and past research in quantitative research and the interpretation of the meaning of findings in qualitative research.
  - Reports tend to use a standard format and present objective and impersonal information in quantitative research and use a flexible format and present subjective and reflexive information in qualitative research.
- *Evaluate the quality of quantitative and qualitative research reports.*
  - The evaluation of a research study is based on criteria that match the overall quantitative or qualitative approach of the study.
  - The evaluation of a research study is also based on the quality of the implementation of the steps of the process of research as described within the major sections of a research report.

✓ **To assess what you've learned to do, click here to answer questions and receive instant feedback.**

Reading Research Articles

Carefully reread the quantitative physical-activity-in-middle-schools study by Xu et al. (2010) found at the end of Chapter 1 (starting on p. 27) and the qualitative physical-activity-at-daycare study by Tucker et al. (2011), also found in Chapter 1 (starting on p. 40).

As you read each article, pay attention to the paragraphs in which the authors conveyed the different steps of the research process for their study. Use the highlighting tool in the Pearson etext to indicate where the authors have provided information about each step, and use the notetaking tool to add marginal notes that name each step you highlighted and note how each one relates to the study's overall approach. Among the steps you will want to find are:

1. Identifying a research problem
2. Reviewing the literature
3. Specifying a purpose
4. Choosing a research design
5. Selecting participants and collecting data
6. Analyzing data and reporting results
7. Drawing conclusions

Note, however, that sometimes authors do not directly state all seven of these steps—for example, they may not explicitly state their research design choice or include a clear purpose. If one of these steps is missing, indicate that in your marginal notes.

 Click here to go to the quantitative physical-activity-in-middle-schools study by Xu et al. (2010) so that you can enter marginal notes about the study.

 Click here to go to the qualitative physical-activity-at-daycare study by Tucker et al. (2011) so that you can enter marginal notes about the study.

Understanding Research Articles

Reflect back on the characteristics of quantitative and qualitative research and apply your knowledge of the content of this chapter.

1. Read the following abstract of a study on the topic of autism by Smith, Greenberg, and Seltzer (2012). List four characteristics of *quantitative* research that you find in the study's abstract.

   > The present study investigated the impact of social support on the psychological well-being of mothers of adolescents and adults with ASD [autism spectrum disorders] (*n* = 269). Quantity of support (number of social network members) as well as valence of support (positive support and negative support) were assessed using a modified version of the "convoy model" developed by Antonucci and Akiyama (1987). Having a larger social network was associated with improvements in maternal well-being over an 18-month period. Higher levels of negative support as well as increases in negative support over the study period were associated with increases in depressive symptoms and negative affect and decreases in positive affect. Social support predicted changes in well-being above and beyond the impact of child behavior problems. Implications for clinical practice are discussed. (Smith et al., 2012, p. 1818)

2. Read the following abstract of a study on the topic of autism by Tozer, Atkin, and Wenham (2013). List four characteristics of *qualitative* research that you find in the study's abstract.

   > Sibling relationships are usually lifelong and reciprocal. They can assume particular significance when a brother or sister has a learning disability. Until recently, adult

siblings of people with disabilities such as severe autism have been ignored by policy, practice and research. This qualitative study contributes to an emerging literature by exploring how adult siblings, who have a brother or sister with autism (plus learning disability) and living in England, give meaning to their family (and caring) relationships and engage with service delivery. We spoke to 21 adult siblings using semi-structured interviews and met with 12 of their siblings with autism. Our analysis, using a broad narrative approach, demonstrates the continuity of the sibling relationship and an enduring personalised commitment. The nature of this relationship, however, is sensitive to context. How non-disabled adult siblings relate to their childhood experience is fundamental when making sense of this, as is their need to fulfil other social and family obligations, alongside their "sense of duty" to support their disabled brother or sister. Sibling experience was further mediated by negotiating their "perceived invisibility" in social care policy and practice. Our work concludes that by understanding the way relationships between siblings have developed over time, adult siblings' contribution to the lives of their brother or sister with autism can be better supported for the benefit of both parties. Such an approach would support current policy developments. (Tozer et al., 2013, p. 480)

✓ **Click here to answer the questions and receive instant feedback.**

Evaluating Research Articles

Practice evaluating the quality of a study, using the quantitative physical-activity-in-middle-schools study by Xu et al. (2010) in Chapter 1 (starting on p. 27) and the qualitative physical-activity-at-daycare study by Tucker et al. (2011), also in Chapter 1 (starting on p. 40).

1. Use the criteria discussed in Table 2.1 to evaluate the quality of the physical-activity-in-middle-schools study. Note that, for this question, the rating form includes advice to help guide your evaluation.

✓ **Click here to open the rating scale form (Figure 2.3) to enter your ratings, evidence, and reasoning.**

2. Use the criteria discussed in Table 2.2 to evaluate the quality of the physical-activity-at-daycare study. Note that, for this question, the rating form does NOT include additional advice.

✓ **Click here to open the rating scale form (Figure 2.3) to enter your ratings, evidence, and reasoning.**

UNDERSTANDING THE INTRODUCTION SECTIONS OF RESEARCH REPORTS

Recall that we started this text by comparing a researcher who conducts a study to a traveler who takes a journey to a new destination. If you are going to travel, what do you do before the trip? You probably complete a number of activities, such as deciding where you want to go, packing a suitcase, and planning your itinerary.

Like planning for a trip, researchers also complete a number of steps in their research studies. They decide on a general "destination" by identifying a topic and problem that needs to be studied. Researchers might not pack a suitcase, but they do "pack up" the knowledge that currently exists on the problem by reviewing the literature. With this background information in hand, they specify the specific goal for their research, which sets the agenda for the study they are going to conduct.

When researchers write their study reports, they start from the beginning of their research "journeys" by describing their preliminary preparations. Researchers' descriptions of these preparations can be found in the Introduction sections of research reports. You should read these passages to learn the context and objectives for reported research studies. That is, a study's Introduction shows why the study was important, the background that informed the study, and the researcher's goal for conducting the study. In the next three chapters, you will learn how to read the information found in the Introduction sections to research reports so that you can understand and critique these key elements of research studies.

The chapters in Part Two are:

- Chapter 3—Statements of the Problem: Identifying Why a Study Is Important
- Chapter 4—Literature Reviews: Examining the Background for a Study
- Chapter 5—Purpose Statements, Research Questions, and Hypotheses: Identifying the Intent of a Study

STATEMENTS OF THE PROBLEM: IDENTIFYING WHY A STUDY IS IMPORTANT

A research report starts by introducing the "problem" that the researcher is addressing. This "statement of the problem" appears in the opening paragraphs of a research report. Researchers use this passage to explain the study's importance and to convince you, the reader, to read the rest of the report. You need to know how to read and interpret this passage to understand the researcher's argument for conducting the study and what makes the study necessary. In this chapter, you will learn how to identify a research problem, what makes a problem important to study, and how to read and assess a "statement of the problem" passage that introduces a research report.

BY THE END OF THIS CHAPTER, YOU SHOULD BE ABLE TO:

- Identify and understand the statement of the problem in a research report.
- List five reasons why researchers need to conduct studies to add to knowledge about research problems.
- Distinguish between the types of research problems that fit quantitative studies and qualitative studies.
- Know how to identify the five elements that comprise a good statement of the problem passage.
- Evaluate the quality of the statement of the problem in a research report.

Suppose someone gives you a research report and suggests that you read it. As you first look at the document, what are you looking for? You probably start at the beginning of the report and quickly decide whether the reported study is of interest to you and whether it merits your reading the full text. In fact, when researchers write their introductions, their primary goal is to convince readers (like you!) that the study described in the report is interesting and important. But what kind of argument should convince you of that? All research reports should answer what we call the "So what?" question— that is, "So what? Why would anyone want to read about this study?" To be able to answer this question, you need to learn how researchers explain:

- the importance of the topic being addressed and
- the importance of the research study for addressing this topic.

Researchers write about a study's necessity in the "statement of the problem" passage of a research report. By learning how to identify and understand this component of research reports, you will be able to identify studies that are important for the topics and problems that interest you.

How Do You Identify the Statement of the Problem in a Research Study?

Recall from Chapter 1 that researchers often begin their process of conducting research by identifying a research problem. During this step in the research process, researchers determine why a study is needed about the general topic that interests them. You can probably imagine, even if you are new to reading research, that there are many possible research studies that could be conducted about any particular topic. Not all of these studies need to be conducted, however. Because the conduct of research entails resources, including the time and effort of the researchers and the participants, research should only be conducted when researchers can make a convincing argument that the study is worth the effort. Well-written research reports therefore include a strong statement of the problem that provides the researcher's justification for why the study was worth conducting. To understand any research study, you need to locate the statement of the problem to learn why the study was conducted.

Locate the Statement of the Problem in the Introduction Section

A **statement of the problem** is an argument at the beginning of a research report that justifies why the research study was needed. It is called the "statement of the problem" because the researcher identifies a problem and argues that a particular research study is needed to address this problem. You can usually find this statement in the opening paragraphs. These paragraphs might have the heading *Introduction*, *Statement of the Problem*, or *The Research Problem*. In some reports, there is no heading, and this passage simply appears as the first few paragraphs of the report. In either case, this passage attempts to generate interest in the study, articulate the importance of the study, argue for the need of the study, and suggest why the study has significance for others. Once you locate this opening passage, read it to learn why the study was conducted and determine whether it interests you.

When you read a well-written statement of the problem, you can quickly decide whether the study pertains to a topic and issue that interests you. However, the function of the statement of the problem goes beyond creating interest in a particular study. You should also expect that the researchers will advance a strong and logical argument that their study is worth your attention. When this argument is done well, it should convince you that, of all the research studies that could possibly have been done, this particular study was interesting, important, needed, and significant. When the argument is not done well, then the reasons why the study was even conducted remain unclear. By learning how to identify and evaluate statements of the problem in research reports, you will understand what makes a study warranted so you can select reports of quality research studies on the topics that interest you.

Identify the Problem That Needs to Be Solved

At the heart of any research study's statement of the problem is the identification of a research problem. A **Research problem** is the issue, controversy, or concern that guides the need for a study. Researchers often identify real problems needing solutions in our society. You encounter potential research problems every week in the media, such as:

- the disruptions to people's lives caused by natural disasters,
- the increase in violence on college campuses,
- the controversy about the positive and negative roles of high-stakes testing, and
- the harmful health consequences of adolescent risk-taking behaviors.

Problems such as these are important because they concern personnel in our schools, clinics, and communities, and affect all kinds of practice. Research generally cannot solve these problems directly; however, researchers study these problems to help policy makers make decisions, to help practitioners solve practical problems, and to provide other researchers with a deeper understanding of the issues. By tying a research study to a real-world problem, a researcher indicates that the study is important because there is something that affects people that needs to be solved. When you identify the research problem a study is addressing, you can consider whether the study pertains to a topic and issue that concerns you.

You can usually find the research problem mentioned in the first or second paragraph of the report as part of the statement of the problem. Although some reports only imply that a problem exists, the research problem in a well-written report is usually stated explicitly as a real problem in need of a solution. To identify the research problem, ask yourself the following questions as you read the opening paragraphs of a research article:

- Is there a sentence like "A major problem is . . . ."?
- Is there an issue, concern, or controversy that the researcher wants to address?
- What real-world problem needs to be solved?

You are probably aware of many educational and societal problems from your own practice and experiences. Even so, it can be difficult to identify them in research articles. As an example, let's consider an excerpt from Xu et al.'s (2010) Introduction section (paragraphs 01–03) in the quantitative physical-activity-in-middle-schools study from Chapter 1. Ask yourself the questions listed above as you reread the following passage:

> Low levels of physical activity (PA) are a major contributor to current overweight and obesity problems in children and adolescent[s] (Fairclough and Stratton, 2005; Lobstein et al., 2004) . . . . Obesity is associated with chronic diseases such as heart disease, type 2 diabetes, stroke, some forms of cancer, and osteoarthritis, premature death or discounted quality of life (USD-HHS, 2001), and high healthcare costs (Wang et al., 2003). There is clearly a need to reduce the impact of this problem, and the school setting appears as a viable intervention venue to promote PA involvement, e.g. tailor an effective exercise intervention program (Edmunds et al., 2001; Wechsler and Devereaux, 2001).
>
> School is considered to be an ideal early intervention institution for PA promotion because it can reach most children and adolescents and has a strong potential effect on children's and adolescents' behaviours (Edmunds et al., 2001; Wechsler and Devereaux, 2001). However, successful school-based PA intervention at the middle school level, grades 6–8, has seldom been reported in comparison to those targeting elementary schoolchildren (Sallis et al., 2002). . . . School-based PA intervention tailored for middle school age children and adolescents therefore might be essential for PA promotion . . . prior studies provided useful guidance; however, there has been no 'best practice' to promote PA in middle school age children and adolescents. Therefore, it seems that, in order to identify effective intervention strategies for this specific population, there is a need to further examine and better understand available school-based PA opportunities and factors that may influence these PA opportunities because it could be thought of as a key in promoting PA among middle school age children and adolescents.
>
> Accordingly, the present study was designed to explore school-based PA opportunities in public middle schools and to examine factors that may be associated with these opportunities from physical education (PE) teachers' perspectives.

The research problem identified in this study is in the first sentence of the above excerpt: "Low levels of physical activity (PA) are a major contributor to current overweight and obesity problems in children and adolescent[s]." That is, youth's low levels of physical activity is the issue that concerns educators and society at large that is identified by the authors of this study. This is a problem because low levels of physical activity contribute to obesity and obesity is related to many serious health outcomes. The researchers argue that we need a study that examines the factors associated with physical activity opportunities for middle school students because we do not know enough about which practices are successful for encouraging physical activity in middle schools.

Here's a Tip!

When identifying the research problem, ask yourself "Why is that a problem?" as a check. You should be able to say, "It's a problem for people because . . . ." If you can't give a reason, then you might not have correctly identified the problem.

Distinguish the Research Problem From the Study's Topic and Purpose

Did you identify the issue of youth's low levels of physical activity as the research problem from the excerpt, or did you focus on another part of the passage? A common pitfall is to confuse a study's research problem with its topic or purpose. As depicted in Figure 3.1, researchers are interested in a broad topic, then identify a research problem within that topic and specify a study purpose to address

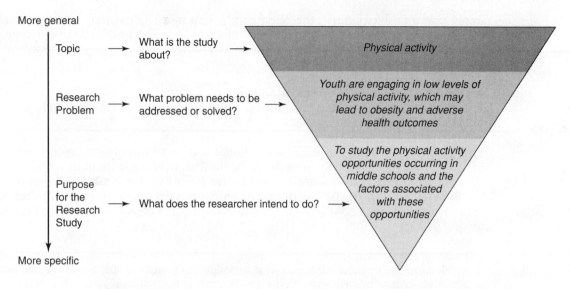

More general

Topic → What is the study about? →

Research Problem → What problem needs to be addressed or solved? →

Purpose for the Research Study → What does the researcher intend to do? →

More specific

Physical activity

Youth are engaging in low levels of physical activity, which may lead to obesity and adverse health outcomes

To study the physical activity opportunities occurring in middle schools and the factors associated with these opportunities

FIGURE 3.1   Distinguishing Among a Study's Topic, Research Problem, and Purpose

the research problem. To better understand research problems, it is therefore helpful to distinguish them from the topics and purposes found in research reports. Let's consider how a study's topic, research problem, and purpose differ from each other.

- *The study's research problem falls under its general topic.* Perhaps you thought the research problem was "physical activity." Notice, however, that this is not really a problem that needs to be solved (in fact, physical activity can be a good thing!). Physical activity is simply the topic of the research report. A research **topic** is the broad subject matter of the study. A study's topic can generally be stated as a short phrase that summarizes what the study is about, such as "physical activity." Within a broad topic, researchers identify a problem related to the topic, such as "low levels of physical activity are a major contributor to current overweight and obesity problems." Recall that the research problem is an issue, controversy, or concern that needs to be solved and guides the need for a study. See how the research problem falls under the topic in Figure 3.1.
- *The study's purpose follows from the research problem.* Perhaps you thought the research problem in the passage was "to explore school-based PA opportunities in public middle schools and to examine factors that may be associated with these opportunities from physical education (PE) teachers' perspectives." That is a very common answer. However, notice that this is not a societal problem that needs to be solved. Instead, this statement describes the researchers' purpose for conducting the study. From the research problem, researchers formulate the specific purpose for the study, as shown in Figure 3.1. This **purpose for research** indicates what the researchers actually intend to do by collecting and analyzing data in the study. The purpose is the goal for one specific research study, not a larger problem in society that is a concern to many. You will learn more about the purposes for research in Chapter 5.

These three aspects of research—the topic, research problem, and purpose—and their application in the quantitative physical-activity-in-middle-schools study are summarized in Figure 3.1. These aspects vary in terms of their breadth from very general (the topic) to more specific (the purpose). As you read the Introduction sections of research reports, distinguish among these parts of research. With this understanding, you can differentiate what the study is about (the topic); the issue, concern, or controversy being addressed (the research problem); and what the author intends to do (the purpose).

What Do You Think?

Consider the following sentences taken from Zerillo and Osterman's (2011) introduction to their research study. As you read the passage, answer the following questions: What is the study's topic? What research problem is identified that falls under this topic? What purpose for research is formulated from this problem?

> Peer bullying is recognized as a significant problem in schools at all levels, with serious consequences for both bully and victim. While there is extensive research on peer bullying, it is only recently that teacher bullying has emerged as an equally, if not more, serious problem. . . . While there is little research on the consequences of teacher bullying per se, our understanding of the immediate and long term effects of peer bullying and other forms of abuse, clearly indicate the potential severity of the problem. . . . Recognizing the importance of teacher bullying, this study, then, offers an exploratory perspective on teachers' understanding of teacher bullying and expands our understanding of this phenomenon. (pp. 239, 242)

Check Your Understanding

The researchers identify bullying as the general, broad *topic* of this study. They do this by mentioning different types of bullying (e.g., peer and teacher) that are of interest. Under this topic, the researchers identify the *research problem* as the serious issue of teacher bullying. This is the larger problem and concern that the authors argue needs to be studied. It is a problem because children likely suffer serious consequences if they experience bullying from a teacher. Narrowing down from the research problem, the researchers end this passage by indicating that the *purpose* of their study is to explore teachers' understanding of teacher bullying.

Why Do Researchers Need to Study Research Problems?

Researchers identify research problems in the introductions to their research studies to make it clear that the study is important because it addresses a problem that needs to be solved. However, the existence of a problem is not enough to argue that a research study is needed. There are many ways that scholars could work to solve a problem, such as writing a play about it, teaching a course on it, or writing an opinion paper about it. There must be a good reason why a research study about the problem is needed. Why should researchers conduct research studies? Recall from Chapter 1 that researchers conduct research studies to contribute to our knowledge base about problems. Therefore, research studies are needed when new knowledge about an important problem is required. When research studies provide this new knowledge, then researchers, policy makers, and practitioners may be able to use that new knowledge to develop solutions.

Although there are countless problems that need to be solved, there are five basic reasons why research studies are needed to provide new knowledge about these problems. New knowledge may be needed to fill gaps in knowledge, to replicate past results, to extend past results, to include voices that have been previously excluded and unheard, and to improve practice. Let's examine each of these reasons that you may find provided in research reports.

- *A research study is needed to fill a gap in the existing literature about the research problem.* Assume that a researcher is concerned with the ethical climate of high schools. An examination of the literature finds that past research has examined the perceptions of students, but not of teachers. The perspective of teachers is a gap or void in the body of knowledge about this issue. Therefore, there is a need to conduct a study about teacher perceptions of the ethical climate because that topic has not been studied in the existing literature.

- *A research study is needed to replicate past results about the research problem by examining different participants and different research sites.* The value of some research increases when the results can apply broadly to many people and places rather than to only the one setting where the initial research occurred. Results of past studies need to be replicated with new participants or settings especially for quantitative experiments. Such replications can determine whether positive effects for a treatment are achieved more than once. In a quantitative study about a program to promote an ethical climate, for example, past research about a program conducted at a private school in an urban setting can be tested (or replicated) at other sites, such as a rural high school or an all-boys' school. Research at such sites would be new to the topic and the information from their study will provide new knowledge.

- *A research study is needed to extend past results or examine the research problem more thoroughly.* Some research problems need to be studied to extend the existing research into a new topic or area, or to conduct research at a deeper, more thorough level. For example, in our illustration on ethical climate, prior research may have examined ethical practices in relation to student demographics such as age and gender. However, there may be a need to extend this topic to examine additional factors such as participation in athletics and attitudes about cheating and fairness. In this way, the knowledge about the problem is extended to include more detail. This extension is different from the previous example of replication because the investigators extend the research to different topics rather than repeating a past study with different participants and research sites.

- *A research study is needed to learn from people affected by the problem whose voices have not been heard, who have been silenced, or who have been rejected in society.* Research can add to a problem's knowledge base by presenting the ideas and the words of marginalized individuals and groups (e.g., individuals who are homeless, women, racial groups). For example, although past studies on ethical climate have addressed students at predominantly white Midwestern schools, we have not heard the voices of Native Americans on this topic. A study of the ethical climate at a tribal school would therefore report and give voice to Native American students and teachers.

- *A research study is needed to improve current practices related to the research problem.* Practitioners may need practical knowledge arising from research to inform their practice. By examining the problem, research may lead to the identification of new techniques or technologies, the recognition of the value of historical or current practice, or the necessity to change current practice. For example, a study of ethical issues in a district's schools may lead to a new honor code, new policies about cheating on exams, or new approaches to administering tests.

You now know five different reasons why researchers need to conduct research studies. Let's use this information to consider why a research study was needed to add to the knowledge base about the problem of youth's low levels of physical activity in the quantitative physical-activity-in-middle-schools study. From the excerpt we read earlier in this chapter, the authors imply that there are two reasons why a study is needed about this issue. First, there is a need to extend past research about physical activity programs in elementary schools by including a new dimension about this topic—namely, the context of middle schools. Second, there is a need to improve practice, but prior research has not been able to identify which practices are most successful at promoting physical activity for middle school students.

As you begin reading any research article, identify the larger research problem being addressed and note why a new study is needed. In addition, from the start of any research report, consider whether the identified research problem is more suited to a quantitative or a qualitative study.

How Do You Distinguish Between the Types of Research Problems Found in Quantitative and Qualitative Studies?

As discussed in Chapter 2, quantitative and qualitative research approaches differ in their basic characteristics. When applied to the step of identifying a research problem, this means that some research problems fit a quantitative approach better and others fit a qualitative approach better. In high-quality research, you should expect to find a clear match between the study's research problem and the approach used to study it. Researchers often provide indications as to whether the study will be quantitative or qualitative from the beginning of the written report, and you should look for this match when reading a study's introduction. What types of research problems are best suited for quantitative and qualitative research? Let's consider research problems as representing two overarching types: those that call for *explanation* and those that call for *exploration*.

Quantitative Research Is Used When the Research Problem Calls for Explanation

Recall the quantitative physical-activity-in-middle-school study from Chapter 1 and highlighted earlier in this chapter. Xu et al. (2010) argued that we know little about the importance of different factors (or variables) that influence the physical activity opportunities available in middle schools. That is, we do not know how *to explain* why some middle schools offer higher levels of physical activity opportunities and others offer lower levels. Why would it be important to know the factors that best explain the different levels? The researchers suggest that by knowing the factors associated with higher levels of physical activity opportunities, middle school personnel would know the best practices to include in their own programs to promote physical activity within their schools. So, there is a need to describe the physical activity opportunities that are occurring and to explain the relationships between these opportunities and other variables. Explaining or predicting relationships among predetermined variables is an important characteristic of quantitative research, as we learned in Chapter 2. Problems that call for new knowledge that explains the effect of a treatment, the extent that groups differ in terms of variables, and the trends for variables in a large group also fit a quantitative research approach.

> ### Here's a Tip!
>
> Be wary of the words that authors include in their statements of the problem. For example, a researcher may state there is a need to "explore" the trends in a quantitative variable. Notice the words used, but more importantly, consider whether the problem calls for an examination of predetermined variables and factors (i.e., an explanation) or an examination of perspectives and experiences that are not predetermined (i.e., an exploration).

Qualitative Research Is Used When the Research Problem Calls for Exploration

Next consider the qualitative physical-activity-at-daycare study from Chapter 1. Although it addresses a topic and problem similar to the quantitative physical-activity-in-middle-school study, we find that Tucker et al. (2011) argue that a different type of study to address the research problem is needed. The research problem in this study called for the researchers *to explore* the unique perceptions of daycare providers about improving physical activity practices without preconceived ideas about what they would find or which variables might be important. In Chapter 2, we learned that exploring a problem is a characteristic of qualitative research. Problems that require new knowledge exploring how a process unfolds, the meaning of a phenomenon, the complexity of a case, or the stories of individuals' lives also fit a qualitative research approach.

What Do You Think?

Consider the following passage from a study about a special peer interaction program at a summer camp. As you read the paragraph, ask yourself the following questions: Why is the study needed? Does the research problem seem to call for a quantitative or a qualitative approach?

> Few research studies have been published regarding attempts to increase social interaction between children with and without disabilities outside of the school setting . . . . There is a demonstrated benefit of social interaction during leisure activities for children with disabilities (Bedini, 2000) . . . . However, these studies did not address improving interactions between children with and without disabilities, which is an extensively studied area in educational settings. Due to the lack of intervention studies in leisure settings, research is needed to determine the impact of peer training at recreation sites. (Boyd et al., 2008, pp. 92–93)

Check Your Understanding

From this paragraph, we see that the study is needed because it will contribute to the knowledge base by filling a gap in the literature about programs that aim to increase interactions between children with and without disabilities. Boyd et al. (2008) note that we do not know whether programs focused on peer interactions in nonschool settings will have a positive impact for children with disabilities. This passage includes indications that the researchers are going to use a *quantitative* approach in the study because they discuss a need for research that determines the impact (an effect) of a program that involves peer training (a treatment) in a recreational setting. Problems that call for explaining the effect of a treatment are generally associated with quantitative research.

How Do You Understand the Elements of a Study's Statement of the Problem?

You can now recognize research problems, understand why researchers need to study these problems, and distinguish problems that call for either a quantitative or a qualitative approach. With this information, you are ready to consider how to read and understand the full statement of the problem passages found in the Introduction sections of research reports. By carefully reading these passages, you can understand researchers' arguments about why their studies are of interest, important, needed, and significant.

When reading a study's statement of the problem, it is helpful to observe that researchers tend to address a common set of elements in their statements of the problem. These elements include:

1. The topic
2. The research problem
3. Evidence for the importance of the problem
4. The knowledge about the problem that is missing
5. The audiences that may benefit from the new knowledge

By recognizing these five elements as you read a study's introduction, you can readily understand why the researchers think that their study is of interest, important, needed, and significant. When well written, these five elements can form a strong argument for the research study and provide an engaging introduction to the research study. Let's consider how you identify these five elements.

Find the Topic

When reading a research article, find the topic first. Remember, a research topic is the broad subject matter that a researcher addresses in a study. Examples of topics are leadership, bullying, world language education, drug use, and family relationships. Look for the topic in the first few sentences of the introduction by asking yourself, "What is this study about?" In many articles, you can find the topic in the article's title or the provided keywords, but often these terms are more narrow and specialized than the overall topic. The opening sentences of a well-written statement of the problem passage, however, should start with a broad topic that is easy to identify. Consider whether these sentences generate your interest in the study and provide you with an initial frame of reference for understanding the topic of the study. A good introduction should encourage you to read beyond the first page.

When reading any research report, you will typically start with the opening sentences. When written well, the first sentence of a research report should encourage you to pay attention and continue reading by eliciting an emotional or attitudinal response and sparking interest. These first sentences often generate interest by including one

---

Here's a Tip!

When reading a report, circle or highlight the words that best identify the topic. This will make it easy for you to quickly recall the topic when you come back to this same report in the future.

of the following types of information: statistical data, a provocative question, a clear need for research, a powerful quote, or a key definition. See how the following examples of each of these strategies introduce the studies' topics in an engaging way.

- *A study about juvenile delinquency started with statistical data:* "In 2006, law enforcement agencies in the United States made an estimated 2.2 million juvenile arrests accounting for 17% of all violent and 26% of property crime arrests (Snyder, 2008)" (Zhang, Hsu, Katsiyannis, Barrett, & Ju, 2011, p. 283).
- *A study about parenting by fathers started with a provocative question:* "What is good fathering?" (Brotherson, Dollahite, & Hawkins, 2005, p. 1).
- *A study about college experiences started with a clear need for research:* "Student employment has long been a cause of concern for educators of American postsecondary institutions" (Cheng & Alcántara, 2007, p. 301).
- *A study about academic dishonesty started with a powerful quote:* "'I think the WorldCom and Enron scandals point to the need for character in our business schools. If the driver at the helm is unethical, so shall the crew be.' —Comments of an MBA student at a large U.S. university" (McCabe, Butterfield, & Treviño, 2006, p. 294).
- *A study about cancer prevention started with a key definition:* "Cancer is used as a generic term to describe over 100 diseases characterized by abnormal cell growth that can affect any part of the body" (Keeney, McKenna, Fleming, & McIlfatrick, 2010, p. 769).

When you begin to read a new study report, examine the first sentence, assess what topic is being introduced, and consider whether this sentence piques your interest and encourages you to read further.

Identify the Research Problem

After introducing the overall topic, most introductions narrow the topic to a research problem. Recall that a research problem is an issue, concern, or controversy that needs to be solved. Researchers conduct studies to help address different problems. Authors may present the research problem as a single sentence or as a few sentences, and it often appears within the first paragraph or two of an article. You can identify research problems as issues or concerns that affect people in real-world settings, such as schools or clinics or families, or problems associated with our knowledge about a topic, such as when a controversy exists in the literature. In either case, a well-written research problem is one that the researcher states clearly as a problem so that it helps to convey a strong sense of importance. See how the following examples from research articles make clear that there is a problem that needs to be addressed.

- *A problem that is a major concern:* "In particular, the career development of African American adolescents has been of major concern in light of literature delineating numerous challenges that affect their personal, educational, and career development . . . " (Constantine, Wallace, & Kindaichi, 2005, p. 307).
- *A problem that affects the lives of many individuals:* "Approximately one third of children and adolescents experience the stress of being bullied by their peers . . . " (Newman, Holden, & Delville, 2011, p. 205).
- *A problem that has serious consequences:* "Not only does lack of participation in physical activity contribute to the rising obesity rates in the United States, but it also directly contributes to the risk for several chronic diseases and leading causes of death in the United States, such as heart disease, hypertension, Type 2 diabetes, and certain cancers . . . " (Harley et al., 2009, p. 97).
- *A problem that is a current issue for practitioners:* "Computer science faculty today face many pressures to integrate collaborative and cooperative learning approaches in courses, increase active participation by students in classes, and increase the participation of under-represented groups in computing . . . " (Barker & Garvin-Doxas, 2004, p. 119).
- *A problem about what is known about a topic:* "Burns (1978) observed that despite the large volume of scholarship on the topic, leadership is not well understood" (Komives, Owen, Longerbeam, Mainella, & Osteen, 2005, p. 593).
- *A problem that arises from conflicting evidence in the literature:* "In the literature on the impact of mobility on children's educational attainment, findings are inconsistent" (Heinlein & Shinn, 2000, p. 349).

Whether the research problem arises from a practical setting, a need in the research literature, or both, by identifying the issue in the Introduction, you can discern the larger problem that the study addresses. Consider whether you find this problem to be a compelling one that needs to be resolved, which helps to argue that the research study is important.

Note the Justification for the Importance of the Problem

It is not sufficient for researchers to merely state a problem or issue in their reports. You should expect that they also provide a justification for the problem's importance. In **justifying a research problem**, researchers present evidence for the importance of the issue being studied. Once you have located the problem, look for evidence justifying the extent that the problem affects real people's lives. In good-quality research reports, researchers regularly provide evidence to support their claims, such as the claim that an important problem exists. The evidence may appear in a few sentences or in several paragraphs, and may include two types: evidence from the literature and evidence from the workplace and personal experience.

- *Evidence from the literature.* Evidence taken from the literature is the most scholarly type of evidence that researchers use to justify the importance of the problem in their reports. Evidence from the literature includes any arguments and results that were previously reported in the literature by experts. Most introductions to quantitative and qualitative research reports include numerous references to the literature to indicate the existence and magnitude of the problem, which justifies its importance. These justifications indicate that not only does the author think the problem is important, but other researchers agree. For example, note how Newman et al. (2011) justify the importance of the problem of youth experiencing stress from being bullied by referencing six other articles that found that such stress is harmful to youth:

  > This stressor has been linked to emotional and behavioral problems, including depression and anxiety (e.g., Bond, Carlin, Thomas, Rubin, & Patton, 2001; Craig, 1998), suicide risk (Klomek, Marrocco, Kleinman, Schonfeld, & Gould, 2007), and increased likelihood of conduct disorders (Wolke, Woods, Bloomfield, & Karstadt, 2000; for reviews, see Griffin & Gross, 2004; Hawker & Boulton, 2000). (p. 205)

- *Evidence from the workplace or personal experience.* You will find that researchers also justify their research problems based on evidence from the workplace or their own personal experiences. There are many issues and concerns that arise in workplaces, such as issues surrounding treating addiction or approaches to classroom discipline. Therefore, problems related to addiction or discipline may be justified because of their impact on professional settings. Likewise, researchers may describe personal experiences from their lives as evidence for the importance of studying a problem. These personal experiences may arise from intense professional experiences or experiences drawn from childhood or family situations. For example, Green (2003) justified the importance of the problem of experiencing stigma for families of children with disabilities by referring to her own family experiences. She wrote:

  > As the mother of a teenager with cerebral palsy, my life has become a case study in the lived experience of courtesy stigma (Green, 2002, 2003). Based on the social scientific literature, I carried into this experience awareness that Amanda would likely be devalued and discriminated against because of the stigma associated with her diagnosis. I also carried an intense, almost unbearable, fear that this stigmatized status would result in a life of rejection, mistreatment, social isolation and loneliness for my daughter (Green, 2002). Many years later, I have learned that stigma is a much more complex phenomenon than I originally anticipated. (pp. 1361–1362)

In many qualitative studies, researchers refer to their personal experiences as evidence for the importance of the problem, especially in those studies with a practical orientation. However, keep in mind that some individuals, particularly those trained only in quantitative research, feel that evidence based on personal experience is not as scholarly as evidence from the literature. Therefore, most articles will emphasize evidence from the literature and, if they include personal experiences, they will combine it with evidence from the literature. When you read a study's Introduction, pay attention to evidence from the literature and from personal and workplace experiences to understand why the researcher believes the study about the identified research problem is important.

Identify the Knowledge About the Problem That Is Missing

Once you have read the problem and the evidence for its importance, look for one or more sentences stating that there is something we currently do not know about this research problem. Recall that a research study is needed when the present state of knowledge about the problem is somehow deficient and a study can add new knowledge that will address this deficiency. There is a **deficiency in knowledge** when past literature or practical experiences of the researchers do not adequately address the research problem. Recall the five reasons why research is needed to study a problem presented earlier in this chapter. These reasons tie directly to the types of deficiencies that may exist in knowledge. For example, deficiencies in knowledge may mean that there is a gap in what is known, that past research has not been extended to certain topics, that past studies have not been replicated in specific settings or with different people, that the voices of marginalized people have been previously excluded, or that individuals have not identified good and workable solutions for schools or other professional settings.

When reading an Introduction section, pay careful attention to any deficiencies in identified by the authors. These deficiencies indicate that a research study is needed to fill the gap, extend past research, replicate a study, lift the voices of marginalized people, or add to practice. In good-quality reports, the researchers enumerate several deficiencies in the existing literature or in practice to make a strong argument for the need for the research study. Here are example statements where researchers indicated the need for their studies by identifying specific deficiencies in what is known about a problem:

- *A statement that there is a gap in knowledge that needs to be filled:* "Despite the broad scope of this literature, there is little scholarship about how leadership develops or how a leadership identity develops over time" (Komives et al., 2005, p. 593).
- *A statement that there are past results that need to be replicated:* "Since parenting processes change in the early adolescent years in the Chinese culture (Shek & Lee, in press), it would be important to replicate the findings of Shek (2006b) in Chinese Secondary 2 students" (Shek, 2007, p. 569).
- *A statement that there are past results that need to be extended:* "While evidence has supported pre-teaching as an effective supplemental instructional approach, its effectiveness in the area of math has yet to be examined" (Lalley & Miller, 2006, p. 748).
- *A statement that the voices of marginalized people need to be heard:* "Little research has been conducted describing the perception of friendship and social experiences of adolescents who have Asperger syndrome, and there has been even less qualitative research incorporating children's own words" (Carrington et al., 2003, p. 211).
- *A statement that practice needs to be improved:* "Further experimental research is needed to provide educators with information that they can use to make sound decisions about selections and implementation of vocabulary instruction programs and strategies" (Apthorp, 2006, p. 67).

Researchers often identify at least two or three reasons why existing research and practice are deficient in addressing the research problem. You can usually find these statements toward the end of the Introduction section. A good statement of a deficiency is one that explicitly identifies a specific type of knowledge that is missing, as done in the listed examples. By locating these statements, you can clearly understand why a research study is needed to add to the knowledge base about the problem.

Note the Audiences Who Will Benefit From the Knowledge Generated by the Study

The final element to look for when reading a statement of the problem passage is the audience for the study. A study's **audience** consists of individuals and groups who the authors expect will read and potentially benefit from the new knowledge provided in the research article. These audiences will vary depending on the nature of the study, but researchers often include practitioners, policy makers, other researchers, and individuals participating in the studies as relevant audiences for their research. For example, note how Churchill and colleagues identified a number of audiences for their study about how rural, low-income families have fun in the following passage:

The findings from this study can be applied in many different areas. Leisure researchers will gain a better understanding of how rural low-income families have fun and the contexts influencing those choices. In addition, policymakers and rural advocates will gain a better understanding of an important aspect of rural and low-income families' lives. Extension educators and rural community service providers will learn about challenges faced by rural low-income families and strategies used by some families to make fun an important part of their life. Finally, play advocates gain an important understanding about what families with young children see as fun. (Churchill, Plano Clark, Prochaska-Cue, Creswell, & Ontai-Grzebik, 2007, p. 272)

As this example illustrates, researchers often name multiple audiences (e.g., leisure researchers, policy makers, rural and play advocates, extension educators, and rural community service providers). In addition, researchers may mention how the specific audiences will be able to use the new knowledge resulting from the research study (e.g., learning challenges and new strategies, which may be useful for professionals working with other families). You will usually find an audience passage near the end of the Introduction section. These passages explain the significance of addressing the deficiencies in the knowledge base about the problem for specific audiences. Such information strengthens the argument for the value of the research study because it implies that it will potentially provide meaningful information and useful results. By identifying the audience for a study as you read the Introduction, you learn who may benefit from the study results and can consider whether the study and its results may be useful for you.

Consider the Five Elements to Understand a Study's Statement of the Problem Passage

You now are familiar with the five elements that are typically included in a statement of the problem passage that introduces a research study: the topic, the research problem, evidence for the importance of the problem, deficiencies in what is known about the problem, and audiences. The order in which authors discuss these ideas can vary, but it often matches the flow of ideas shown in Figure 3.2. This figure shows the five elements as they typically appear within a generic statement of the problem passage. In addition, this figure highlights how each element was applied within Lassetter, Mandleco, and Roper's (2007) Introduction to their qualitative study about parents raising children with disabilities. Although you do not have the full details of their three-paragraph statement of the problem, note how you are able to follow the flow of their argument for their study based just on a summary of these five elements.

As summarized in Figure 3.2, Lassetter et al. (2007) began their study report with the *topic* of children with disabilities. They then narrowed down to the *problem* of parents of children with disabilities experiencing stress and the adverse effects of parent stress on families. The researchers' *justification* of the importance of this problem includes evidence from prior research about the sources of stress for parents of children with disabilities, such as those arising from the various physical and psychological demands of caring for a child with a disability. They next note that the knowledge about this problem is *deficient*. Specifically, the researchers explain that little research has explored the richness of parents' experiences of raising a child with a disability using qualitative methods and that the meanings of the experiences for parents are unknown. A study that addresses these deficiencies will be useful for various *audiences*. Although the authors do not explicitly name the audiences in their Introduction section, they imply that this missing knowledge is important for those who work to develop effective interventions and support systems for parents who are raising a child with a disability. In summary, even without reading the full text of the Introduction section, you can see how these five elements create a compelling argument for a research study.

Look for these five elements when you read any research article's Introduction section. A good strategy is to mark the words *topic, problem, justification, deficiency* (or *gap*), and *audiences* in the article's margin next to the sentences where each element is best addressed. By noting these key elements, it will be easier for you to follow the flow of ideas in the researcher's argument as to why the reported research study is interesting, important, needed, and significant.

FIGURE 3.2
Flow of Ideas in a "Statement of the Problem" Passage

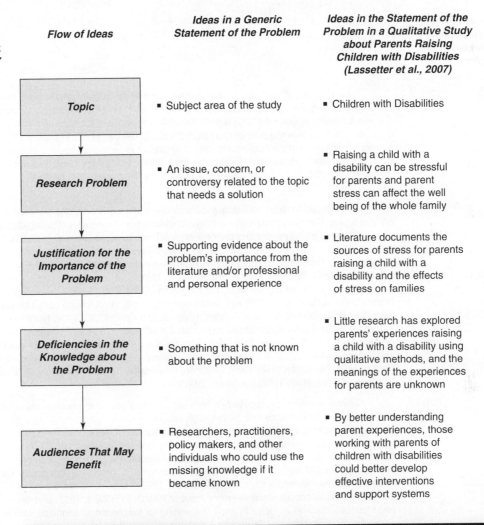

Flow of Ideas	Ideas in a Generic Statement of the Problem	Ideas in the Statement of the Problem in a Qualitative Study about Parents Raising Children with Disabilities (Lassetter et al., 2007)
Topic	▪ Subject area of the study	▪ Children with Disabilities
Research Problem	▪ An issue, concern, or controversy related to the topic that needs a solution	▪ Raising a child with a disability can be stressful for parents and parent stress can affect the well being of the whole family
Justification for the Importance of the Problem	▪ Supporting evidence about the problem's importance from the literature and/or professional and personal experience	▪ Literature documents the sources of stress for parents raising a child with a disability and the effects of stress on families
Deficiencies in the Knowledge about the Problem	▪ Something that is not known about the problem	▪ Little research has explored parents' experiences raising a child with a disability using qualitative methods, and the meanings of the experiences for parents are unknown
Audiences That May Benefit	▪ Researchers, practitioners, policy makers, and other individuals who could use the missing knowledge if it became known	▪ By better understanding parent experiences, those working with parents of children with disabilities could better develop effective interventions and support systems

What Do You Think?

Read the statement of the problem passage from a research article in Figure 3.3. As you read the passage, identify the five elements of a good statement of the problem. Write the words *topic*, *problem*, *justification*, *deficiency* (or *gap*), and *audiences* in the margins to indicate each element. If an element is missing, be sure to note that as well.

Check Your Understanding

In the statement of the problem found in Figure 3.3, the authors introduce the *topic* (tobacco use) and *research problem* (number of expected premature deaths because of teenage smoking) in paragraph 01. This illustrates how the topic and the research problem can sometimes blend. They provide their *justification* for this problem in paragraph 02—for instance, by citing statistics about the magnitude of the problem and summarizing prior research on the problem. Notice how they included many references to the literature to justify the importance of this problem. Following the justification for the problem, they mention the *deficiencies* in the knowledge base about this problem in paragraphs 03 and 04. For example, little research has examined the social context of high schools or explored students' views. In the final paragraph, they indicate various *audiences* (e.g., researchers, administrators, and teachers) who may benefit from the new knowledge generated from the study. Therefore, this passage included all five elements of a statement of the problem.

Identify the Five Elements of the Statement of the Problem

(01)　　　　　Tobacco use is a leading cause of cancer in American society (McGinnis & Foege, 1993). Although smoking among adults has declined in recent years, it has increased for adolescents. The Centers for Disease Control (CDC) reported that the incidence of tobacco use among high school students has risen over the past decade from 27.5% in 1991 to 34.5% in 2000 (CDC, 2001). These figures fall well short of the Healthy People 2010 goal of reducing adolescent tobacco use to 16% (U.S. Department of Health and Human Services, 2000). Unless this trend is dramatically reversed, an estimated 5 million American children will ultimately die a premature death due to smoking related diseases (CDC, 1996).

(02)　　　　　Previous research on adolescent tobacco use in the school context has focused on the following primary topics. Several studies have surveyed public school students, collecting data on initiation of smoking among young people and patterns of escalating tobacco use (CDC, 1998a, 1998b, 1998c; Heishman et al., 1997; Peyton, 2001). Other studies have focused on the prevention of smoking and tobacco use in schools. This research has led to numerous school-based prevention programs and interventions (e.g., Bruvold, 1993; Sussman, Dent, Burton, Stacy, & Flay, 1995). These prevention programs have involved explicit curricular programs (Kolbe et al., 1995; Larsen & Christiansen, 1994; Martin, Levin, & Saunders, 1999) and policy elements, including tobacco bans (Ashley, Northrup, & Ferrence, 1998; Bowen, Kinne, & Orlandi, 1995; Bunch, 1990; CDC, 1994; Northrup, Ashley, & Ferrence, 1998). Fewer studies have examined the schools' role in "quit attempts" or smoking cessation among adolescents. Some investigators have looked at ways to make cessation counseling and support more accessible by offering such services in the school setting (Aveyard et al., 1999; Burton, 1994; Heishman et al., 1997; Pallonen, Prochaska, Velicer, Prokhorov, & Smith, 1998; Pallonen, Velicer, et al., 1998; Sussman, 2001).

(03)　　　　　Minimal research has focused on high schools as a site where adolescents continue to explore and experiment with tobacco use. During high school, students form peer groups that can contribute to adolescent smoking. Often, peers become a strong social influence that reinforces smoking behavior in general (Engels, Knibbe, Drop, & de Haan, 1997; Ennett & Bauman 1993; Gibbons & Eggleston, 1996; Graham, Marks, & Hansen, 1991; Hansen, Johnson, Flay, Graham, & Sobel, 1988), and belonging to an athletic team, a music group, or the "grunge" crowd can influence thinking about smoking (McVea, Harter, McEntarffer, & Creswell, 1999; Sussman, Dent, Stacy, et al., 1990). Schools are also places where adolescents spend most of their day (Fibkins, 1993) and develop sustained attitudes toward smoking. Schools provide a setting for teachers and administrators to be role models for abstaining from tobacco use and for enforcing policies about tobacco use (Brown, Jr., & Butterfield, 1992; Bunch, 1990; CDC, 1994; Tompkins, Dino, Zedosky, Harman, & Shaler, 1999).

(04)　　　　　The vast majority of studies looking at smoking within the context of schools have used quantitative research methods; however, schools are also places to explore qualitatively how students view smoking. Rather than using predetermined concepts and theoretical models derived from the adult tobacco literature (Pallonen, 1998; Prochaska et al., 1994), researchers need also to hear how adolescents talk about tobacco use (Ginsburg, 1996; Moffat & Johnson, 2001). Much can be learned from a qualitative study that involves high school students talking with other students about tobacco use. Employing students as co-researchers to gather data not only provides detailed participant views in qualitative research (Creswell, 2002; Ginsburg, 1996) but also offers the opportunity to gather information without biases and perspectives that adults often bring to the study of adolescent smoking.

(05)　　　　　By examining multiple school contexts, using qualitative approaches, and involving students as co-researchers, we can better understand the complexity of the perceptions held about adolescent tobacco use. This understanding comes from listening to what students have to say about adolescent tobacco use when they talk with other students. With this understanding, researchers can better isolate variables and develop models about smoking behavior. Administrators and teachers can plan interventions to prevent or change attitudes toward smoking, and school officials can assist with smoking cessation or intervention programs.

FIGURE 3.3   A "Statement of the Problem" Passage in a Study About Adolescent Tobacco Use

Source: This passage is reprinted from Plano Clark, Miller, Creswell, McVea, McEntarffer, Harter, & Mickelson, *Qualitative Health Research*, Vol. 12, Issue 9, pp. 1264–1266, 2002. Reprinted with permission of Sage Publications, Inc.

How Do You Evaluate the Statement of the Problem in a Research Study?

Recall that researchers develop a statement of the problem passage to present their argument for why they conducted the research study. By identifying the five elements of topic, problem, justification, deficiencies, and audiences, you can understand and interpret the argument being presented. As you identify the elements in a report's statement of the problem, you should also evaluate the quality of each element as well as the overall argument in order to determine your own assessment of how well the researchers answered the "So what?" question. Table 3.1 lists criteria that are useful to consider when evaluating the elements of a study's statement of the problem as well as its overall argument. This table also provides indicators of higher quality and lower quality for the criteria to help you make your own judgments when evaluating the information provided in a research report.

The rating form in Figure 3.4 provides a convenient means for you to apply the quality criteria to a statement of the problem described in the Introduction section of any research report. For each of the criteria you locate, assign a quality rating from *fair* (1) to *excellent* (3), and document your evidence and/or reasoning behind the rating. If one of the criteria is missing or very poorly stated, then indicate *poor* (0) as your rating.

TABLE 3.1 Criteria for Evaluating the Statement of the Problem in a Research Report

Quality Criteria	Indicators of Higher Quality	Indicators of Lower Quality
The Key Elements		
1. The topic is interesting.	+ The study's subject matter is intriguing and pertinent. + The report begins by introducing the subject matter in a broad way and engages the reader from the first sentence.	− The study's subject matter is boring and irrelevant. − The report begins with detailed and specialized concepts and does not engage the reader.
2. There is a meaningful problem.	+ The study addresses at least one clear problem that needs to be solved. + The problem is stated explicitly and succinctly.	− It is unclear why the identified issue is a problem that needs to be solved. − A problem is merely implied.
3. The importance of the problem is justified.	+ Clear evidence of the importance of the problem is provided by several recent references in the literature as well as with personal experiences.	− The problem seems relatively unimportant and little evidence is offered to justify its importance.
4. There are deficiencies in the knowledge about the problem.	+ Two or more clear deficiencies are stated and supported by the literature such as a gap in knowledge, research that has not been extended, a lack of replication, the omission of the voices of marginalized people, or practices that are not sufficient.	− Only a non-specific statement about a general lack of knowledge is provided with little support from the literature.
5. There are audiences who can benefit from the missing knowledge.	+ Two or more audiences for the missing knowledge are identified. + Specific examples of how the audiences could use the missing knowledge are provided.	− Only a general audience for the missing knowledge is implied. − No examples of how the audiences could use the missing knowledge are provided.
General Evaluation		
6. The passage clearly argues that the study is warranted.	+ The topic, problem, justification, deficiencies, and audiences form a logical, coherent, and convincing argument that the study is of interest, important, needed, and significant.	− The argument that the study is of interest, important, needed, and significant is confusing, unclear, and not convincing.
7. The passage is well written.	+ The passage is engaging, concise, and easy to follow.	− The passage is uninteresting, overly verbose, and hard to follow.

Quality Criteria	Quality Rating				Your Evidence and/or Reasoning
	0 = Poor	1 = Fair	2 = Good	3 = Excellent	
The Key Elements					
1. The topic is interesting.					
2. There is a meaningful problem.					
3. The importance of the problem is justified.					
4. There are deficiencies in the knowledge about the problem.					
5. There are audiences who can benefit from the missing knowledge.					
General Evaluation					
6. The passage clearly argues that the study is warranted.					
7. The passage is well written.					
Overall Quality 0–10 = Low quality 11–16 = Adequate quality 17–21 = High quality	**Total Score =**				**My Overall Assessment =**

FIGURE 3.4   A Rating Scale for Evaluating the Statement of the Problem in a Research Report

Because the goal of a study's statement of the problem is to provide a compelling argument in support of the research study, several of these ratings will be subjective because what rates as very interesting and convincing to one person may not rate so highly for another. Even with this caveat in mind, a good statement of the problem should still score well on most of the items listed in Figure 3.4. By summing the rating scores for each of the criteria and using the suggested cutoff values provided at the bottom of the figure, you will have a quantitative measure that you can use to inform your overall assessment of a study's statement of the problem.

Reviewing What You've Learned To Do

- *Identify and understand the statement of the problem in a research report.*
  - ❑ The statement of the problem is found in the Introduction section of a research report. This passage presents the researchers' argument for why the study is interesting, important, needed, and significant for others.
  - ❑ Researchers identify a research problem as a key part of the statement of the problem passage. A research problem is an issue, controversy, or concern that guides the need for a research study. The research problem is more specific than a study's topic, which is the broad subject matter of the study, and more general than a study's purpose, which is the researcher's specific goal for conducting the study.
- *List five reasons why researchers need to conduct studies to add to knowledge about research problems.*
  - ❑ There is a need to study a research problem when new knowledge about the problem is required. New knowledge about research problems is called for when there is a need to fill a gap in the existing literature, to replicate past results, to extend past results, to give voice to those unheard, and to inform practice.

- ■ *Distinguish between the types of research problems that fit quantitative studies and qualitative studies.*
  - ❑ Research problems that call for explanations about treatment effects, relationships among variables, or trends for many people fit a quantitative research approach.
  - ❑ Research problems that call for explorations about individual perspectives, unfolding processes, or the meaning of phenomena fit a qualitative research approach.
- ■ *Know how to identify the five elements that comprise a good statement of the problem passage.*
  - ❑ A good statement of the problem passage creates interest by identifying the general topic of the study.
  - ❑ The passage conveys the importance of the study by identifying a problem that needs to be solved.
  - ❑ The passage justifies the importance of the research problem by including scholarly and personal evidence.
  - ❑ The passage argues why the study is needed by identifying deficiencies that exist in the knowledge base about the problem.
  - ❑ The passage indicates the usefulness and significance of the study by mentioning audiences that may benefit from learning the missing knowledge.
- ■ *Evaluate the quality of the statement of the problem in a research report.*
  - ❑ The evaluation of a statement of the problem passage begins by considering the extent to which the author effectively considered the five key elements of topic, research problem, justification for the problem, deficiencies, and audiences.
  - ❑ The evaluation of a statement of the problem passage is also based on the extent to which the author's argument for the study is logical, coherent, convincing, and well written.

✓ **To assess what you've learned to do, click here to answer questions and receive instant feedback.**

Reading Research Articles

At the end of this chapter, you will find a research article to help you practice your new skills. Carefully read the quantitative bullying-intervention study by Perkins, Craig, and Perkins (2011) starting on p. 98. First, write a complete, APA-style reference for the article.

As you read the article, pay close attention to the statement of the problem that appears in the Introduction section (paragraphs 01–02). Use the highlighting tool in the Pearson etext to indicate where the authors have provided information about the statement of the problem, and use the notetaking tool to add marginal notes that name each element you highlighted and note how each one is related to the study's importance. Among the elements you will want to find are:

1. Topic
2. Research problem
3. Justification
4. Deficiency (or gap)
5. Audiences

Note, however, that sometimes authors do not directly state all of these elements—they may not explicitly state the topic, research problem, justification, deficiency, or audiences. If one of these elements is missing, indicate that in your marginal notes.

 Click here to go to the quantitative bullying-intervention study by Perkins et al. (2011) so that you can write a complete APA-style reference for the article and enter marginal notes about the study.

Understanding Research Articles

Apply your knowledge of the content of this chapter to the quantitative bullying-intervention study by Perkins et al. (2011) starting on p. 98.

1. Examine the first sentence for this study: "Over the last decade, increased media attention to the characteristics of school shooting and cyberbullying perpetrators and their victims has heightened research interest in bullying among adolescents, particularly in school settings (Dake, Price, & Telljohann, 2003; Elias & Zins, 2003; Reuter-Rice, 2008; Srabstein, 2008)." Evaluate whether it is an effective first sentence for introducing the study's topic.

2. What research problem(s) do the authors identify?

3. How do the authors justify the importance of the research problem?

4. A research study about a problem is needed if knowledge about the problem is lacking. What deficiencies in knowledge did the authors identify?

5. Did the authors mention audiences that may benefit from the new knowledge generated by the bullying intervention study? If so, who are they? If not, what audiences would you suggest?

6. What indications did you note in this Introduction section to suggest the need for a quantitative study to address the research problem?

✓ **Click here to answer the questions and receive instant feedback.**

Evaluating Research Articles

Practice evaluating the quality of a study's statement of the problem, using the quantitative bullying-intervention study by Perkins et al. (2011) starting on p. 98.

1. Use the criteria discussed in Table 3.1 to evaluate the quality of the statement of the problem in the bullying-intervention study. Note that, for this question, the rating form includes advice to help guide your evaluation.

✓ **Click here to open the rating scale form (Figure 3.4) to enter your ratings, evidence, and reasoning.**

An Example of Quantitative Research: The Bullying-Intervention Study

Let's examine another published research article to apply the ideas you are learning. Throughout this book, we will refer to this study as the "quantitative bullying-intervention" study. This journal article reports a quantitative research study conducted and reported by Perkins et al. (2011). Examine this article to practice your skills with reading, understanding, and evaluating research.

 Click here to write a complete APA-style reference for this article and receive instant feedback.

Group Processes &
Intergroup Relations

G
P
I
R

Article

Group Processes & Intergroup Relations
14(5) 703–722
© The Author(s) 2011
Reprints and permission: sagepub.
co.uk/journalsPermissions.nav
DOI: 10.1177/1368430210398004
gpir.sagepub.com

⑤SAGE

Using social norms to reduce bullying: A research intervention among adolescents in five middle schools

H. Wesley Perkins,[1] David W. Craig[1] and
Jessica M. Perkins[2]

Abstract

Bullying attitudes and behaviors and perceptions of peers were assessed in a case study experiment employing a social norms intervention in five diverse public middle schools in the State of New Jersey (Grades 6 to 8). Data were collected using an anonymous online survey (baseline n = 2,589; postintervention n = 3,024). In the baseline survey, students substantially misperceived peer norms regarding bullying perpetration and support for probullying attitudes. As predicted by social norms theory, they thought bullying perpetration, victimization, and probullying attitudes were far more frequent than was the case. Also as predicted, variation in perceptions of the peer norm for bullying was significantly associated with personal bullying perpetration and attitudes. Using print media posters as the primary communication strategy, an intervention displaying accurate norms from survey results was conducted at each of the five school sites. A pre-/postintervention comparison of results revealed significant reductions overall in perceptions of peer bullying and probullying attitudes while personal bullying of others and victimization were also reduced and support for reporting bullying to adults at school and in one's family increased. The extent of reductions across school sites was associated with the prevalence and extent of recall of seeing poster messages reporting actual peer norms drawn from the initial survey data. Rates of change in bullying measures were highest (from around 17% to 35%) for the school with the highest message recall by students after a one-and-a-half-year intervention. Results suggest that a social norms intervention may be a promising strategy to help reduce bullying in secondary school populations.

Keywords

bullying, students, middle schools, violence, social norms, peers, perceptions, misperceptions, norms, adolescents

Paper received 16 June 2010; revised version accepted 05 December 2010.

[1]Hobart and William Smith Colleges, Geneva, New York
[2]Harvard University, Cambridge, Massachusetts

Corresponding author:
H. Wesley Perkins, Hobart and William Smith Colleges, 214 Stern Hall, Pulteney Street, Geneva, New York 14456 USA
Email: perkins@hws.edu

Introduction

(01) Over the last decade, increased media attention to the characteristics of school shooting and cyber-bullying perpetrators and their victims has heightened research interest in bullying among adolescents, particularly in school settings (Dake, Price, & Telljohann, 2003; Elias & Zins, 2003; Reuter-Rice, 2008; Srabstein, 2008). In the United States, a nationally representative survey of youth in Grades 6 to 12 showed that 9%, 9%, and 3% were identified as bullies, victims, and both bullies and victims, respectively, in 2001 (Spriggs, Iannotti, Nansel, & Haynie, 2007). A 2002–2003 study on the prevalence of various forms of victimization in a nationally representative sample of young children and adolescents found that emotional teasing (one form of bullying) occurred among 20% of the sample (Finkelhor, Ormrod, Turner, & Hamby, 2005). Other studies focusing on different areas within the United States have shown a similar prevalence of bullying ranging from 20 to 30% (Carlyle & Steinman, 2007; Juvonen, Graham, & Schuster, 2003; Sawyer, Bradshaw, & O'Brennan, 2008).

(02) Given the potential psychosomatic, violent, and other negative consequences of bullying (Brunstein Klomek, Marrocco, Kleinman, Schonfeld, & Gould, 2007; Klomek et al., 2008, 2009; Lund et al., 2009; Nansel, Craig, Overpeck, Saluja, & Ruan, 2004; Nansel et al., 2001; Nansel, Overpeck, Haynie, Ruan, & Scheidt, 2003; Salmon, James, & Smith, 1998; Sourander, Helstela, Helenius, & Piha, 2000; Srabstein & Piazza, 2008), understanding why some people are at risk of either bullying perpetration or victimization is salient. Numerous studies and reviews have shown many individual, family, peer/social, community, and school risk factors that contribute to bullying and youth violence such as low IQ, antisocial attitudes, weight status, substance use, television viewing, exposure to family violence, low parental involvement, poor family functioning, social rejection by peers, poor academic performance, diminished economic opportunities, socially disorganized neighborhoods, school social environment, school size, and school policy (Bowes et al., 2009; Center for Disease Control and Prevention [CDC], 2008; Department of Health and Human Services [DHHS], 2001; Janssen, Craig, Boyce, & Pickett, 2004; Johnson, 2009; Kuntsche, Knibbe, Engels, & Gmel, 2007; Kuntsche et al., 2006; Lipsey & Derzon, 1998; Resnick, Ireland, & Borowsky, 2004; Smith & Myron-Wilson, 1998; Spriggs et al., 2007). Although several reports on youth violence (American Psychological Association [APA], 1996; DHHS, 2001; Hahn et al., 2007; Murray, Guerra, & Williams, 1997; Srabstein et al., 2008) have signaled the necessity of developing effective prevention programs, many of the aforementioned studies do not fully identify the mechanisms explaining why youth may engage in bullying, knowledge that would help to devise effective prevention.

Conformity to peer norms

(03) Although sociodemographic and contextual factors represent an important consideration when attempting to predict and prevent bullying perpetration and victimization, another set of potential risk factors—peer norms and the perception of peer norms—deserves special attention. Decades of research in social psychology going all the way back to the classic experiments of Solomon Asch (Asch, 1956) and Musafer Sherif (Sherif, 1936, 1937) have demonstrated the strong tendency of people to conform to peer norms as they look to others in their midst to help define the situation and give guidance on expected behaviors in the group or cultural setting. Although many people, and especially adolescents, frequently think of themselves as individuals in their actions, a considerable degree of peer influence is consistently documented in laboratory experiments, social surveys, and observations of crowd behavior. In studies on antecedents of personal health-related behaviors, for example, extensive evidence has supported the theory of reasoned action (Ajzen & Fishbein, 1980) and its extension, the theory of planned behavior, which posits norms as a determinant of personal behavior along with personal attitudes and perceived behavioral control (Ajzen, 2001, 2002; Ajzen & Madden, 1986). Furthermore, research on adolescents' health and well-being has singled out peer influence as crucial in regard to risk behaviors such as alcohol, tobacco, and other drug use. Bullying and victimization in schools are inherently relational processes, relying on domination, subjugation, and bystander apathy, all presumably shaped by peer norms. This type of violence is a demonstration of "peer group power" in which a whole peer group participates in the bullying with individuals fulfilling different roles and acting as moderators of such behavior (Salmivalli, 1999).

(04)   Often, bullying occurs in academic settings, not only because adolescents spend a significant portion of every day in school, but also because schools are such peer intensive social environments where behaviors such as who sits with whom in the lunchroom are rigidly defined by student norms and pervasively communicated in the ways students talk (or not talk) to each other (Eder, Evans, & Parker, 1995). Thus, students form impressions, be they correct or incorrect, about what is going on in the school environment and who is involved in peer social interaction from a context where peer talk frequently dominates the milieu. In turn, these impressions may lead students to participate in bullying, to acquiesce to victimization, or to remain as bystanders to the bullying of others.

(05)   Thus, widely shared practices or behaviors (descriptive norms) and widely shared beliefs or common attitudes (injunctive norms) serve as social cues directing and constraining individuals' behaviors and attitudes in educational environments at various stages of development. For example, among 1,368 female sixth graders, friends' bullying perpetration or victimization was associated with personal bully/victim status (Mouttapa, Valente, Gallaher, Rohrbach, & Unger, 2004). Among college students, peer group ideological beliefs predicted individual members prejudiced attitudes (Poteat & Spanierman, 2010).

Misperceived norms and the social norms approach to reducing problem behavior

(06)   Since its introduction in an initial study of university student drinking (H. W. Perkins & Berkowitz,

1986), the examination of the degree of discrepancy between actual and perceived norms as well as the potential influence of both has received a great deal of theoretical and empirical examination as applied to adolescent and young-adult consumption of alcohol, tobacco, and other drugs (H. W. Perkins, 2003a). Indeed, a consistent and dramatic pattern of misperceptions about peer norms for substance use has been documented in studies conducted in several nations (Hughes, Julian, Richman, Mason, & Long, 2008; Kilmer et al., 2006; Linkenbach & Perkins, 2003; Lintonen & Konu, 2004; McAlaney & McMahon, 2007; Page, Ihasz, Hantiu, Simonek, & Klarova, 2008; Page, Ihasz, Simonek, Klarova, & Hantiu, 2006; H. W. Perkins, 2007; H. W. Perkins & Craig, 2003; H. W. Perkins, Haines, & Rice, 2005; H. W. Perkins, Meilman, Leichliter, Cashin, & Presley, 1999) where the tendency is to overestimate the permissiveness of peers and the extent or prevalence of use, even in peer contexts where use is relatively high. Similarly, adolescent and young adult misperceptions of norms have been identified for other concerns regarding health and well-being including body weight and image (Clemens, Thombs, Olds, & Gordon, 2008; J. M. Perkins, Perkins, & Craig, 2010a), consumption of sugar-sweetened drinks (J. M. Perkins, Perkins, & Craig, 2010b), violence against women (Fabiano, Perkins, Berkowitz, Linkenbach, & Stark, 2003; Neighbors et al., 2010), and sexual behavior (Martens et al., 2006).

(07)   Thus, the various studies consistently show that positive attitudes and behaviors, though most often the norm among young people in schools and communities, are often not perceived to be the peer norm. Adolescents and young adults tend to believe that risky or problem behaviors and attitudes are most common among peers and think protective responsible action is rare. These exaggerated or erroneous perceptions may be the result of (a) attribution error where behavior occasionally observed in others is thought to be typical of them when only incomplete or superficial information about peers is available, (b) social conversation among youth about the most extreme behavior in their midst getting disproportionate attention, thus creating a sense that the extreme behavior is common, and (c) entertainment and news media further amplifying misperceptions by focusing almost entirely on images and stories of the risky or problem behavior (H. W. Perkins, 1997, 2002, 2003a).

(08) It is argued that these misperceptions then contribute to or exacerbate the problem behavior as more youth begin to support and engage in the behavior than would otherwise be the case if norms were accurately perceived. Amidst these widely held misperceptions of problem behavior as "normal" among peers, those who regularly engage in the problem behavior freely do so thinking they are just like most others and are likely to have the greatest commitment to the misperception. Those who are ambivalent about joining in the behavior, nonetheless, by misperceiving the norm, may occasionally do so mistakenly feeling a false majority pressure. Finally, most of those who oppose the behavior (the real majority) remain silent as bystanders to the problem behavior believing that they, as bystanders, are alone in their opposition. They may hold less extreme misperceptions of the problem as the norm and thus feel least pressured to actually engage in the behavior. However, the misperception that does exist among them is still harmful as it spawns apathy and withdrawal from interaction with peers (H. W. Perkins, 2007).

(09) Thus, the strategy of the social norms approach to preventing problem behavior, put simply, is to dispel the myths about the problem being the norm among peers. Social norms interventions seek to turn the process around by intensively communicating the truth about positive norms based on credible data drawn from the target population. In short, social norms theory (H. W. Perkins, 1997, 2003b) predicts that by reducing misperceptions and increasing the proportion of students with more accurate information about existing healthy norms, occurrences of unhealthy or problem behavior will decrease. Several intervention studies regarding alcohol, tobacco, and other drug use have shown that when students are intensively exposed to actual norms, their misperceptions and actual problem behavior

can be reduced (Bewick, Trusler, Mulhern, Barkham, & Hill, 2008; DeJong et al., 2006; Haines & Spear, 1996; Haines, Barker, & Rice, 2003; Hansen & Graham, 1991; Linkenbach & Perkins, 2003; Mattern & Neighbors, 2004; Neighbors, Larimer, & Lewis, 2004; H. W. Perkins & Craig, 2006; Turner, Perkins, & Bauerle, 2008). Interventions using social norms feedback about peer and community attitudes and behavior for other topic areas such as conservation and recycling have demonstrated positive effects as well (Cialdini, Reno, & Kallgren, 1990; Schultz, 1999; Schultz, Khazian, & Zaleski, 2008).

Although limited research has examined the **(10)** relationship between bullying norms and personal involvement in bullying, and some studies have found norms to be important predictors of other health-related behavior among adolescents, no studies have examined the accuracy of students' perceptions of bullying norms (personal perception of the bullying norm in a given group versus the actual extent of bullying behavior and attitudinal support for it in the group). Furthermore, no study has reported an intervention to challenge misperceptions as a means to reduce bullying. Thus, the current study introduces research examining three important questions related to perceived norms of bullying. Specifically, we consider: (a) the extent and direction of misperceptions about bullying as well as how much variation in perceived norms exists, (b) the degree of association between perceptions of the peer bullying norm and personal involvement in bullying, and (c) the impact that might be produced by disseminating actual norms about bullying in adolescent populations. Thus, the objective of the study was to address these three questions with action-oriented research on bullying conducted in five middle-school populations.

Method

Participants

Students in five middle schools located through- **(11)** out the State of New Jersey in the United States provided the data for this research. Each school contained Grades 6 through 8 and almost all students were between the ages of 11 and 14. The five schools were from an initial group of seven middle schools in the state that had chosen to participate in an online survey of their students regarding bullying in late spring of 2006. The five sites providing data for this study were all of the schools from the initial survey group that fulfilled the following criteria: (a) the entire school population served as the sampling frame for the survey; (b) the school subsequently conducted an intervention to challenge misperceptions with data-based messages about actual peer norms in the local school; (c) the intervention campaign included at least the posting of print media in the school with messages that had been created by the research team and displayed with supporting images created or approved by the researchers (additional communication venues were also used by local schools in some instances); (d) the same survey of bullying was again administered as a postintervention assessment with all students as the sampling frame; and (e) demographically comparable pre- and postintervention samples were obtained from the school as a result of the surveys. The two other schools that participated initially were excluded from the study because their response rates for the baseline survey were very low (17% and 22%) and resulted in samples that did not adequately represent the school populations. No schools conducted the survey at two time points without conducting the intervention so no overtime control comparison sites were available. Thus, this study provides

five case studies of the intervention based on representative cross-sectional data collected at each school site at pre- and postintervention time points.

Four schools in this study were very large middle schools (populations between 900 and 1,300 students) and one was midsize (300–400 students). Three were located in suburban settings, one was in a combined urban and suburban area, and one was rural. Three schools were largely homogeneous in racial composition (85% or higher White) and two schools reflected substantial diversity (about 50% minority races). The average response rate across schools from the school populations was 59%. Table 1 provides the pre- and postintervention respondent characteristics for each school. **(12)**

Survey procedures

Data were collected using the "Survey of Bullying at Your School" (Social Norms Surveys Online). The Institutional Review Board of the academic institution hosting the online survey approved the survey procedures and local schools obtained parental consent for student participation. From class sessions or other group assignments in school, students who had parental consent were instructed to go in groups to rooms where a computer was available for each student. Each group was given general information about the online survey and told that the survey was voluntary and anonymous. A student could leave all questions **(13)**

Table 1. Pre- and postintervention sample demographics for five school sites

	School A[a]		School B[a]		School C[a]		School D[b]		School E[b]	
	Pre	Post	Pre	Post	Pre	Post	Pre	Post	Pre	Post
N	180	225	759	681	578	799	484	592	588	727
Response rate (%)	50	70	80	71	47	69	43	50	50	61
Female (%)	58	56	53	53	55	52	53	50	50	52
Mean age	12.5	12.3	12.8	12.3	12.7	12.4	12.8	12.5	12.6	12.5
(SD)	(.9)	(1.0)	(1.0)	(1.0)	(.9)	(1.0)	(.9)	(1.0)	(1.0)	(1.0)
Minority (%)	27	24	21	25	29	29	48	57	57	59

Note. [a]Schools with 1.5 academic-year intervention; [b]Schools with 1.0 academic-year intervention.

blank if they did not want to participate. No personal computing accounts were used. To access the survey all students in a specific group session were publicly given the same password and URL address in order to assure students of their anonymity in completing the survey. However, the password was changed between sessions so that no student could access the survey and submit multiple responses after leaving his or her survey session. There was a teacher or other adult monitor present simply to make sure that students did not speak with each other while taking the survey. The survey data were subsequently checked to screen out submissions with intentionally provided erroneous or random answers. The small number of respondents who submitted multiple answers that were clearly outside of possible ranges or who answered sets of questions with contradictory responses was eliminated.

Measures

(14) **Bullying perpetration**   The survey instrument included a series of questions about what are commonly identified as bullying behaviors in schools including: (a) pushing, shoving, hitting, kicking, hair pulling, or tripping; (b) teasing in an unfriendly way; (c) calling hurtful names; (d) excluding someone from a group to make them feel bad; (e) taking or damaging someone else's belongings; (f) spreading unkind stories or rumors about someone else; (g) threatening to hurt someone; and (h) making someone do something they did not want to do. Specifically, respondents were asked how often in the last 30 days they had done each of these eight behaviors to another student using the response categories of "Not in the last 30 days" (coded 0), "Once" (coded 1), "2–3 times" (coded 2), and "4 or more times" (coded 3). We refer to these behaviors as personal bullying behaviors. An index measure of personal bullying perpetration was subsequently computed by summing scores for responses to all eight items. Scale reliability analyses (Cronbach's alpha) indicated high inter-item reliability for responses in both the preintervention (.82) and postintervention (.83) surveys.

Using the same behavioral items and response **(15)** categories, respondents were also asked how often they thought most other students had done these things at their school. We refer to these responses as perceived peer norms for bullying behaviors. An index measure of the perceived norm for bullying perpetration was subsequently computed by summing scores of responses to all eight items. Scale reliability analyses (Cronbach's alpha) indicated high inter-item reliability for the perceived norm measure in both the preintervention (.91) and postintervention (.91) surveys.

Bullying victimization   Seven items comprised **(16)** measures of personal bullying victimization and the perceived norm for bullying victimization that paralleled the first seven items of the perpetration measures. Respondents were asked how often in the last 30 days each of the following things had happened to them, and also how often in the same 30 days they thought these things had happened to most other students at their school: (a) being pushed, shoved, hit, kicked, hair pulled, or tripped; (b) being teased in an unfriendly way; (c) being called hurtful names; (d) being excluded from a group to hurt feelings; (e) belongings being taken or damaged; (f) unkind story or rumor spread; and (g) threatened to be hurt. The eighth item in the list of perpetration measures—making someone do something they did not want to do—was not converted to a victimization item in the construction of the survey because it was judged that "being made to do something you did not want to do" might be confused with being required to perform legitimate or positive behaviors under the direction of peers or others at school. Thus, the survey only presented seven victimization items. The same response categories and scores as used in the bullying perpetration questions were employed, and again, indices were created by summing responses to the items. Scale reliability analyses (Cronbach's alpha) also indicated high inter-item reliability for personal bullying victimization in both the preintervention (.82) and postintervention (.81) surveys and for the perceived norm for bullying victimization at both times (.86 and .88).

(17) Probullying attitudes   A second set of questions measured personal pro-bullying attitudes and the perceived norm for pro-bullying attitudes by providing four statements and asking respondents to what extent they agreed or disagreed and to what extent they thought most other students agreed or disagreed. Statements were as follows: (a) "Students should NOT tease in a mean way, call others hurtful names, or spread unkind stories about other students"; (b) "Students should NOT shove, kick, hit, trip, or hair pull another student"; (c) "Students should NOT threaten to hit another student even if they don't actually hit the other student"; (d) "Students should always try to be friendly with students who are different from themselves." Response categories for personal beliefs and for what respondents thought most others would say were strongly agree, agree, disagree, and strongly disagree coded 0 to 3, respectively. Indices for personal attitude and the perceived norm were created by summing the response scores for all four items. Scale reliability analyses (Cronbach's alpha) indicated high inter-item reliability for personal probullying attitudes (.82 and .84 for pre- and postsurveys, respectively) and for the perceived norm for pro-bullying attitudes (.82 at each survey time).

(18) Reporting bullying   In a third set of questions students were asked: "Who do you think students should tell if they or someone else are being bullied at school? And what would most other students say?" Respondents could indicate any of several different types of people for their personal opinion with a separate listing of the same types for their perceptions about what would be most others' response (perceived peer norm). Of specific interest for the intervention and for assessment in this study were the three categories: (a) principal, (b) teacher or counselor, and (c) parent or other adult relative.

(19) Poster campaign message exposure   One final measure used in this study was drawn from a set of questions added to the postintervention survey at the end of the survey instrument. The questions asked how often and where during the school year respondents had seen or heard information about what most students or the majority do or think about bullying and unfriendly behaviors based on survey results from students at their school. Given the nature of the intervention described below, the item focusing on how often, if ever, students had seen such material on posters at school was of specific interest for this study. Response categories were "never," "once," and "more than once" (scored 0, 1, or 2, respectively).

Intervention

The basic strategy of the social norms intervention was to provide students in each local school with feedback about the results of the initial survey by conveying actual positive norms, which were widely misperceived. Social norm messages about the prevalence of positive behavior and opinion were created for each school based on their data. Messages indicated the recent survey on bullying at their school as the source of information and noted the large number of students participating. Examples of norm messages (school name deleted) are: **(20)**

> Most ____ Middle School students (9 out of 10) agree that students should always try to be friendly with students who are different from themselves.

> 95% of ____ Middle School students say students should NOT tease in a mean way, call others hurtful names, or spread unkind stories about other students.

> 94% of ____ Middle School students believe students should NOT shove, kick, hit, trip, or hair pull another student.

> 9 out of 10 ____ Middle School students agree that students should NOT threaten to hit another student even if they don't actually hit the other student.

> Most ____ Middle School students (3 out of 4) do NOT exclude someone from a group to make them feel bad.

Most _____ School students (9 out of 10) do NOT take or damage other's belongings.

Most _____ Middle School students (8 out of 10) think that students should tell a teacher or counselor if they or someone else are being bullied at school.

94% of _____ students say they are encouraged to help and respect other students.

Most (4 out of 5) _____ students do NOT spread unkind rumors or stories about other students.

2 out of 3 _____ students think that students should tell a parent or other adult relative if they or someone else are being bullied at school.

7 out of 10 _____ students do NOT get involved in any pushing, shoving, kicking, pulling hair or tripping any other students.

Poster images containing these messages did not display the negative behavior. Rather, they presented scenes of positive student interaction or simply scenes or emblems associated with the local school. Figures 1 and 2 provide examples (with actual school names and survey dates changed or removed). These posters were printed as large (3 by 4 feet) wall posters and as smaller posters for display in the school. In three schools, the campaign was carried out over one and one half academic years before the postintervention assessment and in two schools the campaign ran for one academic year before the postintervention assessment.

Analytic approach

The first hypothesis we examined was that students tend to overestimate the prevalence of and **(21)**

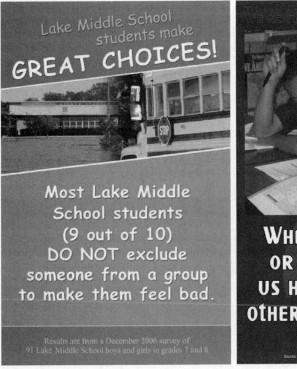

Figure 1. Examples of social norms intervention posters.

Figure 2. Example of social norms intervention poster.

support for bullying behaviors among peers. We assessed this initial assumption by comparing the mean reported personal bullying perpetration, bullying victimization, and probullying attitudes with the corresponding perceived peer-norm mean for perpetration, victimization, and attitudes at each school using a paired sample *t* test of significance for each set of measures in each preintervention school sample. We then tested our second hypothesis that students' personal behaviors and attitudes are associated with what they perceive to be the norm. That is, even though most individuals may overestimate problem behaviors and attitudes, we further hypothesized that those who tend to think bullying behaviors and attitudes are more pervasive than not will also be the ones who engage in more of the actual behavior and more often believe it is acceptable. To test this assumption we calculated the correlation (Pearson r) between the perceived norm and personal behavior or attitude in each initial sample.

(22)   Our third hypothesis was that an intervention providing students with information about actual norms to challenge misperceptions of the peer norm would reduce misperceptions (i.e., lower students' estimates of the prevalence and support for bullying behavior and raise estimates of peer support for reporting bullying to principals, teachers, and parents), and, in turn, reduce the actual levels of bullying and support for bullying and raise levels of personal support for reporting bullying. This prediction was tested for each school site by (a) comparing the pre- and postintervention levels on each of the perception of peer measures of this study, and (b) comparing the pre- and postintervention levels on each of the personal measures. For each of these comparisons, we conducted an independent sample *t* test for a significant pre/postintervention difference in means or proportions in the predicted direction. It is important to note that although the social norms intervention model predicts that perceptions of peers can be shifted in the direction of the actual norms by providing accurate normative information, it does not necessarily predict that the gap between perceived and actual norms will be lessened. Rather, the model predicts that

712   *Group Processes & Intergroup Relations 14(5)*

changing what is perceived as normative will lead to a change in personal attitudes and behaviors. Thus, an equally large gap may still exist in the wake of an effective intervention if both perceptions of norms and personal attitudes or behaviors have shifted toward the actual and subsequently more positive norm. Assessing the pre/post differences in perception and in personal attitude or behavior, and not a change in the gap between perceived peer and personal attitudes or behaviors, is the critical measure of impact.

(23)   Furthermore, it is most appropriate to use an independent samples test of the difference of pre/post means (proportions) in this instance (and not a paired sample test). First, the data were collected anonymously so there are no links between the pre- and postintervention respondent records. Second, the samples measured at baseline preintervention represented mostly different respondents than the respondents in the postintervention survey. The postintervention survey, which took place 12 to 18 months later, was intended to measure the impact of the intervention on perceptions and experiences of bullying for all grade levels in the school including new cohorts that moved into the middle school after such an intervention was underway. Thus, one or two new grade cohorts had moved in (and out) of each school by the time the postsurvey was given. Therefore, posttest samples inherently included from one third to two thirds different respondents who were new in each school. Moreover, some additional students move in and out of the school district every year as families move. Finally, each year a significant portion of the student body did not participate (response rates reported in Table 1) due to absences on the survey days or parental permission slips for participation not being available. The net result is that only a relatively small percentage of students were the same in the pre- and postsamples, and thus very little distortion is created in using the independent samples *t* test. Also, it is important to note that the significance test is fundamentally conservative in identifying true Time 1/Time 2 differences in the population because the sampling frame used was the entire population itself, not a random sample drawn from the population.

An additional prediction associated with our **(24)** third hypothesis was that the degree of success of a social norms intervention is based on achieving widespread and intensive exposure to the campaign messages. Thus, variation among school sites in the prevalences of recalling multiple exposures and no exposure to social norms poster media about bullying at school were examined. The mean exposure level for each school was calculated and then correlated (Pearson r) with the mean rate of pre/post intervention change in all bullying measures at each site.

Results

Baseline findings

Table 2 presents the initial mean scores in all five **(25)** school samples (preintervention surveys) for personal bullying perpetration compared to the perceived norm for bullying perpetration, for personal bullying victimization compared to the perceived norm for bullying victimization, and for personal probullying attitudes compared to the perceived norm for probullying attitudes. Here, the mean of each personal measure provides an estimate of the actual norm existing in each school based on the sample. The mean of each perceived-norm index provides an estimate of students' average subjective perception of how much bullying perpetration, victimization, and attitudinal support for bullying is the peer norm. Perceptions of the peer norm for bullying behavior are three to four times higher than the estimates of the actual norm based on the aggregate of personal behaviors in each sample. Perceived levels of victimization are more than twice as large as what are found in the anonymous personal reports, and peers are perceived to be about twice as supportive of probullying attitudes as what is actually found among students at each school. Statistically significant differences ($p < .001$) were found in the predicted direction in every instance of comparing means in each set of measures at each site.

Table 2. Preintervention bullying perpetration, victimization, and attitude norms compared to perceived peer norms by school site

	School A	School B	School C	School D	School E
BULLYING PERPETRATION					
Personal bullying perpetration mean (SD)	2.3 (2.8)	2.9 (3.8)	2.7 (3.7)	3.0 (3.6)	2.4 (3.3)
Perceived norm for bullying perpetration mean (SD)	10.6 (5.7)	10.7 (6.6)	13.0 (6.8)	11.5 (6.3)	9.4 (6.2)
BULLYING VICTIMIZATION					
Personal bullying victimization mean (SD)	5.0 (4.6)	4.4 (4.4)	4.7 (5.0)	4.5 (4.3)	4.1 (4.2)
Perceived norm for bullying victimization mean (SD)	10.7 (4.9)	10.8 (5.4)	12.7 (5.6)	11.4 (5.1)	10.2 (5.2)
PROBULLYING ATTITUDES					
Personal bullying attitudes mean (SD)	1.7 (2.0)	1.8 (2.2)	1.8 (2.2)	1.8 (2.1)	1.7 (2.0)
Perceived norm for bullying attitudes mean (SD)	3.3 (2.1)	3.5 (2.6)	4.5 (2.7)	3.9 (2.4)	3.5 (2.2)

Note: All personal index means are significantly different from the corresponding perception index means at $p < .001$.

Table 3. Preintervention correlations of personal bullying perpetration and attitudes with the corresponding perceived peer norm index by school site

	School A	School B	School C	School D	School E
BULLYING PERPETRATION					
Personal bullying perpetration by perceived norm for bullying perpetration	0.356	0.407	0.330	0.412	0.474
PROBULLYING ATTITUDES					
Personal bullying attitudes by perceived norm for bullying attitudes	0.465	0.563	0.395	0.503	0.529

Note: All correlations are significant at $p < .001$.

(26)   Table 3 presents correlation coefficients examining the association between students' personal bullying perpetration and their perceived norm for bullying perpetration as well as the association between the perceived norm for probullying attitudes and personal probullying attitude. Clearly one's personal behavior and attitudes regarding bullying are highly linked to how commonplace one thinks such behaviors are and how much support one believes exists for these actions among peers, regardless of the accuracy (or more often inaccuracy) of these perceptions. All correlations are positive as predicted, ranging from .33 to .56 in strength, and all are statistically significant at $p < .001$.

Pre/postintervention comparisons

Table 4 presents the results comparing pre- and **(27)** postintervention data on all perceived norm and personal measures used in this study (all bullying indices as well as the measures of respondents' perceived norms and personal attitudes regarding reporting bullying perpetration). School A demonstrated significant change in the predicted direction on all measures. There was less perception of bullying perpetration and victimization, less personal reporting of being a perpetrator or victim, and less personal and perceived peer support for bullying and more personal and perceived peer willingness to report bullying to

Table 4. Pre- and postintervention perceived norms and personal bullying perpetration, victimization, probullying attitudes, and beliefs about reporting by school site

	School A			School B			School C			School D			School E		
	Pre	Post	Rate (%) change	Pre	Post	Rate (%) change	Pre	Post	Rate (%) change	Pre	Post	Rate (%) change	Pre	Post	Rate (%) change
BULLYING PERPETRATION															
Perceived norm for bullying perpetration mean	10.6	8.1	−24***	10.7	8.4	−21***	13.0	10.7	−18***	11.5	9.2	−20***	9.4	9.4	0
Personal bullying perpetration mean	2.3	1.5	−35**	2.9	2.5	−14*	2.7	2.4	−11	3.0	2.0	−33***	2.4	2.3	−4
BULLYING VICTIMIZATION															
Perceived norm for bullying victimization mean	10.7	8.8	−18***	10.8	8.9	−18***	12.7	10.7	−16***	11.4	9.7	−15***	10.2	10.0	−2
Personal bullying victimization mean	5.0	3.3	−34***	4.4	4.0	−9	4.7	4.2	−11*	4.5	4.0	−11*	4.1	3.7	−10
PROBULLYING ATTITUDES															
Perceived norm for bullying attitudes mean	3.3	2.4	−27***	3.5	3.0	−14**	4.5	3.4	−24***	3.9	3.2	−18***	3.5	3.2	−9*
Personal bullying attitudes mean	1.7	1.1	−35**	1.8	1.5	−17*	1.8	1.7	−6	1.8	1.4	−22***	1.7	1.5	−12
REPORTING BULLYING															
Perceived most peers would say students should tell ____ if they or others are being bullied (%)															
A principal	46	60	30**	36	48	33***	39	48	23***	31	37	19*	30	36	20**
A teacher or counselor	59	69	17*	54	63	17***	48	54	13*	57	63	11*	51	61	20***
A parent/other adult relative	52	61	17*	48	54	13***	41	48	17**	48	53	10	38	48	26***
Personally thinks students should tell ____ if they or others are being bullied (%)															
A principal	55	73	33***	40	53	33***	58	67	16***	37	43	16*	44	44	0
A teacher or counselor	77	89	16**	72	79	10***	74	80	8*	81	83	2	78	80	3
A parent/other adult relative	71	81	14*	68	73	7*	68	76	12**	73	75	3	62	69	11**

Note. *p < .05; **p < .01; ***p < .001 in the predicted direction.

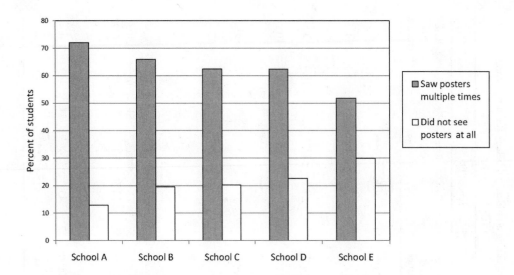

Figure 3. Recollection of seeing posters reporting survey results during the school year by intervention site.

principals, teachers and counselors, and adult relatives. Rates of change ranged from 17% to 35% in the expected direction. Postintervention samples from schools B, C, and D, likewise, displayed change as predicted on all 12 pre/postcomparisons with 11, 10, and 9 of them producing statistically significant results, respectively. Rates of change on the significant items ranged between 7% and 33% in the expected direction. Finally, School E demonstrated the least change after the intervention; only 5 of the 12 measures showed a statistically significant difference in the predicted direction and two items showed no change. Nevertheless, observed differences between the pre- and postintervention samples of School E remained in the predicted direction and there were appreciable rates of change (between 9% and 26%) in the expected direction on the five statistically significant measures for this school with the weakest impact. Thus, overall, four schools provided strong support for the intervention having a positive impact while one school showed a more mixed or weaker positive result.

Exposure to poster message intervention

Figure 3 presents the prevalence of respondents **(28)** recalling having seen multiple poster messages at school about what the majority of peers think and do regarding bullying based on survey data and the prevalence of respondents not recalling seeing any poster with this type of message. Prevalence of exposure and lack of exposure to the poster campaign is broken down by school. The school achieving the greatest postintervention change in the expected direction with significant results on all bullying items (School A) is also the school demonstrating the highest exposure level to the poster campaign with 72% reporting multiple exposures and only 13% reporting no recall. Schools B, C, and D with 11, 10, and 9 measures demonstrating significant pre/postchange, respectively, exhibited multiple exposures for 66%, 62%, and 62% of their students, respectively, and no recall for 20%, 20%, and 23%, respectively. Finally, the school that revealed the least change in perceptions of norms and personal attitudes and behaviors regarding bullying with significant differences on just five measures (School E), also demonstrated the lowest campaign exposure level. Only about half (52%) recalled seeing multiple poster messages and almost one third (30%) recalled no messages.

(29) As a further assessment of the relationship between poster message exposure levels achieved at each school and pre/postchange in school bullying climate, the mean score on the exposure question (scored as 0 for never recalling seeing a poster, 1 for once, and 2 for recalling seeing two or more poster messages) at each school was compared with the mean percentage pre/post-intervention rate of change in all attitudinal and behavioral measures of perceived and personal bullying and victimization. That is, the average of absolute values of all percentage rates of change reported in Table 4 was calculated for each school. Absolute values of rates of change were used because declines were expected based on item wording and scoring for the measures of bullying perpetration, victimization, and probullying attitudes whereas increases were expected for the measures of attitudes about reporting bullying to school officials and familial adults. Absolute values could be used for this computation because all observed change at each school

was in the predicted direction. Table 5 reports these means by school along with the correlation between mean exposure and mean rate of change. Near perfect association is demonstrated here with a Pearson r of .96, which is highly significant in the expected direction at $p < .005$ even taking into consideration the small number of schools in the correlation.

Thus, overall school exposure levels to the **(30)** campaign were strongly related to the overall change experienced at the school. More social norm message exposure was associated with greater change in the school in an almost perfect correlation. This pattern of results provides further evidence supporting the claim that the intervention to reduce misperceptions about bullying was the crucial factor accounting for the postintervention change in bullying.

Discussion

This study expands the realm of research on mis- **(31)** perceptions of peer norms among youth to the phenomenon of bullying in middle schools. Without doubt, participation in bullying behaviors is a serious problem in schools. However, this research finds that middle school students grossly

Table 5. Mean exposure to poster media and mean percentage pre-/postintervention rate of change in all bullying measures by school site

School site	Mean exposure to poster media[a]	Mean percentage rate of change in all bullying measures[b]
A	1.59	25.0
B	1.46	17.1
C	1.42	14.4
D	1.40	15.1
E	1.22	9.7
Pearson r		.96[c]

Note: [a]Mean score was computed from respondent recall of the frequency of seeing posters displaying survey information about what most students think and do about bullying during the school year where 0 = never, 1 = once, and 2 = 2 or more times. [b]Mean percentage pre/postintervention rate of change was computed from the absolute values of the rates of change in all survey measures of perceived and personal bullying as reported in Table 4. Absolute values of rates of change were used because declines were expected for the measures of bullying perpetration, victimization, and probullying attitudes whereas increases were expected for the measures of attitudes about reporting bullying. Absolute values could be used for this computation because all observed change at each school was in the predicted direction. [c]$p < .005$ in the predicted direction.

overestimate the prevalence of bullying, and also overestimate support for it in their perceptions of the norm for peer attitudes (the first hypothesis). The pattern replicates what has been found for other youth risk behaviors, most notably concerning alcohol, tobacco, and other drug use.

(32) Furthermore, variation in personal attitudes and behaviors observed among individual students was highly correlated with variation in their perceptions of the peer norm (the second hypothesis), again a pattern commonly found in research of substance abuse. Although variation in personal behavior may be, in part, a determinant of one's perception (presuming some students will rely on themselves as a referent for establishing a sense of the peer norm), much research as previously discussed, has also indicated that peer norms, and more importantly, the perception of peer norms, are strong determinants of personal attitudes and behaviors. This suggests that interventions to reduce misperceptions can help reduce problem behaviors.

(33) The third hypothesis predicted that an intervention exposing students to accurate positive norms based on local data through a print media campaign at each of the five research sites would reduce perceptions of bullying attitudes and behaviors as the peer norm and concomitantly reduce personal bullying behaviors and attitudes. The predicted result of the intervention was precisely what was observed in the comparison of the pre- and postintervention data. That is, results showed significant reductions in problematic misperceptions of the prevalence of bullying and of peer support for bullying and simultaneous reductions in personal bullying behaviors and experiences of victimization. Students were also more supportive of reporting bullying to school authorities and parents and they came to believe that peers more often supported this behavior than was previously thought to be the case.

(34) Without the availability of control site comparisons, one must be cautious in attributing the change observed to the intervention that was conducted. Other local events or newly introduced programs or policies might have contributed to the observed changes. However, all five schools with differing demographic characteristics and drawn from different areas within the state exhibited significant changes in the predicted direction and none of the schools experienced any changes in the opposite direction. Moreover, variation in the extent of change from pre- to postintervention across sites corresponded highly to the level of message exposure achieved at each school. These facts provide a greater confidence that the results are likely due to the effect of the intervention, but further research employing simultaneous control sites are no doubt needed to more rigorously test our third hypothesis. Use of a multiple baseline design (multiple pretest assessments over time before introducing the intervention) in future research might be considered to strengthen the evidence of any intervention effect if control sites cannot be enlisted.

Another limitation of this study is the reliance **(35)** on self-report measures for an estimate of actual bullying norms. It may be that some students did not fully recall all of the bullying behaviors in which they engaged over the last month or they may not want to reveal the full extent of their actions, and therefore, actual norms might be higher than estimated based on self-reports. If so, then the gap between the actual norm for personal behavior and perceived norms in reality may not be as great as the results of this study suggested. However, at least three points argue against this possibility as significantly accounting for the difference. First, the method employed made clear that the surveys were anonymous for students. Thus, they did not need to hide their behavior for fear of punishment. Second, given that students most often believed that the norm for bullying behavior among other students was so much more than they did, even among those engaging in bullying, then it could be argued that there should be little shame or fear in reporting more behavior if they in fact were doing more bullying. And, if they thought most others were engaging in extensive bullying one might argue that their perceived norm could even encourage them to say they were personally doing more bullying than was actually the case, meaning that the actual gap could be larger than observed. Third, the suggestion that recall error—the possibility that the respondent would tend not to remember all of the bullying behaviors over several weeks time—is not an issue for the measures of attitudes about bullying. One does not forget what one's attitude is, and yet the gap between personal attitudes and perceived attitudinal norms of peers was substantial as well. Although one may not always act in accordance with one's attitudes— and here that may occur precisely because of the pressure one feels to behave in bullying ways because of misperceptions of the peer norm— one's attitude is still presumably what one states unless one is intentionally being evasive.

(36)   The question about the accuracy of self-reporting personal behavior may also arise in the context of assessing the pre- to postintervention change. It is possible that exposure to messages indicating that engaging in bullying is not normative might lead some respondents to simply say they are doing less than what they reported in the initial survey given the new information. However, there were no messages about the prevalence rates of victimization, only messages about volitional behavior. And yet, being a victim of bullying also declined in the wake of the intervention, which strengthens the conclusion that actual bullying had declined.

(37)   To conclude, this research suggests that a social norms intervention may be a promising strategy to help reduce bullying. Future research should examine this approach in a broader range of school settings, consider how misperceptions emerge and are transmitted from cohort to cohort in the school context, determine which groups are most vulnerable to acting in accordance with the erroneously perceived norm, and explore other ways of delivering accurate norm messages that would effectively reduce misperceptions.

Acknowledgments

The authors wish to thank the staff of the Rowan University Center for Addiction Studies for their essential role in the recruitment of schools in this research and for their work at local school sites promoting the implementation of the social norms media intervention. The authors also wish to thank Bernadette van der Vliet of BMT Design for her work designing the poster media and Deborah Herry for administrative assistance in producing print media. Funding for survey development and administration and for poster media production was provided by Rowan University Center for Addiction Studies with support the Center received from the New Jersey Department of Education.

References

Ajzen, I. (2001). Nature and operation of attitudes. *Annual Review of Psychology, 52*(1), 27–58.

Ajzen, I. (2002). Perceived behavioral control, self-efficacy, locus of control, and the theory of planned behavior. *Journal of Applied Social Psychology, 32*, 665–683.

Ajzen, I., & Fishbein, M. (1980). *Understanding attitudes and predicting social behavior.* Englewood Cliffs, NJ: Prentice-Hall.

Ajzen, I., & Madden, T. J. (1986). Prediction of goal-directed behavior: Attitudes, intentions, and perceived behavioral control. *Journal of Experimental Social Psychology, 22*(5), 453–474.

American Psychological Association (APA). (1996). *Reducing violence: A research agenda. A Human Capital Initiative report.* Washington, DC: American Psychological Association.

Asch, S. E. (1956). Studies of independence and conformity: A minority of one against a unanimous majority. *Psychological monographs, 70*(9), 1–70.

Bewick, B. M., Trusler, K., Mulhern, B., Barkham, M., & Hill, A. J. (2008). The feasibility and effectiveness of a web-based personalised feedback and social norms alcohol intervention in UK university students: A randomised control trial. *Addictive Behaviors, 33*(9), 1192–1198.

Bowes, L., Arseneault, L., Maughan, B., Taylor, A., Caspi, A., & Moffitt, T. E. (2009). School, neighborhood, and family factors are associated with children's bullying involvement: A nationally representative longitudinal study. *Journal of American Academic Child and Adolescent Psychiatry, 48*(5), 545–553.

Brunstein Klomek, A., Marrocco, F., Kleinman, M., Schonfeld, I. S., & Gould, M. S. (2007). Bullying, depression, and suicidality in adolescents. *Journal of American Academic Child and Adolescent Psychiatry, 46*(1), 40–49.

Carlyle, K. E., & Steinman, K. J. (2007). Demographic differences in the prevalence, co-occurrence, and correlates of adolescent bullying at school. *Journal of School Health, 77*(9), 623–629.

Center for Disease Control and Prevention (CDC). (2008, August 11). *Youth violence: Risk and protective factors.* Retrieved June 10, 2010, from http://www.cdc.gov/ViolencePrevention/youthviolence/riskprotectivefactors.html

Cialdini, R. B., Reno, R. R., & Kallgren, C. A. (1990). A focus theory of normative conduct: Recycling the concept of norms to reduce littering in public places. *Journal of Personality and Social Psychology, 58*(6), 1015–1026.

Clemens, H., Thombs, D., Olds, R. S., & Gordon, K. L. (2008). Normative beliefs as risk factors for involvement in unhealthy weight control behavior. *Journal of American College Health, 56*(6), 635–641.

Dake, J. A., Price, J. H., & Telljohann, S. K. (2003). The nature and extent of bullying at school. *Journal of School Health, 73*(5), 173–180.

DeJong, W., Schneider, S. K., Towvim, L. G., Murphy, M. J., Doerr, E. E., Simonsen, N. R., ...Scribner, R. (2006). A multisite randomized trial of social norms marketing campaigns to reduce college student drinking. *Journal of Studies on Alcohol, 67*(6), 868–879.

Department of Health and Human Services (DHHS). (2001). *Youth violence: A report of the surgeon general.* Rockville, MD: U.S. Department of Health and Human Services.

Eder, D., Evans, C. C., & Parker, S. (1995). *School talk: Gender and adolescent culture.* New Brunswick, NJ: Rutgers University Press.

Elias, M. J., & Zins, J. E. (Eds.). (2003). *Bullying, peer harassment, and victimization in the schools.* Binghamton, NY: Haworth Press.

Fabiano, P. M., Perkins, H. W., Berkowitz, A., Linkenbach, J., & Stark, C. (2003). Engaging men as social justice allies in ending violence against women: Evidence for a social norms approach. *Journal American College Health, 52*(3), 105–112.

Finkelhor, D., Ormrod, R., Turner, H., & Hamby, S. L. (2005). The victimization of children and youth: A comprehensive, national survey. *Child Maltreatment, 10*(1), 5–25.

Hahn, R., Fuqua-Whitley, D., Wethington, H., Lowy, J., Crosby, A., Fullilove, M., ...Liberman, A. (2007). Effectiveness of universal school-based programs to prevent violent and aggressive behavior: A systematic review. *American Journal of Preventive Medicine, 33*(2), S114–S129.

Haines, M. P., & Spear, S. F. (1996). Changing the perception of the norm: A strategy to decrease binge drinking among college students. *Journal of American College Health, 45*(3), 134–140.

Haines, M. P., Barker, G. P., & Rice, R. (2003). Using social norms to reduce alcohol and tobacco use in two Midwestern high schools. In H. W. Perkins (Ed.), *The social norms approach to preventing school and college age substance abuse: A handbook for educators, counselors, and clinicians* (pp. 235–244). San Francisco, CA: Jossey-Bass.

Hansen, W. B., & Graham, J. W. (1991). Preventing alcohol, marijuana, and cigarette use among adolescents: Peer pressure resistance training versus establishing conservative norms. *Preventive Medicine, 20*(3), 414–430.

Hughes, C., Julian, R., Richman, M., Mason, R., & Long, G. (2008). Harnessing the power of perception: Exploring the potential of peer group processes to reduce alcohol-related harm among rural youth. *Youth Studies Australia, 27*(2), 26–35.

Janssen, I., Craig, W. M., Boyce, W. F., & Pickett, W. (2004). Associations between overweight and obesity with bullying behaviors in school-aged children. *Pediatrics, 113*(5), 1187–1194.

Johnson, S. L. (2009). Improving the school environment to reduce school violence: A review of the literature. *Journal of School Health, 79*(10), 451–465.

Juvonen, J., Graham, S., & Schuster, M. A. (2003). Bullying among young adolescents: The strong, the weak, and the troubled. *Pediatrics, 112*(6), 1231–1237.

Kilmer, J. R., Walker, D. D., Lee, C. M., Palmer, R. S., Mallett, K. A., Fabiano, P., & Larimer, M. (2006). Misperceptions of college student marijuana use: Implications for prevention. *Journal of Studies on Alcohol, 67*(2), 277–281.

Klomek, A. B., Sourander, A., Kumpulainen, K., Piha, J., Tamminen, T., Moilanen, I....Gould, M.S. (2008). Childhood bullying as a risk for later depression and suicidal ideation among Finnish males. *Journal of Affective Disorders, 109*(1–2), 47–55.

Klomek, A. B., Sourander, A., Niemela, S., Kumpulainen, K., Piha, J., Tamminen, T. ...Gould, M. S. (2009). Childhood bullying behaviors as a risk for suicide attempts and completed suicides: A population-based birth cohort study. *Journal of American Academic Child and Adolescent Psychiatry, 48*(3), 254–261.

Kuntsche, E., Knibbe, R., Engels, R., & Gmel, G. (2007). Bullying and fighting among adolescents – Do drinking motives and alcohol use matter? *Addictive Behaviors, 32*(12), 3131–3135.

Kuntsche, E., Pickett, W., Overpeck, M., Craig, W., Boyce, W., & de Matos, M. G. (2006). Television viewing and forms of bullying among adolescents from eight countries. *Journal of Adolescent Health, 39*(6), 908–915.

Linkenbach, J., & Perkins, H. W. (2003). Most of us are tobacco free: An eight-month social norms campaign reducing youth initiation of smoking in Montana. In H. W. Perkins (Ed.), *The social norms approach to preventing school and college age substance abuse: A handbook for educators, counselors, and clinicians* (pp. 224–244). San Francisco, CA: Jossey-Bass.

Lintonen, T. P., & Konu, A. I. (2004). The misperceived social norm of drunkenness among early adolescents in Finland. *Health Education Research, 19*(1), 64–70.

Lipsey, M. W., & Derzon, J. H. (1998). Predictors of violent or serious delinquency in adolescence and early adulthood: A synthesis of longitudinal research. In R. Loeber & D. P. Farrington (Eds.), Serious and violent juvenile offenders: Risk factors and successful interventions (pp. 86–105). Thousand Oaks, CA: Sage Publications, Inc.

Lund, R., Nielsen, K. K., Hansen, D. H., Kriegbaum, M., Molbo, D., Due, P., & Christensen, U. (2009). Exposure to bullying at school and depression in adulthood: A study of Danish men born in 1953. *European Journal of Public Health, 19*(1), 111–116.

Martens, M. P., Page, J. C., Mowry, E. S., Damann, K. M., Taylor, K. K., & Cimini, M. D. (2006). Differences between actual and perceived student norms: An examination of alcohol use, drug use, and sexual behavior. *Journal of American College Health, 54*(5), 295–300.

Mattern, J. L., & Neighbors, C. (2004). Social norms campaigns: Examining the relationship between changes in perceived norms and changes in drinking levels. *Journal of Studies on Alcohol, 65*(4), 489–493.

McAlaney, J., & McMahon, J. (2007). Normative beliefs, misperceptions, and heavy episodic drinking in a British student sample. *Journal of Studies on Alcohol and Drugs, 68*(3), 385–392.

Mouttapa, M., Valente, T., Gallaher, P., Rohrbach, L. A., & Unger, J. B. (2004). Social network predictors of bullying and victimization. *Adolescence, 39*(154), 315–335.

Murray, M. E., Guerra, N. G., & Williams, K. R. (1997). Violence prevention for the 21st century. In R. P. Weissberg & T. P. Gulotta (Eds.), *Healthy children 2010: Enhancing children's wellness* (pp. 105–128). Thousand Oaks, CA: Sage Publications.

Nansel, T. R., Craig, W., Overpeck, M. D., Saluja, G., & Ruan, W. J. (2004). Cross-national consistency

in the relationship between bullying behaviors and psychosocial adjustment. *Archives of Pediatric and Adolescent Medicine, 158*(8), 730–736.

Nansel, T. R., Overpeck, M., Pilla, R. S., Ruan, W. J., Simons-Morton, B., & Scheidt, P. (2001). Bullying behaviors among US youth: Prevalence and association with psychosocial adjustment. Journal of the American Medical Association, *285*(16), 2094–2100.

Nansel, T. R., Overpeck, M. D., Haynie, D. L., Ruan, W. J., & Scheidt, P. C. (2003). Relationships between bullying and violence among US youth. *Archives of Pediatric and Adolescent Medicine, 157*(4), 348–353.

Neighbors, C., Larimer, M. E., & Lewis, M. A. (2004). Targeting misperceptions of descriptive drinking norms: Efficacy of a computer-delivered personalized normative feedback intervention. *Journal of Consulting and Clinical Psychology, 72*(3), 434–447.

Neighbors, C., Walker, D. D., Mbilinyi, L. F., O'Rourke, A., Edleson, J. L., Zegree, J., & Roffman, R. (2010). Normative misperceptions of abuse among perpetrators of intimate partner violence. *Violence Against Women, 16*(4), 370–386.

Page, R. M., Ihasz, F., Hantiu, I., Simonek, J., & Klarova, R. (2008). Social normative perceptions of alcohol use and episodic heavy drinking among Central and Eastern European adolescents. *Substance Use and Misuse, 43*(3–4), 361–373.

Page, R. M., Ihasz, F., Simonek, J., Klarova, R., & Hantiu, I. (2006). Cigarette smoking, friendship factors, and social norm perceptions among Central and Eastern European high school students. *Journal of Drug Education, 36*(3), 213–231.

Perkins, H. W. (1997). College student misperceptions of alcohol and other drug norms among peers: Exploring causes, consequences, and implications for prevention programs. In *Designing alcohol and other drug prevention programs in higher education: Bringing theory into practice* (pp. 177–206). Newton, MA: Higher Education Center for Alcohol and Other Drug Prevention.

Perkins, H. W. (2002). Social norms and the prevention of alcohol misuse in collegiate contexts. *Journal of Studies on Alcohol,* Supplement *14,* 164–172.

Perkins, H. W. (2003a). The emergence and evolution of the social norms approach to substance abuse prevention. In H. W. Perkins (Ed.), *The social norms approach to preventing school and college age substance abuse: A handbook for educators, counselors, and clinicians* (pp. 3–18). San Francisco, CA: Jossey-Bass.

Perkins, H. W. (2003b). *The social norms approach to preventing school and college age substance abuse: A handbook*

Perkins et al.   721

for educators, counselors, and clinicians. San Francisco, CA: Jossey-Bass.

Perkins, H. W. (2007). Misperceptions of peer drinking norms in Canada: Another look at the "reign of error" and its consequences among college students. *Addictive Behaviors, 32*(11), 2645–2656.

Perkins, H. W., & Berkowitz, A. D. (1986). Perceiving the community norms of alcohol use among students: Some research implications for campus alcohol education programming. *International Journal of Addiction, 21*(9–10), 961–976.

Perkins, H. W., & Craig, D. W. (2003). The imaginary lives of peers: Patterns of substance use and misperceptions of norms among secondary school students. In H. W. Perkins (Ed.), *The social norms approach to preventing school and college age substance abuse: A handbook for educators, counselors, and clinicians.* pp. 209–223. San Francisco, CA: Jossey-Bass.

Perkins, H. W., & Craig, D. W. (2006). A successful social norms campaign to reduce alcohol misuse among college student-athletes. *Journal of Studies on Alcohol, 67*(6), 880–889.

Perkins, H. W., Haines, M. P., & Rice, R. (2005). Misperceiving the college drinking norm and related problems: A nationwide study of exposure to prevention information, perceived norms and student alcohol misuse. *Journal of Studies on Alcohol, 66*(4), 470–478.

Perkins, H. W., Meilman, P. W., Leichliter, J. S., Cashin, J. R., & Presley, C. A. (1999). Misperceptions of the norms for the frequency of alcohol and other drug use on college campuses. *Journal of American College Health, 47*(6), 253–258.

Perkins, J. M., Perkins, H. W., & Craig, D. W. (2010a). Peer weight norm misperception as a risk factor for being over- and underweight among UK secondary school students. *European Journal of Clinical Nutrition, 64*(9), 965–971.

Perkins, J. M., Perkins, H. W., & Craig, D. W. (2010b). Misperceptions of peer norms as a risk factor for sugar-sweetened beverage consumption among secondary school students. *Journal of the American Dietetic Association, 110*(12), 1916–1921.

Poteat, V. P., & Spanierman, L. B. (2010). Do the ideological beliefs of peers predict the prejudiced attitudes of other individuals in the group? *Group Processes & Intergroup Relations, 13*(4), 495–514.

Resnick, M. D., Ireland, M., & Borowsky, I. (2004). Youth violence perpetration: What protects? What predicts? Findings from the National Longitudinal Study of Adolescent Health. *Journal of Adolescent Health, 35*(5), 424.e1–424.e10.

Reuter-Rice, K. (2008). Male adolescent bullying and the school shooter. *Journal of School Nursing, 24*(6), 350–359.

Salmivalli, C. (1999). Participant role approach to school bullying: Implications for interventions. *Journal of Adolescence, 22*(4), 453–459.

Salmon, G., James, A., & Smith, D. M. (1998). Bullying in schools: Self reported anxiety, depression, and self esteem in secondary school children. *British Medical Journal, 317*, 924–925.

Sawyer, A. L., Bradshaw, C. P., & O'Brennan, L. M. (2008). Examining ethnic, gender, and developmental differences in the way children report being a victim of "bullying" on self-report measures. *Journal of Adolescent Health, 43*(2), 106–114.

Schultz, P. W. (1999). Changing behavior with normative feedback interventions: A field experiment on curbside recycling. *Basic and Applied Social Psychology, 21*(1), 25–36.

Schultz, P. W., Khazian, A. M., & Zaleski, A. C. (2008). Using normative social influence to promote conservation among hotel guests. *Social Influence, 3*(1), 4–23.

Sherif, M. (1936). *The psychology of social norms.* New York, NY: Harper.

Sherif, M. (1937). An experimental approach to the study of attitudes. *Sociometry, 1*(1/2), 90–98.

Smith, P. K., & Myron-Wilson, R. (1998). Parenting and school bullying. *Clinical Child Psychology and Psychiatry, 3*(3), 405–417.

Social Norms Surveys Online. Retrieved January 17, 2011, from http://www.socialnormsurveys.org/

Sourander, A., Helstela, L., Helenius, H., & Piha, J. (2000). Persistence of bullying from childhood to adolescence – A longitudinal 8-year follow-up study. *Child Abuse and Neglect, 24*(7), 873–881.

Spriggs, A. L., Iannotti, R. J., Nansel, T. R., & Haynie, D. L. (2007). Adolescent bullying involvement and perceived family, peer and school relations: Commonalities and differences across race/ethnicity. *Journal of Adolescent Health, 41*(3), 283–293.

Srabstein, J. (2008). Deaths linked to bullying and hazing. *International Journal of Adolescent Medicine and Health, 20*(2), 235–239.

Srabstein, J., Joshi, P., Due, P., Wright, J., Leventhal, B., Merrick, J., …Riibner, K. (2008). Prevention of public health risks linked to bullying: A need for a whole community approach. *International Journal of Adolescent Medicine and Health, 20*(2), 185–199.

Srabstein, J., & Piazza, T. (2008). Public health, safety and educational risks associated with bullying behaviors in American adolescents. *International Journal of Adolescent Medicine and Health, 20*(2), 223–233.

722   *Group Processes & Intergroup Relations 14(5)*

Turner, J., Perkins, H. W., & Bauerle, J. (2008). Declining negative consequences related to alcohol misuse among students exposed to a social norms marketing intervention on a college campus. *Journal of American College Health, 57*(1), 85–94.

Biographical notes

H. WESLEY PERKINS is Professor of Sociology in the Department of Anthropology and Sociology at Hobart and William Smith Colleges. His research interests include the social psychology of norm misperception, normative influence on health and well-being and evaluation of alcohol abuse and violence prevention strategies for adolescents and young adults in school and community settings.

DAVID W. CRAIG is Professor of Biochemistry at Hobart and William Smith Colleges. His research interests include alcohol, tobacco, and other drug use and violence among youth with an emphasis on how perceptions of peers drive behavior and how educational programs directed toward correcting inaccurate perceptions can reduce harmful behaviors.

JESSICA M. PERKINS is a doctoral candidate in Health Policy at Harvard University. Her research interests include exploring the influence of social capital, social networks, and social norms in developed and developing countries with an emphasis on how perceptions of peers drive behavior as well as examining social determinants of health across a variety of outcomes. (e.g., weight status, depression, alcohol use, and other health and development topics).

Source: This article is reprinted from *Group Processes and Intergroup Relations*, Vol. 14, Issue 5, pp. 703–722, 2011. Reprinted with permission of Sage Publications, Inc.

4 | LITERATURE REVIEWS: EXAMINING THE BACKGROUND FOR A STUDY

Researchers review the literature to learn what is and is not known about a study's topic and research problem. They document this essential information in a "literature review" passage as part of the Introduction section of the report. When you read a study's literature review, you can use this passage to understand the background behind the research study. As a practitioner, you also need to develop your own skills for reviewing literature to learn what is known about the topics that interest you. In this chapter, you will learn how to interpret and evaluate the literature reviews that researchers include in their studies. In addition, you will learn steps that you can use to locate and summarize literature and write your own literature reviews.

BY THE END OF THIS CHAPTER, YOU SHOULD BE ABLE TO:

- Identify and understand the literature review in a research report.
- Describe how researchers use literature in their research studies.
- Describe differences in how researchers use literature in quantitative and qualitative research.
- Take steps for reviewing the literature about a topic of interest to you.
- Identify steps useful for writing a literature review.
- Evaluate the quality of the literature review in a research report.

One of the ways that all of us learn about topics that matter to us is from what others have already done and found. As the expression goes, there is no need to reinvent the wheel if someone else already knows how to make one! This is particularly true in our professional practices where so much is already known about topics such as teaching second language learners, preventing drug use in adolescents, assisting new parents with infant care, and providing effective interventions. In many situations, you can learn about topics such as these by watching what others do and talking to them about it. However, this strategy is only useful for learning from people who are readily accessible. Therefore, one of the best ways to develop comprehensive knowledge about topics is to read the literature that has been prepared by individuals with expertise in the topic area. Learning by reading literature is essential for anyone who wants to know the state of knowledge about a topic.

You have probably been required at some point in your schooling to go to the library building or website, read some literature, and write a report about what you learned. It is likely that you have a "literature review" project assigned as a requirement for the course you are taking right now. Completing a class assignment is one important reason to review the literature, but there are also several additional reasons why individuals choose to review the literature. As we learned in Chapter 1, reviewing the literature is an essential step for researchers to complete in the process of conducting research. Researchers need to be aware of the knowledge that exists about the topic and problem they want to study, and reviewing the literature gives them access to the knowledge available. Knowing how to review the literature, however, is not only important for researchers. Students, practitioners, and policy makers also need to locate, understand, summarize, and critique literature to gain knowledge about important topics.

Therefore, you need to understand the role that literature plays in a research study, *and* you need to develop your own skills for reviewing literature. In fact, developing these skills is probably the main reason you are taking this class and reading this book! We will consider both types of skills in this chapter. We begin by first defining what we mean by a literature review and considering how you can recognize its application in a research report.

How Do You Identify the Literature Review in a Research Study?

Reviewing the literature is the process that individuals use to locate, read, synthesize, and critique the literature available on a topic. The result of this process is usually a written product that is referred to as a literature review. In the process of research, a **literature review** is a written synthesis of journal articles, books, and other documents that summarizes and critiques the past and current state of information about a topic, organizes the literature into subtopics, and documents the background for a study. In the most rigorous forms of research, investigators develop a comprehensive review based on quality sources of literature such as journal articles and government documents. Regardless of the sources of information, individuals conduct literature reviews to learn the state of knowledge about topics.

As introduced in Chapter 1, reviewing the literature is an essential step in the process of research so that researchers ensure that their study will add to the existing knowledge. Simply put, researchers cannot design a study to add to the existing knowledge if they do not know what that knowledge is. Knowing the current state of knowledge keeps them from duplicating research already available. It also informs them as to how their study can be planned so that it will build on what others have learned. In addition, researchers learn about theories and philosophies relevant to their topic areas by reading the literature. They can also examine models of how others have designed their research studies. Therefore, a good review of the literature provides important background information for researchers about what has been done, what still needs to be done, and how best to go about doing it. As you read a research study, you can identify the literature review by finding a specific section about the literature and noticing where the researchers cited the literature throughout the report.

Look for the Literature Review in a Stand-Alone Section

Because the literature review provides the background for a study, you can expect it to appear early in a report as part of the Introduction section(s). In some reports, you can locate a stand-alone section that reports a study's literature review. This section typically is part of the overall Introduction and follows the statement of the problem. Researchers often use a heading of *Literature Review* to designate this section. Other commonly used headings include *Background for the Study* or *Conceptual Framework*. Some authors use a heading that describes the content topic being reviewed, such as *Adolescent Egocentrism and Invulnerability* (Frankenberger, 2004, p. 577). The literature review can vary in length from a paragraph or two to multiple pages, depending on the extent of the literature that the researchers choose to include.

Once you locate a study's literature review, read it to learn what information was available to inform the planning of the research study. Identify the major themes in the reviewed literature as well as the subtopics found within the themes. Look to the headings that appear in the report to help you understand how the literature has been organized. If headings are not used, make your own notes in the margins to identify the topic of each paragraph or section. At the end of the literature review, see if the authors provide their conclusions about the literature and some statement as to how this literature provides a background for the study they are reporting.

Note Where Researchers Refer to Others' Work from the Literature

Not all research reports will include a stand-alone section for the literature review. Even if the researchers do not include a specific section, the reviewed literature is typically quite

Here's a Tip!

Good research reports include many citations to others' work. Do not worry about understanding each one individually as you read. Instead, focus on the major ideas that the author is describing as you read a literature review.

visible because of its importance in research. You can identify when researchers refer to "the literature" when they include citations within the text to other published work. These citations often appear in parentheses and include authors' names and the year of the work being cited, such as (Smith, 2012; Young & Jones, 2008). In some reports, these citations will be indicated with numbers within brackets, such as [1, 2], or superscript numbers, such as[3,8]. No matter the format, researchers will clearly indicate where they are using others' ideas in their reports by providing citations. These in-text citations indicate the authors' use of the literature, and you can use them to identify how the current study is building on what others have found.

How Do Researchers Use Literature in Their Studies?

Now you know a shortcut for finding reviewed literature in a report—look for the researchers' use of citations. Noting citations will tell you *where* a researcher is referring to the literature in their report, but it does not tell you *how* that literature is being used in the study. There are five common ways that researchers use their literature review. These uses include:

- providing a justification for the research problem,
- documenting what is and is not known about the topic,
- identifying the theory or conceptual framework behind a study,
- providing models for the methods and procedures, and
- interpreting results.

Let's examine each of these uses in more detail so you can recognize and understand their application in research reports.

Literature Provides a Justification for the Research Problem

As we learned in Chapter 3, researchers use references to the literature to provide evidence for the importance of a study's research problem. This use of literature is usually found in the study's Introduction section as part of the statement of the problem. Literature may be used to document the extent of the problem or the issues and concerns associated with the problem. For example, read how Poyrazli and Lopez (2007) use literature to provide evidence for a "major problem" in their study about the experiences of international students attending colleges in the United States: "Homesickness, a component of culture shock, is a major problem for college students, particularly those new to the university system (S. Fisher & Hood, 1987; Tognoli, 2003)" (p. 263). Good research reports include multiple references to the literature to substantiate the importance of the research problem.

Literature Documents What Is and Is Not Known About the Topic

Researchers review the literature to document what is known about a topic and to uncover what is not known. Researchers include the literature in their reports to demonstrate that they are sufficiently aware of other research on the study topic. Researchers summarize and report the existing knowledge in the study's Introduction, as part of the statement of the problem and/or in a stand-alone section. Often the key ideas are mentioned in the statement of the problem, but then discussed in detail in a separate section. As discussed in Chapter 3, in well-written reports, the researchers also clearly state the knowledge that is missing in the available literature to convey the need for the study. For example, in a study about hostile conflict in early marriages, Topham, Larson, and Holman (2005) reviewed what was known about four relevant subtopics: (1) parental marital status and offspring marital satisfaction, (2) quality of the parent–child relationship, (3) quality of parental discipline, and (4) quality of family-of-origin environment. They then concluded, "No research was found which specifically suggests a family-of-origin relationship to hostile marital conflict" (p. 108). A good use of the literature occurs when researchers provide a comprehensive summary of the literature on a topic and identify two to three explicit deficiencies in that literature.

Literature Identifies the Theory or Conceptual Framework Behind a Study

In many studies, researchers go beyond simply documenting what is known about a topic by identifying a perspective from the literature that guides how they approach their study of that topic. These perspectives come from theories and conceptual frameworks discussed in the literature. Researchers often mention the guiding theory or conceptual framework for their study in the Introduction sections of the research report. To understand how a researcher uses the literature in this way, we need to consider what theories and conceptual frameworks are and the role they each play in research.

Researchers Use Theories to Identify Key Variables and Expected Relationships Among Them.   A **theory** in research explains and predicts the probable relationship among different concepts (or variables). Theories about variables develop from research over time. For example, researchers test the idea that peer groups have an influence on adolescents' beliefs and behaviors. This relationship is tested over and over, such as with the Boy Scouts, in church groups, in middle schools, in sports teams, and other settings. Repeatedly the relationship of a positive effect holds true. In light of all this evidence, someone calls this relationship a theory and assigns a name to it. "Smith's Theory of Peer Influence" is born, reported in the literature, and tested further by other researchers. The literature includes many well-developed theories on concepts such as how students learn, what motivates people, how new ideas are adopted, and how leadership styles promote certain behaviors.

> **Here's a Tip!**
>
> Theories can also be useful for practitioners because they provide you with a framework for thinking about your practice. Pay attention to the theories mentioned in reports to see if you can find a theory that resonates with you and can inform your practices.

When you read a study in which the researchers planned to test a specific theory, then learning about the theory is important background information for understanding the study. Researchers use the literature to document and describe the important elements of the theory in their report, and they may include a figure that illustrates the theory. The use of theory strengthens the rigor and quality of research because the use of a theory from the literature provides a sound basis for the study's selected variables and predictions about expected results. Therefore, you need to be able to recognize and understand researchers' use of theory in studies. Here are two examples of researchers using theories from the literature to identify the variables in their studies:

- *An example of the use of an existing theory depicted as a figure in the literature.* Brady and O'Regan (2009) used a previously published theory to select the variables for their study of a Big Brothers Big Sisters program. As shown in Figure 4.1, Rhode's Model of Mentoring is a theory that relates several variables important to youth mentoring (e.g., *mutuality, cognitive development, health risk,* and *community context*). This theory predicts that the mentor relationship influences the development of the mentored youth, which then leads to positive outcomes for the youth. The theory also suggests that various contexts and other interpersonal relationships will influence the extent to which the mentor relationship will lead to positive youth outcomes.
- *An example of the use of an existing theory discussed in the literature.* Not all theories are drawn in figures; many are simply described in words. For example, Constantine et al. (2005) discussed the Social Cognitive Career Theory in their literature review passage of their report of a study of African American adolescents' career decisions. They used this theory to make predictions for how they expected *perceived occupational barriers* to be related to *career certainty* in their study.

Researchers Use Conceptual Frameworks to Inform Their Assumptions and Beliefs About the Topic Under Study.   In many studies, the researchers do not intend to test a specific theory, but they do use a theory or conceptual framework to guide how they think about the study's topic. A **conceptual framework** represents a philosophical perspective, an advocacy or social justice stance on behalf of marginalized groups, or a particular way of viewing knowledge that the researcher uses to inform a study. As with the use of theory, researchers' use of a conceptual framework drawn from the literature also strengthens the rigor and quality of research. This is because the use of

Rhodes's Model of Mentoring

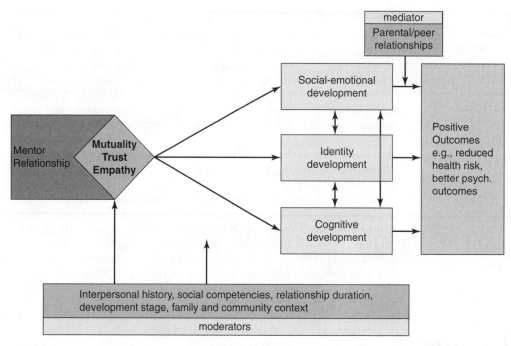

FIGURE 4.1   Example of Using a Diagram to Depict a Theory From the Literature

Source: This figure is reprinted from Brady and O'Regan, *Journal of Mixed Methods Research*, Vol. 3, Issue 3, p. 268, 2009, as adapted from the *Handbook of Youth Mentoring* (p. 32), edited by David L. DuBois and Michael J. Karcher, 2005. Thousand Oaks, CA: Sage. Copyright © 2005 by Sage. Reprinted with permission of Sage Publications, Inc.

a conceptual framework provides researchers with a perspective for thinking about the study topic that is well thought out (as opposed to just using their own personal beliefs). When you identify the conceptual framework that researchers used, then you have a clear idea about how they approached the study. Here are three examples of how researchers use conceptual frameworks from the literature to inform their research studies:

- *An example of the use of a philosophical perspective to inform a research study.* Philosophical perspectives describe how researchers think about abstract concepts such as the nature of reality and how one can gain knowledge about reality. Churchill et al. (2007) noted the philosophical perspective that guided their study of how rural, low-income families have fun when they wrote,

  > An interpretive, constructivist perspective guided this study (Lincoln & Guba, 2000; Newman, 2000). This means that we assumed that multiple views of reality exist, we were interested in learning about ordinary experiences in people's every day lives, and that we openly explored participants perceptions and experiences and the contexts in which they occur (Churchill et al., 2007, p. 276).

- *An example of the use of a social justice stance to inform a research study.* Social justice stances are used when researchers are concerned about inequalities that exist in society and bring an advocacy perspective to their research. For example, Kamphoff (2010) used a feminist perspective to inform her study of why female coaches leave coaching at the college level. She discussed the use of feminism in her report, noting that "feminist research brings women's experiences to the center, aiming to better the lives of those involved (Klein, 1983; Thompson, 1992)" (p. 361).
- *An example of the use of a way of viewing knowledge to inform a research study.* Research studies can also be informed from general ways of viewing knowledge or approaching a topic. For example, Craig (2004) described the following view of knowledge used in her study about the influence of mandated testing. She wrote, "A particular view of knowledge forms a central underpinning of this work. Personal practical knowledge (Clandinin, 1986) is embedded in, and shaped by, situations" (p. 1231).

In each of these three examples, the researchers used literature to describe a perspective that was important in shaping the research study, but not something to be tested. That is, they did not set out to test constructivism, test feminism, or test the idea of personal practical knowledge. Instead, these researchers used these perspectives to guide how they thought about planning, conducting, and interpreting their studies. Therefore, it is essential to identify these perspectives when reading research studies in order to understand how the researchers approached their studies.

Literature Provides Models for the Methods and Procedures Used in a Study

In addition to including literature in the Introduction section(s) of a report, researchers also frequently cite literature when describing their study's methods and procedures in the Method section. Researchers use the literature to provide models for how to design their studies and to collect and analyze their data. For example, when researchers decide to use a certain instrument for collecting data, they may explain where in the literature they found this instrument. They also use literature to justify the choice for the study's research design or decisions about how to select people as participants. This literature may include other published studies that used the same procedures or methodological writings where scholars discuss the procedures that can be used in the research process (like this book). When you note that the researchers used procedures that have been previously discussed in the literature, you are provided with evidence for the quality of the study because it indicates that the researchers used established procedures and did not just "make things up." We will learn more about these procedures in Chapters 6–13.

Literature Helps Researchers Interpret Their Results

A final use of literature that you find in research reports is the use of literature to aid in the researchers' interpretation of the results found from the research study. Researchers cite literature in the final Conclusion section of their reports when they compare the new results with past studies in the literature or examine the overall meaning of the new results for the existing literature. We will discuss this use of the literature further in Chapter 14.

What Do You Think?

Read the following excerpts taken from Smith, Estudillo, and Kang's (2011) quantitative study that investigated racial differences in middle school students' identification with academics (e.g., perceptions of testing) and its association with grade point average (GPA). For each excerpt, determine how the researchers appear to be using the literature.

a. "Ogbu and Simons (1998) described *cultural-ecological theory* as a series of belief systems held among students that influences how they perceive the education system and ultimately the potential for gains attained from engaging in the educational system" (p. 75).

b. "While many studies compare aspirations and achievement between White and African American students, increasingly researchers point to the need to study within group differences (Meece & Kurtz-Costes, 2001)" (p. 78).

c. "Students completed the *Identification with Academics* questionnaire, adapted from Osborne (1997), consisting of 13 items" (p. 80).

d. "Contrary to the literature on teacher expectations going back to Good and Brophy (1986) that suggested that African American students cared less about school, we expected and found that African American students reported higher levels of identification with school" (p. 86).

Check Your Understanding

Each of these passages made reference to the literature as indicated by the citations in the sentences that identify authors' names and years. Excerpt (a) is an example of the researchers using the literature to identify the theory or conceptual framework behind the study—namely, the cultural-ecological theory. Excerpt (b) is an example of the use of literature to establish what is and is not known about a topic to justify the need for the study because the literature needs to be extended to study within group differences. Excerpt (c) is an example of the use of the literature to provide models for the methods that the researchers applied in the study. In this case, the researchers used a measurement instrument that was adapted from one previously employed by others. Excerpt (d) is an example of using the literature to interpret the results found from the study. The researchers noted that their results differed from what others in the literature have found.

How Does the Use of Literature Differ in Quantitative and Qualitative Studies?

When researchers review the literature for their studies, they summarize research articles that use quantitative and qualitative approaches. Both are acceptable and useful. However, as you learned in Chapter 2, the way researchers use the reviewed literature differs in quantitative and qualitative research. There are two primary differences in its application. The use of literature differs in terms of the role it plays in the study (more prescriptive or more informative) and when in the research process it is reviewed (reviewed primarily at the start and remains more static, or reviewed throughout the process and becomes more dynamic).

The Use of Literature Is More Prescriptive and Static in Quantitative Research

In quantitative studies, researchers tend to focus extensive attention on reviewing the literature at the beginning of the study's research process. They use the literature to substantiate the research problem, point to the specific variables of interest in the study, suggest theories that explain the expected relationships among variables, provide a rationale for the study's purpose, and form the basis for the hypotheses to be tested in the study. That is, the literature is used to *prescribe* the direction and intent of the quantitative research study. At the end of the study, the researchers return to the literature when drawing conclusions, but this is typically the same literature reviewed at the start of the study. The researchers compare the study results to the predictions identified at the beginning. In this way, the use of literature is more *static* because it is primarily reviewed at the start of the study to set the quantitative study's direction and variables, which do not change as the study is conducted.

Because of the more prescriptive and static role of the literature in quantitative research, the literature typically has a prominent presence in the Introduction sections of quantitative study reports. In addition to its use in the study's statement of the problem, quantitative researchers typically include a more thorough treatment of the literature in its own section titled *Review of the Literature* to highlight the important role it plays in setting the direction of the study. This literature review is often organized around the major variables of interest in the study and emphasizes how the variables have been found to relate to other variables in past research. The researchers also incorporate the literature in the Method section when they discuss the instruments used to measure the study's variables and in the final section of the report when they interpret how the results found in the study compare to the predictions made based on the literature review.

In the quantitative physical-activity-in-middle-schools study (Xu et al., 2010) from Chapter 1, you find that the citations to the literature cluster around the beginning and the end of the article. In paragraph 01, Xu et al. cite studies to document the importance of the problem: low levels of physical activity lead to serious health consequences. In paragraph 02, the authors provide a short review of literature found on school-based interventions for physical activity and identify deficiencies in this literature (i.e., a lack of research on successful programs at the middle school level). Then, in paragraph 03, the authors explain that a model (or theory) exists in the literature suggesting factors that might explain behaviors of middle school students—the Social Ecological Model. They also present study aims consistent with the factors in this model that are expected to influence physical activity opportunities. In addition, the authors use literature when they discuss the measures they used to collect data for the study's variables (e.g., see paragraph 07). Finally, the authors return to the literature in paragraphs 14–20 by comparing their results to other studies in the literature.

The Use of Literature Is More Informative and Dynamic in Qualitative Research

Similar to quantitative research, qualitative researchers review existing literature at the beginning of their research process to document the importance of the research problem. Unlike quantitative research, qualitative researchers do not use this literature to prescribe specific variables or hypotheses, choosing instead to use it to *inform* their overall approach. Recall that qualitative researchers want to remain open to exploring their topic and learning from participants' perspectives as opposed to testing ideas from the literature. In some qualitative studies, the researchers make little use of the literature at the beginning of their study to keep this openness. Others, however, may use the literature to describe a conceptual framework that informs their stance for the study. This framework does not set the direction of the study or introduce predictions like a theory in a quantitative study; instead, it informs how the researchers think about and approach the topic. Qualitative researchers also may use the literature to document models for their methods, but these tend to focus more on general procedures and not on specific instruments. In contrast to quantitative research, researchers using a qualitative approach often return to the literature as they are conducting the study and new ideas develop from the data. Because of the open nature of qualitative research, new concepts often emerge that were not anticipated at the start and researchers need to examine the literature about these new topics. Therefore, qualitative research involves a more *dynamic* process of reviewing the literature as new ideas emerge from the study. At the end of the study, the researchers use literature to describe the meaning of the results in relation to past studies. Relating qualitative results to the literature is not the same as comparing to predictions in quantitative research. In qualitative inquiry, researchers are more interested in whether the findings of a study support or modify existing ideas and practices advanced in the literature.

Because of the informative and dynamic role of the literature in qualitative research, its presence in qualitative research reports may be minimal, extensive, or somewhere in between. At a minimum, the researcher will use literature in the statement of the problem to justify the importance of the research problem and in the Conclusion section to assist in the interpretation of the results. Many qualitative studies will incorporate extensive literature as part of the Introduction, often in a section titled *Conceptual Framework*, to explain the assumptions and perspectives that inform the researchers' thinking about the topic and approach to the study design.

In the qualitative physical-activity-at-daycare study (Tucker et al., 2011) from Chapter 1, you find that the authors begin their article by citing literature to document the research problem of insufficient physical activity and obesity for preschool-aged children (see paragraphs 01–04). The purpose and research questions (paragraph 04) were not prescribed by the literature. Rather, the researchers' intent is general and open ended—in this way, they can learn from the participants. The authors of this study did not identify any conceptual framework that informed their research approach, so this study is an example of a more minimal approach to using the literature. The authors do cite literature in the Method section (paragraphs 05–07) to explain their procedures. Finally, they also use literature to help interpret the larger meaning of the results of the study. In the Conclusion section (see paragraphs 24–32), the authors discuss how three key findings that emerged from the participants' perspectives both reinforce and depart from past research, and suggest ways that the literature and practice need to further consider the perspectives of daycare providers.

What Are the Steps That You Can Use to Review the Literature?

So far in this chapter, we have focused on how to recognize and interpret researchers' use of literature within their research reports. It is not enough, however, for you to understand how others use literature. You also have to develop your own skills for locating and summarizing literature and writing a literature review. Most of us complete our first literature reviews as class assignments. There are many additional reasons why you should read the research literature beyond fulfilling a course requirement. Recall from Chapter 1 that reading research adds to your knowledge, informs your position in policy debates, and suggests improvements for practice. Practitioners of all professions review the literature for these same reasons. By reading the literature, practitioners keep up to date on the latest developments in their fields. They also learn about new topics that they have not previously examined. For example, a science teacher may want to review information to develop effective strategies for a new student who is visually impaired or a social worker may want to review information relevant to the issues experienced by recent immigrant families. Practitioners who are able to critically read available research studies can develop new ideas and strategies to try in their practice from reviewing literature.

Completing a comprehensive, thoughtful review of the literature is a challenging process that takes determination and perseverance. Like all tasks, it becomes easier with practice and as you learn more information about the process. The good news is that you bring many useful experiences and skills to this process. Today's literature reviews make extensive use of computer-based technologies, and your prior experiences with searching the Internet will provide a helpful starting place. Your skills for keeping records and writing reports on the computer will also be very useful in this process. As we will learn, reviewing the literature also requires you to keep track of sources and sort information into categories. Therefore, your organizational skills will be required. Your process for reviewing the literature is also enhanced by the knowledge and prior experiences you have had related to your topic of interest. This background will serve you well as you begin to think about how to locate literature. Finally, to conduct a good formal literature review, you should be able to identify and understand reports of research. As you learned in Chapter 1, research represents activities where individuals systematically gather and analyze empirical data to answer a question. Therefore, you already know how to identify reports of research, and this entire book is aimed at helping you understand the information that researchers include in these reports.

Regardless of whether you are a researcher planning a study, a practitioner interested in examining the evidence for certain practices, or a student working on a class assignment, there is a set of common steps that individuals use to search for, locate, and summarize literature for a literature review. In this section, we describe the steps in terms that you can directly apply in your own work. Keep in mind as you read that these are the same steps that researchers take when they review the literature for their research studies. Knowing these steps therefore helps you understand the literature discussed in research studies and provides you with a framework for reviewing the literature for your own personal use. These steps are:

- Identify key terms.
- Use search strategies to locate literature.
- Select relevant documents that are of good quality.
- Take notes on the key aspects of each selected document.

Although these steps are relatively easy to describe, you will likely find that reviewing the literature is a little like hunting for hidden treasure: It takes work and you do not always know where to dig. To help you with this process, we will discuss specific strategies for each of these steps. In addition, we will briefly consider how each step could be applied in a literature review conducted to learn about weapon possession and violence in middle schools.

Step 1—Identify Key Terms Related to the Topic of the Literature Review

Today you can easily search for most anything, including literature, from the comfort of your school, home, or work using a computer or smart device. Searching over the Internet is a fantastic strategy, but it only works well if you are able to tell the search programs what you want them to find. Therefore, the first step to take when searching for literature is to identify your topic and narrow it to a few key terms. These key terms should be one or two words or short phrases. Choose these terms carefully because they are important for initially locating literature through an online search. To identify these terms, you can use several strategies, such as:

- Pose a short, general question that you would like answered by reviewing the literature. Select the two or three terms in this question that best summarize the primary concepts.
- Write a preliminary working title for your project and select two to three keywords in the title that capture the central ideas.
- Use words that you find used in the literature. You might be interested in how different students learn and then read a journal article that refers to these differences as "learning styles." You can then use this phrase as a key term for the topic.
- List synonyms for your topic. For example, you might be interested in the supports needed by family members who care for an elderly parent. You might consider synonyms such as *family support, spousal care,* and *caregiver* to access this topic.

> **Here's a Tip!**
>
> Keep a list of all possible key terms that occur to you as you read and think about your topic. This will help you identify a set of best terms to use for your areas of interest.

Let's suppose you are interested in learning about student violence in general and weapon possession by middle school students in particular. Using these strategies, you might start by writing a working title for your project, "Student Violence and Weapon Use by Middle School Students." From this title, you might consider the words *violence, weapon,* and *middle school* as key terms for this topic. You might also start listing some possible synonyms, such as *fighting* and *physical attack* for violence, *guns* and *knives* for weapon, and *junior high* for middle school. A good search of the literature is able to identify all the key research that has been conducted on a topic. This means that you need to be creative and clever about the key terms to use in searching to ensure that you find the relevant literature. Just as a treasure hunter must dig in many spots when looking for treasure, you will likely need to try many key terms when searching for useful literature.

Step 2—Search Databases Using the Key Terms to Locate Literature

Having identified key terms, you can begin the search for literature. There is so much literature available that you need to develop efficient strategies when searching for literature that relates to your topic of interest. Fortunately, you probably have experience searching for information on friends or finding directions using Internet search engines such as Google™. You might be tempted to search for literature in the same way by accessing websites and exploring the information available on a topic. Although this process may be convenient, keep in mind that not all literature posted online is dependable or of high quality, and a lot of information online is not research. To find scholarly research literature on topics, you should search places that are set up specifically to help individuals identify scholarly literature. These places include academic libraries and electronic databases.

Use Academic Libraries to Find an Introduction to Your Topic. A sound approach is to begin your search in an academic library housed at a college or university. By searching an academic library's catalogs and stacks, you will save time because

Here's a Tip!

If you have trouble locating research on your topic, go to an academic library and ask for help from the reference librarians. They are experts at locating scholarly literature and all the ones that we have met have been delighted to help students locate literature.

you will find comprehensive holdings not available through other sources. Although a town or city public library may yield some useful literature, an academic library typically offers the largest collection of materials, especially research studies. Academic libraries typically have online catalogs of their holdings so that you can search the library materials easily to find books and summaries on your topic. Books and summaries typically do not report the details of individual research studies, but they can provide a good introduction to your topic and help you further identify appropriate key terms.

Search Electronic Databases to Find Research Articles on Your Topic. The best sources for literature reviews consist of journal articles written by the individuals who actually conducted the research or originated the ideas. You can find many scholarly journals in the stacks at your academic library, but it would take too much time to review them all by hand. Therefore, to locate journal articles on your topic, you should search the electronic databases that are available. Six useful databases that offer easy retrieval of journal articles and other documents related to educational, social, and health topics are listed in Table 4.1. If you access these databases through your school's library, they may also indicate which documents are directly available from the library for free. Usually you will want to search more than one database to find all relevant literature on your topic.

When you use one of the databases listed in Table 4.1, one possible approach is to simply enter your key terms into the main search box on the database's website. Although this strategy is often successful for everyday searches such as looking for the best pizza restaurant in a neighborhood, it is not a very efficient way to search for research literature. For example, searching for the phrase *violence in middle schools* found more than 39,000 hits in

TABLE 4.1   Electronic Databases Useful for Searching for Research Journal Articles

1. *Educational Resources Information Center* (ERIC, 1991):
   - The ERIC database consists of two parts: (1) major educational and education-related journals; and (2) documents, including conference papers, project and technical reports, speeches, unpublished manuscripts, and books.
   - You can search *ERIC* on the Internet (eric.ed.gov) or online through academic libraries that have purchased access.

2. *Psychological Abstracts* (APA, 1927–):
   - This database provides a comprehensive source of psychological literature. It focuses on peer-reviewed journals, but also includes books and dissertations.
   - You can search the database through *PsycINFO* on the Internet (www.apa.org) or online through academic libraries that have purchased access.

3. *Sociological Abstracts* (Sociological Abstracts, Inc., 1953–):
   - This database provides access to the world's literature in sociology and related disciplines through abstracts of journal articles, books, dissertations, and conference papers.
   - The *Sociological Abstracts* database is available from Cambridge Scientific Abstracts (www.csa.com) or online through academic libraries that have purchased access.

4. *EBSCO Information Services:*
   - This service provides online access to more than 150 databases and thousands of e-journals.
   - Academic libraries purchase the services of *EBSCO* or individuals can purchase articles of interest through the pay-per-view feature (www.ebsco.com).

5. *PubMed:*
   - The *PubMed* database is a service of the U.S. National Library of Medicine and provides access to biomedical and life science publications, including free access to research funded by the National Institutes of Health through *PubMed Central.*
   - You can search the full *PubMed* database (www.ncbi.nlm.nih.gov/pubmed/) and the *PubMed Central* database (www.ncbi.nlm.nih.gov/pmc/) on the Internet or through many academic libraries.

6. *Google Scholar:*
   - Google Scholar is a searchable database that provides access to a wide range of scholarly literature found in academic sources and other online repositories. It includes both peer-reviewed and non-peer-reviewed sources.
   - You can search using *Google Scholar* (scholar.google.com) for free on the Internet.

the ERIC database! A better strategy is to use the "Advanced Search" features available in all electronic databases. These advanced features can help you search for documents that meet a set of specific criteria. Making good use of advanced searches takes practice, but it will be well worth your effort to learn to use the more advanced features. Here are a few tips that we use when searching a database. For each tip, we also describe how we applied it in an advanced search for articles about violence and weapon possession in middle schools through the ERIC website (eric.ed.gov).

■ *Use multiple key terms, but not too many.* Two or three broad key terms (such as "violence" and "middle school") can help you identify literature clearly related to your topic. Using one keyword that is too general (such as "violence") can get you thousands of hits! Using too many key terms or terms that are very specific (such as "bring a knife to seventh grade") may cause you to get too few hits and miss many good documents.

■ *Use "logic" terms to combine multiple key terms.* Most databases will let you use logic terms to combine key terms in specific ways in an advanced search. Consider the use of the following logic terms:

■ The word "AND" is used to indicate that two (or more) terms must appear within a document to satisfy the search criteria. An example of using the AND logic term in a search is:

violence AND school

℘ Search.

This search will only identify literature that includes both the term *violence* and the term *school*. The AND logic term is good to use when you want to ensure that two or more different ideas are present in an article.

■ The word "OR" is used to indicate that at least one of the terms must appear within a document to satisfy the search criteria. An example of using the OR logic term in a search is:

weapon OR gun

℘ Search.

This search will identify all literature that includes the term *weapon*, that includes the term *gun*, and that includes both of these terms. The OR logic term is good to use when you have two or more synonyms for the same idea.

■ Quote marks are used to indicate that an exact phrase of two or more words must appear within a document to satisfy the search criteria. An example of using quote marks in a search is:

violence AND "middle school"

℘ Search.

By putting the words "middle school" in quotes, this search requires a match to that exact phrase. Using quote marks can reduce the number of extra hits that occur for alternative uses of the words *middle* (such as an article about children caught in the middle of their parents' divorce) and *school* (such as home school or elementary school). Quote marks are good to use when terms about your topic are usually used in a specific combination and order (e.g., you are interested in literature about *middle school*, not *school middle*).

■ *Limit your search to recent literature.* A good literature review documents the current state of knowledge about a topic. Therefore, consider limiting your search to research on your topic that has been published recently. What is considered recent depends somewhat on your topic. If your topic is changing quickly (e.g., the use of social media in classrooms), then you may want to keep your search very recent, say the last 5 years. For most topics, a good starting place is to consider the research published in the past 10 years. To find recent research, most database search engines allow you to limit your search to certain publication dates, such as 2009–2013.

■ ***Begin your search by looking for journal articles.*** The best sources for scholarly literature reviews are journal articles that are current and good quality. Therefore, when first starting to look for literature on a topic, consider limiting your search to journal articles. This is often an option in the database search engines. For example, the ERIC database allows you to select a "Publication Type" of "Journal Articles" as a filter in your search of the database. Once you have examined the available journal articles on your topic, you might return and search more broadly to include documents like conference papers and dissertations.

■ ***Keep trying new combinations of key terms to find the best literature.*** You might hope to search the literature once and be done. In a good literature review, that is rarely the case. You will likely need to try several different combinations of key terms to ensure that you find all the relevant literature on your topic. To facilitate this process, it is a good idea to keep a record of the different combination of terms that you use as well as notes about what did and did not work well for finding useful literature. Also keep in mind that new publications are continually becoming available and therefore you might want to repeat your best terms at a later time to check whether anything new has been published.

> **Here's a Tip!**
>
> You may be tempted to limit your search to only results with free full-text access, but you might miss some good articles this way. Keep in mind that your academic library can often help you obtain the literature that is needed for your review for no cost.

Once you conduct a search, the database will display a list of all documents that met your search criteria. When you obtain a list of hits from a search, you can click on the title of each document to view more detailed information. For example, we ran the following search in the ERIC (eric.ed.gov) database:

violence AND "middle school" AND (weapon OR gun)

⁍ Search.

We limited our search to journal articles published in the last five years (2009–2013). Based on this advanced search, we found seven articles in the database that satisfied our criteria. The titles of three of these seven articles are:

■ "Reported Occurrence and Perceptions of Violence in Middle and High Schools" (Algozzine & McGee, 2011)
■ "The Role of Sociability Self-Concept in the Relationship Between Exposure to and Concern About Aggression in Middle School" (Miller, 2013)
■ "Urban Seventh Grade Students: A Report of Health Risk Behaviors and Exposure to Violence" (Dowdell, 2012)

By clicking on a title of one of the articles, the search engine then displays a detailed record for that journal article. Although the format of the detailed records can vary among the different databases, they generally include information such as the article title, authors' names, journal information, publication date, article abstract, and other information about the article such as whether the publication was peer reviewed and in what language the publication was written. You can review these details about each document identified in your search to decide whether it is a good source for you to use in your literature review.

What Do You Think?

Suppose you want to review the literature to learn about research related to teaching science laboratory activities for students with visual impairments. What key terms might you use? What are some synonyms that might also be useful? How might you use logic operators (AND, OR) to combine the terms in an advanced search? In what database would you start searching for literature?

Check Your Understanding

A good place to start thinking about a search is to write down a project title or question that you want answered. An example is: What strategies are available to teach science laboratory activities to students who are visually impaired? To find literature related to this question, key terms might include *visual impairment*, *laboratory*, and *science*. Possible synonyms might include *blind* (for visual impairment) and *physics* or *biology* (for science). One possible combination of these terms in an advanced search might be:

("visual impairment" OR blind)

AND laboratory AND (science OR physics OR biology)

⸮ Search.

Because this is an educational topic, ERIC would be a good database to use for this search. We tried the combination of terms listed above in ERIC and found 35 journal articles published from 1979 to 2012 that met these search criteria.

Step 3—Select Literature That Is Relevant and of Good Quality

Let's return to the major steps in conducting a literature review. After you have identified key terms and searched for resources in a database, your next step is to select the literature that you want to read and include in your literature review. A typical database search will narrow the literature down to 10–40 hits, but you still need to decide which of those potential sources are worth your time. A good strategy to use once you have a list of potential literature is to examine each source and consider two questions: Is it relevant? Is it good quality? Let's consider how you can go about making these decisions for your literature review.

Determining Whether a Source Is Relevant.   When you examine a source identified by your search, your first consideration is whether the source is relevant for your literature review. A research study is relevant when it includes information pertinent to the topic of the review. Individuals new to reviewing the literature often think too narrowly about relevance by wanting to only include studies that are exactly the same as the situation that concerns them. For example, if a principal is concerned with gun possession by rural middle school students, she might be tempted to discount research conducted in urban settings as not relevant, but research on student weapon possession in urban settings could be highly relevant for determining possible strategies to use because it addresses the same problem. Relevance therefore has several dimensions, and your review will be more comprehensive if you are open to including literature that represents more than one of the dimensions. The following criteria can be helpful for considering different dimensions that can be relevant when selecting literature to review:

- Does the source focus on the same topic as the one in which you are interested?
- Does the source examine the same individuals or sites that you want to learn about?
- Does the source examine the same research problem that concerns you?

If you answer "yes" to any of these questions when considering a source, then the source is likely relevant for your literature review. For example, suppose you want to review literature relevant to school-based programs for preventing student weapon possession in rural middle schools. Literature can be relevant if it examines the same topic (student weapon possession), the same context (middle school-based intervention programs), or the same problem (issues faced by children in rural schools). That is, relevant literature for this review might include literature on student weapon possession, literature about any type of prevention programs for middle school students, and literature about issues facing children in rural schools. Keep in mind that both quantitative and qualitative research studies are relevant for your review because each form of research has advantages and provides insight for our knowledge base about any educational or social science topic. A good literature review is comprehensive in that the reviewer locates sufficient literature so that the review includes the many different perspectives and research approaches to the topic that are available in the recent literature.

Determining Whether a Source Is Good Quality. Once you have determined that a source is relevant for your review, your next consideration is whether it is a good-quality source. The best sources for a literature review are those that are original reports of research, are peer reviewed, and come from sources that are known to be reputable. When choosing the sources for a review, it is therefore helpful to consider the following important dimensions:

- *Original vs. secondary sources.* Original sources of research are reports of studies that are written by the people who actually conducted the research. Secondary sources of research are reports in which the author refers to studies published elsewhere. Original sources are best to review because they include the full details of the research reported by the researchers themselves so that you can make your own judgments about the quality of the work and usefulness of the results. Although secondary sources such as literature reviews, theoretical papers, and summaries can provide useful information about your topic, you need to be careful using them to understand the available research because they will not include the full details of each individual study.
- *Peer-reviewed vs. not reviewed.* Peer review is the process by which the quality of research is ensured. Researchers write reports of their studies and then submit the manuscripts to journal editors for consideration. In the peer-review process, the journal editor sends a copy of the report to independent peers (i.e., other researchers not associated with the study) who read and critique the report in an attempt to catch any problems with the research or incompleteness in the report. Although the peer-review process does not remove all problems with research, you can feel more confident in the quality of a report if it has undergone peer review. Reports of research found in journals will typically be peer-reviewed. Other types of reports, such as dissertations, conference papers, and books, typically have not been reviewed so carefully.
- *Reputable sources vs. unknown sources.* Reports of research can come from many different sources. The best sources are academic sources, such as those found through the library of your college or university. Some journals in your field may have a better reputation for their quality than others, and this is something you will learn by talking to others in the field and reading many different reports. In addition, sources associated with reputable organizations such as the federal government, professional organizations, or well-known publishers can often be trusted to maintain a high level of quality. Be cautious using other sources, such as those from organizations that publish reports for a fee paid by the author or sources prepared by for-profit companies. When the source of the information is unknown or promoting a particular agenda, then there is little guarantee that the information will be of high quality.

Recall from Chapter 1 that there are three broad types of literature where research is reported: early stage materials, peer-reviewed journal articles, and books. Table 4.2 considers each of these types of literature along these three dimensions. Examining this information should help make it clear that reports of research published in peer-reviewed journals are the best sources of information for a literature review because they are original reports of research that have been reviewed for quality. Therefore, when reviewing research literature, it is best to select relevant literature that reports original research, is peer-reviewed, and comes from a reputable source. Depending on your topic, you may also find documents like school reports (such as about new programs) of interest, but you have to keep in mind that school report documents are often not reviewed for quality and they may not include any research component.

TABLE 4.2 Comparing Different Types of Literature along Dimensions of Quality

Type of Literature	Original vs. Secondary	Peer-reviewed vs. Not Reviewed	Reputable vs. Unknown
Early Stage Material			
■ Dissertations and theses	Original	Not peer-reviewed	Typically unknown
■ Conference papers	Original	Not peer-reviewed	Typically unknown
■ Technical reports	Original	Not peer-reviewed	Typically unknown, but websites maintained by the government or professional organizations are reputable sources
Journal Articles			
■ Research reports	Original	Peer-reviewed	Varies by journal
■ Literature reviews	Secondary	Peer-reviewed	Varies by journal
■ Theoretical discussions	Secondary	Peer-reviewed	Varies by journal
Books			
■ Handbooks	Secondary	Usually not peer-reviewed, but reviewed by the editors	Varies by publisher
■ Encyclopedias	Secondary	Usually not peer-reviewed, but reviewed by the editors	Varies by publisher
■ Conceptual Books	Secondary	Usually not peer-reviewed	Varies by publisher
■ Books Reporting Research Studies	Original (but often with less detail about the methods used than a journal article)	Usually not peer-reviewed	Varies by publisher

Step 4—Take Notes on the Key Aspects of Each Selected Source

Once you have located literature that is relevant and good, you are ready to read and learn from the sources. Before you begin reading, however, you might want to organize your literature so it is easy for you to use and summarize. Make one copy of each article by photocopying the document, scanning the document, or downloading an electronic copy of the document (e.g., as an .html or .pdf file)—copyright laws permit you to make one duplicate copy of an article without the permission of the publisher. From there, you need to develop a system to easily retrieve the documents and information such as using folders to group documents on your computer or in your filing cabinet. Organize the literature in a way that makes sense to you, such as by author, by topic (e.g., possession of weapons, prevention programs, and effects of weapons), or by participant (e.g., middle school, high school, and college).

In addition to organizing the literature, you also have to read it! Because you will be reading many articles over time about your topic, it is a good idea to make your own set of notes about each of the sources. This process yields a useful record so that you can recall the details of the individual studies without having to keep rereading them in their entirety. A systematic approach for keeping notes when reviewing the literature is to develop a detailed summary for each source (sometimes referred to as an abstract). A detailed article summary should include your notes about the major aspects of an article recorded in a concise way (about 350 words for this purpose). Do *not* use the abstract provided by the author at the beginning of a journal article for this purpose. There are several reasons why this is not appropriate. For one, there are rules about copying the words written by others so that you do not plagiarize others. We will learn more about plagiarism later in this chapter, but for now the key point is that you cannot copy some-one else's words for your own use unless you clearly document that it is a direct quote using quote marks and indicate where in the document you copied the quoted text. Direct quotes are useful for key ideas like a definition, but are not good to use for long passages such as an abstract. The second reason to not use the article abstract is because it is usually too brief to be useful as a summary for a literature review. The third reason is that article abstracts are not written in a uniform way so they will not include consistent information across the articles that you read. The final reason not to use article abstracts is because they do not include your own comments about the articles. It is very important for you to document your reflections and comments about each source and how it applies to your work as you read so that ideas are fresh in your mind. Therefore, you should write summaries of articles in your own words to avoid plagiarizing someone else's words and to prepare notes that are useful for your literature review purposes.

A good strategy for making summary notes about quantitative and qualitative research studies is to systematically record the same set of information. For each source, we recommend that you summarize:

- the complete reference to the source;
- the research problem;
- the purpose, research questions, and hypotheses;
- the data collection procedures;
- the major results and findings; and
- your comments about the study (such as the strengths and weaknesses in the research or the implications of the results for your practice).

Figures 4.2 and 4.3 illustrate examples of two summaries created for articles located in a search for literature about violence and weapon possession in middle

---

Reference:
Wylie, L. E., Gibson, C. L., Brank, E. M., Fondacaro, M. R., Smith, S. W., Brown, V. E., & Miller, S. A. (2010). Assessing school and student predictors of weapons reporting. *Youth Violence and Juvenile Justice, 8*(4), 351–372.

Research Problem:
Wylie et al. (2010) noted that students, parents, and school officials are fearful of school violence, particularly school shootings. Although school personnel are implementing policies to address these concerns, they have not been very successful. Student willingness to report when another student is known to be carrying a weapon is an important prevention mechanism, but there is a gap in the literature about how school contexts combine with student characteristics to predict students' willingness to report weapons.

Purpose, Research Questions, or Hypotheses:
Wylie et al.'s (2010) purpose was to study the relationship of student and school climate variables with willingness to report a weapon. They hypothesized that individual student variables and school climate variables will be significantly related to general willingness to report, but that school climate variables will not be significant predictors for students' willingness to report anonymously.

Data Collection Procedure:
The research took place at 27 middle schools in five diverse U.S. states. A total of 3,197 sixth- to eighth-grade students completed an anonymous survey questionnaire. The questionnaire included items to measure the following variables: likelihood of weapons reporting, demographics, relationship with adults, self-reported delinquency, peer delinquency, school size, and socioeconomic status.

Results:
The results included: (1) Age significantly predicts willingness to report, with older students being less willing. (2) Students who are more involved in delinquency and those who have more delinquent peers are less willing to report. (3) Students who were less bonded to adults were less willing to report. (4) School climate as measured by collective identity and school conflict were both significant predictors of higher willingness to report in general. (5) School climate was not a significant predictor of willingness to report anonymously.

Comments:
Wylie et al. (2010) suggest two implications for schools: (1) work to improve the perceived climate and (2) implement a way for students to report weapons anonymously. That might be useful advice for my school district. The research was limited to middle school students from Florida, Texas, California, New Jersey, and Connecticut, but did include a large, diverse sample.

FIGURE 4.2   Sample Summary Notes for a Quantitative Research Study

Reference:
King, K. A., & Vidourek, R. A. (2010). In search of respect: A qualitative study exploring youth perceptions. *The International Journal on School Disaffection, 7*(1), 5–17.

Research Problem:
King and Vidourek (2010) note that not feeling positively connected to school contributes to negative student behaviors such as violence and carrying a weapon. A lack of positive connection may arise when students experience negative school climates, such as through bullying or feeling unsafe at school. They note that there is little research that has examined school-based respect, despite its relationship to bullying and school climate.

Purpose or Research Questions:
The purpose of the study was to explore students' perceptions of school-based respect. Their specific research questions related to how students define, show, and perceive respect and disrespect at school.

Data Collection Procedure:
King and Vidourek (2010) conducted their qualitative study at nine schools that varied in terms of type (middle, high), setting (urban, suburban, rural), and district (public, nonpublic). A total of 78 students participated in focus group discussions held at the schools. The focus groups were audio-recorded and transcribed.

Findings:
The researchers concluded that students felt there was a "major problem with respect" (p. 12). Their analysis identified seven themes: student definitions of school-based respect, student definitions of school-based disrespect, causes of and contributing factors to school-based disrespect, student disrespect based on sex, disrespect between students and teachers, problems resulting from school-based disrespect, and methods of increasing respect among students. Students defined respect in terms of practicing the golden rule, listening to others, honoring others' property and space, and not talking negatively about others. They defined disrespect in terms of making fun of other students based on their attire, putting others down, not listening to others, gossiping, and bullying and threatening others. Causes of disrespect included pressures from cliques, jealousy and insecurity, wanting revenge, racial and ethnic differences, and social media outlets.

Comments:
This was a fresh approach to the problem of student violence. It was interesting to read the actual words of adolescents! Participants were limited to central Ohio so may not be the same as my location. Students noted how problems related to respect can lead to student violence. Suggestions for practice included: involve students in planning interventions, (2) develop programs that develop cross-cultural understandings, and (3) recognize the increasing role that social media is playing in the school environment.

FIGURE 4.3 Sample Summary Notes for a Qualitative Research Study

---

> **Here's a Tip!**
>
> A good strategy to force yourself to summarize an article in your own words is to write your summary notes on the backside of a printed copy of the article. That way, you can't look at the author's words as you write your summary.

schools. The summary in Figure 4.2 describes the six elements for a quantitative study about middle school students' willingness to report a weapon at school. A complete reference to the article is listed at the top so that the summary is fully documented. (Recall that the format for writing these references was introduced in Chapter 1 and is reviewed in the Appendix.) Notice in this summary that the information about each element is short. In this example, the information is written out in sentences, but some reviewers may choose to use bulleted lists for the key information in their summary notes. Whatever style you prefer for recording your notes, remember that you must record the information in your own words and indicate any direct quotes (e.g., five or more consecutive words taken from the article's text) with quote marks. These six elements were also used to write a summary for a qualitative study about student and staff perceptions of preventing violence in middle schools. As shown in Figure 4.3, this summary also starts with a complete reference to the article and includes brief notes about each element.

The elements summarized for the quantitative and qualitative studies in Figures 4.2 and 4.3 illustrate typical information extracted from research studies. You may also choose to summarize other forms of writing such as theoretical discussions or school reports as part of your review. When summarizing other forms of writing, you may want to include the following points in your summary: the complete reference; the overall problem; the question or concern; the arguments, points, or program components; the implications or importance of the information; and your reflective comments (such as the strengths and weaknesses of the argument or the implications for your practice).

By developing summary notes for all the sources you select for your literature review, you are ready to turn your attention to the process of synthesizing what you learn across the sources and preparing a written document that reports this information. We consider the steps for synthesizing literature and writing a literature review in the next section.

How Do You Synthesize Literature and Write a Literature Review?

In many cases, individuals read literature simply to learn about a topic for themselves. Reading literature and taking notes is sufficient for this purpose. In other cases, however, individuals want to summarize the information to share it with others. If you plan to share the information, then you will probably want to write a literature review that summarizes what you have learned. The nature of this review will differ depending on its purpose. A student preparing a literature review for her class may write it differently from a teacher preparing a literature review report for his principal, who will write it differently from a researcher writing the literature review section of her research article. Each of these individuals, however, will engage in four basic steps:

- Organize the literature into themes.
- Summarize the major themes.
- Document the sources with citations to the literature.
- Provide conclusions about the review.

Let's examine the process of implementing each of these steps to help you learn to write your own literature reviews and to interpret the literature reviews written by others.

Step 1—Organize the Literature into Themes

As you organize and take summary notes on the articles, you will begin to understand the content of your literature review. In other words, a conceptual picture will begin to emerge. This conceptual picture usually involves organizing the studies in themes, or groupings of studies, that discuss similar subtopics within your larger topic. One way to develop this conceptual picture is to create a visual diagram that allows you to organize the literature in your mind. This visual picture results in a map of the reviewed literature. A **literature map** is a figure or drawing that visually organizes the literature on a topic. This visual picture helps you make sense of the literature because it encourages you to think about the larger ideas emerging across all of the relevant literature that you found in your search. It is also useful for conveying a picture of the literature with others, such as colleagues at work or an audience at a conference.

Figures 4.4 and 4.5 provide two examples of literature maps created by students who reviewed literature on their topics of interest. Vlasin-Marty (2011) examined literature about food safety and developed the map pictured in Figure 4.4. At the top of the figure she lists the topic: food safety. Below the top level, she identifies three subtopics: foodborne illnesses; instruments for assessing food safety practices; and knowledge, attitudes, and behaviors. Within the third subtopic, she identifies themes in the literature that she read, such as the knowledge, beliefs, and behaviors of adolescents, low-income individuals, and families. Under each theme that she identified from her literature, she lists the specific research studies that she reviewed. At the bottom of the map, Vlasin-Marty advances her proposed study about the food safety knowledge, attitudes, and behaviors for Native American families with young children in Nebraska, which she believes is needed to extend the literature.

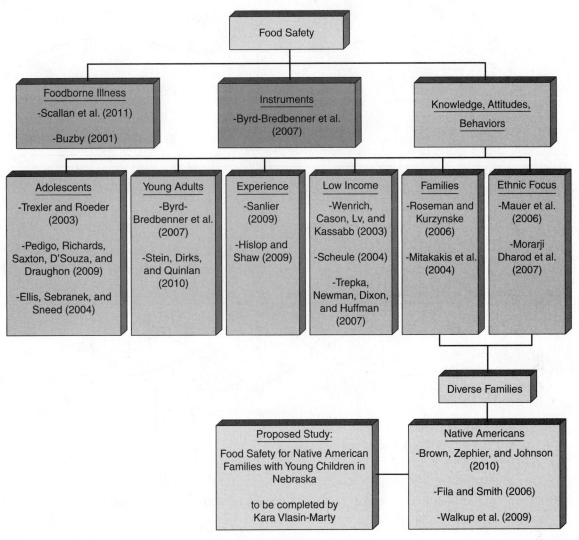

FIGURE 4.4   A Sample Literature Map on Food Safety

Source: Used by permission of Kara Vlasin-Marty, 2011.

In another example, Hermann (2011) developed Figure 4.5 as a result of reviewing literature that described the use of interventions based on art and creativity. She found two categories of interventions: those used as formal therapy (therapeutic art) and those used in educational settings (education creativity). She organized the literature within these two subtopics into themes (e.g., medical, clinical, and K-12) and listed the studies she reviewed that formed each of these groupings. At the bottom of the figure, she identified her interest in understanding the context for these interventions: "the environment/setting at the intersection of art therapy/creative education interventions."

These two literature maps illustrate several useful features that you can include when developing your own literature map. Use the following guidelines when constructing a map of reviewed literature:

- Identify the key term for your general topic and place it at the top of the map. Keep this term broad so that it helps to easily orient anyone who might be reading your literature review.
- Take your reviewed sources and sort them into groups of related topical areas or families of studies. These "families" represent the themes you find in the literature. Your summary notes and comments should be very helpful for recalling the major topics of each article that you read. Think in terms of identifying three to five broad groupings to focus on the big ideas of the literature.

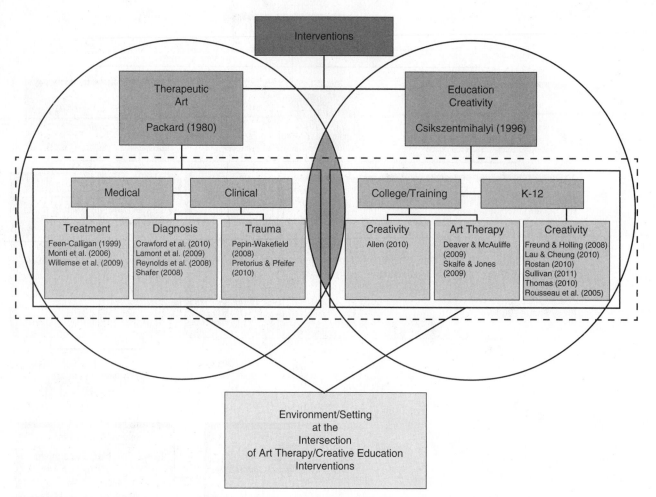

FIGURE 4.5   A Sample Literature Map on Environments for Art/Creativity Interventions

Source: Used by permission of Rita Cihlar Hermann, 2011.

- Provide a name for each of the themes based on the articles in each of the groups. Use these theme names as the labels for the boxes in the figure. In each theme box, list the key sources you found in your literature search that fall within that theme.
- Indicate your own work on the map. For example, if you review the literature to identify a strategy for promoting parent involvement at your school, then indicate where your preferred strategy comes out of the literature. Draw a box near the bottom of the figure that says "our proposed program." In this box, you could describe the program that you think your school should consider adopting based on your literature review. This helps others understand how the proposed program comes out of the literature.

Step 2—Write a Summary of the Major Themes

Once the literature is organized, then the writing process begins. But how do you report what you learned from the literature? Using your literature map as a guide, a good first step is to prepare an outline for your review. Well-written literature reviews are organized so that a reader can easily follow the ideas presented and preparing an outline will help you organize your writing. Therefore, you should develop an outline that follows the logical order of topics and subtopics that you identified in your literature map. For example, see how the outline for a literature review in Figure 4.6 follows the themes presented in the literature map depicted in Figure 4.5.

Another writing strategy is to use the themes in your outline as headings in your written paper. **Headings** are signposts that writers use to designate the topics and subtopics within a written document. Good headings are descriptive of the content, but

The paper title	Design of Conducive Environments at the Intersection of Art Therapy and Creative Education Interventions
Major topics	**Statement of the Problem**
	Therapeutic Art Interventions
Subtopics	**Medical Treatment**
	Clinical
	Diagnosis.
	Trauma.
Another major topic	**Education Creativity Interventions**
More subtopics	**College/Training**
	Creativity.
	Art therapy.
	K-12 Creativity
	Conclusions
	Proposed Study
	References

FIGURE 4.6   A Sample Literature Review Outline

Source: Used by permission of Rita Cihlar Hermann, 2011.

also short; that way, they are easy for the reader to interpret. Good headings are also formatted in a consistent manner so readers can readily differentiate major topics from subtopics. Recall that we were introduced to different style manuals in Chapter 1. These style manuals provide directions for how to format the different levels of headings within a written document. The levels of headings provide logical subdivisions of the text from topics to subtopics. Figure 4.7 summarizes the different styles used for different levels of headings in the APA (2010) style. This style was used to format the headings listed in Figure 4.6 as well as the sample paper found in the Appendix.

Once you have your outline and headings planned, the next step is to write a summary of what you learned from the literature for each of the major themes that you identified. There are two common styles for writing this summary from which you can choose:

- a study-by-study literature review or
- a thematic literature review.

The Title Is Centered and in Title Case
Level 1 Heading Is Centered, Bold, and in Title Case
Level 2 Heading Is Left Justified, Bold, and in Title Case
Level 3 heading is indented, bold, in sentence case, and ends with a period.
Level 4 heading is indented, bold, italicized, in sentence case, and ends with a period.
Level 5 heading is indented, italicized, in sentence case, and ends with a period.

FIGURE 4.7   Title and Headings in the APA Style

Source: APA, 2010, p. 62.

Note: "Title Case" is where every major word is capitalized; "sentence case" is where only the first word is capitalized.

One convenient approach to summarizing literature is to describe each reviewed study one at a time. In this way, a **study-by-study review of the literature** provides a detailed summary of each study grouped under each of the broad themes identified in the review. The detailed summary of each study is usually one paragraph in length and highlights the elements shown in Figures 4.2 and 4.3. This form of literature review typically appears in journal articles that summarize the literature on a topic and in student work, such as class papers, theses, or dissertations. When presenting a study-by-study review, authors link the summaries of the studies using transitional sentences. They also organize the summaries under subheadings that reflect the major themes in the reviewed literature (i.e., the topics identified in boxes of the literature map).

Young et al.'s (2012) review of the literature about video games in education in the journal *Review of Educational Research* illustrates the study-by-study review approach. As you read the following excerpt, note that the authors discuss the research that addresses video gaming in mathematics education one study at a time.

> In our review of the math gaming literature, we initially identified an investigation by A. Harris, Yuill, and Luckin (2008) that addressed how video games may be used to effectively facilitate student collaboration on complex logic problems. The study included 34 primary school students aged 8 to 10 years, and the researchers examined the influence of mastery and performance goals on the nature of children's participation during video gaming. Each student was matched with a partner based on his or her goal orientation, and each pair spent 20 minutes cooperatively playing a logic-development game (The Logical Journey of Zoombinis). A. Harris et al. observed that students with different goal orientations interacted in different ways while solving mathematical problems and concluded that goal-focused instructions could be used to influence the nature and quality of children's partnered interactions, potentially improving long-term academic achievement.
>
> Similarly, Mayo's (2009) study found that although many educators were not open to the idea of using video games in their classrooms, such programs increased achievement (as measured by standardized testing) from 7% to 40%, including high school algebra and college-level numerical methods.... (p. 67)

In this excerpt, the authors first described the study by A. Harris and colleagues in one paragraph. Then, in the next paragraph, they described the study by Mayo. In this way, they discussed one study at a time. They also provided a detailed description of each study, which included the research problem (e.g., whether video games effectively facilitate student collaboration), an implied question (e.g., whether student goals influence the nature of participation with a partner), the data collection (e.g., 34 participants in the study), and a summary of the results (e.g., students with different goal orientations interacted with partners in different ways).

In contrast to the study-by-study approach, you can use a **thematic review of the literature** where you identify a theme and briefly cite literature to document this theme. In this approach, you would discuss only the major ideas or results from studies rather than the detail of any single study. Authors use this approach frequently in journal articles that report research studies. You can recognize this form by locating a theme and noting the references (typically multiple references) to the literature used to support the theme. For example, Musher-Eizenman et al. (2011) reviewed the literature about influences on individuals' eating patterns. The following passage, appearing in an early section in their study report, illustrates a thematic literature review approach:

> Research on the effects of external cues on eating patterns in children has primarily included efforts to reduce food neophobia, or avoidance of unfamiliar foods, particularly for fruits and vegetables. Increased exposure to a food (Birch and Marlin, 1982; Sullivan and Birch, 1994), access and availability (Hearn et al., 1998), and parent and peer modeling (Birch, 1980; Wardle et al., 2003a, 2003b) have all demonstrated success in increasing children's consumption of healthy foods. . . . (p. 192)

In this excerpt, the authors reviewed the literature about the theme "external cues and children's eating patterns" and briefly mentioned multiple references to support the theme. The authors do not discuss the details of each reviewed study separately.

Step 3—Document the Sources by Including Citations to the Literature

Regardless of whether you choose to write a study-by-study or thematic literature review, you must include citations (or references) for all of the sources that you have reviewed. You must give credit to these sources, so as to not plagiarize others' work. To **plagiarize** means to represent someone else's ideas and writings as if they were your own. Examples of plagiarism include copying someone else's words directly without putting them into quotes and giving credit, using someone else's ideas without giving them credit, or using someone else's sentences but changing just a few words. It is not only rude to plagiarize someone else's work, but it is wrong to do. In many cases, plagiarizing someone else's work can result in serious consequences such as failing a class, being dismissed from school, or losing a job. Therefore, you must learn to *always* give proper credit to your sources.

> *Here's a Tip!*
>
> Understanding plagiarism and how to avoid it is challenging. A good resource to learn more about this important topic is http://plagiarism.org/

We have already seen how summary notes can include a complete reference to a source (see Figures 4.4 and 4.5). Documenting your sources for your own use is an important part of the literature review process, but you also have to document these sources in your writing about the literature. Fortunately, style manuals such as the one by APA (2010) provide guidance on including citations in scholarly writing in addition to formatting headings.

There are two approaches related to writing citations found in the APA style that you need to use when writing about the literature on a topic:

- in-text references and
- end-of-text references.

In-text references are references cited in a brief format within the body of the text to provide credit to authors. In-text references should be used in your writing whenever you refer to an idea, procedure, or result from someone else's work. The APA style lists several conventions for citing these in-text references. You can find examples of in-text references using the APA style in Figure 4.8. Key features of this style include the following elements:

Type of Reference	In-Text Examples
Single author	Rogers (2004) compared reaction times for athletes and nonathletes in high schools.
	Previous research has examined differences between athletes and nonathletes (Rogers, 2004).
Two authors	Bacyn and Alon (2008) tested the effectiveness of group learning on reaction times.
	Studies have also tested the effectiveness of group learning (Bacyn & Alon, 2008).
Three to five authors, first mention in a paper	The difficulty of test taking and reaction times has been examined by Smith, Paralli, John, and Langor (2012).
	Reaction times are important considerations for test design (Clark, Peabody, & Johnson, 2008).
Three to five authors, subsequent mention in a paper	The study of test taking and reaction times (Clark et al., 2008). . . .
Six or more authors, any mention	Smith et al. (2012) suggest there is a need for research on test taking to move beyond only considering reaction times.
Multiple references (listed in alphabetical order)	Past studies of reaction times (Clark et al., 2008; Gogel, 1992; Lucky & Jones, 1994; Rogers, 2004; Smith et al., 1994) showed. . . .
Direct quote	Reaction times are defined as "the time to react to an unexpected stimulus" (Mills & Haas, 2007, p. 42).

FIGURE 4.8   Examples of In-Text References in the APA Style

- Use only the last names of authors, listed in the order they appear in the article.
- Include the year of the publication.
- If there is more than one author, write out the word "and" if the names are used as part a sentence text or use "&" if the names are referenced within parentheses.
- If a reference has three to five authors, write all of the authors' last names the first time you refer to the work and then only list the first name followed by "et al." (meaning "and others") subsequently. If a reference has six or more authors, then use the "et al." form each time you refer to the work. An example of the "et al." form is: Xu et al. (2010).
- If you use a direct quote from the source, include the original page number of the quote as part of the in-text reference.

End-of-text references are the references listed at the end of a research report. It is essential that you provide the full details of each reference in this list at the end of your writing. Common forms for these references in the APA style were introduced in Chapter 1. When combined into an end-of-text references list, the APA style includes the following features:

- Start the end-of-text references on a new page and title this section "References."
- List all cited references alphabetically by the last names of the first authors.
- Include *all* the references mentioned in the body of the paper and *only* the references mentioned in the body of the paper in the end-of-text references list.
- Use a hanging indent form for each reference. This means that the first line is left adjusted and the subsequent lines are indented.
- Double space the text in the end-of-text references list.

An example of an end-of-text references list in the APA style is located at the end of the sample paper in the Appendix.

Step 4—Provide Your Conclusions About the Literature

Once you have summarized the literature, you are ready to write an ending for your literature review. A good review concludes with a thoughtful discussion that summarizes the literature and provides commentary about the literature. To write a conclusion for your literature review, first restate the major themes that you found. Ask yourself, "What are the major ideas from all of the studies I reviewed?" Your answer to this question will result in the identification of three to five themes that summarize the literature. With these themes in mind, briefly highlight what you learned about each theme. This discussion should emphasize the big ideas under each major heading in the literature review and point out what the reader should remember from the review. The discussion should also identify strengths and weaknesses you identified about what is known and not known in the literature.

In addition to noting the major themes found from the review, your concluding discussion should also explain how the literature informs your work. For example, if you are a practitioner reviewing the literature to learn what is known about different available programs, then you should conclude the literature review with a statement giving your recommendation for which program should be adopted by your organization based on what you learned. Likewise, when researchers conclude their literature reviews in their study reports, they often explicitly state how information from the literature (such as an identified theory or conceptual framework) was used to shape the research study they conducted.

How Do You Evaluate a Literature Review in a Research Study?

Now that you know how individuals conduct and write literature reviews, you can more easily interpret and evaluate the literature review sections included as part of the Introduction sections of research reports. Recall that the primary purpose of including a literature review in a research report is for the author to inform readers about the background for the study and demonstrate that the research is grounded in the knowledge that exists in the literature. A good, rigorous literature review therefore conveys that the researcher completed a comprehensive review of the literature, organized and synthesized this literature, and made it clear how the literature was used to direct or inform the conducted study. Table 4.3 lists criteria that are useful to consider when

TABLE 4.3   Criteria for Evaluating the Literature Review in a Research Report

Quality Criteria	Indicators of Higher Quality	Indicators of Lower Quality
The Key Elements		
1. The review includes the relevant literature.	+ The review is comprehensive, including numerous sources that clearly relate to the study's topic. + Important subtopics are included in the reviewed literature.	− The review is superficial, including only a small number of sources, some of which does not seem related to the study's topic. − Important subtopics are missing from the reviewed literature.
2. The review examines sources that are recent and of high quality.	+ The reviewed literature focuses on reports of original research published in peer-reviewed journals that are considered recent for the topic (e.g., from the last 10 years for many topics).	− The reviewed literature focuses on books, secondary sources, materials that have not undergone peer review, and materials that are no longer current for the topic.
3. The literature review is appropriately documented.	+ Citations are provided as support for all ideas drawn from the literature. + The citations are correct, complete, and in a consistent style.	− Not all ideas drawn from the literature are supported with citations. − Some citations are incorrect, incomplete, or in an inconsistent style.
4. The literature is thoughtfully synthesized.	+ The literature is organized into major themes and subtopics that make sense in the context of the study's topic. + The major ideas that the researcher found from the literature are clearly identified by headings and/or a visual map.	− The organization of the literature does not make sense in the context of the study's topic. − It is difficult to identify the main ideas that the researcher found from the literature.
5. The literature is critically examined.	+ The researcher critiques the literature by considering issues such as its deficiencies, strengths and weaknesses, and implications for the study's design.	− The researcher only summarizes the literature without offering critical commentary about it.
General Evaluation		
6. The study has a strong foundation in the literature.	+ The study's problem, purpose, approach, methods, and interpretations are clearly connected to and informed by the literature. + The study report includes explicit statements that explain how the literature is being used in the study, such as by providing a guiding theory or conceptual framework.	− There is a lack of connection between the literature and the study's problem, purpose, approach, methods, and interpretations. − The study report does not indicate how the literature is being used in the study.
7. The use of the literature fits the study's overall research approach.	In a quantitative study: + The literature review justifies the problem, provides direction by identifying the major variables and hypotheses from theories, supports the procedures, and is used to compare the results to the predictions. In a qualitative study: + The literature review justifies the problem, informs the researcher's approach and stance through a conceptual framework, is examined further as new findings emerge, and is used to interpret the meaning of the findings.	In a quantitative study: − The literature review is minimal for the topic and does not support the choice of variables and stated hypotheses. In a qualitative study: − The literature review is used to specify variables or make predictions that limit the researcher's openness to learn from participants or remains static even when new findings emerge.

Quality Criteria	Quality Rating				Your Evidence and/or Reasoning
	0 = Poor	1 = Fair	2 = Good	3 = Excellent	
The Key Elements					
1. The review includes the relevant literature.					
2. The review examines sources that are recent and of high quality.					
3. The literature review is appropriately documented.					
4. The literature is thoughtfully synthesized.					
5. The literature is critically examined.					
General Evaluation					
6. The study has a strong foundation in the literature.					
7. The use of the literature fits the study's overall research approach.					
Overall Quality 0–10 = Low quality 11–16 = Adequate quality 17–21 = High quality	Total Score =				My Overall Assessment =

FIGURE 4.9   A Rating Scale for Evaluating the Literature Review in a Research Report

evaluating the contents, organization, and use of the literature review in a research study. This table also provides indicators of higher quality and lower quality for the criteria to help you make your own judgments when evaluating the literature review in a research report.

The rating scale in Figure 4.9 provides a convenient means for you to apply the quality criteria to the literature review in any research report. For each of the criteria you locate, assign a quality rating from *fair* (1) to *excellent* (3), and document your evidence and/or reasoning behind the rating. If one of the criteria is missing or very poorly stated, then indicate *poor* (0) as your rating. Although research reports will vary in the extent of literature they include, good reports should still score well on most of the items listed in Figure 4.9. By adding up the rating scores for each of the criteria and using the suggested cutoff values provided at the bottom of the figure, you will have an indicator that you can use to help you determine your overall assessment of a report's literature review.

Reviewing What You've Learned To Do

- *Identify and understand the literature review in a research report.*
  - ☐ A literature review is a written synthesis of available documents that organizes the information into subtopics, and summarizes and critiques the past and current state of knowledge about a topic. Researchers use literature reviews to provide the background for their research studies.
  - ☐ Literature reviews are often found as a part of the Introductions in research reports. In addition, researchers' use of literature can be identified when they refer to the literature in citations throughout the report's text.

- *Describe how researchers use literature in their research studies.*
  - ❑ Researchers use literature in the Introduction section of their reports to provide evidence for the research problem, to document what is and is not known about the study topic, and to identify the theory or conceptual framework behind the study. They also use the literature to provide models for the procedures used in the study and to interpret the results at the end of the study.
- *Describe differences in how researchers use literature in quantitative and qualitative research.*
  - ❑ In quantitative studies, researchers complete their literature review at the start of the research. They use the literature to help prescribe the variables and hypotheses of interest at the start of the study, and to compare the results with the expectations found in the literature at the end of the study.
  - ❑ In qualitative studies, researchers review the literature at the start of the research and during the research when new topics emerge from the data. They use the literature to inform the researchers' stance and assumptions about the study topic, and to interpret the meaning of the findings as they relate to other studies found in the literature.
- *Take steps for reviewing the literature about a topic of interest to you.*
  - ❑ Four useful steps for reviewing the literature include identifying key terms, searching academic libraries and electronic databases, selecting literature that is relevant and of good quality, and preparing summary notes on each source of information located in the literature.
- *Identify steps useful for writing a literature review.*
  - ❑ Four useful steps for writing a literature review include organizing the literature into themes, summarizing the sources within each of the major themes, documenting the sources with citations, and discussing conclusions about the literature.
- *Evaluate the quality of the literature review in a research report.*
  - ❑ The evaluation of a literature review begins by considering the extent to which the researchers examined literature that is relevant and of good quality and the extent to which they appropriately cited, thoughtfully synthesized, and critically considered the literature.
  - ❑ The evaluation of a literature review is also based on the extent to which the researchers used the literature to provide the background for the study and the extent to which the use of the literature fits the study's quantitative or qualitative approach.

✓ **To assess what you've learned to do, click here to answer questions and receive instant feedback.**

Reading Research Articles

At the end of this chapter, you will find a research article to help you practice your new skills. Carefully read the qualitative adolescent-homelessness study by Haldenby, Berman, and Forchuk (2007) starting on p. 148. First, write a complete, APA-style reference for each article.

As you read the article, pay close attention to the use of literature throughout, particularly in the Introduction section (paragraphs 01–20). Use the highlighting tool in the Pearson etext to indicate where the authors have provided information from their literature review, and use the notetaking tool to add marginal notes that name each use you highlighted and note how each one is related to the study's background. Within the literature review, you will want to look for the ways the authors use literature to specify:

1. Justification for the research problem
2. What is and is not known
3. Theory or conceptual framework
4. Models for the methods
5. Interpretation of results

Note, however, that sometimes authors do not use their literature in all of these ways—for example, they might not include a theory or conceptual framework or they might not use literature to provide models for the methods. If one of these uses is missing, indicate that in your marginal notes.

 Click here to go to the qualitative adolescent-homelessness study by Haldenby et al. (2007) so that you can write a complete APA-style reference for the article and enter marginal notes about the study.

Understanding Research Articles

Apply your knowledge of the content of this chapter to the qualitative adolescent-homelessness study by Haldenby et al. (2007) starting on p. 148. Click here to answer questions and receive instant feedback.

1. There are five ways that researchers tend to use literature in their research reports. For each of the following ways, identify an example of this use in the adolescent-homelessness study. If you do not find an example for any of the listed uses, then state where you would have expected to find this use in the report.
   a. Providing justification for the research problem.
   b. Documenting what is and is not known about the topic.
   c. Identifying the theory or conceptual framework behind the study.
   d. Providing models for the methods and procedures.
   e. Interpreting results.

2. Using Figure 4.3 as a guide, develop summary notes for the qualitative adolescent-homelessness study.

3. Assume that you want to conduct a literature review on the topic of adolescent homelessness. What key terms and logic terms (e.g., AND, OR) would you use to complete an advanced search to locate additional research on this topic? Try your search using the ERIC database (eric.ed.gov) and note how many hits you obtained with these search terms.

4. Write a sentence about the adolescent-homelessness study using an in-text reference in the APA style. Write an end-of-text references list in the APA style that includes the adolescent homelessness study plus two other studies you identified in your ERIC search.

5. Identify the major topics and subtopics that the authors summarized in their literature review in the adolescent-homelessness study. Using Figures 4.4 and 4.5 as a guide, sketch a literature map that represents this literature review.

✓ **Click here to answer the questions and receive instant feedback.**

Evaluating Research Articles

Practice evaluating a study's literature review, using the qualitative adolescent-homelessness study by Haldenby et al. (2007) starting on p. 148.

1. Use the criteria discussed in Table 4.3 to evaluate the quality of the literature review in the adolescent-homelessness study. Note that, for this question, the rating form includes advice to help guide your evaluation.

✓ **Click here to open the rating scale form (Figure 4.9) to enter your ratings, evidence, and reasoning.**

An Example of Qualitative Research: The Adolescent-Homelessness Study

Let's examine another published research article to apply the ideas you are learning. Throughout this book, we will refer to this study as the "qualitative adolescent-homelessness" study. This journal article reports a qualitative research study conducted and reported by Haldenby et al. (2007). Examine this article to practice your skills with reading, understanding, and evaluating research.

 Click here to write a complete APA-style reference for this article and receive instant feedback.

Homelessness and Health in Adolescents

Qualitative Health Research
Volume 17 Number 9
November 2007 1232-1244
© 2007 Sage Publications
10.1177/1049732307307550
http://qhr.sagepub.com
hosted at
http://online.sagepub.com

Amy M. Haldenby
Helene Berman
Cheryl Forchuk
The University of Western Ontario

Despite an abundance of resources, many of the world's wealthiest nations have a large homeless population. People at all stages of development are affected by this problem, but adolescents who are homeless face a unique set of challenges. In this critical narrative study the authors examined the experiences of homeless adolescents with particular attention to the role of gender and public policy, health experiences and perceptions, and barriers to health care services. Six girls and 7 boys participated in semistructured dialogic interviews. Their stories revealed that living without a home had a substantial impact on their health and wellness. The findings from this study support the need for health care professionals to work in collaboration with homeless youth so that more effective care that is sensitive to their unique health needs can be provided.

Keywords: *adolescence; homelessness; health; critical theory; narrative*

(01) Many of the world's wealthiest nations have a large homeless population despite an abundance of natural and material resources. Because of the inherently transient nature of homelessness and few agreed-on definitions, it is difficult to obtain an accurate picture of those who are living without a home (Panter-Brick, 2002). However, there is evidence that a significant proportion is made up of adolescents (City of Calgary, 2006). The leader of the New Democratic Party of Canada, Jack Layton (2000), observed that the word *homeless* conjures up powerful images of people who have no roof under which to reside or individuals and families who live in "substandard" housing. How the term is defined is rooted in ideology (Ensign, 1998) and can influence who is researched and how the findings are interpreted. For the purposes of this study, homelessness includes individuals who live in the streets, are in the shelter system, or are continuously moving between temporary housing arrangements. Throughout this research the terms *homeless*, *street-involved*, and *living on the streets* are used interchangeably.

(02)   The City of Toronto report commissioned by the Mayor's Homelessness Action Task Force (1999) identified youth under the age of 18 as the fastest growing group of users of emergency hostels. Living without a

home, and thus at the margins of society, is thought to create grim consequences for adolescents' health, development, and overall well-being (Panter-Brick, 2002).

Background and Significance

(03)   In the past 10 years changes in the national economy, including socioeconomic restructuring in Canada, have had a substantial impact on adolescents nation-wide (Dematteo et al., 1999). The effects of this restructuring are demonstrated through cuts to social programs and supports as well as drastic reductions to welfare and unemployment insurance. These factors have led to an increase in the number of youth living in poverty. Although there are many other factors, including various forms of abuse and neglect, that play a role in the homelessness of adolescents (Martijn & Sharpe, 2005), such structural changes are also thought to contribute to the rise of street-involved youth in Canada. There is, however, little knowledge regarding how these social and political factors influence the experience of being without a home.

(04)   The gender stratification of contemporary Western society can be characterized by a devaluing of the lives of girls and women (Neysmith, 1995). Consequently, gender is a powerful shaper of an individual's experiences and can therefore influence how young women and men create different meanings out of similar

Authors' Note: This study was funded by the Sigma Theta Tau International Honour Society–Iota Omicron Chapter

circumstances. Because of their lower position in the social hierarchy, it has been suggested that living without a home places adolescent women at a significant disadvantage (Ensign & Panke, 2002). Little research, however, has been conducted to confirm or refute this idea. In the absence of such knowledge, health care professionals are typically limited in their ability to provide care for this population.

(05) It has been well documented that homeless adolescents experience a variety of health-related concerns (Boivin, Roy, Haley, & du Fort, 2005). Despite this fact, many researchers have found that these youth are the least likely to access the available health care services (Barkin, Balkrishnan, Manuel, Anderson, & Gelberg, 2003; Shiner, 1995). It is therefore crucial for health care providers to better understand the health perceptions and experiences of this group in order that more effective approaches to health care can be provided. More specifically, it is anticipated that the findings from this research can be used to assist in the development and implementation of programs and policies designed to meet the needs of homeless adolescents.

Literature Review

Homeless Youth

(06) There is a widely accepted misconception that youth who reside on the streets are there by choice (City of Toronto, 1999). In fact, numerous reports have identified various forms of abuse, including physical, sexual, or emotional, as main factors that can cause young people to flee their homes (Health Canada, 2005; Russell, 1996). It is thought that a comprehensive understanding of homelessness also requires attention to macrolevel factors such as poverty, support networks, and employment (Boydell, Goering, & Morell-Bellai, 2000; Morrell-Bellai, Goering, & Boydell, 2000). In this section, the literature that relates to the health of adolescents once they become homeless, and the barriers that they face when trying to access health care, will be discussed.

Health Sequelae Associated With Homelessness

(07) Many adolescents who are homeless experience a range of physical and emotional health problems (Panter-Brick, 2004). Several quantitative studies have shown that this population has a high rate of suicide ideation (Leslie, Stein, & Rotheram-Borus, 2002; Rew, Taylor-Seehafer, & Fitzgerald, 2001). It is thought that this risk is amplified among gay, lesbian, bisexual, and transgendered youths (Cochran, Stewart, Ginzler, & Cauce, 2002; Noell & Ochs, 2001). Homeless youth have a high prevalence of depression and other psychiatric disorders, which is associated with elevated rates of intravenous drug use (Rhode, Noell, Ochs, & Seeley, 2001). Substance abuse often contributes either directly or indirectly to the homelessness of adolescents (Mallett, Rosenthal, & Keys, 2005). Homeless youth also suffer from an increased rate of acute and chronic respiratory diseases (Clatts, Davis, Sotern, & Attillasoy, 1998; Hwang, 2001). The increase in respiratory disease might be related to exposure to tuberculosis and influenza (O'Connell, 2004), which can result from staying in crowded quarters such as emergency shelters or squats.

In addition to being at risk for various physical and **(08)** emotional problems, homeless adolescents are often forced to engage in "survival sex," whereby sexual activity is traded for money, drugs, or shelter (Rew, Chambers, & Kulkarni, 2002). As a result, these adolescents might have more sexual partners than the adolescent population in general (Anderson et al., 1996; Clatts et al., 1998). They are also likely to be involved in some form of high-risk sexual activity, such as inconsistent condom use and prostitution (Johnson, Aschkenasy, Herbers, & Gillenwater, 1996).

Several large quantitative studies conducted in urban **(09)** centers in North America have shown that homeless adolescents are at high risk for contracting HIV infection (Dematteo et al., 1999; Walters, 1999). It has been estimated that these youth are 6 to 12 times more likely to become infected with HIV than any other group of youth (Rotheram-Borus et al., 2003) and are more likely to contract chlamydia (Shields et al., 2004).

Many researchers have observed that homeless ado- **(10)** lescents are more likely to become victims of many forms of violence than those who are not homeless (Kipke, Simon, Montgomery, Unger, & Iversen, 1997; Whitbeck, Hoyt, & Ackley, 1997). Street involvement has also been found to increase the risk of mortality by 8 to 11 times that of the general population (Hwang, 2000; Roy et al., 2004).

A number of researchers have examined the expe- **(11)** rience of adolescent homelessness (Kidd, 2004; Paradise & Cauce, 2002). In a study with street youth in Brazil, experiences of homelessness varied according to the local context and circumstances (Raffaelli et al., 2000). This finding is important because it highlights the problems inherent in attempts to generalize the experiences of street-involved youth across diverse settings and cultures. The illness experiences

1234 Qualitative Health Research

of urban homeless youth have also been examined (Ensign & Bell, 2004). Of particular interest, Ensign and Bell concluded that health-seeking behaviors differed by gender. Female youth sought care more often and typically preferred to be accompanied by a friend. Another finding of interest was that females reported more safety concerns while ill and living on the streets than their male counterparts.

Barriers to Care

(12)   Although homeless adolescents experience a variety of health-related concerns, they rarely access health care services (Barkin et al., 2003; Shiner, 1995). Some barriers they encounter are fears that they will experience discriminatory attitudes (Gerber, 1997) and be negatively judged by health providers (Ensign, 2001; Reid, Berman, & Forchuk, 2005).

(13)   There is evidence that these concerns among homeless youth might be warranted. In research with medical students, more negative attitudes toward homeless people were found at the end of their courses than at the beginning (Masson & Lester, 2003). Among nursing students care has been declined to homeless clients in certain situations (Zrinyi & Balogh, 2004). It is possible that health professionals' negative attitudes regarding homeless individuals dissuade this population from accessing needed health care and, in turn, contribute to their poorer level of health.

Unique Challenges Faced by Homeless Adolescent Women

(14)   Several investigators have examined the unique challenges faced by homeless female adolescents and have concluded that they are the most vulnerable subculture within the homeless population (Ensign & Panke, 2002). In this section, the research related to young women's risks for sexual victimization and health problems more broadly will be examined.

Sexual Victimization

(15)   There is some evidence that the nature of victimization while residing on the streets differs for women and men. More specifically, several researchers have observed that women and girls are significantly more likely to be sexually assaulted than are men and boys (Kipke et al., 1997; Rew, Taylor-Seehafer, et al., 2001; Tyler, Hoyt, Whitbeck, & Les, 2001). The detrimental effects that result from such violence have been described to include fear, anger, hostility, depression, anxiety, and humiliation (Fontaine & Fletcher, 1999;

Hall, 2000; Nehls & Sallmann, 2005). Sexualized violence can also increase the risk of contracting HIV, a problem that is well documented among this subpopulation (Clements, Gleghorn, Garcia, Katz, & Marx, 1997; O'Connor, 1998).

Health

(16)   Several investigators (Chen, Tyler, Whitbeck, & Hoyt, 2004; Harrison, Fulkerson, & Beebe, 1997) have found that a history of childhood sexual abuse increases the risk of substance abuse among homeless youth. As girls are sexually abused with much greater frequency than are boys (Trocme & Wolfe, 2001), homeless adolescent women are thought to be at considerable risk for substance abuse. There are reports that a relationship between substance abuse and prostitution among homeless female adolescents exists, which are thought to have adverse consequences for the women's physical and emotional health (Weber, Boivin, Blais, Haley, & Roy, 2004). Finally, there is some evidence that suicide is more prevalent among adolescent homeless women than it is among their male counterparts (Leslie et al., 2002; Molnar, Shade, Kral, Booth, & Watters, 1998). Collectively, these research findings offer compelling documentation that homeless young women are at a substantial health disadvantage.

Summary and Critique of the Literature

(17)   Much of the current research related to homeless adolescents focuses on the rates at which disease and violence occur and the barriers faced when trying to access care. With regard to gender, several researchers have brought attention to the sexual victimization and ensuing health problems suffered by young homeless women. Missing from this body of work, however, is consideration of the youths' perceptions about homelessness. As well, there are few studies that explore the experiences of homeless adolescents, or the ways in which gender and public policy influence their experiences. Many researchers have tended to characterize this population as a homogeneous group. In effect, this depiction negates the importance of gender, race, ability, or other social locations and identities. To present a comprehensive analysis, a brief commentary regarding current policy that affects homeless youth is presented.

The Contemporary Policy Context

(18)   Over the past 10 years the Canadian federal government has dissolved its responsibility for homelessness by forcing the funding and implementation of most

affordable housing programs onto the provinces and territories, which have, in some cases, directed the issue onto the municipalities. Each level of government has its own perspective on the issue of homelessness, with little consensus as to possible solutions. Consequently, millions of allocated social housing dollars have been left unspent (Federation of Canadian Municipalities, 2006). With lack of federal leadership, there are limits to what can be accomplished. Failure of the Canadian government to work as a cohesive whole contributes to an inability to meet the unique housing needs of homeless individuals, including adolescents.

(19)   Among the scant social housing programs, only a few have addressed youth as a subpopulation of the homeless, and even fewer have addressed young women in particular. Historically, the Youth Homeless Strategy, which was part of the National Housing Initiative (NHI) established in 1999 by the Liberal government, narrowly focused on adolescents' job training (Government of Canada, 2004). Although employment status contributes to a person's ability to find and maintain housing, this program overlooked major factors that contribute to their homelessness such as poor levels of well-being and lack of affordable housing. All NHI programs have since been dissolved. Currently, there are few remaining policies that relate to housing needs for youth. Of these, the federal government's Shelter Enhancement Program focuses solely on emergency and second-stage housing (Canada Mortgage and Housing Corporation [CMHC], 2007b). Although this type of shelter is needed to initially help those fleeing violent situations, this program fails to address the long-term housing needs of individuals with histories of abuse. Also, individuals who access this program are expected to contribute financially to the operating costs (CMHC, 2007b). With a few exceptions, such as the First Nations Market Housing Fund (CMHC, 2007a), the current government's housing policies fail to consider how a multitude of factors such as poverty, age, ability, race, and gender influence the housing needs of homeless individuals.

Ontario Works Act

(20)   The Ontario Works Act is provincial legislation that provides either employment or financial assistance to those "in need" (Government of Ontario, 2006). Although it varies slightly between municipalities, in most regions it is mandatory for individuals under the age of 18 to be enrolled full time in school or an alternative learning program to be eligible. To have mandatory enrolment in the school system could be viewed as

encouraging adolescents to continue their education. It does not, however, consider a variety of factors that might keep youths from attending school, such as homelessness or a variety of health concerns.

Purpose of the Study and Research Questions

The overall purpose of this study was to explore **(21)** the experience of homelessness among adolescents. More specifically, the research questions that guided this investigation are

1. How is homelessness experienced by adolescents?
2. How does gender shape these experiences?
3. How is health perceived and experienced by homeless adolescents, and what are the barriers they encounter with respect to the health care system? and
4. How does current Canadian policy shape these experiences?

Method

Design

The selected research design was a critical narrative **(22)** analysis. This approach integrates key ideas from critical social theory and narrative inquiry. Critical theory builds on Marxist thought to consider that multiple, often overlapping forms of oppression exist. From an epistemological perspective, knowledge within a critical theory framework is historically constructed and socially situated. Thus, characteristics such as social class, race, age, ability, and gender are considered to be social constructions that afford different access to power and privilege within our society (Browne, 2000). Depending on one's social location, or identity, individuals and groups have unequal ability to fully participate in society. One aim of research that is informed by critical theory is to examine individual experiences but to simultaneously consider how these are shaped by broader social, political, and historical contexts.

As selected study participants were from a group who **(23)** are often in the margins of society, this research created a "space" for the voices and perspectives of homeless adolescents to be heard. At the same time, their individual, subjective experiences were analyzed with particular attention to the manner by which those experiences are shaped by gender and by public policy.

Narrative inquiry is a research method that is **(24)** highly compatible with critical social theory.

Narrative inquiry involves using language as the medium that reflects meanings, which are understood as the groundwork of reality (Riessman, 1993). The participants' stories are rooted in time, place, and personal experience (Lieblich, Tuval-Mashiach, & Zilber, 1998; Riessman, 1993), which provide insight into social patterns as they are seen through the lens of an individual (Patton, 2002; Riessman, 1993). In this research the social patterns and culture that were revealed though the individual's stories can be used to better understand the experiences of living without a home.

Sample

(25)   After ethics approval was obtained through the University of Western Ontario's research ethics board, the study participants were recruited from a community center that works with adolescents who are homeless. This center is located in the downtown area of a southwestern city in Ontario. Information about the study was provided to the agency staff, who assisted with recruitment by allowing discussion about the study during various youth group meetings. The youth who were interested in participating were asked to contact the researcher by phone or e-mail or in person during a visit to the centre. After meeting the adolescent, the researcher provided a letter of information. The main points of the letter were reviewed at the beginning of the interview, and any questions the participants had were addressed. Informed consent was obtained verbally and in writing at the time of the interview.

(26)   All male and female participants had self-identified as being homeless, were able to speak and understand English, and, with one exception, ranged in age from 14 to 19 years. The rationale for the lower age limit is that 14 is the legal age at which individuals can agree to participate in research without parental consent. In recognition of the diversity within the homeless adolescent population, efforts were made to recruit youth from a variety of backgrounds and ethnicities. One Black male participant who was 6 months above the specified age range was granted acceptance to participate. All other youth were White.

(27)   The total sample consisted of 6 female and 7 male participants. All participants were given the choice of taking part in group or individual interviews. Five young women and 4 young men opted to be interviewed individually. Two group interviews were conducted, one consisting of 2 adolescent boys and another consisting of 1 adolescent boy and 1 adolescent woman participant. In both of these interviews

the two participants knew one another and considered each other friends. The final decision regarding sample size was determined during the course of the research according to the criterion of saturation (Patton, 2002). In essence, sampling was discontinued when no new themes emerged from the data.

Data Collection Procedures

The individual and group interviews followed a semi-   **(28)** structured format and were dialogic and interactive in nature. Critical theory assumes that the standards of truth are always social (Campbell & Bunting, 1991). Thus, new knowledge is coconstructed between the nurse researcher and the participants. Field notes were taken after the interviews, which assisted the nurse researcher in revising the interview guide as the study progressed as well as assisting in data analysis (Patton, 2002).

Data Analysis

All interviews were audio-recorded and transcribed   **(29)** verbatim as soon as possible following the interview. Transcripts were reviewed by the interviewer for accuracy. Once transcription was completed, a narrative style of analysis was conducted with the assistance of Atlas-Ti, a qualitative software program. This process involved several readings of the transcripts to capture initial impressions (Lieblich et al., 1998). More focused codes were then developed as ideas surfaced from the narratives. The code list was continuously revised to accommodate new perspectives and to collapse overlapping categories. The focused code list guided the analysis, and more abstract themes evolved from the transcribed stories. Attention was paid to both the content of the story and the way in which it was told (Lieblich et al., 1998).

Zimmerman and West (1987) have argued that   **(30)** society "invisibly" guides people to behave socially within the dichotomous norms of femininity and masculinity. It is therefore thought that gender is embedded in our everyday experiences (Zimmerman & West, 1987), which influence how youth create different meanings out of similar circumstances. Social understandings of gender and their influence on the narratives were therefore considered throughout the analysis. Ideas that emerged from the transcripts that did not fit the evolving code list were recognized as important and considered throughout the analysis. In all cases except for the one boy/girl group interview, young women's and young men's transcripts were

(31)   initially analyzed separately. Finally, dominant themes were identified, and conclusions were made.

Findings

All participants appeared eager to share their stories and did so in an insightful way. From their narratives five themes emerged: (a) the realities of exiting street life, (b) negotiating dangerous terrain, (c) rethinking family, (d) the hazards of being female, and (e) the elusive nature of health and the health care system. Because critical research invites reflection into the contextual factors that shape and influence a person's experience, a separate analysis of current Canadian policy was completed. These findings will be addressed in relation to the participants' stories.

"You're Just Stuck": The Realities of Exiting Street Life

(32)   Several participants expressed the belief that they were unable to change their current situation and obtain stable housing. Seeing few options, many participants stated that they felt "stuck." As one youth who was living at a shelter at the time of the interview explained,

> Um like the fact that I'm just like stuck in my life, there's nothing really I could do right now . . . well just like stuck in a shelter. I can't really—I don't talk to my dad so I don't really want to live with him. I don't really want to live with my mom, plus where she lives it's too crowded anyway.

(33)   One male participant had received assistance from the Children's Aid Society (CAS) and noted that without their involvement, "then you're just stuck. You got no one to help you out pretty much." Thus, feeling stuck meant perceiving few options and little or no support. It was clear, however, that the youths were dissatisfied with their homeless status and aspired to something better. Often, the participants described a strong determination to reach their goals. Throughout their stories, positive images of the future were shared, including their hope that living without a home "does not last a long time." One youth talked about his desire to follow in his brother's footsteps and "try and get college done" and maybe "join the [army] Reserves." Recognizing that this would not be easy, he also asserted that he was determined to get himself "off the streets."

(34)   Although many comments reflected a desire to bring about change, it was acknowledged that achieving personal goals would be extremely difficult. Many spoke about the desire to get off the streets but described various barriers that kept them from doing so. The inability to obtain stable employment, education, or training was commonly mentioned. In one group interview, participants shared that being judged negatively by potential employers because of residing in a shelter could impede finding employment. Another participant, who suffered from chronic fatigue syndrome, explained how her health condition prevented her from finding employment:

> I'd like to have a job, you know. I'd like to be able to be more independent, but I can't um because society doesn't really understand um where—they don't understand chronic fatigue. And I mean a job can't be based around how the employee is feeling, you know, they've got to be you know—if they book you in there, you have to be there, right? And so it's hard. That's tough to deal with.

(35)   Feeling misunderstood, judged, and unsupported while attempting to overcome barriers contributed to a belief among many of the youths that they could rely only on themselves and that reversing their homeless status would be extremely difficult.

(36)   In summary, many of the participants explained that they felt stuck, and meaningful strategies to end their homelessness seemed elusive. They believed that their efforts were thwarted by barriers over which they had little or no control. They described feeling unsupported and judged and ultimately began to rely only on themselves to bring about change.

"I Can't Really Feel Safe": Negotiating Dangerous Terrain

(37)   Several of the participants discussed the desire to have a place for themselves that was safe and comfortable, a place they could call "home." The living circumstances for the homeless youth in this research varied but included couch surfing, staying in shelters, and sleeping in parks, stairwells, or abandoned cars. Residing in public spaces often left the youth exposed to violence, which further threatened their sense of safety. Living in a shelter at the time of the interview, one participant commented,

> I don't know because I can't really feel safe because I'm out here in this world . . . you can't really feel safe because you don't know what's going to happen next. You don't know if this drunk is going to come up and punch you in the face for no reason just because he's drunk or if this guy's going to start something with you, and you can't really feel safe there.

(38)   Several youths explained that they had been robbed, threatened, and ridiculed or forced to witness physical fights. After being beaten to the point of hospitalization by three older men in a back alley, a male participant commented that he "can't feel safe anymore."

(39)   Being exposed to constant threats of violence with no safe place to go, the youth's daily focus was on meeting their urgent safety and physical needs. Many of the youth chose to tell stories that portrayed them as survivors. The fact that they were living on the streets and still alive was something that they were proud of. The participants told about creative strategies they used in an attempt to feel safe. These included being part of a group, which served as a form of protection while sleeping outside. This peer group would also "help you out" in the event of a fight. Others talked about feeling safer when they were a "one-man army" or when they wore neutral colors so as not to be affiliated with a gang. Carrying a weapon such as a knife and using humor to distract a potential "enemy" were also described as ways to create a sense of safety. Although staying within the confines of the shelter afforded some protection, safety seemed to be an unattainable goal when lacking places of their own.

"They're in the Same Situation as You": Rethinking Family

(40)   A multitude of complex factors combined to contribute to the homelessness among the study participants. Most of the participants had grown up in poverty. Several described various forms of violence, including sexual, emotional, and physical abuse by one or more parent or step-parent that occurred during their childhoods. Others told of emotional abuse by a sibling. Some of the participants explained that problems experienced by their parents, including substance abuse, mental health problems, or unresolved grief, led to neglect of them as children. One youth had a cognitively impaired sibling who needed full-time care at home, requiring the full attention of her mother.

(41)   A few participants described their efforts to seek help for the abuse, confiding in an adult or youth pastor. According to them, their concerns were either perceived to be untrue or trivialized. These responses resulted in feelings of abandonment and betrayal. A young female participant who had fled from her home because of emotional abuse by her parents and sister commented, "I just um—I find that—I mean I have parents but in many ways I feel like an orphan."

(42)   In addition to feeling betrayed and abandoned by their families, several participants also felt similarly disconnected from their peers. Many youths explained that they felt like an outcast, "being on the bottom of the list," or "the most made fun of person at school." One youth was forced to quit high school while he was homeless because the only shelters were downtown and he could not afford the necessary bus tokens. He commented,

> I don't really talk to anybody from my high school any more. Things went sour with a lot of them too though, eh, because they found out I was living on the streets. If you know anything about high school kids gossiping and like that are talking behind your back, it kind of starts, "Oh (participant's name) is homeless," blah, blah, blah, and they all have this, you know, impression of homelessness that um— that has stuck with them, I guess. It's not exactly the cool thing to be, the homeless guy in high school, you know what I mean? They like you more if you're the captain of the football team, I think.

Prior to becoming homeless, he had been well liked by his peers but subsequently felt like an outcast.

(43)   The sense of betrayal and abandonment at both the family and the peer levels led to deeper connections with individuals who shared similar experiences. While living on the streets, all of the participants developed meaningful relationships in which they felt supported, cared for, and protected. Some youth found these relationships to be more "real," as they could empathize with one another and talk about their situations without feeling that they were being judged negatively. After living on the streets, one participant was able to establish meaningful relationships with other homeless youth because, as he stated, "they're in the same situation as you."

(44)   Often, street culture provided the youth with the "family" that they felt they never had. Close friends were the people in their lives that could be trusted and on whom they could rely. It was stated that friends would not "blow me off like my family did." After being dropped off at a shelter because her father and stepmother couldn't "deal with her," one female participant commented,

> And when you're homeless too, like you kind of— like because nobody that's living in a shelter really has like close family. It's like everyone kind of like connects and you find your own group and like your own family within that.

(45)   Meaningful relationships were desired by all participants. Sharing similar experiences often allowed

the youths to feel connected and supported after being abandoned and betrayed by family and peers.

"More Things Can Happen to You": The Hazards of Being Female

(46)   Although all of the participants had discussed being exposed to various types of violence while homeless, vulnerability to gender-based violence was particularly pronounced among the female participants. Some told of physical and financial abuse, and one participant was forced to return to living in a shelter after she fled her verbally abusive boyfriend. Other females told about harassment while living on the streets, which is captured in the following comment: "I just feel like if you're a girl like a lot of the older, sort of weird guys at places like that may hit on you and make you feel strange about yourself." It was also shared that women are more likely to sell their bodies as a means to meet their various needs, one of which was a place to sleep.

(47)   Being female meant having more complex health concerns. Money was needed for feminine hygiene products and birth control. Fears of getting pregnant were expressed by several young women. One female participant commented,

> With a girl, with me being a girl there's maybe a biased thing just because I am a girl. But there are more things that can happen to you. Like if you're living on the streets you have to afford feminine hygiene products. You've got to afford like everything that there is to do with that. You've got to worry about if you get pregnant . . . and guys don't have to worry about getting pregnant, they don't have to worry about getting their period. They don't have to worry about getting raped in the middle of the night because usually guys—especially guys who live on the street are tough enough to take care of themselves. There are some girls who can; there are a lot of girls I know who can't.

(48)   There was a common perception that young women living on the streets are unable to take care of themselves:

> I think that sometimes like living in the street especially females need to be a little bit more tough . . . because guys think that we're not that tough so if we stand up for ourselves and show them we are, then like they're not going to mess with you or whatever.

As a result of this perception, some of the young women felt forced to prove otherwise. To one female

participant, it was important that she "not back down when called on to fight," even if the opponent was male and much larger than she. Developing a reputation of being tough, in some cases, helped a woman feel safer.

(49)   In summary, young female adolescents had a multitude of concerns while living on the streets. They experienced a variety of forms of violence, had complex health concerns, and were viewed as unable to care for them themselves. For one participant, being female and homeless equated to feeling "more used than you are appreciated."

"It Takes a Toll on You": The Elusive Nature of Health and the Health Care System

(50)   Many youth spoke about the energy and effort that being homeless demands. A young male participant, who fled from a violent home where he was ridiculed and physically abused for being gay, stated that he was "very fatigued all the time, like not tired but fatigued I think is the right word. I don't know, like not really tired to go to bed but you're just like exhausted by the littlest thing." Another youth spoke about how fatigue prevented him from "getting stuff accomplished." A few participants felt that no one wanted to talk to them. Many others were depressed, lonely, and ashamed to tell people of their current situation. Describing how he feels about himself, one participant stated,

> Really like insecure and like I didn't have like very health—like high self-esteem and like I'd always think that like people thought I was like a bad person and didn't want to like hang out with me because of who I was. And like I'd just sort of like get really depressed and like start thinking that everybody hates you, and really they don't. And like scared to talk to people because you think that they're not going to want to like interact with you, or whatever.

(51)   When hurt or feeling ill, several participants indicated that, if necessary, they would access traditional forms of health care, such as emergency rooms and clinics. However, many described obstacles that kept them from doing so. No longer covered by his father's health insurance, one participant was left feeling as though he would have to pay to use Canada's public system. Others noted their inability to afford expensive prescriptions or eye exams. Another youth commented that she "will do anything and everything to stay out of going to a hospital" after she experienced what she considered insensitive care while being hospitalized following the death of her newborn daughter.

(52)   Whereas some participants described barriers to care, others claimed there was inadequate support available for them to feel healthy. Feeling healthy involved having access to resources such as a place to have a shower and a safe place to live. Others described health as eating each day, living a low-stress life, and being able to support themselves. It was perceived that there was a tendency for some homeless people to "give up" because they were not initially supported. This idea was captured in the following statement:

> Yeah, but the way that happened is because no one would help them in the first place. People that need support and they don't have, if they would just have that support they could like make a whole world of a difference from turning someone from committing suicide and someone turning into a good citizen and having a job, just because they never had support. And they didn't know where to turn, or what to do and they got in with the wrong crowd. They needed money for a place to stay, so they started prostituting themselves or selling drugs and end up in jail or whatever, end up robbing houses, blah-blah-blah, and go down the wrong road all because they didn't know where to turn. They had no help.

According to the participants, lack of support contributed to a more complex situation than they had faced prior to becoming homeless.

(53)   A perception among other participants was that homelessness is hidden from society, a perception that made it difficult to access services. It was explained that before becoming homeless, a male participant viewed the shelter system as a service used by "just old people, like old guys." Similarly, a few other participants said that when initially homeless, they were unaware that there were even shelters available, let alone ones that are primarily for youth or women. This lack of knowledge about available services led them to sleep outside, sometimes in the middle of winter. During one pair interview, participants shared that health services were not publicly advertised because of the negative image it would have on the government.

(54)   Several of the participants spoke about the lack of specific health care services. When reflecting back on her time in a group home, a young female participant commented that the counselors to whom she had access were not trained "to deal with a lot of stuff." She also noted that she "would have liked to have more actual counseling, like on a weekly basis to deal with a lot of my stuff." Recognizing that she needed someone to whom she could talk, this young woman observed that there were not appropriate health care services available to her. Another participant had a similar experience. Trying to come to terms with her history of sibling abuse, she found that the violence that she endured was often dismissed as sibling rivalry. She said there were no resources to help her because the seriousness of sibling violence was not recognized. Dealing with her history was described as being "really hard."

Homelessness and the Public Policy Context

(55)   Public policy regarding housing shaped the lives of homeless youth in subtle and direct ways. Not having the education or the proper training kept many youth from finding employment. Chronic health problems and feelings of being judged negatively also prevented the youth from being able to obtain work. As a result, poverty was a central context in the lives of virtually all of the participants. Some youth noted that small amounts of money were fairly easy to come by, but having enough money for rent and other necessities was much more difficult. According to one, it was "just that large amounts of money where you could, you know, go get your own place and stuff like that, that's you know, that's kind of a bit harder to get." Having this "jump start" was seen as a way to get out of their situation.

(56)   Several youth spoke about the difficulties of continuing their education while homeless. Not knowing where they were going to sleep at night, feeling insecure, and having no income with which to buy food made regular school attendance extremely difficult. Recently discharged from jail to a shelter, a male participant commented on his frustration of not being able to receive Ontario Works:

> No, not really because like there's not much you can really do when you're 17 at all. Like if you're 18 you can get on Welfare, like no big deal but when you're 17 you have to have like—the only way you can get on Welfare is like Student Welfare and it's like too late. . . . It's too late in like the semester to even start school right now.

Not being able to continue their schooling meant that many of the participants were not eligible for Ontario Works.

Discussion

(57)   All of the participants created stories that included ideas and issues that were current in their lives. They discussed the desire for a situation that was "better" than the one they currently had. Although their narratives revealed a sense of determination, the youth encountered many barriers, such as social policies that were not sensitive to their situations, chronic health issues, and perceived judgment of others. These obstacles prevented them from reaching their goals. This analysis shifts the sole blame of a person's homelessness from the individual and captures how public policy contributes to their lack of options. This research challenges the socially accepted idea that homeless youth are "lazy" and cannot be "bothered" to find a job. Exposure to various forms of violence and being forced to focus on their daily survival had detrimental effects on the adolescents' perceptions of their health and well-being. As they observed, having a safe and secure place of their own would allow them to redirect their energies to the fulfillment of other goals, such as completion of their education or finding employment. This brings attention to the fundamental role that affordable housing plays in the well-being of youth. In addition, in this study gender was clearly an important context to homelessness, with homeless adolescent females particularly vulnerable to distinct forms of violence. Although many described a range of physical and emotional health problems, the participants generally perceived little available material or emotional support. The accessibility gap that exists between homeless youth and needed health-related services emerged as an important feature in their lives.

Implications

(58)   Based on the findings from this research, several important implications might be suggested. Of particular importance, this study highlighted the agency of adolescents experiencing homelessness. Health care professionals working with homeless youth have ample opportunity to facilitate group discussions that address their circumstances. Through discussion, health care professionals and the youths can collaboratively identify solutions to their situations. All care providers can invite homeless youth to join them in their lobbying of local governments as a way to initiate change. In addition, health professionals can encourage adolescents to participate in community-based programs that help raise awareness regarding the issue of homelessness. Public health professionals can facilitate peer-led support groups for those who have experienced violence as well as advocate for affordable long-term counseling

services. They can also work with homeless youth to increase the visibility of homelessness in the school system. This awareness will ultimately help link youth in the process of becoming homeless to the needed health-related services.

(59)   This study makes it clear that adolescent females have complex health needs while homeless. To promote the health of young homeless women, all health care providers should consider the fact that being female places homeless adolescents in a position where they are likely to experience various forms of violence such as sexual assault and harassment. For supportive and effective care to be provided, it is crucial to be able to recognize that these events have detrimental effects on the health and well-being of homeless adolescents. Creating "safe spaces" where homeless youth can talk with one another about the challenges they face, and about violence in particular, is a possible avenue for a health promotion intervention.

(60)   With respect to education, inclusion of nursing, medical, and social work curriculum related to the needs and challenges of homeless youth is essential. Offering clinical practice opportunities that would afford exposure to this population, and to street culture more broadly, increases the likelihood that health services can be provided in a compassionate and nonjudgmental manner.

(61)   More research is needed that will examine the perceptions of homeless youth. To understand how youth perceive their health, more effective care programs can be developed and implemented. This study noted an accessibility gap between health care services and those who need them. Research that explores the nature of where adolescents are receiving health-related information would be helpful to better develop care programs. Because the health of lesbian, gay, bisexual, and transgendered individuals is generally considered to be poorer than that of other homeless youth (Cochran et al., 2002; Noell & Ochs, 2001), research that considers their perspectives on health is needed to provide effective health care programs. In addition, more research that attempts to create a deeper understanding of how ability and race influence the health and well-being of homeless youth is needed.

(62)   Social policies that influence an adolescent's homeless situation extend beyond the urgent need to expand our current affordable housing initiatives. Living on the streets often forces adolescents to focus on daily survival, making it difficult to stay enrolled in school or to maintain a job. It is essential that all social policies consider homeless youths' situations

so that those who choose to exit street life have the ability and the resources to do so. Changes to the eligibility criteria for Ontario Works so that homeless youth would be able to receive support under this initiative is an important policy direction.

Limitations

(63)   There are several limitations with regard to this study. First, despite the researchers' efforts, only one community service was used to recruit the participants. Because critical research examines a variety of contextual factors, such as race, gender, and socioeconomic status, lack of a diverse sample inhibits an understanding of homelessness among these groups. Second, in this study gender was examined as a binary concept. To do so limits the involvement of youth who do not self-identify as either one of the two dominantly accepted gender identities, female and male. This further limited the ability to understand how various factors such as gender orientation shape the perceptions and experiences of homeless adolescents. The third limitation of this study was the inability to share emerging findings with many of the participants. Because of the transient nature of homeless adolescents' lifestyle, it was difficult to locate many of the youth following the initial interview. Finally, the findings of this research suggest that adolescent boys do not experience sexualized violence. As there is stigma surrounding this issue, some of the male participants might have chosen not to disclose such information.

Conclusion

(64)   The findings of this study highlight the experiences of homeless youth and offer insights into the complex nature of homelessness. Pulling the issue beyond the individual allows for the consideration of how contextual factors influence the experiences of homeless adolescents. This study draws attention to the fundamental roles that affordable housing policies and gender play in shaping the health of homeless adolescents. The findings from this research can be used to help create more effective social housing policies and care programs for adolescents who are homeless. To recognize an accessibility gap between the current health care services and those who need them, health care professionals can also use the knowledge from this investigation to provide more culturally meaningful and sensitive care to homeless adolescents.

References

Anderson, J. E., Cheney, R., Clatts, M., Farugue, S. Kipke, M., Long, A., et al. (1996). HIV risk behavior, street outreach and condom use in eight high-risk populations. *AIDS Education and Prevention, 8*, 191-204.

Barkin, S. L., Balkrishnan, R., Manuel, J., Anderson, R. M., & Gelberg, L. (2003). Health care utilization among homeless adolescents and young adults. *Journal of Adolescent Health, 32*(4), 253-256.

Boivin, J., Roy, E., Haley, N., & du Fort, G. G. (2005). The health of street youth. *Canadian Journal of Public Health, 96*(6), 432-437.

Boydell, K. M, Goering, P., & Morrell-Bellai, T. L. (2000). Narratives of identity: Re-presentation of self in people who are homeless. *Qualitative Health Research, 10*, 26-38.

Browne, A. J. (2000). The potential contributions of critical social theory to nursing science. *Canadian Journal of Nursing Research, 32*, 35-55.

Campbell, J. C., & Bunting, S. (1991). Voices and paradigm: Perspectives on critical and feminist theory in nursing. *Advances in Nursing Science, 13*(3), 1-15.

Canada Mortgage and Housing Corporation. (2007a). *First Nations housing market fund.* Retrieved July 18, 2007, from http://www.cmhc-schl.gc.ca/en/ab/

Canada Mortgage and Housing Corporation. (2007b). *Shelter enhancement program.* Retrieved July 19, 2007, from http://www.cmhc-schl.gc.ca/en/co/prfinas/prfinas_011.cfm

Chen, X., Tyler, K. A., Whitbeck, L. B., & Hoyt, D. R. (2004). Early sexual abuse, street adversity, and drug use among female homeless and runaway adolescents in the Midwest. *Journal of Drug Issues, 34*(1), 1-21.

City of Calgary. (2006). *Count of homeless persons in Calgary.* Retrieved January 15, 2007, from http://www.calgary.ca/docgallery/bu/cns/homelessness/2006_calgary_homeless_count.pdf#search=%22count%20of%20homeless%20person%20in%20downtown%20calgary%22

City of Toronto. (1999). *Taking responsibility for homelessness, an action plan for Toronto: Report of the Mayor's Homelessness Task Force.* Toronto, Canada: Author.

Clatts, M. C., Davis, W. R., Sotern, J. L., & Attillasoy, A. (1998). Correlates and distribution of HIV risk behaviors among homeless youths in New York City: Implications for prevention and policy. *Child Welfare, 77*, 195-207.

Clements, K., Gleghorn, A, Garcia, D., Katz, M., & Marx, R. (1997). A risk profile of street youth in Northern California: Implications for gender-specific human immunodeficiency virus prevention. *Journal of Adolescent Health, 20*(5), 343-353.

Cochran, B. N., Stewart, A. J., Ginzler, J. A., & Cauce, A. M. (2002). Challenges faced by homeless sexual minorities: Comparison of gay, lesbian, bisexual, and transgender homeless adolescents with their heterosexual counterparts. *American Journal of Public Health, 92*(5), 773-777.

Dematteo, B. A. Major, C., Block, B., Coates, R., Fearon, M., Goldberg, E., et al. (1999). Toronto street youth and HIV/AIDS: Prevalence, demographics, and risk. *Society for Adolescent Medicine, 25*, 358-366.

Ensign, J. (1998). Health issues of homeless youth. *Journal of Social Distress, 7*(3), 159-174.

Haldenby et al. / Adolescent Homelessness and Health 1243

Ensign, J. (2001). "Shut up and listen": Feminist health care without of the mainstream adolescent females. *Issues in Comprehensive Pediatric Nursing, 24*, 71-84.

Ensign, J., & Bell, M. (2004). Illness experiences of homeless youth. *Qualitative Health Research, 14*, 1239-1254.

Ensign, J., & Panke, A. (2002). Barriers and bridges to care: Voices of homeless female adolescent youth in Seattle, Washington, USA. *Issues and Innovations in Nursing Practice, 25*, 166-172.

Federation of Canadian Municipalities. (2006). *Communique: Breaking the log-jam in affordable housing.* Retrieved March 22, 2006, from http://www.fcm.ca/english/media/press/dec12004.html

Fontaine, K., & Fletcher, J. (1999). *Mental health nursing.* Menlo Park, CA: Addison Wesley Longman.

Gerber, G. M. (1997). Barriers to health care for street youth. *Journal of Adolescent Health, 21*, 287-290.

Government of Canada. (2004). *NHI programs: Communities taking the lead.* Retrieved March 22, 2006, from http://www.homelessness.gc.ca/initiative/p1nhiprograms_e.asp

Government of Ontario. (2006). *The Ministry of Community and Social Services.* Retrieved October 29, 2006, from http://www.mcss.gov.on.ca/mcss/english/pillars/social/programs/ow.htm

Hall, J. M. (2000). Core issues for female child abuse survivors in the recovery from substance misuse. *Qualitative Health Research, 10*, 612-631.

Harrison, P. A., Fulkerson, A., & Beebe, T. J. (1997). Multiple substance use among adolescent physical and sexual abuse victims. *Child Abuse and Neglect, 21*, 529-539.

Health Canada. (2005). *The street lifestyle study.* Retrieved November 15, 2005, from http://www.hc-sc.gc.ca/ahc-asc/pubs/drugs-drogues/street_life_vie_la_rue/index_e.html

Hwang, S. W. (2000). Mortality among men using homeless shelters in Toronto, Ontario. *Journal of the American Medical Association, 283*, 2152-2157.

Hwang, S.W. (2001). Homelessness and health. *Canadian Medical Association Journal, 164*(2), 229-233.

Johnson, T. P., Aschkenasy, J. R., Herbers, M. R., & Gillenwater, S. A. (1996). Self-reported risk factors for AIDS among homeless youth. *AIDS Education and Prevention, 8*, 308-322.

Kidd, S. A. (2004). "The walls were closing in, and we were trapped": A qualitative analysis of street youth suicide. *Youth & Society, 36*(1), 30-55.

Kipke, M., Simon, T. R., Montgomery, S. B, Unger, J. B., & Iversen, E. F. (1997). Homeless youth and their exposure to and involvement in violence while living on the streets. *Society for Adolescent Medicine, 20*(5), 360-367.

Layton, J. (2000). *Homelessness: The making and unmaking of a crisis.* Toronto, Canada: Penguin.

Leslie, M. B., Stein, J. A., & Rotheram-Borus, M. J. (2002). Sex-specific predictors of suicidality among runaway youth. *Journal of Clinical Child and Adolescent Psychology, 31*(1), 27-40.

Lieblich, A., Tuval-Mashiach, R., & Zilber, T. (1998). *Narrative research: Reading, analysis and interpretation.* Thousand Oak, CA: Sage.

Mallett, S., Rosenthal, D., & Keys, D. (2005). Young people, drug use and family conflict: Pathways into homelessness. *Journal of Adolescence, 28*, 185-199.

Martijn, C., & Sharpe, L. (2005). Pathways to youth homelessness. *Social Science & Medicine, 62*, 1-12.

Masson, N., & Lester, H. (2003). The attitudes of medical students towards homeless people: Does medical school make a difference? *Medical Education, 37*(10), 869-872.

Molnar, B. E., Shade, S. B., Kral, A. H., Booth, R. E., & Watters, J. K. (1998). Suicidal behaviour and sexual/physical abuse among street youth. *Child Abuse & Neglect, 22*(3), 213-222.

Morrell-Bellai, T., Goering, P. N., & Boydell, K. M., (2000). Becoming and remaining homeless: A qualitative investigation. *Issues in Mental Health Nursing, 21*, 581-604.

Nehls, N., & Sallmann, J. (2005). Women living with a history of physical and/or sexual abuse, substance abuse, and mental health problems. *Qualitative Health Research, 15*, 365-381.

Neysmith, S. M. (1995). Feminist methodologies: A consideration of principles and practice for research in gerontology. *Canadian Journal on Aging, 14*(1), 100-118.

Noell, J. W., & Ochs, L. M. (2001). Relationship of sexual orientation to substance use, suicidal ideation, suicide attempts, and other factors in a population of homeless adolescents. *Journal of Adolescent Health, 29*, 31-36.

O'Connell, J. J. (2004). Dying in the shadows: The challenge of providing health care for homeless people. *Canadian Medical Association Journal, 179*(8), 1251-1252.

O'Connor, M. L. (1998). Unsafe behaviours place street youth, especially women, at risk of HIV. *Family Planning Perspectives, 30*(1), 50-51.

Panter-Brick, C. (2002). Street children, human rights and public health: A critique and future directions. *Annual Review of Anthropology, 31*, 147-171.

Panter-Brick, C. (2004). Homelessness, poverty, and risks to health: Beyond at risk categorization of street children. *Children's Geographies, 2*(1), 83-94.

Paradise, M., & Cauce, A. M. (2002). Home street home: The interpersonal dimensions of adolescent homelessness. *Analyses of Social Issues and Public Policy, 2*(1), 223-238.

Patton, M. Q. (2002). *Qualitative research and evaluation methods* (3rd ed.). London: Sage.

Raffaelli, M., Koller, S. H., Reppold, C. T., Kuschick, M. B., Drum, F. M., Bandeira, D. R., et al. (2000). Gender differences in Brazilian street youth's family circumstance and experiences on the streets. *Child Abuse & Neglect, 24*(11), 1431-1441.

Reid, S., Berman, H., & Forchuk, C. (2005). Living on the streets in Canada: A feminist narrative study of girls and young women. *Issues in Comprehensive Paediatric Nursing, 28*, 237-256.

Rew, L., Chambers, K. B., & Kulkarni, S. (2002). Planning a sexual health promotion intervention with homeless adolescents. *Nursing Research, 51*(3), 168-174.

Rew, L., Taylor-Seehafer, M., & Fitzgerald, M. L. (2001). Sexual abuse, alcohol and other drug use, and suicidal behaviors in homeless adolescents. *Issues in Comprehensive Pediatric Nursing, 24*, 225-240.

Rhode, P., Noell, J., Ochs, L., & Seeley, J. R. (2001). Depression, suicidal ideation and STD-related risk in homeless older adolescents. *Journal of Adolescence, 24*(4), 447-460.

Riessman, C. K. (1993). *Narrative analysis.* London: Sage.

Rotheram-Borus, Song, J., Gwadz, M., Lee, M., Rossem, R., & Koopman, C. (2003). Reductions in HIV risk among runaway youth. *Prevention Science, 4*(3), 173-187.

Roy, E., Haley, N., Leclerc, P, Sochanski, B., Boudreau, J., & Boivin, J. (2004). Mortality in a cohort of street youth in

1244   Qualitative Health Research

Montreal. *Journal of the American Medical Association, 292,* 569-574.

Russell, L. A. (1996). *Homeless youth: Child maltreatment and psychological distress.* Unpublished doctoral dissertation, University of California, Los Angeles.

Shields, S. A., Wong, T., Mann, J., Jolly, A. M., Haase, D., Mahaffey, S., et al. (2004). Prevalence and correlates of chlamydia infection in Canadian street youth. *Society of Adolescent Medicine, 34,* 384-390.

Shiner, M. (1995). Adding insult to injury: Homelessness and health services use. *Sociology of Health and Illness, 17*(4), 525-549.

Trocme, N., & Wolfe, D. (2001). *The Canadian incidence study of reported child abuse and neglect.* Retrieved October 29, 2006, from http://www.phac-aspc.gc.ca/publicat/cissr-ecirc/pdf/cmic_e.pdf

Tyler, K. A., Hoyt, D. R., Whitbeck, L. B., & Les, B. (2001). The effects of a high-risk environment on the sexual victimization of homeless runaway youth. *Violence and Victims, 16*(4), 441-455.

Walters, A. S. (1999). HIV prevention in street youth. *Journal of Adolescent Health, 25,* 187-198.

Weber, A. E., Boivin, J., Blais, L., Haley, N., & Roy, E. (2004). Predictors of initiation into prostitution among female street youths. *Journal of Urban Health, 81*(4), 584-595.

Whitbeck, L. B., Hoyt, D. R., & Ackley, K. A. (1997). Abusive family backgrounds and later victimization among runaway and homeless adolescents. *Journal of Research on Adolescence, 7*(4), 375-392.

Zimmerman, D. H., & West, C. (1987). Doing gender. *Sociologists for Women in Society, 1*(2), 125-151.

Zrinyi, M., & Balogh, Z. (2004). Student nurse attitudes towards homeless clients: A challenge for education and practice. *Nursing Ethics, 11*(4), 334-348.

Amy M. Haldenby, RN, MScN, currently works at the Odette Cancer Centre, which is part of Sunnybrook Health Sciences Centre.

Helene Berman, RN, PhD, holds the Scotiabank Chair at the Centre for Research and Education on Violence Against Women and Children and is an associate professor at The University of Western Ontario, School of Nursing, London, Ontario, Canada.

Cheryl Forchuk, RN, PhD, is a professor at The University of Western Ontario, School of Nursing, London, Ontario, Canada.

Source: This article is reprinted from *Qualitative Health Research*, Vol. 17, Issue 9, pp. 1232–1244, 2007. Reprinted with permission of Sage Publications, Inc.

5 PURPOSE STATEMENTS, RESEARCH QUESTIONS, AND HYPOTHESES: IDENTIFYING THE INTENT OF A STUDY

When you read about the research problem and literature review in the Introduction of a research report, you learn about the importance of and background for a study. This information is necessary, but it does not tell you what the researchers intended to do in their study. Researchers indicate their study's intent by stating the specific goals of their study in one or more sentences. Although these sentences are only a small part of a report, they represent the most fundamental statements for understanding any research study. In this chapter, you will learn how to identify, understand, and evaluate the purpose statements, research questions, and hypotheses that researchers use to convey the intent of their quantitative and qualitative research studies.

BY THE END OF THIS CHAPTER, YOU SHOULD BE ABLE TO:

- Identify and understand the purpose of a study.
- Describe how the purpose differs in quantitative and qualitative research.
- Identify the different types of variables investigated in a quantitative research study.
- Understand the elements included in quantitative purpose statements, research questions, and hypotheses.
- Identify the central phenomenon investigated in a qualitative research study.
- Understand the elements included in qualitative purpose statements and research questions.
- Evaluate the quality of the purpose in a research report.

In statements of problems and in literature reviews, research reports can sometimes suggest several different types of studies that could be carried out to address deficiencies in the literature on a particular topic. Some of this information can be valuable to other researchers. However, usually when we read a report, we do not want to know what *could* be done; we want to know what the particular study we are reading *actually intended to do*. Recall that conducting research consists of the researcher asking a question, collecting information, and analyzing the information to answer the question. Researchers indicate the question they are asking by specifying the purpose for their research in their study reports. You need to locate the statements that convey a study's purpose to learn what a researcher wants to accomplish. By learning how to interpret a study's purpose from these statements, you will be well on your way to understanding any reported research study.

How Do You Identify the Purpose in a Research Study?

Recall from Chapter 1 that one of the essential steps of the research process is for researchers to specify the study's purpose. To understand this step, let's first consider how the purpose is defined, its significance, and how you locate it within a research report. When researchers specify a purpose for their research, they set the direction and goals for their study. This means that the researchers make several key decisions about the study, including:

- *The study's focus*—the specific topic(s) of interest in the study
- *The overall intent*—what the researchers want to learn about the specific topic
- *The framework*—the theory or conceptual framework that guides the researchers' perspectives
- *The participants*—the people or organizations to be examined in the study
- *The setting*—where the study takes place

Specifying a purpose by deciding on these five aspects for a study may be the most important step in the research process. As shown in Figure 5.1, the research problem and literature review lead the researcher to specify the purpose for the research study. The purpose for the study then guides the researchers' decisions for all the steps that follow. Researchers choose their design and decide how to collect, analyze, interpret, and report their data in response to their study's purpose. Therefore, the purpose is a major aspect of all research studies because it connects all of the steps in the research process.

To identify a study's purpose, bear in mind that researchers typically include one or more sentences in their reports that convey the intent for conducting the study. These statements serve as signposts in a written report similar to a thesis statement or objectives in term papers. One way to recognize these statements is to look for descriptions of the essential decisions that the researcher has made about the study, as listed in the bullet points above. That is, when you locate one or a few sentences that identify the study's focus, intent, framework, participants, and setting, you have likely found the researcher's purpose. You will not always find all of these elements in a researcher's statement of purpose, but a few of these are almost always present.

FIGURE 5.1
The Central Role of Specifying the Purpose in the Process of Research

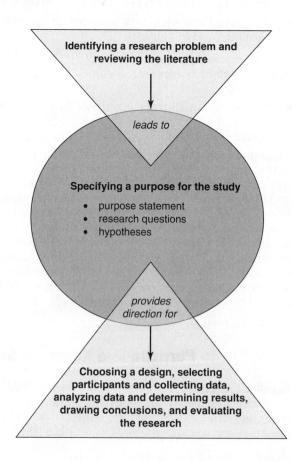

Identifying a research problem and reviewing the literature

leads to

Specifying a purpose for the study
- purpose statement
- research questions
- hypotheses

provides direction for

Choosing a design, selecting participants and collecting data, analyzing data and determining results, drawing conclusions, and evaluating the research

These statements are often placed at the end of the Introduction section, either immediately following the statement of the problem or at the end of the literature review. In some reports, you find the study's purpose stated in both locations. In addition to placing the purpose in different locations within a report, researchers also use different types of statements for describing their research purpose. These different types of statements are referred to as *purpose statements, research questions,* and *hypotheses.* By learning to recognize each of these types of statements, you can readily identify the purpose that a researcher specified in any study report.

Identify the Study's Purpose Statement First

Researchers first specify their research purpose by describing the overall intent of the study in one or more succinctly formed sentences, referred to as a purpose statement. The **purpose statement** is a statement that advances the overall direction for a study. As discussed, these sentences typically identify the focus and intent for the study, and may mention the participants, setting, and the researcher's framework. This sentence is important to identify because it tells you the overall purpose of the study. You can recognize purpose statements because researchers usually start these statements using a phrase such as "The purpose of this study is. . . ." Other common phrases that signal a study's purpose statement include "the goal of the study is . . ." or "this study aims to. . . ." The sentences then continue by providing information about the study's focus, intent, framework, participants, and setting. Two examples of purpose statements are:

- The purpose of this quantitative study is to examine the relationship between cultural awareness and client satisfaction for counselors working in an urban city.
- The purpose of this qualitative study is to explore counselors' stories of developing cultural awareness in one urban support clinic.

Look for Research Questions That Narrow the Study's Purpose

Some research reports only include a purpose statement to indicate the intent for the study. Many quantitative and qualitative research reports, however, also include statements that narrow the overall purpose to questions that the researcher wants to answer. **Research questions** are statements used to narrow the purpose statement to specific questions that the researcher seeks to answer by conducting a study. To locate research questions, look for passages in which authors identify the questions they are addressing. These frequently appear as questions, but in some studies they are phrased as statements or are referred to as objectives. Unlike the single statement found in a purpose statement, researchers typically state multiple research questions so that they can fully examine several dimensions about a topic. In many studies, the researchers provide both a purpose statement and research questions. This is a good presentation style that indicates general as well as specific directions for a study. Two examples of research questions that have been presented in the form of questions are:

- Is counselors' cultural awareness related to client satisfaction with their clinic experience?
- How do counselors experience cultural awareness?

Look for Hypotheses That Narrow the Study's Purpose to Predictions

In some quantitative studies, researchers narrow their purpose to specific hypotheses that they want to test. Used only in quantitative research, **hypotheses** are statements in which the investigator makes a prediction or conjecture about the relationship that exists among two or more attributes or characteristics (i.e., variables). Hypotheses serve to narrow the purpose statement to specific predictions. These predictions are not simply an educated guess. Researchers base their hypotheses on results from past research found during the literature review. If the literature includes studies that have found certain results in the past, then based on these results, investigators can offer predictions on what they expect to find when the study is repeated with new people or at new sites. Usually researchers advance several hypotheses in their quantitative studies in addition to providing a purpose statement. An example of a hypothesis is:

- Counselors who complete a program on cultural awareness will have higher client satisfaction than those who do not complete the program.

How Does the Purpose Differ in Quantitative and Qualitative Studies?

All research reports—quantitative and qualitative—include statements that convey the researcher's intent. Although researchers specify their purpose in all types of research, how they plan and write these statements differs whether the study uses a quantitative or a qualitative approach. Before we learn the details of how quantitative and qualitative researchers compose their purpose statements, research questions, and hypotheses, it is helpful for us to first consider how a research purpose in quantitative research is similar to and different from one in qualitative research. Let's review the ideas that we introduced in Chapter 2 about specifying purposes for quantitative and qualitative research.

Quantitative Researchers Specify Purposes That Are Specific and Narrow

In quantitative research, the investigator specifies a purpose that is specific and narrow in response to a problem that calls for explanation and to the information reviewed in the literature. The purpose is considered specific because the focus of the study is a small set of specific factors, called variables. We will discuss variables a little later in this chapter, but for now recall that they are the particular concepts that researchers want to measure and learn about in quantitative studies. The purpose of a quantitative study is considered narrow because the researcher intends to examine the variables in a certain way. In some quantitative studies, researchers are interested in investigating a causal relationship among variables, such as whether teaching parents about nutrition (one variable) causes better health (another variable) in 5-year-old children. In other quantitative studies, researchers are interested in describing trends for single variables, such as students' attitudes about cheating (a variable), or describing noncausal relationships between variables, such as how computer use (one variable) differs by gender (another variable), how graduation rates (one variable) change over time (another variable), or how school climate (one variable) predicts teacher turnover (another variable).

When you read the purpose statement, research questions, and hypotheses stated in quantitative study reports, you find that they reflect the specific and narrow nature of the purpose in quantitative research. These statements indicate that the researcher is interested in studying only a few variables, which the researcher has determined at the start of the study. Recall from Chapter 4 that quantitative researchers often use theories to predict how variables are related and, when they do, they state hypotheses that convey these predictions. Researchers conducting quantitative studies identify the purpose statement, research questions, and hypotheses about the variables of interest before they collect any data in the study. In addition to being set at the start of a study, quantitative research questions and hypotheses remain fixed and do not change as the data are collected and analyzed during the study.

In the quantitative physical-activity-in-middle-schools study from Chapter 1, Xu et al. (2010) state the purpose for their study in paragraph 03, at the end of the Introduction section. In reading this paragraph, we learn that the *focus* of their study is a set of variables that included the status of physical activity opportunities and social and environmental factors (e.g., school policies and students' family support). Their *intent* is to (1) describe trends in the status of physical activity opportunities and (2) examine the factors that relate to the presence of these opportunities. Therefore, we learn that Xu and her fellow researchers are interested in describing the relationships between the opportunity for students to participate in school-based physical activities (one variable) and social and environmental factors (two other variables). The paragraph also states that the *setting* for the study is middle schools and the *participants* are physical education teachers. As we continue to read paragraph 03, we learn that their *framework* is a theory called the Social Ecological Model. The researchers use this theory to decide which variables to study that may be related to the physical activity opportunities. The authors conclude the paragraph by narrowing their purpose into two specific research questions, which they present as study aims:

> Specific aims of this study were to investigate the status of PA [physical activity] opportunities afforded to public middle school students, and to examine interactions between existing factors and PA opportunities in the middle school setting. (p. 185)

Qualitative Researchers Specify Purposes That Are Broad and General

In qualitative research, the investigator specifies a purpose that is broad and general in response to a problem that calls for exploration and to the information reviewed in the literature. The purpose is considered broad because the focus of the study is on one single complex concept—a central phenomenon—instead of a set of several specific variables. We will also discuss the central phenomenon later in this chapter, but examples of a central phenomenon might be a concept (e.g., trust), an activity (e.g., a citizenship program for new immigrants), or a process (e.g., learning to cope with the loss of a child). The purpose of a qualitative study is considered general because the researcher intends to explore the central phenomenon in an open, comprehensive way to develop a good understanding of it and its complexity. This exploratory intent might be to describe the meaning of a concept, interpret what happens in an activity, or generate a theory about a process.

When you read the purpose statement and research questions in qualitative research reports, you find that they are also typically written in a broad and general way. The purpose statement and research questions focus on one central phenomenon and the intent is very general and nonspecific. Recall that qualitative researchers do not test predictions and therefore hypotheses are generally not used in qualitative research. Instead of testing theories, the qualitative researcher seeks a deep understanding of the views of individuals or a group. To develop a deep understanding in qualitative research, the focus of the study is not predetermined and fixed at the start of the study. The inquirer allows the central phenomenon to emerge during the study and often changes the phenomenon being studied as the data are collected and analyzed. The research questions, therefore, may change based on what is learned from the participants. This means that in some qualitative studies, the research questions reported at the completion of the study may not have been the same ones that the inquirer posed at the start of the study.

In the qualitative physical-activity-at-daycare study from Chapter 1, Tucker et al. (2011) identify their study's purpose at the end of the Introduction section (see paragraph 04):

> The primary purpose of this study was two-fold: 1) to gain insight into the current physical activity levels of preschoolers, with regard to the feasibility of meeting the NASPE physical activity guidelines; and 2) to identify daycare providers' suggestions for improving these pre-schooler's physical activity levels. (p. 209)

In this sentence, the authors identify two topics of interest as the *focus* of their study: insights about current physical activity levels of preschoolers and suggestions for improving these levels. Although two topics are identified, the researchers do not intend to relate them as in a quantitative study that aims to relate two variables. Instead, they *intend* to explore these two ideas in an open way to learn about them from the perspectives of daycare providers without using predetermined variables for these ideas. The authors could have identified one broad central phenomenon—perspectives about physical activity in daycare—and then identified these two subtopics of interest in separate research questions. From this purpose statement we also learn that the *participants* are daycare providers. Although the authors did not explicitly identify the *setting* in this statement, we might guess that the setting for the study includes daycare facilities, and later in the report we learn that is indeed the case.

With these general differences in mind, you are ready to learn the detailed elements that researchers use when specifying the purposes of quantitative and qualitative studies. Because of their important differences, we will examine each approach separately, starting with quantitative research. For each approach, we first consider the focus for the research studies (variables in quantitative research and a central phenomenon in qualitative research). We then examine the different ways that researchers present their purpose statements, research questions, and hypotheses.

How Do You Identify Variables in Quantitative Research?

As just discussed, quantitative research focuses on sets of variables and specifies various intentions for examining those variables. Thus, the key to understanding quantitative purpose statements, research questions, and hypotheses is to learn about variables. We start with a definition of variables, a consideration of the different types of variables, and a discussion of how the variables can be related to each other in a quantitative study.

Variables Are the Measurement of Constructs

Quantitative researchers study important constructs such as academic achievement and mental health. These constructs are complex ideas, and to study them, quantitative researchers specify variables that they can measure as indicators of the constructs of interest. A **variable** is an indicator of a characteristic or attribute of individuals or organizations that researchers measure and that varies among the individuals or organizations studied. Variables are the key ideas for which researchers collect and analyze data to address their quantitative research purpose. Because of their importance, let's consider these three aspects of the definition of variables further.

- *Variables are indicators of characteristics and attributes.* Variables serve as indicators of characteristics and attributes of individuals and organizations that interest researchers. Characteristics refer to personal aspects such as grade level, age, or income level for individuals, or number of employees and total budget for organizations. An attribute represents how individuals and organizations feel, behave, or think. For example, individuals have levels of self-esteem, display the leadership behavior of being well organized, or have opinions about same-sex marriage; similarly, organizations have positions on issues, provide services, or have opinions about the type of training to offer to employees.
- *Variables can be measured.* Researchers define their variables in a specific way so they can be measured. Measurement occurs when the researcher records information from individuals and organizations to assess attributes or characteristics. Examples of measurement include having individuals answer questions on a questionnaire (e.g., a student completes questions on a survey asking about self-esteem) or observing an individual and recording scores on a checklist (e.g., a researcher watches a student playing basketball and records scores on dribbling techniques). We will learn

more about these procedures in Chapter 7. By measuring a variable, the researcher assigns a number or score for the attribute or characteristic of interest for each individual. For example:

- Gender is measured by two possible scores: female = 1 and male = 2.
- Grade point average is measured along a range of scores: scores vary from 0.00 to 4.00.

- ***The scores measured for a variable vary for the participants in the study.*** When researchers measure variables, they expect the scores to vary (hence the name *variable*)—that is, they can assign different scores to different participants in the study. For example, gender would be a variable in a study that includes both girls (gender = 1) and boys (gender = 2). However, if a study only included girls, then gender would not be a variable because the participants' gender would not vary in the study. When researchers measure their variables, they assign the scores in two ways: in categories and along a continuum. *Categorical variables* are a type of variable that occurs when researchers measure the variable by grouping the scores into a limited number of groups (or categories). Researchers may also refer to their categorical variables as *nominal variables* (variables measured in categories with names) or *ordinal variables* (variables measured in categories that are ranked in order). Here are examples of two variables that vary by categories:
  - *A nominal categorical variable*: political status. *Categories*: Democratic = 1, Republican = 2, Independent = 3.
  - *An ordinal categorical variable*: grade level. *Categories*: Freshman = 1, Sophomore = 2, Junior = 3, Senior = 4.

Continuous variables are a type of variable that occurs when researchers measure scores along a continuum of possible scores, from low to high scores and anywhere in between. Two examples of continuous variables are:

- *A continuous variable*: test performance. *Varies*: from low of 0% to high of 100%.
- *A continuous variable*: level of satisfaction. *Varies*: from low of 10 to high of 50.

Variables Are Connected to Other Variables Through Theories

In some quantitative studies, researchers intend to measure and describe trends for single variables such as the likelihood of voting in an upcoming election. More often, however, quantitative researchers intend to measure several variables so they can study how the variables are related to each other. For example, a researcher may conduct a study to determine whether there are differences for men and women in the likelihood to vote. In that case, the researcher is interested in the relationship between two variables: *gender* and *likelihood to vote*. How do researchers identify variables they expect to be related? Recall from Chapter 4 that quantitative researchers identify sets of variables that they expect to be related from theories in the literature. As mentioned earlier, theories explain and predict the probable relationships among different variables. That is, researchers use theories to not only suggest what variables are important to measure, but also to predict how the variables are expected to relate to each other. For example, a theory of math learning might suggest that the variables of *type of math instruction, student self-efficacy,* and student *gender* influence the *final math test scores* that students achieve and their *attitudes about math.*

Theories suggest specific connections among different variables, including how one variable (e.g., type of instruction) may influence another (e.g., final math test scores). Therefore, in many quantitative studies, researchers use a theory from the literature to suggest a "family" of variables to study in which the different variables are related to each other in particular ways like members of a family. Figure 5.2 illustrates the family of variables in a theory that predicts the likely impact of some variables (called independent or predictor variables) on other variables (called dependent or outcome variables). To fully understand variables, you need to understand the different types of variables that occur in a quantitative study and how they relate to each other.

FIGURE 5.2
The Family of
Variables in
Quantitative
Studies

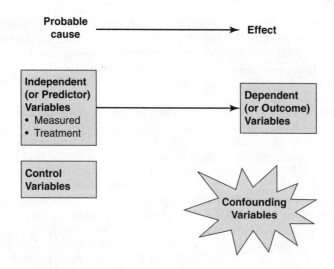

Researchers Study Dependent, Independent, Control, and Confounding Variables

When researchers are interested in how two or more variables are related, they use different types of variables in their quantitative studies' purpose statements, research questions, and hypotheses. A useful way to understand these types of variables is to consider them in a cause-and-effect relationship where the variables on the left side of Figure 5.2 tend to influence (or cause or predict) those on the right side (the outcomes). Keep in mind that the theories we are discussing here deal with humans whose behavior cannot be perfectly predicted because we can never account for all possible variables. Therefore, in quantitative research we say that there is a *probable* cause-and-effect relationship between the independent variables and the dependent variables. *Probable causation* means that researchers cannot prove cause-and-effect relationships, but they can use research procedures to establish that it is likely (or probable) that an independent variable causes an effect in a dependent variable. In Chapters 6–8, we will discuss the procedures that researchers use to be able to make claims of cause and effect.

For now, let's focus on how to identify the different roles that variables play when the intent is to determine how variables are related. To identify the different types of variables in a quantitative study, ask yourself the following:

1. What are the outcomes that the researcher is trying to explain or predict? (the dependent or outcome variables)
2. What are the factors that the researcher expects to influence the outcomes? (the independent or predictor variables)
3. What other variables does the researcher measure (or control) that might also influence the outcomes? (the control variables)
4. What variables might influence the outcomes that the researcher cannot or does not measure in the study? (the confounding variables)

Here's a Tip!

Quantitative research studies can include many variables. To keep track of their role in the study, make a table that reflects the family of variables and list each major variable in the appropriate column:

Independent → (and Control) Variables	Dependent Variables
_____	_____

To help you understand how these different types of variables relate to each other, let's consider how they can be applied to an everyday situation. Take, as an example, a fender-bender. Let's say that you hit another car at a stop sign, which is the outcome (dependent variable). This fender-bender was caused because you were talking on your cell phone (independent variable). It might have been caused by the slick pavement (control variable), but the skies were sunny and it had not rained for days. That you were daydreaming might have contributed to the accident (confounding variable), but this fact would be difficult to measure after the accident. Figure 5.3 illustrates how we might depict this situation using the family of variables. See how

**FIGURE 5.3
An Example of
the Family of
Variables**

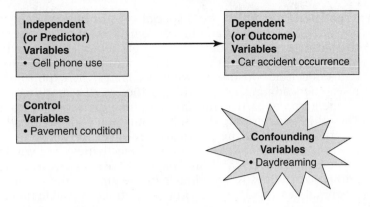

this works? Now take an actual situation in your life from this past week, and list the dependent, independent, control, and confounding variables in your own cause-and-effect situation.

Now let's examine each of these four types of variables in a little more depth. Notice that the independent variables are listed on the left side of Figures 5.2 and 5.3 because logically they must occur first in order to cause an effect in the dependent variables. Therefore, it would be logical for us to start by discussing independent variables. However, we start by discussing *dependent* variables because they are typically the variables of most interest in a quantitative study, which makes them the variables that are easiest to identify when reading a study report.

- *Dependent (or outcome) variables.* Look at Figure 5.2 again. On the right-hand side are the dependent variables. A **dependent variable** is an attribute or characteristic that is dependent on, or influenced by, the independent variables. This is generally the variable that the researcher wants to affect or predict—the variable of most interest in the study. Researchers also refer to their dependent variables as the *outcome variables, effect variables,* or *criterion variables.* Examples of dependent variables are achievement scores on a test, the health of a patient, the organizational climate of an organization, the retention of new social workers, or the satisfaction of clients in a clinic. Researchers often study more than one dependent variable in a quantitative study, such as job satisfaction and job retention. To identify dependent variables in a study, examine the purpose statement, research questions, and hypotheses for the outcomes that the researcher wants to cause, predict, or explain. Ask yourself, "What is the primary outcome that the researcher is trying to explain in this study?"
- *Independent (or predictor) variables.* On the left side of Figure 5.2 are the independent variables. An **independent variable** is an attribute or characteristic that is thought to influence, predict, or affect an outcome or dependent variable. In Figure 5.2, the arrow shows how the independent variables are expected to influence the dependent variables. Researchers also refer to their independent variables as *treatment variables, manipulated variables, predictor variables,* or *factors.* Researchers measure this type of variable distinctly (or independently) from the dependent variable. They select these variables as worthy of study because they expect them to influence the outcomes and they intend to learn what that influence is. For instance, consider this research question: Do students who spend time exercising in the morning behave better at school than students who do not exercise in the morning? From this question, we learn that *student behavior* is the outcome variable that interests the researcher and that *exercising* (that is, *exercising or not exercising*) is the variable that the researcher expects will influence the outcome. Therefore, exercising is the *independent* variable and student behavior is the *dependent* variable.

There are two main types of independent variables: treatment variables and measured variables. Each serves a slightly different purpose in quantitative research and it is important to be able to distinguish between them when you read quantitative study reports.

- **Treatment variables** are a special type of independent variable that are used when researchers administer some kind of treatment or intervention to the participants in a study. Researchers report using an independent treatment variable when they conduct experimental studies to test for a cause-and-effect relationship between variables. In experimental studies, the researchers administer specific activities (e.g., a morning exercise program) to one group of participants and withhold the activities from another group. They then measure the dependent outcome variable for all participants and determine whether the group who receives the activities scores differently than the group that did not receive the activities. (We will learn more about this approach to research in Chapter 6.) Because researchers administer or withhold activities to individuals in the groups, the groups are "treated" or "manipulated" by the researcher. A treatment variable therefore is measured in categories (i.e., received or denied activities) representing the different groups. Experimental researchers often refer to these groups as levels (i.e., level 1, level 2) in their reports. For example, a treatment variable could be the *type of instruction* used in a study of student math achievement. The researcher manipulates the conditions so that one group of students receives instruction with small-group discussions (level 1) and the other group receives traditional lecture-style instruction (level 2). In this example, the independent variable *type of instruction* is a treatment variable because the researcher manipulates the conditions experienced by the groups. As we will discuss in the next chapter, using a treatment variable and manipulating conditions is the best way for a researcher to determine whether a cause-and-effect relationship exists among variables.
- **Measured variables** are independent variables that the researcher measures as they currently exist without doing anything to manipulate the scores on these variables. That is, in contrast to treatment variables, measured variables represent existing characteristics or attributes of participants that a researcher chooses to measure. Measured variables can be scored in categories (e.g., gender or personality type) or on a range of continuous scores (e.g., motivation to change). Researchers measure these factors because they expect them to influence or predict or relate to the dependent variables. Because the researcher does not manipulate the levels of measured variables, the researcher cannot know that they are truly independent from the dependent variables. Therefore, researchers often refer to measured variables as *factors* or *predictors* instead of as independent variables. When researchers use measured variables as the independent variables in their studies, it also limits their ability to make claims of probable cause and effect. You will learn more about these concerns in Chapters 6–8.
- *Control variables.* A **control variable** is a type of independent variable that is not of central interest in the study, but that the researcher measures because it may also influence the dependent variable. A control variable is a variable that must be considered (or "controlled") because the researcher cannot change it or cannot remove it from the participants. Typically control variables are personal attributes or characteristics, such as gender, ethnicity, socioeconomic status, or prior knowledge. These variables are controlled through statistical procedures. (You will learn more about statistical procedures in Chapter 8.) Using special statistical procedures, the researcher is able to account for their effects during the data analysis, which helps the researcher better understand the relationship of interest between the independent and dependent variables. For example, a researcher interested in how the type of math instruction affects student exam scores may decide to measure and control for participating students' grades in the prior math class because prior math achievement will likely also be related to the exam scores. By controlling for prior math class grades, the researcher will be able to better determine the effect of the type of instruction on math exam scores.
- *Confounding variables.* The final type of variable included in Figure 5.2 is the confounding variable. In this illustration, confounding variables are not directly in the probable cause-and-effect sequence, but are extraneous or uncontrolled variables. **Confounding variables** are attributes or characteristics that may

influence the relationship between the independent and dependent variables, but that the researcher does not measure. These variables get in the way of research because researchers may not know that they should be measured. For example, a room used for a math test may be uncomfortably hot one day so that it adversely affects students test performance, but the researcher could not have known that room temperature would be important and should be recorded. Confounding variables may also be too difficult to measure because their effects cannot be easily separated from those of other variables. For example, it may be impossible to separate high school students' race and prior discriminatory experiences as predictors of attitudes toward school. Thus, researchers measure the variables they can identify (e.g., race) and then discuss the limitations of their results in the report (e.g., race was so interconnected with discriminatory experiences that it could not be easily separated as an independent measure). All quantitative studies have the potential for confounding variables because it is not possible for researchers to measure or control for all variables that influence an outcome. Good quantitative studies reduce the threats from confounding variables by carefully selecting the independent and control variables that are measured and by managing the conditions of the study.

What Do You Think?

When you read the following description of a quantitative research study, think about the types of variables being discussed.

> A researcher is interested in adolescents' attitudes about smoking tobacco. She designs a special health curriculum about smoking and has some students complete the special curriculum and other students complete the usual curriculum. At the end of the year she measures the students' attitudes about smoking tobacco by asking about their level of agreement with a series of questions. She also measures their gender and parental smoking status (current smoker, past smoker, or non-smoker) since she expects those may also be important variables to know. Unfortunately she did not know that the theater club had decided to produce a play about smoking this year, so the students who participated in theater were also learning about the issue of smoking.

Answer the following questions based on this passage:

a. What is the dependent variable in this study?
b. What is the independent variable in this study? What were the control variables?
c. What confounding variable was identified?
d. What is an example of a variable measured in categories? What is an example of a variable measured as continuous?
e. What is an example of a treatment variable? What is an example of a measured variable?

Check Your Understanding

This passage illustrates the different variables in the family of variables as follows:

a. The dependent variable is *attitudes about smoking tobacco*. That is the variable that the researcher is interested in affecting as an outcome of the study.
b. The independent variable is the *type of health instruction* that the students complete. The researcher expects the type of instruction will influence students' attitudes about smoking tobacco. The researcher also measures two control variables: *gender* and *parental smoking status*.

> **c.** The passage identifies one confounding variable: *participation in theater*. There could be many other possible confounding variables, such as whether a student knows someone who has lung cancer.
> **d.** Several variables mentioned in this passage are measured in categories, including *type of instruction* (special or usual), *gender* (male or female), and *parental smoking status* (current, past, or nonsmoker). The variable *attitudes about smoking tobacco* is likely measured as a continuous variable because the scores will fall along a range of scores.
> **e.** The *type of instruction* is a treatment variable because the researcher is manipulating what the students experience. All of the other variables that the researcher recorded are examples of measured variables.

How Do You Understand Purpose Statements, Research Questions, and Hypotheses in Quantitative Research?

You now know how to identify the different types of variables that are the focus of quantitative studies. With this information, you can understand the statements that researchers use in their quantitative reports to indicate their study purpose. Recall that researchers write statements that convey the essential elements of the study. Quantitative researchers include this information in the form of purpose statements, research questions, and hypotheses. Let's examine each of these common formats in detail.

Read Purpose Statements to Learn the Overall Quantitative Intent

When you read a quantitative study, look for the purpose statement to learn the researchers' overall intent. When written well, quantitative purpose statements usually

- begin with words such as "The purpose of this study . . ." or "The aim of this study. . . ."; and
- include the five elements for specifying a quantitative purpose: the major variables, overall intent, theory (if applicable), the participants, and research site or setting.

Because the purpose statement provides the overall intent, researchers will often refer to the major variables, participants, and research site in a general way. For example, they might refer to "demographic variables" in the purpose statement and then narrow this down to the specific variables of gender and family income in the research questions and hypotheses. Although the variables, participants, and sites of interest in research will vary greatly across the studies you read, there are four basic intents that researchers have when conducting quantitative research. These intents are summarized in Table 5.1 along with words that typically indicate a researcher's use of these intents. The table also includes models of good purpose statements for each of the intents to help you recognize them. In addition, you can use these models as templates when you want to write a study's purpose statement in your own words. Here we also provide an example of each that demonstrates how these forms may appear in reports:

- *An example of a quantitative purpose statement when the researcher's intent is to describe variables.* The purpose of this study is to describe attitudes about high-stakes testing for special education teachers at U.S. elementary schools.
  In this example, the intent is to describe a trend, the major variable is *attitudes about high-stakes testing*, the participants are *special education teachers*, and the

TABLE 5.1 Models of Purpose Statements for Different Intents of Quantitative Research

Quantitative Intent	Words Commonly Used to Indicate the Intent	Example Models of a Purpose Statement
Describe trends for variables	Describe Frequency Prevalence	▪ The purpose of this quantitative study is to describe [*the variable(s)*] for [*participants*] at [*the research site*].
Describe the relationship among two or more variables	Relate to Correlate with Influence on Predict Associate with	▪ The purpose of this quantitative study is to test [*the theory*] by relating [*the independent variable(s)*] to [*the dependent variable(s)*] for [*participants*] at [*the research site*]
Describe the difference among measured groups in terms of a variable	Compare Differ	▪ The purpose of this quantitative study is to compare [*group 1 of the independent variable*] with [*group 2 of the independent variable*] in terms of [*the dependent variable*] for [*participants*] at [*the research site*].
Test the effect of a treatment variable by comparing the differences among treatment groups for an outcome variable	Compare Impact Effect Differ	▪ The purpose of this quantitative study is to test [*the theory*] by comparing [*group 1 of the independent treatment variable*] with [*group 2 of the independent treatment variable*] in terms of [*the dependent variable*] for [*participants*] at [*the research site*].

research site is *U.S. elementary schools*. We do not find a theory or independent and dependent variables in this example because the researcher is *not* relating or comparing two or more variables, but instead intends to describe trends for one variable.

- ▪ *An example of a quantitative purpose statement when the researcher's intent is to relate variables.* The purpose of this study is to test the theory of caregiving support by relating caregiver confidence to overall well-being for elderly dementia patients living in rural areas of the Midwest.

  In this example, the overall intent is to relate two variables based on a theory (the *theory of caregiving support*). The independent predictor variable is *caregiver confidence*, and the dependent variable is *overall well-being*. In addition, we learn that the participants are *elderly dementia patients and their caregivers* and the research site is *rural areas of the Midwest*.

- ▪ *An example of a quantitative purpose statement when the researcher's intent is to compare existing groups.* The purpose of this study is to compare autocratic leaders with consensus-building leaders in terms of the satisfaction of doctors in New York City hospitals.

  In this example, the researcher identifies one independent measured variable (*leadership style*) with two levels (autocratic or consensus-building), one dependent variable (*satisfaction*), participants (*doctors*), and the research site (*New York City hospitals*). No theory is stated.

- ▪ *An example of a quantitative purpose statement when the researcher's intent is to test the effect of a treatment.* The purpose of this study is to test Smith's theory of parenting by comparing parents assigned to receive communication training, discipline training, or time management training in terms of reported adolescent behavior issues for families in Cherryville.

  In this example, the researcher identifies a theory (*Smith's theory of parenting*), one independent treatment variable (*training type*) with three levels (communication, discipline, and time management), one dependent variable (*adolescent behavior issues*), participants (*families*), and the research site (*Cherryville*).

What Do You Think?

Using the models of good quantitative purpose statements, identify the main features of the following purpose statement from a published research study:

> The purpose of the current study was to use SAT scores and Tracey and Sedlacek's psychosocial variables to predict Asian American students' GPA and retention in the first year of college. (Ting, 2000, p. 444)

Check Your Understanding

Let's first consider the features present in this purpose statement. It included the following elements:

Theory. A theory developed by Tracey and Sedlacek.

Independent variables. SAT scores and psychosocial variables.

Dependent variables. GPA (grade point average) and retention in the first year of college.

Words that indicate the study intent. The purpose of the study was to use independent variables "to predict" the dependent variables. Words like *predict, associate with,* and *influence* all indicate the intent to describe a relationship among variables.

Participants. Asian American college students.

This purpose statement is missing the research site. If you read the full study, you can learn that the study took place at one Southeastern public land-grant research university. It would have been more complete if the author had specified that information in the purpose statement.

Read Quantitative Research Questions to Learn How the Researcher Narrows the Overall Intent Into Specific Questions

Recall that researchers present their overall intent in a purpose statement and then narrow this intent by stating the specific questions they will answer to achieve this intent. Therefore, look for research questions in addition to a study's purpose statement. Good research questions logically follow from the study purpose and are worded so that the key elements are clear and easy to identify. To more easily interpret these questions in quantitative study reports, note that researchers use the following strategies to write their quantitative research questions:

- The research questions are phrased as questions, often beginning with the words *how, what,* and *do,* and ending with a question mark.
- Each research question identifies one or more variables and a specific intent.
- The variables appear in the order as shown in Figure 5.2: independent variables first and dependent variables second. Because control variables are of secondary interest, they typically appear third in the order.

Table 5.2 lists models for how researchers present three types of research questions in quantitative research reports: descriptive questions, relationship questions, and comparison questions. Let's examine examples of these three common forms.

- *An example of a quantitative descriptive research question.* How frequently do African Americans feel isolated on college campuses?

TABLE 5.2 Models of Research Questions in Quantitative Research

Type of Quantitative Research Question	Example Models
Descriptive	■ How frequently do [*participants*] [*variable*] at [*the research site*]? ■ What is [*variable*] for [*participants*] at [*the research site*]?
Relationship	■ How does [*the independent variable(s)*] relate to [*the dependent variable(s)*], controlling for [*the control variable(s)*]? ■ Do [*the independent variable(s)*] predict [*the dependent variable(s)*], controlling for [*the control variable(s)*]?
Comparison	■ How do [*group 1 of the independent variable*] compare to [*group 2 of the independent variable*] in terms of [*the dependent variable*]? ■ What is the difference between [*group 1 of the independent variable*] compared to [*group 2 of the independent variable*] in terms of [*the dependent variable*]?

Researchers use a descriptive question when they intend to describe participants' responses to a single variable. This single variable may be an independent, a dependent, or a control variable. In this example, the intent is to describe one variable, *feelings of isolation*. The question also identifies the participants and site (*African Americans* on *college campuses*).

■ ***An example of a quantitative relationship research question.*** Do feelings of isolation relate to ethnic identity?

Researchers use a relationship question when they want to examine the relationship between two or more variables. Relationship questions seek to answer questions about the magnitude and direction of the relationship among variables. Researchers who pose these questions can be interested in the relationships between different types of variables in their studies. The most common situation occurs when researchers intend to relate the independent variable to the dependent variable, but researchers may also be interested in relating dependent variables to control variables. In the example provided here, we find the researcher is relating an independent variable (*feelings of isolation*) to a dependent variable (*ethnic identity*).

■ ***An example of a quantitative comparison research question.*** How do African Americans and Chinese Americans differ in their perceptions of ethnic identity?

Researchers ask comparison questions when they intend to find out how two or more groups for an independent variable differ in terms of one or more outcome variables. They use these questions for independent variables that are measured variables (e.g., gender) and those that are treatment variables (e.g., type of program). In this example, the researcher is comparing two racial groups, so *race* is the measured independent variable. The dependent variable is *perceptions of ethnic identity*.

What Do You Think?

Read the following examples of research questions taken from research studies. For each, identify the type of research question (descriptive, relationship, or comparison).

a. "Do appropriate duties, inappropriate duties, self-efficacy, frequency of district and peer supervision, and perceived stress correlate with school counselors' career satisfaction?" (Baggerly & Osborn, 2006, p. 199).

b. "Does technology access differ for children attending high-poverty and low-poverty schools?" (Judge, Puckett, & Bell, 2006, p. 53).

c. "What are elementary school principals' perceptions of music learning outcomes as they are currently being met?" (Abril & Gault, 2006, p. 10).

Check Your Understanding

Research question (a) is an example of a relationship research question. The words "correlate with" are equivalent to "relate to." The researchers are interested in whether numerous independent variables (*appropriate duties, inappropriate duties, self-efficacy, frequency of district and peer supervision,* and *perceived stress*) relate to one dependent variable (*career satisfaction*) for school counselors.

Research question (b) is an example of a comparison research question. The word *differ* provides an indication of the intended comparison. The researchers are interested in comparing two groups of schools based on their *socioeconomic status* (high poverty and low poverty) in terms of a dependent variable (*technology access*).

Research question (c) is an example of a descriptive research question. The researchers are interested in describing a single variable (*perceptions of music learning outcomes*) for elementary school principals.

Read Quantitative Hypotheses to Learn How the Researcher Narrows the Overall Intent Into Specific Predictions

Recall that hypotheses are an alternative to research questions that researchers use to narrow the purpose of a quantitative study to specific predictions. When researchers write hypotheses, they advance a prediction about what they expect to find. Researchers use hypotheses to make predictions about two or more variables. For example, a hypothesis may predict how groups are expected to differ, such as predicting that one group will have a more favorable change than other groups, or predicting that there will be no difference among the groups. A hypothesis can also indicate the expected relationships among variables, such as a positive relationship or no relationship. Hypotheses do not apply to single variables because they are predictions about two or more variables.

There are two types of hypotheses you may read in quantitative reports: null hypotheses and alternative hypotheses. Researchers use both types during the data analysis step in a quantitative research study, but they generally only write one or the other into the introductions of their reports. A good hypothesis clearly identifies the independent and dependent variables of interest; in addition, it advances a prediction about these variables that is based on the study's chosen theory and/or based on results of past research found in the literature. Table 5.3 lists models for two types of research hypotheses that you will read in reports. Let's examine examples of how researchers use each of these formats.

- *An example of a quantitative null hypothesis.* There is no difference between third-grade students placed at risk and those not at risk in terms of achievement on math test scores.

    The null hypothesis (often indicated as H_0) is the most traditional form that researchers use to write their hypotheses. Null hypotheses are predictions that there is *no relationship* between independent and dependent variables, or *no difference*

TABLE 5.3   Models of Research Hypotheses in Quantitative Research

Type of Quantitative Research Hypothesis	Example Models
Null	■ There is no relationship between [*the independent variable*] and [*the dependent variable*]. ■ There is no difference between [*group 1 of the independent variable*] and [*group 2 of the independent variable*] in terms of [*the dependent variable*].
Alternative	■ [*The independent variable*] is [*positively/negatively*] related to [*the dependent variable*]. ■ [*Group 1 of the independent variable*] score [*higher/lower*] than [*group 2 of the independent variable*] in terms of [*the dependent variable*].

between groups of an independent variable in terms of a dependent variable. The example provided illustrates a null hypothesis because it predicts "no difference" between two groups of third graders. This example has one independent variable (*at-risk status*) with two levels (placed at risk and not at risk). It also identifies one dependent variable (*achievement on math test scores*).

- **An example of a quantitative alternative hypothesis.** Time spent studying is positively related to reading test scores for athletes in rural high schools.

This example predicts that the two variables (*time spent studying* and *reading test scores*) will be related *and* that they will be related in a certain way, namely "positively." It illustrates an alternative hypothesis because it predicts a specific direction to the relationship for the participants (*athletes in rural high schools*). In contrast to a null hypothesis, researchers write an alternative hypothesis (often indicated as H_A or H_1) so that it predicts the direction of a change, difference, or relationship for the variables being studied. The alternative hypothesis form is more commonly found in research reports than the null hypothesis form.

What Do You Think?

Read the following examples of hypotheses taken from research studies. For each, identify the type of hypothesis (null or alternative) and the study's independent and dependent variables.

a. "We hypothesized that perceived occupational barriers would be negatively predictive of career certainty . . . in a sample of African American adolescents" (Constantine et al., 2005, p. 311).

b. "We hypothesized that women when compared with men would score lower in ethnocentrism, intercultural communication apprehension, prejudice, and ambiguity intolerance" (Kim & Goldstein, 2005, p. 269).

Check Your Understanding

Hypothesis (a) is an example of an alternative hypothesis. The authors identify an independent variable (*perceived occupational barriers*) and dependent variable (*career certainty*). They predict that these two variables will be "negatively" related, thereby predicting the direction of the relationship. If the authors had written a null hypothesis, it might have been: "We hypothesized that there would be no relationship between perceived occupational barriers and career certainty."

Hypothesis (b) is also an example of an alternative hypothesis. The authors are interested in *gender* (women and men) as an independent variable and in several dependent variables (e.g., *ethnocentrism, intercultural communication apprehension, prejudice,* and *ambiguity intolerance*). They use an alternative hypothesis because they predict that women will score lower than men on these dependent variables. If the authors had written a null hypothesis, it might have been: "We hypothesized that there would be no difference between women and men in terms of ethnocentrism, intercultural communication apprehension, prejudice, and ambiguity intolerance."

You now have a basic understanding of the forms that researchers use to convey the purpose of their quantitative studies. The provided models and examples of quantitative purpose statements, research questions, and hypotheses fit the narrow and specific intents of most quantitative research studies. In contrast, recall that *qualitative* studies are generally conducted with a different intent in mind. Researchers conduct qualitative research when the research problem calls for exploration and they specify purposes that are general and broad. Therefore, qualitative researchers write purpose statements and research questions that reflect their intent to explore a central phenomenon in their qualitative studies. We will now switch to considering how to understand the purpose in qualitative research studies. We begin by examining what a central phenomenon is and how it provides the focus in qualitative research.

How Do You Identify a Central Phenomenon in Qualitative Research?

In Chapter 2 you learned that researchers specify intents that call for the exploration of a central phenomenon when they conduct qualitative research. This means that the key to understanding qualitative purpose statements and research questions is first to recognize and understand the role of the central phenomenon in qualitative research.

A Central Phenomenon Is a Concept, Activity, or Process

When researchers conduct qualitative research, they do not specify a set of variables as the focus for their studies. Instead, qualitative researchers focus their attention on a single phenomenon that is central to their inquiry. A **central phenomenon** is the concept, activity, or process explored in a qualitative research study. For example, as a concept, it could be:

- the ethnic identity of Chinese American immigrants.

As an activity it might be:

- a program that helps individuals who are unemployed learn new skills.

As a process it might be:

- the process of negotiation used by a female superintendent with her principals.

These examples illustrate the expression of a central phenomenon in a few words. They also show a focus on a single concept, or a single activity, or a single process. This single focus is different from quantitative research that emphasizes relating two or more variables (e.g., "How do alienation and isolation relate for the female superintendent?") or comparing groups in terms of a variable (e.g., "How do female principals and superintendents compare in their alienation?"). This comment is not to suggest that researchers may not explore comparisons or relationships in qualitative inquiry. Comparisons and relationships may emerge as the qualitative data analysis proceeds (we will discuss qualitative data analysis further in Chapter 11). The qualitative inquirer, however, begins by identifying one single idea to explore as the focus for the study.

> **Here's a Tip!**
>
> Some qualitative studies specify multiple issues as the focus. When this happens, ask yourself what seems to be the one broad concept that the authors are exploring as a way of identifying the study's central phenomenon.

Researchers Study a Central Phenomenon to Learn About Its Meaning and Complexity

To understand the purposes in qualitative research studies, you need to understand why researchers explore a single central phenomenon in their studies. Qualitative researchers focus on one central phenomenon so that they can explore that phenomenon in depth to understand its meaning for individuals and its complexity as it naturally occurs in people's lives. This is very different from the purposes of quantitative research. To better conceptualize the differences between explaining variables in quantitative research and exploring a central phenomenon in qualitative research, see Figure 5.4.

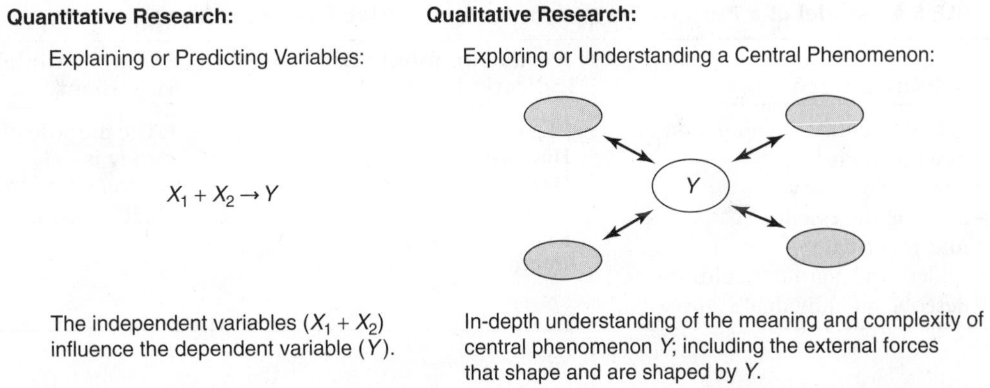

Quantitative Research:

Explaining or Predicting Variables:

$$X_1 + X_2 \rightarrow Y$$

The independent variables $(X_1 + X_2)$ influence the dependent variable (Y).

Qualitative Research:

Exploring or Understanding a Central Phenomenon:

In-depth understanding of the meaning and complexity of central phenomenon Y; including the external forces that shape and are shaped by Y.

FIGURE 5.4 Comparing How Researchers Explain or Predict Variables Versus How They Explore or Understand a Central Phenomenon

This figure contrasts an image of the explanation of how independent variables affect an outcome variable on the left side of the figure with the different image of the exploration of a central phenomenon on the right side of the figure. Rather than using cause-and-effect logic as in quantitative research, the qualitative researcher seeks to explore and understand one single phenomenon in its complexity and in terms of the meaning it has for individuals. To understand the complexity and meaning of a single phenomenon requires the researcher to consider the multiple external forces that shape and are shaped by this phenomenon (as indicated by the double-headed arrows in the figure). At the beginning of a study, the qualitative researcher cannot predict the nature of the external forces (i.e., Which ones will be important? What are their roles?). The qualitative researcher wants to understand the phenomenon in all its complexity instead of limiting the view to a set of predetermined variables. In some qualitative studies, the researchers bring a conceptual framework that informs their stance in the research about the central phenomenon. Recall from Chapter 4, however, that this framework guides the researchers' approach to studying the central phenomenon and does not serve to specify variables or to make predictions in the study.

How Do You Understand Purpose Statements and Research Questions in Qualitative Research?

Although researchers have a different focus and intent when they conduct qualitative research compared to quantitative research, they still convey the essential elements of their qualitative studies by specifying the purpose in their reports. When you read a qualitative study, you should examine the report to locate the purpose statement and research questions that the researchers include. Let's examine how you can understand these different formats in qualitative research reports.

Read Purpose Statements to Learn the Study's Overall Qualitative Intent

Recall that researchers present purpose statements that convey the overall intent of their study. When you read a well-written qualitative study, the purpose statement:

- begins with signal words such as "The purpose of this study . . ." or "The aim of this study. . . ."; and
- includes the elements for specifying a qualitative purpose: the overall intent, the central phenomenon, the participants, and the research site.

Table 5.4 lists examples of qualitative intents as well as the words that researchers often use to indicate their intent in qualitative research reports. Because of the broad

TABLE 5.4   Model of a Purpose Statement for Qualitative Research Intents

Qualitative Intent	Words Commonly Used to Indicate the Intent	Example Model of a Purpose Statement
Explore a central phenomenon to: • describe themes • generate a theory • describe the essence • interpret a case • understand a group's culture • describe an individual's story	Explore Describe Discover Understand Generate Interpret	• The purpose of this qualitative study is to [*qualitative intent*] [*the central phenomenon*] for [*participants*] at [*the research site*].

> **Here's a Tip!**
>
> Recall that when summarizing a study, it is best to put the study's purpose into your own words. A good strategy is to identify the major elements of the study's purpose and use the provided models as templates for writing your own summary statements of a study's purpose.

and general nature of qualitative purpose statements, Table 5.4 lists one qualitative purpose statement that serves as a model for the wide range of purposes that you read in qualitative research reports. As the model illustrates, you can expect a good qualitative purpose statement to identify that the study's intent is to explore one broad central phenomenon. The researchers may also choose to identify their stance (e.g., a feminist perspective) as part of the purpose statement if applicable. Let's examine examples that demonstrate how these elements come together to inform you about a qualitative study's intent:

- **An example of a qualitative purpose statement when the researcher's intent is to explore a central phenomenon.** The purpose of this qualitative study is to describe classroom learning using the Internet for five nurses participating in a sign language class.

  In this example, the overall intent is to explore, as indicated by the word *describe*, and the central phenomenon is *classroom learning using the Internet*. The purpose statement also identifies that the participants are *five nurses* and the research setting is a *sign language class*. In this example, the researchers did not identify a stance for the research study.

- **An example of a qualitative purpose statement that includes the researcher's conceptual framework.** The purpose of this qualitative study is to explore the meaning of academic achievement for African American students attending an urban community college using a critical race theory lens.

  This example identifies one central phenomenon that the researcher wants to explore: *meaning of academic achievement*. This statement also indicates that the participants are *African American students* and that the research takes place at an *urban community college*. In addition, this purpose statement notes that the researcher is using a conceptual framework to inform the study, namely *critical race theory*.

What Do You Think?

Using the characteristics of good qualitative purpose statements, identify the main features identified in the following purpose statement as well as any features that are missing:

The purpose of this study was to understand the processes a person experiences in creating a leadership identity. (Komives et al., 2005, p. 594)

Check Your Understanding

Let's first consider the features present in this purpose statement. It included the following elements:

Central phenomenon. Creating a leadership identity (a process).

Words that indicate the intent to explore. The purpose of the study was to "understand" this process.

This purpose statement is missing a clear identification of the *participants* and the *research site*. If you read the full study, you can learn that the study took place at one large Mid-Atlantic research university. The participants included undergraduate students from this university. This purpose statement also did not identify that the study is qualitative. Putting these elements together, the authors could have written their purpose statement as follows:

The purpose of this qualitative study was to understand the processes for creating a leadership identity that undergraduate students experience at a large Mid-Atlantic research university.

Read the Central Research Question and Subquestions to Learn How the Researcher Narrows the Overall Intent Into Specific Questions

As in quantitative research, researchers include research questions in their qualitative studies that follow from the study's overall purpose. Qualitative research questions are open-ended, general questions that the researcher intends to answer. In a good qualitative research study, the research questions flow logically from the overall intent stated in the study purpose. When you read good qualitative research questions, you find that the researchers:

- Pose only a few, general questions. By using only a few questions, the researchers place emphasis on learning from participants, rather than learning what the researcher expects to find.
- Identify the key elements of the central phenomenon and the intent; the researchers may also identify the participants and research site.
- Phrase them as questions, often beginning with the words "how" or "what."
- Use neutral, exploratory language and refrain from conveying an expected direction or prediction.
- Are open to questions emerging or changing during the study to reflect the participants' views of the central phenomenon and the researcher's growing understanding of it.

There are two types of research questions found in qualitative research reports: central research questions and subquestions. Models for these questions are provided in Table 5.5. As these models illustrate, research questions in qualitative research are broad and open to indicate that the researchers are open to learning from the participants and not limited to their own perspective. Let's consider these two question types further by examining some examples.

- ***An example of a qualitative central research question.*** What is creativity for female athletes at County High School?

    This is an example of a central research question in a study of creativity. The **central research question** is the overarching question that the researcher explores in a qualitative research study. It is the most general question that the researcher can ask, usually a brief and very general question that specifies the central phenomenon.

TABLE 5.5   **Model of Central Research Questions and Subquestions for Qualitative Research**

Type of Qualitative Research Question	Example Models
Central Research Question	▪ What is [*the central phenomenon*] for [*the participants*] at [*the research site*]?
Subquestions	▪ What is [*a subissue of the central phenomenon*]? ▪ What is [*a context*] for [*the central phenomenon*]? ▪ What do [*the participants*] [*do, think, say*] when experiencing [*the central phenomenon*]? ▪ How do [*a subgroup of the participants*] experience [*the central phenomenon*]?

Note how this question begins with the word *what* to signal the need for an exploration. This question also identifies the central phenomenon of *creativity*. The study participants are female athletes and the study takes place at County High School.

▪ ***An example of qualitative subquestions.*** What is creativity during a game? What is creativity during practice? How is creativity experienced by the individual? How is creativity experienced by the team? What are the contexts for creativity?

In addition to reading a central question, many qualitative research reports include subquestions that the researcher has posed. These subquestions refine the central question into subquestions to be addressed in the research. These subquestions contain many of the same elements as central questions (i.e., open-ended, emerging, neutral in language, and few in number), but they provide greater specificity about the study's direction. As these examples illustrate, the central phenomenon, creativity, is divided into five topical areas (or issues) that the researcher explores in the study.

Well-written qualitative central research questions and subquestions provide some direction for the study but do not leave the direction completely wide open. When you read a research question that is too open, you do not have enough information to understand the project. Alternatively, when the research question is too specific or too laden with assumptions, it does not offer enough latitude for the researcher to understand participants' views. Narrow research questions may indicate that the researcher was not sufficiently open to learning about the central phenomenon from participants. If you read qualitative research questions that are too narrow, then you should consider that the researcher may have unintentionally shaped the views of participants in one direction or another.

In Table 5.6, several specific examples illustrate central research questions stated in terms that are too general, too focused, or too laden with assumptions. First a poor example is given, followed by a better, improved version. In the first example, the author states a central question so broadly that readers and audiences do not understand the central phenomenon being studied. This situation can occur when a qualitative researcher takes too literally the concept of open-ended questions to mean anything goes.

In the second example of Table 5.6, the author focuses the question too much. By focusing on specific activities of a committee, the researcher may miss the larger process at work in the committee and lose important information. In the final example, the researcher starts with the assumption that the committee is "alienated" from the school board. Although this may be the case, the specification of a negative direction may severely limit what the inquirer can learn from a situation. A better form is presented when a researcher asks about the "role of the school board," because that includes the possibility that the role may be alienating, supportive, or may serve some combination of roles. Note, however, that some qualitative researchers do choose to use an advocacy approach for their studies and bring to the research assumptions about power imbalances and alienation of groups in society based on issues such as gender, race, disability, sexual orientation, or class. Such perspectives can be appropriate in qualitative research when they are informed by theoretical stances drawn from the literature (as discussed in Chapter 4).

TABLE 5.6 Problems Typically Found in Research Questions in Qualitative Research

Problem	Poor Example of a Central Research Question	Better Example of a Central Research Question
Question is too general	What is going on here?	What is the process being used by the curriculum committee at the elementary school?
Question is too focused	How did the committee make a decision about the curriculum for a new foreign language program?	What is the process of the curriculum committee in making decisions about the curriculum?
Question is too laden with assumptions	How did the curriculum committee address its alienation from the school board?	What was the role of the school board in the curriculum committee's deliberations?

What Do You Think?

Read the following passage from a qualitative study about parents' role in helping their children go to college. What is the study's central phenomenon? What types of research questions did the author pose?

This study draws on 3 years of ethnographic data to illustrate one of many possible alternative typologies of parent roles in the pursuit of educational access. What do parents of color without college experience think and do when they want their high school-age students to go to college? What shapes their beliefs, goals, and support strategies? (Auerbach, 2007, p. 251)

Check Your Understanding

The first sentence in this passage is a purpose statement that provides the general intent of the study. The purpose statement identifies the central phenomenon (parent roles in the pursuit of educational access) and the use of a qualitative ethnographic approach. This statement, however, did not clearly identify the participants or research site. The participants—parents of color—are identified in the first research question. The two research questions are subquestions that serve to focus the purpose to specific issues that will be addressed in the study (what parents think and do and what shapes these beliefs and strategies). They are open-ended, exploratory questions that indicate that the author is open to learning from participants.

How Do You Evaluate the Purpose in a Research Study?

You have now learned the important elements that researchers specify for the purpose in quantitative and qualitative research studies. When you examine a research report, you want to first identify each of these elements to understand what the study is about. If a study's purpose is not clear, then you can only guess what the researcher was trying to do. A good research purpose will not only identify the elements, but these elements will also logically follow from the statement of the problem and literature review advanced by the author. In addition, the purpose should be specified in a rigorous way that is consistent with the quantitative or qualitative approach. Because of the differences between the two approaches to research, Tables 5.7 and 5.8 list criteria that are useful for considering the quality of the purpose in quantitative reports (Table 5.7) and qualitative reports (Table 5.8). That is, although the purpose has similar elements in both types of research, what counts as good quality in the implementation of these elements differs depending on the study approach.

The rating form in Figure 5.5 provides a convenient means for you to apply the quality criteria to evaluate the purpose described in the Introduction of any research report. For each

TABLE 5.7 Criteria for Evaluating the Purpose in a Quantitative Research Report

Quality Criteria	Indicators of Higher Quality in Quantitative Research	Indicators of Lower Quality in Quantitative Research
The Key Elements		
1. The study's purpose is clearly specified.	+ The researcher includes a concise and clear purpose statement in the report's Introduction section that identifies the study's focus, intent, framework, participants, and setting. + The purpose statement includes signal words such as "The purpose of the study is . . ." so that it is easy to identify.	− The researcher includes only a vague statement of purpose or states the purpose somewhere in the report other than the Introduction. − The purpose statement is difficult to locate or the researchers' purpose has to be deduced from what the researchers actually did.
2. The focus of the study is appropriate.	+ The focus of the study is a set of major variables that are clearly identified and worthy of study. + The variables form a "family" of variables including independent, dependent, and control variables as suggested by a theory from the literature. + Relevant confounding variables are identified and studied if possible.	− The focus of the study only refers to general ideas or broad concepts or seems unworthy of study. − The variables seem unrelated to each other or were selected without a theoretical basis. − Important potential confounding variables are not included in the study focus.
3. The overall intent of the study is appropriate.	+ The overall intent of the study is to explain, describe, or predict the major variables. + The intent is stated in a precise manner and indicates what is to be learned about the identified variables.	− The overall intent of the study seems poorly related to explaining the major variables. − The intent is stated in a confusing manner, perhaps including multiple or contradictory purposes.
4. The participants and sites are appropriate.	+ The general people and settings to be studied are clearly identified and clearly fit the study's focus and intent.	− The general people or settings to be studied are unclear and do not clearly fit the study's focus and intent.
5. The purpose is narrowed through appropriate research questions and/or hypotheses.	+ The research questions and hypotheses follow from the purpose by examining specific relationships among the variables and making predictions about the relationships based on the literature.	− The research questions and hypotheses introduce topics that do not clearly follow from the overall purpose, fail to identify possible relationships, or make predictions without a clear basis in the literature.
General Evaluation		
6. The purpose follows logically from the statement of the problem and literature review.	+ The reasons for the study's major variables, intent, theory, participants, and sites are well argued. + The purpose, research questions, and hypotheses clearly build from existing knowledge, address an important problem, will fill a gap in knowledge, and will produce results that may have significance for audiences.	− The reasons for the study's major variables, intent, theory, participants, or sites are unclear or unwarranted. − There is a disconnect between the statement of the problem and literature review and the stated purpose, research questions, and hypotheses.
7. The purpose is consistent with the study's overall approach.	The purpose, research questions, and hypotheses are: + narrow and specific; + based on the literature and applicable theory; + predetermined and remain fixed during the study; and + aimed at describing trends for variables in a large population, describing the relationship among variables, describing the difference between groups, or testing the effect of a treatment.	The purpose and research questions are: − broad and general; − poorly tied to the literature or relevant theory; − stated with open-ended language and allowed to emerge or change during the study; or − aimed at an intent that would be better addressed through a qualitative approach, such as generating a theory.

TABLE 5.8 Criteria for Evaluating the Purpose in a Qualitative Research Report

Quality Criteria	Indicators of Higher Quality in Qualitative Research	Indicators of Lower Quality in Qualitative Research
The Key Elements		
1. The study's purpose is clearly specified.	+ The researcher includes a concise and clear purpose statement in the report's Introduction section that identifies the study's focus, intent, framework, participants, and setting. + The purpose statement includes signal words such as "The purpose of the study is . . ." so that it is easy to identify.	− The researcher includes only a vague statement of purpose or states the purpose somewhere in the report other than the Introduction. − The purpose statement is difficult to locate or the researchers' purpose has to be deduced from what the researchers actually did.
2. The focus of the study is appropriate.	+ The focus of the study is a single central phenomenon that is clearly identified and worthy of study. + The central phenomenon is a broad, general concept, activity, or process that is experienced by individuals.	− The focus of the study includes multiple topics, is unclear, or seems unworthy of study. − The central phenomenon is a narrow topic or multiple topics that are defined by the researcher.
3. The overall intent of the study is appropriate.	+ The overall intent of the study is to explore the central phenomenon. + The intent is stated in a precise manner and indicates what is to be learned about the central phenomenon.	− The overall intent of the study seems poorly related to exploring the central phenomenon. − The intent is stated in a confusing manner, perhaps including multiple or contradictory purposes.
4. The participants and sites are appropriate.	+ The general people and settings to be studied are clearly identified and clearly fit the study's focus and intent.	− The general participants or settings to be studied are unclear and do not clearly fit the study's focus and intent.
5. The purpose is narrowed through appropriate research questions and/or hypotheses.	+ The research questions clearly follow from the overall purpose to explore the central phenomenon and related issues. + No hypotheses are stated indicating that the researcher is open to learning from participants.	− The research questions introduce topics that are not related to the overall central phenomenon or that identify multiple phenomena. − The researcher conveys expected outcomes as hypotheses, indicating a lack of openness for learning from participants.
General Evaluation		
6. The purpose follows logically from the statement of the problem and literature review.	+ The reasons for the study's central phenomenon, intent, conceptual framework, participants, and sites are well argued. + The purpose and research questions clearly build from existing knowledge, address an important problem, will fill a gap in knowledge, and will produce results that may have significance for audiences.	− The reasons for the study's central phenomenon, intent, conceptual framework, participants, or sites are unclear or unwarranted. − There is a disconnect between the statement of the problem and literature review and the stated purpose and research questions.
7. The purpose is consistent with the study's overall approach.	The purpose and research questions are: + broad and general; + consistent with the researchers' conceptual framework; + stated with neutral and open-ended language; + allowed to emerge and change during the study; and + aimed at exploring individuals' perceptions and experiences such as to generate a theory, provide description, and/or identify thematic patterns.	The purpose and research questions are: − narrow and specific; − inconsistent with the researchers' conceptual framework; − stated with non-neutral or leading language; − predetermined and kept fixed; or − aimed at an intent that would be better addressed through a quantitative approach, such as assessing an impact or effect of a variable or treatment.

Quality Criteria	Quality Rating				Your Evidence and/or Reasoning
	0 = Poor	1 = Fair	2 = Good	3 = Excellent	
The Key Elements					
1. The study's purpose is clearly specified.					
2. The focus of the study is appropriate.					
3. The overall intent of the study is appropriate.					
4. The participants and sites are appropriate.					
5. The purpose is narrowed through appropriate research questions and/or hypotheses.					
General Evaluation					
6. The purpose follows logically from the statement of the problem and literature review.					
7. The purpose is consistent with the study's overall approach.					
Overall Quality 0–10 = Low quality 11–16 = Adequate quality 17–21 = High quality	**Total Score =**				**My Overall Assessment =**

FIGURE 5.5   Rating Scale for Evaluating a Purpose in a Research Report

of the criteria you locate, assign a quality rating from *fair* (1) to *excellent* (3) and document your evidence and/or reasoning behind the rating. If one of the criteria is missing or very poorly stated, then indicate *poor* (0) as your rating. Although research reports will vary in the forms used to state the study's purpose, good reports should still score well on most of the items listed in Figure 5.5. By summing the rating scores for each of the criteria and using the suggested cutoff values provided at the bottom of the figure, you have a quantitative measure that you can use to inform your overall assessment of a report's research purpose.

Reviewing What You've Learned To Do

- *Identify and understand the purpose of a study.*
  - ☐ The Introduction section of a research report includes information that indicates the researchers' purpose for conducting the research study, which includes specifying the study's focus, intent, framework, participants, and setting.
  - ☐ Researchers specify their purpose in a purpose statement that conveys the overall intent, and they narrow this purpose into research questions that state the questions to be answered by the study and/or hypotheses that state predictions that will be tested in the study.
- *Describe how the purpose differs in quantitative and qualitative research.*
  - ☐ In quantitative studies, researchers specify a purpose, research questions, and hypotheses that are narrow and specific. The intent focuses on a set of variables and remains fixed during the study.
  - ☐ In qualitative studies, researchers specify a purpose and research questions that are broad and general. The intent focuses on a central phenomenon and may change as the researcher learns from participants during the study.

- *Identify the different types of variables investigated in a quantitative research study.*
  - □ A variable is a characteristic or attribute of an individual or an organization that researchers measure and that varies among the individuals or organizations studied.
  - □ Variables may influence or have an effect on other variables as described by theories. Dependent variables are the outcomes that the researchers are most interested in understanding. Independent variables are the variables that are thought to influence or predict the dependent variables. Control variables are of secondary interest, but researchers measure them because they may also influence the dependent variable.
- *Understand the elements included in quantitative purpose statements, research questions, and hypotheses.*
  - □ In quantitative research, the purpose statement specifies the intent, major variables, theory, participants, and setting for the research study. Quantitative intents include describing trends for single variables, relating variables, comparing groups, or testing the effect caused by a treatment.
  - □ The research questions in a quantitative study narrow the purpose to the specific descriptive, relationship, and comparison research questions that will be answered in the study.
  - □ The null or alternative hypotheses in a quantitative study narrow the study purpose into predictions that will be tested.
- *Identify the central phenomenon investigated in a qualitative research study.*
  - □ A central phenomenon is the concept, activity, or process that researchers explore as the focus of a qualitative research study.
- *Understand the elements included in qualitative purpose statements and research questions.*
  - □ In qualitative research, the purpose statement specifies the intent, central phenomenon, conceptual framework, participants, and setting for the qualitative research study. Qualitative intents include describing, exploring, and understanding the complexity and meaning of the central phenomenon.
  - □ The research questions in a qualitative study narrow the purpose to the specific central research question and subquestions that will be answered in the study.
- *Evaluate the quality of the purpose in a research report.*
  - □ The evaluation of a study's purpose begins by considering the extent to which the author identified a good intent, focus, framework, participants, and setting.
  - □ The evaluation of a study's purpose is also based on the extent to which the purpose stems from the statement of the problem and literature review and the extent to which the purpose is consistent with the study's quantitative or qualitative approach.

✓ **To assess what you've learned to do, click here to answer questions and receive instant feedback.**

Reading Research Articles

Carefully review the quantitative bullying-intervention study by Perkins et al. (2011) found at the end of Chapter 3 (starting on p. 98) and the qualitative adolescent-homelessness study by Haldenby et al. (2007) found at the end of Chapter 4 (starting on p. 148).

As you read each article, pay attention to the statements in which the authors conveyed the intent for their research. Use the highlighting tool in the Pearson etext to indicate where the authors have provided information about the purpose of the study, and use the notetaking tool to add marginal notes that name each element you highlighted and note how each one is related to the study's purpose. Among the elements you will want to find are:

1. Purpose statement
2. Research questions
3. Hypotheses (appropriate only in quantitative studies)

Note, however, that sometimes authors do not directly state all three of these elements—they may not explicitly state their purpose, their research questions, or their hypotheses. If one of these elements is missing, indicate that in your marginal notes.

Click here to go to the quantitative bullying-intervention study by Perkins et al. (2011) so that you can enter marginal notes about the study.

 Click here to go to the qualitative adolescent-homelessness study by Haldenby et al. (2007) so that you can enter marginal notes about the study.

Understanding Research Articles

Apply your knowledge of the content of this chapter to the quantitative bullying-intervention study by Perkins et al. (2011) starting on p. 98 and the qualitative adolescent-homelessness study by Haldenby et al. (2007) starting on p. 148.

1. Consider the quantitative bullying-intervention study. Identify the study's main variables. That is, what are the (a) independent and (b) dependent variables? (c) For each identified independent variable, indicate whether it is a measured variable or a treatment variable. (d) What might be an example of a confounding variable?

2. Using the models provided in this chapter, write a purpose statement for the bullying-intervention study in your own words. How does your purpose statement compare to the statement that the authors provided at the end of paragraph 10?

3. The authors referred to three research questions in paragraph 10 of the bullying-intervention study. For each question, determine whether it is a descriptive, relationship, or comparison research question.

4. The authors stated several hypotheses in the report of the bullying-intervention study (see paragraphs 21–24). Consider the second hypothesis (middle of paragraph 21) and the third hypothesis (start of paragraph 22). Are these hypotheses examples of null and/or alternative hypotheses?

5. Now consider the qualitative adolescent-homelessness study. Identify the central phenomenon explored in this study.

6. Using the model provided in this chapter, write a purpose statement for the adolescent-homelessness study in your own words. How does your purpose statement compare to the one that the authors wrote into the study (see paragraph 21)?

7. Consider the research questions provided in paragraph 21 of the adolescent-homelessness study. Identify each question as either a central research question or a subquestion.

✓ **Click here to answer the questions and receive instant feedback.**

Evaluating Research Articles

Practice evaluating the purpose of a study, using the quantitative bullying-intervention study by Perkins et al. (2011) starting on p. 98 and the qualitative adolescent-homelessness study by Haldenby et al. (2007) starting on p. 148.

1. Use the criteria discussed in Table 5.7 to evaluate the quality of the purpose in the bullying-intervention study. Note that, for this question, the rating form includes advice to help guide your evaluation.

✓ **Click here to open the rating scale form (Figure 5.5) to enter your ratings, evidence, and reasoning.**

2. Use the criteria discussed in Table 5.8 to evaluate the quality of the purpose in the adolescent-homelessness study. Note that, for this question, the rating form does NOT include additional advice.

✓ **Click here to open the rating scale form (Figure 5.5) to enter your ratings, evidence, and reasoning.**

UNDERSTANDING THE METHOD SECTIONS AND RESULTS SECTIONS OF QUANTITATIVE RESEARCH REPORTS

Recall the analogy that the process researchers use to conduct research is like the process travelers use to take a journey. Keeping this analogy in mind can help you understand the information reported about research studies. In Chapters 3–5, you learned how to understand researchers' preliminary considerations for their research "journeys" as discussed in the Introduction sections of reports. These include why they want to go (the research problem), what they know about the destination (the literature review), and their goals for the trip (the purpose). With these decisions in place, researchers take their journeys and implement their studies.

When the preliminary considerations call for explanation and measurement of variables, researchers choose to take a quantitative research "journey." When researchers use a quantitative approach, they plan all the important details of their "itineraries" from the start. Before collecting any information, quantitative researchers set the plan for the study, such as who will be involved, where they will go, and what they will do and see along the way. That is, you can say that all the major decisions for a quantitative study are made before the researcher "leaves home." This type of trip does not permit much flexibility, but quantitative researchers ensure that they cover everything on their "itinerary" in order to gather consistent information about the variables to answer their research questions.

Once the study is complete, quantitative researchers report the details of their research "journeys" in the Method section of a research report. In this section, you can find details about the overall plan for the study, called a research design, and the procedures used to select participants and collect and analyze data. A description of the results of the study can be found in a separate section, called the Results section. While the Method section describes the "path" that the researchers took in their study, the Results section describes what they found along this path, like the pictures and mementos that a traveler acquires during a trip. We now examine the different ways that quantitative researchers design, conduct, and report their methods and results so you can better understand and evaluate the Method and Results sections of quantitative research reports.

The chapters in Part Three are:

- Chapter 6—Quantitative Research Designs: Recognizing the Overall Plan for a Study

- Chapter 7—Participants and Data Collection: Identifying How Quantitative Information Is Gathered

- Chapter 8—Data Analysis and Results: Examining What Was Found in a Quantitative Study

QUANTITATIVE RESEARCH DESIGNS: RECOGNIZING THE OVERALL PLAN FOR A STUDY

You have already learned that researchers use quantitative research when their purpose is to test the effect of a treatment or to describe trends and relationships among variables. Identifying the overall approach of a study as quantitative research is a good start to understanding any quantitative report. A better understanding arises if you also recognize and understand the different quantitative research designs that researchers use to conduct their studies. Quantitative research designs provide overall plans for the methods used to conduct quantitative studies to address different purposes. This chapter first introduces you to two major types of quantitative research. It then focuses on the characteristics of five quantitative research designs that you will likely encounter as you read research. Knowing about different quantitative research designs will help you read the Method sections of quantitative reports and understand and evaluate the research designs used in quantitative studies.

BY THE END OF THIS CHAPTER, YOU SHOULD BE ABLE TO:

- Identify and understand the research design of a quantitative study.
- List the characteristics that differentiate the two major types of quantitative research.
- Distinguish among five common quantitative research designs based on their intents and procedures.
- Recognize the research design used in a quantitative research report.
- Evaluate the quality of the research design in a quantitative research report.

In this chapter, we focus our attention on examining studies that use a *quantitative* approach when implementing the process of research. Recall from Chapter 5 that researchers use quantitative research for different purposes. For example, consider the purposes found in the following brief descriptions of three quantitative studies.

- Musher-Eizenman et al. (2011) wanted to test the effect of an intervention where unusual foods were given fun names to see if the fun names caused young children to eat more of the foods than when they were called by their healthy names. The researchers decided on which days the fun name or the healthy name was used when the target foods were served to the children at one child care setting. They compared the amount of the unusual foods eaten when the group heard the fun names to the amount when the group heard the healthy names.
- Constantine et al. (2005) wanted to describe the extent to which the variables of perceived barriers and parental support predict levels of career certainty and career indecision for a group of African American high schools students. They administered questionnaires to the students to measure the four variables and then analyzed the data to determine whether the variables were related.
- Messinger (2011) wanted to describe the prevalence of intimate partner violence among same-sex couples in the United States. Using a large number of individuals that were representative of the general public, researchers gathered information about individuals' relationship histories and experiences, and analyzed them for overall trends for individuals who had same-sex relationships.

As these three examples illustrate, quantitative research studies can have different purposes, such as explaining the effect of an intervention, the relationships among variables, or the trends in a population. These examples also show that researchers may use different procedures. In one study, the researchers manipulated the conditions that the participants experienced (i.e., labeling food with a fun or healthy name), but the researchers did not manipulate the conditions in the other studies. The selection of participants for the study also differed across the examples: In one study, students at one child care setting participated, and in another a large number of participants were selected so that they were representative of a group (i.e., the general public). There are also some commonalities among the example studies, such as they all measured specific variables (e.g., amount of food eaten, career indecision, and relationship history).

As you read quantitative research reports, you need to understand the different ways that researchers conduct and report their quantitative studies. Quantitative researchers use a wide range of procedures for selecting participants and gathering and analyzing quantitative data, and we will learn more about these procedures in later chapters. To start, it is helpful to learn how researchers design a plan for their methods in quantitative studies. Researchers select an overall plan, called a *research design*, to guide their choices among all possible procedures that they could use. By knowing how to recognize the different research designs used in quantitative studies, you have a better understanding of how the particular methods and results follow from a study's purpose. In this chapter, you will learn about the different quantitative research designs and standards that you can use to evaluate the research designs used in quantitative studies.

How Do You Identify the Research Design in a Quantitative Study?

Recall from Chapter 1 that researchers choose a research design as an important step in the process of conducting research. A **research design** is a logical set of procedures that researchers use to collect, analyze, and report their data in a research study. They are considered logical, because all the different procedures fit together in a coherent way to address a specific kind of research purpose. In Chapter 2, you also learned that when the process of research involves quantitative research, then the researcher's procedures usually include deciding what to study; stating specific, narrow research questions or hypotheses; collecting numeric data from a large number of participants or time points; analyzing the numbers using statistics; and providing objective explanations about group differences, relationships, and trends among variables. From the concepts of research designs and quantitative research, we can advance the following definition: **Quantitative research designs** are logical sets of procedures for collecting, analyzing, and reporting numeric data to answer research questions and test hypotheses about specific variables.

Figure 6.1 summarizes the general characteristics of quantitative research (as introduced in Chapter 2), and indicates how research designs fit within this process of quantitative research. Researchers choose a specific quantitative research design based on their purpose for conducting research, such as to test the effect of an intervention on an outcome variable or to describe trends for certain variables in a population. Quantitative research designs, such as experiments or survey research, provide researchers with blueprints to guide how they select participants and collect, analyze, and report data in their studies so that they can address their specific research purposes.

Research designs are not always easy to identify within quantitative research reports, but in a well-written report, you will often find one or more sentences that explicitly identify the research design for the quantitative study. Because the research design provides the overall plan for the data collection and analysis procedures used in a study, information about the research design can generally be found in the Method section in the report. In some research reports, you find a discussion of the research design in its own subsection with a heading such as *Research Design*, *Study Design*, or *Methodology*. The research design may also be mentioned in the Abstract at the start of

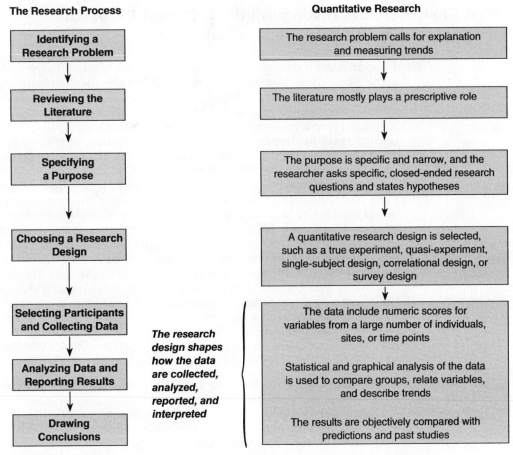

FIGURE 6.1 Research Designs in the Process of Quantitative Research

the study report. As examples, here are four statements where researchers explicitly named their research design (italics added for emphasis):

- "The current study was best characterized as a *quasi-experimental research design*" (Mun, Hew, & Cheung, 2009, p. 854).
- "A *single-subject research design* with a baseline phase (A1), treatment phase (B) and a follow-up phase (A2) was used in the current study (Ottenbacher, 1986; Domholdt, 2000)" (Gustafsson & Nilsson-Wikmar, 2008, p. 19).
- "The design of this study included a combination of *causal-comparative, correlational,* and *descriptive research* methods" (Clayton, 2011, p. 677).
- "Design. A *cross-sectional survey* was used" (Myers et al., 2011, p. 656).

By reading these short sentences, we quickly learn that the researchers used different designs in their studies such as a quasi-experiment design, single-subject design, correlational design, or cross-sectional survey design. Because there are many different research designs, a well-written quantitative research report includes supporting information about the design choice in addition to specifying which design has been chosen. Often this information includes references to literature that discusses the design to indicate that the researcher is knowledgeable about its use and an explanation as to why the particular design was selected.

Not all quantitative research reports specifically name the research design used. If the name is not provided, then you can deduce the type of design based on the procedures that the researcher used to conduct the study. Recall that a quantitative research design includes the procedures for selecting participants and collecting and analyzing quantitative data. The details about these procedures are found in the Method section of a report. Therefore, this section provides you with many clues as to what research design is used in a study. You will learn how to recognize and understand these clues in the rest of this chapter!

What Characteristics Distinguish the Different Research Designs Used in Quantitative Studies?

To understand the different research designs used in quantitative studies, it is helpful to know a little about how quantitative research has evolved over the years. The development of quantitative research designs has grown alongside the developments in statistical and measurement procedures. In the late 1800s, researchers began working out basic statistical procedures for relating variables and comparing groups. During this same time, researchers in fields such as psychology and agriculture developed procedures for using experimental and control groups, and researchers across many fields developed procedures for measuring variables and selecting individuals for research applications such as national polling efforts. By 1963, Campbell and Stanley had identified several major types of quantitative research designs; these designs' procedures, strengths, and weaknesses continue to be refined and expanded today (Campbell & Stanley, 1963; Kerlinger, 1964; Shadish, Cook, & Campbell, 2002). With the more recent invention of computer technology and its developments, quantitative research designs continue to evolve in terms of the sophistication and complexity of their procedures for using experimental groups, selecting participants, and analyzing quantitative data using statistics.

Many quantitative research designs have been developed and are in use today. They fall within two major categories: experimental research and nonexperimental research. **Experimental research** is used when a researcher intends to test the effect of an intervention by manipulating the conditions experienced by participants. **Nonexperimental research** is used when researchers intend to describe variables without manipulating the conditions experienced by participants. Thus, quantitative research designs differ in terms of:

- the intent (e.g., to test for cause and effect of an intervention or to describe variables),
- the use of manipulation (e.g., the researcher does or does not manipulate the conditions experienced by participants), and
- the procedures used (e.g., procedures for selecting participants, assigning them to groups, collecting data, and analyzing data).

These two major categories and the various research designs within each category can be used to identify the type of research design in most quantitative reports. In addition, by understanding the different procedures that are used, it is easier to assess the kinds of claims that can rightly be made at the conclusion of different quantitative research studies (e.g., claims that an independent variable caused an effect in a dependent variable and claims that the results generalize to a larger population). Let's consider these two categories of quantitative research designs in a little more detail.

Experimental quantitative research is used when the research purpose is to determine whether an independent treatment variable (e.g., taking a special medicine or not) causes an effect in a dependent outcome variable (e.g., feelings of depression). Part of the procedures is the manipulation of the conditions experienced by participants (e.g., determining when and how much of the special medicine is taken) and measurement of the dependent outcome variable after the treatment to determine whether an effect occurred. Experimental research is also referred to as *intervention research* because when the researchers manipulate the conditions, they are intervening in participants' lives in some way. Because the goal of experimental research is to make cause-and-effect claims, experimental research designs include procedures to enhance the researchers' ability to conclude that an independent variable caused an effect in a dependent variable at the end of the study. In good experimental research, the conditions experienced by the participants are carefully controlled (e.g., who takes the medicine, when it is taken, how much is taken, and what else is taken) so that the researchers can be more certain that it was the treatment variable that caused the measured effect and not some other confounding variable.

Table 6.1 provides a summary of several different types of experimental research designs found in the literature. As the table highlights, the experimental research designs differ in their specific intent and procedures, such as whether multiple groups are used, and if so, how individuals are assigned to those groups. When well implemented, experimental design procedures and their emphasis on control can provide strong to moderate evidence that an independent treatment variable caused an effect in another variable.

TABLE 6.1 Intent and Procedures for Different Types of Experimental Research Designs

Design Name	Other Names Used	Intent	Key Procedures*
True experiment	■ Experiment ■ Randomized controlled trial (RCT)	Most rigorous test to determine whether an independent treatment variable causes an effect in an outcome variable for many individuals	Individual participants are randomly assigned to the different levels of the treatment variable
Quasi-experiment	■ Experiment	Test whether an independent treatment variable causes an effect in an outcome variable for intact groups	Intact groups are assigned to the different levels of the treatment variable
Factorial design	■ 2 × 2 design ■ Solomon four group design	Test whether 2 or more independent variables (at least one being a treatment variable) cause an effect in an outcome variable	A type of true or quasi-experiment in which multiple independent categorical variables are considered, such as a treatment variable and gender
Pretest–Posttest design	■ One group design	Test whether a treatment causes an effect in an outcome variable for one group of participants	A weak type of quasi-experiment using only one group and in which the outcome variable is measured with a pretest and a posttest to compare the outcome before and after the treatment occurs
Time series design	■ Repeated measures design	Test whether treatment conditions cause an effect in an outcome variable over time for one group of participants	A type of quasi-experiment in which the outcomes for one group of participants are repeatedly measured before and after the treatment(s) occur to compare the outcomes at different time points
Single-subject design	■ N-of-1 research ■ ABA reversal design ■ Multiple baseline design	Test the effect of one or more treatment conditions on one or a few individual participants	The intervention is administered to only one or a few participants and data are repeatedly measured and graphed before, during, and after the intervention

*Because these are all experimental designs, the researcher manipulates the conditions experienced by participants in each design.

There are many research situations when it is not possible for the researcher to manipulate the conditions experienced by participants. For example, a researcher interested in studying race cannot assign participants to be Hispanic or African American. Likewise, a researcher interested in studying drug abuse could not ethically require some participants to abuse drugs. In these situations, researchers conduct nonexperimental research. Nonexperimental quantitative research is used to describe the extent to which specific variables are related to each other or to describe the trends for certain variables in a large population. In nonexperimental research, the researchers measure the variables of interest, but they do *not* manipulate the conditions experienced by participants. Nonexperimental research is also referred to as *descriptive* or *observational research* because the variables are described or observed as they happen to occur. Instead of focusing on manipulating and controlling the conditions, nonexperimental researchers focus attention on such procedures as carefully selecting the participants for the research. To describe trends in a large population, participants are selected so that they are representative of the population; in this way, strong claims can be made that the study results generalize to that population.

Table 6.2 provides a summary of several different types of nonexperimental research designs found in the literature. As the table highlights, these designs differ in their specific intents and procedures, such as how participants are selected and how often data are gathered. Even when the results of a nonexperimental design indicate that different variables are related to each other, you generally *cannot* conclude that one of the variables caused an effect in the other because of the lack of manipulation and lack of control in these designs. However, if the participants were selected to be representative of a larger population, nonexperimental studies do allow you to conclude that the results generalize to the population.

TABLE 6.2   Intent and Procedures for Different Types of Nonexperimental Research Designs

Design Name	Other Names Used	Intent	Key Procedures*
Correlational design	▪ Predictive design	Describe the extent to which predictor variables relate to outcome variables	Multiple variables are measured for each participant and statistics are used to determine the magnitude and direction of the associations among the variables
Causal-comparative design (Note! The name is misleading because this design does not determine cause and effect.)	▪ Comparative design	Describe how subgroups based on categories from a measured categorical variable compare (or differ) in terms of the outcome variables	The use of correlational design procedures to determine whether a categorical variable (e.g., gender) relates to one or more dependent variables (e.g., motivation) by statistically comparing the categories (e.g., men and women) to determine whether they differ in terms of the dependent variable(s)
Instrument validation design		Describe the quality of an instrument used to measure one or more variables	The use of correlational design procedures to determine the extent to which items on an instrument relate to each other and relate to other variables as expected
Meta-analysis	▪ Systematic review	Describe the extent to which variables are related as determined by many separate research studies	The use of correlational design procedures to gather and analyze the results from numerous completed research studies to determine the extent to which specific variables are related based on all of the completed studies
Survey design	▪ Cross-sectional design ▪ Descriptive research	Describe the trends for variables in a population	A sample is selected that is representative of the population and the variables are measured at one point in time
Longitudinal survey design		Describe the trends for variables over time for a population	The use of survey design procedures to select a sample that is representative of the population and measure the variables at multiple points in time
Secondary Analysis		Describe trends for variables in a population using an available large dataset	The use of survey design procedures to analyze data from a large dataset that was previously collected and use statistics to examine trends or relationships among specific variables of interest

*Because these are all nonexperimental designs, the researcher does *not* manipulate the conditions experienced by participants in any of the designs.

Unquestionably, it is a challenge to recognize and understand the many research designs listed in Tables 6.1 and 6.2 in terms of their different intents, uses of manipulation, and procedures. To help you navigate the many different quantitative research designs, we next provide an in-depth examination of five research designs commonly used today.

How Do You Understand Five Common Quantitative Research Designs?

Although many variations in quantitative research designs exist and new ones continue to be advanced and refined, there is a basic set of research designs used in most quantitative research. For this book, we focus on five common quantitative designs. Three of these designs are types of experimental research that involve the researcher manipulating the conditions experienced by participants. The other two are types of nonexperimental research, which do not involve the manipulation of conditions. As summarized in Figure 6.2, the five quantitative research designs that we consider are:

- true experiment design,
- quasi-experiment design,
- single-subject research design,
- correlational research design, and
- survey research design.

For each research design, we describe its intent and the characteristics that identify its use.

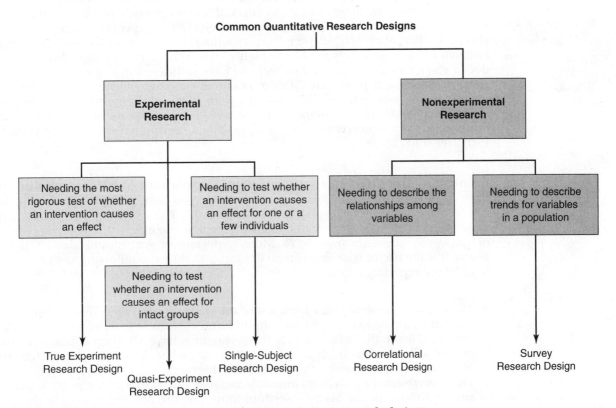

FIGURE 6.2 **Five Common Quantitative Research Designs and Their Use**

The True Experiment Research Design

We will examine three kinds of experimental research, the first of which is called a true experiment. In a **true experiment**, the researcher manipulates the conditions experienced by participants and uses a special procedure called random assignment to assign individual participants to the different levels of the treatment variable. *Random assignment* means that each person who participates in the study has an equal chance of being assigned to the treatment or control conditions. This procedure is used to control for confounding variables that might affect the outcomes. For example, a researcher might use a true experiment to test the use of email messages that encourage parents to read to their children (an intervention). She creates two conditions: one where parents receive weekly email messages about reading to their children (the treatment condition) and the other where parents receive weekly emails about general parenting tips (the control condition). The researcher randomly assigns each participating parent to one of the two conditions. By randomly assigning parents to the conditions, it is most likely that any differences among the parents such as their educational level or how many books they have at home will be evenly distributed between the two groups. Therefore, if the researcher finds that parents in the treatment condition read more to their children over the summer than those in the control condition, she can conclude that this difference is because of the treatment.

Researchers Use True Experiments When They Need to Be Certain That a Treatment Causes an Effect.

All types of experimental research are used when researchers want to establish probable cause and effect between their independent and dependent variables. Researchers use a true experiment when they want to be highly certain that the treatment caused the outcome because true experiments provide the best procedures for controlling all the variables that might influence the outcome. True experiments are sometimes called the "gold standard" for conducting quantitative research because the use of random assignment makes them the best designs for determining whether a treatment causes an effect. If it is not possible for the researchers to randomly assign individual participants to receive an intervention, then they must choose a different research design. True experiments are frequently used in medical research where researchers need to be highly certain that a treatment is effective (e.g., does a vaccine really prevent a disease?) and have sufficient funding to implement the random assignment procedures. Other examples of studies using true experiments include testing whether intensive coaching from caseworkers improves the prospects for employment for new immigrants (Joona & Nekby, 2012) or testing whether a reading summer camp intervention improves reading achievement of first-grade children (Schacter & Jo, 2005).

Identifying the Characteristics of a True Experiment in a Research Report.

True experiments are beneficial to read because you may find strong evidence for interventions to consider applying in your practice. You can note the use of a true experiment when researchers label their design as a *true experiment, intervention trial,* or *randomized controlled trial (RCT)*. More importantly, you should identify that a research study used a true experiment design by finding the following key characteristics in the report:

- **The research problem called for a test of an intervention.** When reading the Introduction of a true experiment, you should find that there is a need for improving outcomes for individuals and that the researchers have an intervention that they believe will cause outcomes to improve. The researcher should state a research purpose that focuses on testing the effect of the intervention.
- **The experimental researcher randomly assigned individual participants to different conditions.** In the Method section, note how the researcher assigns the participants to the different treatment groups. In a true experiment, the researcher uses random assignment to assign each individual to a group (e.g., treatment or

control), which means that each person has an equal chance of being assigned to any group. This random assignment of individuals is essential. If a researcher does not randomly assign each individual participant, then the design is not a true experiment.

- *The experimental researcher manipulated the conditions experienced by participants.* The Method section of a true experiment should also include information describing the intervention (or treatment) and how the researcher manipulates the conditions so that different participants have different experiences. For example, a researcher may provide special nutritional information to new mothers in the treatment group and the standard information about newborn care to new mothers in a control group. A control group is an experimental group that receives the "usual" experience instead of a special intervention.
- *The experimental researcher statistically compared the groups in terms of the outcome variables.* How the researcher gathered and analyzed the data can be found in the Method section. In a true experiment, the researcher measures the outcome variables of interest (e.g., health of infants at 6 months) for each group and uses statistical procedures to test for differences among the groups. The results of these comparisons are placed in the Results section.
- *Strong claims about whether the treatment caused an effect can be made.* Procedures such as random assignment are designed so that a true experiment includes a high level of control for confounding variables. This means that the only difference between the groups is the treatment and everything else is as equal as possible. Therefore, when reading the Conclusion section of a true experiment that found a difference between groups, you can expect the researcher to make strong claims that the treatment caused the measured effect.

An Example of a True Experiment Study.   Unger, Faure, and Frieg (2006) used a true experiment to study the effect of an 8-week training program on gait and perceptions of body image. Their participants included 31 adolescents with spastic cerebral palsy from one school. The researchers randomly assigned the participants to one of two groups: treatment or control. For the 21 individuals assigned to the treatment group, the researchers provided an 8-week program that included specially designed physical exercises. No special training was provided to the individuals in the control group during the study. The researchers measured the participants' gait and perceptions of body image at the beginning of the study and after the 8-week program was complete. They statistically compared the scores for the two groups, and found that the treatment group's scores for gait and perceptions of body image improved more than those from the control group. Therefore, the authors concluded that the school-based strength-training program caused improvements in participants' gait and perceptions of body image.

This true experiment illustrates a study seeking to establish that a school-based strength-training program (the cause) improves gait and perceptions of body image (the effects) for adolescents with spastic cerebral palsy from one school. The authors randomly assigned participants to groups and manipulated the conditions experienced by the participants (some received the program, some did not). They measured the dependent variables after the treatment was complete and used statistical procedures to compare groups based on their scores. They used the differences in the results to conclude that the treatment caused specific outcomes.

What Do You Think?

Suppose you are reading a collection of research articles related to the problem of childhood obesity. Why might one of the studies have used a true experiment to study this topic? What characteristics would you expect to find in the report of this study?

Check Your Understanding

A researcher would use a true experiment to test whether an intervention, such as setting a daily goal of 10,000 steps and wearing a pedometer during the day, causes an effect, such as healthier weights for middle school girls. In this study, we expect the researcher to identify a large number of participants, such as girls from across an urban area. She would randomly assign each participating girl to one of the experimental groups. The researcher would manipulate the experiences of the groups such as (a) by giving a pedometer to the girls in the treatment group and asking them to try to reach a goal of 10,000 steps each day and (b) by not providing a pedometer to the girls in the control group. The researcher would measure the outcome variable by measuring each girl's weight after the intervention was complete and compare the changes in weight between the two groups. From this study, the researcher might conclude that an intervention that asks individuals to set a goal and use a pedometer to track that goal causes the adolescent girls in this study to obtain healthier weights.

How might a true experiment study be used to study a topic of interest to you?

The Quasi-Experiment Research Design

As you read different experimental reports, notice that in some studies the researchers test the effect of an intervention, but are unable to randomly assign individuals to the different treatment groups. This often occurs when researchers use groups that exist naturally (such as residents living in a neighborhood) or are already formed (such as students grouped into classrooms). The research designs in these studies are called quasi-experiments because they lack the random assignment required by true experiments. A **quasi-experiment** is a type of experimental research design in which the researcher tests an intervention using intact groups of individuals. The researcher assigns *existing groups* to the different conditions, but does *not randomly assign individuals* because groups cannot be artificially created for the experiment. For example, in an experimental study of a new math program, the researcher may need to use existing fourth-grade classes and designate one class as the experimental group and one as the control group. Randomly assigning students to the two groups is not possible because it would disrupt classroom learning. Instead, the researcher makes the assignment at the classroom level by assigning which class gets which condition (e.g., treatment or control). Because quasi-experiments make use of existing groups, they are more straightforward for researchers to conduct. The use of intact groups, however, is a weakness of this design because it introduces the possibility of other influences that might affect the outcomes. For example, suppose the teacher assigned to use the new math program also happened to be using a special program to get parents involved with their children's homework. If the students in his class performed better than the control group, we cannot know if it was because of the new math program or because of the parents' involvement. Therefore, quasi-experiments are only able to provide moderate to weak conclusions about the treatment causing a measured effect.

> **Here's a Tip!**
>
> It can be a challenge to distinguish between true and quasi-experiments because authors may use the term *random assignment* in both. If each individual is randomly assigned to a condition, then it is a true experiment. If the random assignment is made to a few existing groups, then it is a quasi-experiment.

Researchers Use Quasi-Experiments to Determine the Effect of a Treatment for Intact Groups. When you read the report of a quasi-experiment, the focus on determining whether a treatment causes the desired effect is readily apparent. The quasi-experiment is used as the research design when the researchers intend to test the treatment with intact groups. Common examples of intact groups include students in specific classes, members of certain clubs, or counselors working in specific clinics. Because many research situations call for using intact groups, quasi-experimental designs are frequently reported. Examples of studies that used a quasi-experiment include a study that tested whether playing live music increased patient satisfaction in the waiting room of a health clinic by comparing patients at the clinic on different days (Silverman, Christenson, Golden, & Chaput-McGovern, 2012), and a study that tested whether a special reading program affected children's alphabet knowledge and vocabulary development by comparing students in one preschool that used the program to those attending another preschool that used usual practices (Gonzalez et al., 2011).

Identifying the Characteristics of a Quasi-Experiment in a Research Report.
You will likely find examples of studies that used a quasi-experiment design while reading the literature. Although quasi-experiments cannot make as strong of claims about cause and effect as can true experiments, they do provide useful evidence of interventions that work within naturally occurring groups like those found in your own practice setting. In some quasi-experiment reports, authors refer to their research design generically as an *experiment*. This means that you need to recognize the identifying characteristics to determine whether it is a true or quasi-experiment. You can identify the use of a quasi-experiment by noting the following key characteristics:

- *The research problem called for a test of an intervention.* In the Introduction of a quasi-experiment, the author argues that a specific intervention is needed to improve the outcomes for groups of individuals. The researcher states a purpose that focuses on testing the effects of the intervention to address this need.
- *The experimental researcher used intact groups of participants.* In the Method section of a quasi-experimental study, you learn that the researcher tested the intervention with participants who were already within existing groups (e.g., members of a class or individuals present in a location) because it is not practical or possible to assign individuals randomly to the different conditions.
- *The experimental researcher manipulated the conditions experienced by the groups.* Although existing groups are used in a quasi-experiment, the researcher still manipulates the conditions that are experienced by the individuals in the groups. For example, a researcher may manipulate conditions by having students in one first-grade class receive healthy snacks at break time and those in another class receive the usual cookie. You can find the description of the different conditions in the report's Method section.
- *The experimental researcher statistically compared the groups in terms of the outcome variables.* The Method section of a quasi-experiment report describes how the researcher measured the outcome(s) of interest (e.g., children's attitudes about fruits and vegetables) and statistically compared the scores for the individuals in the different groups. Because quasi-experiments do not control extraneous variables with random assignment, researchers often report that they measured additional control variables that might influence the outcome, such as parents' attitudes about serving fruits and vegetables. The Results section includes statistical results for comparing the groups in terms of the dependent and control variables.
- *No more than moderate claims about whether the treatment caused an effect can be made.* In the Results and Conclusion sections of a quasi-experiment study, you should notice whether a difference in outcomes was found between the groups. Even if a difference is found, at best the researchers only can make moderate claims that the treatment caused the measured effect because they cannot account for all other variables that may have influenced the outcome.

An Example of a Quasi-Experiment Research Study.
Elliott, Henderson, Nixon, and Wight (2013) used a quasi-experiment design to study the impact of a special school-based sexual health education curriculum on teenage adolescents' sexual health knowledge, attitudes, and behaviors. Students at 12 schools participated in the research. Six schools in one area were selected to receive the intervention and the researchers selected 6 other schools to serve as controls for comparison. Students in the assigned schools completed the special curriculum and those in the comparison schools received the usual health information. The researchers measured a range of dependent variables (e.g., sexual health knowledge, attitudes, and behaviors) and control variables (e.g., gender and socioeconomic level). The variables were assessed the year before

the treatment was implemented as a control and each of 2 years after the curriculum was taught. Using a variety of statistical analyses to compare the students in the two conditions, they found that the curriculum had some positive effects, such as increasing students' sexual health knowledge.

This study illustrates an example of a quasi-experiment study. The researchers assigned students to receive the intervention or control condition by intact groups (i.e., by schools). The researchers compared the groups in terms of the dependent variables, while statistically controlling for other variables that may have also influenced the outcomes. They conducted the research to test whether the curriculum affected students as expected.

What Do You Think?

Suppose you are reading a collection of research articles related to the problem of childhood obesity. Why might one of the studies have used a quasi-experiment design to study this topic? What characteristics would you expect to find in the report of this study?

Check Your Understanding

A researcher might use a quasi-experiment to study the effect of an intervention, such as increasing the amount of weekly recess time, on intact groups, such as students in third-grade classes. In this research, we would expect to find that the purpose of the study is to test the effect of daily recess time on dependent outcome variables, such as student attentiveness and misbehaviors. The study would use intact groups (such as three existing third-grade classrooms), and the researcher would manipulate the conditions by having the classes experience different conditions such as the following: one class receives two recess periods every day, one class receives one recess period every day, and one class serves as the control, receiving the usual two recess periods per week. After the treatment conditions had been applied for several weeks, the researcher measures the dependent outcome variables for the students in each of the groups and compares the groups to determine whether increasing recess time affects student behaviors.

How do you think a quasi-experiment could be used to study a topic of interest to you?

The Single-Subject Research Design

Not all interventions are appropriate to use with large numbers of participants in groups. In some studies, the researcher wants to experimentally test an intervention for just one or a few individuals. **Single-subject research** is a quantitative research design that involves the study of single individuals, the administration of an intervention, and the careful monitoring of the individuals' behaviors before, during, and after the intervention to determine whether the treatment affects the behavior. For example, Cihak, Kessler, and Alberto (2008) tested whether individual students with intellectual disabilities in a community vocational setting who were prompted by a handheld prompting system (an intervention) were able to independently transition between tasks (a behavior). This design does not include random assignment to a group; it focuses on the study of single individuals rather than groups of participants. In contrast to true and quasi-experiments that use a control group for comparison with a treatment group, the individual becomes his/her own "control" in a single-subject experiment in which the researcher collects many measurements of his/her behavior over time.

Researchers Use Single-Subject Designs When They Want to Affect an Individual.   Researchers use single-subject designs when they need to determine whether an intervention affects the behavior of a single participant or a few participants. This design requires that the researcher observe the person's behavior over time, such as before and during the intervention. By observing the individual over a prolonged period of time and recording the behavior before, during, and even after the intervention, the researcher assesses whether the treatment causes a change in the target behavior or outcome. Researchers can use this design to target multiple behaviors of one individual, such as the verbal responses of a student who is selectively mute in three different school settings (Beare, Torgerson, & Creviston, 2008). Researchers may also test the affect of an intervention on several individuals by staggering when the intervention is administered to each one. This approach was used in the study of the handheld prompting system mentioned earlier. Cihak et al. (2008) administered the intervention to each of four individuals over time to show that changes in transition behavior for each individual were clearly associated with the time when the intervention started.

Identifying the Characteristics of Single-Subject Research in a Research Report.   In addition to the term *single-subject research*, you may find that researchers refer to this design as *N-of-1 research*, *applied behavior analysis*, or *multiple baseline design*. Authors also use letters to indicate variants of this design, such as *ABAB single-subject design*, where *A* stands for baseline measurements made without the intervention and *B* stands for measurements made during the intervention. A single-subject research report can also be identified if it has the following characteristics:

- *The research problem called for an intervention to change a behavior that is a problem for an individual.* In the Introduction of a single-subject study, the author argues that one or more individuals have a behavioral problem that requires an intervention to improve their life in some way. The researcher states a research purpose that focuses on testing an intervention for the individual to address this need.
- *The experimental researcher studied a single individual or a few individuals who would benefit from a change in behavior.* The description of the participant(s) in the study is in the Method section of the report. The participants include only a small number of individuals, often as few as one. The participants are individuals who would clearly benefit if the intervention improved the outcomes of interest.
- *The experimental researcher established a baseline of behavior and then manipulated the conditions experienced by the individual.* In the Method section of a single-subject study, note that the researcher usually establishes a stable baseline of information about the individual's behavior before administering the intervention. A stable baseline means that the individual's behavior varies little over several sessions or days. The researcher then administers an intervention and continues to repeatedly measure the outcome behavior for the individual. In some studies, the researcher removes and reapplies the intervention to verify that it is the cause of any measured effects in the outcome behavior.
- *The researcher plotted the individual's behavior over many points of time on a graph and visually inspected the data for change.* In the Method and Results section of a single-subject report, note that the researcher emphasizes using graphs to analyze the gathered data instead of the use of statistics. It is typical for the researcher to have plotted the patterns of behavior over time on a graph and visually inspected the pattern in the data. This pattern may be ascending, descending, flat, or variable. In particular, expect the researcher to note how the behavior of the individual changed during the intervention, after withdrawing the intervention, or during multiple interventions.
- *Strong claims about whether the treatment caused a meaningful change in the individual's behavior can be made.* The conclusions of a single-subject research study focus on whether the participant's behavior meaningfully changed and whether this change was caused by the intervention. Because of the high level of control of when and how the intervention was administered, the single-subject researcher often makes strong claims of cause and effect in the Conclusion section.

An Example of a Single-Subject Research Study.   Kern et al. (2007) used a single-subject research design to study the impact of the use of songs in assisting two young children with autism transition into their inclusive childcare classrooms each morning. The treatment was the use of a morning greeting song composed by a music therapist for each child. The outcomes of interest included five specific behaviors, such as greeting the teacher or indicating goodbye to the caregiver. The researchers established a baseline for each child by measuring the number of successful behaviors completed for 6 days. They continued to monitor the five behaviors when the intervention was administered, removed, and then reinstated. The resulting graphs of each child's behavior clearly demonstrate that their morning routine behaviors were improved on days when the music therapy intervention was in place.

This study illustrates an example of single-subject research. The researchers wanted to affect the behavior of individual children and applied a treatment (the morning song) to each on an individual basis. Numerous observations were recorded before, during, and without the intervention to establish evidence for its effect on each child's behavior. The researchers graphed the resulting data for each child and analyzed it visually, without the use of statistics.

What Do You Think?

Suppose you are reading a collection of research articles related to the problem of childhood obesity. Why might one of the studies have used a single-subject design to study this topic? What characteristics would you expect to find in the report of this study?

Check Your Understanding

A researcher would use a single-subject design to study the impact of an intervention on an individual, such as the effect of a system that requires peddling a bicycle-like machine to turn on a video game for a child who is severely overweight. In such a study, the researcher is interested in increasing the amount of physical activity in which the child engages on a daily basis. Baseline physical activity data could be collected for several days while the child has access to his usual video game. Then the game could be replaced with the version that requires that the child peddle to make the game turn on. The researcher would continue to observe the amount of physical activity on a daily basis with the intervention, then with it removed, and then with it reapplied. The researcher would then graph this data to determine whether the intervention caused a change in the child's physical activity behavior.

How might a single-subject design be used to study a topic of interest to you?

The Correlational Research Design

There are many situations in which researchers are unable or uninterested in manipulating conditions by administering an intervention. In these situations, the researcher has likely used a correlational research design to describe the association or relation between two or more variables without manipulating what individuals are experiencing. **Correlational research designs** are nonexperimental procedures in quantitative research in which investigators measure the degree of association (or relationship) between two or more variables using the statistical procedures of correlational analysis. This degree of association, expressed as a number, indicates the extent to which the two variables are or are not related, or the extent that one can predict another. To study correlations, the researcher studies a group of participants and treats them all in the same way rather than administering different conditions to two or more groups as in most experiments. In this design, researchers do not attempt to control or manipulate the variables; instead, they use correlation statistics to relate two or more scores gathered for each participant, such as a score for motivation and a score for achievement. Correlational researchers can conclude that two variables are related to each other, such as when higher motivation scores tend to be associated with higher performance scores. They cannot, however, conclude cause and effect because these designs lack the control found in experimental research. That is, a correlational design *cannot* determine whether higher motivation causes students to perform better or higher performance causes students to be more motivated; it can only conclude that the two variables are related to each other.

Researchers Use Correlational Research When They Need to Describe the Relationships Among Variables. Researchers choose to use a correlational research design when they aim to describe the relationship between two or more variables. Correlational researchers are interested in the relationships among many different types of variables, such as the relationship between children's use of the Internet and cognitive development (Johnson, 2010), the relationship among attitudinal factors and a person's intentions to recycle at home (Fornara, Carrus, Passafaro, & Bonnes, 2011), and the relationship between violent behaviors and life satisfaction (Valois, Paxton, Zullig, & Huebner, 2006). This design allows researchers to describe the variables that predict a dependent variable. For example, Sciarra and Ambrosino (2011) studied whether student, parent, and teacher expectations gathered during high school predicted the students' postsecondary educational status 2 years later.

Identifying the Characteristics of Correlational Research in a Research Report. Correlational research is probably the most common type of quantitative research. Perhaps because it is so common, researchers often do not refer to this design by name. However, sometimes studies using this design can be identified by correlational terms such as *correlation*, *association*, or *prediction*. Research studies that use a correlational design share the following characteristics:

- *The research problem called for describing the relationship among variables that cannot readily be manipulated.* In the Introduction of a correlational study, note that the author usually argues that there is a need to understand how specific variables are related to, associated with, or predict one another. The researcher states a purpose that focuses on describing the relationships among the variables to address this need.
- *The correlational researcher studied one group of participants.* Information on the study's participants is presented in the Method section. In a correlational study, the researcher selects a group of participants that are convenient and that should provide a wide range of responses for the variables of interest, such as the students in one school or the families in one area. Individuals are not assigned to groups in a correlational research study.
- *The correlational researcher collected information for each variable.* In the Method section, you can find information focused on how each variable of interest was measured. The correlational researcher collects a score for each variable from each of the participants without manipulating the experiences of the participants.
- *The correlational researcher statistically analyzed the data to test for relationships.* A correlational researcher uses a wide range of statistical procedures (e.g., correlation, multiple regression, structural equation modeling) to test for relationships among variables, and these analytic procedures are described in the Method section. The researcher is interested in determining the tendency or pattern for two (or more) variables or two sets of data to vary consistently. For example, when time spent studying goes up, scores on the final exam tend to go up; therefore, these variables covary and have a positive relationship. It might also be true that as students' anxiety about a test increases, their final exam scores tend to go down. These two variables have a negative relationship. When reading the Results section, you can find results about these relationships as well as tables and graphs that display information about the relationships among variables.

■ *Claims are limited to the extent to which variables are related to each other; claims of cause and effect are not warranted.* Researchers that used a correlational design *cannot* correctly conclude that some variables *cause* an effect in other variables because they did not use random assignment or manipulate the conditions (as in an experimental design). Therefore, the Conclusion section in a correlational study report should not imply that one variable caused a change in the other. For example, a researcher could find that an increase in attendance at swimming pools is related to an increase in domestic violence incidences. However, it is not the case that swimming causes domestic violence (or vice versa). Instead, these variables are related because both increase when the temperature goes up. That is, variables can be related without one causing an effect in the other. Unfortunately, some researchers err by making cause-and-effect claims in their correlational reports, which is why you should identify the research design that was used in a study so you can correctly make your own conclusions!

An Example of a Correlational Research Study. Viana et al.'s (2012) study of predictors of nonmedical use of prescription drugs by 6th- to 12th-grade students is an example of correlational research. The study sought to identify if certain variables (such as race, grade level, anxiety, and prior substance use) predict whether students are more likely to have used prescription drugs for recreational purposes. The researchers studied one group of 6,790 students in one state. All participants completed a set of questionnaires that assessed the variables of interest to the researchers. Once the data were gathered, the researchers used correlation and multiple regression statistical procedures to determine that several variables, including delinquency-related behaviors, age, and substance use, together were significant predictors of nonmedical use of prescription drugs by the youth.

This correlational research illustrates a study of the relationships among variables for a group of participants. The researchers did not attempt to change students' drug use behaviors. Instead, they wanted to understand the relationship among various demographic and social variables and nonmedical use of prescription drugs. The researchers used analysis procedures to statistically test for relationships among the variables.

What Do You Think?

Suppose you are reading a collection of research articles related to the problem of childhood obesity. Why might one of the studies have used a correlational research design to study this topic? What characteristics would you expect to find in the report of this study?

Check Your Understanding

A researcher might use a correlational research design to examine the relationship among variables, such as describing the variables that relate to unhealthy weights for children. We would expect the researcher to study a single group (such as second-graders in one school). The researcher would identify variables she expects to be related to a child's weight, such as the child's family income, parent's education status, self-esteem, age, and height. The researcher would gather information about each variable for every child and analyze the data to determine which variables are best at predicting an unhealthy weight. This study would not determine which factors cause obesity, but it could uncover variables useful for identifying children who may be at a greater risk for developing obesity.

How might correlational research be used to study a topic of interest to you?

The Survey Research Design

In some quantitative research, the investigators focus on describing trends in a large population of individuals rather than relating variables or testing an intervention. In this case, it is likely that the researchers used a survey research design. **Survey research designs** are nonexperimental quantitative procedures that researchers use to administer a survey questionnaire to a smaller group of people (called the *sample*) in order to describe trends in attitudes, opinions, behaviors, or characteristics of a larger group of people (called the *population*). A hallmark of this design is that the researchers carefully select people to study to ensure that they are representative of a larger population that is of interest. For example, if researchers want to describe the risky behaviors of high school students in a school district (the population), then they might carefully select boys and girls that represent all high school grades and each school in the district (the sample). By gathering questionnaire data from a sample of individuals who are representative of a population, the researchers are able to make conclusions about trends in the population as a whole based on the results from the sample.

> *Here's a Tip!*
>
> The word *survey* is used extensively in quantitative research reports. Often it refers to a type of questionnaire used to gather data. Any quantitative study can use a survey questionnaire to gather data. In contrast, a *survey research design* includes procedures for who to study, how to collect and analyze data, and how to report results.

Researchers Use Survey Research When They Need to Describe Trends in a Population. Researchers choose to use survey research designs when they need to describe trends in a population to understand a research problem. For example, researchers might study trends such as community opinions about school bond issues or social workers' attitudes about foster care. Researchers also use this design to determine opinions about policy issues, such as whether job training should be a requirement for housing support. Researchers use survey research designs to identify important beliefs and behaviors of individuals at one point in time, such as early adolescents' reading habits (Creel, 2007), interior design students' attitudes toward environmental issues (Ruff & Olson, 2009), and the general public's awareness of and knowledge about palliative care services in Japan (Hirai et al., 2011). Survey research designs are also used to describe trends over time, such as trends in undergraduate students' alcohol consumption measured every 2 years from 2002 to 2008 (Bulmer et al., 2010). Researchers describe trends in attitudes and behaviors by gathering data from a group of individuals and then analyzing that data to identify average opinions, the prevalence of behaviors, or the range of attitudes held by individuals.

Identifying the Characteristics of a Survey Research Design in a Research Report. Researchers use different names to refer to the use of a survey research design, including *descriptive research* or *population study*. Survey research designs can be difficult to distinguish because researchers using any of the quantitative research designs often refer to their questionnaires for gathering data as a "survey." Therefore, locating the term *survey* in a report does not tell you that a study used a survey research design. To identify this design, you need to locate the following key characteristics in the report:

- *The research problem called for describing the attitudes, opinions, or behaviors of a large group.* In the Introduction of a survey research design study, you learn that there is a need to know how a group of people in society (a population) thinks or acts. The researcher states that the purpose of the research is to describe the attitudes, opinions, or behaviors of the identified group.
- *The survey researcher selected a large number of participants who are representative of the group.* In a survey research design, the procedures used to select participants are of utmost importance because the primary goal is to generalize the results from the participants to the whole population of interest. Therefore, the survey researcher wants to obtain a sample of people to study who are representative of the larger group. The Method section indicates how the researcher selected the participants. The best procedure for obtaining a representative sample occurs when the researcher randomly selects participants from a list of all members of the group. A survey researcher also typically selects a large number of participants so that the results are more likely to represent those of the population.

- *The survey researcher used a survey questionnaire to gather information from the participants.* When reading the Method section of a survey research study, you also find extensive information about the survey questionnaire that the researcher used to gather the data from the selected participants. This information describes the items included on the survey questionnaire to gather data about the attitudes, opinions, or behaviors of interest and how it was administered to all of the study participants in a way that encourages a high number of them to respond.
- *The survey researcher analyzed the data for trends.* In the Method and Results sections of a survey research study, you learn that the researcher analyzes the data primarily to describe trends such as the average responses, the most common responses, and the range of responses. The results may also include analyses that compare subgroups or relate variables, but the primary focus is on describing trends in the larger population.
- *Strong claims about trends in the larger population can be made.* A researcher who uses a survey research design is interested in making claims that the results from the study generalize to the larger population. In the study's Conclusion section, expect these claims to be strongly stated if the researcher selected the study sample so that it was representative of the larger population. The strongest claims that the results generalize to the larger population can be made when the researcher used random selection.

An Example of a Survey Research Study.   Abril and Gault (2006) used survey research to describe elementary principals' opinions about elementary music education. They obtained a list of all elementary principals who belong to a major national organization and randomly selected 350 individuals' names from the list. They mailed a survey questionnaire to each selected person and 61 percent of them returned a completed form. The researchers analyzed the data to describe what principals think elementary children should do in music class, what the curricular goals should be, and what barriers they perceive to elementary music education.

This study illustrates a survey research design. The researchers aimed to provide a general description of how elementary principals currently think about music education. They carefully selected a sample using procedures to ensure that participants would likely represent the opinions of all principals. The researchers gathered information about principals' opinions and reported a description of the trends in their responses.

What Do You Think?

Suppose you are reading a collection of research articles related to the problem of childhood obesity. Why might one of the studies have used a survey research design to study this topic? What characteristics would you expect to find in the report of this study?

Check Your Understanding

A researcher might use a survey research design to describe the attitudes, opinions, or behaviors of a group, such as school nurses' attitudes about children's weight within a particular state. In this study, the researcher may begin by acquiring a list of all school nurses in the state and randomly selecting a large number of them to participate in the study. The researcher would design a survey questionnaire that asks questions about the nurses' attitudes, such as "To what extent do you think obesity is a problem for children?" After the data are gathered, the researcher analyses the data to describe the trends in the responses and makes conclusions about how all school nurses in the state think about the issue of children's weight.

Now, how might a survey research design be used to study a topic of interest to you?

How Do You Recognize the Research Design in a Quantitative Research Report?

You have now reviewed five quantitative research designs, including why researchers use them and their key characteristics. With this information, you can figure out the research designs that were used in most quantitative studies. The following four steps can help identify a study's quantitative research design:

1. *Look to see if the author named the design in the title or abstract of the report.* Researchers often name the study's research design in the title and abstract of the study report. For example, note how the following titles indicate the research design that was used:
   - "What Do You Want to Tell Us About Reading? A Survey of the Habits and Attitudes of Urban Middle School Students" (Hughes-Hassell & Lutz, 2006)
   - "Kindergarteners' Entrée Intake Increases When Served a Larger Entrée Portion in School Lunch: A Quasi-Experiment" (Ramsay et al., 2013)
2. *Examine the purpose statement to see if it names or suggests the study's research design.* Researchers select their research designs to match their studies' purposes. When you read the Introduction section, notice whether the authors include the name of the research design in their purpose statement. If not, the purpose statement can provide clues about the study's research design. For example, if the purpose is to test the impact of an intervention, then the researchers likely used an experiment. If the purpose is to identify variables that predict certain behaviors or attitudes, then the researchers likely used a correlational design. If the purpose is to describe trends in a population, then the researchers likely used a survey design.
3. *Read the beginning paragraphs of the Method section and look for a statement that identifies the design.* Sometimes quantitative researchers name and describe the overall research design at the start of the Method section. You can look for a subsection labeled with a heading such as *Study Design* to locate this description if it is included.
4. *Examine the procedures described within the Method and Results sections.* Quantitative researchers often do not name their designs in their reports. When this occurs, look for procedures that suggest a specific research design as you read the Method and Results sections. A good strategy is to first consider whether the study used an experimental or nonexperimental approach, and then consider the specific design within that approach. You can use the following questions to help identify the key procedures. The designs typically associated with the use of each procedure are indicated within parentheses.
   - Did the researcher manipulate the conditions by providing a treatment to individuals (true, quasi-, or single-subject experimental design) or collect data without manipulating the conditions experienced by participants (correlational or survey nonexperimental design)?
   - Did the researcher study two or more groups (true or quasi-experiment), one group (correlational or survey design), or one or a few individuals (single-subject design)?
   - Did the researcher randomly assign individuals to different conditions (true experiment) or assign intact groups to different conditions (quasi-experiment)?
   - Did the researcher randomly select individuals to participate (usually survey design) or use individuals who were conveniently available (usually experiments or correlational design)?
   - Was the focus of the data analysis on comparing groups (usually true or quasi-experiment), inspecting graphs of an individual's data (single-subject design), describing the relationship among variables (usually correlational design), or describing trends (usually survey design)?

Here's a Tip!

Some quantitative studies use procedures that seem to fit multiple designs, such as randomly selecting participants (typical of survey research) and randomly assigning them to treatment conditions (typical of a true experiment). When this occurs, first, focus on the study's intent, second, determine whether the use of manipulation occurred, and third, consider the other procedures when naming the overall design.

What Do You Think?

Consider the following abstract from a published study about African American adolescents' career issues. Which quantitative research design did the authors use and what is your evidence?

This study examined the extent to which perceived occupational barriers and perceived parental support predicted career certainty and career indecision in a sample of African American adolescents. Perceived occupational barriers were positively predictive of career indecision, and perceived parental support was positively associated with career certainty. The results provided support for the importance of considering contextual variables, such as perceived occupational barriers and perceived parental support, in the career decision-making processes of African American adolescents. The results also highlighted the salience of social cognitive career theory in conceptualizing career-related issues in African American high school students. Future research directions are discussed. (Constantine et al., 2005, p. 307)

Check Your Understanding

This study is an example of a quantitative study using a nonexperimental correlational research design. Evidence for this design includes that the researchers: (a) did not manipulate the conditions and did not provide a treatment, (b) studied one group of African American high school students, (c) intended to describe how some variables predict (or relate to) other variables, and (d) discussed results in terms of positive associations between variables.

How Do You Evaluate the Research Design in a Quantitative Study?

Recognizing the design used in a quantitative study is an important step to understanding and evaluating its report. We discuss the details of the procedures used for participant selection, data collection, and data analysis in quantitative research in Chapters 7 and 8. For now you can focus on evaluating the overall design used in a quantitative research study. Keep in mind that in a good, rigorous quantitative study, the research design matches the purpose, and the methods of collecting, analyzing, and reporting data match the selected design. A good, rigorous report makes it clear that the researcher had a reason for selecting the design for the study, and that this design is identified, explained, and provided a good overall plan for conducting the study. In addition, the claims that the researcher makes at the end of the study need to be consistent with the overall research design used. Table 6.3 lists criteria that are useful to consider when evaluating the research design in a report of a quantitative study. This table also provides indicators of higher quality and lower quality for the criteria to help you make your own judgments when evaluating a research report.

Use the rating scale in Figure 6.3 to apply the quality criteria to the research design used in any quantitative research report. For each of the criteria you locate, assign a quality rating from *fair* (1) to *excellent* (3) and document your evidence and/or reasoning behind the rating. If one of the criteria is missing or very poorly stated, then indicate *poor* (0) as your rating. Quantitative research reports vary in the extent of discussion included about the research design, but good reports should still describe the procedures used and score well on most of the items listed in Figure 6.3. By adding up the rating scores for each of the criteria and using the suggested cutoff values provided at the bottom of the figure, you have a quantitative measure to help you determine your overall assessment of a report's quantitative research design.

TABLE 6.3 Criteria for Evaluating the Research Design in a Quantitative Research Report

Quality Criteria	Indicators of Higher Quality	Indicators of Lower Quality
The Key Elements		

1. The choice of the research design is appropriate and justified.	+ The design fits the study's intent, such as:
	  ■ To test the impact of an intervention in a true experiment, quasi-experiment, or single-subject experiment design;
	  ■ To describe the relationship among multiple variables in a correlational design; or
	  ■ To describe trends for variables in a population in a survey design.
	+ A convincing explanation for why the specific research design was selected is provided.
		− There is a mismatch among the study's intent and research design or no logical design appears to have guided the plans for the study's procedures.
		− The explanation for why the specific research design was selected is unconvincing or unclear.

2. Good quantitative procedures are used to select and assign participants.	+ If the researchers want to test for cause and effect, then they randomly *assign* individuals to the treatment conditions when possible. + If the researchers want to generalize the results to a population, then they randomly *select* individuals to participate when possible. (We will learn more about this in Chapter 7.)	− The procedures for assigning participants to conditions are inappropriate for the design. − The procedures for selecting participants are inappropriate for the design. (We will learn more about this in Chapter 7.)
3. Good quantitative data collection procedures are used.	+ The procedures for collecting the data, such as when and how often, are appropriate for the design. + Rigorous quantitative data collection procedures are used. (We will learn more about this in Chapter 7.)	− The procedures for collecting the data are inappropriate for the design. − Poor quantitative data collection procedures are used. (We will learn more about this in Chapter 7.)
4. Good quantitative data analysis procedures are used.	+ The procedures for analyzing the data, such as comparing groups, relating variables, describing trends, or inspecting graphs, are appropriate for the design. + Rigorous quantitative data analysis procedures are used. (We will learn more about this in Chapter 8.)	− The procedures for analyzing the data are inappropriate for the design. − Poor quantitative data analysis procedures are used. (We will learn more about this in Chapter 8.)

5. Good quantitative results and conclusions are reported.	+ The reported results are appropriate and complete for the design. (We will learn more about this in Chapter 8.)
	+ Claims made are appropriate for the design. For example:
	  ■ claims of cause and effect are made in studies with high levels of control (e.g., true experiments) and
	  ■ claims of generalizability are made in studies with representative samples (e.g., survey designs).
		− The reported results are inappropriate or incomplete for the design. (We will learn more about this in Chapter 8.)
		− Inappropriate claims about cause and effect or generalizability are made.

General Evaluation		
6. The study used a rigorous research design.	+ All elements of the study from problem to purpose to methods to results to conclusions fit together in a logical, coherent way.	− There are inconsistencies in how the study's problem, purpose, methods, results, and conclusions fit together.
7. The use of the quantitative research design addressed the study's purpose.	+ The results and conclusions from the research design provide a rigorous explanation of the impact of an intervention or relationships/trends of variables that fulfills the study's intent and answers the study's research questions.	− The results and conclusions from the research provide a haphazard examination of the study's intent and do not adequately answer the study's research questions.

Quality Criteria	Quality Rating				Your Evidence and/or Reasoning
	0 = Poor	1 = Fair	2 = Good	3 = Excellent	
The Key Elements					
1. The choice of the research design is appropriate and justified.					
2. Good quantitative procedures are used to select and assign participants.					
3. Good quantitative data collection procedures are used.					
4. Good quantitative data analysis procedures are used.					
5. Good quantitative results and conclusions are reported.					
General Evaluation					
6. The study used a rigorous research design.					
7. The use of the quantitative research design addressed the study's purpose.					
Overall Quality 0–10 = Low quality 11–16 = Adequate quality 17–21 = High quality	**Total Score =**				**My Overall Assessment =**

FIGURE 6.3   A Rating Scale for Evaluating the Research Design in a Quantitative Research Report

Reviewing What You've Learned To Do

- *Identify and understand the research design of a quantitative study.*
  - ❑ A quantitative research design is a logical set of procedures for selecting participants and collecting, analyzing, and reporting quantitative data to address a specific research purpose.
  - ❑ A study's quantitative research design and its associated procedures are described in the Method section of a quantitative research report; the results of the procedures are found in the Results section.
- *List the characteristics that differentiate the two major types of quantitative research.*
  - ❑ The two major types of quantitative research differ in terms of the researchers' intent for the study, the use of manipulation, and the specific procedures used in the study.
  - ❑ Experimental research is a type of quantitative research in which the researcher intends to test the effect of an intervention by manipulating the conditions experienced by participants.
  - ❑ Nonexperimental research is a type of quantitative research in which the researcher intends to describe the relationships among variables or describe the trends for variables in a population without manipulating the conditions experienced by participants.
- *Distinguish among five common quantitative research designs based on their intents and key procedures.*
  - ❑ The true experiment is an experimental research design in which the researcher tests whether an intervention causes an effect by randomly assigning individuals to receive different conditions (e.g., treatment or control), measuring the outcomes, and using statistics to compare the groups.
  - ❑ The quasi-experiment is an experimental research design where the researcher tests whether an intervention causes an effect by assigning intact groups to

receive different conditions (e.g., treatment or control), measuring the outcomes, and using statistics to compare the groups.

□ The single-subject design is an experimental research design in which the researcher tests whether an intervention causes an effect for one or a few individuals by monitoring each individual's behavior before, during, and sometimes after administering the intervention and graphing the data to determine whether the intervention had an effect.

□ The correlational design is a nonexperimental research design where the researcher describes the relationships among variables by measuring the variables for the group of participants and analyzing the data for associations among variables.

□ The survey design is a nonexperimental research design where the researcher describes trends for variables in a population by selecting a representative sample, measuring the variables, and analyzing the data to identify general trends for the population.

■ *Recognize the research design used in a quantitative research report.*

□ Researchers write statements into the their reports that identify the overall plan for the study by naming the design and by describing procedures that are used. These statements can be found in the title, purpose statement, Method section, and Results section of a quantitative research report.

■ *Evaluate the quality of the research design in a quantitative research report.*

□ The evaluation of a quantitative research design begins by considering the extent to which the researcher selected an appropriate design for the study's purpose and explained why it was selected.

□ The evaluation of a quantitative research design is also based on the extent to which the researcher used good procedures for selecting and assigning participants and for collecting, analyzing, and reporting quantitative data that are consistent with the selected design and together form a rigorous study that addresses the study's purpose.

✓ **To assess what you've learned to do, click here to answer questions and receive instant feedback.**

Reading Research Articles

At the end of this chapter, you will find a research article to help you practice your new skills. Carefully read the quantitative early-intervention-outcomes study by Raspa et al. (2010) starting on p. 216. First, write a complete, APA-style reference for this article. Then, carefully reread the quantitative bullying-intervention study by Perkins et al. (2011) found at the end of Chapter 3 (starting on p. 98).

As you read each article, pay close attention to statements in which the authors conveyed the characteristics of the study's research design. Use the highlighting tool in the Pearson etext to indicate where the authors have provided information about the research design, and use the notetaking tool to add marginal notes that name each element you highlighted and note how each one is related to the study's design. Among the elements you will want to find are:

1. Study purpose
2. Research design name
3. Reason for the research design
4. Participant selection procedure
5. Participant assignment procedure
6. Data collection procedures
7. Data analysis procedures
8. Results
9. Claims about the results (e.g., cause and effect, generalize to a population)

Note, however, that sometimes authors do not use or discuss all of these elements—for example, they may not explicitly state the name of the research design or they may not have assigned participants to groups. If one of these elements is missing, indicate that in your marginal notes.

 Click here to go to the quantitative early-intervention outcomes study by Raspa et al. (2010) so that you can write a complete APA-style reference for the article and enter marginal notes about the study.

 Click here to go to the quantitative bullying-intervention study by Perkins et al. (2011) so that you can enter marginal notes about the study.

Understanding Research Articles

Apply your knowledge of the content of this chapter to the quantitative early-intervention-outcomes study by Raspa et al. (2010) found at the end of this chapter (starting on p. 216) and the quantitative bullying-intervention study by Perkins et al. (2011) found at the end of Chapter 3 (starting on p. 98).

1. Consider the information provided in the quantitative early-intervention-outcomes study's title and abstract, purpose statement, start of the Methods section, and description of the study's procedures and results. Based on this information, which research design did Raspa et al. use in this study? List three pieces of evidence for your answer.

2. What types of claims can the authors make based on the research design used?

3. Return to the quantitative bullying-intervention study. Identify the research design used in that study. List three pieces of evidence for your answer.

4. What types of claims can the authors make based on the research design used?

✓ **Click here to answer the questions and receive instant feedback.**

Evaluating Research Articles

Practice evaluating the quality of a study's research design, using the quantitative early-intervention-outcomes study by Raspa et al. (2010) found at the end of this chapter (starting on p. 216) and the quantitative bullying-intervention study by Perkins et al. (2011) found at the end of Chapter 3 (starting on p. 98).

1. Use the criteria discussed in Table 6.3 to evaluate the quality of the research design in the early-intervention-outcomes study. Note that, for this question, the rating form includes advice to help guide your evaluation.

✓ **Click here to open the rating scale form (Figure 6.3) to enter your ratings, evidence, and reasoning.**

2. Use the criteria discussed in Table 6.3 to evaluate the quality of the research design in the bullying-intervention study. Note that, for this question, the rating form does NOT include additional advice.

✓ **Click here to open the rating scale form (Figure 6.3) to enter your ratings, evidence, and reasoning.**

An Example of Quantitative Research: The Early-Intervention-Outcomes Study

Let's examine another published research article to apply the ideas you are learning. Throughout this book, we will refer to this study as the "quantitative early-intervention-outcomes" study. This journal article reports a quantitative research study conducted and reported by Raspa et al. (2010). Examine this article to practice your skills with reading, understanding, and evaluating research.

 Click here to write a complete APA-style reference for this article and receive instant feedback.

Exceptional Children

Vol. 76, No. 4, pp. 496-510.
©2010 Council for Exceptional Children.

Measuring Family Outcomes in Early Intervention: Findings From a Large-Scale Assessment

MELISSA RASPA

DONALD B. BAILEY, JR.

MURREY G. OLMSTED
RTI International

ROBIN NELSON
Texas Department of Assistive and Rehabilitative Services, Division of Early Childhood Intervention

NYLE ROBINSON
Illinois Department of Human Services, Division of Community Health and Prevention

MARY ELLEN SIMPSON
Graham Hospital School of Nursing

CHELSEA GUILLEN
Illinois Early Intervention Training Program

RENATE HOUTS
Duke University

ABSTRACT: *This article reports data from a large-scale assessment using the Family Outcomes Survey with families participating in early intervention. The study was designed to determine how families describe themselves with regard to outcomes achieved, the extent to which outcomes are interrelated, and the extent to which child, family, and program factors are associated with outcomes. Families reported positive outcomes, but there was variability in their responses. Factor analysis revealed that outcomes clustered in two areas: (a) family knowledge and ability, and (b) family support and community services. Hierarchical linear models indicated race/ethnicity, income, time in early intervention, perception of early intervention, and family-centered services were related to family outcomes. Recommendations for how to best use survey data are discussed.*

(01)

From its inception, early intervention for children with disabilities has been grounded in a fundamental assumption of the value and necessity of working with families. The Individuals With Disabilities Education Improvement Act states that there is a need "to enhance the capacity of families to meet the special needs of their infants and toddlers with disabilities" (Pub. Law No. 108-446, 2004, Sec. 631 (a)). Part C early intervention programs are required to involve families in assessing the needs of the child and in selecting services. Research has shown that children spend the majority of time with their families in everyday routines and activities (Bruder, 2001; Jung, 2003), and their needs cannot be addressed without taking into account the family context (Carpenter, 1997; Sameroff & Fiese, 2000). Other studies have demonstrated the value of using family-centered practices by creating partnerships between professionals and families (Blue-Banning, Summers, Frankland, Nelson, & Beegle, 2004; Dunlap & Fox, 2007; Krauss, 1997; Turnbull,

Turbiville, & Turnbull, 2000), engaging in help-giving practices (Dunst, 2000; Trivette & Dunst, 2005), and using routines-based assessment (McWilliam, 2005).

(02)   Although the field has focused on best practices in working with families (Horn, Ostrosky, & Jones, 2004) and satisfaction with services (McNaughton, 1994; McWilliam, Lang, Vandiviere, Angell, Collins, & Underdown, 1995), relatively little research has addressed the outcomes or benefits that families ought to experience as a result of their child's participation in early intervention. Assessing family outcomes, and not merely documenting professional practices, is the key to evaluating the efficacy of programs (Bailey, 2001; Dempsey & Keen, 2008; Early Childhood Research Institute on Measuring Growth and Development, 1998; Roberts, Innocenti, & Goetze, 1999). But what are the specific benefits or outcomes that families ought to attain?

Assessing family outcomes, and not merely documenting professional practices, is the key to evaluating the efficacy of programs.

(03)   Drawing on an early framework for conceptualizing family outcomes (Bailey et al., 1998), the National Early Intervention Longitudinal Study (NEILS) found that at the end of early intervention, families felt competent in caring for their child's special needs, advocating for services, and obtaining formal and informal supports. However, selected family demographics were associated with outcome attainment, with parents of minority children or single adult households reporting lower outcomes (Bailey et al., 2005). Complementary research on parenting supports (e.g., Dunst, 1999), empowerment (e.g., Thompson et al., 1997), and quality of life (e.g., Park et al., 2003) exists; however, these are more narrowly defined areas of work and do not encompass a broader perspective of family outcomes.

(04)   Recent requirements from the Office of Special Education Programs (OSEP) in the U.S. Department of Education have reinforced the need to examine family outcomes. Following the enactment of the Government Performance Results Act of 1993, federal agencies are mandated to report to Congress on the accountability of programs that receive federal funding. Each year, early intervention programs are required to demonstrate their effectiveness by measuring and reporting both child and family outcomes.

(05)   To assist with this effort, OSEP funded the Early Childhood Outcomes (ECO) Center (www.the-eco-center.org) in 2003 to promote the development and implementation of child and family outcome measures for infants, toddlers, and preschoolers with disabilities that could be used in local, state, and national accountability systems. Because there was no consensus on the most important benefits for families, an evidenced-based process was used to define and recommend a core set of family outcomes that should result from early intervention (Bailey, Bruder, et al., 2006). An extensive literature review was initially conducted by researchers at the ECO Center to create an empirical and theoretical framework for the process. This was followed by repeated consultations with numerous stakeholder groups, including a national advisory board of researchers, Part C and Part B state coordinators, and family members. After multiple drafts and subsequent revisions based on consumer feedback, five family outcomes were identified. As a result of early intervention, families should (a) understand their child's strengths, abilities, and special needs; (b) know their rights and advocate effectively for their children; (c) help their child develop and learn; (d) have support systems; and (e) access desired services, programs, and activities in their community (Bailey, Bruder, et al., 2006).

(06)   Following this process, researchers at the ECO Center constructed a survey instrument, the Family Outcomes Survey (FOS; Bailey, Hebbeler, & Bruder, 2006), to assess the five outcomes in a way that would be relatively easy for large-scale program evaluation. The scale has undergone extensive development, pilot testing, and revisions based on both data and stakeholder feedback (Bailey, Hebbeler, Olmsted, Raspa, & Bruder, 2008). Measurement decisions, such as how the data will be collected and who will provide it, guided the initial development of the survey. After pilot testing the instrument in Illinois and Texas through a collaborative relationship with the ECO Center and cognitive interviews with families participating in early intervention programs, revisions were made to simplify language use, clarify instructions, and provide consistent descriptors in the response

categories. The final version of the FOS was posted to the ECO Center web site for states to use in assessing family outcomes and addressing annual reporting requirements for OSEP. In the spring of 2007, a large-scale assessment of family outcomes was conducted in Illinois and Texas, two states that had received federal funding to explore ways to document family outcomes. Because these two states were not recruited or selected to participate, the study reflects a community-based participatory research design, with input from all participating authors/researchers.

(07)   Using the first available large-scale assessment data on family outcomes, the goals of this study are to expand the literature by understanding (a) how family outcomes should be measured, (b) how outcomes relate to different types of children and families, and (c) how practices used by early intervention programs when working with families are related to outcomes. This article uses data from Illinois and Texas to address three research questions. First, we wanted to evaluate the utility of the FOS as a measure of family outcomes, examining how the instrument described the current status of family outcomes and employing several traditional psychometric analyses to determine measurement properties of the instrument. Second, we were interested in the extent to which selected child, family, and program characteristics were associated with family outcomes. Finally, we wanted to see if data from these analyses provided insights into the ways we think about families, services, and family outcomes in the context of early intervention and provide initial guidance as to which family outcomes are currently being achieved and which ones might need more attention.

METHOD

PARTICIPANTS

(08)   A total of 2,849 families of children enrolled in Part C early intervention programs in Illinois and Texas participated in the study. The majority (61%) of children were male. Children were from a variety of racial and ethnic backgrounds, including Caucasian (66%), African American or Black (13%), Hispanic or Latino (17%), or another race/ethnicity (3%). States also reported eligibility categories, although each state defined eligibility differently. The possible categories for Texas were developmental delay, medical diagnosis, and atypical development, whereas Illinois used developmental delay, clinical judgment, and medical diagnosis. Overall, 67% of the children qualified for services because of developmental delay, 4% because of clinical judgment, 18% for medical diagnosis, and 11% for atypical development. On average, children had been in early intervention for 10.8 months ($SD = 7.2$) and were 23.3 months of age ($SD = 9.2$) at the time the survey was completed. Because the income data were skewed, the family income variable was collapsed into four categories: (a) $10,000 or less (25%); (b) $10,001 to $25,200 (20%); (c) $25,201 to $58,830 (26%); and (d) $58,831 and above (29%). Although the participating families are not a representative sample, the demographic statistics are comparable to national estimates of children and families in early intervention (see Scarborough et al., 2004).

FAMILY AND CHILD INSTRUMENTS

(09)   *Child and Family Demographics.* Texas and Illinois provided demographic information on the children and families receiving early intervention. Each state uses a data system (i.e., Texas Kids Intervention Data System [TKIDS]; Illinois Primary Health Care Association Cornerstone [IPHCA Cornerstone]) that contains information on a variety of child- and family-level variables. The following were used in the current study: child's date of birth, eligibility category (1 = developmental delay, 2 = clinical judgment, 3 = medical diagnosis, 4 = atypical development, 9 = unknown), gender (1 = female, 2 = male), race/ethnicity (1 = Caucasian, 2 = African American, 3 = Hispanic or Latino, and 4 = Other), family income (1 = $10,000 or less, 2 = $10,001 to $25,200, 3 = $25,201 to $58,830, and 4 = $58,831 or more), time in early intervention, and state (1 = Illinois, 2 = Texas).

(10)   *Family Outcomes.* The Family Outcomes Survey (FOS) was designed to assess five broad family outcomes: (a) understanding your child's strengths, needs, and abilities; (b) knowing your rights and advocating for services; (c) helping your child develop and learn; (d) having support systems; and (e) accessing your community. The FOS consists of 15 items across the five outcome areas, with three items per subscale (see Figure 1

FIGURE 1

Sample Item From the Family Outcomes Survey

1. Your child is growing and learning. How much does your family understand about your child's development?						
1	2	3	4	5	6	7
We are just **beginning** to understand our child's development		We understand **some** about our child's development		We understand a **good amount** about our child's development		We understand a **great deal** about our child's development

for sample item). Respondents rate each item using a 7-point scale with descriptors for 1, 3, 5, and 7. Although the descriptors vary by item, similar items use identical descriptors. For example, all items that ask families to rate the *amount* of an outcome use "just beginning," "some," "a good amount," and "a great deal." Likewise, all *frequency* items use "seldom," "sometimes", "usually," and "almost always." Families had the option of selecting "not applicable" for two items (items 14 and 15) and were instructed to skip an item if they were uncomfortable providing an answer. Because of the possibility of missing data at the item level, a mean score on the FOS was calculated using items 1 through 15.

(11)   *Program Variables.* Two measures were used to determine families' perceptions of the early intervention program. Three FOS companion items were created by the authors to address family perceptions of the helpfulness of early intervention. These items were created to help meet the annual reporting requirements for OSEP. States are required to report annually the percentage of families participating in Part C who report that early intervention services have helped them (a) know their rights, (b) effectively communicate their children's needs, and (c) help their child develop and learn. Each item is rated on a 7-point scale, with descriptors for 1 (poor), 3 (fair), 5 (good), and 7 (excellent). A mean score was calculated as a mean of the total number of items completed.

(12)   In addition, a subset of families completed the Family-Centered Services part of the National Center for Special Education Accountability Monitoring Part C Family Survey (NCSEAM, 2005). The Family-Centered Services items provide information on parent perceptions of the way early intervention services are delivered.

Twenty-five items cover areas such as family priorities in planning services, informational support about community services and programs, and the quality of service provision and service providers. Each item is rated on a 6-point scale (1 = very strongly disagree, 2 = strongly disagree, 3 = disagree, 4 = agree, 5 = strongly agree, and 6 = very strongly agree). Families were instructed to skip items that did not apply to their situation. Although the scale authors recommend using Rasch modeling, a mean score was calculated as the average of the total number of items completed. Reliability estimates for the instrument are $\alpha = .90$ based on pilot test data. Additional information on the Part C Family Survey is available at http://www.accountabilitydata.org/parent_family_involvement.htm.

PROCEDURES

Procedures for collecting data were similar for (13) each state. In Illinois, families scheduled to have a 6-month or annual individualized family services plan (IFSP) review were selected to participate (*n* = 3,538). Packets containing the instruments, a cover letter, and a prepaid return envelope were distributed to the service coordinators at 25 local Child and Family Connections offices. No personally identifying information was on the instruments or return envelope, only an identification number that could be linked by state central office personnel to the demographic data. Both English and Spanish versions of the packets were distributed. Packets were sent to local offices in two phases (early May and mid-June). However, for logistical reasons only the packets distributed in the second phase contained the Family-Centered Services items. Packets were sorted by the service coordinators and distributed during the

IFSP meetings. Two weeks later, families were sent a follow-up postcard and a letter from the service coordinator encouraging them to complete the instruments. To increase response rates in certain areas, staff at the Child and Family Connections offices also conducted follow-up phone calls to families. A total of 1,666 surveys were returned (47%) to the state early childhood intervention office.

(14)   Texas distributed packets to families in each of the 58 community-based Early Childhood Intervention (ECI) programs. Families were selected if they had been receiving services for at least 6 months and had an IFSP meeting between mid-March and mid-June. Service coordinators distributed packets to 4,180 families and a total of 1,670 (40%) were returned via mail to the ECI State Office. Similar to Illinois, both English and Spanish versions were distributed and the Family-Centered Services items were sent in the second half of data collection. To increase response rates, programs sent reminder postcards to families and also asked service coordinators to distribute a letter to families if they had not completed the packets. Completed surveys in each language were as follows: 3,338 families completed the FOS (2,849 English, 489 Spanish) and 1,642 completed the Family-Centered Services items on the NCSEAM scale (1,412 English, 230 Spanish). Preliminary analyses showed differences in the Spanish and English findings, leading to a more extensive review of the Spanish version of the instrument and a new cognitive testing protocol to more fully understand how Spanish speakers interpret survey items. These findings are reported in a separate article (Olmsted et al., in press); therefore, this article reports data on the English version of the survey only.

RESULTS

(15) Several sets of analyses were conducted to address the research questions. Descriptive statistics, including means and standard deviations, were calculated for each item on the FOS to describe the outcomes reported by families. Next, a correlation matrix was constructed with the original five subscales and the mean score to determine the extent to which outcomes were interrelated. This was followed by an exploratory factor analysis to ex-

amine whether there were meaningful outcome clusters and an analysis of internal consistency using Cronbach's alpha. Finally, multiple regressions were performed using hierarchical linear modeling (Bryk & Raudenbush, 1992; Singer, 1998) to account for the nesting of families within the programs and the two states. The regressions examined the relationship between selected child characteristics (gender, age, eligibility type), family characteristics (race/ethnicity, family income), program variables (family-centered practices, family's perceptions of early intervention), and family outcomes. A variety of methods were used to account for missing data. For missing item-level data on the FOS or NCSEAM items, a mean score was calculated instead of a total score. This approach allowed for instances when a family did not complete an item that did not apply to their current situation. Subsets of data also were used for different analyses to account for missing data; for example only families who completed the FOS and NCSEAM were included in the hierarchical linear modeling analyses and only families that completed all items on the FOS were included in the exploratory factor analysis.

OUTCOMES REPORTED BY FAMILIES

Table 1 presents descriptive statistics for each of (16) the 15 items on the FOS. Overall, families reported positive outcomes. The means for the three items that measured families' understanding of their child's strengths, needs, and abilities ranged from 5.8 to 6.0. Two of the items that measured families' knowledge of services (4.5) and rights (5.1) were rated lower than the item asking whether families were comfortable participating in team meetings with professionals (6.0). Families scored themselves high on the items that measured their ability to help their child develop and learn (5.8) and practice new skills (6.1); however, they were somewhat less certain of their ability to help their child behave the way they wanted (5.3). Although families reported usually having someone to talk to when they needed (5.6), they rated themselves lower on having someone to call for help when needed (5.1) and being able to do the things they enjoyed together (5.2). Access to medical care (6.1) and child care (5.6) that met their child's needs were rated highly by families. How-

TABLE 1

Means and Standard Deviations for Each Item on the Family Outcomes Survey

Item	Item Description	N[a]	M	SD
1	Understand child's development	2,839	5.8	1.23
2	Understand child's special needs	2,806	5.8	1.35
3	Understand child's progress	2,833	6.0	1.19
4	Know about services	2,814	4.5	1.62
5	Comfortable participating in meetings	2,798	6.0	1.39
6	Know rights	2,803	5.1	1.75
7	Help child develop and learn	2,832	5.8	1.21
8	Help child behave	2,818	5.3	1.43
9	Practice new skills	2,826	6.1	1.19
10	Have support	2,831	5.6	1.71
11	Someone to call for help	2,827	5.1	2.06
12	Able to do things you enjoy	2,830	5.2	1.60
13	Access to medical care	2,807	6.1	1.33
14	Access to child care	1,004	5.6	1.70
15	Child participates in activities	2,616	4.5	1.97

[a]Families were given the opportunity to skip items 14 and 15 if not applicable.

ever, the mean score for how often their child participates in activities was lower (4.5).

(17)   We examined the frequencies of each response for all the items to better understand the distribution of scores. To illustrate, Figures 2 and 3 depict the frequency distribution for two FOS items. Figure 2 shows an example of an item with a relatively normal distribution of responses. Although the modal response was 5, there was tremendous variation in the amount of knowledge families indicated they had about the programs and services that were available. Figure 3 shows a positively skewed distribution. For this item, more than 92% of families responded that they "usually" or "routinely" help their child practice new skills. These distributions demonstrate that for some items, the majority of families reported they had attained the outcome; whereas for other outcomes, families indicated a wider range of outcome attainment.

PROGRAM FEATURES

(18) Table 2 presents descriptive data on the three companion FOS items that measure families' perceptions of early intervention and the NCSEAM Family-Centered Services items. On average, families rated the helpfulness of early intervention as high, with means ranging from 5.7 to 6.2. There was more variability across the means for the

Family-Centered Services items. The lowest mean score was for the item asking families to rate how much the early intervention program helped them get involved in community activities and services (3.3) and the highest mean scores were for the items that rated whether the families' early intervention provider was easy to talk to and good at working with them (5.4).

ASSOCIATIONS AMONG REPORTED OUTCOMES

The 15 items on the FOS were designed to assess (19) the five recommended family outcomes (Bailey, Hebbeler, et al., 2006) and as such might be considered to have five subscales. We wanted to determine the extent to which the items and subscales were independent and whether the instrument was measuring single or multiple constructs. This information would be useful for states that wish to summarize parent ratings in some way. As a preliminary step, we calculated a correlation matrix for each subscale. Results are presented in Table 3. All subscales were strongly correlated with the mean score (Items 1–15), with Pearson r ranging from 0.67 to 0.80. Three of the five subscales were highly correlated with each other: (a) understanding your child's strengths, needs, and abilities; (b) knowing your rights and advocating for services; and (c) helping your child

FIGURE 2

Frequency Distribution for Item 4: Know About Services That Are Available

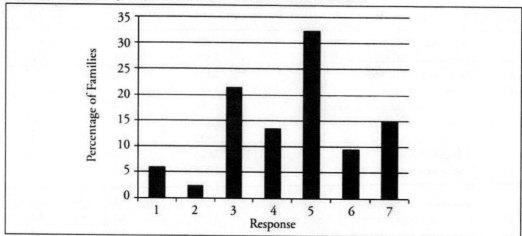

develop and learn. The remaining two subscales (having support systems and accessing your community) were positively related ($r = 0.51$) to each other, but less strongly associated with the other three subscales (r ranging from 0.32 to 0.46).

(20)   Next, an exploratory factor analysis was performed to determine the psychometric properties of the instrument and whether an alternative clustering of items might be more statistically defensible (see Table 4). The analyses was conducted with a subset of families ($n = 917$) who had completed all items on the FOS, including Item 14 (access to child care) and Item 15 (child participates in activities); the survey allows families to skip these items if they do not apply to their situation. The method of extraction was a principle

components analysis with an oblique oblimin rotation (Thompson, 2004). All eigenvalues over 1.00 were retained. Two factors emerged: Factor 1 (eigenvalue = 5.92, 39% of the variance) comprised Items 1 through 9, Factor 2 (eigenvalue = 1.49, 10% of the variance) consisted of Items 10 through 15. The Kaiser-Meyer-Olkin measure of sampling adequacy was large (0.91).

Factor 1 combines three of the five family (21) outcomes into a single factor. The items that measure families' (a) understanding of their child's strengths, needs, and abilities; (b) knowledge of rights and services; and (c) ability to help their child develop and learn all correlated strongly, with standardized regression coefficients ranging from 0.55 to 0.81. This factor appears to

FIGURE 3

Frequency Distribution for Item 9: How Often Practice New Skills

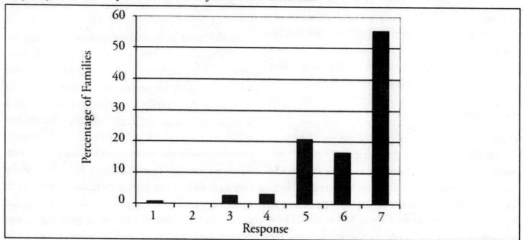

TABLE 2

Means and Standard Deviations for Items Measuring Families' Perception of Early Intervention

Item Description	N	M	SD
FOS Perception Items[a]			
EI helped you to know rights	2,831	5.7	1.39
EI helped you to effectively communicate needs	2,827	6.0	1.18
EI helped you help child develop and learn	2,830	6.2	1.12
Family-Centered Services items[b]			
Offered help when needed	1,071	4.3	1.5
Asked if wanted help with stress	1,228	4.2	1.4
Given choices about services	1,332	4.9	1.1
Daily routines used for planning	1,389	5.1	1.0
Felt part of team	1,382	5.3	0.9
Services provided in timely manner	1,356	5.0	1.1
Given info about modifications	1,353	5.0	1.0
Given info about rights	1,380	5.0	1.0
Given info about community programs	1,324	4.3	1.3
Given info about support programs	1,260	4.3	1.3
Given info about how to participate	1,267	4.2	1.3
Given info about play opportunities	1,276	4.2	1.3
Given info about how to advocate	1,278	4.5	1.2
What to do if not satisfied	1,364	4.8	1.2
Helped me get services	1,014	3.8	1.5
Helped me talk with other parents	1,084	3.6	1.4
Asked if services were meeting needs	1,323	4.9	1.2
Helped us get involved in community	1,044	3.3	1.5
EI provider is dependable	1,401	5.3	1.0
EI provider is easy to talk to	1,402	5.4	0.9
EI provider is good at working with my family	1,404	5.4	0.9
Service coordinator is available	1,391	5.2	1.1
Service coordinator is knowledgeable	1,392	5.3	1.0
Received written info in an understandable way	1,396	5.3	1.0
Given info to prepare for transition	1,259	4.9	1.3

Note. FOS = Family Outcomes Survey. EI = Early Intervention.
[a]FOS perception items rated on a 7-point scale. [b]Family-Centered Services items rated on a 6-point scale.

be measuring families' knowledge and ability as it relates to their child and the early intervention system; therefore, we have labeled it as "Family Knowledge and Ability." Factor 2 consists of the other two types of family outcomes: (a) having support services; and (b) accessing desired services, programs, and activities. The standardized regression coefficients range from 0.49 to 0.80. This factor is labeled "Family Support and Community Services" as it measures families' informal and formal social support, access to quality medical care and child care, and children's participation in community activities. As a follow-up, Cronbach's alpha was calculated for the two factors. Both values were high, with the "Family Knowledge and Ability" factor having an α = 0.86 and the "Family Support and Community Services" factor with an α = 0.79, as was Cronbach's alpha for the total mean score (0.88).

FACTORS ASSOCIATED WITH FAMILY OUTCOMES

Three multiple regressions were conducted to determine the extent to which selected child (gender, age, eligibility type), family (race/ethnicity, family income), or program (length of time in early intervention, family-centered practices, family's perceptions of early intervention) variables were associated with families' reported outcomes (FOS mean score and the two factor scores). Table 5 reports the results of the regression analyses using hierarchical linear modeling (HLM) to

(22)

TABLE 3

Correlation Matrix Among the Five Subscales on the FOS and the Mean Score (n = 2,849)

Subscales	Strength and Ability ($\alpha = 0.73$)	Rights and Services ($\alpha = 0.66$)	Develop and Learn ($\alpha = 0.75$)	Social Support ($\alpha = 0.73$)	Community Access ($\alpha = 0.62$)	Mean Score ($\alpha = 0.88$)
	1	2	3	4	5	Mean
1	1.00	0.50	0.65	0.37	0.33	0.74
2		1.00	0.53	0.38	0.32	0.74
3			1.00	0.46	0.40	0.80
4				1.00	0.51	0.77
5					1.00	0.67
Mean						1.00

Note. All correlations significant at the $p < .001$ level. FOS = Family Outcomes Survey.

account for the nesting of families within local early intervention programs and the two states. Not all families completed the Family-Centered Services items on the NCSEAM scale; thus, fewer families were used in these analyses ($n = 1,392$).

(23) Beta coefficients indicated that race/ethnicity was statistically significant and inversely related to the mean score. A comparison of the means scores for each group showed that Caucasian families reported higher mean family outcomes (5.6) than did African American families (5.3), Hispanic families (5.4), and families of other races/ethnicities (5.2). Family income was also statistically significant but positively related to the mean score. Comparisons of the means on the mean score indicate that families with incomes greater than $58,831 (5.6) reported higher outcomes than did families with incomes less than $10,000 (5.5), between $10,001 and $25,200 (5.4), and between $25,201 and $58,830 (5.5). Child's age and the amount of time spent in early intervention were statistically significant as well. The estimates indicate that the younger the child or the longer the child was in early intervention, the higher the family outcome. Finally, both the FOS perception of early intervention items and the Family-Centered Services items were positively related to family outcomes; that is, families with higher outcome scores were more satisfied with early intervention or rated the delivery of services as more family-centered.

(24) When the same HLM analysis was applied to Factor 1, "Family Knowledge and Ability," the results were similar to those predicting the mean FOS score. Race/ethnicity again was related to family outcomes with Caucasian families (5.7) re-

porting the highest level of knowledge and ability, followed by Hispanic families (5.5), African American families (5.5), and families from other races/ethnicities (5.3). Income, however, was not statistically significant. The same relationship was found for the child's age and amount of time spent in early intervention, with families who had a younger child or families who had been in early intervention longer reporting higher family knowledge and ability. The means of both the FOS perception of early intervention items and the Family-Centered Services items were positively related to Factor 1 as well.

(25) The model for "Family Support and Community Services" (Factor 2) was slightly different. Race/ethnicity was predictive of families' ratings on the "Family Support and Community Services" factor, with a comparison of means indicating the same pattern for Factor 1: Caucasian families reported the highest amount of support and access to services (5.4), followed by Hispanic families (5.2), African American families (5.1), and families from another race/ethnicity (5.0). Family income was a statistically significant predictor of scores on Factor 2. Families with incomes of more than $58,831 reported the highest amount of social support and access to services (5.6), families with incomes between $25,201 to $58,830 and incomes less than $10,000 reported similar levels (5.3; 5.2), and families with incomes of $10,000 to $25,200 reported the lowest level (5.1). Unlike the previous two regression models, child's age and amount of time in early intervention were not predictive of social support and access to services. However, family's perceptions of early intervention (FOS items) and family's

TABLE 4

Standardized Regression Coefficient (and Final Communality) Results of a Principal Components Analysis of the FOS (Items 1–15) Using an Oblimin Rotation (n = 917)

Item	Item Description	Factor 1	Factor 2
1	Understand child's development	0.81 (0.62)	
2	Understand child's special needs	0.76 (0.53)	
3	Understand child's progress	0.64 (0.41)	
4	Know about services	0.55 (0.46)	
5	Comfortable participating in meetings	0.58 (0.30)	
6	Know rights	0.65 (0.43)	
7	Help child develop and learn	0.81 (0.68)	
8	Help child behave	0.66 (0.57)	
9	Practice new skills	0.63 (0.47)	
10	Have support		0.60 (0.52)
11	Someone to call for help		0.80 (0.60)
12	Able to do things you enjoy		0.74 (0.56)
13	Access to medical care		0.49 (0.33)
14	Access to child care		0.74 (0.50)
15	Child participates in activities		0.68 (0.45)

appraisal of whether the services were provided in a family-centered manner were positively related to social support and access to services.

DISCUSSION

(26) This article presents findings from two states that used the FOS to measure outcomes families experienced while their child participated in early intervention. It provides the first look at large-scale assessment data on family outcomes and how they relate to child, family, and program characteristics. There were three central goals of the study: namely, to assess the utility of the FOS as a measure of family outcomes, understand factors associated with family outcomes, and use the findings to reflect on the nature of services and outcomes as a framework for future intervention and evaluation.

SUMMARY OF MAJOR FINDINGS

(27) Overall, families participating in early intervention reported that they have attained or made progress toward important family outcomes, with the average item score on each subscale ranging between 5.2 and 5.9. Families rated themselves highest on their (a) access to high-quality medical care (6.1), (b) ability to help their child practice new skills (6.0), (c) comfort while participating in meetings with professionals (6.0), and (d) understanding of

their child's special needs (6.0). Families felt less positive about (a) knowing what services are available for their child (4.4), (b) having their child participate in activities (4.4), and (c) having someone to call for help when needed (4.9).

(28) The distribution of responses across families was quite variable for some outcomes. For example, only 56% of families responded they knew "a good amount" or "a great deal" (response of 5 or higher) about the services available for their child, whereas 90% of families indicated that their medical care meets "many" or "almost all" of their child's special needs. In general, 27% of families rated themselves as a 1 on at least one FOS item, 88% of families rated themselves as a 3 or lower on at least one item, and 93% of families rated themselves as a 7 on at least one item.

(29) What types of outcomes does the FOS measure? Results from the principle components analysis revealed two factors: "Family Knowledge and Ability" and "Family Support and Community Services." The first factor includes items from three of the five original subscales of the FOS: (a) understanding your child's strengths, needs, and abilities; (b) knowing your rights and advocating for services; and (c) helping your child develop and learn. The second factor, "Family Support and Community Services," consists of items from the other two subscales of the FOS. Although the FOS was designed to measure five family out-

TABLE 5

Summary of HLM Regression Results Predicting Mean Score on the Family Outcomes Survey Using Child, Family, and Program Characteristics (n = 1,392)

Variable	Mean Score β	SE	Factor 1 β	SE	Factor 2 β	SE
Gender	0.068	0.042	0.065	0.044	0.063	0.062
Race/ethnicity	−0.097***	0.024	−0.087***	0.025	−0.116**	0.036
Age in months	−0.006*	0.003	−0.009**	0.003	−0.002	0.004
Eligibility types	−0.006	0.016	−0.006	0.016	−0.007	0.023
Family income	0.072***	0.019	0.017	0.019	0.175***	0.028
Time in early intervention	0.007*	0.003	0.012***	0.003	−0.003	0.005
FOS perception items	0.189***	0.030	0.115***	0.030	0.309***	0.043
Family-Centered Services items	0.350***	0.023	0.412***	0.024	0.248***	0.034

*$p < .05$. **$p < .01$. ***$p < .001$.

comes, the underlying structure of the items group together into two categories. Conceptually, the items on the first factor relate to the family's confidence and competence in parenting a child with special needs and the items on the second factor encompass formal and informal support and community services. Previous research on families has examined these constructs (Brooks-Gunn, Berlin, & Fuligni, 2000; Dunst, Trivette, & Deal, 1994; Koegh, Garnier, Bernheimer, & Gallimore, 2000). The similarity of the FOS with these constructs is not surprising given that the FOS was created after extensive review of the literature on family outcomes (Bailey, Bruder, et al., 2006). In summary, the FOS appears to be measuring two types of family outcomes: those related to the family interacting with the child and those associated with the family and the community.

(30) Hierarchical linear modeling showed that race/ethnicity, family income, age in months, and amount of time in early intervention were statistically significant predictors of the FOS mean score. Race, income, and time in early intervention predicted "Family Knowledge and Ability," whereas race and income were the only variables associated with "Family Support and Community Services." Bailey et al. (2005) found similar results in the NEILS study. Using nationally representative data, the authors found that Caucasian families reported higher scores on a Family Outcome Index than did families who were African American or from other ethnic minority groups. A negative relationship between income and family outcomes has also been demonstrated in past studies. Dunst (1999) reported that family socioe-

conomic status (SES) was inversely related to four types of parenting supports. Data from NEILS also indicated that families with lower incomes tended to have a less positive perception of the impact of early intervention services on their family (Bailey, Nelson, Hebbeler, & Spiker, 2007).

(31) Families of younger children report higher outcomes than those with older children. Yet when time in early intervention is taken into account, we see that children who have just entered early intervention indicated lower family outcomes than did families with children who have received services for a longer amount of time. One possible explanation could be that different types of children enter early intervention at different ages and receive services for various lengths of time, which may explain the relationship between age in months and family outcomes. The NEILS data show that there is a bi-modal distribution of the age at which children enter early intervention: those who enter at a younger age, for example, children who have a diagnosed condition at birth, and those who enter after their second birthday, for example, children who are eligible because of a documented developmental delay (Bailey, Hebbeler, Scarborough, Spiker, & Mallik, 2004; Scarborough et al. 2004). It may be that younger children who received services for a longer amount of time have higher family outcomes than those families whose children entered early intervention later and received services for a shorter period.

(32) The final major finding was the relationship between two measures of satisfaction with services and family outcomes, which were statistically significant in all three regression models. Research

previously has demonstrated that families report high levels of satisfaction with services (McNaughton, 1994; McWilliam et al., 1995). Moreover, families' assessment of the quality of services they and their children received plays a role in their perception of the impact of services (Bailey et al., 2007).

(33)   In summary, results from the factor analysis and internal consistency analyses demonstrated that the FOS is a psychometrically sound instrument. The hierarchical linear models show that the three companion items used to report data to OSEP were strongly related to family outcomes. The descriptive data showed that overall families were reporting high outcomes. This information will be useful for states as they plan for program improvement activities and will help to move the field forward in measuring family outcomes and understanding how early intervention programs can provide the most benefit to the families they serve.

USES OF THE FAMILY OUTCOMES SURVEY

(34)   How can states best use the data from the Family Outcomes Survey? Although the FOS contains the three items on the perception of early intervention that states can use to meet the OSEP reporting requirements, there are multiple uses for the data from the other items. In the following we outline several suggestions for using the FOS for program evaluation and planning. First, however, we discuss the different types of scores that the FOS provides: an item-level score, a factor-level score, and the overall mean score.

(35)   The overall mean score provides summary level information across the five different types of family outcomes. The mean score might best be used to obtain overview information, either at the state or local level, about the outcomes of families participating in early intervention. The factor scores provide additional information about two general types of family outcomes: families' knowledge and ability in interacting with their child and the early intervention system, and families' informal and formal support and access to a variety of services in the community. The factor scores are useful in determining if there are differences between these two types of outcome areas for a given family or program. However, it is likely that the item-level score provides the best

information for states to use for program improvement. Examining item-specific data can indicate if there are outcomes that need to be targeted at the program or state level. The overall mean score or factor scores may indicate high levels of family outcomes, but focusing on the item-level score could show, for example, that three areas have particularly low family outcomes (i.e., families know their rights, families are able to help their child behave, and families have access to child care). States can examine the item-level scores to determine if there are patterns of scores that need to be addressed with systematic improvement strategies.

(36)   There are several ways states can use the FOS for program improvement. First, we recommend states examine subgroups to better understand the different types of families within a state. One way would be to group families by local program or early intervention center and examine the means of the individual items as well as the mean FOS score and the two factor scores. Variations that exist across the programs or centers can be analyzed to determine if changes need to be made to existing practices to improve family outcomes. For example, a subgroup analysis by early intervention programs may identify that families in Program A have a low mean score on Item 4: Know about services for my child. However, families in Program B show higher scores for this item. On examining the practices of Program B, it is discovered that the service coordinators provide families with a brochure on community programs and initiatives once a year during their IFSP meetings. Program A decides to develop a similar brochure that lists community organizations in their city.

(37)   A second way to classify families would be to look at percentages of families in different scoring categories at the item level. For example, families who rated themselves a 5 or higher on all items might be considered the "success stories" of early intervention. On the other hand, families who scored a 3 or lower on more than 5 items might need intensive support or services. These families could be followed over time to determine if improvement was seen in the outcome areas that were more problematic. Families who reported consistent ratings in the 3 to 5 range would be experiencing some benefits of early intervention,

but with additional supports could become "success stories" as well.

(38)   Finally, states could examine other factors that may be associated with family outcomes. Using information in their state database, other child and family characteristics could be explored. For example, previous research has demonstrated that a child's health status is related to outcomes a family experiences (Bailey et al., 2005). Families of children who were in fair or poor health had significantly lower outcomes than families of children whose health was excellent or very good. Another variable that states may want to examine is the amount or type of services a child receives. Families of children who receive much more or less than the average amount of services may have a different pattern of family outcomes. Last, states could look at differences in outcomes between Spanish- and English-speaking families. Although race/ethnicity was found to be predictive of family outcomes, a confounding variable may be language. Spanish-speaking families may have a harder time accessing the services they need and therefore may have lower family outcomes. Moreover, Spanish-speaking families may perceive family outcomes differently than English-speaking families. Because preliminary differences were found in the data between the English and Spanish versions of the FOS, we plan to further explore these issues in a subsequent study.

LIMITATIONS

(39)   The study is the first to report large-scale data on the types of outcomes families experience and factors associated with those outcomes. However, the results should be interpreted while considering three primary limitations. First, the samples are not representative of all families in each state or of those in other states. Although every effort was made to increase response rates from other types of families, the majority of participants were Caucasian and had higher incomes. In addition, some families did not complete the NCSEAM scale. The subset of families that were examined in the last set of analyses, therefore, may be different than those who did not complete the instrument. Second, many items on the FOS are written at a construct level instead of using a measurable indicator (e.g., our family understands our child's special needs vs. our family understands how Down syndrome will affect our child's life). Because families may interpret constructs differently, the data is inherently subjective. Finally, although we measured some aspects of service delivery (i.e., family-centeredness of services), the outcomes data cannot be linked to any specific types of services or the intensity or the frequency of services. Despite these limitations, the findings provide a starting point for understanding how families benefit from services and supports provided by early intervention.

FUTURE RESEARCH

Three main areas of work remain to be completed (40) on the Family Outcomes Survey. First, the validity of the FOS in relationship to other measures of family well-being should be determined. Constructs such as empowerment, social support, parenting self-efficacy, quality of life, hope, and parenting stress are closely related to family outcomes. Part of this process could involve examining the specific items determining whether they are written at the indicator level. Scores on the FOS should correlate with scores on measures of these constructs. Second, in order for the FOS to be a useful tool for state accountability and program improvement, it will need to be sensitive to changes in family outcomes over time. Longitudinal data collection with different types of families needs to be examined to determine the utility of the FOS. Finally, the relationship among family outcomes, characteristics of the early intervention program and types of services delivered, and child outcomes needs to be explored. Research is beginning to examine the relationship in these areas. For example, Dunst (1999) examined the relationships between program practices, parenting supports, and child progress and found that programs that used more family-centered practices had families who reported higher levels of support and children who made more progress than expected on five developmental domains. However, much needs to be studied to determine other factors that relate to family outcomes and whether family outcomes influence child outcomes. Additional studies on the FOS will help to disentangle the relationship between family and child outcomes, program practices, and child and family characteristics.

Beyond this particular instrument, however, (41) our findings suggest that early intervention may have two distinct components—one related to a more traditional view of services (e.g., rights, therapies, assessments, interventions) and one related to social supports and community access. Both types of outcomes are important, but may require different methods to achieve. Future research needs to explore how these two program dimensions can be integrated into a holistic and integrated set of services that maximize both types of outcomes.

REFERENCES

Bailey, D. B. (2001). Evaluating parent involvement and family support in early intervention and preschool programs. *Journal of Early Intervention, 24,* 1–14.

Bailey, D. B., Bruder, M., Hebbeler, K., Carta, J., de Fosset, M., Greenwood, C., . . . Barton, L. (2006). Recommended outcomes for families of young children with disabilities. *Journal of Early Intervention, 28,* 227–251.

Bailey, D. B., Hebbeler, K., & Bruder, M. B. (2006). *Family Outcomes Survey.* Retrieved from http://www.fpg.unc.edu/~eco/pdfs/FOS-PartC_11-16-06.pdf

Bailey, D. B., Hebbeler, K., Olmsted, M., Raspa, M., & Bruder, M. B. (2008). Measuring family outcomes: Considerations for large-scale data collection in early intervention. *Infants & Young Children, 21,* 194–206.

Bailey, D. B., Hebbeler, K., Scarborough, A., Spiker, D., & Mallik, S. (2004). First experiences with early intervention: A national perspective. *Pediatrics, 113,* 887–896.

Bailey, D. B., Hebbeler, K., Spiker, D., Scarborough, A., Mallik, S., & Nelson, L. (2005). Thirty-six month outcomes for families of children with disabilities participating in early intervention. *Pediatrics, 116,* 1346–1352.

Bailey, D. B., McWilliam, R. A., Darkes, L. A., Hebbeler, K., Simeonsson, R. J., Spiker, D., & Wagner, M. (1998). Family outcomes in early intervention: A framework for program evaluation and efficacy research. *Exceptional Children, 64,* 313–328.

Bailey, D. B., Nelson, L., Hebbeler, K., & Spiker, D. (2007). Modeling the impact of formal and informal supports for young children with disabilities and their families. *Pediatrics, 120,* e992–e1001.

Blue-Banning, M., Summers, J. A., Frankland, H. C., Nelson, L. L., & Beegle, G. (2004). Dimensions of family and professional partnerships: Constructive guidelines for collaboration. *Exceptional Children, 70,* 167–184.

Brooks-Gunn, J., Berlin, L. J., & Fuligni, A. S. (2000). Early childhood intervention programs: What about the family? In J. P. Shonkoff & S. J. Meisels (Eds.), *Handbook of early childhood intervention* (2nd ed., pp. 549–588). Cambridge, UK: Cambridge University Press.

Bruder, M. B. (2001). Infants and toddlers: Outcomes and ecology. In M. J. Guralnick (Ed.), *Early childhood inclusion: Focus on change* (pp. 203–228). Baltimore, MD: Paul H. Brookes.

Bryk, A. S., & Raudenbush, S. W. (1992). *Hierarchical linear models: Applications and data analysis methods.* Newbury Park, CA: Sage.

Carpenter, B. (1997). *Families in context: Emerging trends in early intervention family support.* London, UK: David Fulton.

Dempsey, I., & Keen, D. (2008). A review of processes and outcomes in family-centered services for children with a disability. *Topics in Early Childhood Special Education, 28,* 42–52.

Dunlap, G., & Fox, L. (2007). Parent–professional partnerships: A valuable context for addressing challenging behaviors. *International Journal of Disability, Development, and Education, 54,* 273–285.

Dunst, C. J. (1999). Placing parent education in conceptual and empirical context. *Topics in Early Childhood Special Education, 19,* 141–172.

Dunst, C. J. (2000). Revisiting "Rethinking early intervention." *Topics in Early Childhood Special Education, 20,* 95–104.

Dunst, C. J., Trivette, C. M., & Deal, A. (1994). *Supporting and strengthening families, Vol. 1: Methods, strategies, practices.* Cambridge, MA: Brookline Books.

Early Childhood Research Institute on Measuring Growth and Development. (1998). *Family outcomes in a growth and development model* (Technical Report No. 7). Minneapolis, MN: University of Minnesota, Center for Early Education and Development.

Horn, E., Ostrosky, M. M., & Jones, H. (Eds.). (2004). *Family-based practices* (Young Exceptional Children Monograph Series No. 5). Longmont, CO: Sopris West.

Individuals With Disabilities Education Improvement Act, Pub. L. No. 108-446, Sec. 631 (a). (2004).

Jung, L. A. (2003). More is better: Maximizing natural learning opportunities. *Young Exceptional Children, 6,* 21–27.

Koegh, B. K., Garnier, H. E., Bernheimer, L. P., & Gallimore, R. (2000). Models of child–family interactions for children with developmental delays: Child-driven or transactional? *American Journal of Mental Retardation, 105,* 32–46.

Krauss, M. W. (1997). Two generations of family research in early intervention. In M. J. Guralnick (Ed.), *The effectiveness of early intervention* (pp. 611–624). Baltimore, MD: Paul H. Brookes.

McNaughton, D. (1994). Measuring parent satisfaction with early childhood intervention programs: Current practice, problems, and future perspectives. *Topics in Early Childhood Special Education, 14*, 26–48.

McWilliam, R. A. (2005). Assessing the resource needs of families in the context of early intervention. In M. J. Guralnick (Ed.), *A developmental systems approach to early intervention* (pp. 215–234). Baltimore, MD: Paul H. Brookes.

McWilliam, R. A., Lang, L., Vandiviere, P., Angell, R., Collins, L., & Underdown, G. (1995). Satisfaction and struggles: Family perceptions of early intervention services. *Journal of Early Intervention, 19*, 43–60.

National Center for Special Education Accountability Monitoring (NCSEAM). (2005). *Family survey— early intervention.* Retrieved from http://www. accountabilitydata.org/New%20DATA%20FEB% 202006/2005_NCSEAM_PartC_Watermarked_ %20(25196%20-%20Activ.pdf

Olmsted, M. G., Bailey, D. B., Raspa, M., Nelson, R., Robinson, N., Simpson, M., & Guillen, C. (in press). Outcomes reported by Spanish-speaking families in early intervention. *Topics in Early Childhood Special Education.*

Park, J., Hoffman, L., Marquis, J., Turnbull, A. P., Poston, D., Mannan, H., . . . Nelson, L. C. (2003). Toward assessing family outcomes of service delivery: Validation of a family quality of life survey. *Journal of Intellectual Disability Research, 47*, 367–384.

Roberts, R. N., Innocenti, M. S., & Goetze, L. D. (1999). Emerging issues from state level evaluations of early intervention programs. *Journal of Early Intervention, 22*, 152–163.

Sameroff, A. J., & Fiese, B. H. (2000). Transactional regulation: The developmental ecology of early intervention. In J. P. Shonkoff & S. J. Meisels (Eds.), *Handbook of early childhood intervention* (2nd ed., pp. 135–159). Cambridge, UK: Cambridge University Press.

Scarborough, A., Spiker, D., Mallik, S., Hebbeler, K., Bailey, D. B., & Simeonsson, R. (2004). A national look at children and families entering early intervention. *Exceptional Children, 70*, 469–483.

Singer, J. D. (1998). Using SAS PROC MIXED to fit multilevel models, hierarchical models, and individual growth models. *Journal of Educational and Behavioral Statistics, 24*, 323–355.

Thompson, B. (2004). *Exploratory and confirmatory factor analysis: Understanding concepts and applications.* Washington, DC: American Psychological Association.

Thompson, B., Lobb, C., Elling, R., Herman, S., Jurkiewicz, T., & Hulleza, C. (1997). Pathways to family empowerment: Effects of family-centered delivery of early intervention services. *Exceptional Children, 64*, 99–113.

Trivette, C. M., & Dunst, C. J. (2005). DEC recommended practice: Child-focused practices. In S. Sandall, M. L. Hemmeter, B. J. Smith, & M. E. McLean (Eds.), *DEC recommended practice: A comprehensive guide for practical application* (pp. 107–126). Longmont, CO: Sopris West.

Turnbull, A. P., Turbiville, V., & Turnbull, H. R. (2000). Evolution of family–professional partnerships: Collective empowerment as the model for the early 21st century. In J. P. Shonkoff & S. J. Meisels (Eds.), *Handbook of early childhood intervention* (2nd ed., pp. 630–650). Cambridge, UK: Cambridge University Press.

ABOUT THE AUTHORS

MELISSA RASPA (CEC NC Federation), Research Psychologist; **DONALD B. BAILEY, JR.** (CEC NC Federation), Distinguished Fellow; and **MURREY G. OLMSTED**, Research Psychologist, RTI International, Research Triangle Park, North Carolina. **ROBIN NELSON**, Director of Outcomes and System Improvement, Texas Department of Assistive and Rehabilitative Services, Division of Early Childhood Intervention, Austin, Texas. **NYLE ROBINSON**, Statewide Part C Data Manager, Illinois Department of Human Services, Division of Community Health and Prevention, Springfield, Illinois. **MARY ELLEN SIMPSON**, Instructor, Graham Hospital School of Nursing, Canton, Illinois. **CHELSEA GUILLEN** (CEC IL Federation), Statewide Part C Outcomes Coordinator, Illinois Early Intervention Training Program, Tinley Park, Illinois. **RENATE HOUTS**, Research Associate, Department of Psychology and Neuroscience, Duke University, Durham, North Carolina.

Address correspondence to Melissa Raspa, RTI International, 3040 Cornwallis Road, Research Triangle Park, NC 27709 (e-mail: MRaspa@ rti.org).

Preparation of this article was supported in part under a cooperative agreement (#H326L08001) from the Office of Special Education Programs and with support from the Texas Department of Assistive and Rehabilitative Services and the Illinois Department of Human Services. The content, however, does not necessarily represent the policy of these agencies and no endorsement by the federal or state governments should be inferred.

Manuscript submitted August 2008; accepted June 2009.

PARTICIPANTS AND DATA COLLECTION: IDENTIFYING HOW QUANTITATIVE INFORMATION IS GATHERED

You now know how to identify the overall research design used in quantitative studies by recognizing sets of procedures described in reports. Once you have identified a study's overall research design, your next step is to examine the specific procedures that were used in more detail. Two key procedures in quantitative research include how the researcher selected participants and gathered quantitative information from them. Pay careful attention to these specific procedures when reading quantitative research because the quality of a quantitative study's results depends on the quality of the information gathered. In this chapter, you will learn how to understand and evaluate the procedures that researchers report for selecting participants and collecting data in their quantitative research studies.

BY THE END OF THIS CHAPTER, YOU SHOULD BE ABLE TO:

- Identify and understand the participants and data collection of a quantitative study.
- Describe the sample in a quantitative study and identify the strategy the researcher used to select the sites and participants.
- Identify the instruments that a researcher used and recognize evidence that the instruments provided good quantitative data.
- Understand the procedures that researchers used to collect quantitative data in their studies.
- Evaluate the quality of the sample and the collected data in a quantitative research report.

Recall from Chapter 1 that research is a process where researchers pose a question, collect data about the question, and analyze the data to answer the question. A review of this simple definition of research reminds us that the collection of data from participants is at the heart of the research process. Therefore, the procedures that researchers use to select participants and gather data are a key element of any research study. You need to learn how to understand the information that researchers provide about this step in their reports, and to use appropriate standards for considering the quality of this step that reflect the research approach used.

Although the participants and data in a study are important for all types of research, there are particular considerations to keep in mind when the study's purpose called for the researcher to use a quantitative research approach. You were introduced to these considerations in Chapter 2 when you learned that quantitative researchers typically:

- select a large number of participants who are representative of a larger group;
- collect numeric information about the variables of interest using instruments with predetermined questions and responses to obtain objective information; and
- use standardized procedures for gathering the information in an ethical manner.

These elements highlight the major characteristics that describe how researchers typically collect quantitative data. Although these characteristics suggest key attributes of quantitative data collection, they do not tell you how to interpret the information that you find in quantitative research reports. Because of its importance in research, you need to carefully read about how researchers gathered information from participants. The details of this information help you understand the context of the study's results because they tell you what data the researcher collected and from whom. These details also help you assess whether the research procedures were conducted in a rigorous and ethical manner consistent with a good quantitative approach. When a researcher reports good procedures for collecting quantitative data, you can feel more confident in the results that are found based on that data and better understand the claims made based on the results. Let's begin to examine these issues by considering how you locate and read information about data collection in a quantitative report.

How Do You Identify the Participants and Data Collection in a Quantitative Study?

As you learned in the last chapter, researchers describe the procedures that they used (i.e., their method) to conduct their quantitative studies in the Method section of research reports. This section usually has the heading *Method* or *Methods* in quantitative studies, and it follows directly after the Introduction section(s). The Method section often starts with a brief description of the study's research design. However, most of the information you read in the Method section focuses on how the researcher actually gathered information from people or organizations. Because the collection of data is central to conducting research, researchers generally include the same categories of information when discussing their data collection methods.

> **Here's a Tip!**
>
> Authors often include subheadings to organize the information presented in Method sections of reports. Use subheadings such as *Participants* and *Instruments* to help make sense of the information that you read.

Let's consider these categories by first reading an excerpt from a quantitative research report. In this report, Frankenberger (2004) described conducting a correlational study to investigate whether smoking status and gender are related to specific variables, such as egocentrism, for adolescents. As you read this passage, think about what the author conveys about the data collection.

Method

Participants
Participants were 215 male (52%) and female (48%) high school students ranging in age from 14 to 18 ($M = 15.91$, $SD = 1.14$). Because prior research on adolescent egocentrism has historically used White, middle-class samples, data were collected at a high school in the predominantly middle-class neighborhood of a medium-sized city in the Pacific Northwest. Students were predominantly White (77%). Of the original 223 surveys administered, 8 were excluded from the analysis because of missing data.

Procedure
Students completed a self-administered questionnaire during one of their health classes. The questionnaire was titled "You and Your Opinions About Cigarette Smoking" and included measures of adolescent egocentrism, sensation seeking, risk perceptions, and questions regarding smoking behavior. Participants were informed that the results of the survey were anonymous and confidential. Participation was voluntary.

Instruments
Adolescent egocentrism. Adolescent egocentrism was measured with the AES [Adolescent Egocentrism Scale] developed by Enright and colleagues (Enright et al., 1979; Enright et al., 1980). The scale consists of three five-item subscales for the imaginary audience, personal fable, and self-focus. For each item, participants are asked to rate the importance of a statement on a scale ranging from 1 = not important to 5 = very important. The AES has demonstrated acceptable to good levels of internal consistency ranging from Cronbach's alpha = .78 (Enright et al., 1979) to Cronbach's alpha = .83 (Enright et al., 1980). Scores were calculated by summing across the five items for each subscale. . . . (Frankenberger, 2004, pp. 580–581)

As this passage illustrates, you learn about different categories of information regarding how data were gathered in the Method section of a quantitative study. These categories tell you information about the study's sites and participants, general procedures, and instruments.

Look for Information About the Sites and Participants

Frankenberger (2004) began the description of her data collection procedures by telling us where she collected the data (the site) and from whom (the participants). We learn that she collected data from 215 students at one high school in the Pacific Northwest. We also learn why she selected this school because the students had characteristics similar to those used in past research on this topic.

Note the General Procedures for Collecting Data

After telling us about the sites and participants, Frankenberger next described her general procedures for data collection. The procedures included having students complete a questionnaire during health class. In addition, we find that the author was concerned with how she interacted with her participants and made sure she treated them ethically. She noted that she informed the students that their information would be kept confidential and that their participation was voluntary.

Identify the Instruments Used to Gather Quantitative Data

After supplying general information about data collection, Frankenberger provided specific details about the instruments used to collect data. For the description of the one instrument included in this excerpt, she noted its name (Adolescent Egocentrism Scale), who developed it (Enright and colleagues), the types of responses collected with this instrument (rating of importance from 1 to 5), and information about the scores from this instrument (e.g., acceptable to good levels of internal consistency).

From this one example passage, we find there are three categories that provide essential information about how a quantitative researcher collected data during a study. Listing them in their most common order, these include:

- the sites and participants,
- the specific data collection instruments used to measure the variables of interest, and
- the general procedures for administering the instruments to participants.

Although quantitative researchers do not always discuss this information in the same order, these three categories provide you with a framework for reading and evaluating the information included in most quantitative research reports. We will examine each of these categories in more detail in this chapter.

How Do You Understand the Selection of Sites and Participants in a Quantitative Study?

One of the most important elements to consider when reading any research study is the information provided about the study's participants. The participants are the entities who take part in the research. Many studies include individuals as the participants, but you will likely read studies that included other types of participants. Couples, families, organizations, agencies, states, and countries are all examples of "participants" in research. The participants are the ones who provide the data that the researcher uses to answer the study's research questions. Therefore, how well the researcher answers the research questions depends a great deal on who provided the data.

In quantitative research, the way that participants were selected directly affects the kinds of conclusions that you can draw from a study's results. Let's consider an example to illustrate this point. Suppose a researcher conducted a study to describe trends in students' attitudes about science. The study participants included 10th-grade students who had chosen to attend a special science magnet school, and the researcher found very positive attitudes. We might be tempted to conclude that all 10th-grade students have positive attitudes about science. However, if we consider the study participants, we realize that those students likely chose to attend the science magnet school because they have an interest in science, so it makes sense that their attitudes were so positive.

However, another study that measured the attitudes of 10th-grade students at all the schools in a district would likely find a different trend in the attitudes.

Information about the participants in a quantitative study typically appears as one of the first topics discussed in the Method section, often under a subheading such as *Participants* or *Sample*. To understand and evaluate the participants in a quantitative study, you should identify three kinds of information as you read: the study's population and sample, the sampling strategy used, and the size of the sample.

Identify the Population and Sample

Quantitative research typically is about describing trends, relationships, or differences for a group of people or organizations. Therefore, when reading a quantitative study, you should identify the group that the researcher wants to study. The general group of interest in a quantitative study is referred to as the population. A **population** is a group of individuals or organizations who have the same characteristic. Populations can be small, such as all administrators in one school district. Usually the population for a quantitative research study is large, such as all voters in a community, all girls participating in high school sports in a city, or all child services agencies in a state.

Although quantitative researchers conduct their studies to learn about a population, they typically do not collect data from every person or organization in the group. In most situations, it simply would take too long, cost too much, or be too difficult to locate everyone in a group. Therefore, researchers select individuals who are part of the population to participate in their quantitative studies. That is, from all possible people or organizations in the population, they select a sample for study from the population. A **sample** is a subgroup of a population that participates in a study and provides data for the study. As illustrated in Figure 7.1, researchers can select different possible samples from a population of interest. For example, a researcher interested in elementary principals (the population) may select a subset of principals from around the state as the sample for a research study.

It is important to identify the characteristics of the sample when reading quantitative studies. In quantitative research, the best samples are the ones where the researcher selected individuals or organizations that are representative of the entire group of individuals or organizations of interest. *Representative* means that the individuals are typical of the population under study. Therefore, a **representative sample** occurs when the researcher selected individuals for the sample that are typical of the wider population. For example, if the population of elementary school principals is 75 percent female, 70 percent middle class, and 30 percent from rural settings, a representative sample of the population of elementary school principals would be about 75 percent female, about 70 percent of the individuals would be middle class, and about 30 percent of the sample would be assigned to rural schools. When you read about the sample of a quantitative study, you should consider whether the participants are representative of the population so that you can determine whether you are able to use the results obtained from

FIGURE 7.1
A Population and Examples of Possible Samples

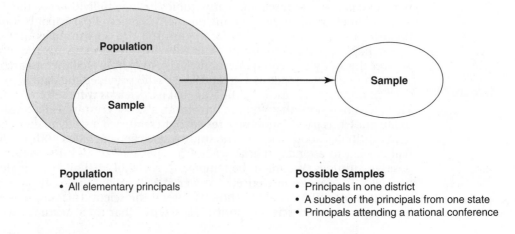

Population
• All elementary principals

Possible Samples
• Principals in one district
• A subset of the principals from one state
• Principals attending a national conference

the sample to draw conclusions about the population as a whole. To help make this determination, you next need to consider the strategies that researchers use to select their samples.

Determine the Sampling Strategy That Was Used

It is important to consider *how* the researcher selected the participants when reading quantitative research because this can tell you whether the study's sample is representative. Researchers employ different approaches for selecting the samples in their studies, which are called **sampling strategies**. There are several different sampling strategies that you may encounter as you read quantitative research studies, several of which are summarized in Table 7.1. When considering the strategy used in a particular study, it is helpful to think of two categories of sampling strategies: probability and nonprobability sampling.

> *Here's a Tip!*
>
> Keep in mind that random *sampling* is a different procedure than random *assignment*. Researchers use random sampling to select participants who are representative of the population. Researchers use random assignment to assign participants to conditions in true experiments to control for confounding variables.

- *Probability sampling.* **Probability sampling** occurs when researchers use a random process to select individuals (or units, such as schools) from the population so that each individual has a known chance (or probability) of being selected. You can think of probability sampling as the researcher putting everyone's name from the population into a hat and drawing out names at random to participate in the study. As listed in Table 7.1, there are several types of probability sampling. The most common type of probability sampling is a strategy called *random sampling*, where the researcher selects participants at random from all the members of the larger group.

When reading quantitative research, look to see whether the researcher used a probability sampling strategy. The use of probability sampling in a study has the advantage that any bias that may exist in the population should have been equally

TABLE 7.1 Types of Sampling Strategies Found in Quantitative Research

Category	Type of Sampling Strategy	Characteristics	Example for a Study About Foster Care
Probability sampling	Random sampling	The researcher randomly selects individuals from a list of all members of the population of interest	A researcher obtains a list of all caseworkers in the state and randomly selects participants from the list
	Systematic random sampling	The researcher randomly picks a starting point within a list of all members of the population of interest and then selects every *n*th individual on the list	A researcher obtains a list of all adults who provide foster care in a county, randomly picks a starting point on the list, and then selects every 5th name on the list to be a participant
	Stratified random sampling	The researcher divides the population into subgroups and randomly selects participants from each group	A researcher obtains a list of all children placed in foster care in the city, divides the list into groups (e.g., infants, toddlers, and preschoolers), and randomly selects participants from each group
Nonprobability sampling	Convenience sampling	The researcher selects participants who are available and accessible	A researcher selects the caseworkers who facilitate foster care placements at one agency near his university
	Purposive sampling	The researcher selects participants "on purpose" because they are considered to be most appropriate for the study	A researcher selects three children in foster care who are in need of an intervention to improve their behaviors

distributed among the selected participants. This is the most rigorous form of sampling in quantitative research because the investigator can make the strongest claims that the sample is representative of the population. This means that when researchers report using probability sampling, you can likely generalize the results found in the study to the larger population. The use of a probability sampling strategy is particularly important in studies using a survey design because the purpose is to describe trends in a population (as discussed in Chapter 6). Despite its advantages, it is not always possible for researchers to use probability sampling in their studies. Probability sampling requires that the researcher obtain a list of *every* person in the population. In many studies, it is not feasible for the researcher to obtain such a list, such as in a study of children who are homeless (no such list exists). Probability sampling is also unusual in experimental studies because it typically is not possible to select participants at random when the researcher plans to manipulate the conditions that the participants experience.

■ *Nonprobability sampling.* In studies where it was not feasible or appropriate for the researchers to use probability sampling, you find that the researchers used nonprobability sampling. **Nonprobability sampling** occurs when researchers select individuals to study because they are available, convenient, and meet some criteria or characteristics that the investigator seeks to study. For example, in the excerpt we reviewed at the start of this chapter, the author conveniently selected participants who were students attending one high school. The two most common types of nonprobability sampling are convenience and purposive sampling, as summarized in Table 7.1.

Many of the quantitative research studies you read made use of nonprobability sampling strategies. They are the most common because they are easier for researchers to implement than probability sampling. Although convenient, their use limits the conclusions that can be drawn about the results from a study. For example, a researcher who studies nurses at one inner city clinic cannot draw conclusions about nurses in general because the participating nurses at that clinic may be different from typical nurses in some important ways (for instance, if all the nurses happen to have less than 5 years clinical experience). In many quantitative experimental and correlational studies, however, the researchers are not interested in generalizing findings to a population, but instead aim to test or describe relationships among variables for a specific group of participants. In such studies, a sampling strategy based on convenience is sufficient.

As you read a Method section of a quantitative report, identify whether the researcher used a probability or nonprobability sampling strategy and look for an explanation as to why the particular strategy was used. Sometimes authors identify these strategies by name, but often they simply describe what they did, and you have to deduce the strategy type from the provided information. Use the information about the sampling, sites, and participants to determine whether the results of the study are representative of a larger population or are limited to the individuals who participated in the study.

What Do You Think?

Consider Perkins et al.'s (2011) quantitative bullying-intervention study found at the end of Chapter 3. Read the following passage from this study. What type of sampling strategy did the authors use? Is the sample representative?

Students in five middle schools located throughout the State of New Jersey in the United States provided the data for this research. Each school contained Grades 6 through 8 and almost all students were between the ages of 11 and 14. The five schools were from an initial group of seven middle schools in the state that had chosen to participate in an online survey of their students regarding bullying in the late spring of 2006. (paragraph 11)

Check Your Understanding

From this passage, we can conclude that the authors used a *nonprobability sampling strategy* to select students who were convenient at a few middle schools. These middle schools were convenient because they were willing to give the researchers access to their students to study bullying issues and were all located in one region. Therefore, the schools and sampled students are likely not representative of all middle school students. This means that the results may not generalize beyond the students that were studied.

Determine Whether the Sample Included a Large Number of Participants

The final essential detail that you should look for when reading about the participants in a quantitative study is the size of the study's sample. The **sample size** is the number of participants (or organizations) that actually participated in the study and provided data. Researchers report their sample sizes by stating the number in the text or using a shorthand such as "$N = 52$," where N stands for the "number of participants" and $=$ stands for "equals."

A general rule of thumb for quantitative research is that the larger the size of the sample, the better. One reason that large sample sizes are important is because a larger sample means that there is less of a chance that the sample that participated in the study is different from the population. In other words, the larger the sample, the less likely there is a sampling error in the results. **Sampling error** is the difference between the result obtained from the data collected from the sample (the sample estimate) and what the researcher would get if data were collected from the whole population (the true population score). Unfortunately, unless researchers collect data from everyone in the population, the true population score cannot be known. This means that you cannot know when reading a report whether the researcher has a large or small sampling error in the study. Let's consider an example to illustrate this idea. Suppose a researcher wants to know how elementary teachers feel about differentiated instruction and selects a small sample that happens to include a few teachers who hate differentiated instruction. If the sample is small, then these few extremely negative views can make the results very negative. If the general population actually has positive feelings about differentiated instruction, then this study has a large sampling error. If the researcher had selected a large number of participants, then the extreme views of a few participants would not have affected the results as much. In good quantitative research, researchers do their best to reduce the chance of sampling error by selecting as many potential participants as possible and encouraging them to agree to participate. When you read that a researcher included a larger number of participants in a study's sample, you can feel more confident that the study reduced the likelihood of having a large amount of sampling error.

The second reason that it is necessary for quantitative studies to have included a large sample size is that it makes it more likely that the researcher, after analyzing the gathered data, can find that variables are related or a treatment made an impact. We will learn more about quantitative data analysis in the next chapter, but simply put, more participants means that the researcher gathers more data, and more data makes it easier to detect relationships and differences that exist among variables. Quantitative researchers refer to their ability to find relationships and differences with their data as *power*, and the more participants in a study means that the study has more "power" to find important results.

When reading quantitative studies, identify the size of the sample and notice if the researchers provided an explanation as to why this size was used. The best way for researchers to pick their sample size is to use precise estimates of the number of participants needed as derived from sample size tables or special formulas that have been developed. You can feel more confident that the sample is large enough when a researcher reports using procedures like a sample size formula to determine the size of their sample. The size of the sample that is appropriate for a particular study depends on many considerations, including the overall size of the population, the number of variables of interest, and the type of quantitative research question that needs to be answered. Therefore, the criteria for good sample sizes also vary for the different research designs discussed in Chapter 6. Here we provide some general guidelines for the minimum sample sizes required for basic versions of the different designs. These guidelines are based on the number of participants needed for typical statistical procedures to provide good estimates of the characteristics of the population (we will learn more about this in Chapter 8). These recommended samples sizes are:

- a minimum of 15 participants in each group in a true experiment or quasi-experiment,
- one participant (or a few) in a single-subject study (with data collected over a large number of points in time),
- a minimum of 30 participants for a correlational study that relates variables, and
- approximately 350 individuals (or more) for a survey study, but this size varies depending on several factors, including the size of the overall population.

What Do You Think?

Consider the following passage from a quantitative survey study. What is the sample size? What sampling strategy appeared to be used to select the participants? What population does the sample represent?

A random sample of 350 was drawn from a list of 8,506 active elementary public school principals enrolled as members of the National Association of Elementary School Principals. . . . Surveys were returned from principals representing various regions of the United States: Midwest (32%), Northeast (27%), South (26%), and West (15%). These proportions closely reflected the membership of the population from which the sample was drawn. . . . Respondents ($N = 214$) reported the length of their service as elementary school administrators to be as follows: under 1 to under 5 years (28.5%), 5 to under 10 years (30.8%), and 10 or more years (40.7%). (Abril & Gault, 2006, p. 11)

Check Your Understanding

From this passage, we learn that Abril and Gault (2006) contacted 350 individuals, but the actual sample size of individuals who participated was 214. That is, $N = 214$. The authors used probability sampling to identify their participants by randomly selecting them from a list of all principals who belong to a national organization. Therefore, the population of this study is all principals who belong to National Association of Elementary School Principals in the United States. Because of the extensive membership of this organization and its representation of all areas of the United States, this sample is likely representative of all U.S. elementary principals. We should, however, be a little cautious about possible sampling error in the results because so many contacted principals did not respond. This could be a problem if the ones who did not respond tend to think differently from those who did respond.

How Do You Understand the Instruments Used to Gather Data in a Quantitative Study?

Once you have examined the information about a study's population and sample, you are ready to consider the quality of the data that the researcher gathered from the participants in the sample. Recall from Chapter 2 that quantitative researchers gather data from participants using instruments with closed-ended items in order to answer their

FIGURE 7.2
The Flow of Activities That Researchers Use to Collect Quantitative Data

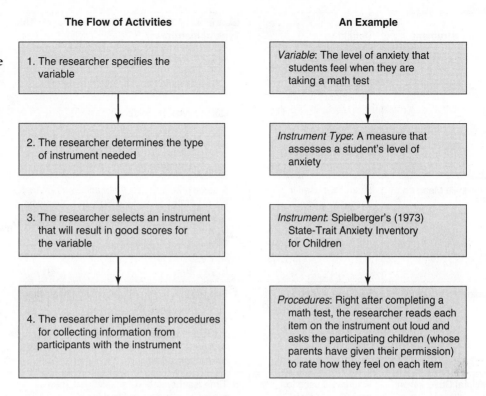

The Flow of Activities

1. The researcher specifies the variable

2. The researcher determines the type of instrument needed

3. The researcher selects an instrument that will result in good scores for the variable

4. The researcher implements procedures for collecting information from participants with the instrument

An Example

Variable: The level of anxiety that students feel when they are taking a math test

Instrument Type: A measure that assesses a student's level of anxiety

Instrument: Spielberger's (1973) State-Trait Anxiety Inventory for Children

Procedures: Right after completing a math test, the researcher reads each item on the instrument out loud and asks the participating children (whose parents have given their permission) to rate how they feel on each item

research questions about specific variables. Therefore, the instruments used to gather data must be considered in quantitative research.

When reading about a quantitative research study, you should expect that the researchers specified their variables, determined the type of instrument needed to collect the information for each variable, and selected instruments that are good quality before gathering any data. The process researchers use to select their instruments is summarized in Figure 7.2 using a variable called "test anxiety." The selection of instruments is a critical step in quantitative research because the quality of the data gathered in a study is only as good as the instruments used to gather them. The process shown in Figure 7.2 provides you with a framework to help you read and evaluate the information that researchers include in their reports about the instruments used in their quantitative studies. Let's examine how to understand each part of this process.

> *Here's a Tip!*
>
> You can identify the major variables in a study by examining the purpose statement, research questions, and hypotheses. You will find that many authors discuss the instruments they used by the variables they measure. Get in the habit of underlining each major variable as you read any quantitative report so you are clear on what the researcher needed to measure.

Identify How the Researcher Specified the Variables

To understand what data are collected in a study, you first need to identify the variables that are of interest from the study's research questions and hypotheses. You learned in Chapter 5 that these variables include independent, dependent, and control variables. Variables represent characteristics or attributes that vary among participants. Researchers must specify each of their variables in a way that can be measured (i.e., assigned a numeric score). For example, a researcher interested in math performance for high school students might define this variable as the grade received in algebra class. By reading that the researcher defined the variable in this way, you learn that the variable can be measured and it can vary among the students (from a low grade of 0.0 to a high grade of 4.0).

Identify the Type of Instrument Used to Gather Information

Once you have identified how the researchers specified the variables in a study, you should next identify how the researchers measured each of the variables. Researchers use various types of instruments to collect quantitative data for their variables.

Type of Instrument	Definition	Examples of Items That Might Appear on This Type of Instrument
Demographic Form	Instrument used to gather facts about or characteristics of participants	1. Gender _____ Male (0) _____ Female (1) 2. Current type of residence _____ Own (1) _____ Rent (2) _____ Temporary housing (3) _____ Homeless (4)
Performance Measure	Instrument used to assess individuals' abilities, achievement, or traits	3. A sample item from a math achievement test: If x is 25% of 40 and y is 50% of x, then what is y? A. $y = 2$ B. $y = 4$ C. $y = 5$ D. $y = 8$ E. $y = 10$

Attitudinal Measure	Instrument used to measure individuals' attitudes and opinions	4. Bullying is a big problem at my middle school.
		  1. Strongly disagree
		  2. Disagree
		  3. Neither agree nor disagree
		  4. Agree
		  5. Strongly agree

Behavioral Observation	Instrument used to record individuals' behaviors	5. Time teacher spends speaking in Spanish during 10 min of Spanish II class: Minute of lesson: 1 2 3 4 5 6 7 8 9 10 — Teacher activity Teacher activity = S = Speaking in Spanish Teacher activity = E = Speaking in English Teacher activity = B = Speaking in both English and Spanish Teacher activity = N = Not speaking
Factual Information	Instrument used to gather information from public records	6. Number of days recorded as absent: _____ 7. Number of days suspended from school: _____

FIGURE 7.3   **Types of Instruments, Their Definitions, and Examples of Items**

An **instrument** is a tool used to gather quantitative data by measuring, observing, or documenting responses to specific items. The instrument may be a test, questionnaire, tally sheet, log, observational checklist, inventory, survey, or assessment instrument. Researchers use instruments to measure achievement, assess individual ability, observe behavior, develop psychological profiles, or interview individuals. There are five general types of instruments that you find when reading quantitative studies. A summary of each type with examples of items that might be included in such an instrument is illustrated in Figure 7.3. Review these types to understand the different information that researchers gather in their studies.

- *Demographic forms.* Researchers use demographic forms to gather basic facts about and characteristics of their participants. Common types of demographic information collected by researchers include gender, age, race, and annual income.
- *Performance measures.* Researchers use **performance measures** to assess or rate individuals' ability to perform in a certain way, such as their achievement, intelligence, aptitude, interests, or personality traits. Examples of performance measures include achievement tests (e.g., the Iowa Test of Basic Skills), intelligence tests (e.g.,

Wechsler Scale), aptitude tests (e.g., Stanford-Binet Intelligence Scale), interest inventories (e.g., Vocational Preference Inventory), and personality assessment inventories (e.g., Myers-Briggs Type Indicator).

- *Attitudinal measures.* Researchers use **attitudinal measures** to measure participants' feelings toward topics (e.g., assessing positive or negative attitudes toward giving students a choice of school to attend). These measures often ask participants to rate their level of agreement for multiple statements on a scale from *strongly agree* to *strongly disagree.* The researcher then adds up the scores on these multiple statements for each individual. This type of attitudinal measure is very common and is often referred to as a "Likert scale" after the person (Rensis Likert) who wrote about its use.

- *Behavioral observation checklists.* Researchers use **behavioral observation checklists** to observe and record specific behaviors of participants, such as paying attention in class or completing a set of prescribed tasks. These checklists identify the behavior(s) of interest and time intervals for observing the behaviors, and provide a space for the researcher to check points on a scale that reflect the behavior(s). Researchers choose to use behavioral observation checklists in their studies when they need to measure an individual's actual behavior, rather than simply record their views or perceptions.

- *Factual information documents.* Researchers gather factual information about participants from documents in the form of numeric, individual data. These documents include available public records. Examples of these types of documents include grade reports, school attendance records, medical records, and census information. As long as these documents are available in the public domain, researchers can access and use them. Some documents, such as grade or health information, can only be accessed if the researcher secures special permission.

Here's a Tip!

Researchers often use the word *survey* to refer to their instruments (particularly when they are attitudinal measures). Keep in mind that using a survey questionnaire to gather data is not the same as using a survey research design. Researchers use survey questionnaires in all types of quantitative research.

You can use these five types of quantitative instruments to understand the instruments that the researchers chose to use to measure their variables. The type is often determined by what variable the researcher wants to measure (e.g., attitudes or behaviors). It also depends on what is feasible in the context of the study. For example, researchers may want to record behaviors to determine how frequently students are bullied on the playground, but observing all students all day may not be feasible. Instead, they may use an attitudinal measure to ask students to indicate their attitudes about how often they feel that they are bullied on the playground. When you read a report, you should note what type of instrument was used for each variable and whether that type seemed appropriate considering what the researcher wanted to learn. More importantly than the types, you also want to consider whether the instruments are of good quality and likely to result in meaningful data. Let's now consider the idea of an instrument's quality.

Assess the Evidence That the Researcher Used a Good Instrument

Once you identify the types of instruments used in a quantitative study, you should note whether there is evidence that good instruments were used. The quality of instruments is important because it determines the quality of the data gathered with them. One of the biggest challenges that researchers face when they conduct quantitative research is obtaining a good instrument to collect data for the variables of interest. Whether the researchers developed the instrument for their study themselves or used an instrument developed by someone else, in a well-written report, they should describe the extent to which the instrument was expected to provide good quality data in the study. Instruments are good if they result in the collection of data that provides a good measure of the variable of interest. What makes an instrument good or bad? Let's start to answer this question by considering a measurement instrument that you probably already know.

Recall that instruments are tools for obtaining quantitative scores that indicate a variable of interest. One variable that interests many of us is our weight, and we often use bathroom scales as our instrument to measure this variable. Suppose you happened to obtain two bathroom scales from a local garage sale. These bathroom scales are now your instruments to measure the variable weight, but you need to determine whether they are good instruments. To test their quality, you decide to try out these bathroom scales with your daughter, who weighs 85 pounds according to her recent visit to the doctor (who you know has a good scale). You ask your daughter to stand on scale 1 three times and you record the following scores: 78 pounds, 103 pounds, and 86 pounds. You ask her to do the same with scale 2 and obtain the following scores: 36 pounds, 36 pounds, and 35 pounds. Knowing that your daughter weighs 85 pounds, are either of these two bathroom scales good instruments?

As the bathroom scale example illustrates, it can be easy for researchers to obtain numbers in their quantitative studies, but it is critically important that they obtain *good* numbers from the instruments they use. If the gathered numbers are not consistent and fluctuate without reason (like scale 1) or if they not accurate (like scale 2), then the numbers are not useful measures of the variables of interest. These problems suggest two criteria that are useful for assessing whether scores from an instrument are good quality:

- the scores need to be reliable (i.e., consistent) and
- the scores need to valid (i.e., accurate).

When you read about the instruments used in a quantitative study, first look for information indicating that the scores from each instrument are reliable. **Reliable** means that scores from an instrument are stable and consistent. The scores should be nearly the same when researchers administer the instrument multiple times to the same participants. For example, if you stand on a bathroom scale once and then again 5 minutes later, you expect to record nearly the same weight because it is unlikely your weight changed in 5 minutes. In our example, scale 2 provided reliable scores that were consistently at about 36 pounds, but the scores from scale 1 were not reliable because they varied from 78 to 103 pounds, even though the girl's weight did not change. Another aspect of reliability is that scores from the multiple items on an instrument need to be consistent with each other. When an individual answers certain questions one way, the individual should consistently answer closely related questions in a similar way.

In good quantitative research, the researchers ensure that the measures or observations are reliable. They do this by including only clearly worded questions on the instrument and using standard procedures for having the participants complete the instrument. In well-written quantitative reports, the researchers include evidence that the scores from their instruments were reliable. You can identify evidence of reliable scores by recognizing the following kinds of information as you read:

- The scores from multiple questions were consistent with each other (called internal consistency or Cronbach's alpha, α). The scores for all questions should relate to each other at a positive, high level (Cronbach's alpha = .7 − 1.0).
- The scores from the instrument were consistent over time when the instrument was administered more than once to the same individuals (called test–retest reliability). The scores from the two times should relate (or correlate) at a positive, reasonably high level (r = .6 − 1.0).
- If multiple raters were used (such as with an observational checklist), the different raters scored items in a consistent way (called inter-rater reliability). Raters in quantitative research should agree 90–100 percent of the time.

When you read about the instruments used in a quantitative study, you should also look for information indicating that the scores from each instrument are valid. **Valid** means that the scores from an instrument are accurate indicators of the variable being measured and enable the researcher to draw good interpretations. That is, the scores should be useful and meaningful measures of the variable of interest. If we consider a bathroom scale, then we expect the measured weight score to accurately indicate a person's weight. That is, if the person weighs 85 pounds, then we expect the scale to record a value around 85 pounds. Likewise, a quantitative instrument should assign scores to individuals that are accurate. For example, if a student excels at reading, then you expect him to obtain a high score on an instrument aimed at measuring reading performance.

In good quantitative research, the researchers ensure that the measures or observations are valid. They do this by carefully developing the instrument, such as by including questions on the instrument that ask about all the important aspects of the variable of interest and writing the questions using language that is at an appropriate level for the participants. In well-written quantitative reports, the researchers include evidence that the scores from their instruments were valid. You can identify evidence of valid scores by recognizing the following kinds of information as you read:

- The authors included a citation to the literature indicating that the instrument was previously developed and used for research purposes.
- If the authors developed their own instrument, they included the text of the items in the report so you can judge whether they addressed the concept being measured in a clear and unambiguous way.
- The researchers used experts to assess that the items on the instrument cover the appropriate content (called content or face validity).
- The researchers tested that the scores from the instrument provided meaningful indicators of the general concept or variable of interest. There are two ways that researchers report testing that scores are meaningful. The researcher may have expected that the scores *are* related to other variables in certain ways (positive or negative) and checked to see that the scores matched these expectations (called construct validity). The researcher may also have expected that the scores *are not* related to certain variables and checked to see that the scores matched these expectations (called discriminant validity).

In summary, when reading information about data collection in quantitative studies, note the major variables and how they were specified to be measured, identify the type of instrument used to measure each variable, and assess the extent to which there is evidence that the scores from the instruments were reliable and valid. Let's apply this set of strategies to the study excerpt that you read at the start of this chapter. Here is the paragraph about one of the instruments in that study. As you read it again, identify the variable, instrument type, and what evidence the researcher provided to indicate that the study used a good instrument.

Adolescent egocentrism. Adolescent egocentrism was measured with the AES [Adolescent Egocentrism Scale] developed by Enright and colleagues (Enright et al., 1979; Enright et al., 1980). The scale consists of three five-item subscales for the imaginary audience, personal fable, and self-focus. For each item, participants are asked to rate the importance of a statement on a scale ranging from 1 = not important to 5 = very important. The AES has demonstrated acceptable to good levels of internal consistency ranging from Cronbach's alpha = .78 (Enright et al., 1979) to Cronbach's alpha = .83 (Enright et al., 1980). Scores were calculated by summing across the five items for each subscale. (Frankenberger, 2004, pp. 580–581)

Here's a Tip!

Researchers are not the only ones who gather information. Practitioners such as teachers, nurses, and social workers also choose to gather information. If someone in your practice setting wants to use a test or survey, be sure to ask whether there is evidence that it will give scores that are reliable and valid with individuals in your setting.

In this paragraph, Frankenberger clearly identified a major construct that she wanted to measure—namely, adolescent egocentrism. We learn as we read that she actually specified three variables related to this construct: imaginary audience, personal fable, and self-focus. She used an instrument called the Adolescent Egocentrism Scale, which can be considered a type of performance measure because it measures the development of certain personality traits (i.e., identity beliefs) in adolescents. In this paragraph, we find that the author provided evidence that the scores from this instrument are reliable (i.e., consistent) to an "acceptable to good" level because Cronbach's alpha is greater than .7. She also provided limited evidence for the validity of the scores by using an instrument that has been previously reported in the literature (see references to the work of Enright and colleagues).

What Do You Think?

Read the following passage about Kim and Goldstein's (2005) data collection in their quantitative study about college students' expectations about studying abroad. (a) What variable is specified? (b) What type of instrument is used? (c) What evidence do you note that the researcher selected a good instrument?

Intercultural communication apprehension. Neuliep and McCroskey's (1997a) Personal Report of Intercultural Communication Apprehension (PRICA) was used to assess anxiety associated with real or anticipated intercultural interaction. The higher the score on this 14-item scale, the greater apprehension indicated. In two studies using this scale with U.S. samples, good internal consistency was obtained, with Cronbach's alpha equal to .92 (Lin & Rancer, 2003; Neuliep & Ryan, 1998). Neuliep and McCroskey (1997a) reported support for the construct and discriminant validity of the PRICA. Lin and Rancer (2003) found significant correlations between the PRICA and a measure of intercultural willingness to communicate. (Kim & Goldstein, 2005, p. 270)

Check Your Understanding

From this passage we note the following: (a) Kim and Goldstein specified a variable called *intercultural communication apprehension.* (b) They used an attitudinal measure for this variable because the instrument measured participants' attitudes about interacting with other cultures. (c) They provided extensive evidence that this was a good instrument. We learned that the scores from this instrument tend to be reliable because they noted that "good internal consistency" was obtained in previous studies (Cronbach's alpha = .92). In terms of the instrument's validity, we learned that this instrument has been previously used, and that its validity has been supported by two studies that examined how its scores related to other measures.

How Do You Understand the Procedures That Researchers Use to Collect Quantitative Data?

It is important to understand both the participants and instruments used when reading any quantitative study, but this information alone does not indicate how the researchers actually obtained scores on the instrument from the participants. Therefore, the third element of quantitative data collection to identify are the procedures that the researchers used to gather the data. The general procedures should be considered because they can have a significant influence on the quality of the data in a research study. For example, suppose a researcher wanted to use the SAT test to measure academic performance, but only gave participants 15 minutes to complete this long test. In that situation, the researcher would be using a good instrument, but because of the poor procedures used, the data would not be high quality because the participants would not be able to complete the test thoughtfully in the time provided. The procedures that researchers use to gather quantitative data differ depending on the research design, the participants, and the instruments used. There are, however, three important aspects for every quantitative data collection process. When you read about the procedures in a quantitative study's Method section, look for information about whether the procedures were ethical, were standardized, and anticipated "threats" to a study's conclusions.

Note Indicators That the Procedures Were Ethical

Above all else, the procedures that researchers use to collect their quantitative data should be ethical and respectful of the participating individuals and sites. In the United States, federal legislation requires that researchers guarantee participants certain rights and request their permission to be involved in a research study. If the data collection procedures in a study are not ethical, then the study should not get published, and it certainly should not receive your attention. Here are some indications that the researcher used ethical procedures during data collection.

- *The researchers obtained approval to conduct their study from their local campus.* Most researchers work for universities that are required to have ethics committees that review the procedures for all research studies. In the United States, these ethics committees are typically referred to as institutional review boards (IRBs). The IRBs are charged with reviewing all planned research procedures before researchers start to conduct their studies. This is to ensure that the procedures represent ethical practices for conducting research involving human subjects. When you read that researchers received approval to conduct the study from an IRB, then you know that an ethics committee reviewed the procedures and found them to be satisfactory.
- *The researchers obtained permission to collect data within an organization.* In many quantitative research studies, the researchers also need to secure permissions to conduct research at a particular site, such as at a school, company, or clinic. When you read that a researcher received permission to access an organization from someone in a position of authority (such as a principal, supervisor, or manager), then you know that the researcher was concerned with ethical practices in conducting the research.
- *The researchers obtained consent from individuals who participated in their study.* Ethical research requires that researchers treat their participants with respect and obtain their consent (or permission) to be included as participants in the study. When reading quantitative research studies, look to see that the researchers informed individuals about the purpose of the research, without deception, and explained the study's procedures to them. Individuals' decisions to participate (or not) should be voluntary, and they should give their informed consent before participating—for example, by signing a form that indicates their consent. If the participants include vulnerable individuals such as minors, then in most instances the researcher must also take steps to secure parental informed consent in addition to having the children agree to participate.
- *The researchers used procedures that did not harm the participants in their study.* In good, ethical research studies, the researchers take steps to make sure that they do not harm their participants and often note these steps as part of their procedures. An example of the kind of procedures that researchers use to protect participants occurs when the researcher takes steps to protect the privacy and confidentiality of individuals who participated in the study, such as by not reporting individuals' names. Protecting participants from harm is especially important in experimental studies because the researchers actually manipulate the conditions experienced by participants. When reading experimental studies, look for information in the report indicating that no matter which condition participants were assigned to, the researcher took steps to assure that the risks would be minimized and they would not be harmed. For example, a researcher might report using the "usual treatment" as the control condition because it would be unethical to not provide any treatment to the participants.

Expect the Data Collection Procedures to Be Standardized

After reading a number of quantitative studies, you learn that researchers use many different procedures for administering their quantitative instruments to participants to gather quantitative data. Examples of different procedures include handing out paper-and-pencil forms, asking questions over the phone or through text messaging, administering questionnaires over the Web, and rating behaviors observed by the researcher. No matter what method is used, researchers in a quantitative study must use standard procedures for collecting all of their quantitative data—that is, the researchers must try to collect their questionnaire, interview, or observation data in a similar way from all participants. If the data collection procedures vary, then it is possible that the researchers may introduce bias into the study and the data being gathered from the participants may not be comparable for analysis. When you read about the procedures used in a quantitative study, look for ways that the researchers standardized the data collection procedures, such as the following:

- All participants were asked the same questions and had the same choices for responding to the questions. Good quantitative instruments include closed-ended questions that have preset response options so that all participants use the same standard set of options for their responses (such as *strongly agree, agree, neutral, disagree,* and *strongly disagree*).

- All participants received the same directions for completing the instruments and they completed the measures under similar conditions. Examples of such standardized procedures include a researcher giving all participants the same amount of time to take a performance test and a researcher making sure participants do not talk to each other while filling out a questionnaire about attitudes.
- All raters involved in conducting the quantitative research were trained so that they recognize and rate the target information in similar and consistent ways. The adequate training of raters is important in studies where the researcher observed behaviors (e.g., time spent paying attention in class) or scored documents (e.g., student portfolios).

Consider the following passage as an example of using standardized procedures in a study involving college students. Kim and Goldstein (2005) wrote: "Between mid-October and mid-November 2000, 1st-year seminar students completed an extensive survey packet during a class period. Volunteer participants were read instructions for completing the questionnaire and then did so at their own pace during the survey administration session" (p. 272). This passage indicates that the researchers collected their data in a standard way because all participants were provided one class period to complete the surveys, data were collected during one month in the semester, and the researchers read the instructions out loud to ensure that participants received the same directions.

Identify How the Researchers Reduced Threats to the Studies' Conclusions

In addition to the use of good instruments and procedures that are ethical and standardized, good quantitative research requires that the researchers collected their data using procedures that allow them to make sound conclusions about their research questions and hypotheses. As introduced in Chapter 6 when you learned about quantitative research designs, there are two special types of conclusions that are frequently desired in quantitative research. These are:

- the researcher wants to claim that the independent variables caused effects in the dependent variables, and
- the researcher wants to claim that the findings from the sample generalize to a larger population.

In good quantitative studies, the researchers design their procedures so that they reduce the threats to one or both of these two types of claims as much as possible. By reducing the threats in their studies, researchers are able to make stronger claims. In fact, being able to make these claims in a valid way is so important that they have been given their own special names in quantitative research: internal validity and external validity. Just as you consider whether there is evidence that the scores from an instrument are valid, you also want to examine the data collection procedures used in the study to determine whether they reduce threats and increase the researchers' ability to draw valid conclusions from the study.

Procedures That Researchers Use to Increase a Study's Internal Validity.   Recall that one reason why researchers conduct quantitative research is to test whether independent variables cause an effect in dependent variables. When you read a quantitative study that was conducted for this purpose, then you should be especially concerned about the study's internal validity. **Internal validity** is the extent to which a researcher can claim that the independent variable caused an effect in the dependent variable at the end of the study. Studies that used rigorous procedures to control for possible confounding variables have a high level of internal validity and can make strong cause-and-effect claims. Studies that did not or could not control for possible confounding variables have low levels of internal validity and cannot correctly make claims of cause and effect based on the results.

As you learned in Chapter 6, researchers conduct different types of experiments (true experiments, quasi-experiments, and single subject experiments) for the purpose of establishing that a treatment causes an effect. Experimental designs provide researchers with sets of procedures aimed at increasing a study's internal validity. One key way that researchers can increase a study's internal validity is by implementing an experimental design instead of using a survey or correlational design. Even when implementing a certain type of experimental design, researchers can be more or less successful at controlling for spurious and confounding variables that may influence the outcome in addition to the independent treatment variable. Good experimental procedures that increase a study's internal validity include:

- manipulating the conditions that participants experience so that the conditions are as similar as possible between groups and across time, except for the treatment related to the independent variable;
- randomly assigning individuals to treatment groups so that existing differences among the individual participants are spread across the groups; and
- measuring other variables that need to be controlled, such as giving a pretest or assessing individuals for attitudes or behaviors that may be relevant to how they respond to a treatment.

Procedures That Researchers Use to Increase a Study's External Validity. Also mentioned earlier is another reason why researchers conduct quantitative research, which is to describe trends for variables for a population. When you read a quantitative study that was conducted for this purpose, then you should be especially concerned about the study's external validity. **External validity** is the extent to which a researcher can generalize the results from the study sample to a population and to other settings. Studies that used rigorous procedures to obtain a representative sample have a high level of external validity and can make strong claims that the results generalize to the larger population. Studies that did not or could not obtain a representative sample have low levels of external validity and cannot correctly make claims that the results generalize beyond the participants in the study.

As a general guideline, studies using a survey design are more generalizable (i.e., have higher external validity) than experimental or correlational studies. This is because survey studies are designed for the purpose of describing trends in a larger population. However, quantitative studies using any of the designs can have high external validity if the sample studied was representative. To conclude that a study's results can generalize from the sample to a larger population, you need to determine that the researchers provided evidence that their sample is representative. Good procedures that increase a study's external validity include the following:

- The researchers randomly select individuals from a list of all members of the population to participate in the study.
- The researchers use procedures that encourage as many participants as possible to respond to the study's measurement instruments. A high rate of response (e.g., 80% or higher) from participants results in a larger sample size and reduces the number of nonrespondents. It is a problem when many people chose to not respond. If the response rate is low (e.g., 60 percent or lower), then the results may not generalize because the people who chose not to respond may be different from those who did respond.
- The researchers examine the demographic information obtained from the participants to determine whether the individuals who participated are similar to the larger group. If the sample is similar to the larger population, then it provides some evidence that the results may generalize.

Both internal and external validity are important to consider when reading any quantitative research study. It is difficult, however, for researchers to achieve high levels of both in a study because they are related to each other in complex ways. Researchers achieve a high level of internal validity by controlling all extra variables. The more that the variables are controlled, however, the less generalizable the results typically become. Let's consider an example to see the relationship between these two ideas.

Suppose researchers wanted to test whether a new reading curriculum causes better reading achievement. They might set up an experiment that compares students randomly assigned to receive the new curriculum to those assigned to receive standard instruction. There are many possible influences on reading achievement—such as the effectiveness of the teacher, available reading materials, and time spent practicing. To control for these effects, the researchers select children from one local magnet school and invite them to attend a special program in their laboratory for 6 weeks during the summer. At the laboratory, the researchers provide instruction to both groups and mandate that all children put in a set amount of time practicing each day with research assistants. Therefore, if the results show better achievement for the students in the experimental group, they can conclude with some certainty that the new curriculum caused this achievement. That is, this study has a high level of internal validity. These results, however, cannot be generalized to all children attending real schools and classrooms, because it is likely that the children at this one magnet school differ from all children in terms of their interests, backgrounds, and teachers, and the laboratory setting likely differs substantially from regular classrooms. Therefore, this study has relatively low external validity.

What Do You Think?

Read the following passage about Xu et al.'s (2010) procedures as described in the quantitative physical-activity-in-middle-schools study from Chapter 1. What procedural issues do the authors discuss?

> Following approval by the University Institutional Review Board, data from participants were gathered between 20 August and 24 November 2006. . . . A convenience sample of 660 middle school PE teachers' email addresses was obtained from 421 middle schools' websites or through phone calls. A promotion email with a web link to the password-protected online survey and a generic cover letter that informed respondents about the purpose of the study, filling instructions, and privacy concerns was delivered to those email addresses. The website remained accessible for data collection for a full two months during which four reminder emails were issued to those people who had not yet responded to our survey. A prize draw after the conclusion of data collection was used as an incentive to stimulate the response rate; in total 43 prizes were given out in the form of gift cards (two $100, six $50, fifteen $20, and twenty $10 gift cards). (paragraph 06)

Check Your Understanding

Xu et al. touch on a number of procedural issues related to their study in these few sentences. First, we find evidence that they employed ethical practices because they received the approval of their IRB for the study and informed potential participants about the study's purpose and how they would be respected, such as having their identity protected. Second, we learn important procedural details, such as when the researchers collected the data and under what conditions participants received a link for the survey questionnaire. Third, we find out that the researchers used a convenience sample of teachers, but did use several procedures to try to ensure a high number of responses to obtain a large sample. Even with these procedures, only 243 participants completed the questionnaire fully. Therefore, the results may be somewhat representative of PE teachers, but the claims for external validity would be stronger if a true probability sample had been obtained.

How Do You Evaluate the Participants and Data Collection in a Quantitative Study?

It is essential to understand and evaluate the basics of quantitative data collection to understand and evaluate any quantitative research report. In all good quantitative research, the researchers use procedures to ensure that they obtain reliable and valid

TABLE 7.2   Criteria for Evaluating the Participants and Data Collection in a Quantitative Research Report

Quality Criteria	Indicators of Higher Quality in Quantitative Research	Indicators of Lower Quality in Quantitative Research
The Key Elements		
1. The sampling strategy is appropriate and justified.	+ If possible, a probability sampling strategy is used to select the sites and participants from the population of interest. + The sampling procedures used are fully described and clear. + Strong reasons are provided that justify why the sampling strategy was appropriate for the study.	− A nonprobability sampling strategy is used to select sites and participants that are convenient. − The sampling procedures are unclear and poorly described. − Weak reasons are provided that do not explain why the specific sampling strategy was used.
2. The sample size is appropriate and justified.	+ The sample size is large, reducing the amount of sampling error. + The sample size meets the minimum size for the selected research design. + The sample size is strongly justified using a procedure such as a sample size formula or power analysis.	− The sample size is small, introducing the likelihood of sampling error. − The sample size barely meets the minimum size for the selected research design. − A weak rationale is provided to justify the sample size.
3. High quality instruments are used to gather data.	+ The instruments used are clearly appropriate for the major variables. + Strong evidence in support of the reliability and validity of the scores from the instruments is provided.	− It is unclear how the instruments align with the study's major variables. − Weak evidence in support of the reliability and validity of the scores from the instrument raises concerns.
4. The data are gathered using ethical quantitative procedures.	+ Appropriate approvals and permissions were secured. + Respectful treatment of the participants is demonstrated. + Adequate steps were taken to prevent the risk of harm to participants.	− Approvals and permissions were not secured. − Procedures demonstrate a lack of respect for participants. − Procedures safeguarding participants are questionable or poorly considered.
5. The data are gathered using standardized quantitative procedures.	+ The researchers used good quantitative procedures such as asking closed-ended questions, giving all participants the same directions, and training raters to ensure that all participants completed the instruments in similar conditions. + The procedures are fully described and explained.	− The researchers varied their data collection procedures across participants and/or time points so participants did not complete the instruments in similar conditions. − The procedures are unclear and poorly explained.
General Evaluation		
6. The study has a high level of internal validity.	+ The researcher measured and/or controlled for all important variables and used experimental design procedures such as random assignment and manipulating the conditions experienced by participants when possible to control for potential confounding variables.	− The researcher did not measure and control for some important variables and did not use experimental design procedures such as controlling conditions or randomly assigning participants to conditions.
7. The study has a high level of external validity.	+ The researcher selected a representative sample, obtained a sample size that is large considering the type of design, used procedures to obtain a high rate of response from participants, and provided detailed information about the characteristics of the sample in the report.	− The researcher selected a convenience sample, obtained a sample size that is small considering the type of design, obtained a low rate of response from participants, and provided little information about the characteristics of the sample in the report.

measures of their major variables. In addition, depending on the study's purpose and research design, they use rigorous procedures for selecting participants and collecting data that position them to achieve the highest possible levels of internal validity and/or external validity. Table 7.2 lists criteria that are useful to consider when evaluating the participants and data collection in a quantitative study. This table also provides indicators of higher quality and lower quality for the criteria to help you make your own judgments when evaluating the information provided in a research report.

Figure 7.4 provides a convenient means for you to apply the quality criteria to evaluate the participants and data collection described within the Method section in any quantitative research report. For each of the criteria you locate, assign a quality rating from *fair* (1) to *excellent* (3), and document your evidence and/or reasoning behind the rating. If one of the criteria is missing or very poorly stated, then indicate *poor* (0) as your rating. Although research reports vary in terms of their overall purpose, the extent of discussion about the participants and data collection, and the type of claims they want to make, a good quantitative study should still score well on most of the items listed in Figure 7.4. By adding up the rating scores for each of the criteria and using the suggested cutoff values provided at the bottom of the figure, you will have a quantitative measure that you can use to inform your overall assessment.

Quality Criteria	Quality Rating				Your Evidence and/or Reasoning
	0 = Poor	1 = Fair	2 = Good	3 = Excellent	
The Key Elements					
1. The sampling strategy is appropriate and justified.					
2. The sample size is appropriate and justified.					
3. High quality instruments are used to gather data.					
4. The data are gathered using ethical quantitative procedures.					
5. The data are gathered using standardized quantitative procedures.					
General Evaluation					
6. The study has a high level of internal validity.					
7. The study has a high level of external validity.					
Overall Quality 0–10 = Low quality 11–16 = Adequate quality 17–21 = High quality	Total Score =				My Overall Assessment =

FIGURE 7.4   A Rating Scale for Evaluating the Participants and Data Collection in a Quantitative Research Report

Reviewing What You've Learned To Do

- *Identify and understand the participants and data collection of a quantitative study.*
  - ☐ The Method section of a quantitative research report contains information about where the study was conducted, who participated, the instruments used to gather data, and the general data collection procedures.
- *Describe the sample in a quantitative study and identify the strategy the researcher used to select the sites and participants.*
  - ☐ The sample in a quantitative study includes the sites and individuals who participated in the research and provided data to the researcher.
  - ☐ Quantitative researchers use probability and nonprobability sampling strategies to select individuals from a larger population to participate in the research. Probability sampling strategies use a random selection process to identify samples that are representative of the population. Nonprobability sampling strategies focus on selecting individuals who are convenient.
  - ☐ Quantitative researchers generally select a large number of participants in order to better learn about the larger population.
- *Identify the instruments that a researcher used and recognize evidence that the instruments provided good quantitative data.*
  - ☐ The types of quantitative instruments that researchers use to measure their variables of interest include demographic forms, performance measures, attitudinal measures, behavioral observation checklists, and factual information documents.
  - ☐ Good quantitative instruments produce scores that are reliable (i.e., consistent and stable). Evidence for good reliability includes the report of a high value of internal consistency among the items on the instrument, high consistency among the scores from the instrument over two time points, and high consistency between two different observers or raters.
  - ☐ Good quantitative instruments produce scores that are valid (i.e., accurate). Evidence for good validity includes the referencing of others' use of the same instrument, asking clear questions on the instrument, using experts to review the instrument's content, and finding that the scores from the instrument relate to other variables in predicted ways.
- *Understand the procedures that researchers used to collect quantitative data in their studies.*
  - ☐ Researchers use procedures that are ethical, such as securing necessary approvals and permissions, treating participants with respect, and making sure that participants are not harmed.
  - ☐ Researchers use procedures that are standardized, such as asking the same questions and providing the same response options to all participants, providing the same directions to all participants, and training the individuals who provide ratings as part of the data collection process.
  - ☐ Researchers use procedures such as random assignment and manipulating conditions to control for possible confounding variables in order to reduce threats to the study's internal validity (the extent to which a study's results can indicate that one variable caused an effect in another).
  - ☐ Researchers use procedures such as random selection and encouraging a high response rate from potential participants to make the sample more representative to reduce threats to the study's external validity (the extent to which a study's results generalize to a larger population).
- *Evaluate the quality of the sample and the collected data in a quantitative research report.*
  - ☐ The evaluation of a quantitative sample considers the sampling strategy used to select the participants, the number of participants in the sample, and the extent to which the participants are representative of the larger population and provide support for making claims that the results generalize to the population.
  - ☐ The evaluation of the quantitative data collection considers the quality of the instruments, the use of ethical and standardized procedures, and the extent to which the data provide accurate and consistent measures of the variables and provide support for making cause-and-effect claims.

✓ **To assess what you've learned to do, click here to answer questions and receive instant feedback.**

Reading Research Articles

Carefully reread the quantitative early-intervention-outcomes study by Raspa et al. (2010) found at the end of Chapter 6 (starting on p. 216) and the quantitative bullying-intervention study by Perkins et al. (2011) at the end of Chapter 3 (starting on p. 98).

As you review each article, pay close attention to statements in which the authors described the participants and data collection in the Method section. Use the highlighting tool in the Pearson etext to indicate where the authors have provided information about the participants and data collection, and use the notetaking tool to add marginal notes that name each element you highlighted and note how each one is related to the study's quantitative approach. Among the elements you will want to find are:

1. Site
2. Participants
3. Sampling strategy
4. Sample size
5. Instruments (e.g., demographic form, performance measure, attitudinal measure, behavioral observation checklist, and factual information document)
6. Instrument quality (e.g., reliability and validity)
7. Data collection procedures (e.g., ethical procedures, standardized procedures, and procedures to reduce threats)

Note, however, that sometimes authors do not describe all of the information about their participants—for example, they might not mention the site or how individuals were selected. In addition, authors may not provide complete information about their data collection—for example, they might not report information about an instrument's quality. If one of these elements is missing, indicate that in your marginal notes.

 Click here to go to the quantitative early-intervention outcomes study by Raspa et al. (2010) so that you can enter marginal notes about the study.

 Click here to go to the quantitative bullying-intervention study by Perkins et al. (2011) so that you can enter marginal notes about the study.

Understanding Research Articles

Apply your knowledge of the content of this chapter to the quantitative early-intervention-outcomes study by Raspa et al. (2010) starting on p. 216.

1. From what sites and participants did the authors collect their quantitative data in the early-intervention-outcomes study? What type of sampling was used? What was the size of the sample?

2. Which of the five types of quantitative instruments did the researchers use in this study? What major variable(s) were measured with each type?

3. Examine the information provided about the instrument to measure Family-Centered Services (paragraph 12). What evidence do you find that the scores from this instrument are good? Explain your thoughts.

4. What procedures did the authors describe indicating that the quantitative data collection was ethical and standardized?

5. Do you think this study has a high, moderate, or low level of internal validity, and a high, moderate, or low level of external validity? Explain your choices.

✓ **Click here to answer the questions and receive instant feedback.**

Evaluating Research Articles

Practice evaluating a quantitative study's participants and data collection, using the quantitative early-intervention-outcomes study by Raspa et al. (2010) starting on p. 216 and the quantitative bullying-intervention study by Perkins et al. (2011) starting on p. 98.

1. Use the criteria discussed in Table 7.2 to evaluate the quality of the participants and data collection in the early-intervention-outcomes study. Note that, for this question, the rating form includes advice to help guide your evaluation.

✓ **Click here to open the rating scale form (Figure 7.4) to enter your ratings, evidence, and reasoning.**

2. Use the criteria discussed in Table 7.2 to evaluate the quality of the participants and data collection in the bullying-intervention study. Note that, for this question, the rating form does NOT include additional advice.

✓ **Click here to open the rating scale form (Figure 7.4) to enter your ratings, evidence, and reasoning.**

DATA ANALYSIS AND RESULTS: EXAMINING WHAT WAS FOUND IN A QUANTITATIVE STUDY

Quantitative research involves more than researchers collecting data. Researchers analyze their quantitative data using statistics and report the results of the analysis to answer their research questions and test their hypotheses. The reason you probably choose to read any quantitative research report is because you are interested in learning the results of the study that was conducted. However, to understand different types of quantitative statistical results, you need to first understand the process that researchers use to analyze their quantitative data. In this chapter, you will learn how to interpret the information that researchers report about their quantitative data analysis process and how to understand and evaluate the results of this process.

BY THE END OF THIS CHAPTER, YOU SHOULD BE ABLE TO:

- Identify and understand the data analysis and results of a quantitative research study.
- List the steps that researchers use to analyze quantitative data.
- Know how to identify quantitative results when reading a quantitative research report.
- Evaluate the quality of the data analysis and results in a quantitative research report.

It is not uncommon for some students to dread reading this chapter as soon as they see the word *statistics*. The use of statistics has a bit of a bad reputation. You might think that statistical procedures are hard to understand and interpret. You might also be concerned that researchers can use statistics to come up with whatever answer they want. In reality, however, statistical procedures are simply mathematical tools that are useful when researchers need to summarize large amounts of numeric data and uncover objective evidence for relationships that exist within the data. Just like a woodworker uses tools such as a hammer, saw, and lathe to make tables, chairs, and bookcases, researchers use different statistics such as a mean, *t* test, and correlation to answer their descriptive, comparison, and relationship research questions. You do not need to be a woodworker to appreciate and use a well-crafted table and chair; likewise, you do not need to be a statistician to appreciate and understand the results of a good quantitative analysis.

Therefore, this book will not teach you how to calculate different statistics. You can take a stats course from a friendly statistician to learn that. Instead, this chapter focuses on understanding the thinking and logic behind researchers' use of statistics in the quantitative data analysis process. By understanding how researchers use statistics and the different kinds of statistical results that they report, you can make sense of most of these results. We will first consider how you identify the information about data analysis and results included in quantitative research reports before we jump into the details of how you understand this process.

How Do You Identify the Data Analysis and Results in a Quantitative Study?

Recall from Chapter 1 that analyzing data and reporting results is an essential step in the process of research. When researchers use a quantitative approach to this process, they collect data in the form of numbers from a large number of participants or time points, and thus they use mathematical analysis procedures, called *statistics*, that help them make sense of this large amount of data. Researchers analyze their quantitative data using statistics and represent the results in tables, figures, and explanations that provide information about their research questions and hypotheses. There are two types of information about quantitative data analysis that you can find when reading a quantitative research report. First are the specific details of the study's data analysis procedures in the Method section. Second are the specific results obtained from the analysis process in the Results section.

Look to the Method Section for a General Description of the Quantitative Data Analysis Process

The first place you can find information about quantitative data analysis is within the Method section. As we learned in Chapter 7, the focus of the Method section is on report-ing the procedures for participant selection and data collection. Many quantitative research reports also include an overview of the data analysis procedures in the Method section, immediately after the discussion of the data collection procedures. You may find this dis-cussion presented under a subheading such as *Data Analysis* or *Statistical Analyses*. In general, authors provide only a brief overview of the specific statistical choices they made to analyze the study's quantitative data. For example, read the following excerpt about data analysis that Ramsay et al. (2013) provided in the Method section of their quasi-experimental study testing the effect of having young children choose their own portion sizes at lunch time compared to serving them predetermined portion sizes without choice:

> Data were analyzed using SPSS Statistical Analysis Software (version 18, IBM Corporation, Somers, NY). Univariate analysis of the distributions indicated strong deviations from normal-ity for all menu items except total food intake. Therefore, Mann-Whitney tests were used to determine a significant difference ($p < .05$) in intake between the choice versus nonchoice lunches. Kruskal-Wallis tests were used to determine if there was a difference in food intake amount among each menu item, sex, whether they attended a school plus program, and whether the children attended AM or PM Kindergarten. . . . A *t* test was used to measure a difference in total food intake. (p. 240)

Note that this excerpt does not provide a full description of the analytic process or statistical calculations that the researchers completed. It does, however, tell us informa-tion such as the software used for the analysis (i.e., SPSS Statistical Analysis Software), the focus on comparing groups (i.e., "determine a significant difference in intake between the choice versus nonchoice lunches"), the name of the tests that were used (i.e., "Mann-Whitney tests," "Kruskal-Wallis tests," and "a *t* test"), and information about criteria for judging the results of the test as significant (i.e., "$p < .05$").

As this passage illustrates, the Method section in quantitative research reports may contain detailed information without much explanation as to what it means. Sur-prisingly, many quantitative research articles do not explicitly discuss any information about data analysis. This lack of description is because all quantitative researchers fol-low the same basic analysis process, with the differences emerging in the choice of the specific statistics that are calculated. In many reports, therefore, the researchers go right from describing their procedures for data collection to presenting their statistical results.

Examine the Results Section to Find the Quantitative Results for the Study's Research Questions and Hypotheses

Almost without exception, results of data analysis are revealed in one of an article's major section—the Results section. In the Results section, researchers report the find-ings obtained for the statistical procedures used to describe the participants, examine the performance of the instruments, and address each of the study's research questions and hypotheses. Thus, it is in the Results section that you learn what researchers found from the collected data. In addition, the Results section also includes key information such as which statistics were calculated during the analysis. So, by learning to understand quantitative results, you can also identify additional details about the analysis process used in a study to obtain the results.

How Do You Understand a Study's Quantitative Data Analysis?

You probably know that analyzing quantitative data involves statistics in some way, but you may not know what this means or how a researcher actually uses statistics. To understand how researchers use statistics, it is helpful to know about the process of quantitative data analysis. You can visualize the major activities in the quantitative data analysis process by examining the top-down approach to quantitative data analysis in Figure 8.1. This process is called top-down (also referred to as *deductive*) because the researcher starts with general explanations by specifying several variables and predicted relationships among them and then works down to all the detailed data and specific

FIGURE 8.1
The Top-Down, Linear Process That Researchers Use to Analyze Quantitative Data

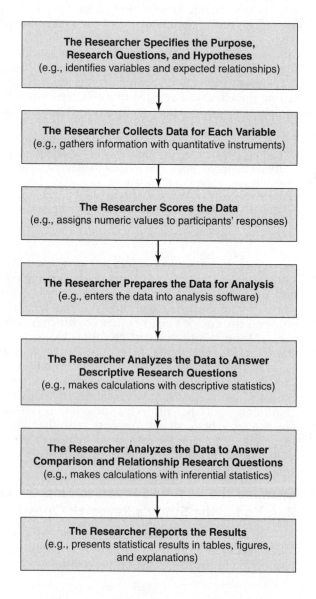

The Researcher Specifies the Purpose, Research Questions, and Hypotheses
(e.g., identifies variables and expected relationships)

The Researcher Collects Data for Each Variable
(e.g., gathers information with quantitative instruments)

The Researcher Scores the Data
(e.g., assigns numeric values to participants' responses)

The Researcher Prepares the Data for Analysis
(e.g., enters the data into analysis software)

The Researcher Analyzes the Data to Answer Descriptive Research Questions
(e.g., makes calculations with descriptive statistics)

The Researcher Analyzes the Data to Answer Comparison and Relationship Research Questions
(e.g., makes calculations with inferential statistics)

The Researcher Reports the Results
(e.g., presents statistical results in tables, figures, and explanations)

analyses. The quantitative data analysis process also unfolds in a very linear fashion. This means that the researcher generally finishes one step pictured in Figure 8.1 before moving to the next.

As shown in the figure, quantitative data analysis begins when researchers state their purpose, research questions, and hypotheses. Recall from Chapter 5 that researchers who use quantitative research are interested in three main types of questions: descriptive, relationship, and comparison. Once the study's direction is specified, researchers collect data for each variable, such as using a questionnaire with items that ask about students' motivation and class grade. After data collection is complete, researchers assign numbers by scoring the responses and prepare the data for analysis. For example, if a student reported his grade as a B, the researcher scores it as 3.0 and enters that score into the database. Researchers then analyze the data to answer their descriptive research questions using procedures called descriptive statistics. For example, from these analyses the researcher finds the average level of motivation in the sample and identifies the high and low motivation scores. After completing descriptive analyses, quantitative researchers move to analyses that use inferential statistics to address their relationship and comparison questions. For example, the researcher tests whether motivation and grade point average are related in the collected data. Finally, researchers represent and report the results of these different analysis procedures.

Although researchers typically include few details about their quantitative data analysis process in their reports, a good strategy for understanding the overall process is to identify how the researcher implemented each of the major steps after data collection as shown in Figure 8.1. The steps to look for include how the researchers:

- scored the data;
- prepared the data for analysis;
- analyzed the data to answer descriptive research questions;
- analyzed the data to test comparison and relationship hypotheses; and
- reported the results.

By using these steps as a framework, you can follow the different procedures that researchers describe in their quantitative reports. Let's consider the kinds of information you can expect to find for the different steps when reading about the quantitative data analysis process.

Step 1—Identify How the Researchers Scored the Data

Researchers cannot analyze their data with statistics unless the data have been recorded in a numeric form. The first data analysis step that researchers complete is to score the data. **Scoring data** is the procedure that researchers use to assign a numeric score (or value) to each participant's response for each question on the instruments used to collect data. In some cases, the score to be assigned is obvious. If the researcher asks a child to indicate her age and she responds 10 years, then the response would be scored as 10. For many quantitative variables, however, the researcher needs to have a plan for how to score different responses. The key is that all participants who respond the same way should end up with the same score. For instance, suppose that parents respond to a survey asking them to indicate their attitudes about choice of a school for children in the school district. One question might be:

> Please indicate the extent to which you agree with this statement:
> "Students should be given an opportunity to select a school of their choice."
>
> _____ Strongly agree
>
> _____ Agree
>
> _____ Undecided
>
> _____ Disagree
>
> _____ Strongly disagree

Assume that a parent checks "Agree." How does the researcher score this response? To analyze the data, the researcher will assign a score that represents each of the response categories, such as *strongly agree* = 5, *agree* = 4, *undecided* = 3, *disagree* = 2, and *strongly disagree* = 1. Based on these assigned numbers, all parents who checks "Agree" would receive a score of 4 for this item. Recall from Chapter 5 that some variables are measured and scored in categories and some are measured along a continuum. In good quantitative research, researchers score their data in consistent ways so that they are reliable and valid indicators of the categorical and continuous variables of interest in the study. You can find information about how the researchers scored the responses in a study in various locations within a quantitative report. In well-written reports, you learn how the researcher scored the responses either as part of the description of data analysis or as part of the information included about the study's instruments. In some studies, you may have to figure out how the variables were scored by examining the results reported in the Results section.

Step 2—Note How the Researchers Prepared the Quantitative Data for Analysis

Once researchers have scored the data, their next procedure is preparing the data for analysis. Researchers select a computer program to use for their analysis and enter the collected data into the program's database. Researchers can choose from several statistical software programs that are available to store data in a study and calculate different statistical quantities from these data. When you read about a study's quantitative data analysis, you often learn the name of the program the researchers used. This detail informs you that the researcher used a sophisticated program to conduct the statistical analyses for the data. Two frequently used programs are SPSS (Statistical Package for the Social Sciences, www.spss.com) and SAS (www.sas.com).

After researchers carefully enter all the scored data into the selected computer program, they take additional steps to prepare the data for formal analysis. You may find they describe details such as examining the dataset for missing data (data that are "missing" because participants did not answer certain items) and checking that no mistakes were made when entering the data into the software program. In addition, researchers prepare the types of scores needed for the analysis. Researchers use different types of scores such as single items, percentages, frequencies, average scores, and summed scores. Many quantitative studies include single-item scores and summed scores, so it is helpful to understand how they differ. Figure 8.2 presents examples of these two types of scores collected for three students.

- *Single-item scores.* Researchers often examine single-item scores. A **single-item score** is a score assigned to each individual question for each participant in a study. These scores can be used to provide a detailed, item-by-item analysis of participants' responses on an instrument. In Figure 8.2, all three participants have single-item scores indicating their level of agreement for questions 1, 2, and 3. Single-item scores are also frequently used for demographic information, such as the variable "gender" in Figure 8.2.

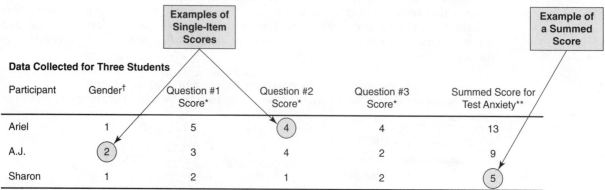

Data Collected for Three Students

Participant	Gender†	Question #1 Score*	Question #2 Score*	Question #3 Score*	Summed Score for Test Anxiety**
Ariel	1	5	4	4	13
A.J.	2	3	4	2	9
Sharon	1	2	1	2	5

†Gender responses scored: 1 = female; 2 = male.
*Question responses scored: 5 = strongly agree; 4 = agree; 3 = undecided; 2 = disagree; and 1 = strongly disagree.
**Test Anxiety: Calculated by summing scores from Questions #1, 2, and 3.

FIGURE 8.2   Two Types of Scores Prepared in Quantitative Data Analysis

- *Summed scores.* Single items often do not completely capture a participant's perspectives and often are not adequately reliable and valid (as discussed in Chapter 7). Therefore, researchers often report that they formed scales based on summing participants' responses to multiple questions as indicators for major variables in the study. **Summed scores** occur when the researcher adds the scores for several items that measure the same variable. As shown in Figure 8.2, the three participants—Ariel, A. J., and Sharon—provided responses to three questions. The researcher summed the three scores for each individual to provide a summed score for the variable "test anxiety," which represents responses to all three questions. Summed scores, especially when they include at least 6–10 similar items, are often more reliable and valid measures of variables than single-item scores. Summed scores are very common when researchers use performance and attitudinal measures in their studies.

Because summed scores provide better measures of variables than single items, you should determine how the researchers prepared the scores for the major variables. As with the procedures for scoring the data, researchers often include information on whether scores were summed in the description of the data analysis procedures or when describing the instruments. You can also often determine whether a researcher used summed scores when you examine the results of the study. For example, suppose a researcher measured *satisfaction* with an instrument that had 10 items, scored each item from 1 to 5, and reported satisfaction scores that went as high as 50. From this information, you can deduce that the researcher summed the scores for the 10 items for the satisfaction variable.

Step 3—Recognize How the Researchers Used Descriptive Statistics to Answer Descriptive Research Questions

Once the researchers have scored and prepared their data, they move to their statistical analyses. Researchers analyze their data to address each of their research questions and hypotheses. Think back to the types of research questions introduced in Chapter 5. Researchers ask descriptive questions to describe trends in the data for single variables. Examples of such descriptive questions are:

- What is the level of self-esteem of new counselors?
- How varied are teachers' level of satisfaction?
- How was a student's performance relative to other students?

Researchers start their statistical analyses by using descriptive statistics to answer questions like these for the independent, dependent, and control variables in their quantitative studies. **Descriptive statistics** are statistical tools that help researchers summarize the overall tendencies in the data, provide an assessment of how varied the scores are in the data, and provide insight into where one score stands in comparison with the rest of the data. These three ideas are called central tendency (overall tendency in the data), variability (how varied scores are), and relative standing (where one score stands relative to the rest of the scores).

The use of descriptive statistics to analyze data is found in almost all quantitative research. Because the use of descriptive statistics is ubiquitous in quantitative studies, researchers often do not explicitly discuss it as part of their data analysis procedures. You can recognize, however, that researchers used descriptive statistics as part of their analyses when they refer to descriptive statistics or report descriptive results in their study. Table 8.1 provides a key for recognizing the most common descriptive statistics found in quantitative research. This table lists the name, symbol, and use of each statistic along with a concrete example of how it might be applied in a study. Because these statistics are so common, researchers often refer to their use by the symbol (e.g., *M* or *SD*) instead of giving the name of the statistic (e.g., mean or standard deviation).

For you to better understand researchers' use of descriptive statistics, let's examine the three types of descriptive procedures (central tendency, variability, and relative standing) in more detail.

TABLE 8.1   A Key for Recognizing Common Descriptive Statistics

Statistic Name	Symbol	Type of Statistic	Use	Example Applications
Mean	M or $\bar{X}$	A measure of central tendency	Describes the average value of a continuous variable	■ The average age of participants was $M = 12.6$ years.
Median	Mdn	A measure of central tendency	Describes the middle response such that when all responses are listed in order from lowest to highest, half of them are above the median and half are below	■ The median age was 13 years.
Mode	(none)	A measure of central tendency	Describes the most common response, usually used for categorical variables	■ Of five possible activities in gym class, the mode was "line dancing."
Range	(none)	A measure of variability	Describes the spread between the highest and lowest score	■ The class test scores had a range of 65 points (from 35 to 100).
Standard deviation	SD	A measure of variability	Describes how dispersed the data points are about the mean	■ The scores on the spelling test ($SD = 12.3$) were more spread out than those on the math test ($SD = 5.5$).
Percentile rank	%	A measure of relative standing	Describes the percentage of participants with scores at or below a particular score	■ The student scored 81 on the test, which is at the 73rd percentile. He scored higher than 73% of the students.
z score	z	A measure of relative standing	Describes the relative standing of a score in units of standard deviations in relation to all the other scores	■ Jennifer's height is very tall for this sample ($z = +3$). Mark is short compared to others in the sample ($z = -2.1$).

The Use of Descriptive Statistics to Describe Central Tendency.   When you read about a study's quantitative data analysis, expect the researchers to use descriptive statistics to describe the central tendency of the collected data for each variable. Descriptions of **central tendency** are single numbers that summarize a set of scores. Researchers choose a particular statistic to describe central tendency based on whether the variable is measured as continuous or in categories. Recall from Chapter 5 that continuous scores fall along a range (such as test scores measured from 0 to 100) and categorical scores fall in distinct categories (such as single, married, or divorced). Two common statistics for central tendency found in quantitative reports are the mean and the mode.

■ The mean is the most common statistic used to describe the responses of all participants for a continuous variable. The **mean** is the total of the scores divided by the number of scores. That is, the mean is the average score for the variable across all the participants. You can recognize the use of the mean when researchers use the symbols M or $\bar{X}$ to report mean values. For example, a researcher uses the mean when reporting the average age of participants as $M = 12.6$ years. You should expect researchers to calculate the mean for variables that are measured as continuous, such as height, self-esteem, or reading achievement.

■ The **mode** is the score that appears most frequently in a list of scores. You should expect researchers to determine the mode when they want to know the most common response for a variable. Researchers mostly use the mode to analyze data for variables with categorical values. For example, a researcher uses the mode to analyze seventh-grade girls' preferred choice from a list of three possible activities for gym class. If 15 girls chose volleyball, 22 girls chose swimming, and 38 girls chose line dancing, then the researcher identifies "line dancing" as the most popular choice. That is, the "line dancing" response is the mode.

The Use of Descriptive Statistics to Describe Variability. When researchers analyze the data gathered for a continuous variable, it is not enough for them to calculate the mean; they also need to consider how much the data vary. Let's examine a practical example to understand this statement. Suppose a researcher gave two classes of third-grade students a spelling test, and both classes had the same mean score: $M = 85.0$. Reading that the means were the same, you might at first conclude that the two classes scored in the same way. However, suppose for one class all of the students' scores fell between 80 and 90, but for the other class the scores fell between 35 and 100. Even though both classes had the same average, their scores differed in terms of how spread out they were. In one class, the scores varied only a little (indicating that all students performed similarly), but in the other class, the scores varied a lot (indicating that performance was not very uniform). Researchers calculate statistics that describe the variability found in the data to address this kind of situation.

When you read quantitative research, expect the researchers to use descriptive statistics to describe the variability of the data collected for each major variable. Descriptions of **variability** are numbers that indicate the spread of scores collected for a variable. Good quantitative data analysis procedures include describing the variability of the data gathered for variables in addition to the means. Recognizing information about the variability of scores is important for understanding the trends found in the data gathered in a study. As shown in Table 8.1, the range and standard deviation are two commonly reported statistics that indicate the amount of variability in a set of scores.

- The range is the most straightforward indication of the variability of scores. The **range** is the difference between the highest and the lowest scores obtained for a variable. In the example of the spelling test just described, one class had a range of 10 points (between a low of 80 and a high of 90) and the other had a range of 65 points (between 35 and 100).
- The standard deviation is the most commonly calculated measure of variability in quantitative research. The **standard deviation** is a measure of how dispersed the data are about the mean value for a continuous variable. As such, it provides useful information about the dispersion or spread of scores in a dataset. This measure of variability is reported almost any time a researcher gives a mean value for a variable. You can recognize its use when researchers refer to the abbreviation *SD* in their reports. The value of a variable's standard deviation is usually reported right after its mean value. For example, a researcher describes the scores on a spelling test as $M = 85.0$, $SD = 5.5$ (where 5.5 is equal to 1 standard deviation).

Because you will encounter the standard deviation frequently when reading quantitative research, it is helpful to understand what it indicates. The meaning of the standard deviation can be illustrated when we graph a theoretical distribution of scores for a variable, as shown in Figure 8.3. If a researcher collected scores for a

FIGURE 8.3
The Normal Curve and Its Relationship to the Standard Deviation

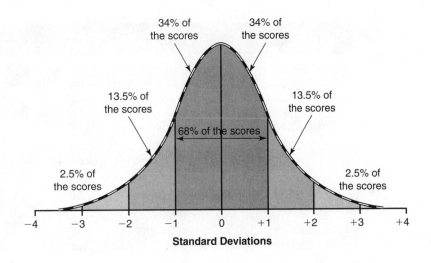

variable from sample after sample of participants and plotted them on a graph, then they would look like a bell-shaped curve—see Figure 8.3. This graph is called a *normal distribution* or *normal probability curve*. Looking at the figure, the shaded areas indicate the percentage of scores for the variable likely to fall within each standard deviation above and below the mean. Therefore, the standard deviation is a useful indicator that describes the spread of the scores for a variable. For example, 68 percent (34% + 34%) of the scores are expected to fall between +1 and −1 standard deviations from the mean. That is, if a researcher analyzed the scores on a spelling test and reported $M = 85.0$, $SD = 5.5$, we can expect that about 68 percent of the scores on this test should fall between 79.5 and 90.5.

The Use of Descriptive Statistics to Describe Relative Standing.   There is one more type of descriptive statistic that researchers include in their quantitative data analysis: descriptions of relative standing. Descriptions of **relative standing** are statistics that describe one score relative to a group of scores. Researchers calculate relative standing scores when they are interested in describing how certain participants' scores compare to those of the larger group. You can recognize a researchers' use of relative standing when they report calculating percentile ranks and z scores.

- The **percentile rank** is a number that describes the percentage of participants in the distribution who have scores at or below a particular score. Researchers use the percentile rank to determine where, in a distribution of scores, an individual's score lies in comparison with other scores. For example, if a student completed a math test and scored at the 73rd percentile, this means that the student scored better than 73 percent of the students who took the test. It also means that 27 percent of the students scored higher.
- The standard **z score** is a measure of relative standing that researchers calculate by converting a participant's score (such as height measured in inches) into a relative score measured in units of standard deviations. The z score has the useful characteristic that when calculated for a set of data, it always has a mean of 0 and a standard deviation of 1. Let's consider an example to understand why this is useful. If you read that a first-grader has a height of 54 inches, you may not know what to make of it. Is this average? Is this tall or short? Suppose instead you read that a first-grader's height had a z score value of +3 standard deviations. If you look back at Figure 8.3, you can find that the expectation is that 97.5 percent of the scores for a variable should be less than +3 standard deviations. Therefore, you can conclude that a student whose height has a z score of +3 is very tall relative to other first-graders! The standard z score has the advantage of making scores easily comparable no matter how they were first measured. For example, if $z = 0$ for a child's height and $z = -2$ for his weight, you can immediately conclude that the child has average height because the mean has a z score of zero and below average weight because the z score is negative.

What Do You Think?

Consider the following results reported in Table 2 of Perkins et al.'s (2011) quantitative bullying-intervention study found at the end of Chapter 3. What variable is being described? What descriptive statistics did the authors use? What do these statistics tell you about the different schools in the study's sample?

	School A	School B	School C	School D	School E
BULLYING PERPETRATION					
Personal bullying perpetration mean (SD)	2.3 (2.8)	2.9 (3.8)	2.7 (3.7)	3.0 (3.6)	2.4 (3.3)

> ### Check Your Understanding
>
> In this excerpt, the authors calculated descriptive information about the variable *personal bullying perpetration*. They reported the values for the mean and standard deviation (*SD*) for this variable for each of the five participating schools. The values of the mean tell us the average scores obtained on the measure of how often students reported exhibiting bullying behaviors. For example, we see that the participants at School D reported the highest number of bullying behaviors on average (*M* = 3.0) and the participants at School A reported the lowest number on average (*M* = 2.3). The values of the standard deviation indicate the spread of the scores about the means. We see that most of the sets of scores had approximately the same amount of variability because the standard deviations are practically equal (2.8–3.8).

Step 4—Identify How the Researchers Used Inferential Statistics to Answer Comparison and Relationship Research Questions

Most quantitative research studies include research questions and hypotheses that call for more than descriptive statistics. Researchers typically ask comparison and relationship research questions in addition to descriptive questions. Comparison and relationship questions go beyond describing single variables. To answer these questions, the researcher must use analysis procedures that involve two or more variables. Examples of comparison and relationship research questions include:

- *Do boys differ from girls in terms of their self-esteem?* This question compares two groups on the independent variable (gender) in terms of the dependent variable (self-esteem). To answer this question, the researcher analyzes the data to determine whether the measured difference between the groups (i.e., between their means) is greater or less than what we would expect to find by chance if the researcher could study the entire population.
- *Does an optimistic attitude relate to satisfaction for daycare providers?* To answer this question, the researcher analyzes the data to determine whether the calculated relationship between the two variables (optimistic attitude and satisfaction) is more than what we would expect to find by chance if the researcher could study the entire population.

When researchers conduct quantitative research to address questions such as these, they use analytic procedures that consider two (or more) variables at a time and that allow them to make inferences about the variables in a population based on the results from the sample. Researchers use **inferential statistics** in their analyses to consider more than one variable and make inferences to a population. The basic idea of inferential statistical procedures is that researchers analyze scores obtained from a sample for two or more variables, and use the results to draw inferences or make predictions about the variables for the population. As a consumer of quantitative research, you may never conduct your own analyses using inferential statistics. However, it is essential for you to understand the basic logic behind researchers' use of inferential statistics in order to understand the analysis (and results) reported in most quantitative research reports. Researchers use a procedure called hypothesis testing when they use inferential statistics during their data analysis. To understand how researchers analyze their data to answer comparison and relationship research questions, you first need to learn about this key procedure.

Hypothesis testing is a quantitative data analysis procedure that researchers use to determine whether a difference or relationship likely exists among variables in a population based on the result obtained from a sample. Researchers start by stating a hypothesis about how the variables are related in the population. They then collect data from a sample of the population and use the information to make a judgment about the hypothesis. That is, researchers use evidence from a sample to make (or infer) a conclusion about the variables for a population. Researchers use hypothesis testing in their quantitative studies, but rarely describe the details of their steps in the description of their data analysis. Therefore, you need to understand this procedure to make sense of the quantitative data analysis process used in the studies that you read.

Let's consider an analogy to help understand the hypothesis testing process. A researcher's use of hypothesis testing is like having a crime scene investigator (a CSI) gather evidence about a crime and go to court to testify. The CSI does his or her best to gather evidence that indicates whether or not a person has a link to a crime. Sometimes the evidence can be overwhelming, and it is easy for the court to conclude that a person is "guilty." In other cases, the evidence can be unclear, and then the court must deliberate and people may not feel very confident in their decision, so they conclude "not guilty" because there is not enough evidence to determine a person's guilt without reasonable doubt. In either case, it is possible that the gathered evidence was misleading or incomplete, although the CSI's job is to try to prevent that from happening. Similarly, in the process of hypothesis testing, the researcher gathers information and determines whether there is sufficient evidence to find the data "guilty," that is, to conclude that a difference or relationship exists.

There are guidelines used in court cases to judge whether a person is found guilty or not guilty. Likewise, hypothesis testing provides researchers with objective guidelines for how to judge whether there is sufficient evidence for or against a hypothesis. These guidelines include five steps that researchers implement whenever they conduct hypothesis testing. For each research question and hypothesis in a study, the researchers

1. identify a null and alternative hypothesis;
2. set the criterion for making a decision, called the alpha value;
3. collect data from a sample;
4. compute a statistic for the sample's data; and
5. make a decision about rejecting or failing to reject the null hypothesis.

Figure 8.4 illustrates these steps along with an example application. Knowing about these steps informs you how researchers analyze their quantitative data. Let's examine each step to help you understand this procedure that is at the heart of most quantitative data analysis.

**FIGURE 8.4
The Five Steps
in the Process
of Hypothesis
Testing**

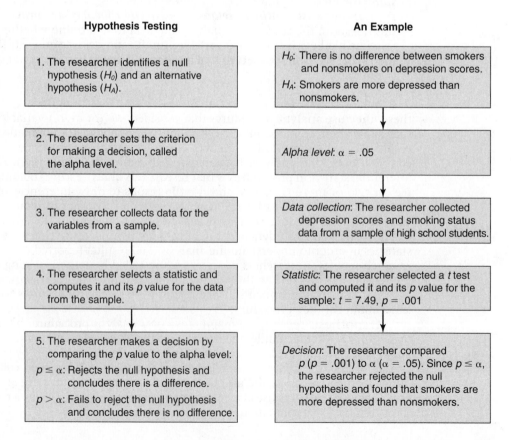

Hypothesis Testing

1. The researcher identifies a null hypothesis (H_0) and an alternative hypothesis (H_A).

2. The researcher sets the criterion for making a decision, called the alpha level.

3. The researcher collects data for the variables from a sample.

4. The researcher selects a statistic and computes it and its p value for the data from the sample.

5. The researcher makes a decision by comparing the p value to the alpha level:

$p \leq \alpha$: Rejects the null hypothesis and concludes there is a difference.

$p > \alpha$: Fails to reject the null hypothesis and concludes there is no difference.

An Example

H_0: There is no difference between smokers and nonsmokers on depression scores.

H_A: Smokers are more depressed than nonsmokers.

Alpha level: $\alpha = .05$

Data collection: The researcher collected depression scores and smoking status data from a sample of high school students.

Statistic: The researcher selected a t test and computed it and its p value for the sample: $t = 7.49$, $p = .001$

Decision: The researcher compared p ($p = .001$) to α ($\alpha = .05$). Since $p \leq \alpha$, the researcher rejected the null hypothesis and found that smokers are more depressed than nonsmokers.

1. **The researcher identifies a null and alternative hypothesis.** As discussed in Chapter 5, a null hypothesis is a prediction about the population and is typically stated using the language of "no difference" (or "no relationship"). An alternative hypothesis predicts that a difference (or relationship) exists, and the direction of this difference may be positive or negative. During data analysis, quantitative researchers actually specify *both* a null hypothesis and an alternative hypothesis for each hypothesis test. Example hypotheses from a study about adolescent smoking and depression are shown in Figure 8.4. Although researchers identify both of these hypotheses as an important part of their hypothesis testing process, they rarely include them in their reports because space is limited.

2. **The researcher sets the criterion for rejecting the null hypothesis, called the alpha level.** Inferential statistics are mathematical tools for estimating the probability that a result (i.e., a difference among groups or a relationship among variables) could have occurred simply by chance instead of because there is a real difference or relationship in the population. Unless a researcher collects data from every person in a population, the true value of the population remains unknown. Researchers thus use inferential statistics to determine whether a difference or relationship found from data collected from a sample provides sufficient evidence to conclude that a difference or relationship really exists. To make certain that a researcher's biases or hopes do not affect the results, researchers set an objective standard for how certain they need to be about the results before they are willing to conclude that there is really a difference or relationship. This objective standard is called the "alpha level" or "level of significance."

The **alpha level (α)** is the criterion that researchers use to determine whether they obtain a statistically significant result. Its value is the maximum level of risk that researchers are willing to take that they incorrectly conclude that they found a significant difference or relationship. As the example in Figure 8.4 illustrates, researchers in education and social sciences traditionally set their alpha at a level of .05 (i.e., α = .05). This .05 value means that researchers are willing to take up to a 5 percent chance that they will be wrong when they conclude that there is a difference or relationship among variables based on the collected data when in reality there is no such difference or relationship. Said another way, for all the quantitative research that finds there is a difference or relationship, the truth is that in as much as 5 percent of those studies, no such difference or relationship actually exists in the population. The problem is that no one knows which studies are the ones that get it wrong. Therefore, the scientific community has decided that, in general, it is acceptable for researchers to risk getting it wrong up to 5 percent of the time. In some studies, researchers want to be more certain about their results (such as when testing a medical procedure) and reduce their risk by choosing a smaller alpha value such as .01 (i.e., they assume a risk of getting it wrong at most 1 percent of the time). Some researchers also reduce their risk by "correcting" their alpha level (i.e., making it lower than .05) because they are running multiple tests with the same dataset and want their total risk across all hypotheses tests to remain no greater than 5 percent. In a few studies, researchers use a higher alpha level (such as .10) when they are more interested in finding a potentially useful result than concerned about making a mistake. When you read about a study's quantitative data analysis, identify the alpha level used and determine whether that was a rigorous, low level of .05 or less and if not, determine whether the researchers had a good reason for using a higher alpha level.

> *Here's a Tip!*
>
> Note that the alpha level (e.g., α = .05) is different from Cronbach's alpha introduced in Chapter 7. The *alpha level* is the criterion that a researcher uses to determine whether a statistical result is significant. *Cronbach's alpha* (also called the alpha coefficient) is a measure of how consistent items are on an instrument.

3. **The researcher collects data from a sample.** As discussed in Chapter 7, researchers collect data for their variables of interest by administering instruments or recording behaviors on a checklist for a sample of participants. Once the data is collected, researchers also score and prepare the data for analysis and complete descriptive analyses, as discussed earlier in this chapter.

4. **The researcher computes the sample statistic to compare groups or relate variables.** Once researchers have collected their data and prepared the data for analysis, they are ready to compute an inferential statistic. Researchers must select the statistical tests that are appropriate for their hypotheses. There are *many* inferential statistics available to researchers. Although there is a great deal of overlap among many of the different statistics, it is helpful for you to think of them as falling into two broad

types: those used to *compare groups* and those used to *relate variables*. Several commonly used statistics for comparing groups are listed in Table 8.2 and several used for relating variables are listed in Table 8.3. These tables can help you to identify the statistics mentioned as part of a study's data analysis procedures.

TABLE 8.2   A Key for Recognizing Common Statistics for Comparing Groups

Statistic Name	Symbol	Use	How to Interpret*	Example Application
t-test	*t*	To test for a difference between 2 groups in terms of 1 dependent variable	■ There is a significant difference between the groups if $p \leq \alpha$	■ Compare boys and girls on time spent reading
Analysis of variance (ANOVA)	*F*	To test for a difference among 2 or more groups in terms of 1 dependent variable	■ There is a significant difference among the groups if $p \leq \alpha$	■ Compare four groups (freshmen, sophomores, juniors, and seniors) on time spent studying
Analysis of covariance (ANCOVA)	*F*	To test for a difference among 2 or more groups in terms of 1 dependent variable, controlling for at least one control variable	■ There is a significant difference among the groups if $p \leq \alpha$	■ Compare three groups (treatment 1, treatment 2, and treatment 3) in terms of their final test score, controlling for scores on a pretest
Multiple analysis of variance (MANOVA)	*F*	To test for a difference among 2 or more groups in terms of 2 or more dependent variables	■ There is a significant difference among the groups if $p \leq \alpha$	■ Compare men and women who are married, single, or divorced in terms of their life satisfaction scores and depression scores
Chi square	χ^2	To test for a difference among groups in terms of a categorical dependent variable	■ There is a significant difference among the groups if $p \leq \alpha$	■ Compare men and women in terms of their political party affiliation (Democratic, Republican, or independent)
Mann Whitney	U	To test for a difference among 2 groups in terms of 1 dependent variable that is non-normal (i.e., the data do not look like Figure 8.3)	■ There is a significant difference among the groups if $p \leq \alpha$	■ Compare boys and girls in terms of amount of food eaten
Kruskal–Wallis one-way analysis of variance	K	To test for a difference among 2 or more groups in terms of 1 dependent variable that is non-normal (i.e., the data do not look like Figure 8.3)	■ There is a significant difference among the groups if $p \leq \alpha$	■ Compare chicken, beef, and fish entrees in terms of the amount of food eaten
Odds ratio	*OR*	To describe the likelihood (or odds) that a trait occurs when an independent/predictor variable is present relative to the odds that the trait occurs when the independent/predictor variable is absent	■ There is a significantly higher or lower likelihood if $p \leq \alpha$, where $OR > 1$ means higher odds of the trait occurring and $OR < 1$ means lower odds of trait occurring	■ Assess the odds of having a trait (e.g., being obese) when a variable is present (e.g., a diagnosis of depression) relative to when the variable is absent (e.g., no diagnosis of depression)
Measures of Effect Size				
Cohen's *d* effect size	*d* or *ES*	To assess the effect size for a significant t test	■ Consider whether the author describes the effect as *small*, *medium*, or *large*	■ Judge whether a statistically significant difference between two groups also has practical significance
Eta squared	η^2	To assess the effect size for a significant ANOVA test	■ Consider whether the author describes the effect as *small*, *medium*, or *large*	■ Judge whether a statistically significant difference among groups also has practical significance

*α refers to the "alpha level." It is set by the researcher, usually at a level of $\alpha = .05$.

TABLE 8.3   A Key for Recognizing Common Statistics for Relating Variables

Statistic Name	Symbol	Use	How to Interpret*	Example Applications
Pearson correlation	r	To test for a relationship between two variables	■ There is a significant relationship if $p \leq \alpha$; the sign of r indicates whether the relationship is positive ($+$) or negative ($-$), and the value of r (0–1.00) indicates the strength of the relationship	■ Determine whether time spent studying is related to grade point average
Multiple regression unstandardized coefficient	b	To provide a measure of the individual contribution of one unit of each independent variable to the dependent variable in a multiple regression analysis	■ Examine the b values for the independent variables found to be significant predictors of the dependent variable $p \leq \alpha$	■ Determine the individual contributions of grade point average, SAT score, and depression for predicting retention in the first year of college
Multiple regression standardized coefficient	(beta)	To provide a standardized measure of each independent variable's individual contribution to the dependent variable in a multiple regression analysis	■ Compare the beta values for each independent variable in a multiple regression equation to see which ones are most important	■ Determine the relative individual contributions of grade point average, SAT score, and depression for predicting retention in the first year of college
Factor analysis	Factor loadings	To use correlational techniques to determine how items on an instrument relate to each other to form different subscales	■ Consider the authors' assessment of the number of factors and how well the items load on the different factors	■ Identify whether an instrument that measures well-being includes different subscales (such as mental, physical, and financial well-being subscales)
Structural equation modeling	SEM	To use correlational techniques to test whether a set of variables are related to each other in a specific causal way as suggested by a theoretical model	■ Consider the extent to which the author notes that there is a good fit between the model and the data	■ Determine whether motivation and parental involvement influence time on task, which then influences achievement
Hierarchical linear and multilevel modeling	HLM	To analyze data that represents multiple nested levels (such as students, their teachers, and their schools) for relationships (or differences)	■ Consider the extent to which each variable is a significant contributor ($p \leq \alpha$) to the model of the dependent variable	■ Determine whether student-, class-, and school-level variables predict student achievement scores

Measures of the Strength of Relationships

Coefficient of determination	r^2	To assess the proportion of variability in one variable accounted for by a second variable	■ Consider this value as the percentage of variance in one variable that is explained by a second variable	■ Time spent studying explained 49 percent of the variability in the final test score ($r^2 = .49$)
R squared	R^2	To assess the proportion of variability in the dependent variable accounted for by the combination of independent variables in the regression equation	■ Consider this value as the percentage of variance in the dependent variable accounted for by the combination of predictor variables	■ Time-on-task, motivation, and prior achievement together predict 34 percent of the variability in student learning ($R^2 = .34$)

*α refers to the "alpha level." It is set by the researcher, usually at a level of $\alpha = .05$.

Researchers carefully select an appropriate statistic, such as those in Tables 8.2 and 8.3, to calculate for their data. Their choice is based on the type of question being addressed (e.g., comparison or relationship). Researchers also must consider factors such as the number of independent and dependent variables in their hypotheses, whether control variables are included in the analysis, whether the data for each variable are measured as continuous or categorical, and whether the distribution of the data is normal (e.g., consistent with the graph in Figure 8.3) or non-normal (not consistent with the graph in Figure 8.3). In well-written reports, the researchers often state the reason why they chose to calculate a particular statistic.

Once researchers select a statistical test, they use the computer software to calculate the statistic that corresponds to that test for their gathered data. Whenever researchers compute a statistic for the data from a sample, they actually obtain two important values. One is the value of the statistic (e.g., t, F, or r) and the other is the p value. A p **value** is the probability (p) that a result (e.g., the value of t, F, or r calculated for the collected data) could have been produced by chance if the null hypothesis were true for the population. For instance, if a researcher finds that $p = .01$, then this indicates that there is a 1 percent chance that the calculated statistical result from the sample is not actually present in the population. Looking back at Figure 8.4, the researcher in the example conducted a t test with the gathered data, and found $t = 7.49$ and that $p = .001$. It is actually the p value that researchers use to make a decision as to whether the data provide sufficient evidence for the alternative hypothesis. Making this decision is the next and final step of hypothesis testing.

5. The researcher makes a decision to "reject" or "fail to reject" the null hypothesis. Once researchers have completed the first four steps of hypothesis testing, they have all the information needed to make a decision. There are two possible decisions for any hypothesis test:

- *The researcher rejects the null hypothesis and concludes there is a difference or there is a relationship.* That is, the analysis finds that the two groups are sufficiently different (or the relationship among variables is sufficiently large) that the researcher is able to conclude that it is very unlikely that the null hypothesis is true. In other words, the data support the conclusion that there is a difference (or a relationship). For example, if the data indicate that girls spend significantly more time reading than boys, then the researcher rejects the null hypothesis and concludes that there is a significant difference and that girls spend more time reading than boys.

- *The researcher fails to reject the null hypothesis and concludes there is no difference or there is no relationship.* That is, the analysis finds that the two groups are not very different (or the relationship among variables is not very large), so the researcher concludes that there is *not* sufficient evidence to reject the null hypothesis. For example, if the data indicate that girls spend about the same amount of time reading as boys, then the researcher fails to reject the null hypothesis and concludes that there is not a significant difference between boys and girls. It is important to keep in mind that researchers never *accept* a hypothesis; they either *reject* or *fail to reject* the null hypothesis, but they do not prove the null hypothesis.

Once the researchers have calculated the statistic, all that remains is for them to apply a criterion to decide whether the evidence supports rejecting or failing to reject the null hypothesis. It turns out that researchers set this criterion level early in the process when they set their alpha level! In the end, the researcher makes an objective decision simply by comparing the p value from their sample statistic to the specified alpha level. If you examine the information from the example study in Figure 8.4, you see that the researcher set $\alpha = .05$ and found $p = .001$. These values tell us that the researcher is willing to take up to a 5 percent risk that the results occurred by chance, but found that there is only a 0.1 percent chance that the observed result from the sample could have occurred by chance. Therefore, because the p value is less than or equal to the alpha value, the researcher concludes that the null hypothesis can be rejected. This means that the researcher is able to conclude that there is a statistically significant difference between the groups. A *statistically significant* result occurs when the p value calculated for the statistic is equal to or less than the predetermined alpha level set by the researcher. If the statistic's p value is greater than alpha, then the researcher concludes that the data do not provide sufficient evidence of a difference of a relationship. Researchers refer to this type of a result as a *nonsignificant* result (sometimes abbreviated as "ns" in reports). When this

Here's a Tip!

Hypothesis testing sets a strict, objective standard for judging whether a result is statistically significant. Close is not good enough. If a *p* value is even a tiny bit higher than the alpha level, the researcher must conclude that there is no difference or no relationship.

happens, the study does not prove that the null hypothesis is true. Instead, a nonsignificant result only means that the study's data do not provide enough evidence to reject the null hypothesis.

As you read quantitative research, keep in mind that researchers use the process of determining statistical significance to determine whether there is evidence of a relationship among variables or a difference between groups, no matter how small the relationship or difference may be. In studies that have very large sample sizes (say, thousands of participants), even a very small difference can be statistically significant because it is unlikely that the difference occurred only by chance. However, determining statistical significance is not the same thing as determining whether a result has any practical significance. Researchers today are often concerned with practical significance in addition to statistical significance. They use a separate indicator, called an effect size, during their data analysis to determine the practical significance of any statistically significant result.

Effect size is a statistic that researchers compute to identify the practical strength of the significant group differences or the relationship among variables in a quantitative study. Effect sizes provide an objective measure that researchers use to judge whether a statistically significant difference or relationship is practically significant based on the researchers' knowledge of practical issues, such as the instruments, the participants, and the data collection efforts. There are many different ways that researchers can calculate effect sizes depending on the type of inferential statistic used to determine statistical significance. Tables 8.2 and 8.3 list a few common forms that you may encounter as you read quantitative research. For each kind of effect size, researchers have adopted a standard for judging whether a measured effect is small, medium/moderate, or large. In well-written reports, the researchers explicitly state what their interpretation of the size of the effect is (e.g., *small*, *medium*, or *large*), so you can determine to what extent the statistically significant result has practical significance.

Here's a Tip!

Statistically significant results are important for adding to knowledge. Results that also have practical significance show promise for being useful for practical applications. If you are looking for research results that can apply to your practice, pay particular attention to results that are associated with large effect sizes.

As an illustration, let's consider the example of a statistically significant difference between smokers and nonsmokers in terms of depression, from Figure 8.4. When examining the difference in the mean scores for the two groups, the researcher reports that, "there is a large effect (*ES* = 1.6)." From this statement, you can understand that the difference likely has important practical significance because the size of the effect is large. Therefore, practitioners working with adolescent smokers may also want to consider monitoring their depression in addition to helping them quit smoking.

What Do You Think?

Consider the following three results from quantitative research articles. Assume that the alpha level is .05 for each study. Based on the ideas of hypothesis testing and Tables 8.2 and 8.3, what do you conclude about the information provided for each study's data analysis procedure? Consider what type of hypothesis was tested, what statistic was selected, what *p* value was determined for the calculated statistic, and whether there was sufficient evidence to reject the null hypothesis in each case.

a. "Females reported greater use of avoidant coping strategies than males; $t(1337) = -2.51, p < .05$" (Newman et al., 2011, p. 207).
b. "Career satisfaction is correlated with appropriate duties ($r = .14, p < .01$) for career counselors" (Baggerly & Osborn, 2006, p. 200).
c. "There was no association between state-anxiety scores and number of test problems answered correctly for the students ($\beta = .11$, ns)" (Weber & Bizer, 2006, p. 281).

Check Your Understanding

Passage (a) is a hypothesis test comparing females and males in terms of their use of avoidant coping strategies. The researchers selected the t statistic and found $p < .05$ for their data. Because p is less than .05, there was sufficient evidence to reject the null hypothesis (i.e., reject that there is no difference). The researchers therefore found a statistically significant difference.

Passage (b) is a hypothesis test relating two variables (career satisfaction and appropriate duties). The researchers selected the r statistic and found $p < .01$ for their data. Because p is less than .05, there was sufficient evidence to reject the null hypothesis (i.e., reject that there is no relationship). The researchers therefore found a statistically significant relationship.

Passage (c) is a hypothesis test relating multiple variables (e.g., state-anxiety scores) to the number of test problems answered correctly. The researchers calculated the β statistic (a type of multiple regression statistic). They did not state the p value, but they did state "ns," which stands for "nonsignificant." This means that p was more than .05. There was not sufficient evidence to reject the null hypothesis, and therefore the researchers conclude that there was no significant result.

How Do You Understand the Results in a Quantitative Study?

Once you have read how researchers have analyzed their quantitative data, you are ready to read the results of the study. The results are the actual products obtained from all the statistical calculations that the researchers made during the data analysis process. In most studies, the results are reported in the Results section, but some quantitative studies include a few preliminary results in the Method section as well. To recognize the different results, it is helpful to know that quantitative researchers often report three types of results as part of their studies:

- **Results about the participants' characteristics.** Researchers present results that describe the participants in the study. These results typically describe the relevant demographic characteristics of the study's sample, such as participants' age, ethnicity, educational background, family status, health status, and so on. You can find results about the participants reported in either the Method or Results sections. Read this information to learn about who participated in the study, and consider whether they seem to be representative of a larger population and whether they are similar to the individuals that you work with in your practice.
- **Results about the instruments' performance.** Researchers present results that describe the performance of the instruments from their use with the study's participants. These results typically include information such as the internal consistency of the instrument's items and the identification of subscales found among the instrument's items. You can find results about the instrument's performance reported in either the Method or Results sections of a report. Read this information to learn about how the instruments performed with the participants in the study.
- **Results in response to the study's research questions and hypotheses.** The major results of any quantitative study are those that address the study's main descriptive, comparison, and relationship research questions and hypotheses. A typical approach is for the researcher to respond to each question or hypothesis one by one in the order in which they were introduced earlier in the study. You can find the major results reported in the Results section. Read this information to learn what the researcher found in response to the research questions and hypotheses.

Here's a Tip!

Keep the study's research questions and hypotheses in mind as you read the results as often the information is organized to address each of these one by one.

When you read the results from quantitative studies, you find that the researchers generally present the information in an objective, impersonal way. They also remain close to the statistical results without drawing broader implications or meaning from them. (We will learn more about how researchers draw conclusions from their results in Chapter 14.) Although quantitative results vary extensively depending on the research questions and variables of interest, researchers generally present their quantitative results in fairly standard ways. By learning to recognize and interpret the typical formats of quantitative results, you can more easily understand what the researchers found in any study you read. Specifically, you can recognize the following three standard formats for the results in quantitative studies:

- tables that summarize statistical information,
- figures that portray variables and their relationships, and
- detailed explanations written about the statistical results.

All these formats are used to present results about the participants, the instruments, and the research questions and hypotheses in quantitative studies. To help you understand the results that researchers include in their reports, let's consider how you should examine each of these formats as you read quantitative results.

First—Examine Tables to Learn a Summary of Major Results

When reading quantitative reports, you frequently encounter the results presented in the form of a table. A **table** is a summary of quantitative information organized into rows and columns. (See an example of a table in Figure 8.2.) Tables that report quantitative results typically contain numeric information, but they often contain text information as well (such as variable names or names of groups). Researchers include tables to summarize key statistical results because they convey an extensive amount of detailed information in a relatively small amount of space. Because of the importance of the results displayed in tables, a good strategy for reading quantitative results is to first examine the tables included in the Results section before reading the information written in the text. Tables serve to highlight the key results from most quantitative studies and, once you learn how to read and understand them, they provide an accessible format for interpreting the major results. Here are some guidelines to help you learn to read tables of quantitative results.

- Researchers give each table a title that describes its contents. Read the title to learn the type of information presented in the table. Determine whether this information seems related to results about the participants, the instruments, or the research questions and hypotheses.
- Researchers generally present one type of statistical test per table. Sometimes, however, they combine data from different analyses into a single table. For example, descriptive results (such as the means, standard deviations, and ranges for variables) are often combined within one table. When you read a table, identify the primary statistics that are included and determine whether the table seems to be presenting results in the form of descriptive statistics and/or inferential statistics. If the table includes inferential statistics (including indications of the p values), then consider whether the statistics test for differences among groups or for relationships among variables.
- Researchers include labels for the columns and rows that name the information included in the cells of the table. Look at the labels for each column and each row to grasp the meaning of the information. These labels will often represent specific variables and computed statistics.
- Researchers often include "notes" that provide important information about the tables. These notes are designated with superscript characters (e.g., *, [a], or $\perp$) and the actual note appears in a small font at the bottom of the table. Often these notes include information about the size of the sample that provided data for a particular variable, the alpha level used in hypothesis testing, and the actual p values obtained.

Let's apply these guidelines to understand three common types of tables found in reports of quantitative statistical results: participant demographic tables, group comparison tables, and variable correlation tables.

Title of the table

Table 1. Pre- and postintervention sample demographics for five school sites

	School A[a]		School B[a]		School C[a]		School D[b]		School E[b]	
	Pre	Post	Pre	Post	Pre	Post	Pre	Post	Pre	Post
N	180	225	759	681	578	799	484	592	588	727
Response rate (%)	50	70	80	71	47	69	43	50	50	61
Female (%)	58	56	53	53	55	52	53	50	50	52
Mean age	12.5	12.3	12.8	12.3	12.7	12.4	12.8	12.5	12.6	12.5
(SD)	(.9)	(1.0)	(1.0)	(1.0)	(.9)	(1.0)	(.9)	(1.0)	(1.0)	(1.0)
Minority (%)	27	24	21	25	29	29	48	57	57	59

Note: [a]Schools with 1.5 academic-year intervention; [b]Schools with 1.0 academic-year intervention.

Variables described

Notes that provide more information

Information about each variable for each time for each school

FIGURE 8.5　A Table Summarizing Participants' Demographic Characteristics

Source: This table is reprinted from Perkins et al., *Group Processes and Intergroup Relations*, Vol. 14, Issue 5, p. 707, 2011. Reprinted with permission of Sage Publications, Inc.

Understanding Tables Used to Describe Participants' Demographics.　Figure 8.5 is an example of a table used to report results that describe participants' demographics. Specifically, this table from the quantitative bullying-intervention study provides information about how many participants provided data (*N*), what percentage (%) of those asked chose to respond, what percentage of those who participated were female and a minority, and what the average (mean) and standard deviation (*SD*) were for the age of the participants. The authors chose to report this descriptive information for each data collection time (pre and post) for each of the five schools. Examining this demographic information gives us a snapshot of the individuals who participated in the study.

Understanding Tables Used to Compare Groups.　Figure 8.6 is an example of a table used to report results from comparing groups. Specifically, this table provides information on six dependent variables for two groups: students who have carried a weapon and those who have not. The authors report descriptive information for each variable (i.e., the mean and standard deviation values) for each group. They also report the value of the *F* statistic, which they used to compare the two groups for each variable. By reading the table notes, we learn that the asterisks (*, **, or ***) that accompany these values indicate the corresponding *p* values. Examining the information carefully, we learn that the two groups were significantly different for five of the variables because *p* was less than .05. We also learn that the groups did not significantly differ in terms of the variable *overall support* because no *F* or *p* values were provided for that variable.

Understanding Tables Used to Relate Variables.　Figure 8.7 is an example of a table used to report results about the relationships between variables. This compact table actually presents the results of 10 different hypothesis tests! The variable names are listed for each row and a shorthand number is listed for these same variables as the column labels. The number that appears in the cell at the intersection of a row and a column represents the *r* correlation statistic for two variables. For example, if you look

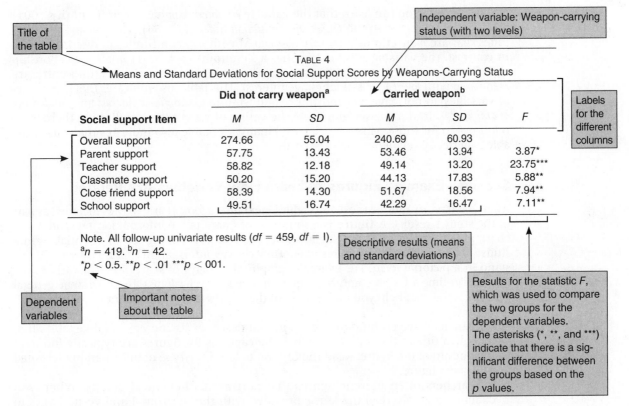

FIGURE 8.6   A Table Summarizing Results Comparing Two Groups

Source: This table is reprinted from Malecki and Demaray, *Journal of Emotional and Behavioral Disorders,* Vol. 11, Issue 3, p. 175, 2003. Reprinted with permission of Sage Publications, Inc.

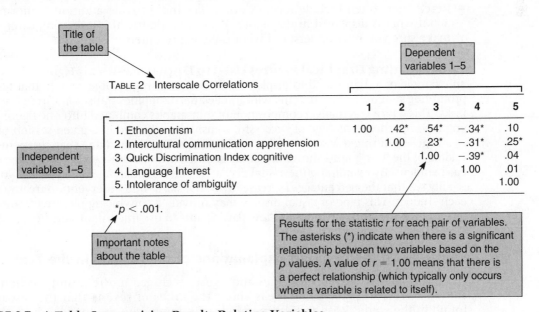

FIGURE 8.7   A Table Summarizing Results Relating Variables

Source: This table is reprinted from Kim and Goldstein, *Journal of Studies in International Education,* Vol. 9, Issue 3, p. 273, 2005. Reprinted with permission of Sage Publications, Inc.

at the first row, you can learn that the variable *ethnocentrism* has a significant ($p < .001$) *positive* relationship with the *Quick Discrimination Index* ($r = .54$). That means that attitudes that are *more* ethnocentric are associated with *higher* attitudes of discrimination. In contrast, the variable *ethnocentrism* has a significant ($p < .001$) *negative* relationship with *language interest* ($r = -.34$). This means that attitudes that are *more* ethnocentric are associated with *lower* levels of language interest. This table also indicates that some pairs of variables do not have a significant relationship (e.g., *language interest* and *intolerance of ambiguity*). In these cases, note that the values of r are near 0, indicating there is no relationship for those pairs of variables. Finally, the table also indicates that each variable is perfectly related to itself ($r = 1.00$).

Second—Examine Figures to Learn How Variables Are Related

After you have examined the results tables, next take a look at any figures included as part of the study's results. A **figure** is a summary of quantitative information presented as a chart, graph, or picture that visually shows the relations among scores or variables in a study. Researchers include figures when they convey information that is easier to understand in a pictorial form. For example, graphical displays of scores for two variables or scores over time are very common in quantitative research reports. Here are some general guidelines that can help you make sense of the figures that report quantitative results.

- Researchers give each figure a caption that describes its contents. Unlike tables that include a title at the top of the table, the captions for figures are typically found at the bottom of the figure. Read the caption to learn the type of information presented in a given figure.
- Researchers often present figures that portray mathematical graphs. When you examine a graph, read the labels provided with the horizontal and vertical axes to learn which specific variables are displayed on the graph. Pay attention to the trend in the plotted scores, such as whether they tend to go up or down or whether there is a sudden change in the trend when an intervention started or was removed.
- Researchers sometimes present visual pictures of the results for the relationships among variables. In these figures, boxes usually represent the major variables and arrows that connect the boxes represent the relationships among the variables. Pay careful attention to the direction of each arrow and any information included with the arrows, such as the indicators of the magnitudes of the relationships.
- Researchers often include legends and notes that provide additional information about what is displayed in the figure. Read this additional information carefully to make sure you fully understand what is being presented.

Understanding Graphical Figures Used to Display Results.   Figure 8.8 presents an example of a figure used to display a graph from a single-subject study that tested a prompting system to help students with intellectual disabilities transition through specific tasks. This figure is actually a composition of four graphs combined into one figure. Each graph shows the percentage of successful transitions achieved in a given session plotted as a function of time (or sessions) for four students. The dashed line that cuts across the middle of the four graphs shows the point in time when the intervention was started for each student. By examining the visual display of the students' scores over time, you can readily see that the percentages increased with the start of the intervention treatment for each student. This type of visual display may provide a convincing picture of cause and effect when the study includes too few participants to use inferential statistics.

Third—Read the Detailed Explanations of the Results in the Text

Once you have reviewed the tables and figures included in the Results section, you should have developed some ideas about the kinds of results that the researcher found in the study. With these general ideas in mind, you are in a good position to read the full text of the Results section to learn all the details of the study's results. As you read, keep in mind that researchers present results about the participants, instruments, and research questions and hypotheses. They also often start with their

**FIGURE 8.8
A Figure
Summarizing
the Results from
a Study Using a
Single Subject
Design**

Source: This figure is
reprinted from Cihak,
Kessler, and Alberto,
*Education and Training
in Developmental Disabil-
ities,* Vol. 43, Issue 1,
p. 107, 2008. Reprinted
with permission of the
Division on Develop-
mental Disabilities of
the Council for Excep-
tional Children.

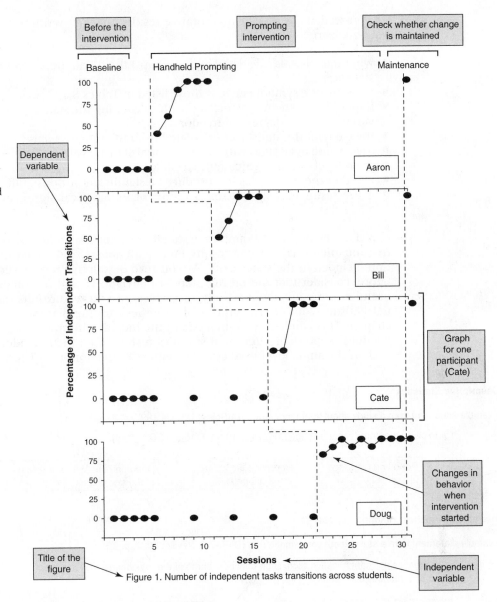

Figure 1. Number of independent tasks transitions across students.

descriptive results and then move to the more sophisticated results that involve
inferential statistics. In some reports of results, you learn that the researchers conducted a series of analyses to answer a particular research question. This is particularly common when researchers are analyzing multiple variables (more than two) at
the same time. When researchers have used a series of analyses, they typically first
report the results of a test that considered all the variables together and, if together
the set of variables produced a significant result, they go on to present results about
individual variables.

As you read the Results section, you need to attend to the researchers' explanations of the central results for each statistical test that they conducted. Typically,
researchers summarize the results from each statistical test in one or two sentences, or
perhaps a short paragraph. They also refer to their specific tables and figures within
the text, and you should review the content of these tables and figures again as you
read the details of the results. Although the exact information that researchers include
about their results will vary depending on the variables of interest, the statistic used,
and the results obtained, researchers generally include the same general types of
information in their explanations in order to provide a complete picture of the results.

As you read about specific quantitative results in a well-written report, it is likely that you will learn:

- what statistic was calculated and (perhaps) the researchers' reasons for selecting that statistic;
- the statistic's symbol (such as those listed in Tables 8.1, 8.2, and 8.3);
- important parameters associated with calculating the statistic, such as the number of variables or the degrees of freedom;
- the value of the statistic as calculated from the sample's data;
- the *p* value associated with the calculated statistic value;
- the α level used to evaluate the *p* value;
- whether the hypothesis test produced a significant or nonsignificant result; and
- if the result was significant, a report of its practical significance in terms of an effect size.

Figure 8.9 shows examples of statements that researchers wrote for both descriptive and inferential statistics results along with notes to help you interpret the information included in the statements. As you read descriptive results such as shown in the figure, consider that the means, standard deviations, and the range of scores provide useful information about a study's variables. As you read results that include inferential statistics, consider the process of hypothesis testing that you learned earlier in this chapter. This will help you understand the included information such as the reported *p* values. Reports of inferential statistics results often include additional information such as the alpha level used and the degrees of freedom (*df*). The value of the degrees

Descriptive Statistics

Example statement from a study about youth mentoring (DuBois & Neville, 1997, p. 228):

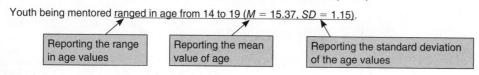

Youth being mentored ranged in age from 14 to 19 (*M* = 15.37, *SD* = 1.15).

Reporting the range in age values | Reporting the mean value of age | Reporting the standard deviation of the age values

Inferential Statistics: Relating Variables

Example statement from a study about youth mentoring (DuBois & Neville, 1997, p. 231):

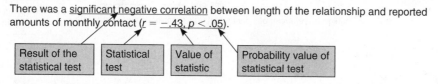

There was a significant negative correlation between length of the relationship and reported amounts of monthly contact (*r* = −.43, *p* < .05).

Result of the statistical test | Statistical test | Value of statistic | Probability value of statistical test

Inferential Statistics: Comparing Groups

Example statement from a study comparing two note-taking interventions: partial graphic organizer (GO) and complete GO (Robinson et al., 2006, p. 105):

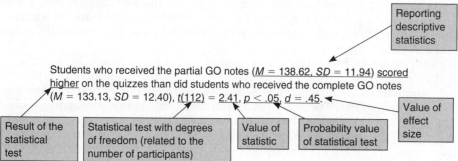

Reporting descriptive statistics

Students who received the partial GO notes (*M* = 138.62, *SD* = 11.94) scored higher on the quizzes than did students who received the complete GO notes (*M* = 133.13, *SD* = 12.40), *t*(112) = 2.41, *p* < .05, *d* = .45.

Result of the statistical test | Statistical test with degrees of freedom (related to the number of participants) | Value of statistic | Probability value of statistical test | Value of effect size

FIGURE 8.9   Examples of Descriptive and Inferential Results Statements

of freedom is related to the number of participants and the number of variables in the calculation. It is listed in parentheses along with the statistic, such as: $F(1, 84)$. Researchers report these numbers because they are important parameters that the computer programs consider when they estimate the p value for the statistic. In this way, the researchers provide key information for other scholars trained in statistics who are then able to better evaluate the quality of the presented information. We will consider the criteria that you can use to evaluate quantitative results in the next section.

One final consideration to keep in mind as you read quantitative results is that researchers report results that match their study's research design (as you learned in Chapter 6). When you read a study that used any of the major quantitative research design types, you can expect the researcher to have analyzed the data and reported results in certain ways, such as the following:

- If the researcher used a *true experiment* or a *quasi-experiment*, then you can expect that the results should emphasize inferential statistics that compare groups in terms of the dependent variables (and possibly taking control variables into account). The presentation of the results usually includes tables (similar to Figure 8.6) and detailed explanations in the text, and occasionally graphs.
- If the researcher used a *single-subject experiment*, then you can expect that the results should emphasize graphical displays in figures showing data over time for single individuals (e.g., Figure 8.8) and explanations in the text. Researchers typically do not use inferential statistics in these designs because they are not attempting to make inferences about a population.
- If the researcher used a *correlational design*, then you can expect that the results should emphasize inferential statistics that test for relationships among variables. Results usually include tables (similar to Figure 8.7) and detailed explanations.
- If the researcher used a *survey design*, then you can expect that the results should emphasize descriptive statistics that describe trends and variability for single variables. Results usually include explanations and tables. In many studies that used a survey design, the researchers also report results from some relationship and comparison analyses.

What Do You Think?

Consider the following excerpt from the results that McCabe et al. (2006) reported in their quantitative study that intended to explain graduate student attitudes about cheating. What type of results did the authors report in this excerpt? What format did they use to report these results? How do you know which results were significant?

Table 1 shows the bivariate correlation analyses for the total graduate student sample. . . . Correlational analysis supports Hypotheses 2, 4, and 5, suggesting that cheating behavior is inversely related to the perceived certainty of being reported by a peer and understanding and acceptance of academic integrity policies and positively related to perceptions of peer cheating behavior. Hypothesis 3, which predicted an inverse relation between academic dishonesty and the perceived severity of penalties, was not supported in any of the samples. (p. 298)

TABLE 1　Intercorrelations of Study Variables

Measures	N	1	2	3	4	5
1. Peer behavior	4457	—				
2. Acceptance of policy	4525	−.29*	—			
3. Severity of penalties	4699	−.28*	.59*	—		
4. Certainty of reporting	5105	−.24*	.31*	.21*	—	
5. Academic dishonesty	3455	.28*	−.11*	−.03	−.13*	—

$*p < .05.　**p > .01.　***p < .001.$

Check Your Understanding

In this excerpt, McCabe et al. present results that respond to their study's hypotheses. Specifically, they are presenting results about how variables are related to (or correlated with) each other. They used two formats to present these results: detailed explanations of the results in the text and a summary table. By examining the table, we see that the authors report how many participants completed each variable (the values of *N*). We also see that they reported results from testing hypotheses about the relationships between five variables. Noting that an asterisk (*) indicates a significant relationship ($p < .05$), we find that all of the presented relationships were significant except one. No significant relationship was found between *academic dishonesty* and *severity of penalties* (as indicated by the absence of an asterisk). Looking at the other values in the table, we find that some relationships are positive (such as *certainty of reporting* and *acceptance of policy*, $r = .31$) and others are negative (such as *peer behavior* and *severity of penalties*, $r = -.28$).

How Do You Evaluate the Data Analysis and Results in a Quantitative Study?

When evaluating the quality of a quantitative study's data analysis and results, keep in mind that these two aspects of the report are strongly tied to each other. You will find information about data analysis and the results in both the Method and Results sections of quantitative reports. Good quantitative research involves the use of a linear and objective process for analyzing and reporting the results about the study's participants, instruments, and research questions and hypotheses. Table 8.4 lists criteria that are useful when evaluating the data analysis and results in a quantitative study. This table also provides indicators of higher quality and lower quality for the criteria to help you make your own judgments when assessing the information provided.

TABLE 8.4   Criteria for Evaluating the Data Analysis and Results in a Quantitative Research Report

Quality Criteria	Indicators of Higher Quality in Quantitative Research	Indicators of Lower Quality in Quantitative Research
The Key Elements		
1. The data were rigorously scored and prepared.	+ Procedures to score the data in a consistent manner were used and clearly described. + The researcher explained how data were prepared, including summing multiple items to create good indicators of major variables and checking the data for errors and missing data. + The researcher named the quantitative statistical software program used and explained why it was a good choice for the analysis.	− The scoring procedures were inconsistent and not adequately described. − The data preparation procedures were limited to single items; procedures to check the data for errors and missing data were not used. − It is unclear whether the researcher used a good quantitative statistical software program.
2. Good descriptive analyses were conducted.	+ The researcher calculated descriptive statistics for all major variables. + The descriptive statistic was appropriate for the variable (e.g., whether it was continuous or categorical).	− The researcher calculated descriptive statistics for only some of the important variables. − The descriptive statistic was not appropriate, such as calculating the mean for a categorical variable.

(Continued)

TABLE 8.4   *(Continued)*

Quality Criteria	Indicators of Higher Quality in Quantitative Research	Indicators of Lower Quality in Quantitative Research
3. Good hypothesis testing procedures were used.	+ The researcher objectively applied the five steps of hypothesis testing to address research questions that involved two or more variables (i.e., stating null and alternative hypotheses, setting the alpha level, collecting data, calculating the statistic and p values, and making a decision). + The alpha level was set at .05 or less and the reason for the selected alpha level was explained. + The selected statistical tests are named; the choice is explained and justified; and the statistic is appropriate for the type of question (e.g., comparison or relationship), type of variables (e.g., continuous or categorical), and whether the data are normal or nonnormal.	− The researcher did not use hypothesis testing to address questions that involve two or more variables (e.g., stopped with descriptive analyses) or did not apply the five steps in an objective manner (such as changing the hypotheses *after* calculating a statistic). − The alpha level was set higher than .05 and no clear explanation for the level was provided. − The selected statistical tests are unnamed; the choice is unclear and not explained; and the statistic is inappropriate for the type of question, variables, or data.
4. The results are comprehensive.	+ There are results reported about the demographic characteristics of the participants, about the performance of the instruments, and about each of the study's research questions and hypotheses. + The results are consistent with the overall research design.	− The results are incomplete and do not include information about the participants, instruments, or all of the study's research questions and hypotheses. − The results are inconsistent with the overall research design.
5. The results include sufficient information.	+ For each result, the researcher reports the statistic, its value, the associated p value, the determination as to whether a significant result was found, and the effect size (if a statistically significant result was found). + The information included in tables, figures, and the text is clear, consistent, and accurate.	− The researcher claims that results are significant without providing sufficient information (e.g., the statistic's value or the p value) as evidence or reports nonsignificant results as if they were significant or almost significant. − There are inconsistencies and errors among the information included in tables, figures, and the text.
General Evaluation		
6. The data analysis represents a good quantitative process.	+ The data analysis was a deductive, objective, and linear process from which statistical results are found based on the gathered data.	− The data analysis included an inductive (i.e., bottom-up), subjective, or dynamic element from which statistical results were produced that do not strongly represent the gathered data.
7. The results provide a good explanation of the study's purpose.	+ It is clear how the reported results address the study's research questions and hypotheses. + Only statistical tests related to the study's purpose were calculated and reported.	− It is unclear how the reported results address the study's research questions and hypotheses. − Some statistical tests were calculated and reported that are not clearly related to the study's purpose.

Figure 8.10 provides a convenient means for you to apply the quality criteria to evaluate the data analysis and results described within the Method and Results sections of any quantitative research report. For each of the criteria you locate, assign a quality rating from *fair* (1) to *excellent* (3), and document your evidence and/or reasoning behind the rating. If one of the criteria is missing or very poorly stated, then indicate *poor* (0) as your rating. Keep in mind that research reports vary in the extent of discussion about the data analysis process and in the different statistics used. Even with this variation, however, a good quantitative study should still score well on most of the items listed in Figure 8.10. By adding up the rating scores for each of the criteria and using the suggested cutoff values provided at the bottom of the figure, you will have a quantitative measure that you can use to inform your overall assessment.

Quality Criteria	Quality Rating				Your Evidence and/or Reasoning
	0 = Poor	1 = Fair	2 = Good	3 = Excellent	
The Key Elements					
1. The data were rigorously scored and prepared.					
2. Good descriptive analyses were conducted.					
3. Good hypothesis testing procedures were used.					
4. The results are comprehensive.					
5. The results include sufficient information.					
General Evaluation					
6. The data analysis represents a good quantitative process.					
7. The results provide a good explanation of the study's purpose.					
Overall Quality 0–10 = Low quality 11–16 = Adequate quality 17–21 = High quality	**Total Score =**				**My Overall Assessment Is**

FIGURE 8.10   A Rating Scale for Evaluating the Data Analysis and Results in a Quantitative Research Report

Reviewing What You've Learned To Do

- *Identify and understand the data analysis and results of a quantitative research study.*
  - ❑ The Method section of a quantitative research report often includes a brief overview of the procedures that the researchers used to analyze the gathered data.
  - ❑ The Results section of a quantitative research report contains the results obtained from the data analysis process in response to the study's research questions.
- *List the steps that researchers use to analyze quantitative data.*
  - ❑ Quantitative data analysis is a process that deductively follows from general explanations about variables to the analysis of the specific data and that unfolds in a linear, step-by-step manner.
  - ❑ Researchers score their data using standard procedures for assigning numeric scores to participants' responses.
  - ❑ Researchers prepare the data by entering it into a computer analysis program and determining the types of scores needed for the analysis.
  - ❑ Researchers calculate descriptive statistics to describe the central tendency, variability, and relative standing of variables to answer their descriptive research questions.
  - ❑ Researchers use a procedure called hypothesis testing to calculate inferential statistics and answer their comparison and relationship research questions. This procedure involves the researcher specifying null and alternative hypotheses, setting the alpha level, collecting data, computing the appropriate statistic and p value from the data, and making a decision to reject or fail to reject the null hypothesis by comparing the p value to the alpha level.
- *Know how to identify quantitative results when reading a quantitative research report.*
  - ❑ The primary types of quantitative results include results about the participants in a study, results about the performance of the instruments in a study, and results that respond to the study's research questions and hypotheses.

- ❑ Quantitative results are found in three different formats: tables that summarize detailed statistical results, figures that display how two or more variables are related, and detailed explanations written into the text of the Results section.
- ■ *Evaluate the quality of the data analysis and results in a quantitative research report.*
  - ❑ The evaluation of a study's quantitative data analysis considers the consistency of the data scoring; the quality of the prepared data; the appropriate use of descriptive statistics to describe variables; and the appropriate use of inferential statistics to compare groups and relate variables.
  - ❑ The evaluation of a study's quantitative results considers the extent to which the reported results are clear, complete, objective, adequately address the study's research questions and hypotheses, and align with the study's quantitative research design.

✓ **To assess what you've learned to do, click here to answer questions and receive instant feedback.**

Reading Research Articles

Carefully reread the quantitative early-intervention-outcomes study by Raspa et al. (2010) found at the end of Chapter 6 (starting on p. 216) and the quantitative bullying-intervention study by Perkins et al. (2011) at the end of Chapter 3 (starting on p. 98).

As you review each article, pay close attention to statements in which the authors described the data analysis process in the Method section and the results in the Results section. Use the highlighting tool in the Pearson etext to indicate where the authors have provided information about the data analysis and results, and use the notetaking tool to add marginal notes that name each element you highlighted and note how each one is related to the study's quantitative approach. Among the elements you will want to find are:

1. Scoring data
2. Preparing data
3. Analysis: descriptive statistics (e.g., calculating means and standard deviations)
4. Analysis: inferential statistics (e.g., calculating an analysis of variance or a correlation)
5. Alpha level
6. Results about participants (e.g., demographics)
7. Results about instruments (e.g., internal consistency, subscale factors)
8. Results for descriptive research questions
9. Results for comparison and relationship hypotheses

Note, however, that sometimes authors do not describe all of the steps of the data analysis process—for example, they might not mention preparing the data or calculating descriptive statistics. In addition, authors do not always report all types of results—that is, they might not report results about participants, about the instruments, or about each possible type of research question or hypothesis. If one of these steps or type of results is missing, indicate that in your marginal notes.

 Click here to go to the quantitative early-intervention-outcomes study by Raspa et al. (2010) so that you can enter marginal notes about the study.

 Click here to go to the quantitative bullying-intervention study by Perkins et al. (2011) so that you can enter marginal notes about the study.

Understanding Research Articles

Apply your knowledge of the content of this chapter to the quantitative early-intervention-outcomes study by Raspa et al. (2010) starting on p. 216.

1. Where in the early-intervention-outcomes study do you find an example of information related to each of the following data analysis steps: (a) data scoring, (b) data preparation, (c) use of descriptive statistics, and (d) use of inferential statistics?

2. Where in the article do you find an example of each of the following types of results: (a) results about the participants' characteristics, (b) results about the instruments' performance, and (c) results about the study's research questions and hypotheses?

3. Examine the information found in Table 1 of the article. What types of scores are reported in this table? Which item(s) had the highest average for the sample and which item(s) had the lowest average? Which item(s) had the most and least variability?

4. Examine the information found in Table 5 of the article. What type of research question is being answered in this table? What alpha level does it appear that the researchers used? What does this alpha level mean?

5. Raspa et al. wrote the following statement in reference to the results presented in Table 5: "Beta coefficients indicated that race/ethnicity was statistically significant and inversely related to the mean score (of the FOS survey)" (paragraph 23). Based on Table 5, what evidence do you find to support this result?

✓ **Click here to answer the questions and receive instant feedback.**

Evaluating Research Articles

Practice evaluating a quantitative study's data analysis and results, using the quantitative early-intervention-outcomes study by Raspa et al. (2010) starting on p. 216 and the quantitative bullying-intervention study by Perkins et al. (2011) starting on p. 98.

1. Use the criteria discussed in Table 8.4 to evaluate the quality of the data analysis and results in the early-intervention-outcomes study. Note that, for this question, the rating form includes advice to help guide your evaluation.

✓ **Click here to open the rating scale form (Figure 8.10) to enter your ratings, evidence, and reasoning.**

2. Use the criteria discussed in Table 8.4 to evaluate the quality of the data analysis and results in the bullying-intervention study. Note that, for this question, the rating form does NOT include additional advice.

✓ **Click here to open the rating scale form (Figure 8.10) to enter your ratings, evidence, and reasoning.**

UNDERSTANDING THE METHOD SECTIONS AND RESULTS SECTIONS OF QUALITATIVE RESEARCH REPORTS

To help us consider the differences we find when reading different types of research reports, let's return to the idea that conducting research is like taking a journey. Recall that researchers take qualitative research "journeys" when they need to explore a topic area and learn from participants' views. As with quantitative research, qualitative researchers use the process of research to guide their journeys. Using this process, they start with a reason for taking the trip (the research problem), a general idea of what is known (the literature review), and an overall goal for the trip (the purpose). Unlike quantitative research, however, qualitative researchers do not preplan all the details of their studies. They learn as they go and often adjust their path during the study based on what they learn. Two benefits of exploring new territory this way when you travel are that you can follow up on unexpected and interesting discoveries and you can better develop an in-depth understanding of the area. You often find that these same benefits have occurred when reading about a qualitative research study that used a good flexible, exploratory approach.

Even though qualitative researchers may travel far and wide during their research journeys, they still keep a detailed record of their path and provide an account of their procedures in their reports. To understand what happened on a researcher's qualitative research journey, you need to understand the information that researchers provide about the path they took as well as what they learned along the way. A record of the researchers' qualitative procedures—the overall design, how participants were selected, and how data were collected and analyzed—can be found in the Method section of the report. You read about what researchers found from these procedures in the Results section. In the chapters that follow, you will learn how to read, understand, and evaluate the information that researchers present in these two major sections of their qualitative research reports.

The chapters in Part Four are:

- Chapter 9—Qualitative Research Designs: Recognizing the Overall Plan for a Study
- Chapter 10—Participants and Data Collection: Identifying How Qualitative Information Is Gathered
- Chapter 11—Data Analysis and Findings: Examining What Was Found in a Qualitative Study

9

QUALITATIVE RESEARCH DESIGNS: RECOGNIZING THE OVERALL PLAN FOR A STUDY

You are already familiar with recognizing study reports where the researchers used qualitative research because their purpose was to explore a central phenomenon. Identifying the overall approach of a study as qualitative research is a good start to understanding any qualitative research report. A better understanding arises if you also recognize and comprehend the types of research designs that researchers report using when conducting their qualitative studies. When discussing the methods in their reports, qualitative researchers describe their research designs as the overall plans they followed when conducting their studies. This chapter first introduces you to a variety of qualitative research designs that you may encounter when reading research. It then focuses on the key features of four common qualitative research designs to help you learn to identify and evaluate the research designs used in qualitative studies.

BY THE END OF THIS CHAPTER, YOU SHOULD BE ABLE TO:

- Identify and understand the research design of a qualitative study.
- List the characteristics that differentiate the various qualitative research designs.
- Distinguish among four common qualitative research designs based on their central phenomena, intents, and procedures.
- Recognize the research design used in a qualitative research report.
- Evaluate the quality of the research design in a qualitative research report.

We now focus our attention on reading studies that use a qualitative approach to the process of research. Recall that researchers conduct qualitative studies for the purposes of exploring, describing, or understanding a central phenomenon. Once you have read a number of qualitative studies, you find there are several different ways that researchers conduct qualitative research studies depending on what they want to explore, describe, or understand. In many qualitative reports, the researchers often simply note that they are using a *basic* qualitative research approach to describe the multiple perspectives held about a topic. When using a basic qualitative research approach, researchers select participants, collect qualitative data, analyze the data to develop themes as results, and discuss general conclusions about the themes in their reports. We will learn more about these general procedures in Chapters 10 and 11.

Although the basic qualitative approach is common, more and more researchers are using *specialized* qualitative research designs to guide their procedures for selecting participants and collecting, analyzing, and reporting data. Researchers who use a design-based approach usually write statements into their reports to help the reader identify the research design used. For example, examine the following statements that appear as the opening sentences in the Method sections of several qualitative research reports and identify the studies' research designs (with italics added for emphasis):

- "This research study incorporated a blending of symbolic interactionism and *narrative inquiry* in order to better understand Julie's journey as she completed her fifth year of teacher's college" (Rushton, 2004, pp. 64–65).
- "The research method that was selected for this study [of information-seeking activities of Web users] was *grounded theory*" (Pace, 2004, p. 332).

- "A *collective case study* of one high school's music department in the Midwestern United States, consisting of four music teachers, served as the focus" (Scheib, 2003, p. 126).
- "To more fully understand the perspective of the adolescent female, I undertook a yearlong *ethnographic study* at one midwestern junior high school. . . ." (Finders, 1996, p. 72).

As these examples illustrate, authors embed special terminology into their reports such as *narrative inquiry, grounded theory, case study*, and *ethnographic study* to identify the research designs that they used in their studies. If you know the meaning of these words and understand the designs they represent, then these single sentences can provide you with important information about the procedures the researchers used and the type of findings that are reported.

As a reader of research reports, then, you need to be familiar with the different types of qualitative research designs. When you recognize the design used in a qualitative study, you immediately have a sophisticated understanding of what the researcher tried to accomplish and the procedures the researcher used to address the stated purpose. This enhanced understanding helps you make sense of the variations found across different qualitative studies and evaluate the studies that interest you.

How Do You Identify the Research Design in a Qualitative Study?

Recall from Chapter 1 that researchers choose a research design for their studies as an early step in the research process. To understand this step in a qualitative research study, let's first consider how a qualitative research design is defined, its importance in the research process, and how you locate it within a research report.

You learned earlier in this book that *qualitative research* is research conducted to explore research problems by collecting text and image data that reflect participants' views about the research problem. You also learned that a *research design* is a logical set of procedures that researchers use to collect, analyze, and report their data in a research study. Putting these two ideas together provides us with the following definition: **Qualitative research designs** are sets of procedures for collecting, analyzing, and reporting text and image data to answer research questions by exploring participants' views. Figure 9.1 summarizes the general process of qualitative research, and indicates how qualitative research designs fit within this process by linking the study's purpose to the study's methods. Researchers choose the research design, such as grounded theory or case study, that best fits their purpose for conducting research. The selected qualitative research design then provides the researchers with a blueprint to guide how they collect data, analyze data, and report results in their qualitative studies. Knowing about the various common research designs, therefore, also provides you with a blueprint for understanding the different types of qualitative studies reported in the literature.

At this point you might be asking yourself, "Why is research so complicated? Isn't it enough just to recognize that a study used a qualitative approach?" It is true that considering different research designs provides you with a more complex picture of research, but considering research designs also provides a far more interesting and useful picture of research studies than just recognizing the overall approach because it helps you better understand and evaluate the specific nuances of each study's procedures. One way to understand the value of different research designs is to think about the value of understanding different styles of music. If you are familiar with different styles of music, you can determine that a song is an example of jazz, country, rock and roll, or classical. Each of these categories represents a different genre of music and each genre has its own history, identifying characteristics, and standards to determine if it is a good example. Knowing about different types of music helps musicians decide what music is appropriate to play in different situations. As a listener, you also have a better understanding of and appreciation for the music you hear if you are able to recognize different styles. Like knowing about different styles of music, learning about different styles of qualitative research designs is an important part of reading, understanding, and evaluating research.

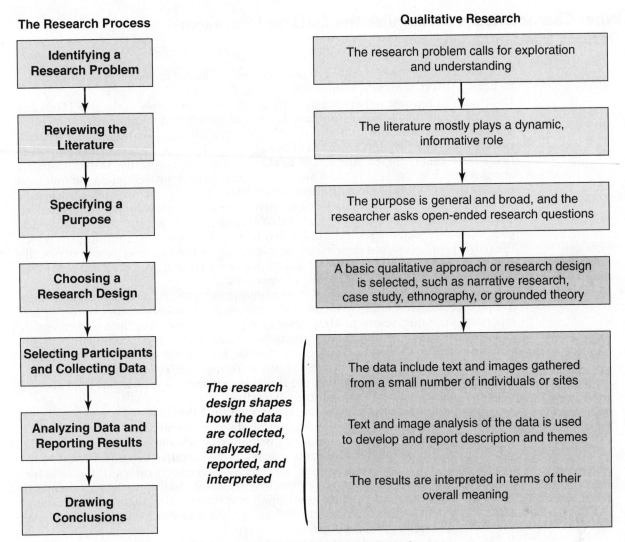

The Research Process

Identifying a Research Problem

Reviewing the Literature

Specifying a Purpose

Choosing a Research Design

Selecting Participants and Collecting Data

Analyzing Data and Reporting Results

Drawing Conclusions

Qualitative Research

The research problem calls for exploration and understanding

The literature mostly plays a dynamic, informative role

The purpose is general and broad, and the researcher asks open-ended research questions

A basic qualitative approach or research design is selected, such as narrative research, case study, ethnography, or grounded theory

The research design shapes how the data are collected, analyzed, reported, and interpreted

The data include text and images gathered from a small number of individuals or sites

Text and image analysis of the data is used to develop and report description and themes

The results are interpreted in terms of their overall meaning

FIGURE 9.1   Research Designs in the Process of Qualitative Research

Well-written research reports always include one or more sentences that identify the researcher's design for conducting the qualitative study. Because the research design should shape all the decisions about the data collection and analysis procedures used in a study, the researcher usually places the sentences that identify the research design at the start of the Method section. In some qualitative research reports, you find the discussion of the research design in its own subsection with a heading such as *Research Design*, *Methodology*, or *Approach*. Because there are many different possible research designs, a well-written report not only names the design, but also includes supporting information about the design choice for the reader. Often this information includes a brief definition of the research design, references to literature that discusses this design to indicate that the researcher is knowledgeable about its use, and an explanation as to why the particular design was selected as the best overall plan for conducting the study to address the study's purpose and research questions. For example, read how Lindstrom, Doren, Metheny, Johnson, and Zane (2007) explained their choice to use a case study design in the Method section of their report:

We used a multiple-method, multiple-case study design to examine the influence of family structure and process variables on career development and postschool employment outcomes for young adults with learning disabilities. Case study research involves a thorough examination of factors within the context of a single case (Stake, 1995; Yin, 2003). This methodology is ideally suited to developing an in-depth understanding of a complex process. (p. 350)

What Characteristics Distinguish the Different Research Designs Used in Qualitative Studies?

To understand different qualitative research designs found in research reports, it may be helpful first to learn why different designs exist and how they differ from each other. Historically, a few researchers began using qualitative procedures in the late 1800s and early 1900s in fields such as anthropology and sociology for qualitative studies of indigenous cultures and immigrants in inner-city Chicago. Although quantitative research was predominant for much of the 1900s, philosophers of education and other fields were calling for an alternative to the traditional quantitative way of thinking about research in the late 1960s. They felt the traditional approach relied too much on the researcher's view of the world and lacked information on the research participant's view. To counter the traditional quantitative approaches, philosophers suggested an alternative way to think about research that emphasized the importance of the participant's view, stressed the setting and context (e.g., a classroom or community) in which the participants expressed their views, and highlighted the meaning people personally held about issues. The principles of qualitative research that we recognize today had their foundations in these alternative perspectives.

As more and more researchers began conducting research based on these alternative perspectives, they began to focus on establishing good procedures for conducting and reporting qualitative research. They developed general procedures for a basic thematic approach such as writing general qualitative research questions, conducting on-site interviews and observations to collect open-ended forms of data, and analyzing data for themes (e.g., Glesne & Peshkin, 1992; Miles & Huberman, 1994; Tesch, 1990). These approaches are aimed at describing the multiple perspectives individuals hold about a topic and finding patterns among these perspectives.

Along with these general efforts, scholars within different disciplines began developing specific procedures for conducting qualitative research to address different research purposes of interest within their disciplines. For example, anthropologists who studied the culture of indigenous groups developed qualitative procedures best suited for describing and interpreting a group's culture. As procedures such as these were further developed and specialized, they went beyond simply analyzing data for themes to forms of analysis that emphasized description and interrelating themes. The development of sets of specific procedures to address specific study purposes started to break qualitative research approaches into different types of research designs (e.g., Creswell, 2013). As these research designs became adopted and formalized across many disciplines, they became distinguished based on the following:

- the central phenomenon of interest (e.g., a group's culture, or an individual's story),
- the intent (e.g., to describe and interpret, or to develop a theory), and
- the procedures (e.g., how data are collected, analyzed, and interpreted; how results are reported).

The many qualitative research designs found in the literature today have evolved from different disciplines, address different central phenomena and research intents, and utilize different procedures for conducting and reporting qualitative research. Because of the flexible nature of qualitative research, however, it is a challenge to say how many qualitative research designs exist in total. There are qualitative books that discuss 3 designs (Richards & Morse, 2007), 8 designs (Denzin & Lincoln, 2005), and even 17 (wow!) designs (Hatch, 2002). In addition, many researchers still choose to use a general thematic approach without a specific research design, although the trend today is for researchers to use a design-based approach to their qualitative studies. To help you navigate this complexity, we provide a summary in Table 9.1, which identifies the basic qualitative research approach and provides the names and a brief overview of 10 qualitative research designs that you will likely encounter. This table introduces you to the variety of qualitative research designs used by researchers and reported in the literature. To help you better understand the differences among the designs, we next provide a more in-depth introduction to the four designs that are most commonly found in qualitative research reports.

TABLE 9.1 Overview of the Central Phenomenon, Intent, and Key Procedures for Different Qualitative Research Designs

Design Name	Central Phenomenon	Intent	Key Procedures
Basic qualitative research approach	■ A topic	■ To explore multiple perspectives	■ Collecting qualitative data, analyzing the data to develop themes, and discussing general conclusions about the themes
Autoethnography	■ The researcher's own personal experiences	■ To understand a larger cultural issue	■ Recording, reflecting on, and analyzing data about one's personal experiences within the larger cultural context
Case study	■ A system of people (a case) bounded by space and time	■ To describe and interpret what is happening	■ Collecting and analyzing multiple forms of data for description, themes, and lessons learned
Discourse analysis	■ How individuals communicate about a topic	■ To examine the use of language	■ Collecting naturally occurring oral or written data and analyzing how language is used in the data (rather than focusing on the content of the data)
Ethnography	■ The language, behaviors, and beliefs (i.e., the culture) of a group of people	■ To describe cultural patterns	■ Collecting data primarily through observations and analyzing the data to describe cultural patterns in the everyday language, behaviors, and attitudes of the group
Grounded theory	■ A process, action, or interaction	■ To generate a theory	■ Collecting data, identifying and relating categories in the data, developing a figure that depicts the theory, and stating predictions that follow from the theory
Historical analysis	■ Events of the past	■ To reconstruct a historical account	■ Collecting artifacts that represent multiple sources of data about the event, assessing the authenticity of the artifacts, and reconstructing the event
Narrative research	■ The experiences of one or more individuals	■ To describe the meaning of experiences through stories	■ Collecting data as field texts in the individual's own words, analyzing the data to organize the story, and retelling the story and identifying the context and themes of the story
Phenomenology	■ An experience	■ To describe the meaning	■ Collecting data from people who have had the experience, analyzing the meaning of significant statements in the data, and describing themes about and the essence of the experience
PhotoVoice	■ Individuals' social circumstances	■ To give voice to individuals through visual and textual forms	■ Providing cameras to participants and asking them to take photos about the topic, interviewing them about the photos, and presenting visual and textual themes
Portraiture	■ Everyday life issues	■ To create an artistically crafted portrait of one or more individuals to gain insight into what is good about an issue	■ Collecting data primarily through interviews, reflecting on the researcher's own role in the research, and creating an engaging portrait of the studied individual(s)

How Do You Understand Four Common Qualitative Research Designs?

In this section, we focus on four designs that are frequently reported in the literature and provide the background you need to understand these common designs. Although these designs are all good examples of qualitative research, they differ in terms of the disciplines where they originated, the intents and central phenomena they address, and the specific procedures and terms that are used and reported. We consider each of these aspects as we examine the following four common designs, which are summarized in Figure 9.2:

- narrative research designs,
- case study research designs,
- ethnographic research designs, and
- grounded theory research designs.

The Narrative Research Design

In some qualitative research, the research purpose is to tell the stories of one or two individuals, and a narrative research design is used. A **narrative research design** is a set of qualitative procedures that the researcher uses to describe the lives of individuals by collecting and telling stories about these individuals' lives, writing narratives about their experiences, and discussing the meaning of those experiences for the individual. *Stories* are descriptions of events and experiences in individuals' lives, organized by how they unfold over time (e.g., what happens first and then what happens next). Researchers have used narrative research deigns to study stories such as the life of a woman who was a successful athlete in the 1930s (Adams, 2012), the story of one principal–student interaction (Cranston, 2012), and stories of parents who completed an international adoption (Pryor & Pettinelli, 2011).

The narrative research design and its focus on telling stories developed from literary approaches used in several disciplines. For example, historians and nonfiction

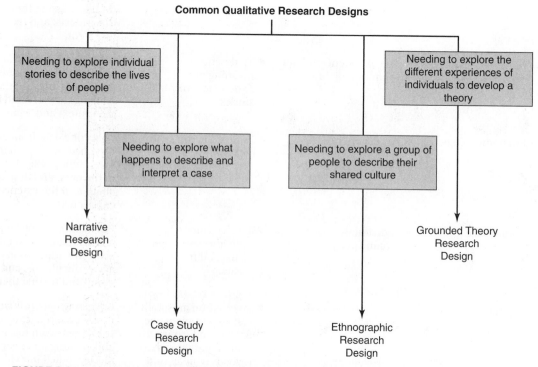

FIGURE 9.2 Four Common Qualitative Research Designs and Their Use

authors developed procedures for writing *biographies* and *autobiographies*, which were adapted by sociologists and anthropologists to collect and analyze *personal experience stories* and by educators to present *teachers' stories.* The use of narrative research designs has become more common as researchers and consumers of research are increasingly interested in learning about individuals' practices, empowering practitioners in their practices, and encouraging reflections about practices. The increased use of narrative research is particularly notable in education, and educational researchers often refer to the writings of educator D. Jean Clandinin (2007; Clandinin & Connelly, 2000) as the basis for their use of a narrative design in their research reports.

Researchers Use Narrative Research to Describe Individuals' Lives Over Time.   Narrative research studies can be engaging to read because they capture and report stories—an everyday form of data that is familiar to most people. Researchers select the narrative research design when they need to learn individuals' stories to help explore a research problem. Narrative research is well suited for studying individuals rather than groups or focusing on abstract patterns across many individuals. This design focuses on events experienced by an individual over time and the settings, actions, contexts, and people involved in these events. It is used when a researcher wants to uncover practical, specific insights that emerge from an individual's personal experiences. A study that used a narrative research design can be especially helpful for practitioners, such as educators and social workers, because the research often produces results that focus on how an individual can change or improve practice. For example, researchers use narrative designs to learn how a father connects to his children (Brotherson et al., 2005), to follow one preservice teacher's placement in an inner-city school (Rushton, 2004), and to describe the lives of older rural women (Terrill & Gullifer, 2010). The readers of these studies can then apply what they learned about these individuals' experiences to their own practice.

Identifying the Characteristics of Narrative Research in a Research Report.   It is useful to identify the overall research design when reading any qualitative research report. Many researchers identify their use of a narrative research design by including terms in their report such as *narrative research, narrative inquiry,* and *story.* Other specialized terms such as *biography* and *autobiography* can also signal its use. In addition to finding the name of the design provided in the report, you can recognize a good example of the narrative research design when the research includes the following key characteristics:

- **The research problem called for an exploration of individual experiences as told through stories.** When reading the Introduction of a narrative research report, you should find that the researcher needed to explore the experiences of individuals to understand the research problem. This need leads the narrative researcher to state a research purpose that focuses on telling and understanding the stories of one or more individuals' lives.
- **The narrative researcher collected field texts that document the individual's story in his or her own words.** When reading the Method section, you should learn that the researcher collected data, sometimes called *field texts*, that provide the story of the individual being studied. The researcher describes gathering data about the individual's life in the form of personal conversations or interviews, journal entries, letters, or other documents, and this often occurs in collaboration with the individual whose story is being documented.
- **The narrative researcher analyzed the data for its story elements.** When reading the Method section of a good narrative research report, you also learn that the researcher used an analytic process to "restory" the data by identifying story elements (e.g., characters, plot, setting) and organizing them in a logical sequence. In addition, the researcher typically reports analyzing the data to identify themes and tensions within the story and to uncover the larger contexts that shape the story.
- **The findings include a chronological retelling of the story, the context for the story, and themes from the story.** The Results and Conclusion sections of the report focus on telling and interpreting the individual's story. As you read about the findings and discussion, you should note that the researcher presents the story in chronological order, including the contexts that provide the setting of the story, identifies themes that emerged from the story, and provides his or her interpretation of the larger meaning of the story.

Here's a Tip!

Because research designs developed in different disciplines, they often use different words to describe their procedures. Special terms like *field texts* for the data gathered in a narrative study and *restory* for the data analysis procedures occur in many of the research designs.

An Example of a Narrative Research Study.   Chan (2010) used a narrative design to study the story of Ai Mei's experience of middle school in Canada. Ai Mei, a Chinese immigrant, experienced tensions, conflicts, and harmonies as she balanced her middle-school life in the context of her peers, teachers, and parents. The researcher collected Ai Mei's story over 2 years through conversations with her, observing her in school, and reading documents such as school announcements, items posted to classroom bulletin boards, and examples of Ai Mei's school work. She analyzed the conversations and stories, and then presented a retelling of Ai Mei's story, described the themes that emerged from the data (including conflicts between teacher and parent expectations), and advanced an interpretation of the story in terms of Ai Mei's sense of identity and its meaning for educators who work with immigrant students.

In sum, this good narrative research example is the study of one individual—Ai Mei—and the story of her experience as a Chinese immigrant youth in middle school. In the report, the researcher told the story as it unfolded in time by using Ai Mei's own words from the data she collected through interview conversations and observations.

What Do You Think?

Suppose you are reading a collection of research articles related to the problem of bullying in schools. Why might one of the studies have used a narrative research design to study this topic? What characteristics would you expect to find in the report of this study?

Check Your Understanding

A researcher could have conducted a study using a narrative design to investigate one high-school student's experiences of being the victim of bullying by a group of classmates. In the report of this study, we would expect to find a focus on the individual and his story. The researcher would describe collecting data from the student that tells the story through conversations and documents, such as his personal diary or artwork. The analysis of the story would include the identification of the story's logical order (e.g., what happens first, second, and third), themes that emerged from the story (such as helplessness or isolation), and the contexts that shape the story (such as school policies or teacher behaviors). The researcher would ultimately retell the story, describe the themes and contexts for the story, and interpret the meaning of the story for the individual.

How might a narrative study be used to study a topic of interest to you?

The Case Study Research Design

As you read qualitative research reports, you find that some researchers intend to examine the complexities of what happens in a system of people, not just with a single individual. Often when they have this purpose, researchers choose to use a case study design. A **case study research design** is a set of qualitative procedures used to explore a bounded system in depth. A *system* can be a program, event, or activity involving individuals, and the system of interest for a particular study is referred to as the *case*. *Bounded* means that the researcher separates out the case in terms of time, place, or some physical boundaries for the purposes of the research study. Examples of cases that could be studied include a third-grade class using a new vocabulary curriculum for a school year, a theater group preparing a theatrical production during the fall semester, or a social work agency establishing budget priorities over 3 years.

Here's a Tip!

Some qualitative research designs are more likely to produce results that suggest direct implications for practice. Look to narrative studies and case studies to find results that might readily apply to your setting.

Case study research is a popular qualitative design because researchers from many different disciplines are interested in understanding what is happening in a system of people. The case study approach has historic roots in the social and behavioral sciences. In the 1920s, sociologists conducted studies to depict and describe ordinary life in U.S. cities, focusing on systems such as Polish-immigrant neighborhoods, the Jewish ghetto, and the taxi-dance hall. Today, case study is a common approach used to study systems within many different disciplines, such as educational systems (e.g., a classroom, a school, or a college campus) or health systems (e.g., a patient and care providers, a clinic, or a hospital). Many scholars write about case study designs, and thus you might read research reports that refer to Robert Stake (1995), Sharan Merriam (1998), or Robert Yin (2009) as support for the researcher's use of this design.

Researchers Use Case Study Research to Describe What Happens in a Case.   Reports of studies that use a case study design can be fascinating because the researchers provide an in-depth exploration of a case to address the research problem. The case may be a single individual (e.g., a teacher or a parent), several individuals separately or in a group (e.g., several teachers or a family), or a program, event, or activity (e.g., the implementation of a new math program or the management of a child's therapy regimen). A case may be selected for study because it is unusual and has merit in and of itself, such as a special professional development program for novice teachers (Clayton, 2007). Alternatively, a case or multiple cases may be selected to illustrate a specific issue. For example, a researcher who wanted to study the specific issue of how eating disorders can affect the family selected four families that included a young person suffering with anorexia nervosa (Dallos & Denford, 2008).

Identifying the Characteristics of Case Study Research in a Research Report.   You can often identify the use of a case study design when researchers use the term *case study* in their report. If the research included multiple cases to provide insight into an issue, then the researchers might refer to their design as a *collective case study* or *multiple case study*. Not all qualitative researchers who use this design choose to refer to it by name, but you can identify the use of a case study design in these reports by finding all or most of the following key characteristics:

- *The research problem called for an in-depth exploration of a case.* When reading the Introduction of a case study report, it should quickly become clear that there is a need to study one or more cases to understand what is happening in a bounded system. The researcher should identify a single case or multiple cases as the object of study in the study's purpose statement, and in a good report the researcher also states how the case(s) are bounded by time, place, and/or physical boundaries.
- *The case study researcher collected multiple forms of data.* Because case study researchers seek to develop an in-depth understanding of the case or cases, they describe collecting multiple forms of data in the Method section of the report. These data forms often include interviews, observations, pictures, documents, videotapes, and e-mails. The use of multiple forms of data is important in case study research so that the researchers can be more certain of capturing the complexity of each case studied with the gathered data.
- *The case study researcher analyzed the data for description and themes.* When reading the Method section of a case study report, you also find that the researcher used procedures to analyze the data for information that describes the case and for themes or patterns that emerge about the case. If the researcher studied more than one case, then he or she typically reports analyzing the data for each case separately before analyzing the data across all the studied cases.
- *The findings include description, themes, and lessons learned.* A well-written case study report includes a rich description of the case or cases as part of the report. In addition, you generally read a presentation of the themes in the Results section and an interpretation of the lessons learned from the case(s) in the Conclusion section.

An Example of a Case Study Research Study.   Wang's (2013) study of three Chinese adolescents is an example of a case study that examined multiple cases. Wang's purpose was to describe how the adolescents experience being Chinese individually, within their families, and within their larger Midwestern communities. During a 4-month period, she interviewed each adolescent, mother, and father twice, and also asked each participant to take photos of their experience being Chinese. She analyzed the gathered data using procedures to produce description and themes. Her findings started with a detailed description of each adolescent. Wang then presented six themes that emerged during the analysis that addressed patterns in the data, such as what it meant to be Chinese for the adolescents, the lack of access to a larger Chinese community, the influences of peers, and the influences of stereotypes. From the individual case analyses, Wang compared the three individuals and found similarities and differences in their experiences of adapting to their Midwestern culture and suggested lessons learned for practitioners who work with Chinese families.

This case study is a good example of a study of three bounded systems—specific individuals bounded by their families and communities—that described the experience of being Chinese for three adolescents. The researcher focused on the central phenomenon of being Chinese and conducted an in-depth examination of the three cases to explore this phenomenon. Multiple forms of data were collected, and the analysis resulted in both description and themes.

What Do You Think?

Suppose you are reading a collection of research articles related to the problem of bullying in schools. Why might one of the studies have used a case study design to study this topic? What characteristics would you expect to find in the report of this study?

Check Your Understanding

A researcher might use a case study design to study bullying events that occur among the children in one sixth-grade classroom during a school year. In this study, we would expect to find the identification of a case (one class bounded by one school during one school year), the collection of multiple types of data (such as observations in the class and during recess; interviews with the teacher, students, and parents; and documents stating the school's policy about bullying), and data analysis focused on developing description and themes from the data. The study's results would include a description of the case, themes that emerged about bullying events, and suggestions of lessons learned from the study.

How might a case study be used to study a topic of interest to you?

The Ethnographic Research Design

When reading qualitative research studies, you may encounter research that investigated a group of individuals but, instead of a focus on what is happening in a particular case, the report presents an exploration of the culture of the group. This type of study is known as an ethnographic study or an ethnography. An **ethnographic research design** is a set of qualitative research procedures for describing, analyzing, and interpreting a culture-sharing group's shared patterns of behavior, beliefs, and language. Central to this definition is culture. *Culture* is "everything having to do with human behavior and belief" (LeCompte, Preissle, & Tesch, 1993, p. 5). It can include language, rituals, communication styles, and economic and political structures that develop over time in the group. Although both the case study design and the ethnographic design focus on groups of people, an ethnographic design is used to study the cultural patterns that form for a group of people who interact with each other enough to develop their own culture. For example, a culture-sharing group might be all personnel and staff that work in an agency, the members of a community church, or the "regular" crowd at a local coffee shop. This focus on a culture-sharing group in an ethnography is different from the focus in a case study, which usually includes a system of people, but that focuses on what is happening in a program, event, or activity that is bounded in time and space.

Although ethnography is used in many disciplines today, its roots lie in the field of cultural anthropology. In the late 19th and early 20th centuries, anthropologists explored indigenous cultures by visiting other countries and becoming immersed in their societies for extensive periods. Educational researchers began to apply these ethnographic strategies to study the culture of educational groups starting in the 1950s. For example, Jules Henry depicted elementary school classrooms and high schools as tribes with rituals, culture, and social structure (LeCompte et al., 1993). The ethnographic research design is now a relatively common approach across many disciplines, including education, health sciences, and sociology. Contemporary ethnographers like David Fetterman (2010) and Harry Wolcott (2008) have written about techniques for using ethnography to study research problems, and researchers using an ethnographic approach often cite their writings in support of the procedures used in their reports.

Researchers Use Ethnographic Research to Explore a Group's Culture.

When you read a report of an ethnographic study, the focus on a group's culture is immediately apparent. Researchers conduct ethnographies when the study of a group can provide a new understanding of a larger cultural issue. The researcher describes a culture-sharing group—one that has been together for some time and has developed shared values, beliefs, and language—and explains why a study of this group is warranted. This culture-sharing group may be narrowly framed (e.g., one committee or team) or broadly framed (e.g., an entire school or community). The researcher aims to study the "rules" of behavior within the culture of the group. Examples of ethnographic designs include the study of how students and instructors behave in the learning environment found within the computer science classrooms at one university (Barker & Garvin-Doxas, 2004), how physicians use electronic health records in a medical practice (Ventres et al., 2006), and the tacit rules for reading teen magazines by a group of best friends at one junior high school (Finders, 1996). Ethnographic research is particularly informative when you want to learn about a group in the setting where they live and work, including a detailed day-to-day picture of the group's thoughts, behaviors, and language.

Identifying the Characteristics of Ethnographic Research in a Research Report.

You can recognize a study using an ethnographic research design by terms such as *ethnography* or *ethnographic*. Unfortunately, some reports include the term *ethnography* to refer to the use of a general qualitative thematic approach instead of the use of an *ethnographic research design*. To correctly identify the use of an ethnographic research design, you should find that the study report includes the following key characteristics:

- *The research problem called for a description of a culture-sharing group.* The Introduction section of an ethnographic study should identify an intact culture-sharing group and explain why it needs to be studied to add to our knowledge about a cultural issue. The members of the selected group, such as students in a class or members of a church, have interacted with each other for sufficient time for the group to have developed its own culture. The researcher generally states that the aim of the study was to understand the language, beliefs, and behaviors—the culture—of this group.
- *The ethnographer conducted extensive field work.* When reading about the methods of a good ethnography, you learn that the ethnographer spent considerable time in the field (e.g., many months or even years) conducting fieldwork with members of the group. This fieldwork typically emphasizes observing the group because that is the best way to learn about cultural patterns that have developed in the group. The data collection methods may also include collecting interviews, documents, and other artifacts, all of which should be described in the report.
- *The ethnographer analyzed the data for shared patterns of behaviors, beliefs, and language.* The Method section describes the procedures that the ethnographic

researchers used to analyze their data. These procedures typically include coding and interpretation to identify shared patterns of behavior, beliefs, and language found within the data gathered from the culture-sharing group. In ethnography, a shared pattern is a common social interaction that stabilizes as a tacit rule or expectation of the group (Spindler & Spindler, 1992). How individuals raise their children, where individuals sit during each committee meeting, and the language used to discuss racial differences are examples of shared patterns.

■ *The findings include a cultural portrait and personal reflections.* In the findings of the research report, the ethnographer presents a cultural portrait of the group—a detailed, rich rendering of individuals and scenes that depict what is going on in the culture-sharing group and the setting, situation, or environment that surrounds the cultural group being studied. In addition, the ethnographic researcher also discusses his or her role in the study in a way that honors and respects the site and participants.

An Example of an Ethnographic Research Study.   An example of an ethnography is Swidler's (2000) study of a one-teacher country school. This researcher considered schools to be cultural settings, and designed this study to examine the shared practices of one specific country school made up of one teacher and 12 students spanning kindergarten through eighth grades. He collected data over 6 months by making extensive observations, conducting interviews, and reviewing artifacts and documents. To present the results of his analysis, Swidler painted a descriptive portrait of life at the school, describing its setting in the community, behaviors and beliefs of the teacher and individual students, and their shared practices during a typical school day. He discussed his views of the teacher's use of a conservative recitation-driven pedagogy, which he interpreted within the cultural contexts in which the school exists. He also provided his interpretation of the community values, including the socialization of the community's children, the desire for children's success in high school, a distrust of youth culture, and defending the community's way of life.

This study is a great example of an ethnographic study of a culture-sharing group—a one-teacher school within a small rural community—that tells us about the shared patterns of beliefs, behaviors, and language. The researcher described the extensive fieldwork he conducted and then presented a rich, detailed portrait of daily life at this school, interpreted within the cultural contexts of the group.

What Do You Think?

Suppose you are reading a collection of research articles related to the problem of bullying in schools. Why might one of the studies have used an ethnographic design to study this topic? What characteristics would you expect to find in the report of this study?

Check Your Understanding

A researcher might use an ethnographic design to study a group of children and parents who frequent one popular park in an inner city neighborhood where bullying occurs, focusing on understanding the cultural patterns that emerge from this group. In a report of this study, we would expect to find an emphasis on the cultural aspects of the group, a description of extensive fieldwork with a focus on conducting observations at the park, and data analysis that identifies shared behaviors, attitudes, and language related to the issue of bullying within the group, such as how parents react to bullying or the language kids use to talk about bullies and victims. The report should end with a rich, detailed description of the setting and typical life at the park and an interpretation of the cultural themes that emerged.

Now, how might an ethnographic design be used to study a topic of interest to you?

The Grounded Theory Research Design

The research designs discussed so far have emphasized description. Narrative designs are used to describe the stories of individuals, case study designs are used to describe what is happening in a case, and ethnographic designs are used to describe the culture of a group. However, many qualitative research reports go beyond description and develop a theory about the central phenomenon. In these situations, the researcher has likely used a grounded theory design. A **grounded theory research design** is a set of systematic, qualitative procedures that researchers use to generate a general explanation (called a *grounded theory*) for a process, action, or interaction among people. Recall from Chapter 4 that a *theory* explains the probable relationships among concepts. A *grounded theory* is an explanation that is developed about a process, action, or interaction through the collection and analysis of qualitative data so that the explanation is built from (or "grounded" in) the experiences and perspectives of participants. For example, researchers might conduct grounded theory studies and report the development of explanations for the process supervisors use to mentor new employees, the actions involved when first-year college students cope with stress, or the interactions among school counselors and parents when working with a child with persistent behavior problems in middle school.

The procedures for conducting a systematic grounded theory design were first developed in the 1960s by two sociologists studying terminally ill individuals (Glaser & Strauss, 1967). These systematic procedures gave researchers a more structured approach to conducting qualitative research that appealed to researchers from many disciplines. From this initial work, grounded theory has become a commonly used research design today because researchers often want to develop general theories that help to explain how a process, action, or interaction unfolds. Grounded theory procedures now may be more structured (such as Corbin & Strauss, 2008) or somewhat more flexible (such as Charmaz, 2006, and Glaser, 1992), and reports should include references to the approach that the researchers used in their study. Both the systematic and flexible grounded theory designs are widely used to develop theories about central phenomena of interest.

Researchers Use Grounded Theory to Develop a Theory.   Grounded theory studies are particularly useful to read when you want to understand a process or to know how to possibly influence the outcomes of the process for others. Researchers use grounded theory designs when there is a need for a broad theory or explanation of a process, action, or interaction because the current existing theories do not adequately address the problem or participants of interest. Because a theory produced from this type of design is "grounded" in the data collected during the study, it works well in

<table>
<tr><td>

Here's a Tip!

Some qualitative research designs are best suited for developing broad patterns across several individuals or larger groups. Read ethnographic studies and grounded theory studies to find results that provide a more abstract description or explanation of the topic to help you understand larger patterns that may be occurring in your practice.

</td><td>

practice, is sensitive to the individuals in the given setting, and represents the complexities found in the specific process, action, or interaction. Thus, it provides a better explanation for the central phenomenon than a theory borrowed off-the-shelf. For instance, theories that address certain populations (e.g., children with attention disorders) may have little applicability to subsets of those populations (e.g., child immigrants from Latin America), and therefore a new or modified theory is needed. In addition, the grounded theory design is used when the purpose of the study is to examine a process, such as how families care for people who had previously attempted suicide (Sun & Long, 2008) or how the careers of high-achieving African American and Caucasian women develop (Richie, Fassinger, Linn, & Johnson, 1997). It also is used to explain specific actions, such as working while enrolled as a college student (Cheng & Alcántara, 2007), or interactions, such as the interactions among high school counselors and gay, lesbian, bisexual, and questioning adolescents (King, 2008).

</td></tr>
</table>

Identifying the Characteristics of Grounded Theory Research in a Research Report.   Good grounded theory studies are usually identified with the term *grounded theory*. Be careful, as many researchers refer to using grounded theory procedures when describing how they developed themes from their data analysis. A good grounded theory design, however, should go beyond identifying themes by relating them to each other to form a theory. You can recognize reports of good grounded theory studies by identifying the following characteristics:

- *The research problem called for an exploration to develop a theory that explains a process, action, or interaction.* When reading the Introduction of a grounded theory report, you should find that the researcher argued for the need for a theory to be developed. The purpose statement in the study should identify a process, action, or interaction that is the focus of the study and state that the intent of the study is to generate a theory about it.
- *The grounded theory researcher collected data in the form of interviews.* When reading the description of the study's data collection methods, you often find that the grounded theory researcher interviewed people who have experienced the process, action, or interaction of interest. Grounded theory studies that focus on an action or interaction may include observations as the primary data source. In either case, the data should be gathered from multiple people who have different experiences with the central phenomenon to provide the most complete data about the process, action, or interaction.
- *The grounded theory researcher analyzed the data using multiple stages of coding.* Grounded theory designs are most easily recognized by the data analysis procedures reported in the Method section. In a systematic grounded theory design, the researcher uses three stages of data analysis: the development of categories from the collected data (known as "open coding"), the identification of one category that is at the heart of the process and its relation to the other categories (known as "axial coding"), and the development of propositions or hypotheses grounded in the data (known as "selective coding"). More flexible grounded theory approaches may not describe specific stages, but they still provide extensive description of how their data analysis led to the development of a theory.
- *The findings include a model of the theory and propositions from the theory.* The Results and Conclusion sections of a good grounded theory report present and interpret the generated theory. The report should clearly describe the categories found in the data and how they relate to each other within the theory that has been developed. The theory is often presented in one or more of these three ways: described in words in the article text, represented in a figure that visually depicts the general relationships among categories, and stated in proposition or hypothesis statements that advance predictions about how specific categories are related.

Here's a Tip!

Grounded theory designs make use of many specialized terms, such as different types of analyses ("open," "axial," and "selective" coding), "categories" for the themes identified during analysis, and "propositions" for the predictions that are advanced at the end of the study.

An Example of a Grounded Theory Research Study.   Komives et al. (2005) used a grounded theory design in their study of how college students develop a leadership identity. They stated the purpose of their study was "to understand the processes a person experiences in creating a leadership identity" (p. 594). To collect their data, the researchers conducted three interviews with each of 13 diverse college students who had been identified as demonstrating leadership qualities. They reported using a systematic process of open coding, axial coding, and selective coding to analyze the data. From this three-stage analysis process, they developed the categories of developmental influences, developing self, group influences, changing view of self with others, and broadening view of leadership; identified the six stages found at the heart of developing a leadership identity; and connected the categories to the six stages to form the theory. Komives et al. presented a visual model showing how the categories related to the stages of the process. In their conclusions, they discussed the implications of the theory for individuals who advise and work with college students.

This grounded theory study demonstrates a good study of a process—the development of a leadership identity—as experienced by a number of individuals. The researchers collected their data through interviews and used a systematic approach to analyze their data, identifying the process and the themes that relate to this process. They brought their findings together into a figure that depicts the developed theory of the process.

What Do You Think?

Suppose you are reading a collection of research articles related to the problem of bullying in schools. Why might one of the studies have used a grounded theory design to study this topic? What characteristics would you expect to find in the report of this study?

Check Your Understanding

A researcher might use a grounded theory design to study the process by which middle school students cope with being bullied. In a report of this study, we would expect the author to discuss why a new theory explaining the coping process is needed. The researcher should collect data from individuals who have experiences this process, such as by interviewing victims of bullying at different middle schools. The researcher should present, in addition, information about the stages of the data analysis. In the results, the researcher should describe the categories that emerged to explain the process, culminating in a figure showing how the themes are interrelated and predictions that result from this new theory.

How might a grounded theory design be used to study a topic of interest to you?

How Do You Recognize the Research Design in a Qualitative Research Report?

You have now been introduced to several different qualitative research designs and know that they differ in terms of their history, the reasons that researchers use them, and their key procedures. With this information in hand, you now have the background necessary to recognize what research design was used when reading a published qualitative research report. To make this determination, we suggest trying four steps to identify the research design used in a qualitative report.

1. *Look to see if the author named the design in the title or abstract of the report.* Researchers frequently identify the specific research design in the title and abstract of their reports. For example, note how the following titles state the research design used:
   - "The Experiences of Parents of Gifted African American Children: A Phenomenological Study" (Huff, Houskamp, Watkins, Stanton, & Tavegia, 2005).
   - "Using Narrative Inquiry to Understand a Student-Teacher's Practical Knowledge While Teaching in an Inner-City School" (Rushton, 2004).

2. *Examine the purpose statement to see if it names or suggests the study's research design.* Some purpose statements in qualitative research reports include the name of the design, such as saying "The purpose of this ethnographic study is. . . ." Unfortunately, many studies do not state the design in the purpose statement. They do, however, state a central phenomenon and intent that suggests a particular design would be most appropriate (e.g., intending to explore an individual's story, describe a system, study a culture-sharing group, or develop a theory about a process). For example, in the grounded theory study by Komives et al. (2005), the purpose statement reads: "The purpose of this study was to understand the processes a person experiences in creating a leadership identity" (p. 594). Although this statement did not identify the study as using grounded theory, we can expect it might be a grounded theory study because it is the study of a process.

3. *Read the beginning paragraphs of the Method section and look for a statement that identifies the design.* Qualitative researchers usually describe the research design at the beginning of the Method section of the research report. For example, Komives et al. (2005) followed up their purpose statement (stated in the

preceding step) with the following sentence at the start of their Method section: "Because the purpose of the study was to understand how a leadership identity develops, a grounded theory methodology was chosen" (p. 594).

4. *Examine the Method and Results sections to identify how the author collected, analyzed, and reported the data.* The surest way to recognize a study's research design is to examine the procedures that the researcher used for collecting, analyzing, and reporting the data and decide whether they match one of the major design types. In fact, this is always the most important step in identifying a design accurately. Some authors mistakenly claim to use a type of design (such as ethnography) when they really mean that they are using a basic qualitative thematic approach. In addition, we have read a few reports that claim to use case study, grounded theory, narrative, and ethnography—all in one study! When in doubt, you should consider the procedures the author actually *used* and not rely on the words they happen to state.

What Do You Think?

Consider the following information from a published study (Asmussen & Creswell, 1995). Which design do you think the researchers used and what is your evidence?

Title: "Campus Response to a Student Gunman"

Purpose Statement: "The study presented in this article is a qualitative case analysis that describes and interprets a campus response to a gun incident." (p. 576)

Excerpt from the First Paragraph in the Method Section: ". . . We also limited our study to the reactions of groups on campus rather than expand it to include off-campus groups (for example, television and newspaper coverage). This bounding of the study was consistent with an exploratory qualitative case study design. . . . We identified campus informants, using a semi-structured protocol that consisted of five questions. . . . We also gathered observational data, documents, and visual materials. . . ." (p. 578)

Check Your Understanding

Using the four steps suggested for determining the research design, we can determine that this study is an example of a qualitative study using a case study research design. (1) The authors do not inform us of the type of design in the report title. (2) When we turn to the purpose statement, however, we find the use of the phrase "case analysis," which suggests the study may be a case study design. (3) In the first paragraph of the Method section, they specifically identify their use of a case study design. (4) As we continue reading, we find several key characteristics of the case study research design in the excerpts. For example, the researchers report wanting to "describe and interpret" the case in their purpose statement. They also note that their study was "bounded," another common feature of the case study design. They report collecting multiple types of data to build an in-depth description. If you review the full study, you will find that the researchers report a detailed description of the event, themes that emerged about the event (such as "fear" and "safety"), and lessons learned for planning a campus response plan.

How Do You Evaluate the Research Design in a Qualitative Study?

Recognizing the design used in a qualitative study is a great step, but you do not want to stop there. When you identify and understand the research design, you can also use the design's characteristics to help evaluate the quality of the study. We discuss the details of qualitative data collection, data analysis, and results reporting procedures in upcoming chapters, but for now, you can focus on evaluating the overall plan described for a study. A good, rigorous report makes it clear that the researcher had a reason for selecting the design for the study, and that this design is identified and explained and provided a good overall plan for conducting the study. Table 9.2

TABLE 9.2   Criteria for Evaluating the Research Design in a Qualitative Research Report

Quality Criteria	Indicators of Higher Quality	Indicators of Lower Quality
The Key Elements		
1. A research design guides the conduct of the qualitative study.	+ The researchers use an overall plan for conducting the study, such as narrative research, case study, ethnography, or grounded theory. + The researchers are knowledgeable about the design and provide indicators such as the correct use of terms and citing up-to-date literature.	− The study approach is simply generic qualitative research or no clear plan for conducting the study is used. − The researchers lack knowledge about the design such as indicated through the incorrect use of terms or lack of supporting literature.

2. The choice of the research design is appropriate and justified.	+ The design fits the study's intent and central phenomenon, such as:
	  ■ To tell the story of an individual's life for a narrative design;
	  ■ To explore one or more cases in a case study design;
	  ■ To describe a group's cultural patterns in an ethnographic design; or
	  ■ To generate a theory about a process, action, or interaction in a grounded theory design
	+ A convincing explanation for why the specific research design was selected is provided.
		− There is a mismatch among the study's intent, central phenomenon, and research design.
		− The explanation for why the specific research design was selected is unconvincing or unclear.

3. Good qualitative data collection procedures are used.	+ The procedures for collecting the data are appropriate for the design. + Rigorous qualitative procedures are used. (We will learn more about this in Chapter 10.)	− The procedures for collecting the data are inappropriate for the design. − Poor qualitative procedures are used. (We will learn more about this in Chapter 10.)
4. Good qualitative data analysis procedures are used.	+ The procedures for analyzing the data are appropriate for the design. + Rigorous qualitative procedures that go beyond identifying themes are used. (We will learn more about this in Chapter 11.)	− The procedures for analyzing the data are inappropriate for the design. − Poor or limited qualitative procedures are used. (We will learn more about this in Chapter 11.)
5. Good qualitative results and interpretations are reported.	+ The reported results are appropriate and complete for the design. + Rigorous qualitative procedures are used. (We will learn more about this in Chapter 11.)	+ The reported results are inappropriate or incomplete for the design. − Poor qualitative procedures are used. (We will learn more about this in Chapter 11.)
General Evaluation		
6. The study used a rigorous research design.	+ All elements of the study from problem to purpose to methods to results fit together in a logical, coherent way.	− There are inconsistencies in how the study problem, purpose, and methods fit together.
7. The use of the qualitative research design addressed the study's purpose.	+ The findings from the research provide a rich exploration that fulfills the study's intent and answers the study's research questions.	− The findings from the research provide a superficial examination of the study's intent and do not provide adequate answers to the study's research questions.

Quality Criteria	Quality Rating				Your Evidence and/or Reasoning
	0 = Poor	1 = Fair	2 = Good	3 = Excellent	
The Key Elements					
1. A research design guides the conduct of the qualitative study.					
2. The choice of the research design is appropriate and justified.					
3. Good qualitative data collection procedures are used.					
4. Good qualitative data analysis procedures are used.					
5. Good qualitative results and interpretations are reported.					
General Evaluation					
6. The study used a rigorous research design.					
7. The use of the qualitative research design addressed the study's purpose.					
Overall Quality 0–10 = Low quality 11–16 = Adequate quality 17–21 = High quality	**Total Score =**				**My Overall Assessment =**

FIGURE 9.3   A Rating Scale for Evaluating the Research Design in a Qualitative Research Report

lists criteria that are useful to consider when evaluating the research design in a report of a qualitative study. This table also provides indicators of higher quality and lower quality for the criteria to help you make your own judgments when evaluating a research report.

The rating scale in Figure 9.3 provides a convenient means for you to apply the quality criteria to the research design used in any qualitative research report. For each of the criteria you locate, assign a quality rating from *fair* (1) to *excellent* (3) and document your evidence and/or reasoning behind the rating. If one of the criteria is missing or very poorly stated, then indicate *poor* (0) as your rating. Although qualitative research reports vary in the extent of discussion about the research design, good reports should still score well on most of the items listed in Figure 9.3. By adding up the rating scores for each of the criteria and using the suggested cutoff values provided at the bottom of the figure, you have a quantitative measure to help you determine your overall assessment of a report's qualitative research design.

Reviewing What You've Learned To Do

- ■ *Identify and understand the research design of a qualitative study.*
  - ❑ A qualitative research design is a set of procedures for collecting, analyzing, and reporting qualitative data in a study to address the research purpose.
  - ❑ A study's qualitative research design and its associated procedures are described in the Method section of a qualitative research report; the results of the procedures are found in the Results section.

■ *List the characteristics that differentiate the various qualitative research designs.*
- ❑ There are many different types of qualitative research designs that originated from different disciplines.
- ❑ The research designs differ in terms of the type of central phenomenon to be addressed, the overall intent, and the specific procedures used for collecting, analyzing, and reporting qualitative data.

■ *Distinguish among four common qualitative research designs based on their central phenomena, intents, and procedures.*
- ❑ Narrative research designs are used to explore individual experiences as told through a story. The procedures include collecting an individual's words through field texts, analyzing the data to restory the story, and reporting the results by retelling the story and describing the context and themes of the story.
- ❑ Case study research designs are used to describe and interpret what is happening in a case (a system bounded by place and time). The procedures include collecting multiple forms of data about the case, analyzing the data for description and themes, and reporting the results by describing the case, themes from the case, and lessons learned about the case.
- ❑ Ethnographic research designs are used to describe the culture (language, behaviors, and beliefs) of a group of people. The procedures include collecting data using observations, analyzing the data for cultural patterns, and reporting the results by presenting a description of the group's culture and personal reflections of the researcher about the group's culture.
- ❑ Grounded theory research designs are used to generate a theory about a process, action, or interaction. The procedures include collecting data through interviews, using multiple stages of analysis to identify and relate categories, and reporting the results by describing the theory in the text, with a diagram, and with predictions (often called propositions) that result from the new theory.

■ *Recognize the research design used in a qualitative research report.*
- ❑ Researchers write statements into the their reports that identify the overall plan for the study by naming the design or by the procedures that are used. These statements can be found in the title, abstract, purpose statement, Method section, and Results section of a qualitative research report.

■ *Evaluate the quality of the research design in a qualitative research report.*
- ❑ The evaluation of a qualitative research design begins by considering the extent to which the researcher selected an appropriate design for the study's purpose and explained why it was selected.
- ❑ The evaluation of a qualitative research design is also based on the extent to which the researcher used good procedures for collecting, analyzing, and reporting the data that are consistent with the selected design and together form a rigorous study that addresses the study's purpose.

✓ **To assess what you've learned to do, click here to answer questions and receive instant feedback.**

Reading Research Articles

At the end of this chapter, you will find a research article to help you practice your new skills. Carefully read the qualitative adoption-of-pedagogical-tools study by Leko and Brownell (2011) starting on p. 306. First, write a complete, APA-style reference for this article. Then, carefully reread the qualitative adolescent-homelessness study by Haldenby et al. (2007) found at the end of Chapter 4 (starting on p. 148).

As you read each article, pay close attention to statements in which the authors conveyed the characteristics of the study's research design. Use the highlighting tool in the Pearson etext to indicate where the authors have provided information about the research design, and use the notetaking tool to add marginal notes that name each element you highlighted and note how each one is related to the study's design. Among the elements you will want to find are:

1. Research design name
2. Central phenomenon
3. Study intent
4. Reason for the research design
5. Data collection procedures
6. Data analysis procedures
7. Results

Note, however, that sometimes authors do not discuss all of these elements—for example, they may not explicitly state the name of the research design or they may not provide their reason for choosing the design. If one of these elements is missing, indicate that in your marginal notes.

 Click here to go to the qualitative adoption-of-pedagogical-tools study by Leko and Brownell (2011) so that you can write a complete APA-style reference for the article and enter marginal notes about the study.

 Click here to go to the qualitative adolescent-homelessness study by Haldenby et al. (2007) so that you can enter marginal notes about the study.

Understanding Research Articles

Apply your knowledge of the content of this chapter to the qualitative adoption-of-pedagogical-tools study by Leko and Brownell (2011) found at the end of this chapter (starting on p. 306) and the qualitative adolescent-homelessness study by Haldenby et al. (2007) found at the end of Chapter 4 (starting on p. 148).

1. Consider the information provided in the adoption-of-pedagogical-tools study. Did the researchers include terms that name the research design in the title or abstract of the report? If yes, what terms did you find?

2. What was the central phenomenon and intent of the study and which research design do they suggest?

3. Did Leko and Brownell identify their research design in the opening paragraph of the Method section (paragraph 12)? If yes, which design did they identify?

4. Consider the procedures that the researchers used to collect data, analyze data, and report the results. Based on these procedures, which research design did the researchers use in this study? What is your evidence?

5. Return to the qualitative adolescent-homelessness study. Identify the research design used in that study. List three pieces of evidence for your answer.

✓ **Click here to answer the questions and receive instant feedback.**

Evaluating Research Articles

Practice evaluating the quality of a qualitative study's research design, using the qualitative adoption-of-pedagogical-tools study by Leko and Brownell (2011) starting on p. 306 and the qualitative adolescent-homelessness study by Haldenby et al. (2007) starting on p. 148.

1. Use the criteria discussed in Table 9.2 to evaluate the quality of the research design in the adoption-of-pedagogical-tools study. Note that, for this question, the rating form includes advice to help guide your evaluation.

✓ **Click here to open the rating scale form (Figure 9.3) to enter your ratings, evidence, and reasoning.**

2. Use the criteria discussed in Table 9.2 to evaluate the quality of the research design in the adolescent-homelessness study. Note that, for this question, the rating form does NOT include additional advice.

✓ **Click here to open the rating scale form (Figure 9.3) to enter your ratings, evidence, and reasoning.**

An Example of Qualitative Research: The Adoption-of-Pedagogical-Tools Study

Let's examine another published research article to apply the ideas you are learning. Throughout this book, we will refer to this study as the "qualitative adoption-of-pedagogical-tools" study. This journal article reports a qualitative research study conducted and reported by Leko and Brownell (2011). Examine this article to practice your skills with reading, understanding, and evaluating research.

 Click here to write a complete APA-style reference for this article and receive instant feedback.

Exceptional Children

Vol. 77, No. 2, pp. 229-251.
©2011 Council for Exceptional Children.

Special Education Preservice Teachers' Appropriation of Pedagogical Tools for Teaching Reading

MELINDA M. LEKO
University of Wisconsin-Madison

MARY T. BROWNELL
University of Florida

ABSTRACT: *This study examined various influences on special education preservice teachers' appropriation of pedagogical tools for teaching reading to students with high-incidence disabilities using an activity theory framework. Interview, observation, and artifact data were collected on 6 preservice teachers, their reading methods course instructors, field supervisors, and practicum cooperating teachers. Using grounded theory methods, 4 concepts emerged as chief influences on participants' appropriation of conceptual and practical reading tools: (a) opportunities to appropriate knowledge in practice, (b) personal qualities, (c) motivation for knowledge assimilation, and (d) access to knowledge. Specific information related to these 4 concepts and their relationships are reported with implications for future research and practice in special education teacher education.*

(01) Learning to teach well is a complicated process—not easily accomplished by simply watching good teachers or having been a student oneself (Lortie, 1975; Munby, Russell, & Martin, 2001). A myriad of personal and contextual factors come into play when one decides to become a teacher and learns how to teach. Motivations for entering teaching, type of preparation program, and incoming knowledge and experiences are just a few of the many factors that typically influence preservice teacher learning (Brookhart & Freeman, 1992;

Richardson & Placier, 2001; Wilson, Floden, & Ferrini-Mundy, 2001).

(02) Moreover, the prior experiences and knowledge preservice teachers bring to their preparation program interact with their coursework and field experiences to either advantage or disadvantage them as learners (Boyd, Grossman, Lankford, Loeb, & Wyckoff, 2006; Humphrey & Wechsler, 2005). The relationship between teacher preparation and what preservice teachers learn, therefore, is not unidirectional; instead, it depends on what preservice teachers contribute to their opportunities to learn. That is, how preservice teachers construct and enact the knowledge they are

acquiring, in turn, affects what they bring back to the learning situation and ultimately what they learn from the preparation program. Without a deep understanding of preservice teacher learning, teacher educators cannot be assured that their efforts will be beneficial to prospective teachers. In other words, given the complex nature of teacher preparation, the study of preservice teacher learning and development is important if teacher educators hope to craft preparation programs that will adequately prepare future teachers to meet the needs of students and silence critics of teacher education.

> *The relationship between teacher preparation and what preservice teachers learn . . . is not unidirectional; instead, it depends on what preservice teachers contribute to their opportunities to learn.*

(03)   Historically, studies of special education preservice preparation have been few in number and scattered in their focus (Sindelar, Bishop, & Brownell, 2006). Further, most studies have not focused on the contributions individual teacher qualities, teacher preparation coursework, and field experiences make to preservice teacher learning. Even when researchers have attempted to study special education preservice teacher learning in greater depth, they often end up examining factors in isolation (e.g., the impact of preservice teacher beliefs, *or* knowledge, *or* specific pedagogical practices) and their influence on knowledge acquired in special education preservice programs (see Brownell, Ross, Colon, & McCallum, 2005; Goe & Coggshall, 2007; Risko et al., 2008, for reviews). Although these studies improve understanding of how special education teachers' learning and beliefs may influence or be influenced by specific aspects of teacher preparation, they do not provide a comprehensive model or theory of special education teacher learning. Experts in the field of teacher education warn that without such models researchers will be unable to explain their mixed findings regarding the effectiveness of teacher education and will encounter obstacles as they attempt to develop a more comprehensive research base (Sindelar, Brownell, &

Billingsley, 2010; Zeichner, 2005). The present investigation is intended to respond to the call for more sophisticated models of teacher learning, particularly in the context of special education preservice preparation.

ACTIVITY THEORY AS A FRAMEWORK FOR UNDERSTANDING THE COMPLEXITIES OF PRESERVICE TEACHER LEARNING

When designing teacher education studies, the research on teacher learning calls for a sophisticated (04) model that accounts for teachers' prior experiences, beliefs, knowledge, and practice (Borko & Putnam, 1996; Humphrey & Wechsler, 2005; Zeichner, 2005). *Activity theory* is a framework for research on teacher learning that holds promise for studying interactions among preservice teacher experiences, knowledge, and practice: It focuses on the interaction of human activity and cognition within relevant environmental contexts (Jonassen & Rohrer-Murphy, 1999; Leont'ev, 1981). A key assumption of activity theory is that cognition and learning are developed through activities carried out in specific settings. Activity theory is an appropriate framework for examining teacher learning because, according to activity theorists, context affects learning—and a person's actions, beliefs, and knowledge affect the context (Fairbanks & Meritt, 1998; Grossman, Smagorinsky, & Valencia, 1999). Thus, activity theory accounts for individual influences on learning such as prior beliefs, knowledge, and experiences, as well as the various contexts in which teacher learning is situated; for example, contexts such as methods courses and internships (Valencia, Martin, Place, & Grossman, 2009).

In 1999, Grossman and colleagues adapted (05) the tenets of activity theory to the field of general education, asserting that how preservice teachers interacted with their teacher preparation context would in turn influence their learning. Specifically, they assumed that contexts (e.g., methods courses and field experiences) would provide preservice teachers with opportunities to acquire either conceptual or practical pedagogical tools.

According to Grossman and her colleagues, *conceptual tools* are broad principles and ideas that help guide teachers' decision making, such as reader-response theory, constructivism, or scaffolding; *practical tools* are specific skills and strategies with immediate utility, such as journal writing, graphic organizers, or daily oral language. Teachers use pedagogical tools "to guide and implement their classroom practice" (Grossman et al., 1999, p. 13).

(06)   The extent to which preservice teachers appropriate or adopt a pedagogical tool, however, depends on the level of congruence between preservice teachers' prior knowledge, beliefs and motivations, and their opportunities to learn in course work and fieldwork (Grossman et al., 1999). Grossman and her colleagues identified five levels at which conceptual and practical tools can be adopted. At the lowest level, preservice teachers do not adopt a tool because they either lack sufficient knowledge of the tool, their beliefs do not support using the tool, or the context is not conducive to utilizing the tool. At the second level, preservice teachers adopt a label for the tool; that is, they can name the tool but cannot describe the tool's important features. When preservice teachers have reached the third level, adopting surface features, they know some of the tool's features, but cannot describe how those features work together to create a holistic picture of the tool. For instance, they might be able to describe all the steps involved in teaching a cognitive strategy, such as summarization, but they cannot explain why those steps are important for helping students learn to regulate their learning. At the fourth level, preservice teachers can appropriate the tool's conceptual underpinnings or describe the theory behind the tool. Thus, a preservice teacher could describe the steps of a summarization strategy and why those steps would promote self-regulation of the comprehension process. Once preservice teachers are able to integrate a tool effectively into their classroom instruction, they have reached the final level: mastery of tool appropriation. Tools that have been adopted at higher levels become accessible practices preservice teachers can draw from during their teaching (Grossman et al., 1999).

ACTIVITY THEORY APPLIED TO GENERAL EDUCATION TEACHER LEARNING

Several general education teacher studies have been conducted using activity theory as a framework. Most notably, Grossman and other researchers at the Center for English Learning and Achievement completed a longitudinal study of 10 preservice teachers' Language Arts instruction, following them from their last year of preservice training through their third year of teaching. Results from a series of studies indicated that the student teaching placement was a valuable setting in which to experiment with the pedagogical tools acquired from the preparation program (Grossman et al., 2000). Grossman and colleagues found that the preservice teachers were able to appropriate tools whether or not their student teaching placement aligned with the teacher preparation program. The key was that teacher educators supported preservice teachers in taking a reflective stance toward their student teaching experiences. Moreover, the preservice teachers drew on pedagogical tools from the preparation program—but not until their second year of teaching when they had more time and energy to devote to reaching their ideal vision of writing instruction (Grossman et al., 2000). In addition, the research team found that the interplay of curricular materials, teacher knowledge, and context resulted in either supportive or inhibitive learning experiences. Teachers who relied solely on structured curricular programs, either by choice or by school mandate, did not experience large knowledge gains and had trouble adapting their instruction based on students' needs (Valencia, Place, Martin, & Grossman, 2006). Finally, competing demands and perspectives among preservice teachers, their cooperating teachers, and university supervisors resulted in several missed learning opportunities for the preservice teachers during their student teaching placements (Valencia et al., 2009). The preservice teachers, excited to try out tools they acquired from their teacher preparation program, often met resistance from cooperating teachers who felt uneasy about relinquishing classroom control or who felt pressured to adhere to district-mandated curricula and content standards (Valencia et al., 2009).

(07)

(08)   Taken together, these studies (Grossman et al., 2000; Valencia et al., 2009; Valencia et al., 2006) point to the utility of activity theory as a framework for studying teacher learning. In particular, the relationships among activity settings, including the pedagogical tools and individuals in these settings, generate an explanatory model that can account for differences in individual preservice teachers' learning outcomes. Although these findings contribute to understandings of teacher learning in general education contexts, they provide little information about special education teacher learning. We can assume that there are similarities between general education and special education teacher learning; both general education and special education preservice teachers bring their prior experiences and knowledge to the teacher preparation context, and they both enter a preparation context that typically comprises course work, field experiences, and internships.

(09)   Despite these similarities, however, there are numerous differences between special education and general education teacher preparation that necessitate the study of special education teacher learning exclusively. For example, cooperating teachers may be special or general educators with discrepant knowledge of reading instruction for students with disabilities, providing disparate opportunities for special education preservice teachers to learn about teaching reading during their field experiences. Unlike general education teacher preparation, special education teacher preparation is designed to prepare preservice teachers to meet the individual needs of students with disabilities as indicated by individualized education programs (IEPs). Ostensibly, a large part of learning to be a special educator is implementing IEPs. Finally, the extensive research base on reading instruction for students with disabilities has demonstrated the importance of systematic, explicit instruction, conducted in small groups with extended opportunities for practice and regular progress monitoring (Chard, Vaughn, & Tyler, 2002; Raskin-Erickson & Pressley, 2000; Taylor, Pearson, Clark & Walpole, 2000)—features that do not always characterize general education reading instruction.

(10)   Given the differences between general education and special education teacher preparation contexts, it is critical that special education teacher education researchers devote time and energy to investigations aimed at unraveling the complex connections among special education preservice teacher preparation, knowledge, and practice (Zumwalt & Craig, 2005). By studying special education teacher education using an activity theory framework, we can better understand the ways in which individual preservice teachers and their teacher preparation experiences interact to influence prospective special educators' learning and practice. Further, studying special education teacher education from this framework helps us understand how a theory that has been used to provide a richer understanding of how general education preservice teachers learn can be translated to the field of special education.

(11)   The purpose of this study, therefore, was to examine various influences on special education preservice teachers' appropriation of pedagogical tools for teaching reading to students with high-incidence disabilities using elements of an activity theory framework. The research questions guiding this study included:

1. What are the individual and contextual influences on special education preservice teachers' appropriation of pedagogical tools in reading for students with disabilities?

2. How do these influences impact the extent to which special education preservice teachers appropriate evidence-based practices in reading for students with disabilities?

It should be noted that these research questions resulted in us focusing on some aspects of activity theory more than others. (For example, to understand how individual and contextual influences impact preservice teachers' appropriation of evidence-based practices in reading, we examined more closely how contexts affect preservice teachers rather than how preservice teachers affect their context.)

METHOD

(12)   The activity theory framework developed by Grossman et al. (1999) served as a foundation for the conceptual framework guiding this qualitative investigation of preservice teacher learning. We chose qualitative methods for this study because

they result in in-depth information that leads to greater understandings about social phenomena (Creswell, 1998). When employing qualitative methods, it is important to acknowledge that the researcher is an integral part of data collection and analysis; thus, a researcher's subjectivities should be acknowledged (Brantlinger, Jimenez, Klingner, Pugach, & Richardson, 2005; Patton, 2002). Our theoretical perspective underlying this study was constructivism. A critical tenet of constructivism is that individuals are viewed as active agents, acquiring knowledge about the world through experiences with their environments (Crotty, 1998); hence, constructivism is well aligned with the principles of activity theory.

PARTICIPANTS

(13) To understand the individual and contextual influences on special education preservice teachers' appropriation of pedagogical tools in reading, it was necessary to secure a sample of participants who had heterogeneous beliefs, knowledge, and prior experiences concerning reading instruction and students with disabilities. Such a sample was needed so that we could discern and explain differences in preservice teachers' interactions with their preparation program, appropriation of instructional tools, and knowledge. To obtain such a sample, we selected participants using purposive criterion sampling techniques grouped into two phases.

(14) *Phase 1 Sample Selection.* In Phase 1 sampling we created a list of preservice teachers whose practicum placement environments fit the study parameters. To participate in this study, preservice teachers had to (a) be first-semester special education Master's-level students in our institution's collaborative preparation program, (b) have completed the program's requisite reading coursework, (c) have fall practicum placements in elementary classrooms that required work with students with high-incidence disabilities, and (d) provide reading instruction to students during practicum. The research team worked in conjunction with the special education field experience supervisor to generate a list of preservice teachers ($N = 18$) who met these selection criteria.

(15) *Phase 2 Sample Selection.* Phase 2 sampling ensured that the final sample was small enough to

allow for in-depth examination of key variables and recruit participants who represented diverse backgrounds and knowledge bases. To secure this sample, we asked the 18 preservice teachers to complete an open-ended survey assessing their beliefs and prior experiences as well as a concept map that assessed their knowledge for reading instruction. Concept maps are useful visual representations that can be used both as learning tools and assessment tools (Novak & Cañas, 2006). On the concept map, preservice teachers generated as many ideas as they could about *reading instruction*. After reviewing the surveys and concept maps, we used a variety of criteria to narrow the sample size to eight preservice teachers.

(16) First, we sorted concept maps into three groups according to level of detail and sophistication. We assessed level of detail by tallying the number of items a preservice teacher included on her concept map. We assessed sophistication by examining how many concepts were linked to one another and the ways they were linked. Four concept maps fell into the low detail and sophistication group, nine were considered medium detail and sophistication, and five were high detail and sophistication. Then, for each group, we evaluated preservice teachers' prior experiences with children with disabilities (i.e., no prior experiences, prior experiences in personal life, or prior experiences in a teaching context), experiences during K–12 schooling (i.e., inclusive schooling or not); and beliefs about reading instruction for students with disabilities (i.e., ideas related to explicit, systematic phonics-based approach or ideas related to whole-language approach) as reported on the open-ended survey, looking particularly for preservice teachers whose prior experiences and beliefs varied. The result was eight preservice teachers who varied in their prior experiences, beliefs, and knowledge.

(17) Before establishing the final sample, we questioned the eight preservice teachers individually about their concept maps and practicum placements. Two preservice teachers were dropped from the final sample because, though their practicum placements were in inclusive classrooms, they reported having little interaction with students with disabilities.

(18) We narrowed the final sample to six preservice teachers, a small enough sample size to allow

TABLE 1

Demographic Information

| Preservice Teacher | Age/ Ethnicity | Practicum Setting | Practicum School Data | | | Cooperating Teacher | |
			Size	Free/Reduced Lunch Rate	Minority Rate	Name (Years Experience)	Position
Anita	22/Asian	Grade 3 inclusive	670	36.6%	43.4%	Mrs. Adams (12)	General educator
Colleen	22/White	K–1 inclusive/ pull-out	800	33.3%	45.7%	Mrs. Carter (14)	Special educator
Kristy	22/White	Multigrade K–2 inclusive	460	45.8%	46.1%	Mrs. Kirk (35)	General educator
Melanie	27/White	Grade 2 inclusive/ pull-out	800	33.3%	45.7%	Mrs. Monroe (10)	General educator
Nancy	25/White	Grade 3 inclusive	468	87.8%	98.4%	Mrs. Nell (7)	General educator
Tricia	22/White	K–3 resource	639	44.8%	42.8%	Mrs. Taylor (32)	Special educator

for in-depth interviewing and observation while also including a representation of various backgrounds, beliefs, and prior knowledge. In addition, the preservice teachers' reading methods course instructors ($N = 5$), field supervisors ($N = 3$), and practicum cooperating teachers ($N = 6$) participated (none of whom were members of the research team). We selected them because they were active agents in facilitating the preservice teachers' acquisition and enactment of knowledge. Table 1 provides demographic information for the six preservice teachers (all identified with pseudonyms), as well as data concerning their practicum placements.

(19)   *Participant Descriptions.* Melanie was placed in an inclusive second-grade classroom with Mrs. Monroe, a general educator who had extensive prior experience as a special educator. Melanie and Mrs. Monroe worked with the lowest ability reading groups, using the Reading Mastery curriculum (SRA/McGraw-Hill, 2008)—a scripted direct instruction curriculum. Colleen was paired with Mrs. Carter, a 14-year special education veteran, who provided push-in/pull-out services for reading and math in kindergarten and first grades also using Reading Mastery. Tricia worked with a special educator with 32 years of experience, who provided a variety of services to students in Grades K–3. Tricia and her cooperating teacher, Mrs. Taylor, had a resource room, but they also

provided small-group instruction in students' general education classrooms, utilizing both Reading Mastery and the basal reading series Harcourt Trophies (Harcourt, 2007). Anita was placed in a third-grade inclusive classroom with Mrs. Adams, a general educator who had 12 years of teaching experience but who was teaching third grade for the first time. For reading, Mrs. Adams relied on the Harcourt Trophies series. Kristy worked with Mrs. Kirk, a general educator with 35 years of teaching experience. Mrs. Kirk used the Harcourt Trophies reading series in addition to ideas she pulled from various teacher resource books on guided reading and holistic teaching practices. Her classroom was a multi-age inclusive class for students in Grades K–2. Nancy was placed in a third-grade inclusive classroom with Mrs. Nell—a general educator with 7 years of teaching experience. Mrs. Nell worked in a high-poverty school that adopted the Success for All (Success for All Foundation, 1987) reading curriculum in conjunction with Harcourt Trophies basal.

READING COURSE WORK IN THE PREPARATION PROGRAM

The backdrop for the preservice teachers' prepara-   **(20)** tion was a collaborative program designed to prepare teachers in both elementary education and high-incidence disabilities. The preparation program included three reading methods courses. The first course was a beginning reading course in which preservice teachers learned about literacy development and evidence-based teaching practices for students in K–3. Although the course included information on all five areas of reading (i.e., phonemic awareness [PA], phonics, fluency, vocabulary, and comprehension), the bulk of the course focused on PA, phonics, and fluency. Preservice teachers learned about (a) the need for systematic explicit reading instruction, particularly for students who struggle in reading, (b) widely adopted basal reading series such as Harcourt Trophies (Harcourt, 2007) and how to provide accommodations for students with disabilities within the structure of the basal, and (c) various reading assessments including Dynamic Indicators of Basic Early Literacy Skills (Good & Kaminski, 2002) and Concepts of Print (Clay, 2002).

(21)   The second reading course was an intermediate grades (3–8) methods course that focused on vocabulary and comprehension instruction. While enrolled in this course, preservice teachers learned about proper text selection, guided reading, the use of questioning, and a variety of comprehension strategies.

(22)   The final reading course was a graduate-level intervention course focused specifically on students with disabilities and their language and reading instruction needs. The course topics included language and reading disorders; assistive technology; assessment and interventions in vocabulary, phonics, comprehension, and writing; and evidence-based practices and interventions. A large component of the course was the administration of reading assessments, analysis of assessment data, and subsequent instruction and accommodations.

(23)   Throughout their preparation program, the preservice teachers engaged in a series of field experiences and practicum/internship experiences in inclusive classrooms. During practicum experiences, the preservice teachers received feedback multiple times throughout the semester from a field supervisor who observed their instruction. After observing a lesson, the field supervisor had a conference with the preservice teacher, providing

her with feedback on strengths and weaknesses of the lesson.

DATA COLLECTION

Observation Field Notes. For each preservice   **(24)** teacher, we conducted three videotaped observations, at the beginning, middle, and end of the semester. The observations were scheduled ahead of time and lasted from 30 to 90 min depending on the length of reading lesson; the intent of these observations was to record participants' reading instruction and classroom practices. The observations enabled us to identify the levels at which preservice teachers were appropriating tools for reading instruction, and also permitted the preservice teachers to view their teaching and reflect on their reading practices during subsequent interview sessions.

While in the field observing the preservice   **(25)** teachers, we took extensive field notes on a laptop computer. When completing field notes, our goal was to focus on tools, knowledge, and strategies used by the preservice teachers and the level to which they were appropriated. These field notes provided rich descriptions of the participants' reading instructional practices and classroom contexts, and proved helpful in triangulating the data. To ensure the trustworthiness and credibility of field notes, we asked an external auditor not affiliated with the study to view four (roughly 22%) of the videotaped observations and to complete field notes. We compared field notes with the external auditor, verifying that we observed the same instructional practices. The majority of our field notes describing the preservice teachers' instructional practices matched the external auditor's. In instances where our field notes differed from the external auditor's, we discussed differences, came to a resolution about how best to describe instruction, and then adjusted notes accordingly. For example, during one observation we noted that the preservice teacher had students engaging in *timed readings*, whereas the external auditor recorded that the students were doing *repeated readings*. We discussed this difference and agreed that the most accurate representation was *timed repeated readings*.

Observation Ratings. As a secondary form of   **(26)** observation data, immediately following each field

TABLE 2

Observation Scores for Participants in the Study

Participant	Observation	PA	Word Study	Vocabulary	Fluency	Comprehension	CM	OCP
				RISE Observation Elements				
Anita	1	—	—	2	—	2	1.5	2
	2	—	—	2	—	2.5	2	2
	3	—	—	—	—	3	2.5	2.5
Colleen	1	2.5	2	—	—	—	1.5	2
	2	2.5	—	—	—	—	2.5	2.5
	3	3	3.5	—	—	—	3	3
Kristy	1	—	2	2	3	1.5	2.5	2
	2	—	2	2	—	1.5	2.5	2
	3	2.5	2.5	2	—	—	2	2.5
Melanie	1	3	3	—	—	—	3	3
	2	3.5	3.5	—	2.5	2.5	3	3
	3	4	4	—	3.5	—	2.5	3.5
Nancy	1	—	—	2	2	1.5	1.5	1.5
	2	—	—	—	2	2	1.5	2
	3	—	2	—	2.5	1.5	1.5	2
Tricia	1	—	—	3	3.5	2	3.5	3
	2	—	—	3.5	2.5	2.5	3.5	3.5
	3	3.5	3.5	—	2.5	—	3.5	3.5

Note. RISE = Reading Instruction in Special Education observation instrument (Brownell et al., 2009); PA = phonemic awareness; CM = classroom management; OCP = overall classroom practice. Dashes indicate the area of reading instruction was not observed during the preservice teacher's lesson.

observation the first author rated the preservice teachers' reading practices using the observation instrument tool that Brownell et al. (2009) modified from Baker, Gersten, Haager, Dingle, and Goldenberg (2004). The Reading Instruction in Special Education (RISE; Brownell et al., 2009) observation instrument consists of 22 items addressing the following areas: instructional practices in the five areas of reading, classroom management, and overall classroom practice. Observers use a 1–4 Likert scale to evaluate a teacher's performance on each of the items, though observers can use midpoint ratings such as 1.5 or 2.5. A score of 1 represents low quality for an item and a 4 represents high quality. The coefficient alpha for the instrument was 0.92. The overall classroom practice scale and classroom management subscale contributed 37% and 59% of the variance to students' oral reading fluency gains, respectively (Brownell et al., 2009). The purpose of using RISE (Brownell et al., 2009) in this study was to provide evidence of the extent to which preservice teachers' appropriated evidence-based practices in

reading, as well as to document changes in their reading practices over time. Table 2 provides participants' scores on overall instructional practices in the five areas of reading, on classroom management, and on overall classroom practice.

(27) To establish interrater reliability, a second external auditor not affiliated with the study but trained in using RISE (Brownell et al., 2009) watched and rated four videotaped observations. The interrater reliability between the external auditor and the first author was 86%. Interrater reliability was calculated by dividing number of "hits" between the external auditor and researcher by the total number of items that were rated. A *hit* was defined as a .5 or less difference between the external auditor's score and the first author's. For example, if the external auditor rated an item on RISE (Brownell et al., 2009) as 3.5 and the first author rated the same item as 3.0, that was considered a hit.

(28) *Interviews.* We conducted three semi-structured, tape-recorded interviews with each preservice teacher: one before any classroom

observations, one conducted in conjunction with classroom observations, and one at the end of the data collection phase. Each interview lasted between 30 and 90 min and was later transcribed. Interviews are important data sources to the activity theory framework because they provide critical insights into potential relationships between preservice teachers and their preparation program. These interviews also provided us with insights concerning the preservice teachers' motivations, concerns, and attributes; we asked the preservice teachers to describe their strengths and weaknesses regarding teaching reading and why they chose to become special educators. Additionally, our questions focused on (a) preservice teachers' perceptions concerning their knowledge, coursework, beliefs, and prior experiences for teaching reading; (b) sources of knowledge and program experiences they drew from as they enacted their practice in reading instruction; and (c) participants' experiences in the various activity systems and how these experiences influenced their knowledge of reading instruction. During the second and third interviews, participants also reflected on video clips from their classroom observations. While the preservice teachers viewed their instruction, the research team asked them to describe the sources of knowledge they drew on during their instruction and why they chose to implement various instructional practices.

(29)   We also interviewed participants' cooperating teachers, reading methods instructors, and field supervisors once each during the study. We asked these participants semistructured questions about their background, reading philosophies, estimations of the preservice teachers' strengths and weaknesses, and goals for the preservice teachers. For example, we asked cooperating teachers to describe their beliefs about reading instruction; we asked field supervisors to describe their approach to evaluating and providing feedback to preservice teachers. These interviews not only served to triangulate data but also assisted us in understanding the types of tools preservice teachers had exposure to during their preparation.

(30)   *Artifacts.* At the beginning and end of the study, each preservice teacher completed a pre- and postconcept map about *reading instruction* and a four-question open-ended survey. The survey questions were: (a) describe your K–12 schooling experiences, (b) describe any experiences you have had teaching children how to read, (c) describe any experiences you have had working with students with disabilities, and (d) what are your beliefs about how best to teach students with learning disabilities how to read? The concept map and the open-ended survey served as informal assessments of participants' prior experiences and knowledge for reading instruction, and were used as part of the sample selection procedure.

We also collected participants' reading methods course syllabi and preparation program plans to serve as data triangulation mechanisms and as discussion pieces during interviews. The program plan helped document various experiences that preservice teachers might have drawn on in their reading instruction. (31)

DATA ANALYSIS

We analyzed data using constructivist grounded theory methods (Charmaz, 2000; Glaser & Strauss, 1967). Grounded theory is a method for systematically analyzing qualitative data by utilizing explicit and analytic procedures (Charmaz, 2000; Strauss & Corbin, 1998). Grounded theory methods are especially useful when studying the microcosm of interactions in particular settings and when new theoretical explanations of a phenomenon are needed (Grbich, 2007). The lack of existing theory to explain interactions involved in special education preservice teachers' appropriation of conceptual and practical tools made grounded theory an ideal method for this study. (32)

The grounded theory process consists of three stages: open, axial, and selective coding (Strauss & Corbin, 1998). We began by open coding interview transcripts and observation field notes line by line. The codes were not identified a priori; rather they emerged from the data and were continually redefined throughout the analysis process. *Differentiate instruction, tension between ideal and reality,* and *open to feedback* are some open-code examples from this study. We completed memoing for secondary data sources such as artifacts, and used these memos as support for the derived codes and categories. For example, we used memos to make notes when observing course content (noted in the syllabi) in (33)

TABLE 3

Influences on Participating Preservice Teachers' Appropriation of Tools

Selective Codes	Axial Codes					
	Anita	Colleen	Kristy	Melanie	Nancy	Tricia
Personal qualities	Rigid adherence to structure (I)	Desire to be liked (I)	Open minded (I)	Accepts challenges (I)	Lacks confidence (I)	Reflective (I)
Motivation for knowledge assimilation	Positive family influence (I)	Sibling w/ disability (I)	Strong dedication to teaching (I)	Wants to implement effective instruction (I)	Sibling w/ disability (I)	Positive family influence (I)
Access to knowledge	Cooperating teacher lacks reading knowledge (P)	Special education cooperating teacher (P)	Lack of opportunities to observe explicit instruction (P)	Negative beginning reading course (U)	Limited access to special education knowledge (P)	Special education cooperating teacher (P)
Opportunities to appropriate knowledge in practice	Few opportunities for intensive reading instruction (P)	Exclusive work w/ students w/ disabilities (P)	Change in reading beliefs (P)	Exclusive work w/ students w/ disabilities (P)	Difficulties w/ classroom management (P)	Little instructional freedom (P)

Note. I = influence of the individual; U = influence of the university; P = influence of the practicum.

various preservice teachers' practice. Finally, a third external auditor open coded a random selection of four interview transcripts to verify open codes and emerging axial codes. In general, the external auditor's codes matched ours. Although there were minor variations in codes, these differences did not seem to change overall emerging themes or outcomes. For example, we coded one data chunk as *congruence between university course work* while the external auditor coded the same chunk *overlap in university courses*. In instances where data chunks were coded differently, we met with the external auditor to discuss differences and bring to light any hidden biases.

(34)   In the second stage, axial coding, we reassembled data by making connections between categories and subcategories. The outcome of the final stage, selective coding, is formal theory development (Strauss & Corbin, 1998). *Personal qualities* and *access to knowledge* were some of the selective codes that emerged. Table 3 provides additional examples of axial and selective codes from the study. Selecting a central category that is consistent across data to represent predominant research theme refines the theory. In this study, the central category or core concept was *opportunities to appropriate knowledge in practice.*

VERIFICATION

In qualitative research, establishing credibility and (35) trustworthiness enhances validity (Brantlinger et al., 2005). We triangulated data by collecting multiple pieces of evidence (interview, observation, and artifact data). We also triangulated interview data from various study participants (preservice teachers, cooperating teachers, field supervisors, and teacher educators). Throughout the interview process we engaged in member checking, presenting initial findings and impressions to participants and asking for feedback on emerging themes. We employed peer-debriefing measures by conferring regularly about emerging themes. Finally, as mentioned previously, we secured a series of external auditors not affiliated with the study.

FINDINGS

MELANIE

According to Melanie, her practicum placement (36) influenced her appropriation of tools the most, as she had few prior experiences with students with disabilities and reported having a negative experience in her beginning reading methods course due to the instructor's disorganization and unclear expectations. Melanie stated,

> Before this semester, I thought phonemes, phonics—aren't they all the same? I had heard all the concepts in my reading course, but I really didn't know what they meant. But now I know what it all means, and I can do it myself. I totally attribute that to Mrs. Monroe.

(37)   Melanie's practicum was an environment rich in opportunities to enact beginning reading knowledge and receive content-specific feedback. Melanie's overall classroom practice rating started at a 3, and by the end of the practicum it was a 3.5. By the final observation, Melanie received a rating of 4 on both phonemic awareness and word study and 3.5 on fluency, some of the highest scores across all participants.

(38)   Classroom observation and interview data indicated that Melanie reached conceptual levels of appropriation regarding reading instruction and classroom management. According to Melanie, observing Mrs. Monroe and teaching reading helped her appropriate knowledge of individual letter sounds and concepts related to phonics instruction. Although Melanie's beginning reading class had covered letter sounds, Melanie reported she did not appreciate this knowledge until her practicum when she had access to a knowledgeable cooperating teacher and a structured curriculum. Observation data confirmed Melanie's knowledge appropriation while teaching in her practicum. During a review, Melanie pointed to the letter *b* and asked one of the students for the proper sound. The student said /bah/ and Melanie corrected him by saying, "it's not /bah/ it's /b/, it's a stopped sound": The practicum provided an opportunity to appropriate knowledge in practice and supported Melanie's appropriation of letter sounds beyond a basic level of understanding.

(39)   From her practicum, Melanie also appropriated tools about positive reinforcement and engaged in active, intensive, explicit, and systematic instruction. Melanie described how one reading group posed formidable behavior problems, thus Mrs. Monroe decided to implement a formal behavior plan. Seeing how well a behavior plan could work, Melanie incorporated it into her in-

struction. When interviewed later about the behavior plan, Melanie's appropriation of tools related to behavior management reached a conceptual level when she said that although she would like the students to exhibit appropriate behavior for intrinsic reasons, she realized that sometimes they needed "something to get their hands on" to let them know they were doing what was expected of them.

The practicum provided an opportunity to appropriate knowledge in practice and supported Melanie's appropriation of letter sounds beyond a basic level of understanding.

Throughout the study, observation and inter- **(40)** view data indicated that Melanie was not bound by the curriculum. Instead, she combined the curriculum's structure with her own knowledge of reading and effective instructional practices. The result was high-quality reading instruction that was engaging and tailored to fit students' individual needs— evidence of Melanie's appropriation of pedagogical tools at conceptual levels of understanding.

COLLEEN

Colleen entered the preparation program with a **(41)** well-defined goal of being a special educator—a goal that resulted from her prior experiences with a sibling with a disability. For Colleen, the Reading Mastery (SRA/McGraw-Hill, 2008) curriculum and her knowledgeable cooperating teacher provided helpful structure and guidance. Colleen's overall classroom rating score started at a 2 and rose to a 3 by the end of the practicum. Guidance from Mrs. Carter contributed to Colleen's improved classroom management skills, as her rating on the RISE (Brownell et al., 2009) increased by 1.5 points.

For Colleen, the most important influence in **(42)** her appropriation of reading instruction tools was the opportunity to situate them in practice. Before this opportunity, Colleen had difficulty seeing the need for various tools presented in her coursework. She described learning about phonemes in her beginning reading course and "not being able to stand it. When I was learning it I was thinking oh my God, I know how to say a /b/!" But Colleen went on to describe how being in her practicum helped her understand the need for knowledge such as phonics: "It took me a while to realize that that stuff was helpful." She described how during one lesson she realized she did not really know to pronounce the sound /x/ even though she thought learning letter sounds was useless during her course work. Upon being responsible for providing beginning reading instruction in her practicum, Colleen developed greater intrinsic motivation for learning about phonics. Colleen's beginning reading course instructor confirmed Colleen's statements: "I don't think [preservice teachers] realize the benefit of the course until they walk away from it. They grumble through it."

(43) Mrs. Carter was a powerful influence on Colleen. Mrs. Carter's extensive knowledge of students with disabilities and behavior management was critical in helping Colleen refine her instruction. Colleen's desire to be liked by her students seemed to influence her willingness to discipline students. During initial observations, Colleen adopted an informal tone with a small group of students, often giggling at their misbehavior rather than correcting them. As a result of these management issues, Colleen spent more time attending to student behavior rather than considering how she might deliver effective reading instruction. Upon seeing Colleen's initial struggles with behavior management, Mrs. Carter provided Colleen with extra feedback, guidance, and support in the area of classroom management. Mrs. Carter said:

> Behavior management is always the hardest for beginning teachers. Colleen and I have talked about managing behaviors of large and small groups, how it is different. It seems like when you do a small group, you tend to back off a little and that's a mistake some people make because those kids can get just as hyper as a large group. So we've talked about setting clear expectations and setting those rules and consequences. And that eliminates that wandering that always leads to trouble.

(44) Mrs. Carter's support benefited Colleen, as her classroom management score on the RISE (Brownell et al., 2009) rose from a 1.5 to a 3. Ad-

ditionally, interview statements indicated Colleen had appropriated behavior management tools to conceptual levels. She was able to describe how strategies such as positive reinforcement and proximity control worked particularly well for specific students and why.

At the end of her practicum, Colleen's (45) knowledge of beginning reading had increased. Whereas her preconcept map included only six broad terms (e.g., *predicting* and *phonics*), her post concept map was more detailed with 28 ideas, including the five major components of reading, as well as their meanings and ways to teach them.

TRICIA

Several characteristics of Tricia's background influ- (46) enced her beliefs and future goals; thus, one of the biggest influences on Tricia was the role of the individual. Tricia's mother was a teacher, and it was clear that her mother's influence was important to her. Tricia credited her mother with many of her ideas about instruction.

Data indicated Tricia's reading instruction (47) improved during her practicum, but she resisted ideas because of the many instructional restrictions she encountered. Tricia reported not having much freedom to plan instruction in her practicum, because Mrs. Taylor told her what needed to be done each day. As Tricia described it, "Mrs. Taylor is really set in her ways."

Although Tricia complained about the rigid- (48) ity of her practicum, it seemed to have a positive influence on her appropriation of reading knowledge and her lesson execution, as her scores on the RISE (Brownell et al., 2009) were some of the highest of all the participants. Her overall classroom rating started at a 3, eventually reaching a 3.5, and her classroom management score remained at 3.5. Tricia was one of the only participants who, over the course of the semester, had opportunities to implement instruction in all five areas of reading, with no score dropping below 2. In fact, many of her scores on the individual reading components were 3.5. Her postconcept map also indicated that she had appropriated conceptual and practical tools about reading instruction, especially for struggling readers. Although her preconcept map only included six terms, one of which addressed the five major reading components, her postconcept map depicted 30 terms, with all five areas of reading, ways to teach them, and concepts about effective instructional practices such as explicit instruction and multiple opportunities to practice.

(49)   Tricia also appropriated tools of various classroom management techniques including the use of a point system. Mrs. Taylor (and subsequently Tricia) awarded students positive points when they followed directions and completed their individual turns during Reading Mastery (SRA/McGraw-Hill, 2008), and negative points when they were off task and disruptive. Tricia stated she did not think the awarding of negative points was as effective because some students got upset and shut down. However, Tricia also described Mrs. Taylor's strategy for avoiding these types of shut-downs: As soon as a child received a negative point, Mrs. Taylor would immediately give the child an opportunity for success, and therefore a positive point that would bring the student back into the instruction. Reflecting on Mrs. Taylor's classroom management, Tricia seemed to be reaching some conceptual understanding behind the use of this type of behavior management system, because she not only knew its label and surface features but she also understood the conditions under which the system could be most effective for students. In addition to the point system, observation data indicated that Tricia appropriated other classroom management tools (e.g., she always reviewed rules and behavioral expectations at the beginning of each lesson).

ANITA

(50)   Anita entered her practicum placement with extensive and varied prior schooling experiences, as well as a developed sense of a personal teaching style, all of which she learned from her mother who was a teacher. She also relied on her university course work to guide her beliefs and teaching practices. As a result, Anita's beliefs about how tools should be appropriated were influenced by her individual experiences as well as her university experiences. In the end, however, Anita's lack of opportunities to appropriate her knowledge of special education and beginning reading instruction in her practicum left her feeling ill-prepared to teach students with disabilities how to read.

(51)   Anita felt that the practicum reading instruction was not explicit or sufficiently individualized for students with disabilities. She said, "There is nothing that the teachers are doing that is making [instruction] more catered to [students'] needs." Data from the RISE (Brownell et al., 2009) supported some of her assertions. Without a model for how to provide explicit, individualized instruction, Anita's initial overall classroom practice score remained relatively low, starting at a 2 and eventually rising to a 2.5 by the end of the practicum.

(52)   Anita's biggest obstacle to instruction was her pacing and classroom management, a concern confirmed by her initial score (1.5) in this area on the RISE (Brownell et al., 2009) and by Anita's own comments and those of her cooperating teacher, Mrs. Adams. After watching a videotape of her instruction, Anita reflected on what she would like to improve in her teaching: "Time management. If someone is answering a question, I get too drawn into that question and I get off from what we are actually doing." Anita's reflections were confirmed by Mrs. Adams who stated, "My biggest goal for [Anita] is time management. She has wonderful, wonderful plans but she gets too deep into one part of the lesson." For example, in one guided reading lesson, Anita and the students were reading about the Gold Rush and got involved in a discussion about gold that lasted several minutes; after that point Anita had difficulty regaining the students' attention. Anita's difficulties could in part be explained by her hesitation to deviate from her original lesson plans and her difficulty managing unexpected events during instruction.

(53)   During classroom observations, Anita did not teach phonemic awareness, word study, or fluency, mostly because she did not have the opportunity, and thus she did not receive any scores on the RISE (Brownell et al., 2009) for these areas. This is an example of the lowest level of appropriation (i.e., lack of appropriation); Anita did not have a context that was conducive to using tools related to phonemic awareness, word study, or fluency. The areas of reading that were emphasized in Anita's placement were vocabulary and comprehension, perhaps because Mrs. Adams had always taught older elementary students and reported feeling more comfortable teaching writing as opposed to reading. Following Mrs. Adams's lead,

Anita was expected to teach reading using the basal reading series, focusing predominantly on vocabulary and comprehension instruction. In comprehension instruction Anita went from a 2 to a 3 perhaps because of her multiple opportunities to apply her comprehension knowledge during guided reading groups. She was observed posing comprehension questions, both lower order and higher order, having students take turns reading, and using vocabulary and comprehension activities with the text. When talking about reading instruction, Anita talked about the importance of small-group instruction to work on skills for which students might need additional practice.

(54) When Anita tried to combine ideas from her beginning reading course about using read-a-louds with prereading strategies, she met with resistance from students not accustomed to such instruction. Anita said, "the students think I am a bit crazy when I tell them to go through and look at the pictures." Anita thought the university provided an ideal model of teaching that was sometimes incongruent with practices she observed in her practicum, which she described as "a gap in what we've learned should be good [instruction] and what we've seen [in classrooms]." This gap was problematic for Anita: Because she rarely saw practices from her course work applied in the classroom, it made understanding and adopting these practices more difficult.

KRISTY

(55) Throughout the study, Kristy encountered several challenges as she tried to integrate her teaching philosophy with ideas from her course work and her practicum. She struggled to reconcile her ideologies, which supported holistic reading instruction, and her course instructors' ideologies about the need for systematic, explicit reading instruction. She also had difficulties executing reading instruction because of her own misunderstandings and lack of knowledge about reading. For Kristy, her ability to appropriate tools concerning reading instruction was contingent upon having opportunities to enact tools in practice, as well as extensive time to reflect on instruction, receive feedback, and receive support from her cooperating teacher and field supervisor.

For Kristy, the practicum was crucial to tool (56) appropriation. It was only after teaching a lesson that Kristy was able to gauge how much she really understood a particular concept or tool. Kristy's interview statements indicated that she was most successful appropriating tools and knowledge when she (a) enacted her knowledge in practice, (b) had time to reflect on the outcome, (c) discussed her performance with someone who could provide her with feedback, and (d) had an opportunity to practice the lesson again. Although drawing on multiple sources of support, Kristy's overall classroom rating score never surpassed a 2.5. It seemed Kristy's personal difficulties understanding the reading process interfered with her delivery of reading instruction for students, thus an instance of individual influences mediating tool appropriation.

Throughout the semester, there were only a (57) few instances illustrating that Kristy had appropriated tools and knowledge about reading instruction to levels higher than surface features. Specifically, her observation and interview data indicated less sophisticated tool appropriation in phonemic awareness and word-study instruction. For example, at the end of the semester, Kristy still did not completely understand irregular words and how they should be taught. During the final observation, Kristy had students sound out the word *could*. In the final interview it was clear Kristy still did not know that *could* is an irregular word.

In another instance, Kristy experienced difficulty (58) when she tried to incorporate phonemic awareness knowledge from her university training into her daily reading instruction during practicum. During a guided reading lesson, Kristy tried to include the use of Elkonin boxes, but her lack of understanding of the underlying concepts of Elkonin boxes foiled her instruction. Several times during the lesson, Kristy's confusion about Elkonin boxes resulted in her changing her directives to students. As students became more confused about what they were being asked to do, they became less engaged in the lesson. In this instance, Kristy was only able to appropriate the Elkonin box tool to the level of labeling: She knew the name of the tool, but she did not seem to understand its features or underlying concepts.

(59)   Kristy's appropriation of tools seemed to be highest in one particular area of reading: fluency. Not only did Kristy understand the three components of fluency (i.e., rate, accuracy, and prosody), but she was also able to translate that knowledge into effective instruction. Kristy's highest score on the RISE (Brownell et al., 2009) was a 3.0 for the fluency instruction she delivered during one observation. While working with one student, observation data indicated that Kristy taught him the meaning of prosody explicitly. She modeled reading with prosody by reading out loud using expression and proper inflection and then used echo reading to have the student practice reading with prosody.

NANCY

(60)   Nancy's family was an especially important influence. Having a brother with a disability prompted Nancy to become a special educator. Her practicum placement also was an important albeit negative influence. Being placed in a challenging classroom, with little guidance or flexibility, had lasting negative repercussions. Nancy ended up questioning her abilities as a teacher, particularly a special educator.

(61)   Nancy reported being a timid person and lacking confidence in her teaching. These personal attributes coupled with an extremely challenging practicum placement had negative effects on her tool appropriation and classroom reading instruction. On the RISE (Brownell et al., 2009), Nancy's initial overall classroom rating score was a 1.5 and by the end of the practicum was a 2. Her classroom management scores remained at 1.5 throughout the semester.

(62)   Classroom management was a consistent problem in Mrs. Nell's class, creating much stress for Nancy. Mrs. Nell herself admitted that "this is a difficult class and at times it's a little difficult even for me." Classroom observations confirmed challenging student behaviors. Students often argued over their assignments, got out of their seats without permission, and shouted across the room. In addition to classroom management problems, Mrs. Nell's mentoring style created stress for Nancy. Nancy reported that she did not get much guidance when planning and preparing for lessons stating, "I didn't really talk to [Mrs. Nell]. She

told me to go to the curriculum room and get the books and I copied off the lesson from the teacher's manual and looked at it and that was about it." Mrs. Nell verified the lack of lesson collaboration:

> Basically [Nancy] plans it on her own because I give her the teacher's book and she has watched me enough to know what to do. So she basically plans it on her own; all I really do is give her the book and she does the rest.

(63)   Nancy also struggled to receive adequate feedback during her practicum. Nancy talked about how she did not get sufficient feedback because "it is such a busy classroom and I am tutoring during [Mrs. Nell's] planning time. It is hard to get her." When Mrs. Nell did provide Nancy with feedback, the feedback was not specific and did not guide Nancy as to how to change or improve her instruction. Because Nancy had to spend so much time and energy trying to maintain class control, she could not focus on refining her reading instruction. After watching one of her videotaped lessons, Nancy noted she had to read from the teacher's manual when providing reading instruction. Moreover, the school in which Nancy completed her practicum instituted a regimented curriculum, so although she learned about reading from university course work, the practicum curriculum did not leave Nancy much room to appropriate any of these ideas.

CORE CONCEPT: OPPORTUNITIES TO APPROPRIATE KNOWLEDGE IN PRACTICE

(64)   Because all of the study participants emphasized needing opportunities to appropriate knowledge in practice, this emerged as the central or core concept in the grounded theory. For example, Colleen, Melanie, and Kristy all spoke about how learning phonics during their beginning reading methods course seemed unimportant and demeaning until they had to draw on this knowledge to instruct struggling readers. Hence, the most influential activity system was the practicum.

(65)   A number of factors determined the extent to which these preservice teachers had opportunities to appropriate reading tools in the practicum, including: (a) grade level, (b) service delivery model, (c) practicum cooperating teacher, (d) stu-

dent characteristics, and (e) curriculum. Anita's practicum in a third-grade general education classroom meant she had multiple opportunities to teach vocabulary and comprehension, but fewer chances to teach phonics or phonemic awareness. As a result, Anita felt more confident in her abilities to teach vocabulary and comprehension; statements from her interviews illustrated how her knowledge of vocabulary and comprehension was more sophisticated than her knowledge of phonics and phonemic awareness. The opposite was true for Colleen, who primarily taught phonics and phonemic awareness to kindergartners. Additionally, the service delivery model and curriculum employed in practicum influenced participants' opportunities to appropriate tools. Participants in inclusive classrooms that used basal reading series (i.e., Anita, Kristy, and Nancy) reported having fewer opportunities to observe intensive reading instruction that was explicit and systematic and that provided feedback and multiple opportunities to practice compared to participants who were placed in resource rooms or push-in, pull-out models that used scripted direct instruction reading programs (i.e., Colleen, Tricia, and Melanie).

(66)   The most important factor in the practicum placement was the cooperating teacher. Colleen, Melanie, and Tricia had multiple opportunities to observe systematic reading instruction because they were paired with cooperating teachers who had extensive knowledge of special education and the instructional needs of students with disabilities. These cooperating teachers were able to provide feedback that was specific to explicit, systematic reading instruction and behavior management, so Colleen's, Melanie's, and Tricia's overall classroom practice and classroom management scores on the RISE (Brownell et al., 2009) were relatively high throughout the study. Anita, Kristy, and Nancy were paired with general educators who had less knowledge about disabilities and special education reading instruction; the feedback they received focused more on general reading knowledge and instructional practices such as instructional pacing and use of specific feedback. Their overall classroom practice and classroom management RISE (Brownell et al., 2009) scores did not surpass a 2.5.

For some of the preservice teachers in this (67) study, the practicum and its opportunities to appropriate conceptual and practical tools during instruction signified the point at which their course work knowledge began coalescing into a meaningful body of knowledge. For these participants, positive relationships between opportunities to appropriate pedagogical tools in practice and component concepts seemed to be associated with higher levels of appropriation. Not all of our preservice teachers had positive experiences. Negative relationships experienced by some participants appeared to have a detrimental effect on the levels to which their appropriation of tools could occur. For the participants in this study, three component concepts interacted in different ways with the core concept of opportunities to appropriate knowledge in practice.

COMPONENT CONCEPT: PERSONAL QUALITIES

The component concept of personal qualities (68) comprises several elements, including personal attributes, personal concerns, and future goals. Positive personal attributes such as reflectiveness, dedication, confidence, and initiative allowed the preservice teachers in this study to appropriate tools at higher levels. Both Colleen and Melanie showed initiative during their practicum placements, actively seeking answers to their questions, which facilitated their appropriation of tools. Nancy, on the other hand, was a particularly shy person who was placed in a practicum characterized by formidable behavior management problems. For Nancy, aspects of her personality did not help her overcome such a difficult practicum situation. Unfortunately, she had few positive teaching experiences during her practicum; her personality disposition coupled with a negative practicum appeared to accentuate a lack of confidence in her abilities.

The preservice teachers whose concerns cen- (69) tered on students' academic needs reached higher appropriation levels. Kristy and Melanie expressed concern over providing students with effective instruction. Kristy talked about wanting to know her students' instructional needs and then respond to those needs with appropriate instruction. Although Kristy struggled to deliver effective reading instruction because of her own misunderstandings about the reading process, her desire to provide proper instruction to students with disabilities fostered a willingness to dedicate extra time in her practicum to improve her instruction. Melanie spoke about the importance of giving students with disabilities the "right kind of instruction" so they could receive reading instruction in the general education classroom eventually. Melanie was open to challenging teaching situations, because she knew they would help her become a better teacher. She spent extra hours learning letter sounds and proper Reading Mastery (SRA/McGraw-Hill, 2008) procedures so she could deliver intensive reading lessons to students. Melanie's and Kristy's desire to be special educators and provide students with effective instruction fostered a commitment to improving their teaching.

COMPONENT CONCEPT: MOTIVATION FOR KNOWLEDGE ASSIMILATION

(70)   These preservice teachers had varying motivations for assimilating knowledge, with some motivations leading to higher levels of appropriation. The participants who had intrinsic reasons for assimilating knowledge reached higher levels of tool appropriation.

(71)   Accountability measures in place at the university, such as exams and course assignments, provided these preservice teachers with motivation for assimilating knowledge—motivations that were fueled by the extrinsic reward of earning a passing grade. As a result, Colleen, Kristy, and Melanie learned phonics to earn a good grade in their beginning reading course, but they were not motivated to draw on this knowledge because they did not see how it was useful. It was not until they were responsible for reading instruction in their practicum experiences that they developed more intrinsic reasons for assimilating phonics knowledge. In an interview Kristy said, "I want to be able to [teach reading] with the lightning speed students need. I don't want to be standing up there thinking and confused." Once Colleen, Kristy, and Melanie were motivated to learn information, they valued their course work content more, spent more time trying to learn it, and began to understand it on higher levels.

Individual experiences also impacted participants' motivation to appropriate tools. Colleen and Nancy both had siblings with disabilities. Witnessing their brothers' struggles in school, particularly as a result of ineffective instruction, fueled their desire to be effective special educators. For Colleen, an encouraging placement intensified her commitment to the field of special education; for Nancy, a discouraging placement squelched her confidence to be a teacher, much less a special educator. Tricia had a different motivation for entering special education. She talked about wanting to be a special educator because she heard she could make more money. Perhaps her extrinsic motivation for becoming a special educator explains why Tricia was so resistant to some aspects of her practicum. (72)

COMPONENT CONCEPT: ACCESS TO KNOWLEDGE

The final component that impacted these preservice teachers' appropriation of conceptual and practical tools was access. Without access to knowledge about pedagogical tools, preservice teachers can not appropriate them. Some of our preservice teachers had prior experiences that provided them with access to knowledge (e.g., mothers who were educators). Others were paired with cooperating teachers who had extensive knowledge of special education and could serve as a valuable source of knowledge. Finally, some participants reported having reading methods courses and field supervisors that helped them acquire knowledge. (73)

Without access to knowledge about pedagogical tools, preservice teachers can not appropriate them.

The individual activity system influenced these preservice teachers' knowledge access, but it did so in limited ways. None of the participants reported having extensive early reading memories. Colleen best summarized the group sentiment when she said, (74)

> Most of us in college probably learned to read easily. You would have no idea how

many kids didn't [have an easy time]. I had no clue; I just thought reading was a natural process and that everyone learns to read.

Similarly, none of the preservice teachers spoke about extensive prior experiences with special education. Colleen, Melanie, and Tricia had all attended K–12 schools that utilized self-contained service delivery models; as young students they had not witnessed special education students being included in general education classrooms, nor observed any accommodations or individualized instruction. As a result of their limited prior experiences and knowledge, they relied heavily on reading methods and special education courses, field experiences, and practicum placements for their special education and reading knowledge.

(75)   All of the preservice teachers in this study had access to knowledge from the university, though sources of this knowledge varied. The field supervisor was viewed unanimously as a helpful knowledge source, even though the usability of this feedback varied depending on contextual factors of the practicum. Nancy's challenges managing classroom behavior presented barriers for implementing her field supervisor's ideas. Tricia also experienced barriers but for a different reason: Her opportunities to inject new ideas into instruction were constrained by her cooperating teacher's inflexibility. It should also be noted that participating in this study was a potential influence on the preservice teachers, as they were asked to watch videos of their teaching practicum and to reflect on their instruction during interviews with the research team.

(76)   Specific courses and course instructors influenced preservice teachers' access to strategies and ideas in both positive and negative ways. Colleen, Melanie, and Nancy perceived their literacy course work negatively. Nancy said she felt "intimidated" after finishing her beginning reading course because so much content was covered. For Nancy, her feelings of being overwhelmed were exacerbated by her negative practicum experience, where she had few opportunities to appropriate knowledge from the reading course. Colleen and Melanie also felt they gained little from their course work, but gave different reasons for their unsatisfactory experiences. They thought their beginning reading course was disorganized and did

not provide sufficient justification for learning phonics. Going further, Melanie stated, "I felt I got a major disservice because I did not learn that much about reading." Colleen and Melanie felt that the information acquired in the beginning reading course would have faded from memory without a practicum that helped them draw upon this knowledge.

In comparison, Anita, Kristy, and Tricia (77) expressed gratitude for their reading methods course work. Tricia felt her beginning reading course was especially beneficial because of the instructor's caring personality and organized manner. Tricia's positive perceptions of her beginning reading course led to her desire to implement her course work knowledge, although she experienced barriers when placed in an inflexible practicum. Anita and Kristy, similarly, spoke about feeling frustrated when they could not appropriate their reading course work knowledge in their practicum experiences.

Thus, preservice teachers' perceptions of (78) their university courses and course instructors interacted with opportunities to appropriate knowledge in their practicum, impacting the extent to which they appropriated conceptual and practical tools. Although some of the preservice teachers in this study viewed course work positively, their appropriation of course work tools was derailed when they were placed in restrictive practicum experiences.

THE GROUNDED THEORY

Figure 1 illustrates the grounded theory, which (79) consists of (a) three activity systems and influences contained therein and (b) interactions between the core concept and three component concepts that impacted appropriation of pedagogical tools. Without opportunities to appropriate knowledge in practice, the preservice teachers' adoption of pedagogical tools (the core concept) reached low levels at best. Component concepts (i.e., personal qualities, motivation for knowledge assimilation, access to knowledge) either supported or hindered preservice teacher tool appropriation. The figure illustrates the two-way relationships between the core concept and the three component concepts; the core concept influenced component concepts, and vice versa.

FIGURE 1

Grounded Theory of Special Education Preservice Teachers' Appropriation of Conceptual and Practical Tools

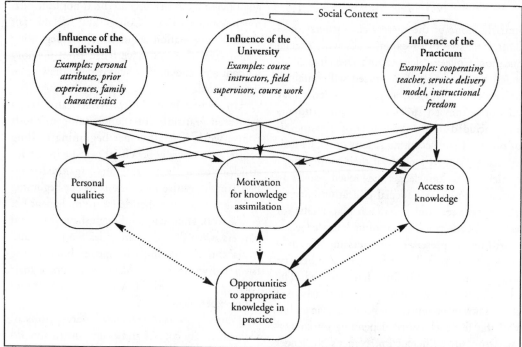

Note. Solid lines indicate one-way relationships. Dotted lines indicate two-way relationships. The bold line signifies the powerful influence of the practicum on preservice teachers' opportunities to appropriate knowledge in practice.

Three activity systems (i.e., individual, university, and practicum) influenced various component concepts, which in turn interacted with the core concept to influence levels at which conceptual and practical tools were appropriated. The link between the practicum activity and the core concept represents the importance of the practicum as an influence on the preservice teachers' appropriation of knowledge in practice.

DISCUSSION

(80) This study resulted in the articulation of a grounded theory explaining the influences on special education preservice teachers' appropriation of pedagogical tools in practice. Based on the results, we theorize that special education preservice teachers will be most likely to appropriate the necessary pedagogical tools to teach reading to students with high-incidence disabilities when the activity systems of the individual, university, and practicum align to provide them with (a) access to

knowledge and tools necessary for teaching reading to students with disabilities; (b) confidence in their abilities as special educators and intrinsic motivations for appropriating the knowledge and tools; and, most important, (c) opportunities to apply the knowledge and tools in practice with adequate support and feedback.

Results from this study illustrate how activity   (81)
theory—a theory traditionally used in general education—could serve as a useful framework when planning future studies of special education teacher learning. Our findings show that special education preservice teachers benefited from having opportunities to apply their knowledge in practical settings that: (a) had a high degree of structure and focus, particularly on the needs of students with disabilities, (b) provided them with opportunities to provide intensive reading instruction to students with disabilities across various components of reading, and (c) included cooperating teachers who were knowledgeable about special education and effective reading

instruction for students with disabilities. The preservice teachers in this study who were paired with knowledgeable special educators teaching in inclusive classrooms that utilized push-in or pullout models and direct instruction reading curricula reported feeling the most confident to teach reading to students with disabilities and were most capable of appropriating tools related to special education reading instruction. These findings support prior research in general education and lend credence to the importance of aligning course work and field experiences and having access to cooperating teachers who can help preservice teachers use knowledge they are acquiring from their teacher education program (Fang & Ashley, 2004; International Reading Association, 2003; Wilson et al., 2001).

(82)   Not all practicum experiences, however, provided our preservice teachers with positive opportunities to appropriate their special education reading knowledge in a supportive environment. In particular, general education practicum experiences that afforded few opportunities to appropriate explicit, systematic reading instruction or that provided limited feedback concerning special education issues hindered participants' appropriation of reading tools for students with disabilities. This finding sheds light on key considerations that emerge when applying activity theory to a special education teacher education context.

Grossman and her colleagues (2000) found that general education preservice teachers were successful in appropriating knowledge despite having student teaching experiences that did not align with the teacher preparation program. The

(83)   key to the preservice teachers' success in the Grossman et al. study was their ability to reflect on their experiences—an ability that had been fostered by a preparation program which emphasized the importance of reflection and supported preservice teachers in taking a reflective stance. This reveals an important difference regarding the activity systems of general education and special education teacher preparation programs. The preservice teachers in our study were in a preparation program in which the emphasis on reflective practice was not as pervasive; rather, the reading preparation program emphasized the acquisition of evidence-based practices for students with dis-

abilities, assessment, and individualized reading instruction.

This difference in the preparation program (84) orientation is not surprising given the conclusions Brownell and colleagues (2005) drew in their review of special education teacher preparation programs. Brownell and her colleagues found that general education preparation programs tended to adopt constructivist epistemologies, thereby encouraging preservice teachers to examine their beliefs, reflect on their practice, and acquire cultural knowledge about students. On the other hand, special education preparation programs had varied epistemological orientations that often blended positivist and constructivist views of knowledge (Brownell et al., 2005). Differences in preservice teachers' individual qualities and philosophical orientations of preparation programs could explain why the preservice teachers in our study benefited when there was congruence among the activity systems of the teacher preparation program and the practicum experience. The preservice teachers in our study entered the special education preparation context with limited prior experiences in special education; they had a lot to learn and little prior knowledge to reflect on as they prepared for the ambitious job of providing high-quality reading instruction to students with disabilities. It seems the complexities that characterize special education reading instruction necessitated practical teaching opportunities in which the preservice teachers could apply the precise knowledge and skill that characterizes effective reading instruction for students with disabilities.

Another difference between findings of this (85) study and those in general education is the impact of pedagogical tools, namely, curriculum. Valencia et al. (2006) found that preservice teachers' reliance on structured curricula or "packed" programs had negative implications for their learning, particularly when the curriculum did not leave room for flexibility in incorporating new ideas. In the current study, the preservice teachers who used a structured, direct instruction curriculum reached the highest levels of appropriation and had the highest scores on the RISE (Brownell et al., 2009). Perhaps this is because the structured direct instruction reading curricula reinforced many of the ideas the preservice teachers were exposed to in their preparation program. Additionally, the direct instruction curricula incorporated behavior management routines. It may be that this supportive structure helped the special education preservice teachers think more deeply about their reading instruction because they had to invest less energy maintaining students' behaviors.

IMPLICATIONS

(86) When the preservice teachers in this study were placed in a practicum that aligned with university course content, they reached higher levels of appropriation. Moreover, when preservice teachers had access to course work content that provided them with practical tools that they perceived as useful, they valued that knowledge more and showed a proclivity towards appropriating it in their practicum. These indicate that course instructors need to provide special education preservice teachers with strong rationales for learning about various aspects of the reading process, though preservice teachers are likely skilled readers themselves. Learning about phonemic awareness and phonics is critical to helping students with disabilities learn to read, as is learning about effective instruction for students with disabilities—instruction that is systematic, explicit, individualized, and intensive. Teacher educators need to make such knowledge relevant through practical teaching experiences, sooner in a preparation program rather than later (Darling-Hammond, 2006). Improving special education teacher preparation programs seems particularly important in light of the current educational context of response to intervention, in which special education teachers are often expected to deliver Tier 3 reading instruction (Fuchs & Fuchs, 2007; Stecker, 2007).

(87)   Although limited by our small, mostly homogeneous sample of preservice teachers from the same preparation program, the results of this study provide implications for future research in special education teacher education. The grounded theory that resulted from this study is an initial step in helping the field of special education teacher education develop sophisticated models that can help explain differences in the complex phenomenon of special education teacher learning and development. Although the grounded theory from this study has the potential to answer a series of questions regarding special education teacher preparation, many questions are left unanswered.

Upon exiting the preparation program, will (88) the grounded theory that emerged from this study continue to influence teachers' appropriation of tools in similar ways? If special education preservice teachers enter contexts that are dissimilar to those experienced in their preparation programs, how will this influence their ability to appropriate tools? It is important to understand how individual qualities and contextual factors interact to enable special education teachers to appropriate tools acquired in their preservice preparation program over time. According to Grossman et al. (2000), general education preservice teachers drew on tools from their preparation program but often not until their second year of teaching. Would a similar longitudinal study of special education preservice teachers have similar findings? How might the key influences from this study interact in other types of preparation programs, such as alternative route programs, which are used widely in the field of special education?

Finally, this study's findings indicate that ac- (89) tivity theory is a viable framework for future investigations in special education teacher education. This is important, because to our knowledge no prior special education teacher education study has utilized activity theory. When applying activity theory to a special education teacher education context it seems particularly important to keep in mind (a) the epistemological orientation of activity systems that comprise the special education preparation program, (b) preservice teachers' limited prior special education knowledge, (c) the pedagogical tools espoused in the preparation program and the extent to which these tools can be situated in the practicum activity system, and (d) cooperating teachers and their level of knowledge regarding special education. We believe future applications of activity theory to special education teacher education investigations will be particularly helpful as the field works to understand and solve complex problems, silence critics, and develop a cohesive research base.

REFERENCES

Baker, S., Gersten, R., Haager, D., Dingle, M., & Goldenberg, C. (2004). *The relationship between observed teaching practice and growth in reading in 1st graders who are English learners* (Report No. 2004-1). Eugene, OR: Pacific Institutes for Research.

Borko, H., & Putnam, R. (1996). Learning to teach. In D. Berliner & R. Calfee (Eds.), *Handbook of research on educational psychology* (pp. 673–699). New York, NY: Macmillan.

Boyd, D., Grossman, P., Lankford, H., Loeb, S., & Wyckoff, J. (2006). How changes in entry requirements alter the teacher workforce and affect student achievement. *Education Finance and Policy, 1*, 176–216.

Brantlinger, E., Jimenez, R., Klingner, J. K., Pugach, M., & Richardson, V. (2005). Qualitative studies in special education. *Exceptional Children, 71*, 195–207.

Brookhart, S. M., & Freeman, D. J. (1992). Characteristics of entering teacher candidates. *Review of Educational Research, 62*, 37–60.

Brownell, M. T., Bishop, A. G., Gersten, R., Klingner, J. K., Dimino, J., Haager, D., . . . Sindelar, P. T. (2009). Examining the dimensions of teacher quality for beginning special education teachers: The role of domain expertise. *Exceptional Children, 75*, 391–411.

Brownell, M. T., Ross, D. D., Colon, E. P., & McCallum, C. L. (2005). Critical features of special education teacher preparation: A comparison with exemplary practices in general teacher education. *The Journal of Special Education, 38*, 242–252.

Chard, D. J., Vaughn, S., & Tyler, B. (2002). A synthesis of research on effective interventions for building reading fluency with elementary students with learning disabilities. *Journal of Learning Disabilities, 35*, 386–406.

Charmaz, K. (2000). Grounded theory objectivist and constructivist methods. In N. K. Denzin & Y. S. Lincoln (Eds.), *Handbook of qualitative research* (2nd ed., pp. 273–285). Thousand Oaks, CA: Sage.

Clay, M. M. (2002). *An observation survey of early literacy achievement.* Auckland, New Zealand: Heinemann Education.

Creswell, J. W. (1998). *Qualitative inquiry and research design: Choosing among five traditions.* Thousand Oaks, CA: Sage.

Crotty, M. (1998). *The foundations of social research.* Thousand Oaks, CA: Sage.

Darling-Hammond, L. (2006). Constructing 21st-century teacher education. *Journal of Teacher Education, 57*, 300–314.

Fairbanks, C. M., & Meritt, J. (1998). Preservice teachers' reflections and the role of context in learning to teach. *Teacher Education Quarterly, 25*(39), 47–68.

Fang, Z., & Ashley, C. (2004). Preservice teachers' interpretations of a field-based reading block. *Journal of Teacher Education, 55*, 39–54.

Fuchs, L. S., & Fuchs, D. (2007). A model for implementing responsiveness to intervention. *TEACHING Exceptional Children, 39*(5), 14–23.

Glaser B., & Strauss, A. L. (1967). *The discovery of grounded theory: Strategies for qualitative research.* New York, NY: Aldine.

Goe, L., & Coggshall, J. (2007). *The teacher preparation → teacher practices → student outcomes relationship in special education: Missing links and next steps.* Washington, DC: National Comprehensive Center on Teacher Quality. Retrieved from http://www.tqsource.org/publications/may2007brief.pdf

Good, R. H., & Kaminski, R. A. (Eds.). (2002). *Dynamic indicators of basic early literacy skills* (6th ed.). Eugene, OR: Institute for the Development of Education Achievement. Retrieved from http://dibels.uoregon.edu

Grbich, C. (2007). *Qualitative data analysis.* Thousand Oaks, CA: Sage.

Grossman, P. L., Smagorinsky, P., & Valencia, S. (1999). Appropriating tools for teaching English: A theoretical framework for research on learning to teach. *American Journal of Education, 108*, 1–25.

Grossman, P. L., Valencia, S. W., Evans, K., Thompson, C., Martin, S., & Place, N. (2000). Transitions into teaching: Learning to teach writing in teacher education and beyond. *Journal of Literacy Research, 32*, 631–662.

Harcourt. (2007). *Harcourt Trophies: A reading/language arts program.* Orlando, FL: Author.

Humphrey, D., & Wechsler, M. (2005). *Insights into alternative certification: Initial findings from a national study.* Retrieved from http://policyweb.sri.com/cep/publications/AltCert_TCR_article.pdf

International Reading Association. (2003). *Prepared to make a difference: An executive summary of the national commission on excellence in elementary teacher preparation for reading instruction.* Newark, DE: Author.

Jonassen, D. H., & Rohrer-Murphy, L. (1999). Activity theory as a framework for designing constructivist learning environments. *Educational Technology Research and Development, 47*(1), 61–79.

Leont'ev, A. N. (1981). The problem of activity in psychology. In J. V. Wertsch (Ed.), *The concept of activity in Soviet psychology* (pp. 37–71). Armonk, NY: Sharpe.

Lortie, D. C. (1975). *Schoolteacher: A sociological study.* Chicago, IL: University of Chicago Press.

Munby, H., Russell, T., & Martin, A. K. (2001). Teachers' knowledge and how it develops. In V. Richardson (Ed.), *Handbook of research on teaching* (4th ed., pp. 877–905). Washington, DC: American Educational Research Association.

Novak, J. D., & Cañas, A. J. (2006). *The theory underlying concept maps and how to construct them* (Report No. IHMC CmapTools 2006-01). Pensacola, FL: Florida Institute for Human and Machine Cognition.

Patton, M. (2002). *Qualitative research and evaluation methods* (3rd ed). Thousand Oaks, CA: Sage.

Raskin-Erickson, J., & Pressley, M. (2000). A survey of instructional practices of special education teachers nominated as effective teachers of literacy. *Learning Disabilities Research & Practice, 15,* 206–225.

Richardson, V., & Placier, P. (2001). Teacher change. In V. Richardson (Ed.), *Handbook for research on teaching* (pp. 905–947). Washington, DC: American Educational Research Association.

Risko, V. J., Roller, C. M., Cummins, C., Bean, R. M., Block, C. C., Anders, P. L., & Flood, J. (2008). A critical analysis of research on reading teacher education. *Reading Research Quarterly, 43,* 252–288.

Sindelar, P. T., Bishop, A. G., & Brownell, M. T. (2006). What is special about special education? Research on the preparation of special education teachers. In B. G. Cook & B. R. Schirmer (Eds.), *What is special about special education: The role of evidence-based practices* (pp. 113–126). Austin, TX: PRO-ED.

Sindelar, P. T., Brownell, M. T., & Billingsley, B. (2010). Special education teacher education research: Current status and future directions. *Teacher Education and Special Education, 33,* 8–24.

SRA/McGraw-Hill. (2008). *Reading mastery signature. edition.* DeSoto, TX: Author.

Stecker, P. M. (2007). Tertiary interventions: Using progress monitoring with intensive services. *TEACHING Exceptional Children, 39*(5), 50–57.

Strauss, A. L., & Corbin, J. (1998). *Basics of qualitative research: Techniques and procedures for developing grounded theory.* Thousand Oaks, CA: Sage.

Success for All Foundation. (1987). *Success for all (SFA).* Baltimore, MD: Author.

Taylor, B. M., Pearson, P. D., Clark, K., & Walpole, S. (2000). Effective schools and accomplished teachers: Lessons about primary-grade reading instruction in low-income schools. *The Elementary School Journal, 101,* 121–165.

Valencia, S. W., Martin, S. D., Place, N. A., & Grossman, P. (2009). Complex interactions in student teaching: Lost opportunities for learning. *Journal of Teacher Education, 60,* 304–322.

Valencia, S. W., Place, N. A., Martin, S. D., & Grossman, P. (2006). Curriculum materials for elementary reading: Shackles and scaffolds for four beginning teachers. *The Elementary School Journal, 107,* 93–120.

Wilson, S. M, Floden, R. E., & Ferrini-Mundy, J. (2001). *Teacher preparation research: Current knowledge, gaps, and recommendations.* Seattle, WA: University of Washington.

Zeichner, K. M. (2005). A research agenda for teacher education. In M. Cochran-Smith & K. M. Zeichner (Eds.), *Studying teacher education: The report of the AERA panel on research and teacher education* (pp. 737–760). Mahwah, NJ: Erlbaum.

Zumwalt, K., & Craig, E. (2005). Teachers' characteristics: Research on the indicators of quality. In M. Cochran-Smith & K. M. Zeichner (Eds.), *Studying teacher education: The report of the AERA panel on research and teacher education* (pp. 157–260). Mahwah, NJ: Erlbaum.

ABOUT THE AUTHORS

MELINDA M. LEKO (Wisconsin CEC), Assistant Professor, Department of Rehabilitation Psychology and Special Education, The University of Wisconsin-Madison. **MARY T. BROWNELL** (Florida CEC), Professor, School of Special Education, School Psychology, and Early Childhood Studies, The University of Florida, Gainesville.

The authors would like to thank Dr. Karen Harris for her helpful feedback on an earlier draft of this manuscript.

Correspondence concerning this article should be addressed to Melinda M. Leko, Department of Rehabilitation Psychology and Special Education, School of Education, 1000 Bascom Mall, Room 409, University of Wisconsin-Madison, Madison, WI 53706-1496 (e-mail: leko@wisc.edu).

Manuscript received June 2009; accepted March 2010.

Source: This article is reprinted from *Exceptional Children,* Vol. 77, Issue 2, pp. 229–251, 2011. Reprinted with permission of Council for Exceptional Children.

PARTICIPANTS AND DATA COLLECTION: IDENTIFYING HOW QUALITATIVE INFORMATION IS GATHERED

*Y*ou have learned that researchers typically indicate their research design in the Method section of a qualitative research report. By recognizing the research design used, you can understand the general plan for the qualitative study, but that does not tell you what the researchers did to gather information. By continuing to read a report's Method section, you find an account of how the researchers collected their qualitative data from participants. The details of these procedures are important to read because the quality of the study's results depends on the quality of the information that the researcher gathered. In this chapter, you will learn how to understand and evaluate the procedures for selecting participants and collecting data described in qualitative research reports.

BY THE END OF THIS CHAPTER, YOU SHOULD BE ABLE TO:

- Identify and understand the participants and data collection of a qualitative research study.
- Describe a qualitative study's sample and identify the strategy used to select the sites and participants.
- Name the types of qualitative data researchers collect in their studies.
- Understand the procedures that researchers used to collect qualitative data in their studies.
- Recognize the issues that occurred during data collection in a qualitative study.
- Evaluate the quality of the sample and collected data in a qualitative research report.

As we learned in Chapter 1, an essential element that separates research from other types of scholarly work is the collection of data. Researchers gather data from participants to address their study purpose and answer their research questions. When you read any research report, you need to pay careful attention to how the data were collected because the extent that a research study is able to address its stated purpose depends on the information that was gathered during the study. Recall that researchers conduct qualitative research to explore a central phenomenon. Thus, when you read a qualitative research report, you need to consider whether the researcher gathered information that provides a good exploration of the study's central phenomenon. The key parameters to identify when reading about qualitative data collection are similar to those that you learned in quantitative research. These include:

- how the sites and participants were selected,
- what types of data were gathered,
- what procedures were used to gather the data, and
- what issues were faced during the data collection.

Although these key parameters are similar to those that we learned for quantitative research in Chapter 7, you need to keep in mind that researchers have special considerations in mind as they implement the data collection step of their qualitative studies because their goal is exploration (not explanation). You were introduced to these considerations in Chapter 2, where we learned that qualitative researchers:

- intentionally select a small number of sites and participants to best learn about the study's central phenomenon;
- collect word (text) and image (picture) data to develop rich detail and in-depth understandings;
- use procedures for collecting data that include open-ended, emerging questions to permit participants to generate their own responses; and
- are sensitive to the ethical issues and challenges of gathering information face to face and in people's homes or workplaces.

These considerations in qualitative research relate to the overall purpose of exploring a central phenomenon and, more specifically, to the particular qualitative research design being used in a study. To be able to understand and appropriately evaluate a study's qualitative data collection, you need to know how to interpret the information that researchers include in their reports about the participants and data collection. Let's begin by examining how to locate and read the information about a qualitative study's process of collecting data.

How Do You Identify the Participants and Data Collection in a Qualitative Study?

To understand any qualitative research study, you need to identify how the researcher selected the participants and collected the data. You can find an author's description of participants and data collection in the Method section of a qualitative research article. This major section usually has a heading such as *Method*, *Methodology*, or *Procedures*. As we discussed in the previous chapter, the Method section often begins with a brief statement introducing the overall qualitative research design in the study, but typically the bulk of the text in this section describes how the researcher implemented data collection during the study. Although every Method section reflects the unique circumstances and procedures used in a study, they do all tend to address a common set of important elements. By learning to look for these elements, you will find it easier to read and understand the information presented within Method sections of qualitative reports.

To learn to identify the elements of qualitative data collection in a report, let's examine an excerpt from the Method section of the qualitative adolescent homelessness study (Haldenby et al., 2007) that we read previously. This passage can be found in Figure 10.1. As you read it, think about the kind of information the researchers are including in their report to identify the sites and participants, the types of qualitative data, the data collection procedures, and the data collection issues.

> **Here's a Tip!**
>
> Look for subheadings when you read the Method section of qualitative reports. Sub-headings such as *Research Site*, *Sample*, *Participants*, and *Data Collection Procedures* can help you quickly understand the information that the author is presenting.

Look for Information About the Sites and Participants

In the passage, Haldenby et al. tell us where they collected the data (the site) and from whom (the participants). The site where they collected the data was a community center that provides services to adolescents who are homeless and is located in a city in Ontario. We also learn that the researchers included 13 adolescents who considered themselves to be homeless as the participants in the study's sample. The researchers worked to recruit adolescents who were male and female, could speak English, and included a range of backgrounds.

Identify the Types of Qualitative Data Gathered

After telling us about the sites and participants, the researchers next identified the types of data that they gathered. Specifically, we learn that they collected interviews with the adolescents. Two of the interviews were group interviews that included

Method

Design

The selected research design was a critical narrative analysis. . . .

Sample

After ethics approval was obtained through the University of Western Ontario's research ethics board, the study participants were recruited from a community center that works with adolescents who are homeless. This center is located in the downtown area of a southwestern city in Ontario. Information about the study was provided to the agency staff, who assisted with recruitment by allowing discussion about the study during various youth group meetings. The youth who were interested in participating were asked to contact the researcher by phone or e-mail or in person during a visit to the centre. After meeting the adolescent, the researcher provided a letter of information. The main points of the letter were reviewed at the beginning of the interview, and any questions the participants had were addressed. Informed consent was obtained verbally and in writing at the time of the interview.

All male and female participants had self-identified as being homeless, were able to speak and understand English, and, with one exception, ranged in age from 14 to 19 years. The rationale for the lower age limit is that 14 is the legal age at which individuals can agree to participate in research without parental consent. In recognition of the diversity within the homeless adolescent population, efforts were made to recruit youth from a variety of backgrounds and ethnicities. One Black male participant who was 6 months above the specified age range was granted acceptance to participate. All other youth were White. The total sample consisted of 6 female and 7 male participants. All participants were given the choice of taking part in group or individual interviews. Five young women and 4 young men opted to be interviewed individually. Two group interviews were conducted, one consisting of 2 adolescent boys and another consisting of 1 adolescent boy and 1 adolescent woman participant. In both of these interviews the two participants knew one another and considered each other friends. The final decision regarding sample size was determined during the course of the research according to the criterion of saturation (Patton, 2002). In essence, sampling was discontinued when no new themes emerged from the data.

Data Collection Procedures

The individual and group interviews followed a semistructured format and were dialogic and interactive in nature. Critical theory assumes that the standards of truth are always social (Campbell & Bunting, 1991). Thus, new knowledge is coconstructed between the nurse researcher and the participants. Field notes were taken after the interviews, which assisted the nurse researcher in revising the interview guide as the study progressed as well as assisting in data analysis (Patton, 2002).

Margin annotations: Ethical issue · Site · Field issue · Ethical issue · Participants · Types of data · Procedures for collecting data

FIGURE 10.1   An Excerpt Describing the Sample and Data Collection in a Qualitative Study

Source: Excerpt from paragraphs 22–28 of the qualitative adolescent-homelessness study (Haldenby et al., 2007, pp. 1235–1236).

more than one adolescent and nine of the interviews were individual interviews with one adolescent.

Discern the Procedures Used to Gather the Data

After identifying the types of data, the researchers provided details about the procedures for collecting the data. These details include the format of the interviews, which were described as using "a semi-structured format and were dialogic and interactive" (p. 1236). This description means that the researchers conducted the interviews in a conversational manner, asking questions based on what the participant had to say as in a normal dialogue between people. We also learn that the researchers recorded notes after each interview, used a guide for the major questions asked during the interviews, and changed these questions based on what was being learned as the study was conducted. Although not stated in this passage, if we keep reading the article we also learn that the authors made audio recordings of each of the interviews.

Note the Issues Related to Collecting Data

In addition to the details about the site, participants, data types, and procedures, in this passage we learn about some of the ethical and field issues that the researchers faced in conducting this study, such as how the researchers received ethical approval for the study, the procedures they used to recruit the participants into the research, and how they obtained the participants' consent to participate in the research.

These categories—the sites and participants, types of data, procedures, and issues—provide essential information about what a qualitative researcher actually did while collecting data during a study. They also provide you with a framework for reading and evaluating a research report. Let's examine each of these categories in more detail.

How Do You Understand the Selection of Sites and Participants in a Qualitative Study?

An important step when reading any research report is identifying the study's sample. Recall from Chapter 7 that a sample is made up of the sites and individuals that actually participate in a study. To understand a study's sample, you need to consider what sites and individuals were included, how the researcher selected them, and how many of them participated. In qualitative research, researchers describe the selected sites and participants, the specific selection strategies used, and the size of the sample in the Method section of the report. In some reports, this information appears in a subsection titled *Participants* or *Sample*, but often it is just discussed in a paragraph or two of the Method section. As you read the information, keep in mind the important features of good qualitative research.

Sites and Participants Are Purposefully Selected

Recall that the intent of qualitative research is to develop an in-depth exploration of a central phenomenon, such as the process of creating community in a clinic or the experience of being a bully. To best explore the central phenomenon, the qualitative researcher reports intentionally selecting sites and individuals who can best help the researcher learn about it. The process of intentionally selecting sites and individuals to participate in research is called **purposeful sampling** (or purposive sampling) because the researcher is purposefully selecting the sites and individuals that they include in the study. This type of sampling is best suited for qualitative research because the researcher is able to select the individuals who are most appropriate for a study of the central phenomenon. The standard used when purposefully choosing sites and individuals is that they are "information rich" (Patton, 2002, p. 230)—that is, they can provide a wealth of information for the study because they have experienced the central phenomenon of interest.

Let's consider a few examples of sites and individuals that could be considered information rich. A qualitative researcher interested in studying the use of culturally relevant curricula may decide to study a site that is known for using this approach (e.g., one elementary school that won an award for its use of culturally relevant materials), several sites actively grappling with this phenomenon (e.g., three urban middle schools with culturally diverse students), individuals or groups who are experiencing the phenomenon (e.g., 15 teachers participating in a professional development program about culturally relevant teaching), or some combination (e.g., purposefully selecting two urban schools and several teachers at those schools who are using culturally relevant materials). Purposeful sampling thus applies to both sites and individuals. Good purposeful sampling is important for a qualitative research study because it indicates that the researcher tried to identify the best sites and participants to learn about the central phenomenon.

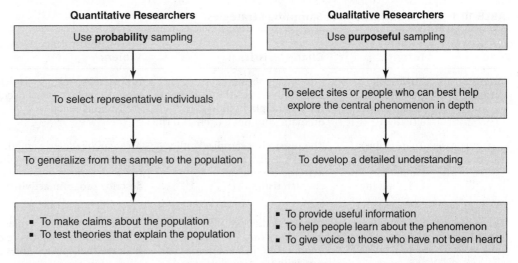

FIGURE 10.2   Differences Between Sampling in Quantitative and Qualitative Research

When reading reports of qualitative research, expect the researchers to have used good purposeful sampling instead of probability sampling, which is a characteristic of good quantitative research. The distinction between quantitative probability sampling and qualitative purposeful sampling is portrayed in Figure 10.2. In quantitative research, the focus is on using probability sampling, selecting representative individuals for the sample, and generalizing results from these individuals to a population. Often this process results in testing theories that explain variables found in the population. In contrast, the qualitative researcher selects sites and people that can best help develop an understanding about a central phenomenon. This understanding emerges through a detailed exploration of the sites and the people. It provides information that is useful and descriptive, that helps us learn about the phenomenon, or that gives voice to individuals who have not been heard.

Specific Strategies Guide the Purposeful Sampling

There are several different specific strategies that researchers use to implement purposeful sampling in their studies. Therefore, in addition to noting the use of purposeful sampling when reading qualitative research reports, you should identify the specific type of purposeful sampling that was used. Table 10.1 summarizes nine different purposeful sampling strategies found in the literature (Patton, 2002). Each of these strategies has a different intent and different characteristics. In a good qualitative study, the researchers choose the strategy that best matches their study's purpose, such as the examples provided in Table 10.1. Each of these sampling strategies can be applied at a single time or multiple times during a study, and researchers use them to sample individuals, groups, or entire organizations and sites. The following examples from published qualitative reports illustrate three of the most frequently used strategies.

- *An example of maximal variation sampling used to describe diverse perspectives.* "We used purposive sampling to ensure that a range of experiences was obtained (Lincoln & Guba, 1985). We selected for interviews (from the 59 students who identified themselves as bullied during the current school term) five children who had a high or low score on the physical, relational, and racial items" (Mishna, 2004, p. 236).

    This research team used the maximal variation sampling strategy to select participants who varied across three characteristics (i.e., physical, relational, and racial scores) in order to best describe different perspectives about bullying.
- *An example of homogenous sampling used to describe a subgroup.* "Students were recommended for participation by their language arts teachers at the end of the previous school year. I asked the teachers to recommend girls who met the definition of a struggling reader and who did not have a history of being absent" (Hall, 2007, p. 134).

TABLE 10.1   Types of Purposeful Sampling Strategies

Type	Intent	Characteristics	Example for a Study About Student Violence
Intensity sampling	To describe cases that dramatically illustrate the situation	The researcher samples exceptional cases that represent the central phenomenon in dramatic (but not extreme) terms	A researcher selects a college campus where a violent event occurs to describe the campus reactions
Extreme case sampling	To describe particularly troublesome or enlightening cases	The researcher samples outlier cases or individuals that display extreme or unusual characteristics	A researcher selects an anti-fighting program in elementary education that has received awards as an outstanding case to describe program activities
Homogenous sampling	To describe a subgroup in depth	The researcher samples individuals or sites based on membership in a subgroup that has defining characteristics	A researcher selects students from rural schools who are members of a gun club to describe their perspectives about gun ownership
Maximal variation sampling	To describe diverse perspectives	The researcher samples cases or individuals that differ on some characteristic or trait	A researcher selects students based on school type (rural, suburban, and urban) and gender (male and female) to explore diverse experiences about student violence
Theory or concept sampling	To generate a theory or explore a concept	The researcher samples individuals or sites because they can help the researcher generate or discover a theory or specific concepts within the theory	A researcher is developing a theory about coping strategies of adolescents incarcerated for weapons charges and identifies students who have experiences that can inform this theory
Typical sampling	To describe cases that are typical	The researcher samples persons or sites that are typical or average	A researcher selects principals that represent schools in a state that report an average number of violent events per school year
Confirming/ disconfirming sampling	To explore cases that confirm or disconfirm emergent findings	The researcher samples individuals to test or confirm preliminary findings	During a study, a researcher finds that Hispanic girls report different experiences with violence than African American girls. The researcher selects additional girls from these two groups to confirm these preliminary findings
Opportunistic sampling	To take advantage of emerging insights	The researcher samples individuals or sites to take advantage of unfolding opportunities that will help answer research questions	While conducting a study of school antiviolence programs, the researcher learns about a special program at another school and decides to select individuals from that school
Snowball sampling	To locate people or sites to study	The researcher samples individuals or sites based on the recommendations of others	A researcher studying the perceptions of gang members about violence asks interviewees to invite other individuals to participate

This researcher used the homogenous sampling strategy to select individuals who are similar (i.e., girls who struggle to read and attend school regularly) in order to describe a subgroup.

■ *An example of snowball sampling used to identify individuals not known to the researcher.* "More than half of the respondents were found through a snowball sample technique. A work colleague in Boulder, a native of Grand Forks, provided two names of women as my initial contacts. At the end of each interview I asked my respondents to recommend someone 'different from themselves' for my next interview, in order to increase diversity of the sample, a strategy that worked well" (Fothergill, 1999, pp. 128–129).

This researcher used the snowball sampling strategy to select individuals after the study began based on the recommendations of participants to identify good potential participants unknown to the researcher.

In a well-written qualitative report, the researchers should describe and defend the specific type of purposeful sampling strategy that they used in their study. Sometimes researchers identify these strategies using the names found in Table 10.1, but often they only describe what they did and you have to deduce the strategy type from this information. As you read a report's Method section, identify the sampling strategy that was used and how the strategy was implemented to understand who participated in the study. Once you have identified information about the sample, consider whether the researcher used a good sampling strategy that led to the inclusion of sites and participants who could best help the researcher learn about the central phenomenon.

What Do You Think?

Read the following excerpt from a qualitative case study about African American students' descriptions of teaching practices and learning environments. Using the purposeful sampling types listed in Table 10.1, determine the purposeful sampling strategy that the author used and state why this would be a good choice for a study on this topic.

> The students ranged from second to eighth grades. A purposeful sample of 30 students was used for the study, 17 girls and 13 boys. A cross-selection of students, based on academic achievement and classroom behavior per their teachers' classifications, were identified to serve as participants for the study. Thus, the students fell into low-, medium-, or high-achievement and behavioral categories. (Howard, 2002, p. 429)

Check Your Understanding

From this passage, we can conclude that the researcher used a maximal variation sampling strategy to select diverse individuals to participate in the study. The sampled students were purposefully selected to vary on the characteristics of gender (girls and boys), academic achievement (low, medium, and high), and classroom behavior ratings (low, medium, and high). The use of maximal variation sampling is a good choice if the researcher wanted to learn about the diverse perspectives held by African American students about teaching practices and learning environments.

A Small Number of Sites and Participants Are Selected

When reading a research report, it is important to pay attention to the number of participants in the study in addition to who participated and how they were selected. Researchers report the *number* of selected sites and participants in addition to the strategy used to select the sample. This number is a study's sample size. You can find the sample size stated in a study's Method section, often in the same paragraph that describes the sampling. Here are some general guidelines to consider when reading about the sample size reported for qualitative research studies:

- It is typical in qualitative research for the researchers to study a small number of sites and individuals or a few cases. This is because the overall ability of a researcher to provide an in-depth exploration diminishes with the addition of each new site and individual. One objective of qualitative research is to present the complexity of a site or of the information provided by individuals and, to fully describe the complexity, qualitative researchers need to focus on a small sample.

■ In some qualitative studies, the researchers study a single individual or a single site. In many studies, the researchers study a sample size of several individuals or sites, ranging from 2 or 3 to 30 or 40. Because of the need to report details about each individual or site, too many cases can become unwieldy and result in superficial perspectives. Often the size of the sample is not set at the start of the study and instead the researchers continue to gather data from participants until they no longer are learning new information about the central phenomenon from new participants. The point in a study when the researchers feel that they are no longer learning new information is called reaching "saturation," and some qualitative researchers report using a criteria of saturation to determine the size of their sample.

■ Researchers consider the specific design (e.g., narrative research, case study, ethnography, and grounded theory) for conducting their qualitative study when deciding the size of their sample. The research design suggests the number of individuals needed to study. Although there are no strict rules for sample sizes in qualitative research, here are some general guidelines for the four common qualitative research designs:

  ■ One or two individuals in a narrative study;
  ■ One case in a case study or two to five cases in a multiple case study, with the number of participants per case depending on the nature of the case (e.g., as few as one if studying an individual as a case or as many as 30 if studying one classroom as a case);
  ■ An entire group of people in an ethnographic study; and
  ■ 20 to 30 individuals in a grounded theory study.

Let's consider some specific examples that were introduced in Chapter 9 to see how many sites and individuals were included in studies that use different qualitative research designs. In Chan's (2010) narrative study of Ai Mei's middle school experience as a Chinese immigrant, there was one participant. In a multiple case study of adolescents' experience of being Chinese, Wang (2013) studied three cases, and each case included three participants (i.e., the adolescent and two parents) for a total of 9 participants. In Swidler's (2000) ethnographic study of a one-teacher country school, there was one culture-sharing group studied that included the teacher, 12 students, and members of the local community, including the 16 parents. In Komives et al.'s (2005) grounded theory study, 13 college students participated (which is a little small for the typical number in a grounded theory approach). As these examples illustrate, the number of participants varies in qualitative research from one to several, depending on the research design used in the study. Researchers need to include enough participants to accomplish the study purpose (such as to fully describe the different perspectives about a case), but should keep it small enough to be able to give rich details from each included participant.

What Do You Think?

Consider the following passage from Auerbach's (2007) qualitative study about the different roles that parents of color construct to support their adolescent children in going to college. What is the sample size in this study? What sampling strategy was used?

A small, purposeful sample of parents of Futures [a college access program] students was selected to explore the role constructions of working-class parents of color who lack a college education but aspire to college for their children. Although not representative of Latino or African American parents at the school or generally, the sample reflects the preponderance of immigrant families in the project and variation on characteristics that could affect parent roles. The sample consisted of 16 working-class parents from 11 families. (Auerbach, 2007, p. 256)

> **Check Your Understanding**
>
> From this passage, we learn that the sample size for this study was 16 parents. These parents appeared to be selected using a homogenous sampling strategy. All of the participants shared the characteristics of being from a working-class background, being a parent of color (African American or Latino), not possessing a college education, and having a child in the Futures program.

What Types of Qualitative Data Do Researchers Collect?

After learning about the sites and participants in a study, you should continue reading to find what types of information the researchers collected. Researchers identify the types of data that they collected to address their research questions in the Method section, often in a subsection titled *Data Collection* or *Data Sources*. You should expect that the researchers name the different types of data that they gathered and explain why these types were appropriate for the specific study and its goals. In good qualitative research, these types of data share several characteristics. The qualitative researcher poses general, broad questions to participants, allowing them to share their views relatively unconstrained by the researcher's perspective. The researcher often collects multiple types of information to capture different dimensions of the central phenomenon and adds new questions and new forms of data during the study to gain greater depth. Further, the researcher engages in extensive data collection, spending a great deal of time at the site where people engage in the phenomenon under study. At the site, the qualitative researcher gathers detailed information to establish the complexity of the central phenomenon.

We can see the varied nature of the different types of qualitative data when they are placed into the following four broad categories:

- interviews,
- observations,
- documents, and
- audiovisual materials.

Table 10.2 lists a definition of different data types, provides examples, and describes the format of the information gathered for each of these major categories of data. Variations on data collection in all four areas are emerging continuously, and you will notice a variety after reading several qualitative research reports, including the many examples listed in the table. Most recently, videos, student portfolios, and the use of social media are increasingly being used as forms of data by qualitative researchers. Researchers choose one or more types of data based on the type of information that will best answer their research questions about the central phenomenon and the type of research design they are using. Some general guidelines of when researchers use each type of data are also provided in Table 10.2, as are some limitations of each data type. Although researchers begin by naming the types of data that they collected in their reports, that is not enough information for you to understand the collected data. You need to also read about the procedures they used to gather each type of data in the study. Now let's take a detailed look at each of the categories to understand the different ways that researchers gather qualitative data.

Here's a Tip!

Good qualitative studies often include several different types of data. As you read the details, it can be helpful to classify each specific data form as an interview, observation, document, or audiovisual material to understand the major types of information gathered in the study.

TABLE 10.2   Characteristics of the Major Categories of Qualitative Data Collection

	Interviews	Observations	Documents	Audiovisual Materials
Definition of the Data Type	Unstructured verbal or written data obtained from participants responding to open-ended questions in conversations or on questionnaires	Unstructured text data and picture data recorded during observations by the researcher	Existing paper and/or electronic records that are available to the researcher	Unstructured data that exists in a visual, audio, or physical form from people or places recorded by the researcher or someone else
Examples of this Data Type	■ Focus group interviews ■ One-on-one interviews ■ Telephone interviews ■ E-mail interviews ■ Open-ended questions on questionnaires	■ Nonparticipant observations ■ Participant observations	■ Public documents (e.g., minutes from meetings) ■ Private documents (e.g., journals)	■ Pictures ■ Photographs ■ Videos ■ Objects ■ Sounds
Format of the Information Gathered	Audiorecordings and text transcriptions	Field notes and drawings	Hand recorded notes about documents or electronic copies of the documents	Images, sounds, or physical objects
Examples of Research Designs in Which Commonly Used	■ Grounded theory ■ Narrative ■ Case study ■ Ethnography	■ Ethnography ■ Case study ■ Some grounded theory	■ Narrative ■ Case study ■ Ethnography	■ PhotoVoice ■ Narrative ■ Ethnography
Advantages of Its Use	Useful for recording information that cannot be observed or providing detailed personal information	Useful for recording information as it naturally occurs and helpful when participants have difficulty verbalizing their ideas	Useful for providing information from public and private records	Useful for providing creative forms of data to supplement text-based data, particularly for topics that are hard to express with words
Limitations of Its Use	Limited by what participants remember or what their perceptions are and may not match what they actually do	Limited to behaviors and actions that can actually be observed by a researcher	Information may be incomplete, not represent all perspectives, or inaccurate because not originally prepared for the purposes of research	Not all participants are comfortable expressing themselves in a creative form and gathered forms are challenging to analyze

How Do You Understand the Common Qualitative Data Collection Procedures?

The Method sections of qualitative research reports include information that goes beyond simply identifying the type of qualitative data that the researcher gathered. When you read reports, you should take note of the details provided about each type of data gathered in the study. These details may be found in a subsection labeled *Procedures* or described in subsections labeled for the type of data (e.g., *Interviews* or *Observations*). When you read about a study's data collection, consider the specific type of data that was gathered and the details about why and how the information was obtained. Let's consider how you read the details about each of the major categories of qualitative data, starting with interviews.

Procedures for Qualitative Interviews

The use of interviews to gather data is probably the most common approach to qualitative data collection that you will find in published reports. A qualitative **interview** occurs when a researcher asks one or more participants open-ended questions and records their answers. An **open-ended question** is a question stated so that it allows the participant to create his/her own options for responding. For example, in a qualitative interview of athletes in high schools, the interviewer might ask, "How do you balance your participation in athletics with your schoolwork?" The athlete then creates a response to this question without being forced to choose from predetermined response options. Qualitative researchers ask good open-ended questions so that the participants can best voice their experiences unconstrained by any perspectives of the researcher or past research findings.

There are many details involved in gathering data through qualitative interviews, and you need to read the researchers' descriptions of this information to understand and evaluate the quality of the data gathered. As you read about the use of interviews, pay attention to

- the reason why the researcher decided to use interviews,
- the type of interviews conducted,
- what questions were asked and whether probes were used, and
- how the interviewer recorded the conversation.

We will now learn more about each of these important considerations.

Examine Why the Researcher Chose to Collect Interviews.   Because there are many possible forms of data that researchers can collect, you should examine the report to learn the reasons why the use of interviews was an appropriate choice for the study. Researchers typically choose to collect data through interviews because they provide useful information when participants cannot be directly observed. This type of data also permits participants to describe detailed personal information. The interviewer has control over the types of information received because he/she can ask specific questions to elicit this information. However, interviews are not the best choice for a study if the participants have trouble expressing themselves verbally or if the central phenomenon is a behavior that would be better observed. Qualitative interviews can be appropriate in studies using any of the available qualitative research designs. They are the primary type of data collected in most grounded theory studies, but are useful for learning from participants in case studies, ethnographies, and narrative studies as well.

Identify the Specific Type of Interview.   There are a number of approaches to interviewing, and they each appear frequently in reported studies. When reading about the use of interviews in a study, identify the specific type used—focus group interview, one-on-one interview, telephone interview, e-mail interview, questionnaire, or some combination—and consider whether the type was the best for learning the participants' views and answering the study's research questions.

- *Focus group interviews.* Researchers use focus group interviews to collect both the views of specific people and a shared understanding from several individuals. A **focus group interview** is the process that researchers use to collect data through conversations with a small group of people, typically four to eight individuals. The researcher asks a small number of general questions and elicits responses from all individuals in the group as well as their reactions to what others have said. A typical focus group interview lasts about an hour. Focus groups are a good type of interview when the interaction among interviewees will likely yield the best information and when interviewees are similar to and cooperative with each other. For example, they would be a good choice in a study of adolescents, who may feel more comfortable talking with the researcher when in a small group and may think more deeply about a topic as they hear what their peers have to say. Because of the group format, focus group interviews are an efficient means of collecting data, but they are not appropriate if the researcher wants to learn about sensitive topics or the details about any one individual's experiences.
- *One-on-one interviews.* A popular, but time-consuming and costly approach is for the researcher to conduct individual interviews. The **one-on-one interview** is a data

collection process in which the researcher asks questions to and records answers from only one participant at a time. Depending on the topic and attention span of the participant, good qualitative one-on-one interviews typically last for at least 30–60 minutes to allow for an in-depth discussion of the person's experiences. The researcher may conduct several one-on-one interviews in the study, such as asking a few teachers and counselors to provide their impressions of a violent event at a school. One-on-one interviews are ideal for studies that include participants who are articulate, who can share ideas comfortably, and who are not hesitant to speak. They are the best way to learn in depth about the perceptions and experiences of single individuals.

- *Telephone interviews.* It may not be possible for a researcher to gather groups of individuals for an interview or to visit one on one with individuals. The participants in a study may be geographically dispersed and unable to come to a central location for an interview. In this situation, a researcher may choose to conduct telephone interviews. Conducting a qualitative **telephone interview** is the process of gathering data from individuals by asking a small number of general questions over the telephone. This form of interview is convenient and the procedures are similar to one-on-one interviews. However, the researcher is unable to observe the participant's behaviors and facial expressions, which can limit how well the researcher interprets the person's reactions during the interview.

- *E-mail interviews.* **E-mail interviews** consist of the researcher collecting open-ended data through typed interviews with individuals using computers and the Internet. They are also useful in studies where the researcher needs to collect qualitative data from participants who are geographically dispersed. This form of interviewing provides rapid access to large numbers of people and a ready-made text database for qualitative analysis. E-mail interviews do limit the amount and timing of follow-up questions, which are easy to ask in the moment during an in-person conversation, but likely require a time delay when using a nonsynchronous form of conversation like e-mail. Although e-mail interviews are still a fairly new type of qualitative data, their use in research studies is growing with the increased availability and use of computers in the population.

- *Open-ended questions as part of a questionnaire.* A final type of qualitative interview found in research reports occurs when a researcher asks open-ended questions as part of a questionnaire that may also include closed-ended items. This type of data collection allows a researcher to net two types of information. The researcher gains quantitative information to support theories and concepts in the literature from the predetermined, closed-ended items. At the same time, the researcher can use the open-ended responses to explore reasons for the close-ended responses and identify comments people might have that are beyond the responses to the close-ended questions. For example, a researcher might ask:

> Indicate the extent of your agreement or disagreement with this statement:
> "Student policies governing binge drinking on campus should be more strict."
> ☐Strongly agree   ☐Agree   ☐Undecided   ☐Disagree   ☐Strongly disagree
> Please explain your response in more detail:

In this example, the researcher started with a closed-ended question and five predetermined response categories. This question is followed with an open-ended question in which the participants indicate reasons for their responses. This type of open-ended data is useful for providing insight into participants' responses on a questionnaire, but it is also very limited because participants often write very little, participants typically do not go into depth about their thinking, and researchers cannot ask the participants for clarifying information.

Note the Way the Researcher Organizes the Interview Questions.   Researchers often have some means for structuring their interviews and taking careful notes, and you should look for information about the interview protocol when reading reports. An **interview protocol** is a form designed by the researcher that contains instructions for the process of the interview, the major questions to be asked, and space to take notes about the responses from the interviewee. This form serves the purpose of reminding the interviewer of the major questions and providing a means for recording notes. Researchers sometimes include their interview protocol as an appendix to the report or they may at least list the main questions in the Method section. This information is an important component of a good qualitative research report, and it is useful for you to determine whether the questions that the researcher asked were truly open-ended, allowing participants to generate their responses, and whether they seemed to be appropriate for learning about the study's central phenomenon.

Examine Figure 10.3 to see an interview protocol that was included as an appendix for a research article. Plano Clark et al. (2002) used focus group interviews to learn about high school students' perceptions of tobacco use. You can find many features that are typical of good interview protocols by reviewing this figure. The protocol begins with a general question to help the participants become at ease (often called an "ice-breaker" question). In addition, it includes only a few questions, which are stated in a broad, open-ended fashion to let the respondents determine their own options for answering the questions. By asking only a few questions, the interview protocol also indicates that the researcher wants the participants to respond with extensive detail and examples for each one. In addition to the main numbered questions, this protocol also indicates probing questions with the bulleted items. **Probes** are subquestions under a main question that the researcher asks to elicit more information. In good qualitative research, researchers use probes to encourage participants to clarify what they are saying and to urge them to elaborate on their ideas. They may be preplanned, but often the researcher uses probes that emerge based on whatever the participant has said in response to the main question. Researchers often refer to this type of an interview protocol as "semistructured" because it has the planned structure of a few open-ended questions, but most of the follow-up questions are not planned ahead of time.

Note How the Researcher Recorded the Data During the Interview. As with all forms of data collection, the researcher needs to make a record of the data gathered during interviews. In a well-written qualitative report, the researcher should note the details of the record making. This record should include basic information such as who the interviewer and interviewee(s) were, where the interview took place, and how long it lasted. In addition, in a good qualitative study the researcher typically records field notes about the interview conversation during the interview and immediately after

---

APPENDIX   **Focus Group Interview Protocol**

1. First, I'd like to go around the room and have each person say their first name and one thing they would like us to know about themselves. (This is an icebreaker and can be modified.)
2. Think back over the course of the past month. Describe for me times when you have or you have seen people using tobacco.
   - Where were you?
   - What was going on?
   - Who was using it?
   - How did you react?
   - Can you give me some examples? (May have to specifically ask: What about chewing tobacco?)
3. Tell me what students at this school think about tobacco.
   - Can you give me an example?
   - Could you tell me more?
   - What do you mean by that?
4. How would you describe the rules for tobacco use at this school?
   - What do students think about the rules?
   - How are they enforced?
5. We've mostly been talking about tobacco use at school. Now I would like for you to tell me what happens outside of school.
   - Other experiences the past month with tobacco?
   - What about the role of advertising, films, television?
   - What about experiences at home, with friends, at work?
6. Could you tell me what you think quitting is like for smokers?
   - How do you think it is different for people who are younger compared to people who are older?

Source: This appendix is reprinted from Plano Clark et al., *Qualitative Health Research*, Vol. 12, Issue 9, p. 1280, 2002. Reprinted with permission of Sage Publications, Inc.

FIGURE 10.3 A Sample Interview Protocol Published as the Appendix of a Research Article

the interview. Because it is difficult to write down all aspects of the interview conversation as it is happening, it is preferable that the interviewer also audiorecord the interview questions and responses with the permission of the participant. Audio recording an interview ensures that the researcher has an accurate and detailed record of the interview's content. In good qualitative research, you should expect that the researcher recorded interview conversations whenever possible.

What Do You Think?

Read the following excerpt from Knesting and Waldron's (2006) study about how at-risk students persist in school. Identify (a) the specific type of interview used; (b) how the questions were organized, including what questions were asked and whether probes were used; and (c) how the data were recorded, including who the interviewer and interviewees were, where the interviews occurred, how long they lasted, and how the interviewer recorded the conversation.

> Individual interviews were conducted with all 17 students recommended for participation. Interviews took place in either a back corner of the school library or an empty classroom. . . . Students were asked four open-ended questions: (a) If I were a new student here, what would you tell me about this school? What would you show me? (b) Tell me some things I might like about this school; (c) Tell me some things I might not like; and (d) If I were a student at this school who was thinking about dropping out, what advice would you give me? Is there anybody here at school that you would suggest that I talk with about my decision?. . . Interviews took place in classrooms or offices and lasted between 45 to 60 min. . . . All interviews were conducted by the first author. They were audiotaped, transcribed, and then returned to participants for feedback and clarification. To help ensure understanding of interviewee responses, during the interviews answers were reflected back and probing questions used to seek clarification. (Knesting & Waldron, 2006, p. 601)

Check Your Understanding

From this passage we learned the following: (a) The study included one-on-one interviews. (b) The interviewer asked four main questions about the participants' ideas about their school. These questions were open-ended and the researcher used probes to obtain clarifying information. (c) The first author (Knesting) conducted the interviews with students. The interviews took place at the students' schools and each interview lasted between 45 and 60 minutes. The interviewer audiotaped the interview conversations.

Procedures for Qualitative Observations

Next to interviews, observations represent a second frequently reported form of qualitative data collection. Qualitative **observation** is the process researchers use to gather open-ended, firsthand information by observing people and places at a research site. This information might include descriptions of the participants, the physical setting, events, activities, and interactions. In observing a daycare, for example, a researcher may report observing and recording the layout of the room, activities by the teacher and children, the interactions between the children and teacher, and the children-to-children conversations. Although classrooms are a common setting where researchers conduct observations, observations occur in many settings beyond schools depending on the topic of the study, such as museums, committee meetings, doctors' offices, homes, community centers, or sporting events.

As with qualitative interviews, there are many decisions that researchers make related to gathering data through observations, and you can look for these in their reports. When reading a study that included the collection of observations, try to find the following details:

- the reason why the researcher decided to gather observations,
- the researcher's role during the observation,
- how the observer recorded the data, and
- how many observations were gathered.

Let's consider each of these aspects in further detail.

Examine Why the Researcher Chose to Collect Observations.   When reading about the use of observations in a qualitative report, look for an indication as to why the researchers chose to collect qualitative observations and an explanation for how the observational data helps to address their study research questions. Examples of reasons why researchers use this type of qualitative data include the following: observations provide the means to record information as it naturally occurs in a setting, are useful to study actual behavior, and work well for studying individuals who have difficulty verbalizing their ideas (e.g., preschool children). Ethnographers often include observations in their studies so that they can observe the shared language, behaviors, and beliefs that are part of the everyday life of the culture-sharing group of interest. Observations are a common type of data collected by case study researchers when they study bounded systems such as classrooms, clinics, or programs. Observations are also useful in grounded theory studies that aim to develop a theory about an action or interaction.

Look for the Researcher's Role as an Observer.   When a researcher gathers data using observations, it requires that he or she adopt a particular role as an observer. Many possible roles exist (e.g., see Spradley, 1980), and no one role is suited for all situations. These observational roles fall along a continuum from the researcher being a complete observer who does not participate in the setting to the researcher actively participating in the setting while observing. In a well-written report, the researcher describes his/her role so that you understand how the observations were gathered in the study. To identify this role when reading a qualitative report, think of the observer having used one of three possible roles:

- *Nonparticipant observational role.* A **nonparticipant observer** is an observer who visits a site and records notes without becoming involved in the participants' activities. Using a nonparticipant observational role, the researcher is an outsider who sits on the periphery or some advantageous place to watch and record the phenomenon under study (e.g., the back of the auditorium during play practice). This role works well in studies where the researcher does not want to disrupt the activities or is not familiar enough with the site and people to participate.
- *Participant observational role.* A **participant observer** is an observational role adopted by researchers when they actually take part in activities in the setting they observe. For example, the researcher might provide tutoring to children while observing in a classroom, assist with meal preparation while observing at a soup kitchen, or participate in celebrations of a community group being studied. As a participant observer, the researcher assumes the role of an observer who engages in activities at the study site and records information at the same time as participating in activities. This role is particularly useful in qualitative studies because it offers opportunities for the researcher to see experiences from the views of participants, which may help the researcher learn about a situation in more depth.
- *Changing observational role.* In many reports of the use of qualitative observations, the researcher may describe shifting or changing roles during the study. A changing observational role is one where researchers adapt their role to the situation. For example, the researcher might enter a site and observe as a nonparticipant in the beginning, needing to simply look around during the early phases of research to become familiar with the setting and people. Then he/she slowly becomes involved as a participant over time to gain a more in-depth observational experience. Sometimes the reverse happens, and a researcher reports moving from a participant role to a nonparticipant role that better supports the recording of detailed notes and reflecting on what is happening at the site. Engaging in both roles permits the researcher to be subjectively involved in the setting and experience, as well as to see the setting and experience more objectively.

Note How Researchers Record Observational Field Notes.   For observations to be useful for research purposes, the researcher uses procedures for recording the data that he/she observes and, in a good report, these procedures are mentioned. The data recorded during an observation are often called *field notes*. **Field notes** are the words and images recorded by the researcher during an observation in a qualitative study. Researchers often record two types of field notes: descriptive and reflective. When making descriptive field notes, observers record a description of the observed events, activities, setting, and people (i.e., what happened). In contrast, when making reflective field notes, observers record personal thoughts that relate to their insights, hunches, reactions, or broad ideas or themes that emerge during the observation (i.e., what sense they make of the site, people, and situation). The field notes become the data that the researcher analyzes in the study. Good qualitative field notes include extensive detail in both the descriptions and reflections that are recorded. Sometimes researchers include excerpts from their field notes in their reports, but more often you have to read about their procedures in the Method section and then look for the presence of extensive details when they report the study results (which you will learn about in Chapter 11).

Assess Whether Researchers Conducted Multiple Observations Over Time.   When people are engaged in a setting and interacting with each other, there is a lot happening all at the same time (e.g., movements, facial expressions, conversations, interactions with objects). It is impossible for researchers to make a record of everything they observe. Therefore, a good use of observations requires that the researcher observe the setting multiple times. Researchers generally start with broad observations, noting the general landscape or activities (such as sketching the layout of a room and the general activities that unfold during the day). As they become familiar with the setting, they narrow their observations to specific aspects (e.g., a small group of parents interacting during a coffee break) that provide insight into the central phenomenon. In a good qualitative research study, the researchers report making many observations over an extended period of time, such as 6 months to multiple years, to gain an in-depth understanding of a setting and individuals.

What Do You Think?

Read the following excerpt from Swidler's (2000) ethnographic study about the culture in a rural, one-room school. Identify (a) the researcher's observational role, (b) how the data were recorded, and (c) whether the observer conducted multiple observations over time.

> My data collection has included participant-observation and narrative fieldnotes from Bighand School for the first 6 months of the 1998–1999 academic year (August–February), at least 2 days/week and in several return visits. (Swidler, 2000, p. 9)

Check Your Understanding

From this passage, we learned the following: (a) Swidler conducted observations at the school using a participant observational role. If we keep reading the full report, we learn that this involved working with the children during school, having lunch with them, and playing games with them during recess. (b) He recorded field notes to document what he observed. (c) He spent considerable time at the site, observing many times (at least twice a week) during a 6-month period of time.

Procedures for the Collection of Documents

A third valuable source of qualitative information that researchers report collecting is documents. **Documents** consist of public and private records that researchers obtain about a site or participants in a qualitative study. Examples of public documents are minutes from meetings, official memos, published program handbooks, and records in the public domain. Private documents consist of personal journals and diaries, letters, medical charts, personal notes, and jottings individuals write to themselves. Other materials such as e-mail comments or Web site data illustrate both public and private documents, and they represent a growing source of qualitative data used in research reports. Documents are useful in a qualitative study when they provide information to help the researchers understand the central phenomenon of interest, and they are often used in ethnographies, case studies, and narrative studies. For example, in a case study of a high school music department, Scheib (2003) noted his collection of documents important for understanding the case by writing: "School policy publications (e.g., student handbooks, teacher handbooks, job descriptions, mission statements), documents sent to students and parents, and concert programs were also collected for analysis" (p. 126). When reading about the use of documents, look for the researcher to report information about what specific types of documents were collected and consider whether these documents provide useful information about the study's central phenomenon.

Procedures for the Collection of Audiovisual Materials

The final form of qualitative data that you will likely find mentioned in qualitative research reports is audiovisual materials. **Audiovisual materials** consist of images, sounds, or objects that researchers collect to help them understand the central phenomenon under study. Used with increasing frequency in qualitative research, images and visual materials include photographs, videos, digital images, paintings, and unobtrusive data forms (e.g., evidence and physical traces found in a setting, such as footsteps in the snow). These forms may be included in most qualitative designs, such as narrative studies and ethnographies. When reading about these types of data, identify the form of the data, note whether the forms were created for the purposes of the research or some other purpose, and consider how the forms provide insight into the study's central phenomenon.

One growing approach for using photographs in qualitative research is the technique of photo elicitation. In this approach, the researchers show participants pictures (their own or those taken by the researcher) and ask them to discuss the contents of the images. These pictures might be personal photographs or albums of historical photographs. The usefulness of this approach has evolved into its own research design, referred to as PhotoVoice (Wang & Burris, 1994), where participants take and discuss photos as a means to self-understanding and empowerment. The photo elicitation method is useful when pictures are able to capture facets of the central phenomenon, but the researcher's understanding of these images is enhanced by a participants' description of the meaning of the images. Here is an example of how one research team described their procedures for collecting photographs with interviews in a qualitative study about parents' experiences raising a child with a disability:

> During the first home visit, lasting approximately an hour, researchers explained the study, obtained informed consent, and gave the parents disposable cameras with 24 to 27 color exposures. Researchers asked parents to photograph images of life that were important to them over a 2-week period. . . . At the end of 2 weeks, researchers retrieved the camera and scheduled a second home visit. During the second home visit, lasting approximately $1^1/_2$ to 2 hours, participants described the significance of each image. Grand tour questions included (a) "Tell me about photograph #1" and (b) "Why did you take this photograph?" Follow-up probes occurred spontaneously. (Lassetter, Mandleco, & Roper, 2007, p. 459)

These researchers combined the collection of photographs with interviews to best learn about the parents' experiences with raising a child with a disability and the meaning of those experiences.

What Do You Think?

Consider the following passage from Clayton's (2007) qualitative case study about a professional development program for new teachers called the Beginning Teachers' Program (BTP). What types of data did the researcher report collecting?

Multiple data collection methods included at least three classroom observations, observation of 15 BTP sessions and the final professional development presentations, three semistructured individual interviews and one group interview, and analysis of all relevant documents and archival materials, including videotape, offered by the teachers and available through the BTP. (Clayton, 2007, p. 219)

Check Your Understanding

From this passage we learn that the author collected: (1) interviews (one-on-one interviews and a focus group interview), (2) observations (in classrooms and in the program sessions), (3) documents from the program, and (4) audiovisual materials (videotaped materials). Recall from Chapter 9 that the use of multiple types of data is an indicator of a good case study approach.

How Do You Understand the Issues That Are Reported About Qualitative Data Collection?

You can now recognize the basics of any study's qualitative data collection by identifying the sites, participants, and types of collected data. In addition, researchers describe important procedural issues related to their qualitative data collection in the Method sections of their reports. In Chapter 2, we learned that ethical issues are an essential consideration in all research studies. Ethical issues often require special attention in qualitative studies because the researcher actually goes to the site, spends considerable time there, and asks detailed questions about participants' lives. In addition, gathering data out in the field (i.e., at the research site) can be complicated as researchers interact with the participants in their natural settings. Therefore, researchers often describe issues from the field that occurred and how they were resolved in their reports. By reading about the ethical and field issues that occur in a qualitative study, you learn important details about how the researcher interacted with the site and participants during data collection, which gives you a more complete picture of the nature of the data that were gathered.

Pay Attention to How the Researchers Handled Ethical Issues

Researchers report information about the ethical issues associated with their study to convey to readers that they treated participants in an appropriate manner. By including this information, the researcher is reporting all the important details of the study and providing you with the necessary information to assess to what extent the study used ethical procedures. Because of the intimate, personal nature of most qualitative research, numerous ethical issues must be anticipated and handled appropriately by researchers.

- *Researchers may note that they adhered to ethical guidelines.* Conducting research ethically is a complex matter that can involve much more than the researcher merely following a set of rules. The key principle that should guide what researchers do in their studies is that concern for the welfare of their participants is paramount. However, what this means can vary depending on the nature of the participants and the topic under study. For example, in many studies it is appropriate for the researchers to ask participants to sign a form that documents that they were fully informed about the research study before they chose to participate in it. However, in some studies, it may be an ethical risk to the participants for the researcher to keep a record of participants' names. If a study is about an illegal behavior, for example, then different procedures need to be used to secure participants' consent to participate so there is no record of the participants' names. Therefore, different procedures may be more ethical for researchers to use depending on the details of the specific study.

Because of the complexity of ethical issues in qualitative research, researchers often report following the ethical guidelines as advanced or monitored by a professional group outside of the research study. Most academic research is monitored by members of a special board who are charged with ensuring that research is ethical. As introduced in Chapter 7, these boards are often referred to as human subject review boards or institutional review boards (IRBs). Researchers often indicate which board reviewed and approved their study's procedures in their reports. Researchers may also refer to guidelines for ethical standards that have been advanced by professional associations such as the American Educational Research Association (*Ethical Standards of the American Educational Research Association,* Strike et al., 2002) and the American Psychological Association (*Ethical Principles of Psychologists and Code of Conduct,* 2003). Researchers use these guidelines to guide the decisions they make about how to interact with participants in their studies. When researchers mention information about review boards and guidelines in their reports, you learn that the researchers were concerned about ethical issues and likely took steps to safeguard participants in their studies.

- ■ *Researchers often use procedures indicating that they respected participants' rights.* In all steps of the research process, researchers need to engage in ethical practices, particularly during data collection. Individuals who participate in a study have certain rights, and researchers often report procedures that demonstrate that they respected these rights for the participants in their study. For example, participants have the right to understand the purpose and aims of the study, how the results will be used, and the likely social consequences the study will have on their lives before they decide whether to participate. They also have the right to freely refuse to participate in a study and to withdraw at any time. When they participate and provide information, their anonymity is usually protected and guaranteed by the researcher. Individuals are not to be coerced to participate, such as by being offered excessive financial inducements to participate in a project. Participants also have the right to gain something from a study. Some researchers actively look for ways to give back (or reciprocate) to participants in a study because the participants have freely provided their time. For example, in one study involving individuals with HIV, the author shared book royalties with the participants in the study. In another study, a researcher volunteered to help supervise lunchroom activities to give back for learning information from students in the school. When reading about data collection in a good, ethical qualitative study, you can expect the researchers to describe procedures such as these that indicate how they protected the rights of their participants.

- ■ *Researchers take steps to protect participants' anonymity.* Researchers need to protect the anonymity of the participants, and this need influences the information they report about their studies. In many qualitative studies, researchers assign pseudonyms to participants or develop a composite picture of the group rather than focus on any single individual to protect the anonymity of participants. Researchers often also choose not to identify the specific research site in the report, such as referring to a school simply as a "Midwestern elementary school," as an additional way to protect participants' identities. Taking steps to mask the identity of sites and participants is a good ethical procedure in qualitative research.

Learn About the Challenges That Occurred in Gaining Access and Gathering Data

In addition to reading for ethical issues in the Method section, you can expect to learn about other types of issues that occurred while the researcher gathered data in the qualitative study. Qualitative researchers negotiate a wide range of issues in the field and discuss these issues in their reports to provide a full account of their data collection process. One such field issue is gaining access to the research site. In qualitative research, the researcher often needs to seek and obtain permissions from individuals and sites at many levels. Because of the in-depth nature of extensive and multiple interviews with or observations of participants, many researchers report making use of a gatekeeper. A **gatekeeper** is a person who assists in the identification of a place to study, has an official or unofficial role at the site, provides entrance to a site, and helps researchers locate people at the site. For example, a gatekeeper may be a teacher, a director, or the informal leader of a special program who has insider status at the site the researcher plans to study. Working with a gatekeeper is advantageous in qualitative research because it helps ensure that the researcher has good access to the site for the study. Another field issue that arises is successfully recruiting participants. Researchers often provide details about how they contacted participants, what information was shared with them, and whether an incentive was provided to participating individuals. This information helps you to judge whether the best participants were recruited into the study.

Researchers may also describe special circumstances that arose during data collection as an important field issue in their report. For example, consider the following statement about issues faced by an ethnographer as she gathered participant observations from a few students during her one-year study of junior high girls' literacy practices:

> Early, there were moments in which I was tested by focal students. On several occasions, a girl would not allow me to see a note that she deemed "too obscene." I did not report such incidents as writing on a restroom wall or faking illness to avoid an exam. I avoided conveying any negative judgment, and as the study progressed, I slowly gained their trust and was permitted to receive literacies still deemed "too gross" for parents or teachers. (Finders, 1996, p. 74)

In this passage, this researcher is sharing information about how she interacted with her participants and the challenges she faced in collecting her data. These details provide evidence that the researcher successfully negotiated field issues and was able to work with participants to engage with the study's central phenomenon at an in-depth level.

How Do You Evaluate the Participants and Data Collection in a Qualitative Study?

When evaluating the quality of a qualitative study's participants and data collection, you need to keep in mind that qualitative research requires different standards than quantitative research. Recall from Chapter 7 that quantitative research is concerned with drawing valid conclusions about how independent and dependent variables are related and generalizing results to larger populations. In contrast, qualitative research is concerned with drawing conclusions that provide in-depth descriptions about a central phenomenon and that are credible. Good qualitative research, therefore, involves the researcher selecting the best sites and participants and gathering data in the best ways to gain an in-depth and credible understanding of the study's central phenomenon. An in-depth understanding comes from procedures such as limiting the number of participants to a small number, collecting extensive datasets that include rich details, spending a long time in the field, and changing the data collection forms as needed during the study to learn more about the central phenomenon. The credibility of a study is enhanced when the selected participants have direct experience with the central phenomenon, the data represent different perspectives and types of sources, and accurate records of the data are made during data collection. Table 10.3 lists criteria that are useful to consider when evaluating the participants and data collection in a qualitative study. This table also provides indicators of higher quality and lower quality for the criteria to help you make your own judgments when evaluating the information provided in a research report.

TABLE 10.3   Criteria for Evaluating the Participants and Data Collection in a Qualitative Research Report

Quality Criteria	Indicators of Higher Quality in Qualitative Research	Indicators of Lower Quality in Qualitative Research
The Key Elements		
1. The sampling strategy is appropriate and justified.	+ A good purposeful sampling strategy is used to select the sites and participants. + The sampling procedures used are fully described and match the selected sampling strategy. + Strong reasons are provided that justify why the sampling strategy was appropriate for the study.	− The sampling strategy for selecting sites and participants is convenient or random. − The sampling procedures are unclear or do not match the selected sampling strategy. − Weak reasons are provided that do not fully explain why the specific sampling strategy was used.
2. The sample size is appropriate and justified.	+ The sample size is sufficiently small so the researcher can capture rich detail. + The sample size is consistent with the selected research design. + A sound rationale is provided to justify that the sample size is appropriate to answer the research questions.	− The sample size is large, limiting the detail that the researcher can capture. − The sample size is not consistent with the selected research design. − A weak rationale is provided to justify the sample size.
3. The data types are appropriate.	+ The data types are clearly well suited for learning about the central phenomenon with the selected participants.	− There are concerns that the data types are poorly suited for learning about the central phenomenon with the selected participants.
4. The data are gathered using rigorous qualitative procedures.	+ The researchers gather information using open-ended forms to learn about participants' perspectives and experiences. + The researchers use emergent procedures to gain a thorough understanding, such as using probing questions, spending a lot of time at the site, or developing new data collection forms. + The researchers create an accurate record of the data such as an audiorecording or detailed field notes.	− The researchers convey their expectations about participants' perspectives and experiences by using closed-ended forms for gathering data. − The researchers use procedures that lead to a superficial understanding, such as asking many narrow questions, spending little time at the site, or keeping data collection forms fixed. − The researchers do not make an accurate, detailed record of the data, but only create summaries of the information.
5. Data collection issues are handled ethically and thoughtfully.	+ Appropriate permissions were secured. + Respectful treatment of the participants is demonstrated. + Field issues are thoughtfully discussed and indicate quality interactions between the researchers and participants.	− Permissions were not secured. − Procedures safeguarding participants are questionable and show lack of respect for participants. − Field issues are not thoughtfully considered and poor interactions occur between the researcher and the participants.
General Evaluation		
6. The selected participants are information rich.	+ The sites and participants clearly fit the study purpose. + The participants are clearly able to provide rich information about the central phenomenon under study.	− The sites and participants are a weak fit for the study purpose. − The participants can only provide limited information about the central phenomenon under study.
7. The database provides extensive and credible information about the central phenomenon.	+ The database is extensive, including detailed information gathered over a long time from multiple types of open-ended data, all clearly related to the central phenomenon and the study's intent.	− The database is limited, including superficial information gathered quickly from a single type of data, some of which is not clearly related to the central phenomenon or study intent.

Quality Criteria	Quality Rating				Your Evidence and/or Reasoning
	0 = Poor	1 = Fair	2 = Good	3 = Excellent	
The Key Elements					
1. The sampling strategy is appropriate and justified.					
2. The sample size is appropriate and justified.					
3. The data types are appropriate.					
4. The data are gathered using rigorous qualitative procedures.					
5. Data collection issues are handled ethically and thoughtfully.					
General Evaluation					
6. The selected participants are information rich.					
7. The database provides extensive and credible information about the central phenomenon.					
Overall Quality 0–10 = Low quality 11–16 = Adequate quality 17–21 = High quality	Total Score =				My Overall Assessment Is

FIGURE 10.4   **A Rating Scale for Evaluating the Participants and Data Collection in a Qualitative Research Report**

Figure 10.4 provides a convenient means for you to apply the quality criteria to evaluate the participants and data collection described within the Method section in any qualitative research report. For each of the criteria you locate, assign a quality rating from *fair* (1) to *excellent* (3), and document your evidence and/or reasoning behind the rating. If one of the criteria is missing or very poorly stated, then indicate *poor* (0) as your rating. Although research reports vary in the extent of discussion about the participants and data collection, a good qualitative study should still score well on most of the items listed in Figure 10.4. By adding up the rating scores for each of the criteria and using the suggested cutoff values provided at the bottom of the figure, you will have a quantitative measure that you can use to inform your overall assessment.

Reviewing What You've Learned To Do

- *Identify and understand the participants and data collection of a qualitative research study.*
  - ☐ The Method section of a qualitative research report contains information about where the study was conducted, who participated, the types of data gathered, and the data collection procedures and issues.
- *Describe a study's sample and identify the strategy used to select the sites and participants.*
  - ☐ The sample in a qualitative study includes the sites and individuals who were selected and agreed to participate in the research.
  - ☐ Qualitative researchers use a wide range of purposeful sampling strategies to select the best sites and participants for learning about their central phenomenon.
  - ☐ Qualitative researchers select a small number of sites and participants to learn about each one in depth.

- *Name the types of qualitative data researchers collect in their studies.*
  - ☐ The types of qualitative data include interviews, observations, documents, and audiovisual materials.
- *Understand the procedures that researchers used to collect qualitative data in their studies.*
  - ☐ When researchers gathered interviews, the key information includes why interviews were appropriate, the type of interviews used, how the questions were organized, and how the data were recorded. The types of interviews include focus groups, one-on-one interviews, telephone interviews, e-mail interviews, and open-ended questionnaire items.
  - ☐ When researchers gathered observations, the key information includes why observations were appropriate, the role of the observer, how the observational field notes were recorded, and how many observations were conducted. The different observational roles include a nonparticipant role, a participant role, and a changing role.
  - ☐ When researchers gathered documents, the key information includes the types of documents that were gathered and how they related to the central phenomenon. Documents may be public or private forms of information.
  - ☐ When researchers gathered audiovisual materials, the key information includes the types of materials that were gathered and how they related to the central phenomenon. Audiovisual materials may include videos, pictures, sounds, and objects.
- *Recognize the issues that occurred during data collection in a qualitative study.*
  - ☐ Ethical issues concern the welfare of a study's participants and include the researcher following ethical guidelines, respecting the rights of participants, and protecting participants' anonymity.
  - ☐ Field issues concern the challenges faced during data collection, such as the researcher working with a gatekeeper to gain access to a site, recruiting individuals to participate in the study, and interacting with participants during the research.
- *Evaluate the quality of the sample and collected data in a qualitative research report.*
  - ☐ The evaluation of a qualitative sample considers the sampling strategy used to select the participants, the number of participants in the sample, and the extent to which the participants can provide rich information about the central phenomenon.
  - ☐ The evaluation of the qualitative data collection considers the types of data gathered, the use of rigorous qualitative procedures, the way ethical and field issues are handled, and the extent to which the data provide extensive and credible information about the central phenomenon.

✓ **To assess what you've learned to do, click here to answer questions and receive instant feedback.**

Reading Research Articles

Carefully reread the qualitative adoption-of-pedagogical-tools study by Leko and Brownell (2011) found at the end of Chapter 9 (starting on p. 306) and the qualitative adolescent-homelessness study by Haldenby et al. (2007) at the end of Chapter 4 (starting on p. 148).

As you review each article, pay close attention to statements in which the authors described the participants and data collection in the Method section. Use the highlighting tool in the Pearson etext to indicate where the authors have provided information about the participants and data collection, and use the notetaking tool to add marginal notes that name each element you highlighted and note how each one is related to the study's qualitative approach. Among the elements you will want to find are:

1. Site
2. Participants
3. Sampling strategy
4. Sample size
5. Interviews
6. Observations

7. Documents
8. Audiovisual materials
9. Data collection procedures
10. Data collection issues (e.g., ethical issues and field issues)

Note, however, that sometimes authors do not describe all of the information about their participants—for example, they might not mention the site or how individuals were selected. In addition, authors often do not gather all possible forms of qualitative data—that is, they might not gather interviews, observations, documents, and/or audiovisual materials. If one of these elements or type of data is missing, indicate that in your marginal notes.

 Click here to go to the qualitative adoption-of-pedagogical-tools study by Leko and Brownell (2011) so that you can enter marginal notes about the study.

 Click here to go to the qualitative adolescent-homelessness study by Haldenby et al. (2007) so that you can enter marginal notes about the study.

Understanding Research Articles

Apply your knowledge of the content of this chapter to the qualitative adoption-of-pedagogical-tools study by Leko and Brownell (2011) starting on p. 306.

1. From what sites and participants did the researchers collect their qualitative data in the adoption-of-pedagogical-tools study? Did they purposefully sample a small number of participants and sites?

2. What type(s) of data did the authors collect to learn about the process of adopting pedagogical tools? In what ways did these types of data fit (or not fit) the study's purpose?

3. What procedures did the researchers describe related to their qualitative data collection?

4. What are some examples of ethical and field issues that confronted the researchers in this study?

✓ **Click here to answer the questions and receive instant feedback.**

Evaluating Research Articles

Practice evaluating a qualitative study's participants and data collection, using the qualitative adoption-of-pedagogical-tools study by Leko and Brownell (2011) starting on p. 306 and the qualitative adolescent-homelessness study by Haldenby et al. (2007) starting on p. 148.

1. Use the criteria discussed in Table 10.3 to evaluate the quality of the participants and data collection in the adoption-of-pedagogical-tools study. Note that, for this question, the rating form includes advice to help guide your evaluation.

✓ **Click here to open the rating scale form (Figure 10.4) to enter your ratings, evidence, and reasoning.**

2. Use the criteria discussed in Table 10.3 to evaluate the quality of the participants and data collection in the adolescent-homelessness study. Note that, for this question, the rating form does NOT include additional advice.

✓ **Click here to open the rating scale form (Figure 10.4) to enter your ratings, evidence, and reasoning.**

11 DATA ANALYSIS AND FINDINGS: EXAMINING WHAT WAS FOUND IN A QUALITATIVE STUDY

If you are similar to most consumers of research, then the main reason you read research is to find out what researchers have learned about topics and problems that are important to you. You are therefore probably most interested in examining the findings when you read qualitative research reports. To understand qualitative findings, however, you need to know how researchers describe their qualitative analysis process in the Method sections of their reports in addition to understanding the forms by which they report their qualitative findings in the Results sections. In this chapter, you will learn to interpret information about how researchers analyze data and present their findings in qualitative research studies.

BY THE END OF THIS CHAPTER, YOU SHOULD BE ABLE TO:

- Identify and understand the data analysis and findings of a qualitative research study.
- List the steps that researchers report using to analyze qualitative data.
- Know how to identify results in the form of description and themes when reading a qualitative research report.
- Evaluate the quality of the data analysis and findings in a qualitative research report.

Research would not be research without the analysis of collected data. It is an essential step and, in qualitative research in particular, it can be the step in the research process that requires the most time and effort from the researcher. Despite all the work that researchers put into their qualitative data analysis, they often report only a paragraph or two about *how* they analyzed the data and instead focus much attention in their reports on the actual *findings* that emerged from the analysis. As a reader of research, however, you need to understand both the process researchers use to analyze qualitative data and how the results of this process are reported to fully appreciate and evaluate the findings presented in a qualitative research report. Let's start by considering how you identify data analysis and results when reading qualitative research.

How Do You Identify the Data Analysis and Findings in a Qualitative Study?

Recall from Chapter 1 that data analysis is the process that researchers use to make sense of and summarize the data that they gathered in order to address their research questions. In Chapter 8, you learned that quantitative researchers use procedures such as descriptive and inferential statistics to analyze the numeric data that they gathered in their studies. Because qualitative researchers gather extensive amounts of text and image data as part of their studies, they use qualitative analytic procedures that are appropriate for analyzing open-ended text and visual data. You can find information about the procedures that a researcher used to analyze the data by reading the Method section of the report. The qualitative data analysis process results in products such as descriptions of people and themes about the study's central phenomenon. These products are the findings of the qualitative study, which you can locate by turning to the report's Results section. That is, you need to look in two sections of the report to learn about data analysis and findings.

Look to the Method Section for an Overview of the Qualitative Analysis Process

You can find authors' discussions of the data analysis process in the Method section of a qualitative research article, usually immediately following the discussion of the data collection procedures. In many studies, the authors use a subheading of *Data Analysis* to help you find the information, but in other studies you need to figure out where in the Method section data analysis is discussed. Generally, authors provide only an overview of the steps they took to analyze the data. Although this description may be brief, it informs you about key steps that occurred in the analysis process. Read the following information that Haldenby et al. (2007) provided in the Method section of the qualitative adolescent-homelessness study for a description of their study's data analysis process. As you read, think about the different steps that the researchers report taking to analyze the data they gathered in the study.

> ### Data Analysis
> All interviews were audio-recorded and transcribed verbatim as soon as possible following the interview. Transcripts were reviewed by the interviewer for accuracy. Once transcription was completed, a narrative style of analysis was conducted with the assistance of Atlas-Ti, a qualitative software program. This process involved several readings of the transcripts to capture initial impressions (Lieblich et al., 1998). More focused codes were then developed as ideas surfaced from the narratives. The code list was continuously revised to accommodate new perspectives and to collapse overlapping categories. The focused code list guided the analysis, and more abstract themes evolved from the transcribed stories. Attention was paid to both the content of the story and the way in which it was told (Lieblich et al., 1998).
>
> Zimmerman and West (1987) have argued that society "invisibly" guides people to behave socially within the dichotomous norms of femininity and masculinity. It is therefore thought that gender is embedded in our everyday experiences (Zimmerman & West, 1987), which influence how youth create different meanings out of similar circumstances. Social understandings of gender and their influence on the narratives were therefore considered throughout the analysis. Ideas that emerged from the transcripts that did not fit the evolving code list were recognized as important and considered throughout the analysis. In all cases except for the one boy/girl group interview, young women's and young men's transcripts were initially analyzed separately. Finally, dominant themes were identified, and conclusions were made. (paragraphs 29–30)

This passage conveys details about the general steps used by researchers to analyze qualitative data. These steps included:

- *Preparing the data.* The researchers transcribed the interview conversations from the audiorecordings made during each interview. The person who conducted the interview checked to make sure that each transcription was accurate. The transcripts were loaded into a special computer software program (called ATLAS.ti) that was used during the analysis.
- *Exploring the data.* Once the transcripts were prepared, the researchers then read through them several times to become familiar with the information and to form some initial ideas about the data.
- *Coding the data.* The researchers next began to assign "codes" to the data and worked to develop a refined list of codes that identified the major ideas and perspectives in the data. They also describe how their conceptual framework about the importance of gender informed aspects of their analysis and coding.
- *Developing description and themes.* As a result of their coding, the researchers identified "abstract themes" that emerged from the analysis of the data. Themes are the larger patterns or ideas found across different sources of qualitative data. The major themes found in the data became the major findings of the study.
- *Validating the findings.* The researchers also provided a little information about how they ensured that the findings were credible and trustworthy. Specifically, they noted that they actively attended to any ideas found in the data that did not seem to

fit their list of codes. By stating that they were open to considering information that was contrary to their early results, the researchers are assuring readers that they can trust that the final results represent the perspectives that were in the data, not just what the researchers were expecting to find.

Look to the Results Section for the Qualitative Findings Produced by the Analysis Process

Authors typically devote a great deal of attention to describing what was found as a result of the qualitative data analysis process. Because of the importance of the results in a qualitative research article, they are reported in their own major section, immediately after the Method section. This section may be called *Results* like in most quantitative studies, but qualitative investigators often prefer to use the word *Findings* as the heading for this section because they feel it better conveys that the researcher was open to having learned from participants. A good strategy for reading a Findings section is to look at the opening paragraph for an overview of what was learned in the study to help you understand the details presented in the section. For example, read how Haldenby et al. (2007) provided an overview of their major findings at the start of the Findings section in the qualitative adolescent-homelessness study:

Findings
All participants appeared eager to share their stories and did so in an insightful way. From their narratives five themes emerged: (a) the realities of exiting street life, (b) negotiating dangerous terrain, (c) rethinking family, (d) the hazards of being female, and (e) the elusive nature of health and the health care system. Because critical research invites reflection into the contextual factors that shape and influence a person's experience, a separate analysis of current Canadian policy was completed. These findings will be addressed in relation to the participants' stories. (paragraph 31)

> *Here's a Tip!*
>
> Look for subheadings to help you identify the major results of a qualitative study when you read the Findings section of a report. Often researchers use a subheading for each major theme that was found.

From reading this short paragraph, we can expect to locate information about five themes in the Findings section. In addition, we learn that the researchers describe the contexts (e.g., being poor and having trouble continuing their education) that emerged as important for understanding the participants' homeless experiences. If we keep reading, we will find six subheadings in the Findings section—one for each of the five themes and one for the contexts. Description and themes are the typical products that result from the qualitative analysis process. To understand and evaluate the results that authors report in their qualitative studies, you next need to know more about the qualitative analysis process.

How Do You Understand a Study's Qualitative Data Analysis?

Individuals who are unfamiliar with qualitative data analysis procedures often think that it must be very simple: The researcher talks to a few individuals and then writes up a summary of what was said. Good qualitative data analysis, however, is *not* simply summarizing what people had to say. Qualitative data analysis should be a systematic, rigorous, and thoughtful process that researchers use to uncover detailed descriptions of and larger patterns about the central phenomenon from the collected data. You need to be able to recognize the different activities involved in this process as they are described in reports and to assess whether the reported information indicates the use of good qualitative procedures.

You can visualize the major activities in the qualitative data analysis process by examining the bottom-up approach to qualitative data analysis in Figure 11.1. This process is called bottom-up (also referred to as *inductive*) because the researcher works from all the detailed data (e.g., typed interview texts or observational field notes) up to a

**FIGURE 11.1
The Bottom-Up
Approach to
the Process of
Qualitative
Data Analysis**

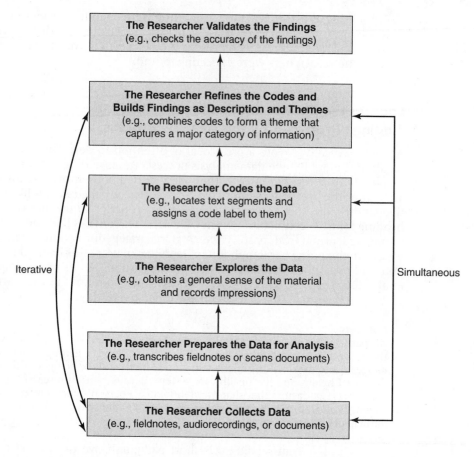

few general patterns (e.g., codes and themes). As shown in the figure, once qualitative researchers collect data, they implement several activities to inductively build up from the data. These activities include preparing the data for analysis, developing a general sense of the data, coding the data, developing findings in the forms of description and themes from the codes, and using strategies to ensure the accuracy of the findings.

The activities shown in Figure 11.1 can be challenging to identify in many qualitative reports because a good qualitative analysis process is an interpretive and dynamic process that is not easily reported in clearly defined steps. The process is *interpretive* because qualitative researchers make personal assessments throughout the process to determine a description that fits the situation or themes that capture the major categories of information. This means that each qualitative researcher brings his/her own perspective to all aspects of the qualitative analysis process. The process is considered dynamic because qualitative researchers often implement the different activities *simultaneously* and *iteratively*. Implementing the process simultaneously means that researchers are involved in more than one activity at any point in time (e.g., preparing the data from one interview while building results from an earlier interview). Implementing the process iteratively means that researchers cycle back and forth between data collection and analysis to ensure they develop the best understanding. For example, researchers might have collected stories from individuals, and as the analysis of the stories proceeds, they may return to the participants for more information to fill in gaps in their stories.

Knowing that qualitative data analysis is inductive, interpretive, simultaneous, and iterative should help you identify some important differences between how researchers report analyzing qualitative data compared to analyzing quantitative data. For example, in quantitative research the investigator completes data collection first and then moves to data analysis. The traditional quantitative process is much more linear than the simultaneous and iterative process used in most qualitative studies. In quantitative research, the researcher also works to remove him- or herself from the process by using procedures such as objective criteria to determine the outcomes of hypothesis tests, which differs from the interpretive and inductive process used in good qualitative research. Keeping these features in mind as you read about how researchers analyzed their qualitative data helps you understand that qualitative researchers use a data analysis process that is different from that used in quantitative research.

Although the qualitative data analysis process reported in a study can be complicated because of its inductive, interpretive, simultaneous, and iterative nature, a good strategy for understanding the overall process is to identify how the researcher implemented each of the major steps shown in Figure 11.1. The steps to look for include how the researchers:

- prepared the data;
- explored the data;
- coded the data;
- refined the codes and developed findings from the codes; and
- validated the findings.

Let's consider key elements that appear during each of these steps and what kinds of information you can learn when reading researchers' reports of their qualitative data analysis process.

Step 1—Identify How the Researchers Prepared Their Data

The first step to look for is data preparation. Because of the vast amount of open-ended information collected in most qualitative studies, researchers must take steps to prepare an accurate and detailed record of the data that can be used during the analysis process. You should remember from Chapter 10 that qualitative researchers obtain images and sounds from documents or audiovisual materials and obtain words through interviewing participants or by writing field notes during observations. When researchers collect images, audiovisual materials, or documents, they usually prepare these data by creating digital copies (such as by scanning a document) that can be used for analysis purposes. When the data are in the form of words, such as from interviews or field notes, then data preparation is more involved. In these situations, researchers need to convert the collected words into typed text.

When considering the preparation of text data in a research study, read carefully to learn how the data were prepared and who did the preparation; also, ascertain the accuracy of the data preparation and the completeness of the data preparation. The most common procedure that researchers use to prepare text-based data from interviews and observations is called transcription. **Transcription** is the process of converting audio recordings or field notes into typed text. Researchers may transcribe the information themselves or they may use a transcriptionist to type the text files. It is best if the person who gathered the data prepares the transcription, but it is not always feasible, particularly in large projects with extensive databases. The most accurate procedure is for the researcher to type the transcriptions verbatim. *Verbatim* means that the researcher types *all* spoken words as well as unspoken events such as [*pause*] to indicate when interviewees take a lengthy break in their comments or [*laughter*] when the interviewee laughs. A verbatim transcript of a 30-minute interview typically results in 10–15 pages of single-spaced text, and qualitative studies that include several interviews include the preparation of hundreds of pages of verbatim transcripts. The most complete procedure occurs when the researcher transcribes all of the gathered interviews and observational notes so that all the data can be included in the formal analysis. In some studies, researchers report that they prepared summaries of the collected data instead of verbatim transcriptions. The use of summaries may occur when a recorder failed to record an interview because of mechanical problems or when the researcher's resources for transcription are limited. Although summaries are sometimes necessary, verbatim transcription of the entire database is best because that provides the researcher with the most accurate and complete record of the collected data.

When reading about data preparation, also note how the researcher organized the database to facilitate the analysis process. Qualitative researchers organize their database in order to analyze the data by hand or by using a computer. Researchers report this detail so that readers better understand how they worked with the data during the full analysis process. Here is an overview of how researchers implement these two options so you can recognize them when reading reports:

- *Analyzing qualitative data by hand* indicates that researchers read the data, mark them by hand, and divide them into parts by hand. Traditionally, analyzing text data by hand involves using colored highlighting markers to mark parts of the text or cutting and pasting (with scissors and tape!) text sentences onto cards. For example, note how Rushton (2004) described analyzing his data by hand in a study of one preservice teacher's experience: "I began to index themes with various highlighted colors and with notes in the margins" (p. 65). For this style of analysis, the researcher prepares printed copies of the transcripts so they are available for marking. A hand analysis is most appropriate in projects with relatively small databases (e.g., less than 500 pages of text).
- *Analyzing qualitative data by using a computer* indicates that researchers use a computer program to facilitate the process of analyzing qualitative data. Unlike the statistical computer programs used to analyze quantitative data, qualitative computer programs *do not* analyze the data for researchers. They do, however, provide several features that help researchers analyze qualitative databases. These features include storing data, enabling the researcher to assign labels or codes to the data, and facilitating searching through the data and locating text assigned to specific codes. (We will learn more about coding shortly.) Computer-assisted analysis is ideal for studies that have large databases. For this style of analysis, the researcher prepares the transcripts and uploads them into a qualitative data analysis program. You can note that researchers analyzed the data by using a computer when they name a specific software program in their reports. For example, Churchill et al. (2007) identified the particular software program (called MAXqda) used for data analysis in their study on rural family well-being by stating: "The qualitative portions of the one-on-one interviews were audiotaped and transcribed verbatim and entered into a MAXqda database for analysis" (p. 278).

Step 2—Note Whether the Researchers Explored Their Data

Once you know how the researchers prepared the qualitative data for their analysis, you should expect to find that they started the formal analysis by exploring the data. A **preliminary exploratory analysis** in qualitative research consists of the researcher reading through the data to obtain a general sense of the data, recording initial ideas, thinking about the organization of the data, and considering whether more data are needed. This step is important in qualitative research because the researcher should have an understanding of the data as a whole before starting to break the data into the different perspectives and ideas. Look for evidence of this exploratory analysis in research reports. For example, Landreman, Rasmussen, King, and Jiang (2007) noted this step in their study about multicultural educators when they wrote: "Each team member read every transcript to gain a sense of the whole experience communicated by participants" (p. 279).

A key strategy that researchers use when exploring the data is to keep records of their thoughts and ideas. These records are often referred to as *memos* in qualitative research. Researchers write memos in the margins of transcripts, under photographs, in personal journals, or with their computers or tablets to help in initially exploring the data. These memos are short phrases, ideas, concepts, or hunches that occur to the researcher. In a good qualitative analysis, researchers continue to memo their ideas during the entire data analysis to document their interpretations throughout the process; these memos often become many pages or files of the researcher's personal reflections. Because the use of memos is indicative of good qualitative analysis procedures, you should note their use when reading about a study's data analysis. For example, read how Havstam and colleagues (2011) mentioned their use of memos when describing the data analysis in their qualitative study of young adults who had been born with a cleft lip: "Memos were written by the first author during the analysis process and shared with the co-writers" (p. 25).

Step 3—Discern the Researchers' Use of Coding

After reading about how the data were prepared and explored in a qualitative study, you should next look for information about how the researchers coded the data. **Coding** is a procedure where a researcher identifies segments of text (or images), places a bracket around them or highlights them, and assigns a code that describes the meaning of the text segment. **Codes** are labels that the researcher uses to describe the meaning of a segment of text or an image in relation to the study's central phenomenon. Codes can address many different topics, including participants' feelings, perspectives, strategies, contexts, behaviors, or language. For example, in a study about how patients manage their chronic pain, the researcher might identify the following text segment from an interview with a participant: "I am so worried about what will happen if my pain gets any worse. How will I continue to work and support my family if that happens?" When considering the meaning of this segment, the researcher might choose to use a code label of *anxiety about the future* because the participant is expressing his concern about future events. As the researcher continues to code the data in the study, she uses this code whenever patients describe concerns about the future. She also develops several different codes including, for example, codes about participants' feelings (e.g., *anxiety about the future* and *frustration*), perspectives (e.g., *the role of physicians* and *medication preferences*), strategies (e.g., *using a pillbox* and *resting*), and contexts (e.g., *home environment* and *work setting*). Coding is at the heart of qualitative data analysis and is used in all qualitative research designs. It helps to make qualitative data analysis rigorous because the researcher considers all the ideas in the data by coding all of the gathered information; because the codes represent the researcher's interpretations of the data, these interpretations are necessarily linked to and build from the data.

Researchers determine their codes in different ways. You should therefore look for information about how they chose their codes when reading reports of the data analysis process. In some qualitative projects, researchers start with specific topics of interest, and they use these topics as codes to identify the data that relates to those topics. For example, in a study about student learning, the researcher's approach might be informed by a theory of motivation based on students' expectations of success, perceptions of the value of the information, and interest in the information. In this case, the researcher might plan to use three codes based on this theory, such as (1) *success expectations*, (2) *value perceptions*, and (3) *interest*. In many qualitative analyses, however, the researchers do not start with predetermined codes. These researchers read the data and create codes based on their interpretation of the meaning of the data. This is often referred to as *open coding* in reports because the researcher is open to the ideas that occur in the data. In open coding, the codes can be phrased in standard academic terms (e.g., a researcher referring to "academic achievement") or expressed in the researcher's own language (e.g., a statement about "teachers working together"). Researchers also state codes in the participant's actual words, which are called *in vivo* codes. For example, in a study of teacher evaluation where a participant noted that she feels like "big brother is watching," the researcher may choose to use *"big brother is watching"* as a code in the analysis for data that represents this perspective of the teacher evaluation process. Researchers may use all of these types of codes when analyzing their data.

To help you understand the process that researchers use to code their data, Figure 11.2 shows a sample transcript from an interview that has been coded by a researcher who used open coding to develop codes from the data. This transcript resulted from an interview for a project exploring changes in the curriculum in a rural high school (Jones, 1999). Overall, the interviewee talks about changes in the high school from a school based on a traditional curriculum to a school based on service learning in the community. Jones asks questions during the interview and "LU," the interviewee, provides responses. Notice the following features of the coding process illustrated in this figure.

- The researcher located sentences that seem to "fit together" to describe one idea and drew a bracket around them. These represent text segments.
- The researcher assigned a code label to each text segment and recorded the codes on the left side. The researcher used only two or three words for each code label. In

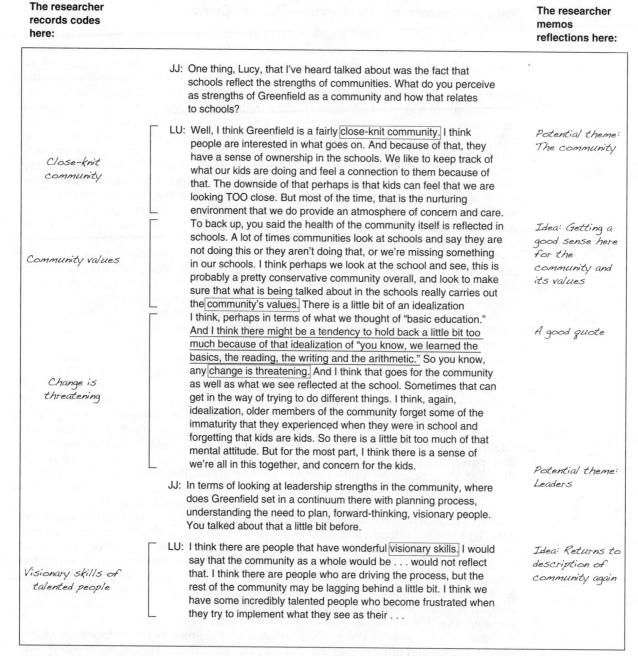

The researcher records codes here:

The researcher memos reflections here:

JJ: One thing, Lucy, that I've heard talked about was the fact that schools reflect the strengths of communities. What do you perceive as strengths of Greenfield as a community and how that relates to schools?

Close-knit community

LU: Well, I think Greenfield is a fairly close-knit community. I think people are interested in what goes on. And because of that, they have a sense of ownership in the schools. We like to keep track of what our kids are doing and feel a connection to them because of that. The downside of that perhaps is that kids can feel that we are looking TOO close. But most of the time, that is the nurturing environment that we do provide an atmosphere of concern and care.

Potential theme: The community

Community values

To back up, you said the health of the community itself is reflected in schools. A lot of times communities look at schools and say they are not doing this or they aren't doing that, or we're missing something in our schools. I think perhaps we look at the school and see, this is probably a pretty conservative community overall, and look to make sure that what is being talked about in the schools really carries out the community's values. There is a little bit of an idealization

Idea: Getting a good sense here for the community and its values

I think, perhaps in terms of what we thought of "basic education." And I think there might be a tendency to hold back a little bit too much because of that idealization of "you know, we learned the basics, the reading, the writing and the arithmetic." So you know, any change is threatening. And I think that goes for the community as well as what we see reflected at the school. Sometimes that can

A good quote

Change is threatening

get in the way of trying to do different things. I think, again, idealization, older members of the community forget some of the immaturity that they experienced when they were in school and forgetting that kids are kids. So there is a little bit too much of that mental attitude. But for the most part, I think there is a sense of we're all in this together, and concern for the kids.

JJ: In terms of looking at leadership strengths in the community, where does Greenfield set in a continuum there with planning process, understanding the need to plan, forward-thinking, visionary people. You talked about that a little bit before.

Potential theme: Leaders

Visionary skills of talented people

LU: I think there are people that have wonderful visionary skills. I would say that the community as a whole would be . . . would not reflect that. I think there are people who are driving the process, but the rest of the community may be lagging behind a little bit. I think we have some incredibly talented people who become frustrated when they try to implement what they see as their . . .

Idea: Returns to description of community again

FIGURE 11.2   Example of How a Researcher Coded a Page from an Interview Transcript
Source: Reprinted with permission of Jean E. Jones, Ph.D.

some cases, these were the actual words used by the participant, "LU," which are examples of in vivo codes.

■ The researcher also recorded reflections (e.g., "getting a good sense here for the community and its values") and potential big ideas (e.g., "community") on the right side as memos.

Although qualitative researchers almost always code their data, they seldom include examples of coded transcripts or list all of their codes in their reports. By understanding what it means to code, however, you can better understand the process that the researcher describes using in a study. It is often helpful to note whether the author provided examples of codes that were used because even a few examples can help you to understand the types of codes in a study. For example, Whitney et al. (2012) listed several codes used in their qualitative data analysis in their study of how teachers wrote reports for publication. These codes included *environments, audience, authority, confidence, identity,* and *risk-taking* (pp. 418–419).

Step 4—Examine How the Researchers Refined Their Codes and Used Them to Build Their Results

Although coding is a key part of qualitative data analysis, simply coding all of the data does not provide useful results in qualitative research. Researchers use procedures to refine their codes and group them together into larger ideas to build their results. As you read the Method section of a qualitative report, you should look for information that explains how the researchers built their findings from the codes and coded data. The visual model in Figure 11.3 will help you understand the process that researchers use. The overall objective of this process is for the inquirer to make sense of the database by dividing it into many text or image segments, labeling the segments with codes, examining codes for overlap and redundancy, and grouping these codes into broad themes. This is why qualitative data analysis is considered to be an inductive process because the researcher starts with lots of data segments and builds up from the data to several codes and then to a few themes.

As Figure 11.3 indicates, in addition to coding the data, qualitative researchers continually evaluate the list of codes they have generated. As they code more of the data, they work to combine codes that represent redundant ideas. For example, a researcher who initially has the codes *happiness* and *enjoyment* might decide they actually represent the same idea in the data and combine the text segments under one code of *happiness.* Researchers also work to group similar codes together during the coding process. For example, the codes of *happiness, feeling at peace,* and *excitement* might be grouped together by the researcher, who then labels this group as *positive emotions* found in the data.

As the researchers make sense of the data, they try to reduce the total number of codes to a manageable number, such as 20 or 30, which represent the most important ideas about the central phenomenon. As the list of codes is refined, the researcher uses the codes to build the study's findings to form answers to the research questions. **Describing and developing themes from the data** consists of answering the major research questions and forming an in-depth understanding of the central phenomenon through description, thematic development, and relating themes. You will find researchers using an assortment of terms to refer to variations of the process of refining codes and building findings, such as *analytic induction, constant comparison,* or *thematic development,* but each of these can be understood by considering the same general procedure

**FIGURE 11.3
A Model of the
Process of
Coding, Refining
Codes, and
Building
Qualitative
Findings**

Source: Adapted from
Creswell (2008).

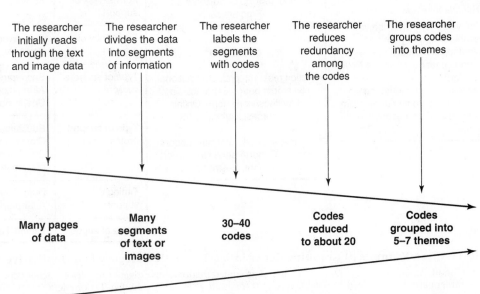

depicted in Figure 11.3. By understanding this general qualitative procedure, you can make sense of the specific process described in the Method section as well as the findings included in the report's Results section. Let's examine how researchers build these three types of qualitative findings in more detail.

Researchers Build Description.   A **description** in qualitative research is a detailed rendering of people, places, or events that provide the context for a qualitative research study. The researcher uses codes that include descriptive information about the people, events, and places to access the text segments in the data that provide the descriptive information. For example, in a study about classroom learning environments, the researcher might use descriptive codes such as *seating arrangements, teaching approach,* or *physical layout of the room* to locate all the text in the database that specifically relates to the classroom in order to build a description of the classroom where instruction takes place. Building description is an important type of result in many qualitative research studies. In providing a detailed description as part of the results, the researcher aims to transport the reader to a research site or help the reader visualize a person. In some forms of qualitative research design, such as in ethnography or in case studies, the researcher pays careful attention to building a description of the setting during the data analysis. Developing detail is important for these designs, and the researcher analyzes data from all sources (e.g., interviews, observations, documents) to build a portrait of individuals and events.

Researchers Build Themes.   In addition to description, the development of themes is another way that researchers build results as they analyze qualitative data. **Themes** (also called *categories*) are similar codes aggregated together to form a major idea about the central phenomenon in the database. They form a core result from qualitative data analysis. Like codes, themes have labels that typically consist of only a few words (e.g., "self-tensions" or "science identities"). They represent larger patterns in the data that emerged from the analysis. Examine Figure 11.4 for an example of how Kirchhoff and Lawrenz (2011), in a study about the role of teacher education in the careers of science

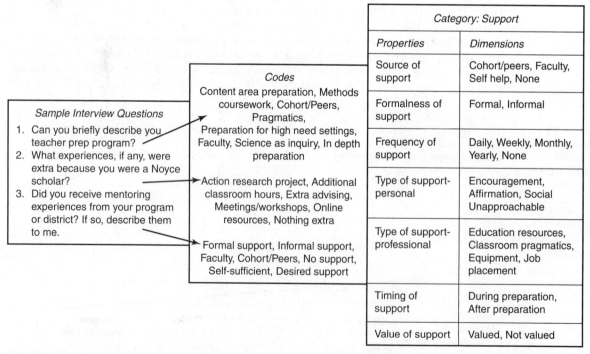

FIGURE 11.4   An Example of Grouping Codes into a Thematic Category in a Qualitative Research Study

Source: Kirchhoff, A., & Lawrenz, F. (2011). The use of grounded theory to investigate the role of teacher education on STEM teachers' career paths in high-need schools. *Journal of Teacher Education, 62*(3), 250, Fig. 1. Copyright © 2011 by Sage Publications. Reprinted by permission of Sage Publications, Inc.

teachers, aggregated many codes together into the thematic category of "support" during their analysis. In the left box in Figure 11.4, the authors give examples of some of the questions that were asked during interviews to gather data from the participating science teachers. In the middle box, they list many of the codes (e.g., "Content area preparation," "Cohort/Peers," and "Pragmatics") that emerged as they initially analyzed the data from these questions. Upon reflecting on the many codes, the authors refined the codes and grouped several of them together to form a category that they named "support." In the right box of the figure, the authors identify this larger category (i.e., "support") as well as list the subthemes (or "properties") and different perspectives (or "dimensions") found within the data for the "support" category. They used a similar process to develop several categories during their analysis, including "preparation for high-need settings," "desire to make a difference," and "educational role models."

When reading about how a researcher developed themes in a qualitative study, try to identify how many themes emerged from the data analysis. A good rule of thumb is to expect qualitative researchers to develop five to seven themes from their codes as their qualitative results. The development of a small number of themes is appropriate so that the researcher can provide detailed information about a few themes rather than superficial information about many themes. The reason that the number of themes is typically not less than five is so that the results include a sufficient number of major ideas to adequately convey the complexity of the central phenomenon under study.

Researchers Relate Multiple Themes.   Many qualitative studies in the literature stop their data analysis with the development of description and themes. In more sophisticated studies, however, the authors discuss using procedures for relating the themes to each other. The researchers may describe these procedures in their Method section, such as in many grounded theory studies where the researchers report using specific procedures (called axial and selective coding) to relate the themes into a theory. In many studies, however, the researchers do not provide much detail about how they related multiple themes, and you have to deduce the use of these procedures by examining the results reported in the Results section (we will learn more about qualitative results later in this chapter). Two examples of how researchers relate multiple themes are layering the themes and interconnecting the themes. Understanding these two approaches will help you make sense of the procedures reported in many qualitative studies.

- *Layering the themes* means that the researcher represents the data using embedded levels of themes. This occurs when the researcher subsumes minor themes within major themes and then includes major themes within broader themes. The entire analysis becomes more and more complex as the researcher works *upward* toward broader levels of abstraction. For example, Asmussen and Creswell (1995) layered their themes in their case study about a campus reaction to a gunman incident by subsuming their five major themes (denial, fear, safety, retriggering, and campus planning) within two broader themes (organizational and psychological/social-psychological). In an ethnographic study of how parents of color support their children's preparation for college, Auerbach (2007) subsumed her six major themes (e.g., mode of support and locus of support) within three types of parent roles that she named "moral supporters," "struggling advocates," and "ambivalent companions" (p. 260).
- *Interconnecting the themes* means that the researcher connects the themes into some sort of a larger order of ideas. For example, this larger order might be a chronology, such as when researchers connect the themes to tell a larger story found in the data. Plano Clark et al. (2002) interconnected their five major themes in a larger story in their study of adolescent tobacco use. Note how the following statement explains these connections:

> As we report these themes in the next section, we organize them into a story line about adolescent use of tobacco. This story line reports how individuals begin smoking; how smoking becomes a pervasive influence in school lives; how attitudes are formed about smoking at school and in personal lives; how these attitudes, in turn, shape what it means to be a smoker; and, ultimately, how these experiences influence student suggestions for tobacco use prevention. (p. 1269)

Connecting themes into a chronology can be useful in different forms of qualitative research, including narrative research in particular. Researchers also interconnect themes into a sequence of relationships, such as when qualitative researchers generate a theoretical model in grounded theory studies. These interconnections convey how certain themes are found to influence or relate to other themes and researchers often develop a visual model to depict the connections. For example, Churchill and colleagues (2007) described interconnecting their themes about how rural low-income families have fun during analysis with the following statement:

> As the thematic categories emerged from the data, we proceeded to the step of theory development. We continually refined the organization and interrelation of the thematic categories during the coding process and a conceptual visual model was developed based on the qualitative findings of this analysis. (p. 278)

Step 5—Identify the Strategies the Researchers Used to Validate Their Results

Once you have identified the previous aspects of the qualitative data analysis process, the last step is to look for evidence that the researchers used strategies to validate the quality of their findings. **Validating findings** means that the researchers use strategies to ensure the accuracy and credibility of the findings as part of the analysis process. In qualitative research, the findings that emerged from the data analysis process should be *accurate* and *credible* representations of the gathered data and participants' experiences. Other terms that authors use to convey the quality of their results are *trustworthiness* and *dependability*. All of these terms aim to ensure that the researchers used a good data analysis process while also acknowledging that this process is very interpretive and subjective. Therefore, qualitative researchers use strategies to validate their findings that emphasize the nature of qualitative data and the qualitative data analysis process. Although you may find authors describing many different strategies for validating their qualitative findings in reports, our attention here is on four forms frequently reported by qualitative researchers: bracketing, triangulation, member checking, and auditing.

- Because qualitative data analysis is an interpretive process, researchers reflect on their personal viewpoints and how they shape their interpretations of the data. One way that researchers address this issue is through bracketing. **Bracketing** is a process by which a researcher reflects on his or her own views and experiences related to the study's central phenomenon, describes these perspectives in writing, and then works to set them aside (or "bracket" them) during the analysis process. Although personal bias can never be totally eliminated, bracketing helps to ensure that the researcher's perspectives do not overwhelm the perspectives of the participants and therefore enhances the credibility of the study's findings.
- Qualitative inquirers also triangulate information from different data sources to enhance the credibility of a study. **Triangulation** is the process of corroborating evidence about a finding from different individuals (e.g., a principal and a student) or types of data (e.g., observational field notes and interviews). The inquirer examines each information source and finds evidence to support a theme. This helps to ensure that the themes found in a study are credible representations of people's experiences and perspectives because the information draws on multiple sources of information or individuals.
- Researchers check their findings with participants in the study to determine whether their findings are accurate. **Member checking** is a process in which the researcher asks one or more participants to check the accuracy of the findings. This process involves taking the findings back to participants and asking them (in writing or in an interview) about the accuracy of the report. Researchers ask participants about many aspects of the study, such as whether the description is complete and realistic, the themes are appropriate, and the interpretations are fair and representative of their perspectives.
- Researchers may also ask a person *outside* the project to conduct an **audit** of the procedures used in a study. This can be as simple as having a second researcher independently code some of the data to see whether there is agreement on the major

ideas found in the data. Some studies may include a peer review of the entire study's methods. A researcher using peer review discusses his/her research process with a knowledgeable colleague to review the data collection and analysis procedures as they unfold during the study. The most formal procedure occurs when a researcher obtains the services of an individual outside the study to review different aspects of the research and report back, in writing, the strengths and weaknesses of the project. This formal process is called an external audit and is the most extensive of the audit strategies.

What Do You Think?

In a qualitative study aimed at understanding women's experiences of divorce, Thomas and Ryan (2008) provided the following information about their data analysis process. As you read the passage, consider which sentences relate to each of the five steps for understanding a study's data analysis process: (1) data preparation, (2) data exploration, (3) data coding, (4) code refinement and building results, and (5) validation strategies. Each sentence is labeled [A, B, and so on] to make it easier to refer to the individual statements.

[A] Following the interviews the researcher transcribed the audiotapes verbatim. . . . [B] The data analysis was completed using a method similar to Strauss and Corbin's (1998) microanalysis techniques and procedures for grounded theory. [C] This method required the researcher to read the transcriptions line by line several times to become immersed in the data. [D] Notes were made to identify specific words or phrases that stood out to construct the initial categories that are termed microanalysis. [E] Specific themes were identified from the phrases to construct initial categories based on the coding process. [F] Validity was addressed in this study through checking the responses with the participants and by creating an atmosphere of openness for the researcher and participants. [G] Evidence was weighed with existing literature to validate findings. [H] Contrasts and comparisons were made based on feedback sought from informants to validate findings as recommended by Miles and Huberman (1994). (Thomas & Ryan, 2008, p. 213)

Check Your Understanding

The authors provided information that relates to each of the five steps for understanding a qualitative data analysis process.

1. *Data preparation.* They indicated that the data were transcribed verbatim in [A], but did not provide any indication as to whether the analysis was conducted by hand or assisted by a computer in this extract.
2. *Data exploration.* They indicated the use of a preliminary exploratory analysis in [C] by referring to reading each transcript "to become immersed in the data."
3. *Data coding.* They mentioned that they constructed "categories" in [D] and specifically referred to their use of a "coding process" in [E].
4. *Code refinement and building results.* The authors indicated the development of themes from the categories in [E]. If we keep reading the full article, we learn that this process identified eight themes that are reported as the study's findings.
5. *Validation strategies.* The authors also discussed several strategies that they used to ensure the quality of the study's findings. In [F] and [H], they referred to forms of member checking in which they had participants react to and provide feedback about the results of the analysis. In [G], they mentioned the use of a strategy of comparing the emergent findings with the existing literature.

How Do You Understand the Findings in a Qualitative Study?

Once you have read how researchers analyzed their qualitative data in the Method section of a qualitative report, you should next read their findings in response to their research questions. As mentioned earlier in this chapter, the section of a qualitative report where you can locate the findings of the study is typically labeled as *Results* or *Findings*. Although the use of one of these terms is most common, as you learned in Chapter 2, qualitative research reports tend to be more flexible in their structure than are quantitative research reports. This flexible structure means that you may read qualitative studies where the results are not so clearly labeled. In some qualitative reports, you may find that the researchers titled the results section based on the content of the findings and/or included more than one results section. For example, in a study of a high school theater program, Larson and Brown (2007) used both of these approaches and followed their description of the study's methods with two sections where they reported the results of their analysis. They titled these results sections "The Experiential Setting of *Les Misérables*" (p. 1087) and "What Youth Learned and How" (p. 1091). There are even a few qualitative reports that include some results *before* the Method section. Although unusual, this may occur when a description of the people, setting, or event that is the focus of the study needs to be included early in the report so that the reader can understand the study's context. For example, in a case study of the reaction of a campus to a specific gunman incident, Asmussen and Creswell (1995) reported their description of the event in a section titled "The Incident and Response" before they discussed the methods used in the study.

Once you have located the findings reported in a qualitative study, your next step is to read and understand these findings. Researchers report their qualitative findings in order to answer their qualitative research questions about the study's central phenomenon. Therefore, it can be helpful to reread the study's research questions before reading the results because knowing what questions are being answered may help you to understand the findings that are reported. It is also useful to specifically look for several key characteristics of qualitative research findings as you read. These characteristics include:

- findings that report description,
- findings that report themes,
- tables and figures that convey additional details and complexity, and
- findings that fit the study's research design.

Let's learn about each of these characteristics, which should help you understand the findings reported in a qualitative research study.

Read Descriptive Findings to Learn the Context of the Study and the Central Phenomenon

When researchers analyze their databases for description, they report this description as part of their results. Recall that description is a detailed rendering of people, places, or events that are examined in a qualitative research study. You may find description reported as part of the results of any qualitative study, but you should particularly expect to find it when reading a case study or ethnography because those approaches describe a case or a culture-sharing group. When you read a good qualitative description, it should effectively transport you into the context of the research and help you get to know the people, setting, or events that are important in the study. These descriptions are key results to read because they provide you with information about the context for the study so that you can better understand the study's central phenomenon and better consider whether the results might be relevant to and useful for your own context.

When you read description about people in a qualitative study, you learn about the participants involved in the research. For example, in an ethnographic study about home literacy practices of Chinese Canadian families with young children, Li (2006) provided a description about the three families who were the focus of the study. These descriptions included many details, such as when each family immigrated to Canada, the background and professions of the parents, and the parents' language proficiency and attitudes toward living in Canada. Likewise, when you read the description about a study's setting, you learn about the environment in which the research took place. In a study about the stress experienced by music teachers at one high school, for example, Scheib (2003) included a description of the school that illustrated the larger community in which the school was located, including details such as the school's size, student demographics, and how each school day is structured. You will also find that researchers report descriptions of events important to research studies, such as specific programs, a typical school day, or a particular activity. Padilla (2003) conducted a qualitative study about one woman's experience of disability and included in his report a dramatic description of the events surrounding the accident that caused her serious head injury. In all of these examples, the descriptive results provide important contexts for more fully understanding the qualitative studies and their central phenomena.

Qualitative researchers use several features for reporting description. Knowing these features can help you read descriptive passages in reports, and understand and assess the presented information. To learn how to read qualitative description, examine part of a descriptive passage from a qualitative study about a professional development program for new teachers (Clayton, 2007). The passage in Figure 11.5 describes one of the teachers in the study, as taken from the author's report. The discussion of this teacher and events in her classroom illustrates several features of description used in good qualitative research reports, which have been highlighted with the labels in the margin of the figure. The features of good qualitative description include:

- *A broad-to-narrow description.* The descriptive passage starts with a broad focus of the day and teacher's context; then the focus narrows to the classroom's details and finally to the events in the classroom on this one day. Look for a broad-to-narrow description to understand the broader context of the study and to develop a sense of the real place where the study is located.
- *Vivid details.* The author uses vivid details to create the description. We know, for example, what is posted on the bulletin boards and what announcements are written on the chalkboard. Noticing the vivid details helps you better understand the uniqueness of the particular people and setting in a study.

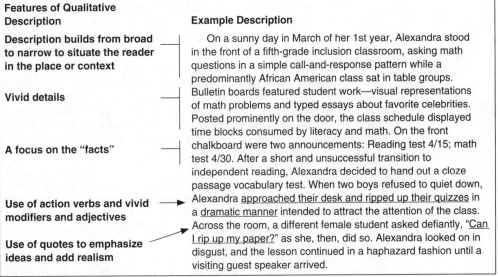

Features of Qualitative Description	Example Description
Description builds from broad to narrow to situate the reader in the place or context	On a sunny day in March of her 1st year, Alexandra stood in the front of a fifth-grade inclusion classroom, asking math questions in a simple call-and-response pattern while a predominantly African American class sat in table groups.
Vivid details	Bulletin boards featured student work—visual representations of math problems and typed essays about favorite celebrities. Posted prominently on the door, the class schedule displayed time blocks consumed by literacy and math. On the front
A focus on the "facts"	chalkboard were two announcements: Reading test 4/15; math test 4/30. After a short and unsuccessful transition to independent reading, Alexandra decided to hand out a cloze passage vocabulary test. When two boys refused to quiet down,
Use of action verbs and vivid modifiers and adjectives	Alexandra approached their desk and ripped up their quizzes in a dramatic manner intended to attract the attention of the class.
Use of quotes to emphasize ideas and add realism	Across the room, a different female student asked defiantly, "Can I rip up my paper?" as she, then, did so. Alexandra looked on in disgust, and the lesson continued in a haphazard fashion until a visiting guest speaker arrived.

FIGURE 11.5 An Example of Description as a Finding in a Qualitative Report
Source: Clayton (2007, pp. 221–222).

- *Focus on facts and what occurred.* The author does not make an interpretation or evaluate the situation—she simply reports the facts as recorded in the data sources. Keep in mind that descriptive results are different from the themes that researchers report as their interpretations of larger patterns in the data. (We will learn more about themes in the next section.)
- *Action words.* The action comes alive with the use of action verbs and movement-oriented modifiers and adjectives. The teacher did not simply take the papers; she "ripped up" the papers. Good description should make you feel like you are in the setting as you as read, and action words help to bring the description to life.
- *Participant quotes.* The passage includes quotes (i.e., the exact words of participants) to provide emphasis and realism in the account. These quotes are usually short because researchers are typically limited in the amount of space they have available to report their study. However, you should notice that good qualitative description includes specific details like quotes that are drawn from the researcher's data collection.

By paying attention to these features of good qualitative description, you can consider to what extent the researcher has provided you with a compelling picture of the people, places, and events that illustrate the context for the qualitative research study.

Examine Themes to Learn the Larger Ideas Found About the Study's Central Phenomenon

The most common form of qualitative results that you will find are themes. Recall that themes are major ideas about the central phenomenon that emerge when the researcher groups several codes together during the analysis. You will find themes reported as the results of qualitative studies using all of the common designs, including grounded theory, case study, ethnography, and narrative studies. Typically, researchers report five to seven themes in the Results section of their study to convey both the major ideas and the complexity of the central phenomenon under study. Remember that a key characteristic of qualitative research is to explore the complexity of topics and that complexity should be evident in the themes because they describe several major aspects of the central phenomenon. The themes that emerge from a qualitative study are the key results to examine to discern what the researchers discovered about the study's central phenomenon. As you read about the themes in a qualitative study, consider whether each theme clearly relates to the study's central phenomenon and represents a major idea about it.

Because themes are the primary findings of most qualitative studies, researchers typically state how many themes resulted from the analysis in their reports and give a name to each theme in the Findings section. When reading the Findings section, look at the major headings that are included, as they most often represent the name of the themes. For example, in the qualitative physical-activity-at-daycare study (Tucker et al., 2011) from Chapter 1, the authors used headings in their Results section to name the four major themes that emerged about ways to enhance preschoolers' activity levels at daycare, including: "Enhanced staff training/workshops" and "Additional equipment and resources." The names of themes can take many different forms, but a good theme name provides you with a clear sense of the larger idea that it represents in the researchers' interpretation of the analyzed data. Theme names might be stated as nouns, verbs, phrases, or even questions. The names of themes can be as short as a single word. Brown and colleagues (2006) used this form for several themes in their study of patients waiting for a liver transplant. Their themes included "Transformation," "Loss," and "Coping." Another common form occurs when researchers include participants' own words in the name of their themes. We read an example of this strategy in the qualitative adolescent-homelessness study at the end of Chapter 4. Haldenby et al. (2007) combined participants' quotes with their own interpretations to derive theme names, such as "'I Can't Really Feel Safe': Negotiating Dangerous Terrain" and "'They're in the Same Situation as You': Rethinking Family."

As you learned for descriptive findings, qualitative researchers also use several features for reporting themes, and knowing these features can help you understand and assess results reported as themes. To learn how to read qualitative themes, examine the discussion of the "students' experiences" theme found in a study about adolescent perceptions of tobacco use (Plano Clark et al., 2002) that is provided in Figure 11.6.

This passage describes one of five themes reported in the study. The theme passage illustrates several of the features used in good qualitative research reports, some of which have been highlighted with the labels in the margin of the figure. The features of good qualitative themes include:

- *Subthemes within each major theme.* Recognize that authors report major themes as well as subthemes subsumed under each major theme. These subthemes often represent the different codes aggregated together to form the theme during the analysis process. In Figure 11.6, the major theme is "What Are the Students' Experiences with Tobacco in High Schools?" Under this major theme, the authors discuss the following

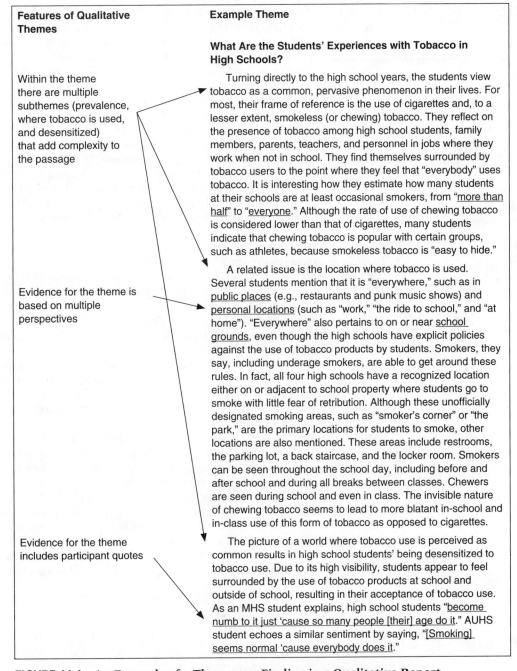

Features of Qualitative Themes

Within the theme there are multiple subthemes (prevalence, where tobacco is used, and desensitized) that add complexity to the passage

Evidence for the theme is based on multiple perspectives

Evidence for the theme includes participant quotes

Example Theme

What Are the Students' Experiences with Tobacco in High Schools?

Turning directly to the high school years, the students view tobacco as a common, pervasive phenomenon in their lives. For most, their frame of reference is the use of cigarettes and, to a lesser extent, smokeless (or chewing) tobacco. They reflect on the presence of tobacco among high school students, family members, parents, teachers, and personnel in jobs where they work when not in school. They find themselves surrounded by tobacco users to the point where they feel that "everybody" uses tobacco. It is interesting how they estimate how many students at their schools are at least occasional smokers, from "more than half" to "everyone." Although the rate of use of chewing tobacco is considered lower than that of cigarettes, many students indicate that chewing tobacco is popular with certain groups, such as athletes, because smokeless tobacco is "easy to hide."

A related issue is the location where tobacco is used. Several students mention that it is "everywhere," such as in public places (e.g., restaurants and punk music shows) and personal locations (such as "work," "the ride to school," and "at home"). "Everywhere" also pertains to on or near school grounds, even though the high schools have explicit policies against the use of tobacco products by students. Smokers, they say, including underage smokers, are able to get around these rules. In fact, all four high schools have a recognized location either on or adjacent to school property where students go to smoke with little fear of retribution. Although these unofficially designated smoking areas, such as "smoker's corner" or "the park," are the primary locations for students to smoke, other locations are also mentioned. These areas include restrooms, the parking lot, a back staircase, and the locker room. Smokers can be seen throughout the school day, including before and after school and during all breaks between classes. Chewers are seen during school and even in class. The invisible nature of chewing tobacco seems to lead to more blatant in-school and in-class use of this form of tobacco as opposed to cigarettes.

The picture of a world where tobacco use is perceived as common results in high school students' being desensitized to tobacco use. Due to its high visibility, students appear to feel surrounded by the use of tobacco products at school and outside of school, resulting in their acceptance of tobacco use. As an MHS student explains, high school students "become numb to it just 'cause so many people [their] age do it." AUHS student echoes a similar sentiment by saying, "[Smoking] seems normal 'cause everybody does it."

FIGURE 11.6 An Example of a Theme as a Finding in a Qualitative Report

Source: Plano Clark et al. (2002, pp. 1270–1271). Reprinted with permission of Sage Publications, Inc.

subthemes: prevalence of tobacco use, where tobacco is used, and students feeling desensitized. In some reports, the authors use subheadings to indicate the subthemes, but often you need to recognize the different ideas within the theme passage as you read. The use of subthemes helps to convey the complexity of the findings, and you should look for the different concepts included when you read any theme.

■ *Multiple perspectives and contrary evidence.* Researchers include multiple perspectives about a theme (and subthemes) in their qualitative findings. The term **multiple perspectives** means that the researcher provides several viewpoints for a theme based on different individuals, different sources of information, or different views held by one person. In Figure 11.6, for example, the authors report the perspectives of many students, including those from different school settings. For instance, we learn different locations where participants perceive tobacco is used, such as public places, personal places, and school grounds. Multiple perspectives are important features of good themes because they convey the complexity of the central phenomenon in qualitative research. Good qualitative themes should include examples of the many different perspectives held by participants, not just the most common or popular perspective.

> **Here's a Tip!**
>
> Good qualitative findings include multiple perspectives and points of view. This means that the researcher has learned about the complex perspectives that people hold about the topic. This is different from quantitative research that emphasizes determining average trends.

The use of different perspectives might also include contrary evidence, such as when participants or the information from different data sources disagree with each other. Although the theme presented in Figure 11.6 did not include contrary evidence, we can imagine what such evidence might have been. For example, had the authors found that some students perceived that very few people use tobacco at their school, they would have included that perspective as contrary to the general idea of tobacco use being prevalent. When reports include contrary evidence, you learn a complex and realistic picture of the central phenomenon through different individuals' experiences. Good qualitative themes highlight the different perspectives that the author found in the data; by noticing these perspectives as you read, you learn about the range of views held about the study's central phenomenon.

■ *Participant quotes as evidence.* As with qualitative descriptive findings, authors include the exact words from participants as quotes when reporting their qualitative themes. The presence of quotes in themes provides you with the actual words of participants, which makes the results seem more real and informs you of the language that participants use when talking about the topic. Researchers select quotes that capture feelings, emotions, and ways people talk about their experiences, such as learning that students refer to a place to smoke tobacco as "smoker's corner."

In addition, and perhaps more importantly, authors include quotes as their evidence for the information about a theme that they are reporting. Recall that themes emerge during data analysis based on the personal interpretations of the researchers. Therefore, researchers include actual excerpts from their data to support the interpretations that they report in their themes. For example, at the end of the passage in Figure 11.6, the authors report their interpretation that students are desensitized to tobacco use and provide two students' quotes as supporting evidence for this claim. Therefore, when you read quotes reported about a theme, consider whether the information from participants supports the interpretation made by the authors.

The form of the quotes can vary across different reports. The passage in Figure 11.6 uses short quotes as evidence throughout the theme. In some reports, however, you may find that the authors include long quotes or even actual dialogue from participants to provide support for themes. For example, in a study about students' perceptions of effective teachers, Howard (2002) provides this dialogue between a teacher (Hazel) and one of her students to support the theme "making school seem like home."

HAZEL [SPEAKING TO STUDENT]:	Where's your book report?
STUDENT:	I don't have it. (long pause) I didn't finish it.
HAZEL:	You didn't finish it? (with emphasis) What are you waiting for to get it done? Christmas?
STUDENT:	No.
HAZEL:	Alright then, get it done! (p. 433)

No matter the form of the quotes, pay close attention to quotes included for each theme to learn how participants talk about the theme and to judge whether the author has included sufficient evidence for you to feel that the theme represents participants' experiences and perspectives.

■ *Inclusion of literary devices such as metaphors, analogies, and tensions.* Literary devices are useful for conveying the richness of qualitative findings, and you will read many qualitative reports that incorporate literary forms such as highlighting tensions and contradictions as part of their results. For example, in the study about adolescent perceptions of tobacco use in Figure 11.6, the authors go on to discuss "a number of contradictions" (p. 1276) that they found in the data and themes, such as adolescents perceiving that their schools support tobacco use despite the fact that all the schools had clear policies against its use. Another common literary device used in qualitative findings is the use of metaphors and analogies. For example, in reporting on the competition and concerns surfacing during the implementation of distance education in the state of Maine, Epper (1997) writes metaphorically about how student and citizen support is a "political football" game:

> As the bickering went on, many students stood by watching their education dreams tossed around like a political football. Some were not content to sit on the sidelines. From the islands, valleys, backwoods, and far reaches of the state came letters to the faculty senates, legislators, and newspapers. (p. 566)

Noting the use of such literary devices when you read about a theme helps you to develop a more rich and in-depth picture of the theme and central phenomenon. The presence of such devices in a report of qualitative themes can help convince you that the researcher completed an in-depth exploration of the central phenomenon and has provided rich information about it.

By looking for these features of good qualitative themes when you read qualitative findings in a report, you can consider to what extent the themes seem based on the views of participants and have provided you with a rich understanding of the complexity of the central phenomenon of the study.

What Do You Think?

Consider how Haldenby et al. (2007) reported the findings in the form of themes in the qualitative adolescent-homelessness study from Chapter 4. Specifically, read the theme titled, "'They're in the Same Situation as You': Rethinking Family," located in paragraphs 40–45 and starting on page 148. List four features of good qualitative themes that you find in the discussion of this qualitative finding.

Check Your Understanding

This theme includes many good features of qualitative findings. Examples are as follows: (a) The larger theme includes several subthemes (e.g., feeling betrayed by their families, feeling disconnected from peers, and feeling connected with other homeless youth). (b) The theme includes multiple perspectives of participants (e.g., several types of violence experienced by the youth mentioned in paragraph 40). (c) The theme incorporates quotes from participants' interview data for richness and as evidence for the researchers' interpretations (e.g., short and long quotes included in paragraph 42). (d) The theme uses a metaphor to convey a key idea (e.g., referring to other homeless youth as "family" in the theme name).

Read Tables and Figures to Learn More About the Details and Complexity of the Findings

In addition to describing the findings in sentences and paragraphs, qualitative researchers often display their findings visually by using tables and figures that augment the discussion (Miles & Huberman, 1994). These displays provide important information about the findings in qualitative studies, often including details beyond what is provided in the text and conveying the complexity of the findings in a way that is difficult to do with words only. As you read qualitative findings, pay close attention to the displays included in the report to develop the most complete understanding of what the researchers found in their study. Although no two displays from different studies are exactly alike, there are a few common types of displays that researchers include in their qualitative reports. Learning to recognize these types makes it easier for you to understand the information presented visually. Five common visual displays that you will encounter include demographic tables, map figures, comparison tables, hierarchical tree figures, and thematic figures.

- *Demographic tables.* Researchers include demographic tables in their reports to describe personal or demographic information for each person or site in the research. Demographic tables provide key information about the participants and settings to help you further understand the study's context. Although demographic tables often appear in the Findings section of qualitative reports, some authors include them when describing the participants in the Method section. In either case, they enhance the description of the study's participants and setting. For example, in a study of how high school teachers use technology in their classrooms, the researcher described each instructor and his or her primary delivery style in a demographic table, shown in Table 11.1. The seven participants in this qualitative study demonstrated different personal characteristics as well as diverse approaches to using technology, which the researcher wanted to highlight for the readers. This table provides readers with various demographic information for each teacher, such as number of years teaching, gender, class level of instruction, instructional approach used in the class, and his or her primary form of technology use. Use demographic tables like this to understand the important characteristics of the settings and participants in qualitative studies.
- *Map figures.* Researchers may include maps to depict the physical layout of the study's setting. Maps provide important details such as the relative placement of objects and how people interact within the study's setting. As shown in Figure 11.7, Miller et al. (1998) display the physical setting of a soup kitchen in their study. The authors provided this figure so that readers could visualize where different activities happened as they were described in the report. Use figures that display maps to understand the important details of a setting and, as you read the results, examine how those details relate to the study's description and themes.

TABLE 11.1   A Sample Demographic Table Used to Present Descriptive Information in a Qualitative Report

Name	Years Teaching	Gender	Class Level of Instruction	Instructional Approach in the Classroom	Primary Form of Technology in the Classroom
Amanda	25	Female	12	Discussion	Internet
Debbie	20	Female	11	Critique	Not used
Michelle	5	Female	11	Discussion	Tablets
Nancy	10	Female	12	Interactive	Wireless laptops
Theresa	6	Female	11	Discussion	Electronic whiteboard
Tim	4	Male	10	Lecture	Internet
Yuchun	12	Female	10	Small Groups	Electronic whiteboard and tablets

FIGURE 11.7
A Sample Map Figure of the Physical Layout of a Setting in a Qualitative Report

Source: Miller, D. M., Creswell, J. W., & Olander, L. S. (1998). Writing and retelling multiple ethnographic tales of a soup kitchen for the homeless. *Qualitative Inquiry,* 4(4), 475. Copyright © 1998 by Sage Publications. Reprinted by permission of Sage Publications, Inc.

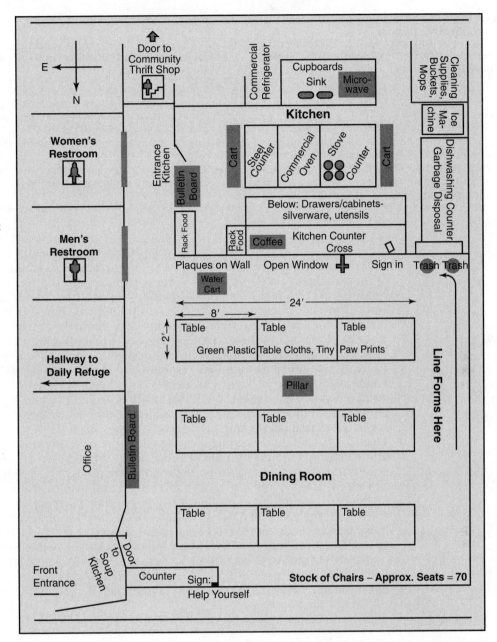

- *Comparison tables.* In some studies, researchers create visuals of the information in the form of a comparison table, a table that compares groups on one or more of the study's themes (e.g., freshmen and seniors in terms of "students' experiences with tobacco"). These tables are particularly useful when they highlight different perspectives found in the data. For example, in a qualitative study of teachers, one theme that emerged was the meaning of "professionalism." In developing this theme, the researcher analyzed statements gathered from both female and male teachers in a school and noticed that there were differences in the perspectives based on the gender of the participants. The table depicted in Table 11.2 compares the statements made by the female and male participants about their approaches to professionalism so that the reader can examine how they differed. When you find a comparison table in a qualitative report, use it to understand the different perspectives that the researcher found in the data about a theme and how those differences related to a certain grouping characteristic, such as gender.

TABLE 11.2 A Sample Comparison Table Used to Compare Two Groups for a Theme in a Qualitative Report

Statements About "Professionalism" From Female Participants	Statements About "Professionalism" From Male Participants
■ Helping fellow teachers is part of my day. ■ When another teacher asks for advice, I am generally a good listener. ■ It is important, once I achieve a certain level of experience, that I become a mentor to other teachers, especially new ones. ■ Caring about how other teachers employ high standards in their classroom is a sign of my own professionalism.	■ Being concerned about following the coordinator's advice about curriculum shows a high level of professionalism. ■ It is important to be in charge in the classroom and to be aware of student off-task behavior. ■ I set standards for myself, and try to achieve these goals each year. ■ It is necessary that each teacher "pull" his or her weight in this school—a sure sign of professionalism.

- *Hierarchical tree figures.* Recall that researchers often relate multiple themes as part of their qualitative analysis. Because these relationships can be difficult to describe clearly in words, researchers may include figures that convey the relationships among the themes as part of the results. One type of figure that relates multiple themes is the hierarchical tree. Researchers use hierarchical tree figures to visually represent themes and the multiple layers among the themes. The hierarchical tree diagram in Figure 11.8 illustrates the major themes (layer 1) and broader categories (layer 2) that describe a campus's response to a gunman incident (layer 3) found in a case study of the incident (Asmussen & Creswell, 1995). Use the information displayed in hierarchical tree figures such as this example to understand how themes relate to each other, particularly which ideas combine together to form larger ideas about the central phenomenon.

- *Thematic figures.* In some qualitative studies, researchers relate multiple themes by interconnecting them into a larger order. It is very common for researchers to use a thematic figure to display how the themes are interconnected by using boxes to convey the themes and arrows to convey the relationships among them. This type of figure is common in studies using a grounded theory design because the researcher analyzes the data with the explicit purpose of developing a theory of how ideas are interconnected. For example, Figure 11.9 depicts the findings from a grounded theory study by Harley and colleagues (2009) that examined the process by which African American women who are physically active adopt and maintain their physical activity practices. The authors identified numerous categories in the boxes, organized the categories within larger phases, and used arrows to show the

**FIGURE 11.8
A Sample Hierarchical Tree Figure to Portray Thematic Layers in a Qualitative Report**

Source: Adapted from Asmussen & Creswell (1995).

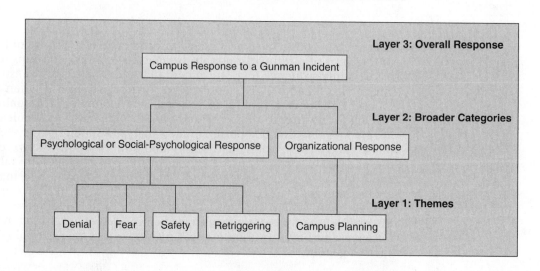

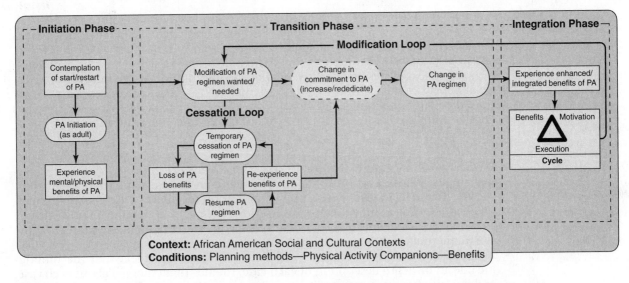

FIGURE 11.9   A Sample Thematic Figure That Interconnects Themes in a Qualitative Report

Source: Harley, A. E., Buckworth, J., Katz, M. L., Willis, S. K., Odoms-Young, A., & Heaney, C. A. (2009). Developing long-term physical activity participation: A grounded theory study with African American women. *Health Education and Behavior, 36*(1), 102, Fig. 1. Copyright © 2009 by Sage Publications. Reprinted by permission of Sage Publications, Inc.

connections among the boxes. When describing the results, the authors discussed each of the phases (i.e., initiation, transition, and integration), the two "loops" that describe how the process was ceased or modified, and the context and conditions for the overall process.

Another way that researchers use thematic figures is to show the interrelationships that exist among themes instead of a sequential order. In Auerbach's (2007) study of parent roles, for example, she identified a typology of parent roles that emerged from the different perspectives across the major themes in her study. In Figure 11.10, she portrayed how these different roles (moral supporters, ambivalent companions, and struggling advocates) overlapped with each other as well as differed along important dimensions (such as how proactive the parents were in their role). When you find thematic figures such as these in reports, use them to not only identify the major themes of a qualitative study, but to also understand how the multiple themes relate to each.

Consider the Form of the Findings in Relation to the Research Design

All qualitative research reports include findings in the form of description, themes, and/or the relationships among multiple themes. As you read reports, you will notice that some studies tend to emphasize one of these types of findings (e.g., description)

FIGURE 11.10   A Sample Thematic Figure That Relates Themes in a Qualitative Report

Source: Auerbach, S. (2007). From moral supporters to struggling advocates: Reconceptualizing parent roles in education through the experience of working-class families of color. *Urban Education, 42*(3), 259, Fig. 1. Copyright © 2007 by Sage Publications. Reprinted by permission of Sage Publications, Inc.

and others emphasize another type (e.g., the relationships among multiple themes). Some of this variation reflects the style of different researchers and their disciplines, but it also reflects the different qualitative research designs that researchers use. Recall from Chapter 9 that reports tend to include different types of findings depending on the research design. Because of the flexible nature of qualitative research, there are no strict rules for how results are reported for each specific research design. Each of the major qualitative design types, however, tends to emphasize certain types of results. Here are some guidelines to keep in mind as you read different types of qualitative research:

- If you are reading a study that used a *general qualitative approach*, expect that the findings simply include a report of the themes that emerged from the study. The report of basic themes is probably the most common form for qualitative research findings.
- If you are reading a study that used *narrative research*, expect that the findings include a chronological retelling of the participant's story, a description of the context for the story, and themes that emerged from the story.
- If you are reading a study that used *case study research*, expect that the findings include an in-depth description of each case, themes that emerged about each case, and if multiple cases were studied, another layer of themes that emerged across all the cases.
- If you are reading a study that used *ethnographic research*, expect that the findings include a detailed description of how a group behaves, thinks, and talks as well as the context, or setting, of the group.
- If you are reading a study that used *grounded theory research*, expect that the findings include the themes (or categories) that emerged, a display of the interconnections among the themes, and a discussion of the theory that emerged about the interconnections and the hypotheses (or propositions) suggested by these connections.

How Do You Evaluate the Data Analysis and Findings in a Qualitative Study?

When evaluating the quality of a qualitative study's data analysis and findings, keep in mind that these two aspects of the report are strongly tied to each other. Researchers describe how they implemented the data analysis process in the Method section and the results of that process in the Findings section. Good qualitative research involves the researcher systematically analyzing the qualitative data using a process that is inductive, interpretive, and dynamic to ensure results emerge that provide an accurate and credible portrayal of the information found within the collected data. Identifying the use of key aspects of the qualitative analysis process such as memoing and coding helps you judge the extent to which the researchers used good procedures in their study. Likewise, recognizing the features of good qualitative findings helps you assess the quality of the presented results as you consider whether they provide detailed and in-depth answers to the study's research questions. Table 11.3 lists criteria that are useful to consider when evaluating the data analysis and findings in a qualitative study. This table also provides indicators of higher quality and lower quality for the criteria to help you make your own judgments when evaluating the information provided in a research report.

Figure 11.11 provides a convenient means for you to apply the quality criteria to evaluate the data analysis described within the Method section and findings presented in the Results section of any qualitative research report. For each of the criteria you locate, assign a quality rating from *fair* (1) to *excellent* (3) and document your evidence and/or reasoning behind the rating. If one of the criteria is missing or very poorly stated, then indicate *poor* (0) as your rating. Keep in mind that research reports vary in the extent of discussion about the data analysis process and that the nature of the qualitative findings varies depending on the study's purpose and research design. Even with this variation, however, a good qualitative study should

TABLE 11.3 Criteria for Evaluating the Data Analysis and Findings in a Qualitative Research Report

Quality Criteria	Indicators of Higher Quality in Qualitative Research	Indicators of Lower Quality in Qualitative Research
The Key Elements		
1. The analysis process used rigorous qualitative procedures.	+ The researcher prepared verbatim transcripts and electronic scans of all gathered data. + The researcher read the data to get a sense of the whole and recorded personal interpretations in memos. + The researcher developed and assigned codes to segments based on the meaning of the data. + The researcher refined the list of codes during the analysis and built results from the refined codes.	− The researcher prepared summaries of the gathered data or did not prepare all of the gathered data. − The researcher started coding without first reading through the data and did record personal interpretations. − The researcher used predetermined codes that did not come from the data. − The process by which the researcher built results from the data is unclear.
2. Strategies were used to validate the findings.	+ The researcher used at least three strategies to ensure the accuracy and credibility of the findings such as bracketing, triangulation, member checking, or audits.	− The researcher did not employ multiple strategies to ensure the accuracy and credibility of the findings.
3. The findings include a description of the people, places, or events in the study.	+ The important context of the study is described with rich detail using a broad-to-narrow form, factual information, action words and modifiers, participant quotes, and tables or figures that provide additional details.	− The description of the context of the study is boring and dry, provides little detail, or is not even included.
4. The findings include appropriate themes about the central phenomenon.	+ There are five to seven themes reported. + The themes convey both major ideas about and the complexity of the central phenomenon using sub-themes, multiple perspectives and contrary evidence, participant quotes as evidence, literary devices to suggest the researcher's interpretations, and comparison tables.	− There are too few (i.e., too simplified analysis) or too many (i.e., not enough analysis) themes. − The themes lack subthemes within the larger themes, include only the common perspectives, have insufficient evidence in the form of quotes, or do not include literary devices that suggest the researcher's interpretations.
5. The findings relate multiple themes to each other.	+ The researcher reports the relationships among the themes, such as the multiple layers of categories or interconnecting the themes into a sequence or larger order, conveys the relationships in the text and with a figure, and develops theme relationships that are consistent with the overall research design.	− The researcher reports themes without explaining how they relate to each other, does not adequately describe or depict the relationships, or relates the themes in a way that is inconsistent with the overall research design.
General Evaluation		
6. The data analysis represents a good qualitative process.	+ The data analysis was an inductive, interpretive, and dynamic process from which credible and accurate results emerged based on the gathered data.	− The data analysis was a deductive (top-down), objective, fixed, or linear process from which results were produced that are not strongly tied to the gathered data.
7. The findings provide a good exploration of the central phenomenon.	+ The findings provide rich and detailed information that answers the study's research questions.	− The findings provide superficial answers or do not clearly answer the study's research questions.

still score well on most of the items listed in Figure 11.11. By adding up the rating scores for each of the criteria and using the suggested cutoff values provided at the bottom of the figure, you will have a quantitative measure that you can use to inform your overall assessment.

Quality Criteria	Quality Rating				Your Evidence and/or Reasoning
	0 = Poor	1 = Fair	2 = Good	3 = Excellent	
The Key Elements					
1. The analysis process used rigorous qualitative procedures.					
2. Strategies were used to validate the findings.					
3. The findings include a description of the people, places, or events in the study.					
4. The findings include appropriate themes about the central phenomenon.					
5. The findings relate multiple themes to each other.					
General Evaluation					
6. The data analysis represents a good qualitative process.					
7. The findings provide a good exploration of the central phenomenon.					
Overall Quality 0–10 = Low quality 11–16 = Adequate quality 17–21 = High quality	**Total Score =**				**My Overall Assessment Is**

FIGURE 11.11   A Rating Scale for Evaluating the Data Analysis and Findings in a Qualitative Research Report

Reviewing What You've Learned To Do

- *Identify and understand the data analysis and findings of a qualitative research study.*
  - ◻ The Method section of a qualitative research report contains information about the process that the authors used to analyze their qualitative data, which includes how they prepared the data, explored the data, coded the data, developed findings from the data, and validated the findings.
  - ◻ The Results section of a qualitative research report contains the findings that emerged from the data analysis process in response to the study's research questions.
- *List the steps that researchers report using to analyze qualitative data.*
  - ◻ Qualitative data analysis is a process that inductively builds from the data to larger patterns, that involves the researcher making personal interpretations, where several steps occur simultaneously, and that takes place iteratively with data collection as early results point for the need for more data.
  - ◻ Researchers prepare their data using procedures such as transcription to develop complete and accurate records of the gathered data.
  - ◻ Researchers explore the data by reading the information to get a sense of the whole and memoing their ideas about the data.
  - ◻ Researchers code the data by breaking the information into segments and assigning code labels to the segments that represent the meaning of the information in the segment.

□ Researchers refine their codes, aggregate them into larger ideas, and use the codes and coded data to build description, themes, and relationships among themes as the findings.

□ Researchers use strategies to validate their findings to ensure that they are credible and accurate.

■ *Know how to identify results in the form of description and themes when reading a qualitative research report.*

□ Description is a type of qualitative finding where the researcher reports a detailed description of the setting, people, or events that provide the context for the study.

□ Themes (or categories) are a type of qualitative finding in which the researcher reports a small number of major ideas that emerged about the study's central phenomenon from the gathered data.

□ Tables and figures augment the descriptive and thematic findings by providing more detail or depicting the complexity within the findings, such as the layers or interconnections among themes.

□ The findings may emphasize description, themes, and/or relationships among themes, depending on the study's overall qualitative research design.

■ *Evaluate the quality of the data analysis and findings in a qualitative research report.*

□ The evaluation of a study's qualitative data analysis considers the completeness and accuracy of the data preparation; the extent to which the researcher developed emergent findings by exploring, coding, and refining the codes about the data; and the strategies used to validate the accuracy and credibility of the findings.

□ The evaluation of a study's qualitative findings considers the extent to which the description is rich and detailed so that readers feels like they were present within the setting; the extent to which the themes and interconnections among the themes convey major ideas about the central phenomenon as well as the complexity of the central phenomenon; and the extent to which the findings answer the study's research questions.

✓ **To assess what you've learned to do, click here to answer questions and receive instant feedback.**

Reading Research Articles

Carefully reread the qualitative adoption-of-pedagogical-tools study by Leko and Brownell (2011) found at the end of Chapter 9 (starting on p. 306) and the qualitative adolescent-homelessness study by Haldenby et al. (2007) at the end of Chapter 4 (starting on p. 148).

As you review each article, pay close attention to statements in which the authors described the data analysis process in the Method section and the results in the Findings section. Use the highlighting tool in the Pearson etext to indicate where the authors have provided information about the data analysis and findings, and use the notetaking tool to add marginal notes that name each element you highlighted and note how each one is related to the study's qualitative approach. Among the elements you will want to find are:

1. Preparing the data
2. Exploring the data
3. Coding the data
4. Developing findings
5. Validating the findings
6. Results as description
7. Results as themes
8. Results as relationships among themes

Note, however, that sometimes authors do not describe all of the steps of the data analysis process—for example, they might not mention preparing the data or exploring the data. In addition, authors do not always report all types of results—that is, they might not report description, they might not report themes, or they might not report relationships among themes. If one of these steps or type of results is missing, indicate that in your marginal notes.

 Click here to go to the qualitative adoption-of-pedagogical-tools study by Leko and Brownell (2011) so that you can enter marginal notes about the study.

 Click here to go to the qualitative adolescent-homelessness study by Haldenby et al. (2007) so that you can enter marginal notes about the study.

Understanding Research Articles

Apply your knowledge of the content of this chapter to the qualitative adoption-of-pedagogical-tools study by Leko and Brownell (2011) starting on p. 306.

1. What evidence can you find about how the authors prepared the gathered data for analysis in the adoption-of-pedagogical-tools study?

2. What evidence can you find that the authors explored the data, coded the data, and refined the codes and developed findings from the codes?

3. What strategies did the authors use to validate their findings?

4. The major types of qualitative findings include description, themes, and relationships among themes. Which of these types of findings did the authors report?

5. Consider the findings in paragraphs 46–49 under the heading of "Tricia." What type of finding is this? What features of good qualitative research did the authors use in these paragraphs?

6. Consider the findings in paragraphs 68–69 under the heading of "Component Concept: Personal Qualities." What type of finding is this? What features of good qualitative research did the authors use in these paragraphs?

7. Consider the tables and figures that appear in this article. (a) How does Table 1 help you learn more about the study's findings? (b) How does Figure 1 help you to learn more about the study's findings?

✓ **Click here to answer the questions and receive instant feedback.**

Evaluating Research Articles

Practice evaluating a qualitative study's data analysis and findings, using the qualitative adoption-of-pedagogical-tools study by Leko and Brownell (2011) starting on p. 306 and the qualitative adolescent-homelessness study by Haldenby et al. (2007) starting on p. 148.

1. Use the criteria discussed in Table 11.3 to evaluate the quality of the data analysis and findings in the adoption-of-pedagogical-tools study. Note that, for this question, the rating form includes advice to help guide your evaluation.

✓ **Click here to open the rating scale form (Figure 11.11) to enter your ratings, evidence, and reasoning.**

2. Use the criteria discussed in Table 11.3 to evaluate the quality of the data analysis and findings in the adolescent-homelessness study. Note that, for this question, the rating form does NOT include additional advice.

✓ **Click here to open the rating scale form (Figure 11.11) to enter your ratings, evidence, and reasoning.**

UNDERSTANDING REPORTS THAT COMBINE QUANTITATIVE AND QUALITATIVE RESEARCH

Throughout this book we have used the analogy of taking a journey to think about how researchers conduct their research. Recall that some journeys are highly structured with set agendas of what to see and do, like many quantitative research studies that focus on explanation. Other journeys are like qualitative research, focusing on exploration. They are flexible and emerging, where people's decisions about where to go next are based on what they have learned along the way. This analogy helps to explain differences in the reports of studies that used quantitative research compared to the reports of studies that used qualitative research.

Thinking about how people take journeys, it will probably come as no surprise to learn that some people like taking trips that include both set agendas as well as time to explore in order to get the most out of their travel plans. Likewise, many of today's research problems call for both explanation *and* exploration. Whether focusing on contributing to knowledge or solving local problems, some researchers studying these complex problems choose to combine *both* quantitative *and* qualitative research to best understand their research problems and questions, and this combination is described in their research reports. To understand these reports, you will now learn about two different research approaches that scholars, including many practitioners, use to combine quantitative and qualitative information in their studies. This knowledge will help you understand research reports using some of the most up-to-date approaches to research and provide you with an approach that you may want to apply to solve problems in your own practices.

The chapters in Part Five are:

- Chapter 12—Mixed Methods Research Designs: Studies That Mix Quantitative and Qualitative Approaches
- Chapter 13—Action Research Designs: Studies That Solve Practical Problems

MIXED METHODS RESEARCH DESIGNS: STUDIES THAT MIX QUANTITATIVE AND QUALITATIVE APPROACHES

*Y*ou now have experience reading reports of both quantitative and qualitative research. As you read research on the topics that interest you, you will likely also encounter reports that combine or "mix" these two approaches. More and more researchers are reporting mixed methods studies that combine quantitative data and qualitative data to understand their research problems. The increasing use of these mixed approaches is one of the newest developments in research. Reading studies that mix methods can be a challenge because of the complexity that occurs when researchers report two types of methods and results in one study. By learning about the different mixed methods designs, you will have a framework for understanding how researchers conduct and report their mixed methods studies. In this chapter, you will learn how to identify mixed methods reports and to understand and evaluate the four major types of mixed methods designs.

BY THE END OF THIS CHAPTER, YOU SHOULD BE ABLE TO:

- Identify and understand the use of mixed methods research in a research study.
- Note the reasons why researchers use mixed methods research in their studies.
- List three characteristics that distinguish the different mixed methods research designs.
- Recognize four different research designs when reading mixed methods reports.
- Evaluate the quality of a mixed methods research report.

As we write this book, researchers' interest in combining quantitative and qualitative research within single studies is growing across all disciplines including education, the social sciences, and the health sciences. Studies that "mix" these two approaches are called "mixed methods research." There are many mixed methods studies published in the literature. By definition, mixed methods studies include:

- two datasets (one quantitative and one qualitative),
- two types of analyses (statistical and thematic), and
- some way of combining or mixing what is learned from the quantitative and qualitative components of the study.

For example, here is how one author described her mixed methods study about the different modes of communication used by college students:

> This study investigated how the Internet is integrated into university students' communication habits . . . . Using a mixed methods approach that combined survey data from 268 Canadian university students with focus group data, a rich description was obtained of what modes of communication students use, how they integrate them to fulfill communication needs, and the implications of this integration for the maintenance of social ties. (Quan-Haase, 2007, p. 671)

Notice how this example refers to quantitative research ("survey data from 268 Canadian university students") *and* qualitative research ("focus group data"). The author combined these two datasets to develop a more complete understanding of the different modes of communication, including what modes are used, how they are used, and the consequences of the use. Because mixed methods studies use more than one data collection and analysis procedure, you need to make sense of a lot of information when reading any mixed methods report. Learning about mixed methods research designs gives you a framework for understanding published reports that make use of this increasingly popular approach to research.

How Do You Determine Whether a Study Used Mixed Methods Research?

To understand any mixed methods report, you must first recognize that the study used a combined approach. The use of mixed methods is considered a distinctive approach to research that has its own designs, procedures, and standards of quality. For this reason, it is essential to identify when a reported study used a mixed methods research approach. As with quantitative and qualitative research, you can learn to identify mixed methods research by recognizing key terms used in reports and identifying the use of two forms of data collection and analysis.

Note Key Terms That Signal the Use of Mixed Methods

Researchers use special words in their reports to signal that they used a mixed methods approach in their study. Although it is becoming more common for researchers to refer to their studies as *mixed methods* when using this approach, this term is still relatively new and not all researchers use it. Other terms that you may encounter include *multimethod*, *mixed methodology*, *integrated*, or *combined*. Sometimes researchers convey their use of mixed methods with phrases that include *quantitative and qualitative* or other related terms to signify the collection and analysis of both quantitative and qualitative data.

You can often find terms indicating a mixed methods approach in the titles of mixed methods studies. For example, see how the following titles signal to the reader that the study mixed quantitative and qualitative research:

- "Preservice Teachers' Culturally Responsive Teaching Self-Efficacy-Forming Experiences: A Mixed Methods Study" (Siwatu, 2011)
- "Young Families Under Stress: Assessing Maternal and Child Well-being Using a Mixed Methods Approach" (McAuley, McCurry, Knapp, Beecham, & Sleed, 2006)
- "Unwritten Rules of Talking to Doctors About Depression: Integrating Qualitative and Quantitative Methods" (Wittink, Barg, & Gallo, 2006)

Not all mixed methods articles include signal terms in their titles, but they do include mixed methods terms in other locations in the report. For example, many authors include terms that identify their use of mixed methods in the Abstract of the study. Some authors also include terms that refer to their use of mixed methods in the purpose statement located at the end of the Introduction section or when discussing the research design at the beginning of the Method section. No matter where in a report they appear, pay close attention when you read terms that indicate the authors' use of mixed methods research.

Note the Collection and Analysis of Both Quantitative and Qualitative Data

You can also identify studies as mixed methods research when the authors report collecting and analyzing both quantitative data and qualitative data. Mixed methods studies include forms of quantitative data (i.e., numbers) and qualitative data (i.e., words or images) as part of the data collection. They also include forms of quantitative data analysis (i.e., statistics) and qualitative data analysis (i.e., coding and theme development).

As with other forms of research, you can learn the forms of data collected in a mixed methods study by examining the Method section of the report. In mixed methods studies, the Method section includes information about both quantitative and qualitative data forms. In many studies, the authors use headings in the Method section to make it clear that different forms of data were gathered in the study (e.g., "Quantitative Survey Data" and "Qualitative Focus Group Data"). These headings can be very useful in helping you identify a study as mixed methods. In other studies, you have to read about the procedures used in the study to identify that both quantitative and qualitative data were gathered and analyzed. Often this information is highlighted in the Abstract of a report, but the details are provided in the Method section. Examine the following excerpts from the Abstracts of three mixed methods studies. Although these studies did not include "mixed methods" in their titles, the authors clearly identify the collection of both quantitative and qualitative forms of data in the following statements.

- "A total of 32 Latino participants completed quantitative surveys before the high school transition and then participated in qualitative interviews 1 year later" (Sánchez, Esparza, Berardi, & Pryce, 2011, p. 225).
- "A population-based survey was conducted among adults in the three study districts [located in Kenya, Tanzania, and Zambia], and qualitative data were obtained from 344 focus group discussions and 18 in-depth interviews" (Njeru, Blystad, Shayo, Nyamongo, & Fylkesnes, 2011, p. 1).
- "To explore ethnic and racial variation in attitudes toward physical activity, semi-structured interviews ($n = 80$) and physical activity checklists ($n = 130$) are conducted with African American, Hispanic, and Caucasian middle school girls in six locations across the United States" (Grieser et al., 2006, p. 40).

Statements such as these that identify the use of both qualitative procedures (e.g., focus group interviews or one-on-one interviews) and quantitative procedures (e.g., surveys or structured checklists) inform you that a study was conducted by mixing methods.

When Is It Appropriate for Researchers to Have Used Mixed Methods Research in Their Studies?

Learning that a researcher collected both quantitative and qualitative data in a study probably sounds pretty good to you. It just makes sense to include both types of data to have the best of both worlds, so to speak. However, for many research purposes a quantitative approach *or* a qualitative approach works best. In addition, collecting both types of data requires special considerations by the researcher compared to conducting a study that is quantitative *or* qualitative. In this book, we have emphasized important differences between quantitative and qualitative research. These differences range from the types of research problems (e.g., those that call for explanation or exploration), to the types of purposes (e.g., narrow and specific or broad and general), to the forms of gathered data (e.g., closed-ended forms or open-ended forms), and even to the role of the researcher (e.g., objective or subjective). There are many differences associated with these two approaches, so it is actually quite challenging for researchers to combine both types of research in one study.

Because of these challenges, researchers need to have a good reason for choosing to combine quantitative and qualitative research. Researchers who used mixed methods research should explain their rationale in their reports and the rationale should be appropriate for using mixed methods. You can typically find the rationale near the purpose statement in the Introduction section and/or at the beginning of the Method section. When reading a mixed methods study, you should look for the researcher's reason for mixing methods and consider whether it provides an appropriate rationale for combining the two different methods. Let's consider several rationales that are appropriate for using mixed methods.

Mixed Methods Is Appropriate If the Researcher Needed to Combine the Strengths of Quantitative and Qualitative Data

In general, researchers conduct mixed methods studies when both quantitative and qualitative data, together, provide a better understanding of the research problem than either type by itself. Mixed methods research allows a researcher to build on the separate strengths of both quantitative and qualitative data. Quantitative data, such as scores on instruments, yield specific numbers that can be statistically analyzed, can produce results to assess the frequency and magnitude of variables, and can provide useful information to describe trends about a large number of people. In contrast, qualitative data, such as open-ended interviews that provide the actual words of a small number of people, offer in-depth perspectives on the study topic and provide a complex picture of the situation. By combining quantitative and qualitative data, therefore, researchers argue that the study can develop a more complete picture of social phenomena that includes both trends and individuals' experiences. For example, in a study of stress experienced by graduate students, Mazzola and colleagues (2011) presented the following statement as their reason for using mixed methods:

> By employing both data collection methods in stress research, the data can be analyzed from the two different perspectives. The quantitative methods can uncover the frequency with which individuals experience stressors and strains being investigated, whereas the open-ended measures can provide detailed information about specific stressor incidents and the resulting strains. Additionally, direct comparisons between the two types of data collection (qualitative and quantitative) can be made, allowing researchers to look at relationships within the stress process in novel ways. (p. 200)

Mixed Methods Is Appropriate If the Researcher Needed to Build From One Type of Data to the Other

Investigators also conduct mixed methods studies when the results of one type of research (qualitative or quantitative) are inadequate to fully address the research problem. In such cases, the researcher needs to collect a second database that builds on the initial results to extend, elaborate on, or explain the initial results. For example, a researcher might engage in a mixed methods study when she needs to build on initial quantitative results with a qualitative exploration to obtain more detailed, specific information that can help explain the results of statistical tests. In this situation, the researcher provides a rationale for why she needs to build on the quantitative results. Ivankova and Stick (2007) provided this type of rationale in their study of persistence in an online doctoral program where they needed qualitative information to explain the initial quantitative results. They wrote:

> The quantitative data and results provided a general picture of the research problem, while the qualitative data and its analysis refined and explained those statistical results by exploring the participants' views regarding their persistence in more depth. (p. 97)

Another researcher may first explore a topic qualitatively to build themes, but then argue for the need to build on those themes with a quantitative assessment. In this case, he may develop an instrument that builds on those themes and then collect quantitative data with that instrument to extend the initial qualitative findings. Here is an example of a researcher stating this type of rationale in a study of the use of alternative medicine by African American adults diagnosed with the AIDS virus:

> This mixed methods study used . . . . a combining of qualitative and quantitative approaches for the purpose of developing and/or refining a measurement tool. This type of model in which initial qualitative data inform the development of a new, culturally appropriate quantitative measure has been successful in prior research. (Owen-Smith, Sterk, McCarty, Hankerson-Dyson, & DiClemente, 2010, p. 570)

Mixed Methods Is Appropriate If the Researcher Needed to Answer Two Questions

Sometimes researchers decide to use a mixed methods approach when they have two different but related questions that they want to answer. For example, a researcher might be conducting an experiment to test the effectiveness of an intervention. In addition to measuring group differences, she might also want to explore the process that the participants experience during the intervention. Therefore, the experiment may yield useful information about outcomes, but the additional collection of qualitative data develops an enhanced understanding of how the experimental intervention actually worked. Brady and O'Regan (2009) provide an example of this rationale when discussing why they mixed methods in their study of a mentoring program. They wrote: "We saw the opportunity to bridge these two traditions [quantitative and qualitative research] in a study that could address questions of impact as well as of process and implementation" (p. 270).

What Characteristics Distinguish the Different Mixed Methods Designs?

Once you have identified a study as mixed methods and have located the reason why the authors chose to mix methods, you next need to consider how they implemented the mixed methods research procedures. Figure 12.1 provides a general framework for understanding the conduct of a mixed methods study using the process of research. As this figure illustrates, the use of mixed methods influences all steps in the process of research. As you have previously learned for quantitative and qualitative research, researchers also use particular research designs when mixing methods in their studies. A **mixed methods research design** is a set of procedures for collecting, analyzing, and mixing both quantitative and qualitative methods in a study to understand a research problem (Creswell & Plano Clark, 2011).

From Figure 12.1, you might imagine that there are numerous ways that researchers can combine quantitative and qualitative procedures in their studies. For example, they might collect one type of data (e.g., qualitative) before the other type (e.g., quantitative) or they might collect them both at the same time. Mixed methods research designs are distinguished by the different ways that researchers relate the quantitative and qualitative components to each other in the study (Creswell & Plano

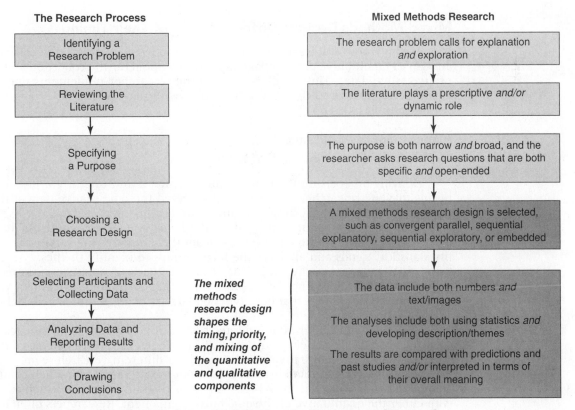

FIGURE 12.1 Mixed Methods Research Designs in the Process of Research

Notations:

+	indicates the concurrent collection of quantitative and qualitative data.
→	indicates the sequential collection of quantitative and qualitative data.
QUAN	indicates a high priority for the quantitative data.
QUAL	indicates a high priority for the qualitative data.
quan	indicates a lower priority for the quantitative data.
qual	indicates a lower priority for the qualitative data.
( )	indicates that a component is embedded within a larger framework.

Sample Study Notations:

Study #1: QUAN + QUAL
Study #2: QUAL → quan
Study #3: QUAN(qual)

FIGURE 12.2 A Notation System for Mixed Methods Studies
Source: Adapted from Morse (1991) and Plano Clark (2005).

Clark, 2011; Teddlie & Tashakkori, 2009). To understand the different mixed methods research designs, you need to first learn about three different ways that the quantitative and qualitative components of a mixed methods study are related, which are referred to as *timing, priority,* and *mixing.* Because of the importance of these characteristics in mixed methods studies, scholars have developed a notation system that is widely used to convey the major characteristics (Morse, 1991). This notation system is summarized in Figure 12.2. As you read mixed methods reports, you will find that researchers often discuss these three characteristics and use the notation system to describe their use of mixed methods. Let's learn a little more about these characteristics so you will be able to understand the different approaches used in mixed methods reports.

Mixed Methods Designs Differ in Terms of Their Timing

All mixed methods studies include both a quantitative component (the collection and analysis of quantitative data) and a qualitative component (the collection and analysis of qualitative data). Timing refers to *when* the researcher implements one of these components relative to the other. There are two basic options for timing in mixed methods studies:

- concurrent (+) timing and
- sequential (→) timing.

Concurrent (or simultaneous) timing, which is indicated by a plus sign (+), means that the researchers collected and analyzed the quantitative data at the same time that they were collecting and analyzing the qualitative data. For example, a research team might gather survey data and focus groups from students during the fall semester. In the spring semester, the team then analyzes the survey data to identify statistical trends and analyzes the focus groups to identify themes. "At the same time" does not necessarily mean that the two types of data are gathered at the same moment on the same day because often that is simply not feasible. What the "same time" does mean is that both types of data are being gathered before the analysis of either one is complete.

Sequential timing, which is indicated by an arrow (→), means that the researchers collected and analyzed one type of data (e.g., qualitative) *before* they collected the other type of data (e.g., quantitative). For example, a different research team might first gather and analyze quantitative survey data; once that is done, they then conduct and analyze qualitative interviews. When using sequential timing, the researchers can start with either the quantitative or the qualitative component. Researchers often explicitly identify the timing of their mixed methods study in the Method section of the report. If not identified explicitly, you can figure it out as you read about the study's procedures for collecting and analyzing the quantitative and qualitative datasets.

Mixed Methods Designs Differ in Terms of Their Priority

Priority refers to the relative importance of the quantitative and qualitative components for addressing a study's purpose. There are two basic options for priority in mixed methods studies:

- equal priority (QUAN, QUAL) and
- unequal priority (QUAN, qual or QUAL, quan).

Equal priority means that the quantitative and qualitative components of a mixed methods study are both equally important for addressing the study's purpose. For example, a research team might gather qualitative observations about what people do along with quantitative surveys about their attitudes, and feel that both are equally important for developing a more complete picture of the topic. In the mixed methods notation system, equal priority is indicated by writing QUAN (shorthand for "quantitative") and QUAL (shorthand for "qualitative") in all uppercase letters.

Unequal priority means that one of the components of the mixed methods study (i.e., the quantitative *or* the qualitative component) has a greater importance for addressing the study's purpose and the other component has a lesser priority. Studies with unequal priority are often referred to as having a quantitative priority or a qualitative priority, depending on which method is emphasized. For example, a researcher might be conducting a quantitative experiment study and decide to add a small, secondary qualitative component to learn about the process of the intervention in addition to assessing the outcomes. This is an example of a study that has a quantitative priority. In the mixed methods notation system, unequal priority is indicated by writing the primary method in uppercase letters (e.g., QUAN) and the secondary method in lowercase letters (e.g., qual). Some researchers explicitly identify the priority of their mixed methods study in the Method section of the report using words or the notation system. Often, however, you have to deduce the study's priority by considering the study's purpose, the relative extent of the quantitative and qualitative components, and the emphasis that the researcher places on each set of results in the Results and Conclusion sections.

Mixed Methods Designs Differ in Terms of Their Mixing

Mixing refers to the procedures that the researchers use to combine or interrelate the quantitative and qualitative data and results of a mixed methods study. A mixed methods study is not mixed unless the authors combine the two datasets in some meaningful way. At a minimum, all mixed methods studies should "mix" the quantitative and qualitative components in the final Conclusion section of a report. When mixing occurs in this way, you read the researchers' interpretation as to what they learned by combining the two different methods in the study. In good mixed methods studies, however, the researchers also mix the two components before the final Conclusion. For example, the researchers might collect and analyze the two forms of data separately and then *merge* the results during the analysis by combining or contrasting the two sets of results. Another type of mixing occurs when the researchers *connect* from one set of results to a second type of data collection. For example, the researchers might use qualitative thematic results to develop the scales and items used in a quantitative instrument. This is an example of connecting from qualitative results to a quantitative data collection. The researchers also might mix the components during the study planning by *embedding* one component within a framework based on the other component, such as embedding qualitative methods within the framework of a quantitative experimental design or embedding quantitative methods within the framework of a qualitative case study design. Although mixing takes on many different forms within mixed methods reports, you can identify when it occurs by noting places where the quantitative and qualitative datasets seem to "talk" to each other, that is, when they are being directly compared, linked, or shaped by each other.

What Do You Think?

Read the following excerpt taken from a mixed methods study. Based on this information, identify the timing, priority, and mixing for this study, and then summarize this study's characteristics using the mixed methods notation system in Figure 12.2.

> This study employed a mixed methods design . . . in which quantitative methods were conducted at T1 [Time 1] followed by qualitative methods at T2 [Time 2]. Through this design, qualitative methods are used to build on the quantitative results collected during T1. Data from the qualitative phase is dominant in this study due to our focus on the qualitative interview data about the development of [natural mentoring relationships] and participants' social networks at T2. (Sánchez et al., 2011, pp. 229–230)

Check Your Understanding

This study used *sequential timing* because the researchers collected and analyzed the quantitative data before collecting the qualitative data. This study had a *qualitative priority*, which we learn because the researchers inform us that the qualitative phase was "dominant in this study." Although there is not much detail about mixing in this short excerpt, we do learn that the researchers *mixed by connecting* from the quantitative results to the qualitative data collection. We might also assume that the authors *mixed in their interpretations* of the study. Using the mixed methods notation system, we can summarize this study's characteristics as: quan → QUAL. This notation conveys that the study used sequential timing (→), with the quantitative component occurring first, and used an unequal priority, with the qualitative (QUAL) component being prioritized and the quantitative (quan) component having lesser priority.

How Do You Understand the Common Mixed Methods Research Designs?

The three characteristics of timing, priority, and mixing and their options are at the heart of the different mixed methods designs being used and reported in research today. As such, they provide you with a framework for understanding and recognizing the ways that researchers combine quantitative and qualitative research within published mixed methods reports. Although there are options for each of the characteristics, they fit together best in certain combinations, which form the major mixed methods research designs that scholars write about and researchers use (Creswell & Plano Clark, 2011; Greene, 2007; Morse & Niehaus, 2009; Teddlie & Tashakkori, 2009). Table 12.1 provides a brief overview for nine mixed methods designs that you will likely encounter when reading research. This table introduces you to the variety of mixed methods designs, why they are used, and their typical characteristics, which researchers discuss in their reports.

To help you better understand the different mixed methods designs, we provide an in-depth introduction to the designs most commonly found in mixed methods research reports. We focus on four mixed methods designs that are frequently reported in the literature and provide the background you need to understand reports of studies that used these common designs. These designs are all good examples of mixed methods research where the researchers mix quantitative and qualitative research within a single study. However, they also all differ in terms of why they are used, the design name that researchers include in their reports, the type of research problem that researchers indicate needed to be addressed, and the way the researchers describe the

TABLE 12.1   Overview of the Intent and Characteristics of Nine Different Mixed Methods Research Designs

Mixed Methods Design Name	Design Intent	Typical Characteristics
Convergent parallel	■ To develop a complete and valid understanding	■ Concurrent timing ■ Equal priority ■ Merging the quantitative results and qualitative findings during analysis and/or interpretation
Sequential explanatory	■ To explain the mechanisms or reasons behind quantitative results	■ Sequential timing ■ Unequal priority ■ Connecting from the quantitative results to shape the qualitative data collection
Sequential exploratory	■ To test or generalize qualitative findings	■ Sequential timing ■ Unequal priority ■ Connecting from the qualitative findings to shape the quantitative data collection
Embedded experiment	■ To enhance a quantitative experimental study by including a secondary qualitative component to explore the procedures or process of the experiment	■ Concurrent or sequential timing ■ Quantitative priority ■ Embedding a qualitative component into a quantitative experimental design
Embedded case study	■ To enhance a qualitative case study by including a secondary quantitative component to enrich the interpretation of the case	■ Concurrent or sequential timing ■ Qualitative priority ■ Embedding a quantitative component into a qualitative case study design
Concurrent conversion	■ To identify quantitative relationships among variables that include at least one variable that is a quantification of qualitative findings	■ Concurrent timing ■ Quantitative priority ■ Converting qualitative findings into a new quantitative variable and analyzing that new variable statistically with other quantitative data
Concurrent multilevel	■ To examine multiple levels (e.g., students, teachers, principals, and districts)	■ Concurrent timing ■ Equal or unequal priority ■ Merging the quantitative results and qualitative findings from each level during analysis and/or interpretation
Multiphase	■ To conduct a program of studies aimed at achieving an overall objective such as developing and evaluating a program	■ Concurrent and sequential timing ■ Varies for each study in the program ■ Connecting from each study to inform the later steps of the program development
Transformative	■ To conduct research that empowers individuals and advocates for social justice	■ Concurrent or sequential timing ■ Equal or unequal priority ■ Embedding a mixed methods design in a social justice framework, which shapes all the design decisions

methods and results in the report, such as the study's timing, priority, and mixing. We consider each of these aspects as we examine the following four common designs, which are summarized in Figure 12.3:

- convergent parallel design,
- sequential explanatory design,
- sequential exploratory design, and
- embedded design.

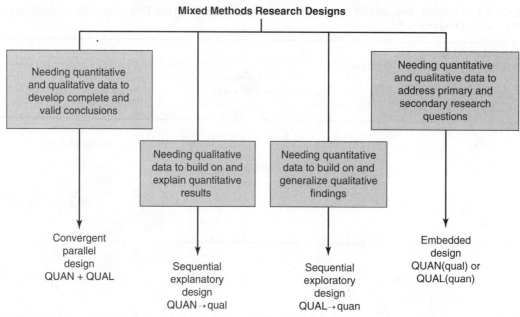

FIGURE 12.3   Four Common Mixed Methods Research Designs and Their Use

The Convergent Parallel Mixed Methods Design

The most common approach to mixing methods occurs when researchers gather and analyze both types of data at the same time. The **convergent parallel mixed methods design** is a set of procedures that researchers use to concurrently collect both quantitative and qualitative data, analyze the two datasets separately, compare and/or synthesize the two sets of separate results, and make an overall interpretation as to the extent to which the separate results confirm and/or complement each other. The way these steps unfold in a study is shown in Figure 12.4, where the two different types of research are implemented "in parallel" and then merged in some way to generate a better understanding of the phenomenon (the interpretation). This mixed methods design is the most intuitive approach and has been applied by researchers the longest. In 1979, for example, Jick described how he combined quantitative research (e.g., surveys of employee anxiety) and qualitative research (e.g., nonparticipant observations) to develop a more complete understanding of how individuals experienced a merger in their place of employment. He referred to his approach as a "triangulation" design, building from the same logic of triangulation of multiple sources of information that we learned about from qualitative research in Chapter 11. Looking back at Figure 12.4, you can see the analogy of the triangle where the two different types of research "point to" a better understanding of the topic under study.

**FIGURE 12.4
The Convergent
Parallel
QUAN + QUAL
Mixed Methods
Design**

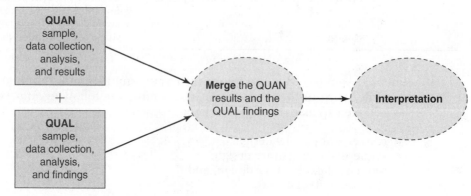

Studies Using the Convergent Parallel Design Develop Valid and Complete Conclusions About a Topic. The basic rationale for the convergent parallel design is that all data forms have strengths and weaknesses, but if combined thoughtfully, then the strengths of one data form may be able to offset the weaknesses of the other form. For example, quantitative scores on an instrument from many individuals provide overall trends (a "strength" of quantitative data) that may offset the weakness of qualitative observations of a few people. Alternatively, qualitative, in-depth observations of a few people provide important details about setting and context (a "strength" of qualitative data) that may offset the weakness of quantitative scores that do not adequately provide detailed information.

In a good application of the convergent parallel design, you find that the researchers carefully combined the quantitative and qualitative data forms to develop results and conclusions about the topic that are more complete and/or more valid. More complete results are obtained when the researchers use the different methods to examine different facets of the study's topic. For example, in a study of parent involvement, researchers gathered quantitative data to measure the extent of parent involvement and qualitative data to describe reasons for parent involvement. They then combined the two sets of results to develop a more complete picture that includes both the extent to which and reasons why parents are involved. More valid results are established within a convergent parallel design when researchers have corroborated a result with both quantitative and qualitative information. By comparing quantitative and qualitative results, this design can also discover inconsistencies in the results when the quantitative and qualitative information do not agree. For example, results from a quantitative survey may indicate low community support for a new community program for teenage mothers, but qualitative focus group interviews might show that individuals are highly supportive of the new program. Some researchers view such a disagreement as troubling. Others, however, see it as an ideal opportunity to learn even more about the phenomenon by examining why the inconsistent results emerged. Further examination in this example study could show that the disparate attitudes about the program for teenage mothers result from the community knowing little about the program specifics.

Identifying the Characteristics of the Convergent Parallel Design in a Research Report. It is important to identify the overall design when reading any mixed methods report. Many authors using the convergent parallel design name it explicitly when describing the overall design for their study. In addition to *convergent parallel*, researchers may use terms such as *triangulation*, *concurrent*, and *simultaneous* to signal the use of this design. If the design is not named, you can still recognize a good application of the convergent parallel design by identifying the following key characteristics of this design in a written report:

- *The research problem called for the strengths of quantitative and qualitative research to be combined.* When reading the Introduction section, you should find that the researchers needed to combine the different strengths of quantitative and qualitative research to provide a complete and valid picture of the phenomenon being studied. Both methods are called for so that the researchers can describe generalizations and trends about variables along with individual perspectives and contexts.
- *The quantitative and qualitative components of the study occurred concurrently.* When reading the Method section of the report, you should learn that the researchers collected and analyzed both types of data during the same phase of the research process, often at the same time. For example, qualitative documents about what students learn in preschool are gathered and examined at the same time that the researcher collects and analyzes quantitative observations on student behavior using a checklist. This concurrent timing is indicated with a "+" in Figure 12.4.
- *The quantitative and qualitative components of the study had equal priority for addressing the study's purpose.* Although different priorities are possible, most convergent parallel studies use an equal priority. When reading the Method and Results sections, you should infer that the researchers value both quantitative and qualitative data and use them as approximately equal sources of information in the

study. For example, interview data are as important as the scores gathered on an instrument. This equal priority is indicated by the uppercase "QUAN" and "QUAL" designations in Figure 12.4. Although you will read reports of convergent parallel studies that used an unequal priority, the standard for this design is for the researchers to prioritize both components of the study equally to address the study's purpose.

■ *The quantitative and qualitative results of the study were combined and compared to produce conclusions that are complete and valid.* When reading the report's Results and Conclusion sections, you should find that the researchers first described quantitative statistical and qualitative thematic results separately (i.e., in parallel) and then directly compared or related the two sets of results to each other. For instance, researchers might report statistical results from a survey, qualitative themes from interviews, and then a comparison of how the statistics and themes agree and disagree on specific concepts that occurred in both sets of results.

An Example of the Convergent Parallel Design.

In a convergent parallel mixed methods study, Hoffman and Nottis (2008) collected quantitative and qualitative data at the same time to understand eighth-grade students' perceptions of preparing for a high-stakes test that they were required to complete at one school. To study these perceptions, they used quantitative surveys with 215 students to gather demographic information and data about how influential students perceived different school-initiated strategies to be in helping them perform on the test. In addition to completing the survey, students were also asked to write a letter to their principal in which they described what they felt helped them perform successfully on the test. After statistically analyzing the quantitative survey responses and thematically analyzing the qualitative letter documents, the researchers compared the results from the two sources of data. From the comparisons, they found areas of agreement (e.g., strategies that scored highest in the quantitative analysis were supported by positive comments in the qualitative letters) and disagreement (e.g., the letters noted that parents were important influences, but the role of parents had not been included in the survey). Hoffman and Nottis (2008) combined the two sets of results to develop a more complete picture of students' perceptions and they concluded, "These [combined] findings suggest that there are multiple ways for administrators to encourage optimal test performance results" (p. 220).

What Do You Think?

Suppose you are reading a collection of research articles related to the problem of alcohol abuse by adolescents. Why might one of the studies have used a convergent parallel mixed methods design to study this topic? What characteristics would you expect to find in the report of this study?

Check Your Understanding

A researcher might use a convergent parallel design to provide a complete picture of adolescents' reasons for using alcohol. To address this purpose, we would expect the researcher to collect both forms of data concurrently and with equal priority. She could ask high school students to complete a survey indicating whether they have used alcohol and, if so, their reasons for the use. During the same semester, the researcher could also conduct focus group interviews with small groups of high school students to learn about their perceptions of why adolescents use alcohol. As the researcher analyzes the results, she would consider both sets of data as equally important for helping her understand adolescents' reasons. She would also compare the trends obtained through the surveys with the themes that emerged from the interviews and interpret the extent to which they confirm each other.

How might a convergent parallel design be used for a topic of interest to you?

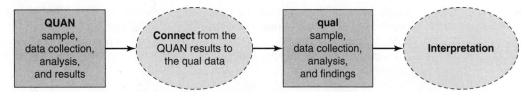

FIGURE 12.5 The Sequential Explanatory QUAN → qual Mixed Methods Design

The Sequential Explanatory Mixed Methods Design

Instead of collecting data at the same time, a mixed methods researcher might collect and analyze quantitative information first and then collect qualitative information in a second phase. This design, shown in Figure 12.5, is a sequential explanatory mixed methods design. A **sequential explanatory mixed methods design** is a set of procedures that researchers use to collect and analyze quantitative data in a first phase, plan a second phase based on the quantitative results, and then collect and analyze qualitative data in the second phase to help explain or elaborate on the quantitative results. The sequential explanatory design captures the best of both quantitative and qualitative data—to obtain quantitative results from a population in the first phase, and then refine or elaborate these findings through an in-depth qualitative exploration in the second phase. This is usually a straightforward design to understand in reports because researchers only implement one component at a time (see Figure 12.5). This means that the report usually unfolds in two distinct phases (i.e., first quantitative, then qualitative), with each phase clearly identified with headings in the Method and Results sections.

> *Here's a Tip!*
>
> One trick for remembering that the sequential explanatory design starts with a quantitative phase is to note that both qua*n*titative and expla*n*atory have an *N* in the words and the researcher aims to *explain* why quantitative results occur.

Studies Using the Sequential Explanatory Design Explain Quantitative Results with Qualitative Data. The rationale for the sequential explanatory design is that quantitative data and results are needed to provide a general picture of the research problem, but that the quantitative results by themselves are inadequate. Specifically, there is a need to build on the quantitative results, through qualitative data collection, in order to refine, extend, or explain the general picture. Quantitative results that are "inadequate" are statistical results (e.g., significant relationships or group differences) that the researchers are unable to fully explain with the existing theory or quantitative data. For example, quantitative survey results may describe significant predictors for high and low levels of parental involvement in school athletics, but the researchers may not understand *why* certain factors are associated with low involvement for some parents. By conducting qualitative interviews with noninvolved parents, the researchers then have information to help explain the specific quantitative results.

In a good application of the sequential explanatory design, you find that the researchers carefully connected from their quantitative results in the first phase to the second, qualitative phase to develop the best explanations. For example, in a study of the rates of child immunizations in a community, the researchers might have quantitatively identified a certain neighborhood in the community that had significantly higher rates of child immunization. To explain why that part of the community scored so high, the researchers could build on those results by deciding to conduct focus group interviews about why and how parents immunize their children with parents of young children who live in that specific neighborhood. The sequential explanatory design is particularly appropriate in studies where the researchers obtained unexpected quantitative results because they then collect a second set of qualitative data to help explain why the unexpected results occurred. This design also works well when the researcher needed to collect quantitative information first to identify the best participants to include for the qualitative data collection. For example, a researcher could use quantitative data to identify individuals who have high achievement to participate in qualitative interviews about the experiences of high achievers.

Identifying the Characteristics of the Sequential Explanatory Design in a Research Report. You can identify mixed methods studies that report the use of a sequential explanatory design by noting the terms *explanatory*, *sequential*, or *two-phase* *design* and determining that the researcher collected and analyzed quantitative data first. For studies that do not provide a specific name for their mixed methods design, you can identify that the researchers used the sequential explanatory design by noting its key characteristics. Specifically, look for the following characteristics when reading a mixed methods report:

- ■ ***The research problem called for quantitative results that are explained.*** When reading the Introduction section of the report, you should learn that the researchers wanted to provide a complete explanation of the research problem and questions, but that quantitative results alone were not enough. A second, qualitative phase was needed that builds on the quantitative results so that the researchers can explain the reasons behind the quantitative results or elaborate further about the quantitative results.
- ■ ***The quantitative and qualitative components of the study occurred sequentially, with the quantitative data collected and analyzed first.*** When reading the Method section of the report, you find that the researchers began the study by first collecting and analyzing quantitative data. The qualitative data collection and analysis then followed after the researchers analyzed the quantitative data so that it built on the quantitative results. This sequential timing is indicated with an "→" in Figure 12.5.
- ■ ***The initial quantitative component of the study had the priority for addressing the study's purpose.*** Although different priorities are possible, most sequential explanatory studies use an unequal priority. When reading the Method and Results sections of the report, you likely infer that the researchers used a quantitative emphasis in the study. A quantitative priority is indicated by a study purpose that aims to measure and understand quantitative results, the quantitative phase occurring first and representing a major aspect of the data collection, and having an overall goal of explanation. The second phase of the research study is then a smaller qualitative component that builds on the quantitative results. The "QUAN" and "qual" shorthand in Figure 12.5 indicates this typical quantitative priority.
- ■ ***The quantitative phase of the study built to the qualitative phase in order to produce qualitative findings that help to explain the quantitative results.*** When reading the Method section of the report, you should determine that the researchers connected the qualitative data collection to the initial quantitative results. This connection occurs when the researchers design the qualitative component of the study based on the quantitative results. For example, they might select a few typical cases based on the quantitative results, follow-up with outlier or extreme cases from the quantitative dataset, or focus the qualitative data collection on the key concept(s) from the quantitative results. Then, when reading the Results and Conclusion sections, you should note that the researchers first present and discuss the quantitative results of the study, and then present the qualitative results and discuss how they help explain the quantitative results.

An Example of the Sequential Explanatory Design.   A two-phase project by Ivankova and Stick (2007) is a good example of a sequential explanatory design. Their research examined the persistence of students enrolled in an educational leadership doctoral program that was delivered using online technology. They described their purpose:

> [T]o identify factors contributing to students' persistence in the [program] by obtaining quantitative results from a survey of 278 current and former students and then following up with four purposefully selected individuals to explore those results in more depth through a qualitative case analysis. (p. 95)

The authors began their study with a quantitative phase. They collected and analyzed survey data to determine the factors (e.g., self-motivation and faculty) that predicted students' persistence in the program. Once these results were obtained, they used the quantitative data to select one typical individual (in terms of the quantitative data) from each of four groups studied (students beginning, matriculated, graduated, or withdrawn from the program). The authors felt that these individuals could best provide detailed information about different perspectives of each group in a second, qualitative phase. Ivankova and Stick then collected qualitative information about each individual, including interview data, program records, and documents such as coursework.

The qualitative descriptions and themes resulting from the four cases helped to explain the quantitative statistical results. For example, the quantitative results pointed to self-motivation as a predictor of persistence in the program and the qualitative results helped to explain the different ways that self-motivation was experienced by participants in the program.

What Do You Think?

Suppose you are reading a collection of research articles related to the problem of alcohol abuse by adolescents. Why might one of the studies have used a sequential explanatory mixed methods design to study this topic? What characteristics would you expect to find in the report of this study?

Check Your Understanding

A researcher might use a sequential explanatory design to provide a better explanation of why adolescents first start to drink alcohol. To address this purpose, we would expect the researcher to begin with a quantitative phase and use those results to connect to a qualitative phase. The researcher might first ask high school students to complete a quantitative instrument indicating at what age and in what circumstances they had their first alcoholic drink. He could then analyze the quantitative data to test a hypothesis that children who start drinking at a young age are more likely to do so at home. The quantitative results may include a surprising finding, such as there is a difference in the circumstances of first drinks for boys compared to girls. The researcher then decides to collect qualitative data to learn girls' stories of having their first alcoholic drinks. The researcher would use this qualitative data to help explain the surprising quantitative results.

How could a sequential explanatory design be used to study a topic of interest to you?

The Sequential Exploratory Mixed Methods Design

In contrast to the sequential explanatory design, some two-phase mixed methods studies begin with the collection and analysis of qualitative data. As illustrated in Figure 12.6, a **sequential exploratory mixed methods design** is a set of procedures that researchers use to collect and analyze qualitative data to explore a topic in a first phase, plan a second phase based on the qualitative findings, and then collect and analyze quantitative data in the second phase to help extend or generalize the qualitative findings. This design gets its name because the researcher begins with a qualitative *exploration* of the topic in the study. A common application of this design is to explore a phenomenon, identify themes, develop an instrument based on the thematic findings, and subsequently administer the instrument to many people to determine the extent to which the themes generalize to the larger group. Because of its two-phase approach, the sequential exploratory design is a straightforward design to understand in reports because researchers only discuss the implementation of one component at a time (see Figure 12.6). This means that the report usually unfolds in two distinct phases (i.e., first qualitative, then quantitative), with each phase clearly identified by headings in the Method and Results sections of the report.

> **Here's a Tip!**
>
> One trick for remembering that the sequential exploratory design starts with a qualitative phase is to note that both qua*l*itative and exp*l*oratory have an *L* in the words and the researcher starts the study by *exploring* the phenomenon.

Studies Using the Sequential Exploratory Design Generalize Qualitative Results with Quantitative Data. The rationale for the sequential exploratory design is that the qualitative data and results are needed to provide an exploration and

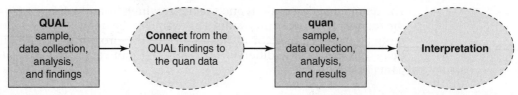

FIGURE 12.6   The Sequential Exploratory QUAL → quan Mixed Methods Design

description of the research problem, but then a quantitative data collection is needed to expand on, generalize, or test the qualitative findings with a larger sample. That is, the researcher starts with a qualitative exploration, but argues that the exploration alone is insufficient to address the study's research problem and purpose. One advantage of this approach is that it allows the researcher to identify quantitative measures that are actually grounded in the qualitative data obtained from study participants. Therefore, this design is particularly useful when existing instruments, variables, and theories are not known or are unavailable for the population under study. For example, a researcher may want to study stress for new fathers who identify as gay, but finds that existing theories and instruments of paternal stress have only been developed from the perspective of fathers who identify as heterosexual. By using a sequential exploratory design, the researcher can initially explore the views of fathers who identify as gay by listening to participants rather than approach a topic with a predetermined set of variables. The researcher may also develop a model by collecting and analyzing qualitative data from a few individuals. This model can then be quantitatively tested in a secondary quantitative phase.

As with the sequential explanatory design, you find that the researchers carefully connect the two phases in a good application of the sequential exploratory design. However, this connection is different because in the sequential exploratory design the researchers need to connect from qualitative findings in the first phase to the collection of quantitative data in the second phase. This connection is most often made when researchers build on initial qualitative findings by using them to select the variables, to state hypotheses for testing, and to select or design the instruments for the quantitative phase. For example, in a study of how nurses cope with emotional stress at work, a researcher might begin by gathering nurses' stories of stressful events at work. By analyzing these stories, the researcher identifies several themes about coping strategies, including *physical activities, blowing off steam,* and *seeking support from others.* Building on these findings, the researcher decides to quantitatively assess the prevalence of different coping strategies and develops and administers an instrument that asks many nurses to indicate how often they use each of the strategies within the themes identified in the qualitative phase.

Identifying the Characteristics of the Sequential Exploratory Design in a Research Report.   You can identify mixed methods studies that report an application of the sequential exploratory design with the terms *exploratory, instrument development, sequential,* or *two-phase design,* and checking to see that the researcher implemented a qualitative phase first. If the design is not clearly named, you can recognize a good use of the sequential exploratory design by identifying the following characteristics as you read the report:

- *The research problem called for qualitative findings that are generalized or tested.* When reading the Introduction section, you should find that the researcher argued for the need for a detailed exploration of the research problem and questions, but also included an indication that qualitative findings alone are not enough. A second, quantitative phase is needed so that the researcher can test or generalize the initial qualitative findings with a larger number of participants.
- *The qualitative and quantitative components of the study occurred sequentially, with the qualitative data collected and analyzed first.* When reading the Method section, you learn that the researcher conducted the study in two phases. The first phase involved the collection and analysis of qualitative data (e.g., open-ended interviews, observations) gathered from a small number of purposefully selected individuals. This phase was followed by quantitative data collection (e.g., a survey) with a large

number of participants in a second phase. The arrow (→) in Figure 12.6 indicates this sequential timing.

- ■ *The initial qualitative component of the study had the priority for addressing the study's purpose.* Although different priorities are possible, most sequential exploratory studies use an unequal priority. When reading the Method and Results sections of the report, you often find indications that the authors used a qualitative priority. This emphasis occurs through presenting the overarching research question as an open-ended question, discussing the qualitative results in more detail than the quantitative results, and having an overall goal of exploration. This typical qualitative priority is indicated by the "QUAL" and "quan" designations in Figure 12.6.
- ■ *The qualitative phase of the study connected to the quantitative phase in order to produce quantitative results that help to generalize or test the initial qualitative findings.* When reading the Method section of the report, you should learn that the researchers built on the initial qualitative findings to shape the quantitative data collection, such as by specifying the variables and informing the development of an instrument. Then, when reading the Results and Conclusion sections, you should find that the researchers first present and discuss the qualitative findings (e.g., themes or theory). Once the qualitative findings are described, they then present the quantitative results and discuss the extent to which they generalize or provide a test of the qualitative findings for a larger population.

An Example of the Sequential Exploratory Design. In a sequential exploratory mixed methods study, Cinamon and Dan (2010) wanted to understand parents' perceptions of career development programs in the context of preschool education. Little previous work had examined this topic, so they needed to begin their study by exploring the topic in a first phase before they could attempt to measure it in a second phase. The authors wrote:

> The objective of the qualitative step is to explore and understand the authentic perceptions and attitudes of parents toward a developmental approach to careers and their attitudes toward the implementation of career education in preschools. . . . Along with the rich descriptions of the parents with regard to their perceptions, these interviews also helped develop two parental attitude questionnaires that were applied in the second step of the study—the quantitative step. (p. 523)

The qualitative first phase of the study consisted of interviews with 15 parents representing both high and low socioeconomic status in the central region of Israel. From this data, the researchers identified that parents had complex attitudes about this topic that grouped into four broad categories (e.g., "relevance of the world of work to children's development" and "parents' activities with children relating to work and career"). From the qualitative findings, the researchers developed questionnaires to measure the different parent attitudes. In the second phase of the study, they then gathered survey data from 140 parents who had a child in preschool. They analyzed the survey data statistically and determined that in general parents' positive attitudes about career education in preschool were significantly higher than their negative attitudes, but that there were significant differences in attitudes depending on whether parents were of high or low socioeconomic status. They concluded by discussing what they learned from the connected results and offering suggestions of how preschool programs interested in including career development activities might work to gain parent support based on the results.

What Do You Think?

Suppose you are reading a collection of research articles related to the problem of alcohol abuse by adolescents. Why might one of the studies have used a sequential exploratory mixed methods design to study this topic? What characteristics would you expect to find in the report of this study?

Check Your Understanding

A researcher might use a sequential exploratory mixed methods design to develop and test a model of how parents come to seek help for their adolescent children's drinking problems. To address this purpose, we would expect the researcher to begin the study with a qualitative phase and then connect to a quantitative phase. The researcher might start by interviewing a few parents across the county who have enrolled their children in a local treatment program. He would analyze the qualitative data to develop a model of the process parents undergo to seek help for their child. Next, he would want to expand these results by seeing if the model generalizes to many parents' experiences. He could develop a questionnaire that includes items about each step identified in the model and administer it to a large number of parents in the region who have enrolled their children in similar programs. From the two sets of results, he could describe the steps and also discuss the trends for how often each step occurs across a large number of parents.

How might a sequential exploratory design be used to study a topic of interest to you?

The Embedded Mixed Methods Design

A fourth form of mixed methods design is similar to the previous designs, with some important exceptions. The **embedded mixed methods design** is a set of procedures that researchers use to collect a secondary set of data (qualitative or quantitative) in a study that is guided by a traditional quantitative design (e.g., a true experiment) or a traditional qualitative design (e.g., a case study) where the secondary dataset addresses a different question than the primary dataset and is used to augment the implementation and/or interpretation of the primary method. You can see the embedded nature of this mixed methods design in Figure 12.7. For example, during a quantitative experiment to compare the outcomes of a treatment to those from a control condition, the investigator decides to collect qualitative data at the same time as the intervention to examine how participants in the treatment condition are experiencing the intervention. The primary aim of this study is to examine the impact of the experimental treatment on the outcome. The addition of qualitative data enables the researcher to *also* explore how participants are experiencing the process of the intervention. As another example,

FIGURE 12.7
Two Examples of the Embedded Mixed Methods Design: QUAN(qual) and QUAL(quan)

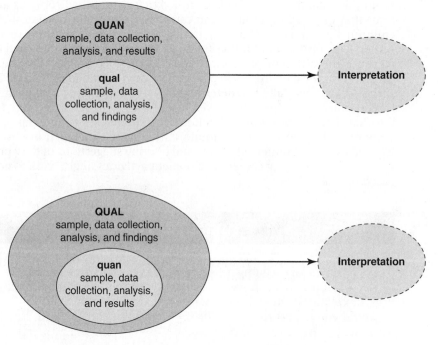

a researcher could embed quantitative data into a qualitative design. For example, a researcher conducting a qualitative case study gathers secondary quantitative data to help explain attitudes in a community that enrich the description of the case and its context. It can be a challenge to distinguish the embedded design from the other mixed methods designs, but when you read embedded studies, it typically feels like you are reading a study that used a specific quantitative or qualitative design and included the other type of data in order to enhance the implementation of the design.

Studies Using the Embedded Design Enhance a Larger Study with a Secondary Dataset. The rationale for the embedded design is that a researcher needs to enhance a traditional quantitative or qualitative design (such as those we learned in Chapters 6 and 9) by asking a secondary question that calls for a different type of data embedded within the traditional design. This mixed methods design enables a researcher to use different methods to address primary and secondary research questions that are different, but related. To date, the most common examples of this design in the literature are those where a researcher embedded qualitative data into an experimental design to enhance the implementation or interpretation of the experiment. Although quantitative data are most effective for testing the outcomes of an experiment, qualitative data can augment an experiment by exploring how different individuals engage with the intervention or how the intervention is delivered to the participants in different contexts. In this case, the qualitative component of the study is assuming a secondary role and fits within the larger quantitative experiment.

In a good application of the embedded design, you find that the researchers clearly note the primary and secondary aspects of their study and design the supplemental method so it fits within the larger design. Continuing with the example of qualitative data embedded in an experiment, we might find that the qualitative component "fits within" the larger experiment by following procedures that are more in line with a quantitative approach such as a large sample, using random assignment, and using a fixed approach to keep from affecting the outcome of the experiment. Whether the researcher is enhancing a quantitative design with qualitative data or a qualitative design with quantitative data, when researchers have used a mixed methods embedded design, you find that they place their focus on the primary method. They then enhance their understanding of the overall research problem by examining a secondary question with a different method.

Identifying the Characteristics of the Embedded Design in a Research Report. You can identify mixed methods studies that report an embedded design with the terms *embedded* or *nested*. Other key terminology that you may notice includes the terms *primary* and *secondary* to indicate the relative status of the research questions and two datasets. Authors name a specific quantitative or qualitative design (e.g., a quantitative experiment or qualitative case study) while also mentioning the collection of the other type of data (e.g., qualitative or quantitative). If the designation of the design is unclear in the report, you can also recognize an embedded approach by identifying the following main characteristics:

- *The research problem called for a secondary dataset to support the primary design.* When reading the Introduction of the report, you should learn that the researcher has a primary research question that requires a typical quantitative or qualitative approach. In addition, the researcher has the need to ask a secondary question that calls for the other type of data. This secondary research question is asked to augment the implementation or understanding of the primary research question and its method.
- *The quantitative and qualitative components were embedded within a larger design concurrently or sequentially.* You learn the timing of the implementation of the embedded design when reading the Method section. In most embedded designs, the researcher collects both the quantitative and qualitative data at roughly the same time. In some embedded designs, however, the researcher may collect the secondary form of data before or after the primary data collection. The researcher often discusses the two methods in separate sections of the report or even in two separate reports that refer to each other. Whether concurrent or sequential, the collection of the secondary data is embedded within a larger design. This embedded aspect of this design is illustrated by the concentric circles and parentheses "( )" in Figure 12.7.

- *The primary component of the study had the priority for addressing the study's purpose and the secondary component had a lesser priority.* As you read all sections of an embedded report, you find clear indications of an unequal priority. The larger design of the embedded mixed methods study provides the overall framework and sets the priority of the study as either quantitative or qualitative. The secondary form is less important in relation to the overall purpose, and often is collected in service of the primary method. The priority of the primary form is indicated by the "QUAN" and "QUAL" designations in Figure 12.7, and the lesser priority of the secondary form is indicated by the "qual" and "quan" designations.
- *The secondary results augmented or provided additional sources of information for the primary component of the study.* When reading the Results and Conclusion sections, you find that the researchers discuss how the primary goals of the study were enhanced by the inclusion of the secondary dataset. The augmentation arises from the second dataset because it addresses a research question that supports the primary question investigated in the study. For example, the qualitative results from an experiment may describe the *process* the participants experience as part of the treatment, which can augment the interpretation of the quantitative results about the *impact* of the treatment on the outcomes.

An Example of the Embedded Design.   Plano Clark et al.'s (2013) report of a study about a psychoeducational intervention aimed at helping cancer patients better manage their pain illustrates the embedded mixed methods design. The primary intent of the study was to compare the impact of two doses of the intervention in terms of various patient outcomes (e.g., level of pain and self-efficacy). To address this purpose, the researchers used a randomized clinical trial (a type of true experiment) where participants were randomly assigned to one of the two treatment conditions (i.e., high dose or low dose). To better understand how the nurses implemented the treatment and participants experienced the treatment, they were also interested in describing the process of the intervention. Therefore, the team included a qualitative component as part of the larger experiment by having the nurses make audio recordings of their interactions with participants as they delivered the intervention. This form of qualitative data collection did not interfere with the conduct of the experiment, but provided supplemental data to address secondary questions about participants' experiences, such as how they interacted with their assigned intervention nurse. This study is a good example of an embedded design with a major quantitative experimental design that included a secondary, supportive qualitative component.

What Do You Think?

Suppose you are reading a collection of research articles related to the problem of alcohol abuse by adolescents. Why might one of the studies have used an embedded mixed methods design to study this topic? What characteristics would you expect to find in the report of this study?

Check Your Understanding

A researcher might use an embedded mixed methods design to test the effectiveness of a new alcohol treatment program aimed at teaching adolescents alternative strategies for dealing with stress and to understand how the program is experienced. To address this purpose, we would expect the researcher to conduct an experiment and gather qualitative data during the experiment. The researcher might conduct a true experiment where adolescents who have been cited for alcohol possession are randomly assigned to either the new program or to the usual punishment of community service. She would have participants in both groups complete a quantitative measure about their attitudes about and recent experiences with alcohol consumption before the treatment, and then 6 months later test for differences between the groups. At the same time as this quantitative experiment, the researcher might also gather qualitative interview data with individuals completing the new program to understand how they are experiencing the program materials. Therefore, the quantitative dataset would be of primary importance to test the effectiveness of the program, and the qualitative dataset provides secondary information about the program's process.

How might an embedded design be used to study a topic of interest to you?

You now know how to recognize the four major mixed methods designs commonly discussed in research reports. Although other mixed methods designs exist (refer back to Table 12.1 for additional examples), most other mixed methods designs are variations of these four major designs. For example, the transformative mixed methods design occurs when a researcher uses one of the basic mixed methods designs within a transformative (or social justice) theoretical framework. Recall that in Chapter 4 we learned some researchers use a social justice stance to guide their research. When the social justice stance shapes the use of a concurrent, sequential, or embedded mixed methods approach, then it

> *Here's a Tip!*
>
> When reading a mixed methods report, look for a diagram of the study's procedures to help you understand the flow of activities in the study. If such a diagram is not present, sketch out the sequence of activities using the figures in this chapter as models.

is often referred to as a *transformative mixed methods design*. For example, Hodgkin (2008) used a feminist theoretical lens and concern for gender inequalities to shape her use of mixed methods to study how women experience social capital (participation in social, civic, and community activities). She began her study with a quantitative phase to determine whether men and women exhibit different social capital profiles, and specifically used a quantitative instrument thought to include items that represent issues that may be important for women. Finding significant gender differences, she then implemented a qualitative phase where she interviewed women to give them voice as to how they experience social capital in order to explain why women's experiences differ from those of men. This study therefore demonstrates many of the same characteristics as the sequential explanatory design, but it can be called a transformative mixed methods design because the use of mixed methods was shaped by the researcher's social justice stance. By recognizing the key characteristics of the four major designs within any mixed methods report, you are able to understand how the researcher is using the quantitative and qualitative methods to best address the study's purpose.

What Do You Think?

Consider the following excerpts from four published studies. Which mixed methods design do you think each of the authors used? What evidence do you have from the passages? How can you represent the design using the mixed methods notation system in Figure 12.2?

a. "Findings from a qualitative analysis provided complex and rich information about young adults' perceptions of mattering to their current romantic partners. Responses were used to develop a scale that was administered in Study 2 to a sample ($N = 99$) of young adults in romantic relationships" (Mak & Marshall, 2004, p. 469).

b. "Locating our project within the mixed methods framework provided by Hanson et al., our longitudinal data were collected concurrently throughout the project; equal weight was given to the quantitative and qualitative data; and data were analyzed separately, compared, and contrasted" (Bikos et al., 2007, p. 30).

> **c.** "The study included two stages: first a quantitative stage, consisting of self-administered questionnaires addressing each of the hypotheses; and second, a qualitative stage, including interviews focused on a more limited set of issues" (Vittersø et al., 2003, p. 207).
>
> **d.** "A design proposal was circulated to the EAG [expert advisory group] that placed the RCT [randomized controlled trial] study as primary, with a [qualitative] process study taking a secondary role, examining issues of implementation, process, and meaning" (Brady & O'Regan, 2009, p. 275).

Check Your Understanding

Each of the study excerpts mentions the collection of quantitative and qualitative data. Therefore, we can conclude that all four represent mixed methods studies. Excerpt (a) comes from a study that used a sequential exploratory mixed methods design. The authors first collected and analyzed a set of qualitative data. They then used the qualitative results to develop a scale, which was subsequently used to collect quantitative data in a second phase. This study can be represented as: QUAL → quan. Excerpt (b) comes from a study that used a convergent parallel mixed methods design. The authors collected the two datasets concurrently, gave them equal priority, and analyzed them separately before comparing them. This study can be represented as: QUAN + QUAL. Excerpt (c) is from a study that used a sequential explanatory mixed methods design. The authors discuss using two stages, with the quantitative stage first followed by a qualitative stage. This study can be represented as: QUAN → qual. Excerpt (d) comes from a study that used an embedded mixed methods design. The authors note that the primary design of their study was a quantitative randomized controlled trial (RCT) and that they incorporated a secondary qualitative component within the randomized controlled trial. This study can be represented as: QUAN(qual).

How Do You Evaluate a Mixed Methods Research Study?

Like other research approaches, mixed methods studies are based on specific designs that address certain types of research problems and have key characteristics that differentiate them from other designs. With the information you have learned in this chapter, you now have the knowledge needed to identify the design used in a mixed methods study and evaluate the authors' use of that design. Evaluating a mixed methods study requires you to assess a study in different ways. Because the study includes both quantitative and qualitative data, you should assess the quantitative procedures using criteria presented in Chapters 6–8 and the qualitative procedures using criteria presented in Chapters 9–11. In addition to evaluating the two parts, you also need to consider how well the author implemented and reported the major mixed methods design characteristics. Table 12.2 lists criteria that are useful for evaluating the use of mixed methods in a study report. For each of the criteria, the table also provides indicators of higher quality and lower quality to help you make your own assessment when evaluating the information provided in a mixed methods research report.

Figure 12.8 provides a rating form that you can use to apply the quality criteria to evaluate the use of mixed methods research within a study's research report. For each of the criteria you locate, assign a quality rating from *fair* (1) to *excellent* (3) and document your evidence and/or reasoning behind the rating. If one of the criteria is missing in the report or very poorly stated, then indicate *poor* (0) as your rating. Keep in mind that research reports vary in the extent of discussion about the mixed methods procedures and the procedures differ depending on the mixed methods design used. Even with this variation, however, a good mixed methods study should still score well on

TABLE 12.2 Criteria for Evaluating the Use of Mixed Methods in a Research Report

Quality Criteria	Indicators of Higher Quality in Mixed Methods Research	Indicators of Lower Quality in Mixed Methods Research
The Key Elements		
1. The rationale for needing mixed methods research is appropriate and justified.	+ The researcher explicitly articulates why quantitative or qualitative research alone is inadequate. + A sound reason is provided to justify the use of mixed methods.	− The researcher only implies that one research type alone is not adequate. − A weak reason is provided to justify the use of mixed methods.
2. The choice of the mixed methods design is appropriate and justified.	+ A good mixed methods design is used to plan and implement the study. + The mixed methods design is fully described, including the decisions for timing, priority, and mixing. + Strong reasons are provided that justify why the specific design was appropriate for the study.	− The use of mixed methods seems haphazard and not well thought out. − The mixed methods design and its associated decisions are unclear and poorly explained. − Weak or inappropriate reasons are used to justify why the specific design was used in the study.
3. The quantitative methods are of good quality based on the standards of quantitative research.	+ The quantitative component includes a large, representative sample; valid and reliable scores from closed-ended measures; and good statistical analytic procedures. + See Chapters 6–8 for further indicators of higher quality for the quantitative component of the study.	− The quantitative component includes a small, convenience sample; poor quality measures; or inappropriate statistical analytic procedures. − See Chapters 6–8 for further indicators of lower quality for the quantitative component of the study
4. The qualitative methods are of good quality based on the standards of qualitative research.	+ The qualitative component includes a small, purposeful, information-rich sample; extensive and credible open-ended data forms; and good analytic procedures for developing description and themes. + See Chapters 9–11 for further indicators of higher quality for the qualitative component of the study.	− The qualitative component includes a large, convenience sample; superficial and limited data forms; and minimal interpretive analysis. − See Chapters 9–11 for further indicators of lower quality for the qualitative component of the study.
5. The quantitative and qualitative components of the study are meaningfully mixed.	+ The quantitative and qualitative components of the study are explicitly merged, connected, or embedded. + The type(s) of mixing is consistent with the overall mixed methods design. + The quantitative, qualitative, and mixed results are explicitly discussed at the end of the study.	− The quantitative and qualitative components of the study are kept separate. − The type of mixing is inconsistent with the overall design. − Only the separate results are discussed at the end of the study with little to no interpretation of the combination of results.
General Evaluation		
6. The study used a rigorous application of mixed methods research to address the purpose.	+ The mixed methods design is a good fit to the study's research problem and purpose. + The quantitative, qualitative, and mixed aspects of the study fit together in a logical way to address the study's purpose.	− There is an unclear or poor fit between the mixed methods design and the study's research problem and purpose. + There is no clear logic for how the quantitative, qualitative, and mixed aspects of the study fit together to address the study's purpose.
7. The use of mixed methods produced a good understanding of the research purpose.	+ The findings provide complete, valid, and in-depth answers to the study's research questions. + The integrated findings go beyond what was learned from the separate quantitative results and qualitative findings.	− The findings provide superficial answers or do not clearly answer the study's research questions. − The findings are limited to what was learned from the separate quantitative results and qualitative findings.

Quality Criteria	Quality Rating				Your Evidence and/or Reasoning
	0 = Poor	1 = Fair	2 = Good	3 = Excellent	
The Key Elements					
1. The rationale for needing mixed methods is appropriate and justified.					
2. The choice of the mixed methods design is appropriate and justified.					
3. The quantitative methods are of good quality based on the standards of quantitative research.					
4. The qualitative methods are of good quality based on the standards of qualitative research.					
5. The quantitative and qualitative components of the study are meaningfully mixed.					
General Evaluation					
6. The study used a rigorous application of mixed methods research.					
7. The use of mixed methods produced a good understanding of the research purpose.					
Overall Quality 0–10 = Low Quality 11–16 = Adequate Quality 17–21 = High Quality	**Total Score =**				**My Overall Assessment Is**

FIGURE 12.8   A Rating Scale for Evaluating a Mixed Methods Study

most of the items listed in Figure 12.8. By adding up the rating scores for each of the criteria and using the suggested cutoff values provided at the bottom of the figure, you will have a quantitative measure that you can use to inform your overall assessment.

Reviewing What You've Learned To Do

- *Identify and understand the use of mixed methods research in a research study.*
  - ☐ The title, Abstract, and text of a mixed methods report include signal words that indicate the use of mixed methods research.
  - ☐ The Method section of a mixed methods report indicates that the authors collected, analyzed, and mixed both quantitative and qualitative forms of data to best understand a research problem.
- *Note the reasons why researchers use mixed methods research in their studies.*
  - ☐ Mixed methods research is appropriate when the researchers' reasons included needing both quantitative and qualitative data to combine the different strengths of each; to build from one to the other; or to answer two different but related research questions.

- *List three characteristics that distinguish the different mixed methods research designs.*
  - ❑ Mixed methods research designs differ in terms of the timing, priority, and mixing of the quantitative and qualitative components of the study.
  - ❑ Timing refers to when the quantitative and qualitative components of the study are implemented, and it can be concurrent (one phase) or sequential (two phases).
  - ❑ Priority refers to the relative importance of the quantitative and qualitative components for addressing the study's purpose, and it can be equal, quantitative, or qualitative.
  - ❑ Mixing refers to how the researcher explicitly combines the quantitative and qualitative data and results of the study. Strategies include interpreting both sets of results in the Conclusion, merging the two sets of results in the analysis, connecting from one set of results to the collection of the other form of data, or embedding the methods in a larger framework.
- *Recognize four different research designs when reading mixed methods reports.*
  - ❑ The convergent parallel design has concurrent timing, usually has equal priority, and merges the two sets of results during the analysis and/or interpretation. It is used to develop complete and valid conclusions about a topic.
  - ❑ The sequential explanatory design has sequential timing starting with a quantitative phase, often has quantitative priority, and connects from the quantitative results to the collection of the qualitative data. It is used to explain why quantitative results occurred using qualitative data.
  - ❑ The sequential exploratory design has sequential timing starting with a qualitative phase, often has qualitative priority, and connects from the qualitative results to the collection of the quantitative data. It is used to test or generalize qualitative findings using quantitative data.
  - ❑ The embedded design often has concurrent timing, has unequal priority, and embeds one component of the study within a design framed by the other component, such as embedding qualitative data into a quantitative experiment design. It is used to answer primary and secondary questions with different methods.
- *Evaluate the quality of a mixed methods research report.*
  - ❑ The evaluation of a mixed methods study includes assessing the quantitative component using the standards of quantitative research and assessing the qualitative component using the standards of qualitative research.
  - ❑ The evaluation of a mixed methods study includes evaluating its mixed methods features in addition to the separate components. The evaluation considers the rationale for using mixed methods and a particular mixed methods design; the quality of the implementation of the mixed methods design, including the mixing of the two components; and the extent to which the combined results and conclusions go beyond the separate components to answer the study's research questions.

✓ **To assess what you've learned to do, click here to answer questions and receive instant feedback.**

Reading Research Articles

At the end of this chapter, you will find a research article to help you practice your new skills. Carefully read the mixed methods student-note-taking study by Igo, Kiewra, and Bruning (2008) starting on p. 410. First, write a complete, APA-style reference for this article.

As you read the article, pay close attention to statements in which the authors conveyed the quantitative, qualitative, and mixed methods elements of the study. Use the highlighting tool in the Pearson etext to indicate where the authors have provided information about the study's use of mixed methods, and use the note-taking tool to add marginal notes that name each element you highlighted and note how each one is related to the study's mixed methods design. Among the elements you will want to find are:

Quantitative (or "Quan" for short) elements:

1. Quan sample
2. Quan data collection
3. Quan data analysis
4. Quan results

Qualitative (or "Qual" for short) elements:

5. Qual sample
6. Qual data collection
7. Qual data analysis
8. Qual results

Mixed methods elements:

9. Reason for mixing methods
10. Priority (i.e., equal, quantitative, or qualitative)
11. Timing (i.e., concurrent or sequential)
12. Mixing (i.e., interpreting, merging, connecting, and/or embedding)
13. Mixed methods design

Note, however, that often authors do not discuss all of these elements—for example, they may not explicitly state the priority of the mixed methods research design, they may not provide their reason for choosing the design, or they may not provide a name for their design. If one of these elements is missing, indicate that in your marginal notes.

 Click here to go to the mixed methods student-note-taking study by Igo et al. (2008) so that you can write a complete APA-style reference for the article and enter marginal notes about the study.

Understanding Research Articles

Apply your knowledge of the content of this chapter to the mixed methods student-note-taking study by Igo et al. (2008) found at the end of this chapter (starting on p. 410).

1. Give three pieces of evidence for identifying the student-note-taking study as an example of mixed methods research.

2. Why did the researchers choose to conduct a mixed methods study instead of a quantitative or qualitative study?

3. Identify this study's mixed methods design and indicate the priority and timing of this design using the mixed methods notation system.

4. In what way(s) did the authors combine or mix the two datasets?

✓ **Click here to answer the questions and receive instant feedback.**

Evaluating Research Articles

Practice evaluating the quality of the use of mixed methods, using the mixed methods student-note-taking study by Igo et al. (2008) starting on p. 410.

1. Use the criteria discussed in Table 12.2 to evaluate the quality of the use of mixed methods in the student-note-taking study. Note that the rating form includes advice to help guide your evaluation.

✓ **Click here to open the rating scale form (Figure 12.8) to enter your ratings, evidence, and reasoning.**

An Example of Mixed Methods Research: The Student-Note-Taking Study

Let's examine another published research article to apply the ideas you are learning. Throughout this book, we will refer to this study as the "mixed methods student-note-taking" study. This journal article reports a mixed methods research study conducted and reported by Igo et al. (2008). Examine this article to practice your skills with reading, understanding, and evaluating research.

 Click here to write a complete APA-style reference for this article and receive instant feedback.

Journal of Mixed
Methods Research
Volume 2 Number 2
April 2008 149-168
© 2008 Sage Publications
10.1177/1558689807313161
http://jmmr.sagepub.com
hosted at
http://online.sagepub.com

Individual Differences and Intervention Flaws

A Sequential Explanatory Study of College Students' Copy-and-Paste Note Taking

L. Brent Igo
Clemson University, South Carolina
Kenneth A. Kiewra
Roger Bruning
University of Nebraska–Lincoln

In this study, qualitative themes and quantitative findings from previous research were used to justify the exploration of four experimental, note-taking conditions and the impact of those conditions on student learning from Web-based text. However, puzzling results obtained from dependent measures of student learning were quite inconsistent with the previous research. With no adequate theoretical explanation for these results, a follow-up explanations phase of qualitative investigation was conducted. Analyses of interview data indicated that certain experimental conditions imposed upon students an unexpected distraction. Furthermore, quantitizing students' note-taking documents showed that many students in this study used a more effective note-taking strategy than did students in a similar condition in previous research.

Keywords: *Internet learning; note taking; cognitive processes; sequential explanatory*

(01)   In research addressing cognitive approaches to learning, experiments typically are conducted and subsequent statistical results are used to discuss support or lack of support for predetermined, theoretical hypotheses. Mixed methods research might offer cognitive researchers a path toward deeper understanding of their experimental results, however. The primary purpose of this article is to present the findings of an in-depth study of college students' Web-based note taking. As shall be seen, an experiment yielded some results that were not hypothesized and other results that were, in fact, contradictory to previous research. A qualitative follow-up phase of study provided data that allowed us to make sense of the puzzling experimental results. Thus, secondarily, this study illustrates the value of the sequential explanatory mixed method design in cognitive research.

The Preference to Paste

(02)   Most students seem to prefer copying and pasting their notes to typing their notes while they gather text information online. Studies have shown that roughly 80% of general

Authors' Note: Please address correspondence to L. Brent Igo, Clemson University, Educational Foundations, 407b Tillman Hall, Box 340705, Clemson, SC 29634-0705; e-mail: ligo@clemson.edu.

education high school students (Igo, Bruning, McCrudden, & Kauffman, 2003), as well as 80% of middle school students with learning disabilities (Igo, Riccomini, Bruning, & Pope, 2006), will choose copy and paste if the option is offered. Why students prefer to paste their Web-based notes seems to differ among students, however. Whereas high school students' tendency to paste their notes might be a function of diminished motivation, middle school students with learning disabilities report that pasting reduces anxiety associated with monitoring spelling and grammar during note taking.

(03)   Not all students share this preference for copy and paste, however. In one particular study, high school students in advanced placement courses overwhelmingly preferred to type their notes from Web-based sources (Igo et al., 2003). Similarly, middle school students with learning disabilities, but with higher spelling and grammar achievement, seemed to prefer writing notes to copying and pasting notes (Igo et al., 2006). But to date, little research has addressed how learning is affected by the use of copy and paste while students read and note Web-based text. In this report, we first synthesize the limited copy-and-paste note-taking literature. Next, we present a cognitive learning study driven by this research question: How do different copy-and-paste note-taking interventions affect college students' learning of Web-based text ideas? The first two words in this question indicate that a mixed methods approach is warranted, with *do* indicating the need for an experiment and *how* indicating the need for a qualitative follow-up. Thus, in this sequential explanatory mixed methods study (Creswell & Plano Clark, 2007), a cognitive experiment was followed by interview and document analyses intended to help explain results obtained in the experiment. As shall be seen, this study exemplifies the need for the follow-up explanations model in educational research when cognitive experiments yield puzzling results.

How Copying and Pasting Notes Affects Learning From Text

(04)   Despite its apparent appeal to most students, there is an educational problem associated with copy-and-paste note taking. Students' initial learning of text ideas suffers (Igo et al., 2003, 2006), as do students' abilities to transfer text information later (Katayama, Shambaugh, & Doctor, 2005). One explanation for this negative effect on learning is that many students take copy-and-paste notes in a decidedly mindless way—selecting and pasting large amounts of text at any given time with little evaluation of which text ideas are critical to their notes. Upon testing of the information they have noted, then, those students tend to recall little, if any, of the information in their notes. This behavior and subsequent impact on initial learning was documented in studies that examined copy-and-paste note taking with high school students (Igo, Kiewra, & Bruning, 2004) and college students (Igo, Bruning, & McCrudden, 2005b; Katayama et al., 2005), alike.

(05)   Other students (albeit far fewer, based on the extant research) are more selective while taking copy-and-paste notes. They evaluate which text ideas are essential to their notes and paste smaller amounts of text, and consequently, they learn more (Igo et al., 2005b). For example, in a study by Igo et al., students who pasted fewer words per cell of a note-taking chart remembered more ideas from Web-based text, and students who pasted more words per cell (most students) remembered successively fewer ideas. In short, there seems to be an upside and downside to students' default copy-and-paste note-taking strategies; some students are selective and learn more, but most students are not selective and learn little.

(06)   Research also suggests that students can be prompted to be more selective in their pasting and think more deeply about text as they take notes (Igo et al., 2005b). Subsequently, they can achieve dramatic improvements in learning, as described by levels-of-processing theory (Craik & Lockhart, 1972). For example, a computer program that restricts the amount of text students may paste into their notes (an electronic chart that limits the content of each cell to 7 words) has been shown to increase students' text-pasting selectivity and prompt students to engage in evaluative and metacognitive processes while reading and taking notes.

(07)   But there seems to be both benefits and drawbacks to students' restricted copy-and-paste note taking. A study by Igo, Bruning, and McCrudden (2005a) showed that under the 7-word restricted copy-and-paste conditions, roughly one third of students were compelled to make minor modifications to their notes—to tinker or fine-tune. The authors concluded that this behavior led students' attention away from the meaning of the text, focusing it instead on certain note characteristics. Ultimately, learning decreased; students who modified their notes recalled fewer facts and inferred fewer relationships from text than students who did not make modifications. In short, a 7-word level of restriction from previous research, although beneficial to most students, might be too restrictive for others.

(08)   The key to learning through the copy-and-paste note-taking process, then, seems to be selectivity in one's pasting decisions (and the requisite mental processes), whether such selectivity is simply the note taker's personal approach or strategically imposed by a computer note-taking program. A similar theme is found in related text-learning literature. For example, the extent to which students learn text ideas through the underlining or the paper-and-pencil note-taking processes is related to how selective students are and how deeply they process text during the activities (Anderson & Armbruster, 1984; Blanchard, 1985; Hidi & Anderson, 1986; Johnson, 1988; Marxen, 1996; Mayer, 2002; McAndrew, 1983; Peterson, 1992; Rickards & August, 1975; Rinehart & Thomas, 1993; Slotte & Lonka, 1999).

(09)   To date, however, relatively little is known about how students use copy and paste to take notes from Web-based text. The research synthesized above leaves important questions unanswered. First, only one study has deeply explored students' unrestricted copy-and-paste note taking. How might another population of students approach unrestricted copy-and-paste note taking? Also, previous research has tested only the learning effects of a 7-word copy-and-paste restriction. What effects do different levels of copy-and-paste note-taking restriction have on learning from Web-based text, and how are those effects manifested? This study seeks to answer these questions.

(10)   The purpose of this sequential explanatory mixed methods study (Collins, Onwuegbuzie, & Sutton, 2006; Creswell & Plano Clark, 2007; Greene 2006; Tashakkori & Teddlie, 1998) is to explore the impact of different levels of copy-and-paste note-taking restriction on learning from Web-based text. In the quantitative, first phase of this study, college students took notes in one of four experimentally imposed copy-and-paste conditions and then were tested for the learning of facts, concepts, and relationships among text ideas they noted.

The experimental findings and previous research then guided the data-gathering and analysis stages of a qualitative phase of study in which two kinds of data were collected and analyzed (student notes and interviews) to help explain and extend the findings from the experiment.

Quantitative Phase

(11)   The quantitative phase of this study addresses how different levels of copy-and-paste note-taking restriction affect learning from Web-based text. Whereas previous research has investigated the impact of a 7-word restricted copy-and-paste condition on learning, the present study investigates differing levels of restriction.

(12)   In true pragmatist, mixed methods fashion (Tashakkori & Teddlie, 1998), two other levels of copy-and-paste restriction were created for exploration based on learning theory and qualitative themes from previous studies. First, previous research indicates that when students attempt to learn prose, making more difficult decisions (which might require analysis of text) yields better learning of the prose material than making less difficult decisions (which might require only recall of text; see, e.g., Benton, Glover, Monkowski, & Shaughnessy, 1983). As such, the superior learning effect of restricted copy and paste over unrestricted copy and paste in previous research might have been due to the increased difficulty required to make 7-word pasting decisions (where fewer words must be selected) over unrestricted pasting decisions (where any number of words can be pasted). If so, perhaps other levels of pasting restriction might affect the difficulty of note-taking decisions and, in turn, affect learning.

(13)   Qualitative evidence helps determine which levels of restriction should be tested. Participant interviews and an analysis of notes stemming from the Igo et al. (2005b) study suggest that the 7-word restriction be doubled and tripled to create two new experimental groups that differ in how much restriction is imposed upon students' copy-and-paste capabilities (14- and 21-word restrictions). Simplistically enough, students who created 7-word restricted copy-and-paste notes stated that they believed they would have been able to "do a better job" if they had twice as many words with which to work. This is not to say, however, that they would have encoded twice as many ideas with a 14-word restriction, but it is possible that they may have encoded as many or even more. Thus, interview data provide a justification for doubling the allowed number of words.

(14)   The last piece of evidence that justifies different copy-and-paste restrictions stems from the performances of certain unrestricted pasters in the Igo et al. (2005b) study. Some students in the unrestricted copy-and-paste group were highly selective in their copy-and-paste decisions, choosing to paste approximately 21 words per cell in their note-taking charts (where the average unrestricted paster chose 42 words per cell). They exhibited this preference fairly consistently, and they performed better on each of the three tests (fact, concept, skill) than other members of the unrestricted group who chose to paste more words.

(15)   Thus, qualitative interview data suggest that students believed 14 words would have allowed them the flexibility to more efficiently construct notes. Furthermore, an analysis of notes coupled with test performances suggests that students who restrict themselves to 21 words per cell in their charts learn more than students who do not restrict their own pasting. The quantitative phase of this study tests how four note-taking conditions affect learning from Web-based text: the new 14-word and 21-word restricted copy and paste and the former 7-word and unrestricted copy and paste (which were retained for purposes of replication and comparison to the new conditions).

Hypothesis and Prediction

(16)   The restriction hypothesis was created based on previous research and levels-of-processing theory (Craik & Lockhart, 1972). The restriction hypothesis postulates that more learning will occur when students are assigned to restricted copy-and-paste conditions because restricted pasting leads to deeper mental processing of the text. As such, this hypothesis predicts that students assigned to the 7-word, 14-word, and 21-word copy-and-paste conditions will perform better on tests assessing (a) cued recall of facts, (b) recognition of concepts, and (c) inferences regarding relationships among text ideas than students in the unrestricted copy-and-paste condition.

Method

(17)   Ninety-three students from a large Southeastern university volunteered to participate to receive extra credit in their introductory educational psychology class or in a psychology class. Students who participated (a) were judged to have minimal background knowledge of the experimental content (based on a pretest score of the content), (b) ranged from sophomore to senior standing at the university (juniors > seniors > sophomores), (c) had self-reported grade point averages ranging from 2.6 to 4.0, and (d) had an average Scholastic Aptitude Test score of 1,240 (self-reported). Participants were assigned randomly to one of four conditions in which the copy-and-paste feature of a note-taking tool was either restricted to 7, 14, or 21 words or was unrestricted. Students drew slips of paper from a box, with the slips numbered 1 through 4 and corresponding to the experimental conditions. Twenty-two students were assigned to the unrestricted group, 24 to each of the 21-word and 14-word restricted groups, and 23 to the 7-word restricted copy-and-paste group. Of the participants, 23 were men and 70 were women. Among the sample, 8 students reported being African American, 3 Asian, 2 Latino, and the rest Caucasian.

Materials

(18)   For purposes of across-study comparison, materials were identical to the Igo et al. (2005a, 2005b) studies. Students took notes from a text passage was that was 1,796-words long. The text described three learning theories (behavioral, social, and constructivist) and was presented on a single, continuous Web page (HTML document) and accessed through Microsoft Internet Explorer. Describing each learning theory along parallel lines, the text identified each theory's (a) definition, (b) view of the importance of the environment, (c) view of the importance of mental activity, (d) key assumptions, (e) impact on curriculum, (f) impact on instruction, (g) impact on assessment, and (h) criticism.

(19)   The note-taking tool used was an electronic matrix (or chart) fit with the text's structure. It contained three columns corresponding to the three text topics and 11 rows corresponding to the 11 text categories. The three columns were labeled from left to right as *behavioral theory, social theory,* and *constructivist theory.* The eleven rows were labeled *definition, environment,*

mental activity, key assumptions 1-4, impact on curriculum, impact on instruction, impact on assessment, and *criticism.* Thus, at the outset, the tool presented students with 33 blank cells, 11 for each learning theory, with cues directing students to find information intersecting topics and categories. The tool itself could be minimized, maximized, or reduced in the same way as other computer programs. The students could choose to have the tool appear on the screen as they engaged in copy-and-paste decisions with the text, or they could expand the text to cover the screen and hide the chart.

(20)   Students' ability to enter information into the tool by typing was disabled. Thus, students were obliged to copy and paste information into the tool (under either restricted conditions or an unrestricted condition). Students could paste words that appeared together in the text or combine words from disparate areas of the text, as long as the total number of words pasted per cell did not exceed their level of restriction (if one was indeed assigned). They also were permitted to change or delete part or all of their selections as they saw fit.

(21)   Three tests assessed recall of facts, concept recognition, and relational inferences. In the facts test, students filled in a cued paper chart (analogous to the online note-taking chart) with all, or any part of, the information they could remember reading or pasting into their notes. The columns and rows were labeled in the same way the note-taking chart was labeled; the cells were blank. The test was scored by awarding 1 point per idea recalled and placed in the correct, cued cell corresponding to an idea from the text, whether the idea was originally noted or not. There were 33 possible points. Two raters scored the quiz, blind to experimental conditions, with a clearly acceptable level of interrater reliability (Cohen's $K = .87$).

(22)   A 13-item multiple-choice concept test ($\alpha = .64$) required students to recognize novel examples of information presented in the text (e.g., "How would a teacher who subscribes to social learning theory use praise during instruction."). One point was awarded for each correct response.

(23)   Relational inferences were measured with a single essay test item requiring students to compare and contrast ideas presented in the text. Students were asked, "Describe how each theory's views of the importance of the environment and the importance of mental activity are related." These descriptions were scored using a rubric that included eight idea units. A total of eight points were possible—one for each idea. Maximum points were given if a student's complete answer described the opposite relationship of each theory's emphases on the environment and mental activity, as well each theory's position on the importance of the environment and mental activity (e.g., behavioral theory places a greater emphasis on the environment and tends to discount mental activity, whereas constructivist theory is just the opposite). Two scorers rated the essays based on the rubric, blind to experimental conditions, with a clearly acceptable level of interrater reliability (Cohen's $K = .83$).

Procedure

(24)   The experiment occurred over two days. On Day 1 (in four separate sessions), students met in a university computer lab and were assigned randomly to one of the four experimental groups. Next, they were given an overview of the note-taking task and completed informed consent forms. In the overview, the students were informed that the experiment

was going to be conducted on two separate days. The primary researcher told the students that on Day 1 they were going to read and take notes over material that would later be covered in their course and that on Day 2 (two days later) they would be given tests of facts, concepts, and relationships. They then read a brief two-paragraph statement describing the note-taking chart and a written explanation of the version of the chart they were supposed to use (7-, 14-, or 21-word restriction or unrestricted). Next, participants logged on to their computers and created user names and passwords (which permitted their notes to be saved and printed). The students were instructed by the primary researcher to take notes using the cues provided in the chart—for example, *definition* and *criticism*—(which they also read in the two-paragraph statement), to read and take notes at a pace that was comfortable to them, and to take as much time as they needed to complete their notes. Students then read, completed their notes, and saved their notes on the computers. All students completed the note-taking task in approximately 42 to 51 minutes. Students were not forced to conform to identical time on task because the researchers wanted to most closely approximate typical student behaviors, as prompted by the different versions of the note-taking tool.

(25)   On Day 2 (two days later), participants took the three tests. The fact test was administered first because it contained the fewest retrieval cues (i.e., hints about what the students were supposed to have learned), ensuring that students' recall of the text ideas was not prompted by the other tests, which contained additional cues. The relational test then was administered, as it contained the second fewest retrieval cues. Finally, the concept test, which contained the most cues, was administered last. Each test was collected before the next test was given.

Results

(26)   A multivariate analysis of variance (MANOVA) and three separate analyses of variance (ANOVAs) were conducted to evaluate the effects of the copy-and-paste restrictions on student performances on the (a) fact test, (b) relational test, and (c) concept test. Table 1 displays a summary of the means and standard deviations for each of the three tests.

Multivariate Analysis of Variance

(27)   A one-way MANOVA was conducted to determine the effect of the copy-and-paste conditions on student learning, as measured by the three tests. Significant differences were obtained, Wilk's $\Lambda = .76$, $F(9, 211) = 2.80$, $p < .005$. The relationship between copy-and-paste condition and test performance was moderate, as assessed by multivariate η^2 based on Wilk's Λ, accounting for 8.9% of the variance in performance. ANOVAs were conducted on each of the three tests to follow up the MANOVA.

Fact Test ANOVA

(28)   The purpose of the fact test was to measure the learning of facts from the Web-based text. The ANOVA for the main effect of copy-and-paste conditions on cued recall of facts was significant, $F(3, 89) = 5.33$, $MSE = 50.36$, $p < .005$. The strength of the relationship

156   Journal of Mixed Methods Research

Table 1
Means and Standard Deviations for Experimental Groups

	Unrestricted	21-Word Restricted	14-Word Restricted	7-Word Restricted
Fact test				
M	4.77	2.63	2.00	4.87
SD	3.79	2.44	1.84	3.84
Relational test				
M	2.73	1.00	0.54	2.39
SD	2.41	1.45	0.88	2.21
Concepts test				
M	8.05	6.96	6.67	7.87
SD	2.88	2.42	2.44	2.32

between level of copy-and-paste restriction and cued recall was strong as assessed by η^2, with level of restriction accounting for 15.2% of the variance in cued recall.

(29)   Although the performances of the four copy-and-paste groups had significantly different standard deviations (based on Levene's test), an error bar analysis revealed that the differences were acceptable. Nonetheless, Dunnet's C was the procedure used in follow-up post hoc comparisons because it does not assume equal variances and is a more conservative basis for comparison. Dunnet's C indicated that the unrestricted copy-and-paste group and the 7-word restriction group each recalled significantly more text ideas than did those in the 14-word restricted copy-and-paste group.

Relational Inferences ANOVA

(30)   The purpose of the essay test was to measure student ability to compare the three theoretical viewpoints from the text. A one-way ANOVA for the main effect of copy-and-paste restriction on relational learning was significant, $F(3, 89) = 7.8$, $MSE = 25.923$, $p < .001$. The strength of the relationship between level of copy-and-paste restriction and relational inferences was strong as assessed by η^2, with level of restriction accounting for 20.8% of the variance in relational inferences.

(31)   As was the case on the cued recall measure, the variances in performance on the relational inferences measure were significantly different among the four copy-and-paste groups (as assessed by Levene's test). Another error bar analysis, however, again showed that the differences were acceptable. As a conservative precautionary measure, Dunnet's C was again the procedure used in post hoc comparisons. The unrestricted copy-and-paste group made more relational inferences than the 21-word and 14-word restricted groups. Also, the 7-word restricted group made more relational inferences than the 14-word group.

Conceptual Recognition ANOVA

(32)   The purpose of the multiple-choice test was to measure student ability to recognize novel examples of the concepts that were in the text. The ANOVA for this conceptual test was not significant, $F(3, 89) = 1.66$, $MSE = 44.026$, $p = .181$. Although the analysis indicated that there were no significant differences among group performances, the groups' performances

nonetheless differed in ways analogous to the performances on the cued fact and essay tests. That is, the performances of the groups varied in ways similar to the other tests: the 14- and 21- word groups performed worse than the 7-word and unrestricted groups.

Need for Follow-up Explanations

(33)   The results of this experiment do not support the restriction hypothesis. Based on previous research, this hypothesis predicted that the restricted copy-and-paste groups would learn more than the unrestricted group. Instead, the results indicate that the unrestricted copy-and-paste group actually outperformed two of the other groups and performed similarly to the 7-word group.

(34)   Although two of the groups (7-word and unrestricted) seemed to have learned more than the other two (14- and 21-word), the higher performances were not made by the groups that one might assume would do better in light of previous research (Igo et al., 2005b). The most restricted group and least restricted group, oddly, performed the best. The middle-restricted groups performed the worst. This finding is somewhat puzzling, as in previous research the 7-word group learned significantly more than the unrestricted group. Why did this happen?

(35)   A preliminary analysis of notes revealed that all participants completed the note-taking chart and that all participants conformed to their copy-and-paste assignment. That is, all cells were filled in each note chart, and each student filled the cells with an appropriate number of words as per experimental condition. In addition to containing the correct amount of text, the cells also contained information appropriately addressing the note-taking cues. These characteristics of the notes, however, provide no insight into our experimental findings.

(36)   In particular, the answers to two questions seem critical to understanding our results. The first question is, Why did students in the unrestricted pasting group perform as well as those in the 7-word restricted pasting group? A clear and definitive answer to this question is beyond the scope of the experimental findings. More data are needed to resolve the contradictory findings. The second unanswered question is, Why did the 14- and 21-word pasting groups perform worse than the 7-word and unrestricted pasting groups? Students seemingly were able to learn with an unrestricted tool and a highly restrictive tool (7-word), but learning was impeded somehow by a tool that was only moderately restrictive (14- and 21-word). This question, too, is elusive—unanswerable in light of the experimental results alone. Again, more data are needed to determine why there were discrepancies in learning. Together the two questions posed above can be categorized under the same qualitative question: How did the different note-taking conditions affect students during the experiment? The aim of the follow-up component of this study is to provide an explanation to this question.

Qualitative Phase

(37)   In cases where experimental inquiry does not provide enough description of a phenomenon, researchers can use qualitative follow-up procedures to aid understanding (Creswell, 2003; Creswell & Plano Clark, 2007; Tashakkori & Teddlie, 1998). Two types of qualitative

data were used to address the unanswered questions above. Note-taking documents were collected and analyzed to address why the unrestricted pasting groups and the restricted pasting groups performed comparably. Interview data were collected and analyzed to address why the 14- and 21-word pasting groups learned less than the 7-word and unrestricted pasting groups.

(38)   Following the data analyses, which are described below, a researcher outside of the present study performed an external audit of the qualitative analyses and general inferences made from the findings. She was chosen to perform the audit because she had adequate knowledge of both qualitative analysis techniques and cognitive research. In her oral report to the primary researcher, she communicated that the themes were justified by the data and that our inferences stemming from those themes (and from the quantitative data) were logical.

Note-Taking Data Collection and Analysis

(39)   After the experiments, the students' notes were printed and analyzed. The notes were checked for both content and text length. Content was checked by comparing each set of notes with a master set of notes that contained the correct ideas in each cell. Text length was measured by calculating an average number of words used per cell in each student's note chart.

(40)   As mentioned earlier, each student's notes were appropriately constructed in terms of both word count (as per experimental condition) and appropriateness of ideas (where the cued cells contained the correct information). However, within each group there were discrepancies in word count (see range in Table 2). Although no members of the restricted groups (7, 14, or 21) exceeded their words-per-cell limits (as the assigned version of the tool would not permit it), some did use fewer words per cell than their imposed limits (which the tool did permit). Certain students within each experimental group pasted fewer words than other students did.

(41)   For example, students in the 14-word group chose to paste an average of about 11 words per cell. Across students within that group, word pasting ranged from about 9 words to just under 14 words per cell. So whereas some students pasted fewer words than their version of the tool permitted, other students chose to paste as many as their imposed limit would allow. Similarly, although the average words per cell of students restricted to the 21-word group was 15, some students pasted only 13, and other students pasted more than 19 words per cell. In short, within each pasting restriction group, student preferences in how much text to paste varied.

(42)   This variance in word count per cell was, of course, also evident among students in the unrestricted pasting group. Although the average number of words per cell pasted by the unrestricted group was 24, certain students in the unrestricted group chose to paste an average of 16 words per cell, and still other students pasted more words—as many as 52. Again, students' preferences in how much text to paste varied among members of the unrestricted group.

(43)   Interestingly, the notes taken by students in the unrestricted group in this study differed from the notes taken by unrestricted students in previous research (Igo et al., 2005b).

Table 2
Quantitized Note Documents From the Experiment

	Unrestricted $n = 22$	21-Word Restricted $n = 24$	14-Word Restricted $n = 24$	7-Word Restricted $n = 23$
Mean words per cell	24.42	15.08	10.54	6.87
Range	16.23-52.44	12.82-19.40	8.75-13.79	6.54-6.94

In the present experiment, members of the unrestricted group pasted an average of 24 words per cell of their note-taking charts. However, the average number of words pasted by the unrestricted group in previous research was 42 per cell, despite use of the same materials and procedures.

(44)   This discrepancy in apparent selectivity regarding how much text to paste had a bearing on test performance in the previous research (Igo et al., 2005b). Consistently, the students who pasted the fewest words remembered the most, and the students who pasted the most words remember the least of what they had read or noted. But in that study, relatively few unrestricted students were highly selective. In the present study, many were.

(45)   When one considers that students in the present study were, overall, much more selective in what they pasted than were students in the previous research (choosing on average 24 words rather than 42) and that choosing fewer words has positive consequences for learning and recall, a plausible answer to the first qualitative subquestion emerges. Why did the unrestricted and 7-word restricted pasting groups perform similarly, when in the previous research they did not? Because in the present study, more of the unrestricted pasters imposed a self-restriction, were highly selective, chose to paste fewer words, and benefited from that strategic approach.

Interview Data Collection and Analysis

(46)   Two to three days after the tests were graded and the statistical analyses were completed (approximately five to six days after tests were administered), interviews were conducted with 12 participants. The interviewees were students from two different educational psychology classes, and they were chosen at random to participate. Five students were unable to meet for the interviews, at which time 5 other participants were chosen at random. Three participants represented each of the four experimental groups (7-, 14-, 21-word pasting and unrestricted pasting).

(47)   This part of the investigation began with a priori assumptions regarding students' note-taking behaviors and the effects those behaviors have on learning. The assumptions were based on a study by Igo et al. (2005a), which documented that note-taking decisions and note-modifying decisions affect learning differently. In that study, students who took copy-and-paste notes (making only note-taking decisions) learned more than students who took copy-and-paste notes and frequently distracted themselves by making minor note changes (note-taking decisions plus note-modifying decisions). Consequently, an interview

protocol was designed to prompt students for a description of the processes they used to take their notes:

- Describe how you decided what information to include in your notes.
- (Student is given his or her printed notes.) Are there any cells that you remember filling in, and could you describe how you decided which information would be placed in that/those cell/cells?
- How often, if at all, did you change your notes once you filled in a cell, and how did your notes change?
- If you did change your notes, what were your reasons for doing so?

Additional questions were asked to further prompt answers from interviewees who at first gave brief or nondescript answers to one or more of the questions. The interviews were conducted individually by the primary researcher, were audiotaped, and lasted from 5 to 10 minutes, in general.

(48)   Verbatim transcriptions were made of the audiotaped interviews, and then an analysis of the interview data was conducted. First, the transcriptions were read and then reread. Next, descriptive, meaningful statements made by each participant were extracted. A predetermined set of coding schemes—based on note taking versus note modification—then was used to sort the statements into three categories: two addressing a student's tendency to change or not change the notes and one addressing note taking with note modification (see Table 3).

(49)   Following the prescriptions of Miles and Huberman (1994), an effects matrix was constructed to serve three purposes: organization of the interview data, explanation of effects, and drawing conclusions. Several themes emerged from the matrix once the data were organized—themes that plausibly answer the question, Why did the 14- and 21-word pasting groups perform worse on the tests?

Organization of the Interview Data

(50)   The interview data were sorted and then compared and contrasted. Two researchers, blind to experimental condition, sorted the statements into the categories with a high degree of agreement (Cohen's $K = .97$). First, the statements made by the participants were sorted into categories indicative of note-taking changes or no note-taking changes. The statements then were cross-sorted into the categories *note taking* and *note modification* (see Table 3).

(51)   *Note taking* involved choosing ideas from the text while the text was being read or reread. This included the student's decisions that led to the original selection of ideas in the pasting groups (the first words chosen to be pasted into each cell). Note-taking decisions also included choices made while reading or rereading the text that led to alterations in one's notes—where an entire original idea was replaced with a new idea. A student described making such decisions this way: "Sometimes I would get farther along [in the reading] and go back and paste a different part [of the text] instead." In each case, a decision regarding note construction was made while students read the text, and the pasted product was either entered into an empty cell or was used to replace an idea already in the cell.

Table 3
Coded Categories Used to Sort Interview Statements

	No Note Changes	Note Changes
Note taking	Student kept the original note selections. Student selected an idea from the text and placed the idea in the appropriate cell of the chart.	Student did not keep the original note selection. Student selected an idea from the text, placed the idea in the appropriate cell of the chart, and then later deleted that idea from the cell, replacing it with an entirely new idea.
Note modification	By definition, students who did not change their notes also did not modify their notes.	Student selected an idea from the text, placed the idea in the appropriate cell of the chart, and then modified that idea within the cell by deleting certain words or by combining disparate areas of the text.

(52)   *Note modification* involved decisions that were made while students read or reread their notes that led them to modify the contents of a cell. That is, modification involved decisions made after students had entered information into their notes, then examined their notes, and finally altered the contents of a cell. For example, one participant explained, "I wasn't sure what the best parts were, or how many words I had [selected] so I would read what I already had [in the cell] and take some parts out." Hence, note-modifying decisions focused on noted ideas, whereas note-taking decisions focused on text ideas that may or may not have been noted. Table 4 shows the number of interviewees per experimental group who described note taking and note modification.

Explanation of Themes

(53)   Based on the interview data, five note-taking themes are evident (see Table 4). These themes are manifest in the note-taking decisions made by the experimental participants, which differed from group to group. Unrestricted pasters made similar decisions, 14- and 21-word pasters made similar decisions, and 7-word pasters made decisions somewhat different from the other groups. Each of the note-taking themes is now distinguished and discussed.

(54)   The first theme in the effects matrix concerns students who took notes without making any subsequent changes to their notes. That is, they decided what information to note while they read the text and then they noted it without second-guessing their decisions.

(55)   As can be seen in Table 4, unrestricted pasters who were interviewed described that they were likely to take notes and not change them. In fact, all three participants from this group who were interviewed described their note-taking process this way. For example, an unrestricted paster described her choices saying, "I just put in the [sentence] that I thought fit the category best .... I didn't want to change what I had .... I just went with my instinct about it." Apparently, the unrestricted paste condition allowed students to make a decision about which information to note and then move to the next set of cues in the note-taking tool. As such, these students saw no need to change their notes and were perhaps able to focus their mental efforts on the text ideas. Clearly, such focus could have

Table 4
Effects Matrix for Coded Interview Statements

	Number of Interviewees per Group Who Described Note Taking	Number of Interviewees per Group Who Described Note Modification	Themes	Exemplar Quotes
Number of interviewees who described making no note changes	3 unrestricted pasters	None	1. Unrestricted pasters were likely to engage in note taking and not change their notes after entering information into the cells.	"While I was reading I would think about the [cues in the matrix] and when that part of the reading was done I would summarize the paragraph." "I just put in the [sentence] that I thought fit the category best."
Number of interviewees who described making note changes	Two 7-word pasters One 21-word paster	Three 14-word pasters Two 21-word pasters One 7-word paster	2. 7-, 14-, and 21-word pasters were likely to change their notes.	"I always had to fix the things I put in my notes . . . . I usually [pasted] too much."
			3. 7-word pasters were likely to replace whole ideas with other ideas.	"A lot of times I'd find something better [for my notes] the more I read."
			4. 14- and 21-word pasters tended to modify their notes within the cells of the chart.	"In some cells, there were things that didn't need to be in there . . . . I would take them out."
			5. 14- and 21-word pasters counted the number of words they were using several times and found it difficult to count while scrolling through the cells.	"It was frustrating to narrow things down to the right number of words because I had to scroll- up while I counted."

Note: Three members of each group were interviewed.

resulted in their relatively high test performance (as compared to the 14- and 21-word groups).

(56) The second note-taking theme concerns note taking coupled with making note changes. Students displaying this theme were likely to insert information into their charts and then change the information before finally saving their notes. The 7-, 14-, and 21-word pasters were likely to change their notes. Nine participants from these three groups were interviewed, and 8 of them described making frequent changes in their charts while taking notes. For example, one participant assigned to the 14-word paste condition said, "I always had to fix the things I put in my notes . . . . Some of the things that seemed right were too long . . . . I usually [copied] too much . . . [and] had to get rid of some of it." On a similar note, a 7-word paster described filling a note-taking cell this way: "I usually pasted the first thing that sounded like it was supposed to go in there . . . but then other things would come along, too . . . so I changed the things I put in [the cell]."

(57) Each restricted copy-and-paste condition, then, seemed to prompt students to evaluate their notes as well as the text ideas. Recall that unrestricted pasters described only evaluation of the text, not note evaluation. Still, the performances of the restricted pasting groups differed, with 7-word pasters outperforming the 14- and 21-word pasters. So although the second theme distinguishes the unrestricted pasters from the restricted pasters, it does little to explain the performance differences among the restricted groups. The next three note-taking themes help to explain our experimental results by distinguishing the 7-word pasters from the 14- and 21-word pasters.

(58) The third theme concerns making note changes without minor alterations within cells. When students changed their notes this way, they did so because they encountered new, perhaps better, ideas in the text. That is, they changed their notes when, while reading further in the text, a different piece of information was deemed more representative of the cues in the note-taking chart. This theme relates solely to the 7-word pasters. In fact, of the three 7-word pasters interviewed, two described making changes based on further reading in the text. "A lot of times I would find something better [for my notes] the more I read," was how one participant described how she chose to change her selections. In the 7-word paste condition, then, students may have been prompted to be critical of their selections but only when the text presented them with additional information worthy of being noted. This theme is supported by Igo et al. (2005a). Of 34 students assigned to the 7-word pasting group in their study, 21 changed their notes in Theme 3 fashion—a proportion consistent with the 2 of 3 interviewees from the present study.

(59) Finally, the fourth and fifth themes further distinguish the three restricted pasting groups, and they relate to the note-taking decisions made by participants assigned to the 14- and 21-word paste conditions. The fourth theme concerns note modifications, or making minor note alterations within the cells of the chart. When a participant modified notes in some way, it was done in a fine-tuning fashion, where the note cells were reread, examined, and then changed by deleting certain pieces of information from the cells.

(60) The 14- and 21-word pasting groups tended to modify their notes—the distracting behavior mentioned earlier in this report (Igo et al., 2005a). Consider the similarities between these two descriptions made by a 14-word paster and a 21-word paster: "In some cells, I had things that didn't need to be there . . . . I took them out" and "I usually took a couple of sentences that sounded good and then put them in [the cell] and trimmed them down to 14 words."

(61)   Whereas the 7-word group made changes based on new information in the text, the 14- and 21-word paste groups made changes based on the information that was already in the notes. They may, at some level, have moved their attention away from the actual text meaning, focusing instead on certain qualities of their notes.

(62)   The fifth and last theme suggested by the interview data follows from the fourth theme, as it more specifically addresses the note modification of the 14- and 21-word pasters. Whereas all experimental groups were mindful of the text ideas they were pasting into their notes, the 14- and 21-word groups were, in addition, particularly mindful of the number of words they were using. In fact, the interviewees described actually counting the number of words they were pasting in each cell. For example, one participant said, "I didn't really need 14 words but I still counted how many words I was using to make sure it wasn't going to get cut off." This statement refers to how the restricted copy-and-paste tool functions, and it needs some qualification: When a student first pasted information into the chart (in any paste condition), the tool would accept an unlimited number of words in the cell. However, when the student then left that cell and returned to the text, the tool would, by default, save only the initial 7, 14, or 21 words from the pasted segment. The remainder of the text would be cut off.

(63)   Another practical, yet distracting, phenomenon described by the 14- and 21-word groups was their tendency to use the scrolling feature of the note-taking tool. This feature works the same way as the scrolling feature of any word-processing or Internet program. When an electronic document is too long to fit on the screen at one time, a button on the side of the window allows the user to scroll down a page—as if pulling down a window shade—exposing the text on the lower part of the document. In the note-taking tool, each cell of the chart is in fact a separate window with its own scroll button. Students who put large amounts of text into a cell would not be able to view the entire contents of the cell without using the scrolling feature. Interviewees from the 14- and 21-word groups described using this feature with some frequency while making changes to their notes. For instance, one student said, "It was frustrating to narrow things down to the right number of words because I had to scroll-up while I counted."

(64)   Although the 7-word pasters also made changes to their notes, they did not describe counting words or using the scroll button. This is perhaps because the size of the note-taking cells allowed for 7 words to be viewed in each cell without scrolling (provided they were not excessively long words).

(65)   It seems that participants in the 14- and 21-word groups chose to paste more than the allowed number of words (temporarily) in each cell and then made decisions about which parts of the text should stay and which other parts should be removed, all the while keeping count of how many words they were using and scrolling through the cells. Clearly, this is a task more different than selecting consecutive words from the text, pasting them, and then proceeding onward, as described by the unrestricted and 7-word pasters.

(66)   Thus, the second unanswered question from the experiment seems to have a practical answer, in light of cognitive psychology: Why did the 14- and 21-word pasting groups perform worse than the other pasting groups on the tests? Because the versions of the tool they were using prompted them to engage in different note-taking activities than did the unrestricted or 7-word paste tools. In addition to guiding them through the note-taking process (based on the cues and organization of the chart), the 14- and 21-word versions of the tool imposed a distraction from the meaning of the text. As students began to modify their note-taking choices, they were forced to move attention away from the meaning of the text and focus instead on the physical characteristics of their notes (the number of words they had in each cell). Given the limited nature of human attention and the dependence of attention on learning, then, it makes sense that they would learn less than the other note-taking groups who did not experience the same distraction.

Drawing Conclusions, Data Mixing, and Instructional Impact

(67)   Although copy-and-paste note taking is still a relatively unexplored research area, this study, along with previous studies by Igo and colleagues (2003, 2004, 2005a, 2005b, 2006), helps illuminate how copy-and-paste note taking affects learning from Web-based text. The extent to which students encode (or learn) ideas through the pasting process seems related to the subsets of behaviors in which they engage, the selectivity with which they paste, and the kinds of mental processes requisite for those behaviors and such selectivity.

(68)   In a previous study (Igo et al., 2005b), unrestricted pasters were, in general, not at all selective in what they chose to paste into their notes. Whereas the bulk of those students learned little from Web-based text, there were certain students who were more selective in their pasting and who learned considerably more. The present study, however, extends the previous findings, showing that among a different population of students, default copy-and-paste strategies can be much more productive. Unrestricted students in the present experiment performed as well on dependent measures of learning as did students in a condition designed to prompt deeper thinking (7-word paste). The follow-up component of this study then explained how those students approached learning in the supposed disadvantaged condition—strategically and selectively. Thus, we can conclude that students' personal approaches to copy-and-paste note taking vary considerably in terms of effectiveness, with the type of approach relating to how much is learned from Web-based text.

(69)   Similarly, previous research indicated that restricting students' pasting capability to 7 words can positively affect learning for many students (Igo et al., 2003, 2005b), but it also can impose a minor distraction (Igo et al., 2005a). The present study extends this theme. Students assigned to the 14- and 21-word restricted condition performed poorly on the dependent measures of learning. The qualitative follow-up then showed how those conditions affected learning. Students described the imposition of severe distractions that were, in fact, quite antithetical to learning.

(70)   In essence, the key to learning while taking copy-and-paste notes is to approach the task selectively while maintaining one's focus on the meaning in the text and not on the characteristics of one's notes. As such, student learning through the copy-and-paste note-taking process realistically might be influenced by simple teacher-given instructions. Although a restrictive note-taking tool is not currently available to teachers for use in classrooms, students could follow certain guidelines that would simulate the benefits of a restrictive tool. When students take notes from the Web, prompting them to be more selective in their pasting might produce similar gains in learning. For example, a teacher might prompt students to copy and paste main ideas from paragraphs in lieu of pasting entire paragraphs. Or students could be instructed to identify the sentences most valuable to a set of notes. In each case, the directions might function as prompts for productive monitoring.

Contribution to Mixed Methods Literature

(71)   This study evinces the value of the follow-up explanations model in experimental, cognitive research. Consider, for example, the American Psychological Association's requirement that researchers report effect sizes related to their experimental findings. An effect size suggesting that treatment conditions explain 15% of the variance between groups in an experiment would be considered a strong effect size (Green, Salkind, & Akey, 2000). But from a practical standpoint, such as that of a teacher who wants to know as much as possible about student learning, the remaining 85% of the variance might be of great interest. The follow-up explanations model can help researchers fill this need.

(72)   For instance, the experimental phase of this study indicated effect sizes of roughly 21%, 15%, and 9%. These measures perhaps indicate the extent to which the copy-and-paste conditions influenced learning outcomes. But the qualitative phase provided evidence of varying ways in which students behaved within those conditions and how the treatments influenced students' behaviors. This level of understanding would not have been possible without a mixed methods approach to research. Whereas the experiment provided evidence solely of learning differences among students assigned to the four conditions, the qualitative phase clarified the impact of two important factors related to those differences. First, interview data revealed design flaws antithetical to learning (that were present in two of the experimental conditions) and that reduced certain students' capacity to learn during the experiment. Second, analyses of students' note documents showed that the effectiveness of students' personal strategies can vary between samples of a population (as the present study and past research sampled the population of college students, with more effective strategies being employed in the present study).

(73)   In short, given only the experimental findings, we merely could have concluded that (a) two of the treatments yielded better learning than the other two and (b) particular aspects of the present study were inconsistent with previous research. But given the mixing of qualitative and quantitative data, we can explain why we obtained these results. As exemplified by this study, the collection and analysis of qualitative data relevant to the goals of a cognitive experiment can illuminate important nuances that might otherwise remain hidden.

Limitations

(74)   In the present study, sampling participants from a different population than that of the previous studies yielded unexpected results. The findings of this study may only generalize to the type of student who participated. The few studies that have addressed copy-and-paste note taking have produced results that are in some ways consistent and yet in other ways inconsistent.

(75)   Another limitation of this study is its use of a single text. This might raise a serious question of generalizability of the findings. Consider that texts differ in their complexity and density of ideas, as well as in readability, grade level, and content. Future research

should include multiple texts to ensure that present findings can truly affect instruction and learning.

Future Research

(76)

Given the present and previous research, at least two avenues of future research are pertinent. First, future research should explore the use of instructions to students regarding how they should approach copy-and-paste notes. Finally, the present and previous copy-and-paste studies have failed to address the complete benefits of note taking. Until now, studies have addressed only the encoding function of note taking, neglecting to address the external storage function (where notes are studied). This leaves several important questions unanswered. For example, does a level of copy-and-paste restriction perhaps boost initial encoding but then result in an inferior set of notes from which to study? It is possible that a student who pastes large amounts of information, and then performs poorly on measures of initial encoding, might in fact have produced a more complete set of notes and might then be at an advantage when study time is allowed? On the other hand, a student might have only produced a more lengthy set of notes, whereas a restricted paster may have created a more concise record from which to study. In any event, many topics related to copy-and-paste note taking remain unexplored.

References

Anderson, T. H., & Armbruster, B. B. (1984). Studying. In P. D. Pearson (Ed.), *Handbook of reading research* (pp. 657-679). New York: Longman.

Benton, S. L., Glover, J. A., Monkowski, P. C., & Shaughnessy, M. (1983). Decision difficulty and recall of prose. *Journal of Educational Psychology, 75,* 727-742.

Blanchard, J. S. (1985). What to tell students about underlining . . . and why. *Journal of Reading, 29,* 199-203.

Collins, K., Onwuegbuzie, A., & Sutton, I. (2006). A model incorporating the rationale and purpose for conducting mixed methods research in special education and beyond. *Learning Disabilities: A Contemporary Journal, 4*(1), 67-100.

Craik, F., & Lockhart, R. (1972). Levels of processing: A framework for memory research. *Journal of Verbal Learning and Verbal Behavior, 11,* 671-684,

Creswell, J. W. (2003). *Research design: Qualitative, quantitative, and mixed methods approaches* (2nd ed.). Thousand Oaks, CA: Sage.

Creswell, J. W., & Plano Clark, V. L. (2007). *Designing and conducting mixed methods research.* Thousand Oaks, CA: Sage.

Green, S. B., Salkind, N. J., & Akey, T. M. (2000). *Using SPSS for Windows: Analyzing and understanding data* (2nd ed.). Upper Saddle River, NJ: Prentice Hall.

Greene, J. C. (2006). Toward a methodology of mixed methods social inquiry. *Research in the Schools, 13*(1), 93-99.

Hidi, S., & Anderson, V. (1986). Producing written summaries: Task demands, cognitive operations, and implications for instruction. *Review of Educational Research, 56,* 473-493.

Igo, L. B., Bruning, R., & McCrudden, M. T. (2005a). Encoding disruption associated with copy and paste note taking. In L. M. Pytlik-Zillig, M. Bodvarsson, & R. Bruning (Eds.), *Technology-based education: Bringing researchers and practitioners together* (pp. 107-119), Greenwich, CT: Information Age.

Igo, L. B., Bruning, R., & McCrudden, M. T. (2005b). Exploring differences in students' copy and paste decision-making and processing: A mixed-method study. *Journal of Educational Psychology, 97*(1), 103-116.

168   Journal of Mixed Methods Research

Igo, L. B., Bruning, R., McCrudden, M. T., & Kauffman, D. F. (2003). InfoGather: Six experiments toward the development of an online, data-gathering tool. In R. Bruning, C. A. Horn, & L. M. Pytlik-Zillig (Eds.), *Web-based learning: What do we know? Where do we go?* (pp. 57-77) Greenwich, CT: Information Age.

Igo, B., Kiewra, K., & Bruning, R. (2004, April). *Further explorations in online, copy and paste note taking: Mixed methods evidence for how levels of restriction affect encoding.* Paper presented at the annual conference of the American Educational Research Association, San Diego, CA.

Igo, L. B., Riccomini, P. J., Bruning, R., & Pope G. (2006). How should middle school students with LD take Web-based notes: A mixed methods study. *Learning Disability Quarterly, 29*(2), 112-121.

Johnson, L. L. (1988). Effects of underlining textbook sentences on passage and sentence recall. *Reading Research and Instruction, 28,* 18-32.

Katayama, A. D., Shambaugh, R. N., Edmonds, T., & Doctor, T. (2005). Promoting knowledge transfer with electronic note taking. *Teaching of Psychology, 32,* 129-131.

Marxen, D. E. (1996). Why reading and underlining a passage is a less effective strategy than simply rereading the passage. *Reading Improvement, 33,* 88-96.

Mayer, R. R. (2002). *The promise of educational psychology: Volume 2. Teaching for meaningful learning.* Columbus, OH: Merrill Prentice Hall.

McAndrew, D. A. (1983). Underlining and note taking: Some suggestions from research. *Journal of Reading, 27,* 103-08.

Miles, M. B., & Huberman, A. M. (1994). *Qualitative data analysis.* Thousand Oaks, CA: Sage.

Peterson, S. E. (1992). The cognitive functions of underlining as a study technique. *Reading Research and Instruction, 31,* 49-56.

Rickards, J. P., & August, G. J. (1975). Generative underlining strategies in prose recall. *Journal of Educational Psychology, 67,* 860-865.

Rinehart, S. D., & Thomas, K. A. (1993). Summarization ability and text recall by novice studiers. *Reading Research and Instruction, 32,* 24-32.

Slotte, V., & Lonka, K. (1999). Review and process effects of spontaneous note taking on text comprehension. *Contemporary Educational Psychology, 24,* 1-20.

Tashakkori, A., & Teddlie, C. (1998). *Mixed methodology: Combining qualitative and quantitative approaches.* Thousand Oaks, CA: Sage.

Source: This article is reprinted from the *Journal of Mixed Methods Research*, Vol. 2, Issue 2, pp. 149–168, 2008. Reprinted with permission of Sage Publications, Inc.

13 | ACTION RESEARCH DESIGNS: STUDIES THAT SOLVE PRACTICAL PROBLEMS

Throughout this book, we have examined how to understand formal research that was conducted to add to our collective knowledge about research problems. Not all research, however, uses this formal research approach. Sometimes, researchers conduct research to solve real problems that are currently occurring in local settings. Action research designs are best suited for situations where a real local problem needs to be solved. Action researchers study a practical problem with the goal of developing a solution. As a consumer of research, you need to learn to read and understand reports of action research studies. As a practitioner, you also need to learn about the process of conducting action research because it provides you with a framework for developing solutions to problems that you face in your own practice. This chapter introduces two types of action research, provides steps for planning action research studies, and suggests strategies for evaluating action research reports.

BY THE END OF THIS CHAPTER, YOU SHOULD BE ABLE TO:

- Identify and understand the use of action research in a research study.
- Recognize two different research designs when reading action research reports.
- Plan an action research study in response to a problem in your own practice setting.
- Evaluate the quality of an action research report.

Before reading further, stop and think about some practical problems that you have faced in the past year or that you can imagine facing in your profession in the future. Try to list at least three problems that matter to you and your professional practice:

1.

2.

3.

Perhaps you came up with problems similar to ones that others have faced, such as:

- Children at school are not getting enough to eat over the weekends.
- There is a history of alcohol abuse associated with the high school prom each year.
- Students in the tenth-grade English class are struggling with the concept of plagiarism.
- Community members are not making use of the local library.
- Children in one neighborhood are being placed into foster care at an unusually high rate.
- Immigrant parents have difficulty participating in their children's wellness visits at the clinic.

Each of these important problems could call for researchers to conduct formal quantitative, qualitative, and mixed methods research studies. Individuals can also gain knowledge about these problems by reading literature that reports relevant research. Any one of these problems, however, may also be facing you and your community at this moment. In addition to reading research to gain knowledge about the problem, you may want to develop a plan and take action to try to bring about a workable solution. Action research provides practitioners like you with a process to not only learn about a practical problem, but to plan and take actions to solve the problem using the process of research.

Based on the knowledge you have developed about the research process, you possess the tools to develop plans using an action research design. Research does not have to be something that someone else does, but can become part of *your* repertoire of skills and strategies that you bring to address problems that are important to you. By repeatedly identifying a problem, gathering information, acting on that information, and reflecting on what you learn, you can use the process of research to help find solutions to problems that matter to you. That is the goal of action research. In this chapter, you will learn how to read reports of action research and how to apply the process of action research in your own setting.

How Do You Identify That a Study Used Action Research?

Action research is a distinctive approach to conducting research that has its own key characteristics. Authors of action research reports often refer to their approach as a type of *action research* or *participatory research*. In addition, you can learn to identify reports as examples of action research by recognizing key features, such as who conducted the research, why it was conducted, and the cyclical process used in the study.

Recognize That Action Researchers Include Practitioners

When reading an action research report, you find that the researchers who conducted the study included practitioners as researchers. Action researchers can be teachers, administrators, specialists, counselors, nurses, social workers, therapists, and community leaders, to name a few possibilities. Action research provides an opportunity for practitioners to further their own professional development while at the same time working on improving their practices by taking action and participating in research. For example, within school settings, action research offers a means of professional development for teachers and staff and of addressing school-wide problems. Action research studies often also include active partnerships among practitioners, university researchers, and community members, such as parents. This means that a report of an action research study may discuss a variety of individuals who are involved in the conduct of the research, not just as participants, but as partners in the planning and implementation of the reported study. For example, Ditrano and Silverstein (2006) describe how they collaborated with a school psychologist and a small number of parents who had children diagnosed with emotional disabilities in their action research study to improve the relationship between parents and the special education system. The school psychologist and parents were co-researchers who were actively involved in all aspects of the project.

Identify That the Focus Is on a Real Problem in a Local Setting

When reading an action research report, you learn that the problem of interest in the study is a practical problem occurring in a specific setting. This problem needs to be solved because it is currently affecting individuals' lives and practices. Recall from Chapter 3 that formal research typically uses the literature to identify and justify a research problem that affects many individuals. In contrast, the problem in an action research study is one that is being faced by a single practitioner or a single organization. For example, read how one teacher-librarian described the problem occurring at her middle school in the Introduction to her action research study:

> The school year has begun and research projects are underway, but the library shelves are quiet and unused. A quick survey of the computer area shows once again that the students are using the Internet as their first source to locate information. As I watch this scene day after day, I ask these questions: Why do students find the Internet so appealing? Do students know the credibility of sites on the Internet? Do students know how to evaluate sites before using them? Would a unit on how to critically evaluate Internet sites increase the information literacy of the students? I decided to do action research to answer these questions. (Heil, 2005, p. 26)

FIGURE 13.1
**The Action
Research
Process Cycle**

Source: Adapted
from Stringer
(2008).

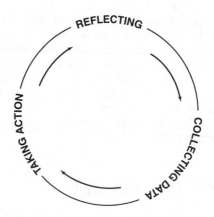

Notice That the Action Researcher Used a Cyclical Process of Research

When action researchers describe their methods in their reports, you notice that it is different from the more linear process of other research designs. Action researchers engage in a dynamic, cyclical process involving iterations of activities. The key idea is that the action researcher cycles or spirals back and forth among reflection about a problem, data collection, and action, as depicted in Figure 13.1. A school-based team, for example, may try several actions after reflecting on the best time for high school classes to begin. Reflecting, collecting data, trying a solution, and spiraling back to reflection are all part of the process of action research. For example, notice how a team of action researchers who worked to improve the emergency services provided in their hospital described their study as including three cycles of research:

> Action research, comprising three action/reflection cycles conducted with participants, was used. Data were collected using retrospective patient record review, interviews with staff members, observation of patient pathways, and measurement of team climate with literature reviews also informing each cycle of data collection. (Endacott, Cooper, Sheaff, Padmore, & Blakely, 2011, p. 203)

How Do You Understand Action Research Designs?

Once you have identified that a research report is an example of action research, you need to understand and evaluate the authors' use of action research as described in the report. Similar to mixed methods research, action research uses data collection based on either quantitative methods or qualitative methods or both methods. However, it differs in that action research addresses a specific, practical issue and works to obtain solutions to a problem. Thus, **action research designs** are systematic procedures done by practitioners (e.g., teachers, social workers, nurses) to gather quantitative and/or qualitative data to improve the ways their particular professional setting operates (e.g., a school, agency, clinic), their practice (e.g., their teaching, counseling, treating), and their impact on others (e.g., student learning, family well-being, children's health).

Although action research is one of the newer approaches to research, it has developed from a long history. The social-psychologist Kurt Lewin coined the term *action research* in the 1930s (Mills, 2007). He developed a process for groups to use to address societal issues. This group process consisted of four steps: planning, acting, observing, and reflecting. Lewin's approach introduced many of the modern ideas of action research: a process of steps, participation, the democratic impulse of involvement, and the contribution to social change (Kemmis, 1994). The development of action research continued in the 1970s with the recognition of the importance of involving practitioners in the solution to their own problems. For example, the Fort Teaching project in England focused on teachers studying their own practices. Another recent development has been the participatory, emancipatory, or community-based action research approach in which groups assume responsibility for their own emancipation and change

FIGURE 13.2
Types of Action Research Designs and Their Use

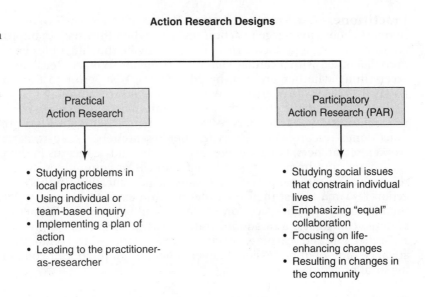

(Kemmis & Wilkinson, 1998). Scholars have used ideological foundations such as feminism and critical race theory to develop action-oriented advocacy means of inquiry that occurs in collaboration with participants for social justice purposes.

From these developments, two distinct types of action research have emerged based on the research having either a practical focus or an emancipatory focus. Although these two designs share many characteristics, they also differ in some important ways. Learning about these two approaches helps you understand the different reports of action research that you may read. As summarized in Figure 13.2 and discussed below, these two action research designs are:

- practical action research and
- participatory action research.

The Practical Action Research Design

One common type of action research that you will read is action research conducted by practitioners. Practitioners across fields seek to address research problems in their own settings so that they can improve their own professional performance and the outcomes from their practices. Teams comprised of teachers, students, counselors, clinicians, parents, and administrators engage in action research to address common issues, such as escalating violence in school or the challenge of providing services to immigrant families in a community. In these situations, practitioners seek to enhance their practice through the systematic study of a local problem. This form of action research is called practical action research, and its purpose is to research a specific professional situation with a view toward improving practice. **Practical action research** involves a small-scale research project, narrowly focuses on a specific problem or issue, and is undertaken by individual practitioners or teams within a practice setting such as a school or clinic. Examples of practical action research studies include:

> *Here's a Tip!*
>
> The best way to recognize the difference in the two action research designs is by considering the intent of the action research. Practical action research addresses a practical problem in one's professional practice. Participatory action research addresses larger injustices in one's community and society.

- A literacy teacher studied the use of differentiated instruction as a means to meet the needs of students at her urban elementary school (Ravitch & Wirth, 2007).
- A team composed of teachers, administrators, and aides working with children studied innovative approaches to early childhood development at two Head Start programs (Haigh, 2007).
- Staff, including nurses and therapists, at a care setting studied strategies for helping patients with dementia move from sitting to a standing position (Varnam, 2011).

Practitioners Use Practical Action Research to Solve Local Problems.   Practitioners choose to engage in action research when they seek to improve specific, local issues by solving a problem. This problem may be the difficulties experienced by children diagnosed with a cardiac condition (Dengler, Wilson, Redshaw, & Scarfe, 2012), ascertaining whether problem-based learning is superior to the traditional lecture (Dods, 1997), or discovering how to promote critical thinking and critical literacy in teachers and students at an urban elementary school (Cooper & White, 2008). Action research calls for practitioners to be researchers. That is, this is a procedure used by practitioner-researchers such as teacher-researchers, nurse-researchers, and social worker-researchers. For example, teachers can study concerns in their own schools or classrooms, and implement site-based councils or committees in schools to enhance research as an integral part of daily classes and education. In this spirit, educators use action research to test their own theories and explanations about learning, examine the effects of their practices on students, and explore the impact of approaches on parents, colleagues, and administrators within their schools. With an emphasis on self-reflection and learning, practitioners also choose to conduct action research to advance their own professional development as an important component of addressing local problems.

Practical Action Research Reports Describe a Spiral Approach to the Process of Research.   When reading practical action research reports, you find that there is no set process that practitioners use when conducting a practical action research study in their setting. Mills (2007), however, advances a model called the dialectic action research spiral, which can help you understand the overall process described in many reports. This model, shown in Figure 13.3, provides teachers, social workers, nurses, and other practitioners with a four-step guide for their action research project. Mills emphasizes that it is a model for practitioners to use to study themselves, not a process of conducting research on practitioners. It is a spiral because it includes four stages where investigators cycle back and forth between data collection and a focus, data collection and analysis and interpretation, and data collection and action.

In this spiral procedure, the practitioner-researcher identifies an area of focus, such as increasing parent involvement in an elementary classroom. This process of defining an area of focus involves doing *reconnaissance*, where the practitioner-researcher engages in self-reflection and description and explanation of the situation. During this stage, the practitioner-researcher also reviews the literature to inform his/her thinking and writes a plan to guide the action research.

With the area of focus defined, then the practitioner-researcher collects data by gathering multiple sources of information (quantitative and qualitative) and by using a variety of inquiry tools, such as interviewing other teachers or sending questionnaires to parents. Data collection also consists of attending to issues of validity, reliability, and ethics, such as provisions for informed consent.

**FIGURE 13.3
Mills' (2007)
Dialectic Action
Research Spiral**

Source: From Geoffrey E. Mills, *Action Research: A Guide for the Teacher Researcher* (3rd ed.). Published by Merrill, an imprint of Pearson Education. Copyright © 2007 by Pearson Education. All rights reserved.

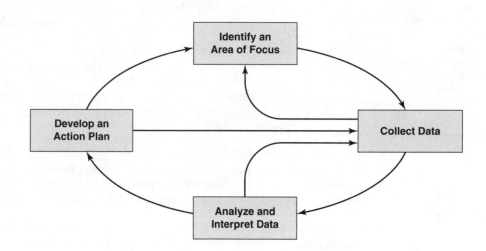

The practitioner-researcher follows this phase with analysis and interpretation. This stage of the process includes coding surveys, interviews, and questionnaires; identifying themes; doing an organizational review; engaging in concept mapping (i.e., visualizing the relationship of ideas); analyzing antecedents and consequences; and displaying findings. For example, the practitioner-researcher might summarize the strategies described by other teachers alongside the opinions of parents. Interpretation involves extending the analysis by raising questions, connecting findings to personal experiences, seeking the advice of critical friends, and contextualizing the findings in literature and theory.

In the final stage, the practitioner-researcher completes an action plan or chart. This chart includes a summary of findings, recommended actions, and the identification of individuals responsible for action and who need to be consulted and informed. Perhaps a few teachers will team up to start a new program of sending weekly updates home to parents, or one parent will work with the teacher to help communicate goals to all parents. The chart also indicates who will monitor and collect the data, the timeline for data collection, and the resources needed to carry out the action (e.g., cookies and coffee available for an evening parents' meeting at the school).

Overall, this spiral process emphasizes practical action research centered on studying a local problem, engaging in inquiry by an individual practitioner or a team, and focusing on professional development in order to plan and take action to address the problem.

Identifying the Characteristics of the Practical Action Research Design in a Research Report.   Although we use the name *practical action research* here to emphasize the practical focus of this design, you will not always find that term used in research reports. Many authors reporting their use of this design refer to it as *action research* or *practitioner action research*. Although practical action research can be used in any practice setting (e.g., a health clinic or a state service agency), many examples appear in the education literature, using the term *teacher inquiry* for this approach. The format of practical action research reports vary because they are intended to be useful for other practitioners instead of serving as formal reports of research. Nonetheless, you can usually identify these study reports because they include the following characteristics:

- **The research problem focused on the need to solve a practical problem.** When reading the Introduction of a practical action research report, you find that the author's focus is clearly on an actual problem in a specific professional setting. Action researchers study practical issues that have immediate benefits for their professional practice. These issues may be a concern of a single teacher in a classroom or a problem involving many employees in an organization. Action researchers do not undertake this form of research to advance knowledge for knowledge's sake, but to solve an immediate, practical problem.
- **The action researcher gathered information using a dynamic process.** When reading about the methods used, you notice that the action researcher engaged in a dynamic process involving iterations of activities. As illustrated in Figure 13.3, this process includes iterations among reflecting and learning about a problem, collecting quantitative and/or qualitative information, interpreting this information, and taking action. A school-based team, for example, may try several actions after reflecting on the best time for high school classes to begin, and gather and interpret information after each action.
- **The action researcher worked to improve his/her own practices.** When reading the report, you learn that the action researcher took steps to develop and improve his/her own professional practice. As action researchers study their own situations, they reflect on what they have learned—a form of self-development—as well as what they can do to improve their practices. In addition, they examine and adjust their own practices during the study. Action researchers deliberately experiment with their own practices, monitor the actions and circumstances in which they occur, and then retrospectively reconstruct an interpretation of the action as a basis for future action.
- **The action researcher used the information to develop a plan of action.** When reading a practical action research report, you find that the author not only gathered data

and reported results, but also prepared to take action. At some point in the process, the action researcher formulates an action plan in response to the problem. This plan may be presenting the data to important stakeholders, establishing a pilot program, implementing new practices, or establishing an ongoing agenda to explore new practices. This plan is shared in the practice setting, but may also be shared more broadly in a report or website or at a conference to share the lessons learned with other practitioners.

An Example of a Practical Action Research Study.   Dicker (1990), an experienced high school teacher, used an action research study to examine her response to being assigned to teach a new communications course that was outside of her expertise in math and drama. She clearly faced a very practical problem in her high school setting in terms of how to cope with this assignment to teach a new course in an unfamiliar content area. The author reflects on her experiences and discusses her situation with another former teacher of English. She used four sources of data in this project: her own reflective journals (the major source), student journals, comments from the former teacher, and tape recordings of class sessions. Throughout the study, a dynamic process unfolds, with this teacher trying out an idea, making adjustments, examining the collected data, and exploring another idea. A series of mini action plans ensued throughout the school year as this author shared her personal frustrations and successes in teaching this unfamiliar subject. Dicker (1990) concludes, "Teaching Communications 11 was a professional development activity that contained as much learning for me as for the students" (p. 208).

What Do You Think?

Suppose you are reading a collection of research articles related to the problem of students' lack of motivation. Why might one of the studies have used a practical action research design to study this topic? What characteristics would you expect to find in the report of this study?

Check Your Understanding

A middle school math teacher may be concerned that her students are not motivated in her pre-algebra class. She decides to implement a practical action research study to focus on developing strategies to improve her students' motivation. We expect that she will gather information, such as talking with other teachers, reviewing papers written about teaching math, and surveying the students about the types of activities they find motivating. She develops a plan to try two different strategies: Having students bring to class examples of math that they find in their everyday lives and asking students to work in groups on a math problem that represents a real-world application of math. She documents the number of questions asked during each class and the percentage of students who complete each activity. Throughout the year, she keeps a journal of the new strategies she has learned, the activities she tries, and how well they worked so she can continue to refine the strategies she uses.

How might you use a practical action research design to address a problem you face?

The Participatory Action Research (PAR) Design

Instead of having a focus on individual practitioners solving immediate problems or members of organizations addressing internal issues, some action research that you will read focuses on social change in communities and organizations. This form of action research is often referred to as participatory action research. **Participatory action research**, often referred to as **PAR**, is a research design that has a social and community orientation and an emphasis on research that contributes to emancipation or change in our society. PAR has a long history in social inquiry involving communities, industries and corporations, and other organizations. Drawing on the ideological works of the Brazilian Paulo Freire, the German critical theorist Jürgen Habermas, and more recently Australians Stephen Kemmis and Ernest Stringer (Schmuck, 1997), this approach is used as an action-oriented advocacy means of inquiry to work for social change.

Researchers Use PAR to Improve the Quality of People's Lives.

Researchers conduct PAR (that is, *participatory* action research) when their goal is to improve the quality of people's organizations, communities, and lives (Stringer, 1999). Although espousing many of the same ideas of practical action research, PAR studies differ because they incorporate an emancipatory aim of improving and empowering individuals and organizations in community settings. Applied to education, for example, the focus of PAR is on improving and empowering individuals in schools, systems of education, and school communities. PAR researchers study issues related to a need to address social problems that constrain and oppress the lives of people. Individuals have engaged in PAR studies to empower parents whose children have been classified as having emotional disabilities to improve family–school relationships (Ditrano & Silverstein, 2006), to improve economic and educational opportunities of street-life oriented Black men (Payne, 2008), to engage a rural community in better understanding their children's health (Campbell, 2010), and to provide for the information needs of diverse parents of preschool children who have asthma (Garwick & Seppelt, 2010).

Researchers also report choosing PAR when they have a distinct social justice theoretical foundation that shapes the direction of the process of inquiry. This foundation may include principles of ideologies such as feminism, critical race theory, or disability theory. These theories encourage PAR researchers to engage in a process of research that promotes egalitarian and democratic aims. PAR researchers strive for an open, broad-based involvement of participants in their studies by collaborating in decisions with participants as consensual partners and engaging participants as equals to ensure their well-being. For example, PAR researchers emphasize the importance of establishing contacts, identifying stakeholder groups, identifying key people, negotiating the researcher's role, and building a preliminary picture of the field context in their inquiries (Stringer, 1999). The social values of liberation and life-enhancing changes also are important. PAR researchers seek to bring about a new vision for schools, agencies, and ethnic groups within communities.

PAR Reports Describe a Social Research Process Emphasizing Collaboration.

Although all types of action research utilize a dynamic research process, when you read about a PAR study, you find that the PAR process emphasizes a social process and collaboration among researchers, stakeholders, and participants. Stringer (2008) provides one model for understanding the action research process within a participatory context. His model portrays the action research process as a helix, which you can see in Figure 13.4. This helix model contains three cyclical phases: look, think, and act.

Let's examine the components of the action research process for looking, thinking, and acting more closely. In this model, Stringer (1999, 2008) places emphasis on the importance of looking to build an understanding so that the researchers help stakeholders understand issues they are experiencing. The "look" phase consists of the PAR researchers working with stakeholders and participants, collecting data (e.g., through interviews, observation, and documents), analyzing and interpreting the information, and reporting to stakeholders about the issue. Often researchers who are conducting PAR emphasize the collection of qualitative forms of data, but they may also include quantitative data collection. The researchers may examine the situation for injustices or ways in which certain individuals are being oppressed. The "think" phase then moves into interpreting the issues in greater depth and identifying priorities for action in collaboration

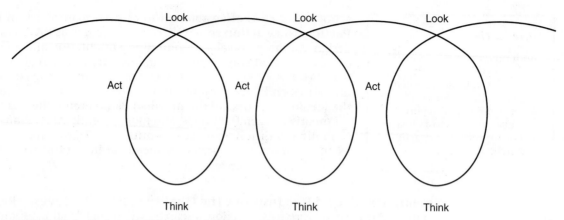

FIGURE 13.4   Stringer's (2008) Action Research Helix

Source: From Ernie Stringer *Action Research In Education* (2nd ed.). Published by Merrill, an imprint of Pearson Education. Copyright © 2008 by Pearson Education. All rights reserved.

with stakeholders and participants. From there, the researchers plan the "act" phase—working with participants to devise solutions to the problems. This involves developing a plan and setting direction, such as objectives, tasks, and persons to carry out the objectives and securing needed resources. It also means implementing the plan, encouraging people to carry it out, and evaluating it in terms of its effect and achievements for improving lives. Good PAR studies report implementing multiple cycles of these phases, as depicted in Figure 13.4, to bring about meaningful social change.

Identifying the Characteristics of the PAR Design in a Research Report.

When reading a research report, you can identify a study that used a PAR design by finding terms such as *participatory action research, critical action research,* or *community-based participatory research.* Keep in mind that many authors refer to their participatory action research design as *PAR* in their reports. In addition to the use of these key terms, you can also identify reports of PAR studies by noting the following key characteristics:

- **The research problem focused on the need to help individuals in the community free themselves from constraints.** When reading the Introduction of a PAR report, you learn that the authors want to empower individuals in the community to help improve their lives. PAR is emancipatory in that researchers use it to help unshackle people from the constraints of irrational and unjust structures that limit self-development and self-determination. These constraints may be found in the media, in language, in work procedures, and in the power relationships that exist among members of a community setting. The intent of a PAR study, for example, might be to change the bureaucratic procedures in a school so that low-income parents have more opportunity to be involved in their children's education.

- **The PAR researcher collaborated with community members.** When reading the Method section of the report, a PAR study describes how the researchers collaborated with others throughout the study. Collaboration in PAR studies often involves the researchers working with participants as co-researchers in the research. These co-researcher participants may be parents, practitioners, community leaders, or policy makers. This collaboration involves establishing respectful and cooperative relationships, communicating in a manner that is sincere and appropriate, and including all individuals, groups, and issues. Many aspects of the research process are open to collaboration in a PAR project, such as determining the study focus, data collection forms, and action plans. During this collaboration, roles may vary and be negotiated, but the concept of collaborating is central to the PAR process.

- **The PAR researcher gathered information using a recursive process.** When reading the Method section of the report, you also find that the research process is recursive (reflexive or dialectical) and focused on bringing about change in social practices in the community. This recursive process occurs through spirals of examination, reflection, and action. When researchers and community members reflect on their roles, they try one action and then another, always returning to the central question of what they learned and accomplished because of their actions.

- **The PAR researcher shared the research in formats to bring about change.** Although you will read examples of PAR studies published in scholarly journals, PAR researchers are typically more interested in sharing the information locally with individuals who can promote change. PAR researchers report their research to individuals who can immediately use the results, such as local school, community, and government personnel. PAR researchers may also use innovative forums to perform what they have learned in order to encourage change. These performances might be a play, a poem, a reading of text, art exhibits, slides, or music. For example, Tofteng and Husted (2011) described how their PAR study resulted in a play that was created and performed to convey the struggles of unemployed members of their community.

An Example of a PAR Study.   Valdez, Dowrick, and Maynard (2007) used PAR as a framework to empower Samoan parents at one middle school. The researchers felt that the school did not adequately understand the cultural perspectives on education held by the Samoan parents. The researchers collaborated with parents, teachers, administrators, and community members (e.g., a minister and a state official) to design and conduct the study. The data collection included primarily qualitative methods, including interviews and observations. As the data were analyzed, the authors continued to share and refine their results with participants representing each role (parents, teachers, and so on). The findings uncovered many cultural misperceptions that existed in the community, such as perceptions about parents' role in education. From the increased understanding of all stakeholders' perspectives, the school developed new programs and policies that better aligned with the cultural values of all ethnic groups represented at the school, thereby reducing barriers against Samoan parents' involvement.

What Do You Think?

Suppose you are reading a collection of research articles related to the problem of students' lack of motivation. Why might one of the studies have used a PAR design to study this topic? What characteristics would you expect to find in the report of this study?

Check Your Understanding

Perhaps a teacher notices that two students have recently become unmotivated in his high school classes. Through conversations with other teachers and the students, the teacher learns that the students are members of the school's gay, lesbian, bisexual, and transgender (GLBT) community, and that other students have recently begun harassing them. The teacher discusses his concerns with the principal and, with her support, they initiate a PAR project to improve the culture for all GLBT students at the school. We might expect the report of this study to emphasize collaboration, such as having the research team include the principal, teachers, GLBT and non-GLBT students, and community activists. Together, they will gather information such as surveying all members of the school (staff and students) and interviewing representatives of different groups. The research team of adults and adolescents together develop an action plan that includes creating a committee on diversity at the school. In addition, the research team may use the results of their research to develop a play that illustrates the injustice of harassment and is performed by the school drama club for the school and members of the community.

How might a PAR design be used in your community?

How Do You Plan Your Own Action Research Study?

You can now recognize and understand action research studies that you find reported in the literature. In addition to reading about others' projects, you can design and implement your own action research design in your own setting. By using an action research approach, you can apply the tools of research to gather information about, reflect on, and take action in response to problems that you want solved in your local setting. Completing an action research project will also encourage and support your own professional development, and help you relate your professional practices to the scholarship of practice in your field.

Drawing from numerous books available on conducting action research (e.g., Mills, 2007; Stringer, 2008), we provide eight steps in Table 13.1 that you can take to conduct your own action research study. As you read about the steps, remember that action research is a dynamic, flexible process and that no precise blueprint exists for how to proceed. However, these steps found within the cyclical action research process can illustrate a general approach for your use.

Step 1—Determine Whether Action Research Is Possible in Your Setting and With Your Colleagues

Start by considering whether it is appropriate and feasible for you to conduct an action research study. You should consider using action research when you want

> **Here's a Tip!**
>
> Remember that in an action research study, you participate in your own research project. You are not studying someone else; instead, you are examining and changing your own practices to solve a problem you face.

to systematically address a problem in your work situation or community, and to advance your own professional development. You need to be open to learning new ideas about your practices, and willing and able to experiment with different options for solving the problem. To help with the process of reflection, you ideally need colleagues with whom you can collaborate and who can potentially serve as co-researchers on the project. Action research also requires some familiarity with the many types of quantitative and qualitative data collection procedures (as introduced in this book and that you may already be using in your professional practice). It requires that you have the time to collect and analyze data so you can use these procedures to gather information and evidence in order to devise a plan of action.

TABLE 13.1 Steps for Planning Your Action Research Study

Planning Step	Your Action Research Study Plans
1—Determine whether action research is possible in your setting and with your colleagues	
2—Specify the problem you want to study	
3—Locate resources to help you address the problem	
4—Identify information you need to examine the problem	
5—Implement the data collection	
6—Analyze the data	
7—Develop a plan for action	
8—Implement the plan and reflect	

Step 2—Specify the Problem You Want to Study

The most important factor in action research is that you need to solve a practical problem. This problem is one that you face in your own practice or in your community (Kemmis & Wilkinson, 1998). Start a record of your thoughts about the problem in a journal or computer file, and note your reflections as they occur. After reflecting and talking with others about the situation, write down the problem or phrase it as a question to answer. In some situations, action researchers may begin with collecting data, evaluating existing information, or even planning an action to help determine the area of focus. Viewing action research as a spiral of activities (recall Figures 13.3 and 13.4) introduces several points in the spiral in which you might begin your action research study.

Step 3—Locate Resources to Help You Address the Problem

Explore several resources to help study the problem. Literature and existing data may help you formulate a plan of action. You may need to review the literature (as discussed in Chapter 4) and determine what others have learned about solving the issue and what possible solutions you may want to try. Asking colleagues for advice also helps initiate a study. Teaming with colleagues, university personnel, or knowledgeable people in the community can provide a resource base for your action research project. These individuals may help you with the action research in different ways, such as with developing potential solutions, gathering and analyzing data, or assisting with putting a plan into action. Individuals who have previously conducted action research projects can also help you navigate the action research process during your research study.

Step 4—Identify Information You Need to Examine the Problem

Plan a strategy for gathering data as part of the action research study so that you have evidence on which to base your action plans. This means that you need to decide who can provide data, how many people you will study, how you will access individuals, and what level of rapport and support you can expect to obtain from them. Because you plan to conduct this action research in your local setting, you should inform your supervisor (e.g., your principal or your manager) and other constituents about your research plans and seek their approval. In addition, if you plan to use this research for part of your graduate program, you may need to have your project formally reviewed and approved by your advisor and others at your institution or agency.

Another important consideration is what type of data you need to collect. Your choices are to collect quantitative data (e.g., attendance data, test scores, or a short survey) or qualitative data (e.g., reflection journals or in-person interviews) or both. The choice of data sources depends on your questions, time and resources, availability of individuals, and sources of information that are accessible. Consider your available resources, such as access to a photocopy machine or a digital recorder on your cell phone, but mostly focus on determining what kind of information you think will help you best understand and monitor the problem that you want to address. In general, the more sources used, the more you will be able to understand the problem and develop viable action plans. It is wise, however, to limit the amount of data collection in your first action research study so that you have a manageable amount of information to analyze.

Step 5—Implement the Data Collection

Implementing data collection takes time, especially if you gather multiple sources of information. In addition, your participants may have limited time to complete instruments or engage in interviews. Keeping an accurate record of the information collected, organizing it into data files for numeric or theme analysis, and examining the quality of the information are important data collection steps. Develop a system to systematically store, organize, and label the information you gather, such as making photocopies of documents and putting them into file folders, or making digital copies of audio recordings and storing them in one folder on your computer. You should also keep a record of your own actions and reflections throughout the process, as these notes will become another source of useful data.

Here's a Tip!

Research is a systematic process, even in action research. This means you should keep records of your reflections, ideas, and actions throughout the project. Record your notes in whatever format is most convenient for you.

Step 6—Analyze the Data

You may decide to analyze the data yourself or enlist the help of other scholars or data analysts to help with that part of the process. Quantitative data should be organized into tables to facilitate calculations with a calculator or a spreadsheet program like Microsoft Excel. Qualitative data should be organized by type (e.g., reflection journals, documents, and interviews). In most situations, descriptive statistics about the trends in the quantitative data (as discussed in Chapter 8) and general themes in the qualitative data (as discussed in Chapter 11) will suffice for your analysis. The major idea is to keep the data analysis manageable so that you can identify useful information in formulating a plan of action. In addition to finding results from your data, also think about how you interpret the results and what you learn from them. Pay particular attention to results that show change or that provide information that you were not expecting. You might show your results to others to find out how they interpret the findings to gain different perspectives on the problem.

Step 7—Develop a Plan for Action

In action research, it is not enough to produce results from your data, you need to use those results to develop a plan for action. Think creatively to develop your action plan, but also be sure to base your ideas on the resources and data that you gathered (not just on your personal preferences!). You may decide to try a completely new strategy that was suggested in the literature or by talking with colleagues, or you may decide that it is best to simply refine existing practices. In any case, an action plan may be an informal statement about the implementation of the new practice. It might be a plan to reflect on alternative approaches to addressing the problem, or to share what you have learned with others, such as other practitioners, individuals in other offices of your organization, or other schools, agencies, and communities. You might formally write out this plan or present it as an outline. You can develop it yourself or collaborate with other personnel in writing it. The important point is that you now have a strategy for trying out some ideas to help solve your problem.

Here's a Tip!

Action research is a great way for you to enhance your professional development, but it also takes time and can be challenging. Do not expect to develop a perfect plan on the first attempt. By focusing on the spiral approach, you can continue to learn and improve over time.

Step 8—Implement the Plan and Reflect

In many action research projects, you will implement your plan of action to see whether it makes a difference. This involves trying out a potential solution to your problem and monitoring whether it has an impact through your reflections and data gathering. To determine this difference, you might consult your original objectives or the research question that you sought to answer in the action research project. Keep in mind that action research is a cyclical process, and that you should plan to gather data, analyze and interpret that data, and reflect for each action you try.

You also need to reflect on what you have learned from implementing your plan and sharing it with others. You may need to share it broadly with school colleagues, school committees, university researchers, or policy makers. In some cases, you will not achieve an adequate solution, and you will need to try out another idea and see whether it makes a difference. In this way, one action research project often leads to another.

What Do You Think?

Suppose you are a third grade teacher who is concerned about the increasing obesity levels found among the children in your classroom. How might you use the steps of action research to address this problem?

Check Your Understanding

You could implement the eight steps of an action research study to address the problem of obesity among the children in the third-grade classroom. Although the details will necessarily vary depending on your background and context, the study steps might be something like the following:

1. Decide that an action research study is feasible. This might be because you have the time available, you have the opportunity to make changes in your classroom, and the school nurse and physical educator have agreed to collaborate with you.
2. After reflecting on the problem and talking with others, specify the problem. This might be: the children are not engaging in enough physical activity each week.
3. Locate and read literature about increasing physical activity in elementary classrooms and talk with the school nurse, physical education teacher, and other classroom teachers for ideas.
4. Discuss the idea of an action research study with the principal and gain her support. Select the types of data to gather in addition to keeping your research journal. These might include: (1) log of the types of physical activity that occur during the school day (e.g., walking to the music room, running laps in physical education class), (2) student documents about physical activity (e.g., stories, drawings), and (3) number of daily steps measured with a pedometer.
5. Gather the forms of data and organize them. This might include putting the logs and pedometer data for each day into a three-ring binder, making copies of the documents (artwork, stories), and organizing them in file folders by week.
6. Analyze the quantitative and qualitative data. This might include creating a table of the activities that occurred and the number of steps taken by the selected children for each day and developing a graph of the data over time. This could be done as part of the math unit, where the children help interpret what happened on days when the numbers went up or down. For the qualitative data, this might include analyzing the student physical activity documents (e.g., stories, pictures) for themes (e.g., hard work, fun, boring).
7. Develop a plan to increase physical activity such as integrating physical activity into primary content areas (such as graphing in math or stories for reading), incorporating 5 minutes of activity before recess, having the children walk the long way through the building to get to the music and art rooms, and encouraging children to increase their number of steps as measured by the pedometer.
8. Implement one or two strategies at a time and monitor how children react. Keep records of each strategy and analyze the data for its impact. Reflect on the results as well as any unintended consequences (such as children selected to wear the pedometer becoming disruptive in class). Regularly discuss what is happening with the school nurse and physical education teacher for ideas to refine the action plan.

How Do You Evaluate an Action Research Study?

Action research has gained support across many disciplines including education, nursing, and clinical work. There are, however, critics who are reluctant to view it as a legitimate form of inquiry (Stringer, 1999). Some view it as an "informal" process of research, conducted by practitioners who are not formal academic researchers. The practical aspect of action research also suggests an applied orientation to this form of inquiry that some view as a less-than-scientific approach. Action researchers typically report results of their studies in informal venues, such as conferences, websites, or local groups in the community. The methods are adapted and changed in response to the practitioners' objectives to understand a practical problem. Hence, the design may not have the rigor and systematic approach found in other designs. However, it is precisely this flexibility and responsiveness that makes action research studies among the best source of information to learn about potential solutions to real problems because they are conducted in real professional settings by real practitioners. Therefore, when evaluating an action research study, you need to keep in mind the intent and standards for this particular form of research.

As the name *action research* implies, there are two aspects you should consider when evaluating any action research study. First, it is a form of research and therefore the action researcher should report using sound procedures for gathering and analyzing quantitative and qualitative information. We have provided quality criteria for these methods already in this book (see Chapters 7–8 and 10–11). Second, the application of this research design and its cyclical process should result in actions that help to solve real problems. Therefore, you should also consider the quality of the process and actions that result from any action research project. Table 13.2 provides criteria that are useful for assessing an author's implementation of an action research design with an emphasis on the features specific to action research. For each of the criteria, the table also provides indicators of higher quality and lower quality to help you make your own assessment when evaluating the information provided in an action research report.

Figure 13.5 provides a rating form that you can use to apply the quality criteria to evaluate the use of action research within a study's research report. For each of the criteria

TABLE 13.2   Criteria for Evaluating the Use of Action Research in a Research Report

Quality Criteria	Indicators of Higher Quality in Action Research	Indicators of Lower Quality in Action Research
The Key Elements		
1. The research focuses on a real problem in practice or the local community.	+ A clear problem with current practices or a clear need for social change is indicated. + The problem arises from one's own practice or from the needs of community members more than from the literature.	− The problem or need for change is unclear or seems unrelated to individual's practices or lives. − The researcher determines the problem from outside the setting and initiates the research based on formal gaps in knowledge.
2. The researcher is a practitioner and/or collaborates with community members.	+ The research is led by a practitioner-researcher who wants to study his/her own practices. + The researcher actively collaborates with others in the setting in a respectful way. + Community members and participant co-researchers are involved throughout the research process.	− The research is led by formal academic researchers. − The researcher involves others in only superficial ways. − Community members and participants have little input into the research process.
3. The research process includes careful reflection about the problem.	+ The area of focus is informed by examining current practices, talking with others in the setting, reading available literature, and gathering relevant information. + The researcher actively reflects on his/her own professional development.	− The area of focus is selected without much thought or examination of what is needed to address the problem. − There is little evidence of the researcher being reflective or developing as a professional.
4. Multiple sources of good information are used.	+ The researcher gathers several sources of information. + The researcher uses good qualitative and quantitative procedures to collect and analyze data. (See Chapters 7–8 and 10–11 for indicators of higher quality.) + The data provide adequate and useful evidence about the problem.	− The researcher gathers only one source of information. − The researcher uses poor or inappropriate procedures for data collection and analysis. (See Chapters 7–8 and 10–11 for indicators of lower quality.) − The data are not clearly useful for examining the problem or provide limited and biased information about the problem.

Quality Criteria	Indicators of Higher Quality in Action Research	Indicators of Lower Quality in Action Research
5. A good action plan is advanced.	+ The researcher develops a clear plan for addressing the problem. + There is a clear link among the elements of the plan and what the researcher has learned from the reflection and gathered data.	− No clear plan is developed or it is unclear how the plan addresses the problem. − The elements of the plan seem disconnected from what the researcher has learned.
General Evaluation		
6. The study used a good action research process.	+ The research process includes reflecting and thinking, looking and gathering information, and acting. + The research process includes multiple cycles or spirals through these phases.	− The research process is linear and fixed or it is haphazard and poorly planned. − The research process includes only one pass through the cycle.
7. The study results in meaningful actions to address the problem.	+ Actions that are based on the research provide workable solutions to the problem. + The actions enhance individuals' lives by improving practice, empowering them, or solving the problem.	− Little to no action is taken or the actions are not clearly based on the research and do not provide workable solutions to the problem. − The actions are superficial and do not change the quality of individuals' lives.

Quality Criteria	Quality Rating				Your Evidence and/or Reasoning
	0 = Poor	1 = Fair	2 = Good	3 = Excellent	
The Key Elements					
1. The research focuses on a real problem in practice or the local community.					
2. The researcher is a practitioner and/or collaborates with community members.					
3. The research process includes careful reflection about the problem.					
4. Multiple sources of good information are used.					
5. A good action plan is advanced.					
General Evaluation					
6. The study used a good action research process.					
7. The study results in meaningful actions to address the problem.					
Overall Quality 0–10 = Low quality 11–16 = Adequate quality 17–21 = High quality	**Total Score =**				**My Overall Assessment Is**

FIGURE 13.5 A Rating Scale for Evaluating an Action Research Study

you locate, assign a quality rating from *fair* (1) to *excellent* (3) and document your evidence and/or reasoning behind the rating. If one of the criteria is missing in the report or very poorly stated, then indicate *poor* (0) as your rating. Keep in mind that action research reports vary in their style and in the extent to which they discuss the research procedures. Even with this variation, however, a good action research study should still score well on most of the items listed in Figure 13.5. By adding up the rating scores for each of the criteria and using the suggested cutoff values provided at the bottom of the figure, you will have a quantitative measure that you can use to inform your overall assessment.

Reviewing What You've Learned To Do

- *Identify and understand the use of action research in a research study.*
  - ☐ Action research is a research approach used by practitioners and community members to address a real problem in their local setting by using a cyclical process of research that involves reflection, data collection, and action.
- *Recognize two different research designs when reading action research reports.*
  - ☐ The practical action research design focuses on a spiral research process for trying to solve a practical problem in one's professional practice.
  - ☐ The participatory action research (PAR) design focuses on a collaborative research process to bring about social change to improve the quality of people's lives.
- *Plan an action research study in response to a problem in your own practice setting.*
  - ☐ The steps of conducting action research assist practitioners with solving problems in their practice through professional development and systematic examination of one's practices.
  - ☐ Although the steps rarely unfold in a linear fashion, the action researcher often begins with determining whether action research is possible, specifying the local problem that needs to be studied, and locating resources to help address the problem.
  - ☐ With the area of focus determined, the action researcher next identifies the quantitative and qualitative information that will help examine the problem, gathers the data forms, and analyzes and interprets the gathered data.
  - ☐ The action researcher uses the information and results to develop a plan of action to address the problem, and implements and reflects on the impact of the actions. Often these reflections lead to another cycle of the research process that includes refining the area of focus, gathering and analyzing information, and planning further actions.
- *Evaluate the quality of an action research report.*
  - ☐ The evaluation of an action research study includes assessing the procedures used to collect and analyze both qualitative and quantitative data.
  - ☐ The evaluation of an action research study includes evaluating its action research features in addition to the data collection and analysis methods. The evaluation considers the importance of the problem for the setting, the extent of collaboration, the cyclical/recursive nature of the research process, and the quality of the actions taken as a result of the research.

✓ **To assess what you've learned to do, click here to answer questions and receive instant feedback.**

Reading Research Articles

At the end of this chapter, you will find a research article to help you practice your new skills. Carefully read the action research learning-by-talking study by Cain (2011) starting on p. 449. First, write a complete, APA-style reference for this article.

As you read the article, pay close attention to statements in which the author conveyed the action research elements of the study. Use the highlighting tool in the Pearson etext to indicate where the author has provided information about the study's use of action research, and use the notetaking tool to add marginal notes that name each element you highlighted and note how each one is related to the study's action research design. Among the elements you will want to find are:

1. Focus on a practical problem
2. Practitioner as researcher
3. Professional development
4. Collaboration with others
5. Cyclical research process
6. Reflection
7. Data collection (i.e., quantitative and/or qualitative)
8. Data analysis (i.e., quantitative and/or qualitative)
9. Action plan development
10. Take action and change practices

Note, however, that authors may not discuss all of these elements—for example, they may not explicitly discuss professional development, they may not describe the development of the action plan, or they may not discuss taking action in the report. If one of these elements is missing, indicate that in your marginal notes.

Click here to go to the action research learning-by-talking study by Cain (2011) so that you can write a complete APA-style reference for this article and enter marginal notes about the study.

Understanding Research Articles

Apply your knowledge of the content of this chapter to the action research learning-by-talking study by Cain (2011) found at the end of this chapter (starting on p. 449).

1. What problem did the author want to solve in his local setting in the learning-by-talking study?

2. What evidence do you find that the action researcher used a cyclical approach to his study?

3. In what ways did the action researcher collaborate with others?

4. What actions did the researcher take as a result of his study?

5. Which type of action research design does this study illustrate? What is your evidence?

6. This action research study was reported as a "formal" research article. How else might the author have shared his project?

✓ Click here to answer the questions and receive instant feedback.

Evaluating Research Articles

Practice evaluating the quality of the use of action research, using the action research learning-by-talking study by Cain (2011) starting on p. 449 and by developing your own action research study plan.

1. Use the criteria discussed in Table 13.2 to evaluate the quality of the use of action research in the learning-by-talking study. Note that the rating form includes advice to help guide your evaluation.

✓ Click here to open the rating scale form (Figure 13.5) to enter your ratings, evidence, and reasoning.

2. Now think about a problem that matters to you because it is occurring or might occur in your own practices. Keeping the quality criteria discussed in Table 13.2 in mind, use the eight steps for planning your own action research study to develop an outline for a good-quality action research study that you might conduct on this problem.

✓ **Click here to open the planning form (Table 13.1) to enter your study plan.**

An Example of Action Research: The Learning-by-Talking Study

Let's examine another published research article to apply the ideas you are learning. Throughout this book, we will refer to this study as the "action research learning-by-talking" study. This journal article reports an action research study conducted and reported by Cain (2011). Examine this article to practice your skills with reading, understanding, and evaluating research.

 Click here to write a complete APA-style reference for this article and receive instant feedback.

Article

International Journal of
Music Education
29(2) 141–154
© The Author(s) 2011
Reprints and permission: sagepub.
co.uk/journalsPermissions.nav
DOI: 10.1177/0255761410396961
ijm.sagepub.com

⑤SAGE

How trainee music teachers learn about teaching by talking to each other: An action research study

Tim Cain
University of Southampton, UK

Abstract

This article presents an action research study into how trainee music teachers in England use a structured discussion process called 'Collegial Consultation' to learn about teaching. The research shows that, in Collegial Consultation, trainees learn from each other by offering several solutions to a problem, offering reasons for their ideas, trying to understand other people's ideas, signalling agreements with each other, disagreeing and building on each other's ideas. The article argues that the structure of Collegial Consultation promotes an ethos of equality that supports high-quality educational discussion, allowing trainee teachers to think together about teaching music within the classroom.

Keywords

action research, collegial consultation, initial teacher education

Conversation as a means of learning

(01) For a long time I have understood that the trainee teachers I teach learn from each other, sometimes better than they learn from me. Therefore I have often tried to instigate whole-group discussions but these have rarely been helpful; they tend to be stilted and uncomfortable and few trainees contribute, unless specifically asked to do so. There are successful aspects of my teaching but group discussions are not amongst them. I therefore wanted to explore how I could encourage trainees to learn from each other in stimulating, educational discussions.

(02) Engaging trainees in talk about teaching is not necessarily educational; as one student teacher said:

Corresponding author:
Tim Cain, School of Education, University of Southampton, Highfield, Southampton, SO17 1BJ, UK.
Email: t.cain@southampton.ac.uk

[in formal conversations] I'll be asking about things like workload or what a good class is like … and I'll think 'I sound like such a geek' … But if I'm out with a friend and we're talking about teaching, we just bitch about it. (Cook-Sather, 2001, p. 27).

Discussions around 'what a good class is like' might be educational but 'just bitching' probably isn't, and there is a growing literature around what makes talk educationally more, or less, productive, in the sense of generating learning for participants. Mercer (1995, 2000) characterized types of classroom talk as 'exploratory', 'cumulative' and 'disputational'. He described these types of talk as 'distinctive social modes of thinking', distinguishable by their differing linguistic structures, psychological intent and cultural functions (Mercer, 1995, p. 104). Exploratory talk is educationally useful because: 'It typifies language which embodies certain principles – of accountability, of clarity, of constructive criticism and receptiveness to well-argued proposals – which are valued highly in many societies' (Mercer, 1995, p. 106). Cumulative talk, 'in which speakers build on each other's contributions, add information of their own and in a mutually supportive, uncritical way construct shared knowledge and understanding' (Mercer, 2000, p. 31), is useful for establishing common ground and bonding people ('just bitching'?) but is educationally less worthwhile; it is characterized by repetitions, confirmations and elaborations (Mercer, 1995, p. 104). Disputational talk is 'characterized by disagreement and individualized decision making' (Wegerif, Mercer, & Dawes, 1998, p. 201) in which the speakers treat each other as threats to their individual interests and work to, 'keep their identities separate, and to protect their individuality' (Mercer, 2000, p. 173). In it, people adopt entrenched positions and close their minds to alternative views.

(03)   Other typologies of talk include Cavazos & the members of WEST (2001), a self-study of conversations between a group of women science teachers. This distinguished between talk ('anecdotal stories and snippets shared by teachers in informal contexts for the purposes of sharing frustration, joy and information'), narrative ('a story a teacher tells that integrates intuition, practical experience, reading and knowledge'), conversation ('a highly active and engaged form of talk where participants learn through and from the talk by sharing opinions, ideas and references') and dialogue ('a conversation directed towards discovery and new understanding, where the participants question, analyze, and critique the topic or experience') (Cavazos et al., 2001, pp. 157–162). These types imply a continuum, from 'anecdotal stories and snippets' to 'question, analyze, and critique': 'talk' and 'narrative' appear similar to 'cumulative talk', whilst 'conversation' and 'dialogue' explicitly include learning and new understanding, and are congruent with 'exploratory talk'. Cavazos et al. (2001) discussed the absence of confrontation in their discussions:

> Our commonly shared understanding of confrontation implies opposition in a hostile manner … focusing our attention on developing skills in collective problem solving and continuous inquiry may be a more natural path to deeper thinking and professional growth than introducing confrontation. (p. 168)

Conflict and resistance in teachers' conversation groups were studied by Zellermayer (2001) who saw them as helpful in stimulating learning. A structural analysis of conversations between (female and male) veteran teachers revealed that educationally worthwhile conversations typically consisted of three parts: (1) a teacher risked sharing an account of a teaching experience, exposing problems and difficulties; (2) one or more teachers challenged this account in some way; (3) teachers decontextualized the account and generalized about it. This process led to a 'reframing' of the matter under discussion (Zellermayer, 2001, p. 45).

(04)   Gruenhagen's (2009) study of a music teachers' inquiry group described its development from the early stages ('although many of the teachers routinely told stories from practice … they didn't necessarily talk about their music teaching practice. They told stories about places, contexts, children, classroom teachers, aides and parents') to its later development ('over time, conversations became more focused and deeply reflective. The teachers began to take more risks by telling personal stories from practice about both triumphs and disappointments') (pp. 135–137). The participating teachers reported being challenged by the group and encouraged to voice their views, and to evaluate what they were doing and why. The multiple perspectives of other group members helped them to solve problems related to teaching and learning, and teachers were prompted to change their practice as a consequence of listening to others. Gruenhagen found no previous studies of teachers' conversation groups in music education.

(05)   A meta-analysis by Clark (2001) found that, when teachers engaged in conversation groups, their learning included articulating their implicit theories, seeing the world through the eyes of others, developing a sense of personal and professional authority, reaffirming ideals and commitments and developing specific solutions to problems (p. 173). According to Clark: 'Good conversations … deal with worthwhile content; resist narrow definition; are voluntary; flourish on common ground, in an atmosphere of safety, trust and care; [and] develop over time, drawing on a shared history and anticipating a shared future' (p. 176). He suggested ground rules for good conversations, including, 'no unsolicited advice giving … Allow the speaker to explore and describe the situation without rushing into a problem-solving mode' (p. 179).

(06)   Taken together, this literature confirms that teachers and student teachers can learn through talking together. My research question was: 'How can I encourage educational talk among the trainee music teachers I teach?'

Methods

(07)   I adopted an action research approach to the question. Action research is undertaken by practitioners in their own practice in order to improve it; it is sometimes referred to as 'practitioner research' (McNiff with Whitehead, 2002). It is prompted by questions such as: 'how can I improve what I am doing?' (Whitehead, 1999). Practitioners, including teachers, answer such questions by systematically investigating their own practice, planning and implementing interventions and evaluating the intended and unintended consequences of these interventions, interrogating data in order to ground their evaluations in evidence. They reflect on each stage in order to generate new plans, in a process that is often described as a cycle, involving planning, acting, observing and reflecting (e.g., Zeichner & Noffke, 2001) although I prefer the term 'evaluate' to 'observe', which, in music, does not adequately describe the essential element of listening (Cain, 2008). Some models of action research also include a 'reconnaissance' phase, which involves an investigation into the situation that is to be improved (Elliott, 1991; Lewin, 1946). Action research is usually seen as collaborative – research with people, rather than on them (Heron and Reason, 2001) and it can help form communities of inquiry. Reflection, which is central to action research, usually includes reflexivity, understood as 'the process of reflecting critically on the self as researcher' (Guba & Lincoln, 2005, p. 210) and a consideration of the researcher's values because, in action research, the researchers are always part of the phenomenon under study (Cochran-Smith & Lytle, 1993). Action research generates practical change and knowledge that can inform the work of practitioners in contexts similar to those researched (Cain, 2010). I hope that the research reported here might inform teacher educators and others who, for educational purposes, engage students in discussions.

(08)   The research was carried out over a period of five years, with cohorts of trainee teachers on a secondary (11–18) Post-Graduate Certificate in Education (PGCE) course. This course was 36 weeks long, of which 60 days were spent in a university and 120 days were spent teaching in school music departments, on two placements: one in the period October–December, and another in the period February–May. The PGCE groups ranged in size from 15 (2009–10) to 19 (2008–09). In each year, the trainees worked together for most of the university days so they knew each other well, and generally felt comfortable with each other. Approximately halfway through each placement, they had a 'university return day'; the research took place on these days.

Reconnaissance

(09) In 2005–06 I started to investigate how I carried out discussions in seminars with my trainee teachers. With their permission, I recorded and transcribed some seminar discussions. Analysis of these transcripts revealed that I tended to dominate discussions, speaking far more than any other person. I controlled the discussions by deciding who would speak when; I responded to trainees by giving information, advice or opinions. When questioning them, I usually had some possible answers in my head; the trainees might have legitimately interpreted these questions as having an assessing function. The usual structure of the discussions could be described as a rondo (me, Trainee A, me, Trainee B, me, Trainee C, etc.) Unless specifically asked to do so, around half the trainees did not contribute to the discussion, so I did not know what they thought.

Intervention

(10) In 2006, I was introduced to a structured approach to discussion, called Collegial Consultation (henceforth, CC). This has its roots in psychotherapy; it is a procedure in which,

> … a therapist invites a colleague (another clinician) into a session to direct a dialogue between therapist and client about their work together … a) to identify if treatment is meeting the client's needs, b) to assess what about treatment has been helpful to the client and c) to elicit and explore suggestions from the client and/or therapist about how treatment could be improved. (Bischoff & McKeel, 1993; see also Seidel, 1998.)

The last of these purposes has the most relevance to teacher education because I envisaged that, with appropriate adaptations, CC might provide a tool for trainee teachers to elicit and explore suggestions about how their teaching on placement can be improved. CC starts when each member of the class writes down a problem they face, and the class democratically chooses one problem for discussion. Thereafter the discussion moves through several, timed stages.[1] The person who raised this problem (the owner of the problem) describes the problem in as much detail as possible, without interruption (the description stage – 3 minutes). Each person in the class asks one question in turn, to which the owner responds (the Q&A stage – as long as it takes). Then, as the owner listens, writing notes as appropriate, the class discusses the problem (the discussion stage – 10 minutes). Finally, class members write down a message to the owner of the problem (3 minutes), who responds to the messages (as long as it takes). The facilitator's role, which I undertook, is to manage the selection of the problem and the transition between stages, but not to contribute to the discussion *per se*.

(11)   In 2006–07 I used CC twice on each return day, once with the whole class and once when the class split into smaller groups of seven or eight trainees. On both occasions CC seemed effective;

the trainees were highly focused on solving the problem and their talk seemed educational. However, trainees reported some uncomfortable silences, and fewer shared ideas during the small group discussions, so I subsequently abandoned them. At this stage, I felt that CC 'worked' but was unsure of my ground; I wondered whether, no longer holding responsibility for leading the conversation, I simply enjoyed it more. To examine CC in detail, I obtained my classes' permission to record and transcribe six instances of their CC discussions between November 2007 and March 2010. Because the focus of my research was the content of the talk, I did not transcribe utterances such as 'uh' and 'um'; rather, I deleted everything from the text that did not convey meaning, including occasional repetitions of words or phrases. I entered the transcripts into Atlas.ti (available from Atlas.ti Scientific Software Development GmbH), and coded each utterance as to its content (i.e., the subject matter referred to) and its function (e.g., 'ask question' or 'offer advice'). Comparing different utterances with the same codes enabled me to find patterns in the talk, and to pick out recurring features. In 2007–08 and 2009–10 I gave the trainees copies of the transcripts and asked them what they had learned from the process. When preparing this report for publication, I changed their names, for ethical reasons.

Findings

(12) Close examination of each transcript revealed six features of the discussions, which related to the features of educational talk, noted in the literature: the trainees, (1) offered several solutions to the problem; (2) offered reasons for their ideas; (3) tried to understand other people's ideas; (4) signalled agreements with each other; (5) disagreed with, or challenged each other; and (6) built on each others' ideas. These features appeared in the discussions with a frequency shown in Table 1, below. (The number of occurrences of each feature varied according to factors such as the topic under discussion, and the make-up of each group. The purpose of this table is not to compare different topics or groups but to show how many times each feature occurred.)

Trainees offered several solutions to the problem

(13) Unsurprisingly, since this is its stated purpose, trainees used CC to offer solutions to the problem under discussion. For example, in March 2008, the group chose to discuss peer assessment of performing; how a trainee teacher could ensure that a class listened attentively and responded critically whilst each pupil in turn performed music they had spent several lessons learning. Antony, the owner of the problem, described it as follows:

Table 1. The frequency of features in six cases of Collaborative Consultation

Trainee teachers:	Nov 07	Mar 08	Nov 08	Mar 09	Nov 09	Mar 10
Offered different solutions	10	14	12	15	9	7
Offered reasons for ideas	13	31	22	23	15	15
Tried to understand others	2	2	0	2	0	0
Signalled agreements	4	7	6	13	6	7
Disagreed/challenged	2	2	5	4	2	3
Built on each others' ideas	7	11	4	8	6	8

Antony: I have to do a lesson where everyone's [peer-]assessed. It's not a situation where I can go round and see one group at a time. So everyone's going to be sat there. What I've tended to do in the past is the usual thing of, [hands up] who can think of something which is really good about the performance, [and] something which can be improved. But, if you've got 30 children in the lesson, once you get before half way, most people are not listening any more … so I find it very difficult to keep them motivated. And tomorrow I've got to do an assessment and everybody's playing the same tune. It's just a melody; it's not going to be that interesting.

During the Q&A session, Simon suggested a means to involve the listeners actively:

Simon: Have you tried, instead of 'hands up', 'put your finger on your nose if you think it's something' or 'put your finger on your ear if it's something else'? It's a good way of getting everybody involved.

Antony: I haven't actually, but that's a good idea.

This idea was reiterated and developed during the discussion stage. I have chosen to include a 2-minute extract from this, to show some of the solutions and to provide a feel for the discussion as a whole:

Ralph: I really like Simon's idea of doing things like that (demonstrates putting his finger on his nose) but I wonder if they might get bored of doing the same thing. So maybe it's a case of doing four performances and saying, 'right, for the next four let's do something different'. So keep the tasks really novel …

Simon: Moving on from that … you could make a recording of one person while everyone else was still working with headphones … then [during] the next lesson you could have each group or individual listen back to the recordings. That could be quite effective if you've got the equipment to do that.

Ellie: I think that the pupils need to understand why it is important … if you implement peer assessment into the lesson, with clear, focused tasks, not necessarily the same tasks for all of them, they will understand that they're getting something out of listening to other people's performances. They need to understand that it's important to peer-assess …

Alfie: It depends on the class how well that works, though. I've tried that; with some classes it works fine. But even when you articulate how important it is to listen, they still don't care.

Ralph: I guess it's about knowing your learners.

Alfie: By the second half of the group they're not doing anything at all, so it depends.

Ellie: I think something like that takes a long time to implement.

Simon: But going along with that, you've got to get them to respect the performer who's playing. Because a lot of kids … don't perform in front of others, it's hard for them to do.

Nikki: I think pace is the main thing, whipping around quickly. And also as you said, the students are being assessed for their ability to show respect to the performer. Perhaps names could be put on the board if you hear anyone speaking during a performance. Sanctions, and rewards for those that aren't on the board.

Ralph: I wonder … could you assess the class on their skills as an audience? Quite difficult to implement if you've got a class of 30, and you've got two people playing and you've got to assess those two. You could also assess them on other criteria when they're listening, to see how much they've been listening. Then they've actually got to listen.

Ellie: What's wrong with a written task? Because that way, they have to do it; [you can set] questions that they have to answer. So they have to maintain their focus. ...

Hayley: Because you assess their answers?

Ellie: Yes.

Hayley: In this way, they know that they can't just write blah blah [rubbish].

Ellie: Or not write. Yes.

In this excerpt, suggested solutions to Antony's problem included asking pupils to put their fingers on their noses (and other actions) to signal hearing particular aspects of the music; recording individuals whilst others work with headphones; teaching pupils why it is important to peer-assess; teaching them to respect to the performer; having a fast pace; applying sanctions for speaking during a performance; and assessing listening skills by means of a written task. Trainees were highly focused on offering solutions; the only loss of focus, in any of the transcripts occurred either because the nature of the problem was interpreted slightly differently by different trainees or occasionally because they told stories from their own experience, which diverted them from the specific problem under discussion.

Trainees offered reasons for their ideas

(14) Mercer (1995) sees the offering of reasons as a characteristic of exploratory talk. Indeed, forming connections between ideas, as occurs when reasons are given (if this, then that) is essential to thinking. This linking of ideas occurs in the above extract. For example, Antony suggests that, '*if* you've got 30 children in the lesson, [then] most people are not listening any more *so* I find it very difficult to keep them motivated', linking the motivation problem with the perceived reasons for the problem. Reasons were not always given; in the above extract, Nikki's statement, 'pace is the main thing' and her suggestions of using sanctions and rewards, were not supported by reasons. However, it was often the case that, when opinions were presented without reasons they were often ignored in the subsequent discussion. At other times, the trainee teachers seemed to exert a pressure on each other, to explain their statements. For example, in March 2009, the group discussed a problem of motivating disengaged students:

Jade: I found a similar problem ... when I was going round the groups, they'd just say, 'I'm not doing music next year. I don't like performing in front of people, I don't want to do it.' And a couple actually didn't turn up on the final lesson because they didn't want to perform it. But the rest of them, the boys enjoyed it ... they actually got up and performed.

Katie: How did you get them to do it?

Jade: It wasn't me, it was the teacher. I think she said to them it was what they had to do, and they would then be assessed on it, and it was kind of, do it or get a 'fail' and get a detention.

Beth: I think having that motivation can be really important, especially when they get to Year 9. Hormones are going crazy ... a lot of them know, 'I'm not going to do music next year, why should I bother?'

Scott: There needs to be an incentive there, somewhere.

Beth: There needs to be that incentive.

Jade: She did give them a reward, I'm sorry ... She gives sweets out.
Scott: because a lot of them really don't want to perform.
Beth: ... they need to be told, 'it's not an option. You've got to perform and actually, you're going to look a bit of a prat [idiot] if you stand up in front of the class and you haven't got anything.'
Scott: If you say 'you've got to perform', that makes the situation pressured. It's a case, I imagine, of making the atmosphere more relaxed.
Linda: So it's a safe environment.

In this excerpt, it seems that, in order to present their views persuasively, individuals gave reasons for their statements. Thus, although the discussion started as a simple narrative (many students don't like performing, although some do) the group explored possible reasons for the students' behaviour (they are in the final year of compulsory music, and don't like performing) and the reasons why they might be persuaded to perform (rewards, compulsion, or a relaxed environment).

Trainees tried to understand other people's ideas

(15)   In the transcripts, I found no clear instances of trainees misunderstanding each other. However, half the transcripts included instances of trainees explicitly seeking clarification. In March 2008, the exchange between Hayley and Ellie ('because you assess their appraisals?') showed Hayley explicitly trying to understand Ellie's meaning. Similarly, in November 2007, the group discussed a problem of explaining complicated instructions clearly:

Jenny: I started off planning, word by word, how I was going to explain something ... I would actually think about every word I was going to say and that would help me because I'd got it clear in my head, so they should be clear about it.
Ralph: Like a speech?
Jenny: Yeah, like a speech.

These and other instances suggest that trainees had a strong commitment to understanding each other.

Trainees signalled agreements with each other

(16)   All transcripts included the word, 'yeah', by which people signal agreement, although it was not always clear what was being agreed to. The figures in Table 1 relate to longer utterances such as the following, extracted from various points in the November, 2008 transcript:

Katie: I like Jack's idea.
Jo: Yeah, that's exactly what I've done.
Scott: I do that a lot, yeah.
Carla: Let's all write that [previous idea] down.
Jack: Yeah, absolutely. Definitely.
Scott: It works well. It works beautifully.

Clearly, such utterances have the effect of affirming previous speakers and building safety, trust and care (Clark, 2001) but I think they also signal a recognition of common ground between two or more speakers.

Trainees disagreed with, or challenged each other

(17) Disagreements occurred in each instance of Collegial Consultation. In March 2008 (above), when Ellie said 'the pupils need to understand why it is important ... to peer-assess', Alfie disagreed, saying 'it depends on the class'. Ralph's comment, 'it's about knowing your learners' attempted to resolve the problem, suggesting that some learners (but not all) were capable of understanding the importance of peer assessment. Nevertheless Alfie still demurred, citing his own experience. A second attempt to resolve the disagreement occurred when Ellie stated, 'it takes a long time to implement'. In this instance, the pattern of conversation followed that identified in Zellermayer (2001): following Alfie's challenge, both Ralph and Ellie made generalized statements about the matter under discussion. However, this pattern was not always followed. In March 2009 (above) the disagreement between Beth ('you've got to perform') and Scott ('that makes the situation pressured') was resolved differently. After Linda had said 'So it's a safe environment', Beth re-configured her own viewpoint and effectively resolved the disagreement, saying:

> Beth: I wonder whether, seeing that there is a recording studio at the school, rather than getting up and performing in front of people, which is very scary, ... they actually record their song [in the studio] so the class are played the recording. It removes that pressure of them having to do it in front of the class.

A different resolution of disagreement occurred in March 2010. The group was discussing Al's problem that he felt he was cloning himself on the teachers at his school, who used independent learning in a way he was uncomfortable with. At the beginning of the discussion stage, trainees expressed empathy with Al, and rationalized reasons for his problem. Then came the disagreement:

> Cathie: I think it's easy to mould into the school's way of teaching ... it's not your school, it's not your class, it's not your job, so you go with the flow of what that school's doing, what that teacher's doing. And you end up adapting their style. And I'm the same.
>
> Sam: I agree. I think it will be different, once we've got our own jobs. It's hard. We're all training and we're in someone else's department and someone else's class.
>
> Cathie: Exactly ...
>
> Rebecca: I don't agree.
>
> Clare: Yeah, same here.
>
> Rebecca: I think, at the end of the day the schools know that we're coming here to train, and we have to try out our own way of doing things. Yeah, we have to fit in with their schemes of work and their behaviour policy and things like that, but the whole point of training is that you're finding out your own way; you're finding out who you are. At the end of the day, if you're trying to be someone else, you're not being you ... I'm finding that I've forgotten who I am, now ... I'm turning into something that I wasn't, and it's not good.
>
> Tanya: In Al's place ... the whole independent learning thing could be quite good.

In this instance, instead of resolving the disagreement by generalizing, Tanya brought the talk back to the actual details of the specific case under discussion (Al's, not Rebecca's). These and similar exchanges suggest that in CC, disagreements do not necessarily result in 'disputational talk' (Mercer, 1995). Often, a stated disagreement opens up a dialectical space: when a 'thesis' is answered with an 'antithesis' the group is challenged to find a 'synthesis', which can involve broadening the focus of the conversation as Zellermayer (2001) demonstrated, or narrowing it down to the details of the particular problem under discussion, or participants can reconfigure their own stance.

Trainees built on each others' ideas

(18) Often, after a solution had been suggested by one trainee, one or more other trainees commented on it, sometimes developing it by relating it to their own experience. In the following extract (November 2009) the problem under discussion, raised by Tamsin, was behaviour management. Shortly after the discussion began, the trainees started to discuss rewards, rather than sanctions:

> Tanya: [The students] are probably completely disaffected by the whole behaviour management system. For most of their lives, they've probably been punished for one thing or another. So they don't actually care. This is their life. So perhaps the use of sanctions … is not as effective as things that will happen if you're good.
>
> Lee: Yeah, I think reward is the best way …
>
> Rachael: I think having positive rewards, really bringing out the positives. Lots of praise, because there seems to be a fairly major lack of self-esteem in a lot of kids … If you give lots of praise, they haven't got that need any more to always be 'me, me, me'.
>
> Maggie: Another way possibly is to try and get on their wavelength, see what does interest them musically, at the moment. What do they listen to? And somehow try and relate that to what you're trying to teach them.
>
> Rebecca: … it's worth doing something they want. Don't make them learn about violins when really they don't care and they're not going to learn anything from it.

The matter of reward, raised by Tanya and agreed by Lee, was developed first as praise, then as choosing music that appeals to the students. This extract exemplifies a common thread throughout the CC transcripts: trainees picked up and developed each other's ideas.

Trainees' perspectives

(19) On two occasions I gave transcripts of the discussion to the class, and discussed these with them. On both occasions they reported trying out the proffered suggestions in their teaching. In 2008, I also asked trainees to write down which ideas, voiced in the discussion, they had used; each person reported using at least one idea, and two people had used five; the mean average was 2.8. Asked 'how useful did you find this discussion?' half the group gave a response such as 'very useful' or 'really useful' and one person wrote, 'extremely thought-provoking'. Only one person voiced reservations, writing: 'useful if the area of discussion was a common problem, less useful if the area was not an issue'. When I asked them verbally, 'why do you think the discussion was useful?' they reported: (1) it was reassuring to know that other people had problems, and that these problems could be addressed by thinking them through;(2) that ideas would spark off other ideas; (3) that everyone brought their different experiences of teaching to the discussion; and (4) because I did not participate, the discussion was between equals. (A written response concurred with this, saying, 'It's also nice to give advice'; I inferred from this that trainees are more often the recipients of advice).

Reflections

(20) Collegial Consultation generated seminar discussions among trainee teachers that had the attributes of 'conversation' and 'dialogue' (Cavazos et al., 2001) and 'exploratory talk' (Mercer, 1995). One reason for their educational quality is that I became a facilitator but not participant so the power relationships, present in previous seminar discussions, were not present in the CCs, which, as one trainee said, constituted 'a discussion between equals'. Their structure supported this: the voting procedure established a sense of democracy; the Q&A stage encouraged everyone to participate at least once, partly because of its turn-taking structure and partly because asking a question is an unthreatening means of entering the discussion; and the individual notes, written after the discussion stage, reinforced the importance of each person's contribution. Having voted for a topic, trainees discussed it more enthusiastically than if I had chosen it. They were keen to suggest solutions to problems and to offer reasons for these solutions, in Mercer's (1995) phrase, 'to think together'. In each case, the owners of the problem were able to express themselves frankly, and their peers responded in ways that were largely non-judgemental.

(21) Zellermayer (2001) found that conversations that led to learning began when a teacher risked sharing a teaching experience; CC incorporates precisely this. During CC, the trainees in this study articulated their own theories, shared other people's perspectives and developed specific solutions to problems, features identified as characteristics of 'good conversations' (Clark, 2001). Furthermore, they fulfilled Clark's criteria for good conversations because they dealt with content that the participants had selected as worthwhile, and took place on the common ground of learning to teach music. Although they were not voluntary, participation in them was unforced and, although they contradicted Clark's 'no unsolicited advice giving' rule, the structure allowed the owner of the problem to describe and explore the situation fully, before others started problem-solving.

(22) The question 'How can I encourage educational talk among trainee music teachers?' is not trivial. Indeed, Ballantyne (2006) reported that the most important aspect of an Initial Teacher Education course, according to newly qualified secondary music teachers, is 'the knowledge and skills that apply specifically to teaching music within the Secondary classroom' (p. 41). Ballantyne (2007) found that student teachers saw their school placements as 'very important' in contrast to the theoretical aspects of their course, and suggested that such courses should be better integrated so that 'the links between education and music, university, schools and the community, can be made clearer to future music teachers' (p. 129). Drawing on interviews with student teachers she suggested that initial teacher education might be improved if 'guided reflection (at university) could take place alongside the school experience' (p. 125). The present study shows one way in which this can be facilitated.

(23) This study has influenced my own practice. Having learned that conversations are more educational when I facilitate them but do not participate, I try to teach less and listen more. In the past, when trainees have presented practical demonstrations, I have evaluated them myself. Now, I encourage them to evaluate each other, and I add substantive comments only if I think there are important matters that they don't mention. I have also instigated structured conversations about reading matter. The trainees read and summarize an article and discuss it in small groups, basing their discussions around: (1) the main points in the article; (2) their responses to the article; (3) their group's responses; and (4) implications for teaching. This agenda encourages them to share their responses to the reading matter in a more informal way than previously and, although I have not researched the process, I have observed them talking a great deal about their reading. Obviously discussions are only one way to learn; there is also a need to impart information and teach specific skills. However, I think I have improved my use of discussion, as a learning tool.

152   *International Journal of Music Education 29(2)*

(24)   This study has increased my personal knowledge of my trainees, the problems they face and how they think about these problems. It has also increased my skills, of managing discussions whilst withholding advice that might be unwelcome and unnecessary. Additionally, it has led to knowledge that might be useful for the research and teacher education communities. Researchers are offered evidence of conversational devices (offering several solutions to a problem, offering reasons for ideas, etc.) that develop a theoretical understanding of educational talk (Cavazos et al., 2001; Clark, 2001; Mercer, 1995). Teacher educators are offered a framework (CC) that can help trainee teachers to learn about teaching through structured discussion.

(25)   Taken together, the theoretical and practical findings of this study help to provide one answer to the question 'how can worthwhile learning be nurtured and recognized?' If education is understood as a practical attempt to stimulate learning, this question is maybe one of the most significant, overarching questions that educational research can ask. Although the matter of 'worthwhile learning' is essentially philosophical, in this study the learning can be said to be worthwhile because it was based around real-world problems that the participants had voted to discuss – they thought them worth discussing. Learning was nurtured through the CC process, as participants offered solutions, built on each other's ideas, offered and explored reasons for their ideas, and resolved disagreements. Learning was recognized through a literature-informed analysis of CC transcripts.

(26)   This study also provides evidence that teachers' action research can address important educational questions. Although the main purpose of action research is practical improvement (Elliott, 1991), this study has demonstrated that action research can also lead to knowledge that has potential to be useable by others. A future study might reveal how trainees use the learning they gain from CC in their own teaching. Research might also investigate CC discussions further, to discover what they reveal about how trainees view themselves, their teaching, their pupils and their schools. In this way, CC data might shed a powerful light on how trainees think, and what they think about when they are learning to teach music in schools.

Notes

1. During the period of the research I experimented with different timings; the ones given here appeared to work well for groups of 15–19 people.

References

Ballantyne, J. (2006). Reconceptualising preservice teacher education courses for music teachers: The importance of pedagogical content knowledge and skills and professional knowledge and skills. *Research Studies in Music Education, 26*(1), 37–50.

Ballantyne, J. (2007). Documenting praxis shock in early-career Australian music teachers: The impact of pre-service teacher education. *International Journal of Music Education, 25*(3), 181–191.

Bischoff, R. J. & McKeel, A. J. (1993). Collegial consultations. *Journal of Systemic Therapies, 12*, 50–60.

Cain, T. (2008). The characteristics of action research in music education. *British Journal of Music Education, 25*(3), 283–313.

Cain, T. (2010). Music teachers' action research and the development of big K knowledge. *International Journal of Music Education, 28*(2), 1–17.

Cavazos, L., & the members of WEST (2001). Connected conversations: Forms and functions of teacher talk. In C. Clark (Ed.), *Talking shop: Authentic conversation and teacher learning* (pp. 137–171). New York: Teachers College Press.

Clark, C. M. (2001). Good conversation. In C. M. Clark (Ed.), *Talking shop: Authentic conversation and teacher learning* (pp.172–182). New York: Teachers College Press.

Cochran-Smith, M., & Lytle S. (1993). *Inside-outside: Teacher research and knowledge*. New York: Teachers College Press.

Cook-Sather, A. (2001). Translating themselves: Becoming a teacher through text and talk. In C. M. Clark (Ed.), *Talking shop: Authentic conversation and teacher learning* (pp.16–39). New York: Teachers College Press.

Elliott, J. (1991). *Action research for educational change.* Milton Keynes: Open University Press.

Gruenhagen, L. M. (2009). Developing professional knowledge about music teaching and learning through collaborative conversations. In L. K. Thompson & M. R. Campbell (Eds.), *Research perspectives: Thought and practice in music education.* Charlotte, NC: Information Age Publishing.

Guba, E. G., & Lincoln, Y. S. (2005). Competing paradigms in qualitative research. In N. Denzin & Y. Lincoln (Eds.), *Handbook of qualitative research.* Thousand Oaks, CA: Sage.

Heron, J., & Reason, P. (2001). The practice of co-operative inquiry: Research with rather than on people. In P. Reason & H. Bradbury (Eds.), *Handbook of Action Research: Participative Inquiry and Practice* (pp. 179–188). London: Sage.

Lewin, K.(1946). Action research and minority problems. *Journal of Social Issues, 2*(4), 34–46.

McNiff, J. with Whitehead, J. (2002). *Action research: principles and practice.* London: Routledge/ Falmer.

Mercer, N. (1995). *The guided construction of knowledge.* Clevedon: Multilingual Matters.

Mercer, N. (2000). *Words and minds.* London: Routledge.

Seidel, S. (1998). Wondering to be done: The collaborative assessment conference. In D. Allen (Ed.), *Assessing student learning: From grading to understanding.* New York: Teachers College Press.

Wegerif, R., Mercer, N., & L. Dawes (1998). Software design to support discussion in the primary classroom. *Journal of Computer Assisted Learning, 14*(3), 199–211.

Whitehead, J. (1999). Educative Relations in a New Era. *Pedagogy, Culture & Society, 7*(1), 73–90.

Zeichner, K. M., & Noffke, S. E. (2001). Practitioner research. In V. Richardson (Ed.), *Handbook of research on teaching* (4th edn.; pp. , 293–330). Washington, DC: American Educational Research Association.

Zellermayer, M. (2001). Resistance as catalyst in teachers' professional development. In C. M. Clark (Ed.), *Talking shop: Authentic conversation and teacher learning* (pp.40-63). New York: Teachers College Press.

Author biography

Tim Cain has taught music to pupils from 5–19. He has been Head of Music in two comprehensive schools in the UK. He has a PhD from the University of Southampton, where he teaches on Initial Teacher Education courses, lectures in music education and carries out research on both topics.

Abstracts

Comment les professeurs de musique en formation apprennent-ils l'enseignement en se parlant : une étude recherche-action

Cet article présente une étude recherche-action sur la manière dont les enseignants en musique en Angleterre se servent d'un processus de discussion structurée appelée 'Consultation Collégiale' pour apprendre comment enseigner. Les recherches montrent que, dans le cadre de la Consultation Collégiale, les apprentis se soutiennent en proposant plusieurs solutions à un problème, en expliquant leurs idées, en essayant de comprendre les idées d'autrui, en signalant des accords et désaccords idéologiques entre eux, et en bâtissant un cadre intellectuel sur les idées de leurs collègues. Il est démontré que la structure de la Consultation Collégiale promeut un ethos d'égalité qui permet une discussion sur l'enseignement de haute qualité, autorisant les professeurs de musique en formation à réfléchir ensemble à l'enseignement de la musique au lycée.

154   *International Journal of Music Education 29(2)*

Wie in Ausbildung stehende Musiklehrer in gemeinsamem Gespräch das Unterrichten lernen. Eine Aktionsforschungsstudie

Dieser Artikel berichtet über eine Aktionfurschungsstudie wie in Ausbildung stehende Musiklehrer in England einen stukturierten Gesprächsablauf, genannt 'Collegial Consultation' benützen um zu lernen, wie man Unterrichtet. Die Forschungsstudie zeigt auf, wie die Lernenden in der 'Collegial Consultation' voneinander lernen, in dem sie sich verschiedene Lösungen zu einem Problem aufzeigen, ihre Ideen begründen, versuchen anderer Leute Ideen zu verstehen, gegenseitiges Einverständnis zu signalisieren aber auch andere Meinungen zu vertreten und auf den Ideen anderer aufzubauen. Der Artikel vertritt die Auffassung, dass das Aufbauen einer 'Collegial Consultation' ein Ethos von Gleichwertigkeit fördert, das Unterstützung für hochqualifizierte Unterrichtsdiskussion bietet, und den auszubildenden Lehrern ermöglicht, gemeinsam über Musikunterricht in der Sekundarstufe nachzudenken.

Cómo aprenden sobre la enseñanza los profesores de música en formación hablando entre ellos: Un proyecto de investigación-acción

Este artículo presenta un proyecto de investigación-acción acerca de cómo los profesores de música en formación en Inglaterra usan un proceso de conversación estructurado, denominado 'consulta colegial', para aprender sobre la enseñanza. La investigación muestra que a través de la consulta colegial los estudiantes aprenden los unos de los otros ofreciendo diversas soluciones a un problema, tratando de entender las ideas de los demás, haciendo acuerdos entre ellos, discrepando y apoyándose en las ideas de los demás. Este artículo sostiene que la estructura de la consulta colegial promueve un espíritu de igualdad que apoya debates educativos de alta calidad, permitiendo a los profesores en formación pensar juntos sobre la enseñanza de la música dentro del aula de educación secundaria.

Source: This article is reprinted from the *International Journal of Music Education*, Vol. 29, Issue 2, pp. 141–154, 2011. Reprinted with permission of Sage Publications, Inc.

UNDERSTANDING THE FINAL SECTIONS OF RESEARCH REPORTS

Throughout Parts One through Five, we have used the analogy of a journey to think about how researchers conduct and report their studies. Now we will use this analogy to help us understand what happens at the end of a study. Think for a moment about what you do when you reach the end of a journey. If you are like many people, you might put together a scrapbook or post information to a website so you can show the pictures you have taken and the mementos you picked up along the way. At the very least, you probably recap what happened on the trip by telling people about it. Perhaps you start by sharing the trip's highlights. These might include the best sights, the tastiest food, or the scariest moment. You might also compare your trip to those you have taken previously or even those taken by others. As you reflect, you will probably think of things that you wish you had done differently, like wishing you had taken a train instead of a bus. If you like to travel, you may also be thinking about where you want to go on your next trip!

These end-of-journey reflections are the same kinds of issues that researchers consider when they reach the end of their research studies and write their reports. They reflect on issues such as the highlights of the results, how the results compare to other studies, the limitations of what they did, and the studies that are needed next. These reflections are shared in the Conclusion sections of research reports. Researchers make interpretations about and suggest implications from their research study in the Conclusion section, which is the final major section of any research report. Information that you find after the Conclusion section is usually just supplemental information that is needed as support for the written report. This Back Matter section includes information that is useful but not essential to include in the report's main sections. You will learn how to recognize and understand the elements that researchers report in their Conclusion and Back Matter sections of quantitative, qualitative, mixed methods, and action research reports.

The final chapter is:

- Chapter 14—Conclusions: Identifying the Interpretations and Implications of a Study

14

CONCLUSIONS: IDENTIFYING THE INTERPRETATIONS AND IMPLICATIONS OF A STUDY

You now know how to read and understand the Introduction, Method, and Results sections of study reports that use a wide range of different research approaches. No matter the research approach used, researchers end their reports with statements that convey their conclusions about the study. These conclusions appear in the final paragraphs of a research article. In a good conclusion discussion, the researcher thoughtfully interprets and evaluates the procedures and results of the study. Therefore, the Conclusion section does not simply summarize the study—it provides a discussion about the implications, limitations, and significance of the study, often returning full circle to the initial research problem stated in the Introduction. In this chapter, you will learn how to read and evaluate the Conclusion sections of quantitative, qualitative, mixed methods, and action research studies. You will also learn about the information that is included at the end of study reports.

BY THE END OF THIS CHAPTER, YOU SHOULD BE ABLE TO:

- Identify and understand the conclusions and supporting information for a research study.
- Know how to recognize the elements of a Conclusion section when reading a research report.
- Recognize the similarities and differences in conclusions among the different research approaches.
- Identify the types of back matter found in research reports.
- Evaluate the quality of the conclusions and back matter in a research report.

You might feel like researchers have said all they need to say about any research study once they have reported the Introduction, Method, and Results sections. After all, you know why the study is important, what they did, and what they found—what else is there to learn? In actuality, researchers have a number of loose ends to tie up at the end of their reports. You may have already noticed a pattern to the ending of reports from those you have read in this book. This pattern usually includes two features: a Conclusion section and a Back Matter section.

How Do You Identify the Conclusions and Supporting Information in a Study Report?

Referring back to the process of research introduced in Chapter 1, you may recall that researchers do not end their research process by analyzing data and reporting results. Once the results are known, researchers then take the step of drawing conclusions about the results and the overall study. Drawing conclusions involves the researcher making interpretations about the results and evaluating the procedures and results that occurred in the study. Because of the importance of this step in the process of research, most researchers report their conclusions as the final major section at the end of the report. In addition, as you read the end of a research report, you frequently find that the researchers provided important supporting information about the study's procedures and context. Learning to identify and understand these features of research reports will help you understand how researchers conclude their study reports.

Look for the Conclusion Section to Learn How the Researcher Interpreted and Evaluated the Study

You can find a discussion of the researcher's reflections about the study in the Conclusion section. This section immediately follows the section where the researcher presented the results of the study. You can usually identify this section because the researchers used a heading of *Conclusions* or *Discussion* to indicate that they are presenting their reflections and comments about the study in this part of the report. When reading this section, you will notice that the researchers provide their *interpretation* of the results. That is, they do not present new results in this section, but instead present information to help make sense of the results found and reported in the Results section. In the Conclusion section (or sections), the researchers often return to the original purpose and research questions or hypotheses, and discuss how the study answered the questions and what are the implications of these results. They also discuss the strengths and weaknesses of the study to help readers understand what conclusions they can and cannot draw about the results. In some study reports, you may find that the researchers include headings or subheadings that help you identify the types of conclusions they are drawing, such as *Implications for Practice*, *Recommendations*, *Future Directions*, *Limitations*, and *Significance*. We will examine these many elements of a good Conclusion section in more detail in this chapter.

> **Here's a Tip!**
>
> Research articles often include multiple headings in the Conclusion section. When present, use these headings to help you identify the key elements being discussed.

Read the Back Matter to Find Supporting Information for the Study Report

As you read to the end of a study report, you find that the researchers have provided a collection of additional information about the study right at the end. As introduced in Chapter 1, this material is called "back matter." The back matter information is related to the article's content, but is not an essential part of the report's major sections. All articles include a list of references at the end of the report, which you can usually identify by the heading *References*. Other common headings used to label supporting back matter include *Notes*, *Comments*, *Acknowledgments*, and *Appendices*. We also examine the common elements found in the back matter of an article in this chapter.

How Do You Understand the Elements Discussed in a Study's Conclusion Section?

Reading the Conclusion sections of research articles can be challenging. In these sections, the researchers interpret their studies by stepping back from the results and making sense of what was found. **Interpretation** means drawing conclusions about the results and explaining how the results answer the study's research questions. When researchers make interpretations, they go beyond simply reporting what was found in the study to making arguments about the meaning, importance, and implications of the specific results that were found. For example, consider a quantitative experiment that tested a new stress reduction intervention for new mothers by comparing two groups of mothers: those who received the intervention and those who did not. A result of this study could be that mothers in the treatment group had significantly lower levels of stress than the mothers in the control group. From this result, the researchers might draw the conclusion that the intervention is an effective approach for helping mothers deal with the stress of being a new mother and recommend that clinics working with new mothers start up their own treatment programs.

No two Conclusion sections are exactly alike because researchers use this section to pull together, interpret, and evaluate the specific research problem, purpose, methods, and results of the study. Despite the variations found across research studies, in a good research report, the researchers tend to address a common set of topics when interpreting their research results. These interpretations include the following elements:

- a summary of the major results,
- a discussion relating the results to the literature,
- personal reflections of the researcher about the meaning of the research,
- implications for practice,
- limitations of the study,
- future research needs, and
- the overall significance of the study.

There is no set order for how researchers discuss these elements in their reports. However, by learning to recognize researchers' use of these seven elements, you will be able to identify and understand the information that you read in the Conclusion sections of quantitative, qualitative, mixed methods, and action research studies. Let's examine each of these elements.

A Summary of the Major Results

When reading a Conclusion section, a good first step is to look for statements where the researchers summarize the major findings of the study. These summary statements generally provide a recap of the key results that the researchers found in response to each of the research questions or hypotheses. These are very useful to read because they provide you with an indication of which results the researcher concluded to be most important to highlight and summarize. For example, in the quantitative early-intervention-outcomes study from the end of Chapter 6, Raspa et al. (2010) included a section labeled "Summary of Major Findings" (paragraphs 27–33), where they summarized several key results such as "Families of younger children report higher outcomes than those with older children" (paragraph 31). Similarly, Leko and Brownell (2011) summarized the findings of the qualitative adoption-of-pedagogical-tools study by starting their Discussion section with: "This study resulted in the articulation of a grounded theory explaining the influences on special education preservice teachers' appropriation of pedagogical tools in practice" (paragraph 80).

> **Here's a Tip!**
>
> Researchers often organize the summary of their results by their purpose statement, research questions, and hypotheses. It can be helpful to review those important statements before reading the Conclusion section.

The summary of the results is different than the presentation of the actual results: It represents general, rather than specific, information. For example, in quantitative research the specific results include details about statistical tests, significance levels, and effect sizes. General summary conclusions state overall whether the null hypothesis was rejected or how the research question was answered. Likewise, in qualitative research, the specific results include description and theme passages. The form of the qualitative summary passage often varies, from a restatement of the major themes, to answering the research questions, to providing general learnings. Mixed methods and action research studies can include both types of specific results, and therefore authors also state both types of general summary conclusions.

Relating the Results to Other Literature

Researchers do more than just summarize the results in their final discussion; they also relate these results to the larger literature. Recall that a goal of research is to add to knowledge about a topic. One way that researchers conclude that their study adds to the knowledge is by interpreting how their results are similar to, are different from, or extend ideas already found in theories or bodies of literature. As you read a Conclusion section, identify places where the researcher interprets the findings in view of past research and discusses how the findings support and/or contradict results from prior studies. For example, in the quantitative physical-activity-in-middle-schools study from Chapter 1, Xu et al. (2010) compared their findings to the literature when they wrote:

Results obtained from this study also confirm findings of Powers et al. (2002) that students' lower participation rate in extracurricular physical activity is a considerable concern, given that on average only 50 students participated per school with the mean enrollment of 911 students per school. (paragraph 15)

Interpretations of results in relation to the literature often include explanations as to why the results turned out the way they did based on predictions made from a theory or conceptual framework that guided the development of the research questions or hypotheses. For example, returning to the quantitative physical-activity-in-middle-schools study (Xu et al., 2010), we learn that the factors that were found to be significant in the results were "in line with the Social Ecological Model" (paragraph 19), which was the theory that the researchers discussed as the foundation for this study in the article's Introduction. When reading a well-written Conclusion section, you should find several points discussing how the results of the study relate to the larger body of knowledge and literature, including theories and past research studies.

The Personal Interpretation of the Researcher

In some reports, you find that the researchers offer their own personal reflections about the results in addition to bringing in prior literature. This is common in qualitative and action research and in some mixed methods research. Because qualitative researchers may believe that the researcher's personal views can never be kept separate from interpretations, personal reflections about the meaning of the results are included in the study's discussion. Researchers base these personal interpretations on hunches and insights. Because they have been to the field and visited at great length with individuals, they are in a good position to reflect and remark on the larger meaning of the study findings. The two examples that follow illustrate the diversity of personal reflections found in studies that emphasized the qualitative approach.

In the action research learning-by-talking study from the end of Chapter 13, Cain (2011) reflected about how the experience of the study had affected him personally: "This study has influenced my own practice. Having learned that conversations are more educational when I facilitate them but do not participate, I try to teach less and listen more . . ." (paragraph 23). The next example shows how researchers can offer personal commentary about the meaning of results for society as part of their personal interpretations. In the discussion at the end of the qualitative adolescent-homelessness study from Chapter 4, Haldenby et al. (2007) remarked: "This research challenges the socially accepted idea that homeless youth are 'lazy' and cannot be 'bothered' to find a job" (paragraph 57).

Implications for Practice

One type of interpretation that you will likely find of particular interest occurs when researchers present the broader implications of the research for audiences such as practitioners, parents, and policy makers. **Implications** are the researchers' recommendations for audiences based on the results obtained in the study. That is, implications go beyond the results by arguing for useful actions that individuals might take in response to the new knowledge that resulted from the study. Researchers often elaborate on the implications of their study for audiences that were initially identified in the statement of the problem as part of the Introduction (discussed in Chapter 3). In effect, once the study has been completed, the researcher is in a position to reflect and remark on how the different audiences may benefit from and use the results.

Although researchers may offer implications for different types of audiences, you are probably most interested in the implications and suggestions for practice. Implications for practice include suggestions that practitioners might use in their practice settings (e.g., in classrooms, in health clinics, or with certain people, such as adults or teenagers). Researchers often suggest implications of the results for practice situations, and you can find these implications either mentioned throughout the Conclusion section or sometimes in their own subsection. For example, in the conclusion of the qualitative adolescent-homelessness study from Chapter 4, Haldenby et al. (2007) included a section labeled "Implications" where they advanced several implications of the study's results for health professionals. These suggestions for practice included having health professionals use group discussions with homeless youth to identify potential solutions to problems they are experiencing, advocating for the availability of appropriate counseling services, and addressing the needs of homeless youth during training opportunities (see paragraphs 58–60). In the mixed methods student-note-taking study from Chapter 12, Igo et al. (2008) provided specific suggestions for teachers who want to promote better practices when their students are taking notes from the Web. The implications of their study included: "A teacher might prompt students to copy and paste main ideas from paragraphs in lieu of pasting entire paragraphs. Or students could be instructed to identify the sentences most valuable to a set of notes" (paragraph 70).

The Limitations of the Present Study

The reality is that no research study is perfect; this is why you need to be a critical reader when you read any research study. However, readers are not the only ones who critique research studies. Researchers provide a critical evaluation of their research by interpreting the limitations or weaknesses of the study that may have affected the results. **Limitations** are potential weaknesses or problems with the study identified by the researcher. Researchers enumerate these weaknesses one by one as part of their study's conclusions. These limitations are useful to other potential researchers who may choose to conduct a similar or replication study. You should also pay close attention to the limitations identified in a study to help judge in what ways a study's findings may be limited because of its procedures and to what extent the researcher provided a thoughtful critique of his or her study. The limitations do not mean that the study is bad; they do, however, inform you about how the results are limited. In a well-written report, the researchers identify and discuss all important limitations of the study.

> **Here's a Tip!**
>
> When evaluating research studies, the limitations provide you with useful information to consider. However, not all researchers will discuss the important limitations. This is why you need to use your own judgment to evaluate the procedures of any research study.

In studies that used quantitative procedures, you often find limitations that relate to the lack of random sampling for selecting participants, small sample sizes, inadequate measures of variables, lack of control of confounding variables, and other issues typically related to quantitative designs, data collection, and analysis. For example, in the quantitative physical-activity-in-middle-schools study, Xu et al. (2010) noted three limitations of their study when they wrote:

> First, the participants in this study were conveniently selected from easily available sources such as school websites and emails and the schools were located in the southeastern region of United States, which might decrease the extent to which the results could be generalized to all middle schools in United States. Secondly, the measures (e.g. PA opportunities) were based on perception of PE teachers, thus exposing questions related to respondents' subjectivity. Lastly, the questionnaire did not assess students' PA participation; the absence of these data hinders our understanding of the association between PA opportunities and student PA participation. (paragraph 18)

From this passage, we learn that they had important limitations in their study's sample (not randomly selected), data collection instrument (an important variable for each school was based on one individual's perspective), and variables (they did not measure a variable that is likely important to this topic).

In studies that used qualitative procedures, you often find that researchers mention limitations related to the data collection, questions answered by participants, or the selection of individuals or sites for the study. In good qualitative studies, the limitations address issues important to qualitative research such as purposeful sampling, rich data sources, and validation strategies. For example, in the qualitative adolescent-homelessness study, Haldenby et al. (2007) discussed the following limitations in their study:

> First, despite the researchers' efforts, only one community service was used to recruit the participants . . . . Second, in this study gender was examined as a binary concept . . . . The third limitation of this study was the inability to share emerging findings with many of the participants . . . . Finally, the findings of this research suggest that adolescent boys do not experience sexualized violence. As there is stigma surrounding this issue, some of the male participants might have chosen not to disclose such information. (paragraph 63)

From this passage we learn that they had important limitations in their study's sample (included only one service context), description of the complexity of the central phenomenon (unable to fully describe the complexity of gender), validation strategies (unable to complete member checking with many participants), and accuracy in one result (they are unsure if male participants told them the full story about violence).

Future Research Needs

Another type of interpretation to look for when reading the conclusion of a research study is the direction needed for future research that the researcher advances. **Future research directions** are suggestions made by the researcher about additional research studies that need to be conducted based on the results and limitations of the present research. For example, Haldenby et al. (2007) provide their suggestions for future research needed about the perceptions of homeless youth that stemmed from the results of their study in paragraph 61 of their report. Note how they referred to a result and then made a future research suggestion in the following passage from the qualitative adolescent-homelessness study:

> This study noted an accessibility gap between health care services and those who need them. Research that explores the nature of where adolescents are receiving health-related information would be helpful to better develop care programs. (paragraph 61)

You often find that researchers link their suggestions for future research directions directly to the limitations of their study. Xu et al. (2010) used this strategy in their suggestions for future research from the quantitative physical-activity-in-middle-schools study. Recall from the previous section that these researchers noted three limitations of their study related to their sample, data collection instrument, and variables. They followed these limitations with three suggestions for future research:

> Future research should attempt to replicate these findings using a randomly selected nationwide sample. Furthermore, researchers should continue to refine survey instrument and other data collection methods to be used in this line of research. Objective measures of PA opportunities and student PA participation on campus are necessary to strengthen the association between PA opportunities and students' level of PA. (paragraph 18)

These suggestions for future research provide useful direction for researchers who are interested in investigating needed areas of inquiry. For those reading a study, future research directions highlight areas that are unknown and provide boundaries for using the study's information. You can use these research directions to help identify important knowledge that is still missing for your topic of interest.

The Overall Significance of the Study

The final element that you might find in a study's Conclusion section is a statement about the overall significance and unique contributions of the study. This is typically a brief and final passage that researchers include to create the effect of leaving a research report on a positive note. Researchers include these passages as strong statements of the conclusions of their studies. When written well, the overall significance provides a wrap-up of what the study accomplished, what new knowledge was generated, and why this knowledge is important. For example, see how the authors of the qualitative adolescent-homelessness study (Haldenby et al., 2007) state the importance of their research in the final paragraph of their report:

Here's a Tip!

Some reports use the heading *Discussion* for the whole Conclusion section and the heading *Conclusion* just for the final statement of the overall significance. By focusing on what interpretive elements are being discussed in which paragraphs, you can figure out how the authors are using the different headings.

> The findings of this study highlight the experiences of homeless youth and offer insights into the complex nature of homelessness . . . . This study draws attention to the fundamental roles that affordable housing policies and gender play in shaping the health of homeless adolescents. The findings from this research can be used to help create more effective social housing policies and care programs for adolescents who are homeless . . . . (paragraph 64)

What Do You Think?

Examine the following four excerpts taken from the Conclusion section of a quantitative correlational study about African American adolescents' career decision status conducted by Constantine et al. (2005). What elements of interpretation do you find in the excerpts?

a. "Findings revealed that African American adolescents who perceived greater career barriers tended to report higher degrees of career indecision. This finding, however, seems somewhat inconsistent with results indicated by some previous researchers. For example, Rollins (2001) reported that African American adolescents perceiving higher degrees of racism reported greater self-efficacy for career decision-making tasks . . ." (p. 314).

b. "In light of the aforementioned issues, it is important that career counselors first identify the extent to which some African American adolescents perceive certain occupational barriers and then process with these students the potential consequences of harboring these barriers in terms of their current and future educational and career development . . ." (p. 315).

c. "The study must be tempered in light of several potential limitations. First, generalizability of the findings is cautioned because the study's participants may differ somehow from other African American adolescents residing in a large urban city in the northeastern United States . . ." (p. 316).

d. "Additional research is needed concerning the career development experiences of African American adolescents. For example, research on the intersections of race, gender, and racial and gender identity in the context of various career development tasks might help to identify and address African American adolescents' perceived career barriers, particularly with regard to stereotypes they might possess about perceived options available to them based on their race and/or gender (Gainor & Lent, 1998; Swanson et al., 1996; Swanson & Woitke, 1997) . . ." (p. 316).

Check Your Understanding

These excerpts each illustrate a different interpretation element. In excerpt (a), the authors relate their results to the literature by comparing one of their results to a prior study. In this case, they note that the current result is inconsistent with a previous finding. In excerpt (b), the authors offer implications of their study results for practice by providing suggestions for career counselors. Excerpt (c) is an example of discussing limitations of a research study. The authors note that the findings are limited to the sample studied and may not generalize to a larger population of all African American adolescents. In excerpt (d), the authors make suggestions for future research directions needed about the topic of career development with African American adolescents.

How Are Conclusions Similar and Different Among the Different Research Approaches?

You now are familiar with seven types of interpretations typically found in the Conclusion sections of research study reports. By recognizing these elements, you can better understand the information that is included in an article's conclusion. It is possible for any research report to include any or all of these elements. The elements typically found in the Conclusion sections of quantitative and qualitative research studies are listed in Figure 14.1. The order of the elements indicates one way that you may find the topics discussed in an article, but you will find that different authors often use a different order

Quantitative Research	Qualitative Research
Conclusion Section	Conclusion Section
■ Summary of major results organized by research questions/hypotheses	■ Summary of major findings organized by themes
■ Explanations of results in terms of predictions and prior studies	■ Comparison of findings with existing studies
	■ Personal reflections about the study
■ Implications and suggestions for practice	■ Implications and suggestions for practice
■ Limitations of the study in terms of the quantitative intent	■ Limitations of the study in terms of the qualitative intent
■ Suggestions for future research	■ Suggestions for future research
■ Overall significance of the study	■ Overall significance of the study

FIGURE 14.1   Conclusion Sections in Quantitative and Qualitative Research Reports

Note: Mixed methods and action research studies use a combination of these two approaches.

depending on the interpretations they are offering. Looking at the two lists, you can see that many similarities exist in how researchers interpret their studies no matter which approach they chose to use. In general terms, the interpretations address the same topics. One exception is that qualitative researchers tend to include personal reflections because they are using a more subjective approach to conducting research. Quantitative researchers usually do not include personal reflections because they are using more objective approach to conducting research.

Whereas the same general topics are typically found in the interpretations of studies using different research approaches, there are important differences in the details of the interpretation elements. Learning to anticipate these differences helps you understand the Conclusion sections and to use appropriate considerations when evaluating the final interpretations provided for a research study. These differences stem from the different purposes for and reasons why researchers choose the different approaches at the start of their research processes. Let's examine the differences in the interpretive elements among the different research approaches, starting with quantitative research.

When you read quantitative studies, you find that the researchers typically interpret their results in terms of their overall goal to explain the trends in a population, the relationships among variables, or the effect of a specific treatment condition. They often organize their summary of the major results in terms of their original predictions or hypotheses and compare and contrast these results to other studies in the literature. Quantitative researchers are often most concerned with interpreting the extent to which their results can apply (or generalize) to a larger population or to another context and the extent to which their results provide evidence for a cause-and-effect relationship among certain variables. As such, quantitative researchers report weaknesses in their studies that limit the representativeness of the study's sample, the adequacy of the measures for key variables, and the ability to control for confounding variables.

In contrast, when you read qualitative studies, you find that the researchers interpret their results in terms of their overall goal to explore a central phenomenon to describe its complexity and meaning. They may organize their summary of the major results in terms of their research questions, but as the questions often change during the study, it is more likely to be organized by the major themes. Because qualitative researchers do not make predictions or state hypotheses, you do not find comparisons to predictions as is common in many quantitative studies. Qualitative researchers are often most concerned with interpreting the extent to which their results accurately captured the complexity of the central phenomenon and provided a credible, full description of it. As such, qualitative researchers report weaknesses in their studies that limit the information richness of the sample, the extensiveness of the database, and the adequacy of the validation strategies.

When reading a mixed methods or action research study, you often find that the researchers use a combination of the interpretation elements found in quantitative and qualitative reports, depending on whether the study emphasized a quantitative or qualitative approach, or used both equally. Mixed methods researchers might or might not include personal reflections, but often do discuss both quantitative and qualitative limitations along with those that arose when they attempted to mix the two components. Action researchers tend to focus on personal reflections, implications for practice, and the overall significance of the action plan. These differences relate back to the very reason that researchers chose to use a specific research approach at the beginning of their research study.

What Do You Think?

Examine the following excerpts taken from the Conclusion sections of four different research articles. For each excerpt, decide whether it likely came from a quantitative or a qualitative research study.

a. "First, the correlational nature of the study meant that we did not study effects, but rather relations" (Walker & Greene, 2009, p. 469).
b. "[The] analysis was limited because the database was collected as part of a larger study, limiting the extent of the follow-up probing to the question about family fun . . ." (Churchill et al., 2007, p. 291).
c. "The . . . approach I've used here has allowed me to experience a critical practice in health and physical education, use this as a reference point for critical discussions and also to be part of spontaneous conversations about how students grapple with issues of power, gender, and racialization" (Fitzpatrick, 2011, p. 191).
d. "Contrary to the literature on teacher expectation going back to Good and Brophy (1986) that suggested that African American students cared less about school, we expected and found that African American students reported higher levels of identification with school . . ." (Smith et al., 2011, p. 86).

Check Your Understanding

These examples of interpretive elements demonstrate attributes of both quantitative (excerpts a and d) and qualitative (excerpts b and c) research. Excerpt (a) discusses a limitation from a quantitative research study because the authors acknowledge that they did not use experimental procedures and therefore cannot conclude that there was a cause-and-effect relationship, a typical concern of quantitative research. Excerpt (b) discusses a limitation from a qualitative research study because the authors acknowledge that they did not gather an extensive database, which limits the complexity of their description, a typical concern of qualitative research. Excerpt (c) discusses a researcher's personal reflection about a study, which is a typical feature of qualitative research. Excerpt (d) discusses how a study's results compare to the researchers' predictions and other literature, a typical interpretation found in quantitative research.

What Information Is Included in the Back Matter of a Research Report?

Once you have finished reading the Conclusion section(s) of a research report, you have reached the end of the report's text. However, you have not reached the actual end of the report document. Researchers include end notes, reference lists, author notes, and appendices as back matter to their research reports. These items provide additional information for the reader of a research report that goes beyond a description and interpretation of the study. This additional information might be as short as part of a page or as long as many pages. When you read research, it is important to be able to locate and decipher the information that researchers include in their back matter so you can recognize the information that is relevant for understanding the conducted study. Although many types of information can be included as back matter, we highlight four types that you will frequently encounter: end notes, references, author notes, and appendices.

End Notes

Some research reports include end notes. **End notes** are specific notes that researchers include to provide extra information about specific statements made within the article's text. Authors usually indicate their use of end notes by a superscript number (e.g.,[1] or [6]) at the end of a sentence within the article text. This superscript number informs you which end note you should read to learn more about the point that the author is trying to make. You can then find the text of the end note listed by number at the end of the article. These numbered end notes appear after the Conclusion section under a heading of *End Notes* or *Notes*.

Let's consider an example of the use of notes. The action research learning-by-talking study (Cain, 2011) from the end of Chapter 13 provides an example of the use of end notes. Under the heading *Notes* after the last paragraph, Cain included the following comment, which provides additional information about how he experimented with his practices during each loop of the action research cycle. This note is indicated with a superscript 1 in paragraph 10 of the article.

1. During the period of the research I experimented with different timings; the ones given here appeared to work well for groups of 15–19 people.

References

Research articles might or might not include end notes, but they always include a list of references after the Conclusion section. Almost without exception, you find this list under the heading *References*. In a **reference list**, researchers provide detailed information about all the sources they used in writing the report. An important rule to remember is that every source cited in the article should appear in this list and every source in the list should be cited somewhere in the article. In good research reports, this list is complete, prepared using a good style (such as the APA style), and includes accurate information. By examining the list of references in an article, you can quickly get a sense of whether the researchers included current references from good sources (i.e., peer-reviewed journals). You can also use the information in the references lists to help you more easily identify and locate other studies on your topic that may be of interest.

The format and ordering of the references in the list depends on the style used for the report. (Recall the discussion of style manuals in Chapter 1.) In educational research reports, references are usually listed in alphabetical order based on the last names of the first author. Therefore, if you want to see the full reference for "Adams and Johnson (2004)," you know to look near the beginning of the list since the first author's last name begins with the letter "A." You may find some reports that list the references in the order in which they appear within the reports' text. In these reports, the references are usually numbered (1, 2, 3, and so on) so readers can identify them. This is more common in research reports from the health sciences. All of the studies included in this book used an alphabetical listing for the reference lists.

Author Notes

Many articles that you read include author notes in addition to the end notes and references. **Author notes** are general notes that researchers include to provide general information about the overall study such as how to contact the author, what agency funded the study, or who the author thanks for assisting with the study. In some reports, some or all of this information may also appear as a footnote on the title page. Most often, you find author notes listed under a wide variety of headings at the end of a research article before and/or after the references list. Examples of author note headings include *Author Information*, *Funding*, and *Acknowledgments*. These notes are particularly interesting to read because you can learn about the researchers who conducted the study and the context for the research study.

As you read many research reports, you notice variation in the format and kinds of information included in the author notes. This variation is often determined by the journal and authors provide the information that has been requested in the journal. You can see this variation in the articles included within the book. For example, several of the articles included information about the authors as part of the back matter, but in different ways. Xu et al. (2010) provided the professional affiliations and locations of each author under the heading *Biographical details* in the quantitative physical-activity-in-middle-schools study. In contrast, Cain (2011) included a brief paragraph describing his background and interests under the heading *Author biography* in the action research learning-by-talking study. We also find author information under the heading *About the Authors* in the qualitative adoption-of-pedagogical-tools study and simply listed at the end of the article with no heading in the qualitative adolescent-homelessness study. Another interesting variation can be found in the back matter of the action research learning-by-talking study where the journal included copies of the study abstracts in French, German, and Spanish to meet the needs of their international audience.

Appendices

The final feature that you may find at the end of a research report are appendices. Researchers use **appendices** to provide detailed information to supplement the main report. The most common types of information found in the appendices of research reports are examples of questions used during data collection (e.g., a qualitative interview protocol or a quantitative survey) and details about or examples of data analysis procedures. For example, Figure 10.3 shows the appendix from a qualitative research study where the authors included the interview protocol used in their focus group interviews. If an author includes more than one appendix, then they are generally identified by letters such as "Appendix A" and "Appendix B." A new trend that is starting is for authors to sometimes place appendix information online as a supplement. In this case, the report simply refers you to a location on the Web where you can read the supplemental information if it interests you. Although this is currently a new and relatively uncommon practice, it is likely that more and more research reports will start to include online appendices to share supporting information.

> *Here's a Tip!*
>
> If you plan to conduct your own research, you might find good questions to ask when collecting data by looking at the appendices of articles published on the topic. Before using these items, however, you should contact the authors and request their approval. You should also be sure to give credit to the source of the items in your work.

How Do You Evaluate the Conclusions and Back Matter in a Research Report?

You have now learned the important elements that go into the interpretation discussions and back matter for quantitative, qualitative, mixed methods, and action research studies. When you read the end of a research study, you should first identify these elements to understand the information presented. Once you have identified these elements, you also need to evaluate how well the authors addressed them. Although there are differences in the details of the elements depending on the research approach used, the conclusions and back matter in high-quality research also share several common features. In a good research study, the interpretations stated by the researcher should thoughtfully address the study's purpose and research questions, should not contradict or overstep the results obtained in the study, and should not go beyond the limits of the study's methods and procedures. The use of back matter varies, but in a good study the included supplemental information should be complete, relevant, and accurate. Table 14.1 lists criteria that are useful to consider when evaluating a study's conclusions and back matter. This table also provides indicators of higher quality and lower quality for the criteria to help you make your own judgments when evaluating the information provided in a research report.

Figure 14.2 provides a convenient means for you to apply the quality criteria to evaluate the conclusions described within the Conclusion section and supplemental information presented as back matter in any research report. For each of the criteria you locate, assign a quality rating from *fair* (1) to *excellent* (3) and document your evidence and/or reasoning behind the rating. If one of the criteria is missing or very poorly stated, then indicate *poor* (0) as your rating. Keep in mind that the details of research reports vary depending on the study's research approach. Even with this variation, however, a good research study should still score well on most of the items listed in Figure 14.2. By adding up the rating scores for each of the criteria and using the suggested cutoff values provided at the bottom of the figure, you will have a quantitative measure that you can use to inform your overall assessment.

TABLE 14.1   Criteria for Evaluating the Conclusions and Back Matter in a Research Report

Quality Criteria	Indicators of Higher Quality	Indicators of Lower Quality
The Key Elements		
1. The major results are identified and summarized.	+ The results that are key for answering the research questions are highlighted in the Conclusion section without introducing new results. + The summary of the key results is organized logically such as by research questions, hypotheses, or themes.	− Many detailed results are restated and/or new results are presented in the Conclusion section. − The logic behind the organization of the summary of the results is not apparent.
2. The results are thoughtfully examined in relation to the literature and personal reflections.	+ The current results are explicitly related to prior research in terms of how they compare to, contrast with, or extend the prior research. + The researcher compares the results to predictions in quantitative research and some mixed methods research reports. + The researcher includes personal reflections about the results in qualitative research, action research, and some mixed methods research reports.	− The current results are only superficially considered in light of prior research. − The researcher inappropriately compares qualitative results to predictions. − The researcher inappropriately includes personal reflections as part of an objective, quantitative study.
3. Appropriate implications of the results for practice are identified and justified.	+ Suggestions for practice that clearly stem from the study results are advanced. + Specific audiences that might benefit from knowing the results of the study are clearly noted.	− Suggestions for practice are stated that seem to contradict or be unrelated to the study results. − The researcher does not interpret the study results in terms of how they might apply to specific audiences.
4. Thoughtful critiques of the study's limitations are provided and appropriate for the research approach.	+ If the study emphasizes quantitative procedures, the stated limitations focus on specific shortcomings in the representativeness of the sampling, quality of the measures, and extent confounding variables were controlled in the study. + If the study emphasizes qualitative procedures, the stated limitations focus on specific shortcomings in the extent the sample was information rich, extensiveness of the database, and use of validation strategies in the study.	− The stated limitations are superficial and general and not specific to the study's approach or identify issues that relate to a different research approach (such as discussing a small purposeful sample as a limitation in a qualitative study when it is really a good feature of a qualitative study but would be a limitation in most quantitative studies).
5. Suitable implications of the results for future research are identified and justified.	+ Suggestions for future research that clearly build from the study's results and limitations are advanced.	− Suggestions for future research are stated that seem to contradict or be unrelated to the study results and limitations.

General Evaluation

6. The interpretations are consistent with the study.

+ The researcher draws conclusions that are a logical extension of the results to address the study's purpose and research questions.
+ The researcher draws conclusions that do not go beyond the limits of the study's procedures. Examples of conclusions that *are* consistent with a study are:
  - concluding only that variables are related when confounding variables were uncontrolled;
  - concluding that results apply only to the study sample when a sample was convenient or purposeful; or
  - concluding that dimensions of a central phenomenon are described when analysis was limited to theme development.

− The researcher draws conclusions that are not clearly warranted from the results or do not address the study's purpose or research questions.
− The researcher draws conclusions that go beyond the limitations of the study's procedures. Examples of conclusions that *are not* consistent with a study are:
  - concluding a causal relationship exists without controlling confounding variables;
  - concluding the results generalize to a larger population without using a representative sample; or
  - concluding that a theory was developed without relating multiple themes during analysis.

7. The back matter is appropriate for the study report.

+ Information included in the list of references, notes, and appendices is complete, relevant to the study and report content, and accurate.

− Information included in the list of references, notes, and appendices is incomplete, not clearly related to the study and report content, or includes inaccuracies and mistakes.

Quality Criteria	Quality Rating				Your Evidence and/or Reasoning
	0 = Poor	1 = Fair	2 = Good	3 = Excellent	
The Key Elements					
1. The major results are identified and summarized.					
2. The results are thoughtfully examined in relation to the literature and personal reflections.					
3. Appropriate implications of the results for practice are identified and justified.					
4. Thoughtful critiques of the study's limitations are provided and appropriate for the research approach.					
5. Suitable implications of the results for future research are identified and justified.					
General Evaluation					
6. The interpretations are consistent with the study's results and limitations.					
7. The back matter is appropriate for the study report.					
Overall Quality 0–10 = Low quality 11–16 = Adequate quality 17–21 = High quality	**Total Score =**				**My Overall Assessment Is**

FIGURE 14.2   A Rating Scale for Evaluating the Conclusions and Back Matter in a Research Report

Reviewing What You've Learned To Do

- *Identify and understand the conclusions and supporting information for a research study.*
  - ☐ The Conclusion section is the last major section of a research report. It contains information about the researchers' interpretations and evaluation of the results and procedures of the study and how the study addressed the purpose and research questions.
  - ☐ The Back Matter section of a research report is located after the Conclusion section. The back matter includes supplemental information that the researcher includes to augment and reinforce the information contained in the report.
- *Know how to recognize the elements of a Conclusion section when reading a research report.*
  - ☐ The elements of a Conclusion section represent different types of interpretations and evaluations that researchers draw about their studies. These elements typically include a summary of the major results, a discussion relating the results to the literature, personal reflections on the meaning of the research, suggested implications for practice, limitations of the study, suggestions for future research needs, and the overall significance of the study.
- *Recognize the similarities and differences in conclusions among the different research approaches.*
  - ☐ Quantitative, qualitative, mixed methods, and action research reports tend to address similar topics in their Conclusion sections, with the exception of including personal reflections, which only appear in qualitative and action research studies and some mixed methods studies.
  - ☐ Quantitative and qualitative reports differ in how they make interpretations in terms of their overall purpose, which affects how they organize their summaries, compare results with predictions, and interpret the limitations of their procedures.
- *Identify the types of back matter found in research reports.*
  - ☐ The types of back matter typically found at the end of research reports include end notes with comments about specific statements in the text, reference lists for all sources used in the text, author notes about the authors and their context for conducting the study, and appendices that include supplemental information about procedures or results.
- *Evaluate the quality of the conclusions and back matter in a research report.*
  - ☐ The evaluation of a study's conclusions considers the extent to which the interpretations address the study's purpose and research questions, are consistent with the study's results, and are consistent with the study's research approach.
  - ☐ The evaluation of a study's back matter considers the extent to which the supplemental information is complete, relevant to the study, and accurate.

✓ **To assess what you've learned to do, click here to answer questions and receive instant feedback.**

Reading Research Articles

Carefully reread the quantitative bullying-intervention study by Perkins et al. (2011) found at the end of Chapter 3 (starting on p. 98) and the qualitative adoption-of-pedagogical-tools study by Leko and Brownell (2011) at the end of Chapter 9 (starting on p. 306).

As you review each article, pay close attention to statements in which the authors described their interpretations in the Conclusion section and the supporting information in the Back Matter section. Use the highlighting tool in the Pearson etext to indicate where the authors have provided information about the conclusions and back matter, and use the notetaking tool to add marginal notes that name each element you highlighted and note how each one is related to the study's approach. Among the elements you will want to find are:

Conclusion section elements:

1. Summary of results
2. Relating results to literature
3. Personal reflections

4. Implications for practice
5. Limitations
6. Future research
7. Overall significance

Back Matter section elements:

1. End notes
2. References
3. Author notes
4. Appendices

Note, however, that sometimes authors do not describe all of these types of conclusions—that is, they might not summarize results, relate results to the literature, include personal reflections, identify implications for practice, state limitations, suggest future research, or state the overall significance. In addition, authors do not always include all types of back matter—that is, they might not include end notes, author notes, or appendices. If one of these elements is missing, indicate that in your marginal notes.

Click here to go to the quantitative bullying-intervention study by Perkins et al. (2011) so that you can enter marginal notes about the study.

Click here to go to the qualitative adoption-of-pedagogical tools study by Leko and Brownell (2011) so that you can enter marginal notes about the study.

Understanding Research Articles

Apply your knowledge of the content of this chapter to the quantitative bullying-intervention study by Perkins et al. (2011) starting on p. 98.

1. Consider the interpretations that Perkins et al. drew from their bullying-intervention study. Which of the following interpretative elements did you locate in their Conclusion section? Provide an example of how the authors addressed each element type that you were able to locate.
   - A summary of a major result
   - A discussion relating a result to other literature
   - A personal reflection
   - An implication of the results for practice
   - A limitation of the study
   - A suggestion for future research
   - A statement of the overall significance of the study

2. Consider the back matter that Perkins et al. included in their study report. What types of back matter are present in the article?

✓ **Click here to answer the questions and receive instant feedback.**

Evaluating Research Articles

Practice evaluating a study's conclusions and back matter, using the quantitative bullying-intervention study by Perkins et al. (2011) starting on p. 98 and the qualitative adoption-of-pedagogical-tools study by Leko and Brownell (2011) starting on p. 306.

1. Use the criteria discussed in Table 14.1 to evaluate the quality of the conclusions and back matter in the bullying-intervention study. Note that, for this question, the rating form includes advice to help guide your evaluation.

✓ **Click here to open the rating scale form (Figure 14.2) to enter your ratings, evidence, and reasoning.**

2. Use the criteria discussed in Table 14.1 to evaluate the quality of the conclusions and back matter in the adoption-of-pedagogical-tools study. Note that, for this question, the rating form does NOT include additional advice.

✓ **Click here to open the rating scale form (Figure 14.2) to enter your ratings, evidence, and reasoning.**

Example of a Paper Written in the APA Style

The following paper provides some general guidance on using the APA style for writing scholarly papers. In addition, it is written using the APA (2010) style, so it also provides a model for what the style looks like when applied in a written paper. Use these style formats to organize and present your written work in the APA style.

You can find additional information about the APA style for references in Chapters 1 and 4 and for headings in Chapter 4. If you want further information on all the details of the APA (2010) style, a good free online resource is the Purdue Online Writing Lab (owl.english.purdue.edu).

Source: Plano Clark, V. L. (2014). *A guide to key features for writing papers in the APA style*. (Unpublished manuscript). University of Cincinnati, Cincinnati, OH. Reprinted with permission.

A Guide to Key Features for Writing Papers in the APA Style

Vicki L. Plano Clark

University of Cincinnati

January 1, 2014

KEY FEATURES FOR THE APA STYLE   2

A Guide to Key Features for Writing Papers in the APA Style

Knowing how to write about research requires learning about research and learning about the conventions for scholarly writing. In this book, we have adopted the conventions of the sixth edition of the APA *Publication Manual* (American Psychological Association, 2010). This brief paper highlights several key features of using this style when preparing written papers about research and provides a guide to writing and formatting three major sections of a scholarly paper: the title page, the main text of the paper, and the references.

The Title Page of the Paper

Formal written papers include a title page that identifies the content and author of the paper. The title page should include a title that summarizes the content of your writing. That is, the title should tell the reader what your paper is about. A generic title such as "Assignment" does not convey a good description of your paper's content, whereas a specific title such as "A Literature Review of Strategies for Preventing Obesity" conveys the content and approach of the paper. The title page should also include your name and affiliation. In the APA style, title pages should be double spaced with centered text, use only 12-point font, and not include any boldface text. The APA style recommends the use of a short (no more than 50 characters) running head that identifies the paper with a consistent header.

The Main Text of the Paper

The main text of the paper is where you write the actual content of your paper. As you write, you need to consider the format, use of headings, and use of references.

Formatting the Main Text of Your Paper

Like the title page, the text of your paper should be double spaced and written using a 12-point font. Start the main text of the paper by repeating the full title from the title page. The title should be centered, use title case, be double spaced, and be in regular font (i.e., not bold). Indent the start of each paragraph and do not leave blank lines between paragraphs. The margins for the paper should be one inch on all sides and each page should be numbered.

Using Headings to Organize Your Writing

Headings are very useful in writing because they provide an organizing framework for the reader. Use them to organize the big ideas of your writing, but do not overuse them so they take away from the flow of your writing.

The headings that appear within the text of your paper and organize your thoughts can appear as different levels. Levels 1, 2, and 3 are most common. Think of the levels of headings like the levels in an outline where secondary headings fall under major headings and, if needed, third-level subheadings fall under secondary headings. The APA style uses a different format for each of the heading levels. The number of levels you use is a personal choice that depends on the length of the paper as well as the details of the information that you are conveying. This paper uses three levels to demonstrate the different formats of each.

Major headings are the first level. Use a level 1 heading style for your major headings. The level 1 headings should be bold, centered, title case, and double spaced. An example of a level 1 heading is the heading "The Main Text of the Paper" used above. I recommend always using level 1 headings in your formal writings to convey the major ideas in your writing.

Secondary subheadings are the second level. Use a level 2 heading if you need subheadings under one of your major headings. The level 2 heading should be bold, left justified, title case, and double spaced. An example of a level 2 heading is the heading "Using Headings to Organize Your Writing" above.

KEY FEATURES FOR THE APA STYLE   4

Tertiary subheadings are the third level. Use a level 3 heading if you need further subheadings under one of your secondary headings. The third level of heading should be bold, indented, in sentence case, end with a period, and flow into the start of the paragraph's text. An example of this format is the heading "Tertiary subheadings are the third level" used at the start of this paragraph.

Using In-Text References to Give Credit to Others' Work

To avoid the serious offense of plagiarism, you must give credit by providing an in-text citation whenever you refer to ideas that have been published elsewhere by yourself or others. This is done through in-text references in the main body of your paper. APA in-text citation style consists of author name(s) and year of publication. Here are four pieces of advice for in-text references.

"And" versus ampersand ("&"). If a reference appears as part of the sentence and there are two or more authors, write out the word "and." If the reference appears as a parenthetical comment, then use the ampersand symbol ("&"). For example, we can say that Creswell and Plano Clark (2011) defined mixed methods as integrating quantitative and qualitative approaches. We could also say that mixed methods research is defined as research that integrates quantitative and qualitative approaches (Creswell & Plano Clark, 2011).

Listing names versus using "et al." If a reference has two authors, always list them both (e.g., Plano Clark & Wang, 2011). If a reference has three, four, or five authors, list all the names the first time you refer to the work in your paper (e.g., Churchill, Plano Clark, Prochaska-Cue, Creswell, & Ontai-Grzebik, 2007) and then use the "et al." format all subsequent times you refer to the work (e.g., Churchill et al., 2007). If an article has six or more authors, then always use the "et al." format (e.g., Plano Clark et al., 2002).

KEY FEATURES FOR THE APA STYLE   5

Ordering multiple references. If you provide multiple references for an idea, order them alphabetically by the first authors' last names and separate them with a semicolon. For example, much has been written about mixed methods research (Creswell & Plano Clark, 2011; Greene, Caracelli, & Graham, 1989; Plano Clark, 2010).

Direct quotes. If you directly quote words from a source, then you must indicate the direct quote with quote marks and include the page number of the original quote in the source. For example, it has been said that the APA manual is "the most popular style guide in educational research" (Creswell, 2012, p. 98).

The References List for the Paper

At the end of your paper, start a section for the references on a new page. Title this section as "References." Like the paper's title, this should be centered, use title case, be double spaced, and not boldface. In this section, you must provide full information on all references that you cited in the main text of your paper. All citations in your paper *must* appear in the list at the end. Likewise, all citations listed at the end *must* appear somewhere in your paper. Each type of reference needs to be formatted carefully (see examples at the end of this paper for books, chapters, and articles), including the hanging indent. The references are listed in alphabetical order based on the first authors' last names.

Conclusion

The APA manual is a complex document with many rules. Some of the rules are logical, but others you have to follow simply because those are the manual's instructions. This paper demonstrates the key aspects of the APA style that should be of concern when preparing scholarly written papers and assignments.

KEY FEATURES FOR THE APA STYLE   6

References

American Psychological Association (APA). (2010). *Publication manual of the American Psychological Association* (6th ed.). Washington, DC: Author.

Churchill, S. L., Plano Clark, V. L., Prochaska-Cue, M. K., Creswell, J. W., & Ontai-Grzebik, L. (2007). How rural low-income families have fun: A grounded theory study. *Journal of Leisure Research, 39*(2), 271–294.

Creswell, J. W. (2012). *Educational research. Planning, conducting, and evaluating quantitative and qualitative research* (4th ed.). Boston, MA: Pearson.

Creswell, J. W., & Plano Clark, V. L. (2011). *Designing and conducting mixed methods research* (2nd ed.). Thousand Oaks, CA: Sage.

Greene, J. C., Caracelli, V. J., & Graham, W. F. (1989). Toward a conceptual framework for mixed-method evaluation designs. *Educational Evaluation and Policy Analysis, 11*(3), 255–274.

Plano Clark, V. L. (2010). The adoption and practice of mixed methods: U.S. trends in federally funded health-related research. *Qualitative Inquiry, 16*(6), 428–440.

Plano Clark, V. L., Miller, D. L., Creswell, J. W., McVea, K., McEntarffer, R., Harter, L. M., & Mickelson, W. T. (2002). In conversation: High school students talk to students about tobacco use and prevention strategies. *Qualitative Health Research, 12,* 1264–1283.

Plano Clark, V. L., & Wang, S. C. (2010). Adapting mixed method research to multicultural counseling. In J. G. Ponterotto, J. M. Casas, L. A. Suzuki, & C. M. Alexander (Eds.), *Handbook of multicultural counseling* (3rd ed., pp. 427–438). Thousand Oaks, CA: Sage.

Glossary

Abstract is a brief summary of an article's content written by the article's author and placed at the beginning of the article.

Action research designs are systematic procedures done by practitioners to gather quantitative and/or qualitative data to improve the ways their particular professional setting operates, their practice, and their impact on others.

Alpha level (α) is the criterion that researchers use to determine whether they obtain a statistically significant result in quantitative data analysis. Its value is the maximum level of risk that researchers are willing to take that they incorrectly conclude that they found a significant difference between groups or relationship between variables in the population.

Analyzing data consists of the researcher taking the data apart to determine individual responses and putting it together to summarize the information within the data.

Appendices appear at the end of a research report and authors use them to provide detailed information (e.g., data collection questions) to supplement the main report.

Attitudinal measures are instruments that researchers use to gather data in quantitative research to measure participants' feelings toward topics.

Audience consists of individuals and groups who the authors expect will read and potentially benefit from the information provided in the research article.

Audiovisual materials consist of images, sounds, or objects that qualitative researchers collect to help them understand the central phenomenon under study.

Audit consists of researchers asking a person outside the study to conduct an audit or review of the procedures used in a qualitative study.

Author notes are general notes that researchers include in their reports to provide information about the overall study such as author contact information, funding information, and acknowledgments.

Back matter consists of the information included at the end of an article such as a list of references and appendices.

Behavioral observation checklists are instruments that researchers use to gather data in quantitative research to observe and record specific behaviors of participants.

Bracketing is a process by which a researcher reflects on his or her own views and experiences related to a qualitative study's central phenomenon, describes these perspectives in writing, and then works to set them aside (or "bracket" them) during the analysis process.

Case study research designs are sets of qualitative procedures used to explore in depth a program, event, or activity involving individuals within a bounded system.

Central phenomenon is the concept, activity, or process explored in a qualitative research study.

Central research question is the overarching question that the researcher explores in a qualitative research study.

Central tendency is a type of descriptive statistic that is a single number that summarizes a set of scores.

Choosing a research design involves the researcher designing an overall plan for the study's methods including selecting participants, collecting data, analyzing data, and reporting the results.

Close-ended questions are questions that researchers ask in quantitative data collection that include preset options from which the participant can respond.

Codes are labels that researchers use to describe the meaning of a segment of text or an image during qualitative data analysis.

Coding is a procedure used in qualitative data analysis where the researcher identifies segments of text or images, places a bracket around them or highlights them, and assigns a code that describes the meaning of the segment.

Collecting data means the researcher gathers information by asking participants questions or observing their behaviors.

Combined research is a type of research in which the researcher studies a problem that calls for explanation and exploration; asks narrow, specific questions and broad, general questions; collects data consisting of numbers and words; analyzes these data for statistical trends and themes; and combines the two sets of results into an overall understanding of the topic.

Conceptual framework represents a philosophical perspective, an advocacy or social justice stance on behalf of marginalized groups, or a particular way of viewing knowledge that the researcher uses to inform a study.

Conclusion section is a major section in a research report where the researcher discusses the interpretation of the results and research study.

Confounding variable is an attribute or characteristic that may influence the relationship between the independent and dependent variables, but that the researcher does not directly measure.

Control variable is a type of independent variable that is not of central interest to the researcher, but that the researcher measures because it may also influence the dependent variable.

Convergent parallel mixed methods design is a set of procedures that researchers use to concurrently collect both quantitative and qualitative data, analyze the two datasets separately, compare and/or synthesize the two sets of separate results, and make an overall interpretation as to the extent to which the separate results confirm and/or complement each other.

Correlational research designs are sets of nonexperimental procedures in quantitative research in which investigators measure the degree of association (or relationship) between two or more variables for a group of individuals.

Deficiency in knowledge means that the past literature or experiences of the researchers do not adequately address the research problem.

Demographic forms are instruments that researchers use to gather basic facts about and characteristics of their participants.

Dependent variable is an attribute or characteristic that is dependent on or influenced by the independent variables; it is the outcome in which the researcher is most interested.

Describing and developing themes from the data consists of the qualitative researcher answering the major research questions and forming an in-depth understanding of the central phenomenon through description, thematic development, and relating themes.

Description is a detailed rendering of people, places, or events that provide the context for a qualitative study.

Descriptive statistics are statistical tools that help researchers summarize the overall tendencies in the data, provide an assessment of how varied the scores are, and provide insight into where one score stands in comparison with the rest of the data.

Disseminating research consists of the researcher developing a written report about the study and distributing it to researcher and practitioner audiences.

Documents consist of public and private records that researchers obtain about a site or participants in a qualitative study.

Drawing conclusions about the research consists of researchers interpreting the results that they obtained and explaining how the results provide answers to the research questions.

Effect size is a statistic that researchers compute to identify the practical strength of the significant group differences or the relationship among variables found in a quantitative study.

E-mail interviews are a type of qualitative data collection in which the researcher collects open-ended data through interviews with individuals using computers and the Internet.

Embedded mixed methods design is a set of procedures that researchers use to collect a secondary set of data (qualitative or quantitative) in a study that is guided by a traditional quantitative design (e.g., a true experiment) or a traditional qualitative design (e.g., a case study) where the secondary dataset addresses a different question than the primary dataset and is used to augment the implementation and/or interpretation of the primary method.

End notes are specific notes that researchers include at the end of report to provide extra information about specific statements made within the article's text.

End-of-text references are the references listed at the end of a research report with the full information about all sources cited from the literature.

Ethnographic research designs are sets of qualitative research procedures for describing, analyzing, and interpreting a culture-sharing group's shared patterns of behavior, beliefs, and language.

Evaluating research involves individuals (e.g., researchers and practitioners) assessing the quality of a research study.

Evidence-based practices are personal and professional practices that have been shown to be effective through research.

Experimental research is a category of quantitative research designs that researchers use when they intend to test the effect of an intervention by manipulating the conditions experienced by participants.

External validity is the extent to which a researcher can generalize the results from the sample to a population and to other settings.

Factual information documents consist of public and private records from which researchers gather factual information about participants in the form of numeric, individual data.

Field notes are the words and images recorded by the researcher during an observation in a qualitative study.

Figure is a summary of information presented as a chart, graph, or picture that shows relations among scores or variables.

Focus group interviews are a type of qualitative data collection in which the researcher collects data through conversations with a small group of people.

Front matter of an article consists of the title, author information, and an abstract.

Future research directions are suggestions made by the researcher in the Conclusion section about additional research studies that need to be conducted based on the results and limitations of the present study.

Gatekeeper is a person who assists in the identification of a place to study, has an official or unofficial role at the site, provides entrance to a site, and helps qualitative researchers locate people to study at the site.

Grounded theory research designs are sets of systematic, qualitative procedures that researchers use to generate a general explanation (called a *grounded theory*) that explains a process, action, or interaction among people.

Headings are signposts that writers use to designate the topics and sub-topics within a written document.

Hypotheses are statements used only in quantitative research in which the investigator makes a prediction about the relationship expected to exist among two or more variables.

Hypothesis testing is a quantitative data analysis procedure that researchers use to determine whether a difference or relationship likely exists among variables in a population based on the result obtained from a sample.

Identifying a research problem consists of the researcher specifying an issue that needs to be studied, developing a justification for studying it, and suggesting the importance of the study for select audiences who will read the report.

Implications are the researchers' recommendations for audiences based on the results that were obtained in the study and stated in the Conclusion section of a report.

In-text references are references cited in a brief format within the body of the text to provide credit to authors of other sources.

Independent variable is an attribute or characteristic that is thought to influence, predict, or affect an outcome or dependent variable.

Inferential statistics are statistical tools that researchers use in their quantitative data analysis to consider more than one variable such as comparing groups or relating variables and to make inferences from a sample to a population.

Instrument is a tool to gather quantitative data by measuring, observing, or documenting responses to specific items. Examples include demographic forms, performance measures, attitudinal measures, behavioral observation checklists, and factual information.

Internal validity is the extent to which a researcher can claim that the independent variable caused an effect in the dependent variable at the end of a quantitative study.

Interpretation means researchers draw conclusions about the results and explain how the results answer the study's research questions in the Conclusion section of a research report.

Interview is the qualitative data collection method of asking one or more participants general, open-ended questions and recording their answers.

Interview protocol is a form designed by the researcher in a qualitative research study that contains instructions for the process of the interview, the major questions to be asked, and space to take notes about the responses from the interviewee.

Introduction section is a major section in a research report where the researcher reports information about the first three steps of the research process: identifying a research problem, reviewing the literature, and specifying a purpose.

Journal articles are polished, short research reports that have been sent to an editor of a journal, accepted for inclusion, and published in a volume of the journal.

Justifying a research problem means that researchers present evidence for the importance of the issue or concern identified in the Introduction of a study report.

Limitations are potential weaknesses or problems with the study identified by the researcher in the Conclusion section of a report.

Literature map is a figure or drawing that visually organizes the literature reviewed on a topic.

Literature review is a written synthesis of journal articles, books, and other documents that summarizes and critiques the past and current state of information about a topic, organizes the literature into subtopics, and documents the background for a study.

Mean is the average score for a variable across a group of participants. It is a measure of central tendency that researchers calculate by dividing the total of the scores by the number of scores.

Measured variables are independent variables that the researcher measures as they currently exist without doing anything to manipulate the scores on these variables.

Member checking is a process in which the researcher asks one or more participants in a qualitative study to check the accuracy of the findings.

Method section is a major section in a research report where the researcher describes the procedures used to implement three steps of the research process: choosing a research design, selecting participants and collecting data, and analyzing data and reporting results.

Mixed methods research design is a set of procedures for collecting, analyzing, and "mixing" both quantitative and qualitative methods in a study to understand a research problem.

Mode is a measure of central tendency that identifies the score that appears most frequently in a list of scores.

Multiple perspectives mean that the researcher provides several viewpoints from different individuals and sources of data as evidence for a theme in a qualitative study.

Narrative research designs are sets of qualitative procedures that researchers use to describe the lives of individuals by collecting and telling stories about these individuals' lives, writing narratives about their experiences, and discussing the meaning of those experiences for the individual.

Nonexperimental research is a category of quantitative research designs used when researchers intend to describe variables without manipulating the conditions experienced by participants.

Nonparticipant observer is an observer who visits a site and records notes without becoming involved in the activities of the participants.

Nonprobability sampling means that the researcher selects individuals to study because they are available, convenient, and represent some characteristic the investigator seeks to study.

Observation is the process that researchers use to gather open-ended, firsthand information in qualitative research by observing people and places at a research site.

One-on-one interviews are a type of qualitative data collection in which the researcher asks questions to and records answers from only one participant at a time.

Open-ended questions are questions asked in qualitative data collection that that the researcher states so that it allows the participant to create his/her own options for responding.

Participant observer is an observational role adopted by researchers in qualitative research when they take part in activities in the setting they observe.

Participatory action research (PAR) is a research design that has a social and community orientation and an emphasis on research that contributes to emancipation or change in our society.

Peer-reviewed journals are journals that only publish research reports after they have undergone a review process where experts in the field independently evaluate each study before the journal will publish it as an article. This is the most rigorous type of research publication.

Percentile rank is a measure of relative standing that describes the percentage of participants in the distribution who have scores at or below a particular score.

Performance measures are instruments that researchers use to gather data in quantitative research to assess or rate individuals' ability to perform in a certain way, such as their achievement, intelligence, aptitude, interests, or personality traits.

Plagiarize means to represent someone else's ideas and writings as if they were your own, without giving proper credit.

Population is a group of individuals or organizations that have the same characteristic and that a quantitative researcher wants to learn about by studying a sample from the population in a study.

Practical action research involves a small-scale research project, narrowly focuses on a specific problem or issue, and is undertaken by individual practitioners or teams within a practice setting such as a school or clinic.

Preliminary exploratory analysis in qualitative research consists of the researcher exploring the data to obtain a general sense of the data, recording initial ideas, thinking about the organization of the data, and considering whether more data are needed.

Probability sampling means the researcher uses a random process to select individuals (or units, such as schools) from the population so that each individual has a known chance (or probability) of being selected. Examples of probability sampling include random sampling and stratified random sampling.

Probes are subquestions under each main question that the researcher asks to elicit more information during a qualitative interview.

Process of research consists of eight steps used by researchers when they conduct a research study. The steps include: identifying a research problem, reviewing the literature, specifying a purpose, choosing a research design, selecting participants and collecting data, analyzing data and reporting results, drawing conclusions, and disseminating and evaluating the research.

Purpose for research indicates the researcher's major intent or aim for conducting the research study.

Purposeful sampling means that researchers intentionally select sites and individuals to participate in a research study to learn about or understand the central phenomenon. Examples of purposeful sampling include maximal variation sampling and homogenous sampling.

Purpose statement is a statement of one or more sentences that advances the overall direction or focus for the study in a research report.

p **value** is the probability (*p*) that an inferential statistical result could have been produced by chance if the null hypothesis were true for the population.

Qualitative research is a type of research in which the researcher studies a problem that calls for an exploration of a phenomenon; relies on the views of participants; asks broad, general questions; collects data consisting largely of words (or text) from participants; describes and analyzes these words for themes; and conducts the inquiry in a subjective and reflexive manner.

Qualitative research designs are sets of procedures for collecting, analyzing, and reporting text and image data to answer research questions that call for exploring participants' views. Examples include narrative research, grounded theory, case study, and ethnography.

Quantitative research is a type of research in which the researcher studies a problem that calls for an explanation about variables; decides what to study; asks specific, narrow questions; collects quantifiable data from participants; analyzes these numbers using statistics and graphs; and conducts the inquiry in an unbiased, objective manner.

Quantitative research designs are sets of procedures for collecting, analyzing, and reporting numeric data to answer research questions and test hypotheses about specific variables. Examples include true experiments, quasi-experiments, single-subject designs, correlational designs, and survey designs.

Quasi-experiment is a type of experimental research design in which the researcher tests an intervention using intact groups of individuals.

Range is a measure of variability that reports the difference between the highest and the lowest scores obtained for a variable.

Reference list is a list of detailed information about all the sources the author used in writing the report that appears at the end of a research report.

Relative standing is a type of descriptive statistic that describes one score relative to a group of scores.

Reliable means that scores from an instrument are stable and consistent.

Reporting results involves the researcher representing the results of the analyses in tables, figures, and discussions that summarize the patterns they found in the data and the results they obtained from the data.

Representative sample means that the researcher selected individuals for the sample that are typical of the wider population so that study's results can be generalized to the population.

Research is a process of steps used to collect and analyze information in order to increase our knowledge about a topic or issue.

Research design is a set of quantitative, qualitative, or combined procedures for collecting, analyzing, and reporting data in a research study.

Research problem is an issue, controversy, or concern that guides the need for a study and indicates the importance of a study.

Research questions are questions in quantitative and qualitative research that narrow the purpose statement to specific questions that the researcher seeks to answer by conducting the study.

Results section is a major section in a research report where the researcher reports the results from analyzing the data collected in a study.

Reviewing the literature means that the researcher locates books and journal articles on a topic; chooses which literature to include in their review; and then summarizes and critically evaluates the included literature.

Sample is a subgroup of the population that participates in a research study and provides data for the study.

Sample size is the number of participants (or organizations) that participate in the study and provide data.

Sampling error is the difference between the result obtained from the data collected from the sample (the sample estimate) and what the researcher would get if data were collected from the whole population (the true population score).

Sampling strategies are approaches that researchers use to select individuals or organizations for the samples in research studies.

Scoring data is the procedure that researchers use to assign a numeric score (or value) to each participant's response for each question on the instruments used to collect data.

Selecting participants and collecting data means that the researcher selects settings and individuals for a study, obtains necessary permissions to study them, and gathers information by asking people questions or observing their behaviors.

Sequential explanatory mixed methods design is a set of procedures that researchers use to collect and analyze quantitative data in a first phase, plan a second phase based on the quantitative results, and then collect and analyze qualitative data in the second phase to help explain or elaborate on the quantitative results.

Sequential exploratory mixed methods design is a set of procedures that researchers use to collect and analyze qualitative data to explore a topic in a first phase, plan a second phase based on the qualitative findings, and then collect and analyze quantitative data in the second phase to help extend or generalize the qualitative findings.

Single-item score is an individual score assigned to each individual question for each participant in a study.

Single-subject research is a quantitative experimental research design that involves the study of single individuals, the administration of an intervention, and the careful monitoring of the individuals' behaviors before, during, and after the intervention to determine whether the treatment affects the behavior.

Specifying the purpose for research consists of the researcher identifying the major intent or objective for a study and narrowing it into specific research questions to be answered or hypotheses to be tested.

Standard deviation is a measure of variability that reports how dispersed the data are about the mean value for a continuous variable.

Statement of the problem is a passage that researchers write into the Introduction of their studies that conveys the importance of a report by addressing: the topic, the research problem, evidence for the importance of the problem, deficiencies in the knowledge about the problem, and the audiences that will benefit from a study of the problem.

Study-by-study review of the literature is a literature review written to provide a detailed summary of each study grouped under broad themes identified in the review.

Style manuals present formats for writing research reports by providing a structure for citing references, labeling headings, and constructing tables.

Summed scores are used when the researcher adds the scores of a participant for several items that measure the same variable.

Survey research designs are nonexperimental quantitative procedures that researchers use to administer a survey questionnaire to a smaller group of people (called the sample) in order to identify trends in attitudes, opinions, behaviors, or characteristics of a larger group of people (called the population).

Table is a summary of information organized into rows and columns.

Telephone interview is the process of gathering qualitative data from individuals by asking a small number of general questions over the telephone.

Thematic review of the literature is a literature review written so that it presents the literature in broad categories or themes and provides citations to the literature to document the major results from studies about this theme without providing the details of any single study.

Themes (also called categories) are the results found during qualitative data analysis where the researcher aggregates similar codes together to form a major idea about the central phenomenon in the database.

Theory explains and predicts the probable relationship among different concepts (or variables).

Topic is the broad subject matter that a researcher wishes to address in a study.

Transcription is the process of converting audio recordings or field notes into typed text.

Treatment variables are a special type of independent variable that researchers use in quantitative research when they administer some kind of treatment or intervention to the participants in a study.

Triangulation is the process of corroborating evidence about a finding from different individuals (e.g., a principal and a student) or types of data (e.g., observational field notes and interviews) in qualitative research.

True experiment is an experimental research design where the researcher manipulates the conditions experienced by participants and uses a special procedure called random assignment to assign individual participants to the different levels of the treatment variable.

Valid means that the scores from an instrument are accurate indicators of the variable that is being measured and enable the researcher to draw good interpretations.

Validating findings means that the researcher uses strategies to ensure the accuracy and credibility of the findings as part of the analysis process in qualitative research.

Variability is a type of descriptive statistic used to indicate the spread of scores in the data collected for a variable.

Variable is an indicator of a characteristic or attribute of individuals or organizations that researchers measure and that varies among the individuals or organizations studied.

z **score** is a measure of relative standing that researchers calculate by converting a participant's score into a relative score measured in units of standard deviations.

References

Abril, C. R., & Gault, B. M. (2006). The state of music in the elementary school: The principal's perspective. *Journal of Research in Music Education, 54*(1), 6–20.

Adams, C. (2012). (Writing myself into) Betty White's stories: (De)constructing narratives of/through feminist sport history research. *Journal of Sport History, 39*(3), 395–413.

Algozzine, B., & McGee, J. R. (2011). Reported occurrence and perceptions of violence in middle and high schools. *Clearing House: A Journal of Educational Strategies, 84*(3), 91–97.

Amatea, E. S., Smith-Adcock, S., & Villares, E. (2006). From family deficit to family strength: Viewing families' contributions to children's learning from a family resilience perspective. *Professional School Counseling, 9*(3), 177–189.

American Psychological Association. (1927–). *Psychological abstracts.* Washington, DC: Author.

American Psychological Association (APA). (2010). *Publication manual of the American Psychological Association* (6th ed.). Washington, DC: Author.

American Psychological Association. (2003). *Ethical principles of psychologists and code of conduct.* Washington, DC: Author.

Apthorp, H. S. (2006). Effects of a supplemental vocabulary program in third-grade reading/language arts. *Journal of Educational Research, 100*(2), 67–79.

Asmussen, K. J., & Creswell, J. W. (1995). Campus response to a student gunman. *Journal of Higher Education, 66*(5), 575–591.

Auerbach, S. (2007). From moral supporters to struggling advocates: Reconceptualizing parent roles in education through the experience of working-class families of color. *Urban Education, 42*(3), 250–283.

Baggerly, J., & Osborn, D. (2006). School counselors' career satisfaction and commitment: Correlates and predictors. *Professional School Counseling, 9*(3), 197–205.

Barker, L. J., & Garvin-Doxas, K. (2004). Making visible the behaviors that influence learning environment: A qualitative exploration of computer science classrooms. *Computer Science Education, 14*(2), 119–145.

Beare, P., Torgerson, C., & Creviston, C. (2008). Increasing verbal behavior of a student who is selectively mute. *Journal of Emotional and Behavioral Disorders.* doi:10.1177/1063426608317356

Bellows, L., Spaeth, A., Lee, V., & Anderson, J. (2013). Exploring the use of storybooks to reach mothers of preschoolers with nutrition and physical activity messages. *Journal of Nutrition Education and Behavior, 45*(4), 362–367.

Bikos, L. H., Çiftçi, A., Güneri, O. Y., Demir, C. E., Sümer, Z. H., Danielson, S., . . . Bilgen W. A. (2007). A longitudinal, naturalistic inquiry of the adaptation experiences of the female expatriate spouse living in Turkey. *Journal of Career Development, 34*, 28–58.

Boyd, C. M., Fraiman, J. L., Hawkins, K. A., Labin, J. M., Sutter, M. B., & Wahl, M. R. (2008). Effects of the STAR intervention program on interactions between campers with and without disabilities during inclusive summer day camp activities. *Education & Training in Developmental Disabilities, 43*(1), 92–101.

Brady, B., & O'Regan, C. (2009). Meeting the challenge of doing an RCT evaluation of youth mentoring in Ireland: A journey in mixed methods. *Journal of Mixed Methods Research, 3*, 265–280.

Brotherson, S. E., Dollahite, D. C., & Hawkins, A. J. (2005). Generative fathering and the dynamics of connection between fathers and their children. *Fathering, 3*(1), 1–28.

Brown, J., Sorrell, J. H., McClaren, J., & Creswell, J. W. (2006). Waiting for a liver transplant. *Qualitative Health Research, 16*(1), 119–136.

Bulmer, S. M., Irfan, S., Mugno, R., Barton, B., & Ackerman, L. (2010). Trends in alcohol consumption among undergraduate students at a northeastern public university, 2002–2008. *Journal of American College Health, 58*, 383–390.

Cain, T. (2011). How trainee music teachers learn about teaching by talking to each other: An action research study. *International Journal of Music Education, 29*, 141–154. doi: 10.1177/0255761410396961

Campbell, B. (2010). Applying knowledge to generate action: A community-based knowledge translation framework. *Journal of Continuing Education in the Health Professions, 30*(1), 65–71. doi:10.1002/chp.20058

Campbell, D. T., & Stanley, J. C. (1963). Experimental and quasi-experimental designs for research. In N. L. Gage (Ed.), *Handbook on research in teaching* (pp. 1–80). Chicago, IL: Rand-McNally.

Carrington, S., Templeton, E., & Papinczak, T. (2003). Adolescents with Asperger syndrome and perceptions of friendship. *Focus on Autism and Other Developmental Disabilities, 18*(4), 211–218.

Chan, E. (2010). Living in the space between participant and researcher as a narrative inquirer: Examining ethnic identity of Chinese Canadian students as conflicting stories to live. *Journal of Educational Research, 103*(2), 112–122.

Charmaz, K. (2006). *Constructing grounded theory.* London, UK: Sage.

Cheng, D. X., & Alcántara, L. (2007). Assessing working students' college experiences: A grounded theory approach. *Assessment & Evaluation in Higher Education, 32*, 301–311. doi:10.1177/0255761410396961

Churchill, S. L., Plano Clark, V. L., Prochaska-Cue, M. K., Creswell, J. W., & Ontai-Grzebik, L. (2007). How rural low-income families have fun: A grounded theory study. *Journal of Leisure Research, 39*(2), 271–294.

Cihak, D. F., Kessler, K., & Alberto, P. A. (2008). Use of a hand-held prompting system to transition independently through vocational tasks for students with moderate and severe intellectual disabilities. *Education and Training in Developmental Disabilities, 43*(1), 102–110.

Cinamon, R. G., & Dan, O. (2010). Parental attitudes toward preschoolers' career education: A mixed-method study. *Journal of Career Development, 37*(2), 519–540. doi:10.1177/0894845309357050

Clandinin, D. J. (Ed.). (2007). *Handbook of narrative inquiry: Mapping a methodology.* Thousand Oaks, CA: Sage.

Clandinin, D. J., & Connelly, F. M. (2000). *Narrative inquiry: Experience and story in qualitative research.* San Francisco, CA: Jossey-Bass.

Clayton, C. D. (2007). Curriculum making as novice professional development: Practical risk taking as learning in high-stakes times. *Journal of Teacher Education, 58*(3), 216–230.

Clayton, J. K. (2011). Changing diversity in U.S. schools: The impact on elementary student performance and achievement. *Education and Urban Society, 43*, 671–696.

Connelly, F. M., & Dukacz, A. S. (1980). Using research findings. In F. M. Connelly, A. S. Dukacz, & F. Quinlan (Eds.). *Curriculum planning for the classroom* (pp. 24–34). Toronto, Ontario, Canada: OISE Press.

Constantine, M. G., Wallace, B. C., & Kindaichi, M. M. (2005). Examining contextual factors in the career decision status of African American adolescents. *Journal of Career Assessment, 13*(3), 307–319.

Cooper, K., & White, R. E. (2008). Critical literacy for school improvement: An action research project. *Improving Schools, 11*(2), 101–113. doi:10.1177/1365480208091103

Corbin, J., & Strauss, A. (2008). *Basics of qualitative research: Techniques and procedures for developing grounded theory* (3rd ed.). Thousand Oaks, CA: Sage.

Craig, C. L. (2004). The dragon in school backyards: The influence of mandated testing on school contexts and educators' narrative knowing. *Teachers College Record, 106*(6), 1229–1257.

Cranston, J. (2012). Honouring roles: The story of a principal and a student. *Brock Education, 22*(1), 41–55.

Creel, S. L. (2007). Early adolescents' reading habits. *Young Adult Library Services, 5*(4), 46–49.

Creswell J. W. (2008). *Educational research: Planning, conducting, and evaluating qualitative and quantitative research* (3rd ed.). Upper Saddle River, NJ: Pearson Education.

Creswell, J. W. (2012). *Educational research: Planning, conducting, and evaluating quantitative and qualitative research* (4th ed.). Upper Saddle River, NJ: Pearson Education.

Creswell, J. W. (2013). *Qualitative inquiry and research design: Choosing among five approaches* (3rd ed.). Thousand Oaks, CA: Sage.

Creswell, J. W., & Plano Clark, V. L. (2011). *Designing and conducting mixed methods research* (2nd ed.). Thousand Oaks, CA: Sage.

Dallos, R., & Denford, S. (2008). A qualitative exploration of relationship and attachment themes in families with an eating disorder. *Clinical Child Psychology and Psychiatry, 13*, 305–322.

Damico, J. S., Muller, N., & Ball, M. J. (Eds.). (2010). *The handbook of language and speech disorders*. Oxford, UK: Blackwell Publishers.

Dengler, K. A., Wilson, V., Redshaw, S., & Scarfe, G. (2012). Appreciation of a child's journey: Implementation of a cardiac action research project. *Nursing Research and Practice, 2012*, 1–7. doi:10.1155/2012/145030

Denzin, N. K., & Lincoln, Y. S. (Eds.). (2005). *The Sage handbook of qualitative research* (3rd ed.). Thousand Oaks, CA: Sage.

Dicker, M. (1990). Using action research to navigate an unfamiliar teaching assignment. *Theory into Practice, XXIX*, 203–208.

Ditrano C. J., & Silverstein, L. B. (2006). Listening to parents' voices: Participatory action research in the schools. *Professional Psychology Research and Practice, 37*(4), 359–366.

Dods, R. F. (1997). An action research study of the effectiveness of problem-based learning in promoting the acquisition and retention of knowledge. *Journal for the Education of the Gifted, 20*(4), 423–437.

Dowdell, E. B. (2012). Urban seventh grade students: A report of health risk behaviors and exposure to violence. *The Journal of School Nursing, 28*(2), 130–137. doi:10.1177/1059840511425678

Educational Resources Information Center (U.S.). (1991). *ERIC directory of education-related information centers*. Washington, DC: Author.

Elliot, L., Henderson, M., Nixon, C., & Wight, D. (2013). Has untargeted sexual health promotion for young people reached its limit? A quasi-experimental study. *Journal of Epidemiology and Community Health, 67*, 398–404.

Endacott, R., Cooper, S., Sheaff, R., Padmore, J., & Blakely, G. (2011). Improving emergency care pathways: An action research approach. *Emergency Medicine Journal, 28*, 203–207. doi:10.1136/emj.2009.082859

Epper, R. M. (1997). Coordination and competition in postsecondary distance education. *Journal of Higher Education, 68*(5), 551–587.

Fetterman, D. M. (2010). *Ethnography: Step-by-Step* (3rd ed.). Thousand Oaks, CA: Sage.

Finders, M. J. (1996). Queens and teen zines: Early adolescent females reading their way toward adulthood. *Anthropology and Education Quarterly, 27*(1), 71–89.

Fitzpatrick, K. R. (2011). A mixed methods portrait of urban instrumental music teaching. *Journal of Research in Music Education, 59*, 229–256. doi:10.1177/0022429411414912

Fornara, F., Carrus, G., Passafaro, P., & Bonnes, M. (2011). Distinguishing the sources of normative influence on proenvironmental behaviors: The role of local norms in household waste recycling. *Group Processes & Intergroup Relations, 14*, 623–635. doi:10.1177/1368430211408149

Fothergill, A. (1999). Women's roles in a disaster. *Applied Behavioral Science Review, 7*(2), 125–143.

Frankenberger, K. D. (2004). Adolescent egocentrism, risk perceptions, and sensation seeking among smoking and nonsmoking youth. *Journal of Adolescent Research, 19*(5), 576–590.

Garwick, A. W., & Seppelt, A. M. (2010). Developing a family-centered participatory action research project. *Journal of Family Nursing, 16*(3), 269–281. doi:10.1177/1074840710376175

Glaser, B. G. (1992). *Basics of grounded theory analysis*. Mill Valley, CA: Sociology Press.

Glaser, B., & Strauss, A. (1967). *The discovery of grounded theory.* Chicago, IL: Aldine.

Glesne, C., & Peshkin, A. (1992). *Becoming qualitative researchers: An introduction*. White Plains, NY: Longman.

Gonzalez, J. E., Goetz, E. T., Hall, R. J., Payne, T., Taylor, A. B., Kim, M., & McCormick, A. S. (2011). An evaluation of Early Reading First (ERF) preschool enrichment on language and literacy skills. *Reading and Writing, 24*, 253–284.

Green, S. E. (2003). "What do you mean 'what's wrong with her?'": Stigma and the lives of families of children with disabilities. *Social Science & Medicine, 57*, 1361–1374.

Greene, J. C. (2007). *Mixed methods in social inquiry*. San Francisco, CA: Jossey-Bass.

Grieser, M., Vu, M. B., Bedimo-Rung, A. L., Neumark-Sztainer, D., Moody, J., Rohm Young, D., & Moe, S. G. (2006). Physical activity attitudes, preferences, and practices in African American, Hispanic and Caucasian girls. *Health Education & Behavior, 33*(1), 40–51. doi:10.1177/1090198105282416

Groton, D., Teasley, M. L., & Canfield, J. P. (2013). Working with homeless school-aged children: Barriers to school social work practice. *School Social Work Journal, 37*(2), 37–51.

Gustafsson, J., & Nilsson-Wikmar, L. (2008). Influence of specific muscle training on pain, activity limitation and kinesiophobia in women with back pain post-partum—A 'single-subject research design.' *Physiotherapy Research International, 13*(1), 18–30.

Haigh, K. M. (2007). Exploring learning with teachers and children: An administrator's perspective. *Theory into Practice, 46*(1), 57–64.

Haldenby, A. M., Berman, H., & Forchuk, C. (2007). Homelessness and health in adolescents. *Qualitative Health Research, 17*, 1232–1244. doi:10.1177/1049732307307550

Hall, L. A. (2007). Understanding the silence: Struggling readers discuss decisions about reading expository text. *Journal of Educational Research, 100*(3), 132–141.

Harley, A. E., Buckworth, J., Katz, M. L., Willis, S. K., Odoms-Young, A., & Heaney, C. A. (2009). Developing long-term physical activity participation: A grounded theory study with African American women. *Health Education & Behavior, 36*(1), 97–112. doi:10.1177/1090198107306434

Harr, N., Dunn, L., & Price, P. (2011). Case study on effect of household task participation on home, community, and work opportunities for a youth with multiple disabilities. *Work, 39*, 445–453.

Hatch, J. A. (2002). *Doing qualitative research in education settings*. Albany, NY: State University of New York Press.

Havstam, C., Laakso, K., & Ringsberg, K. C. (2011). Making sense of the cleft. Young adults' accounts of growing up with a cleft and deviant speech. *Journal of Health Psychology, 16*(1), 22–30.

Heil, D. (2005). The internet and student research: Teaching critical evaluation skills. *Teacher Librarian, 33*(2), 26–29.

Heinlein, L. M., & Shinn, M. (2000). School mobility and student achievement in an urban setting. *Psychology in the Schools, 37*(4), 349–357.

Hermann, R. C. (2011). *Exploring design of conducive environments at the intersection of art therapy and creative education interventions.* (Unpublished literature review). University of Nebraska–Lincoln, Lincoln, NE.

Hirai, K., Eguchi, K., Kudo, T., Akiyama, M., Matoba, M., Shiozaki, M., . . . , Morita, T. (2011). Public awareness, knowledge of availability, and readiness for cancer palliative care services: A population-based survey across four regions in Japan. *Journal of Palliative Medicine, 14,* 918–922.

Hodgkin, S. (2008). Telling it all: A story of women's social capital using a mixed methods approach. *Journal of Mixed Methods Research, 2*(3), 296–316.

Hoffman, L. M., & Nottis, K. E. K. (2008). Middle school students' perceptions of effective motivation and preparation factors for high-stakes tests. *NASSP Bulletin, 92*(3), 209–223.

Howard, T. C. (2002). Hearing footsteps in the dark: African American students' descriptions of effective teachers. *Journal of Education for Students Placed at Risk, 7*(4), 425–444.

Huff, R. E., Houskamp, B. M., Watkins, A. V., Stanton, M., & Tavegia, B. (2005). The experiences of parents of gifted African American children: A phenomenological study. *Roeper Review, 27*(4), 215–221.

Hughes, R. G. (Ed.) (2008). *Patient safety and quality: An evidence-based handbook for nurses.* Rockville, MD: Agency for Healthcare Research and Quality.

Hughes-Hassell, S., & Lutz, C. (2006). What do you want to tell us about reading? A survey of the habits and attitudes of urban middle school students toward leisure reading. *Young Adult Library Services, 4*(2), 39–45.

Igo, L. B., Kiewra, K. A., & Bruning, R. (2008). Individual differences and intervention flaws: A sequential explanatory study of college students' copy-and-paste note taking. *Journal of Mixed Methods Research, 2*(2), 149–168.

Ivankova, N., & Stick, S. (2007). Students' persistence in a Distributed Doctoral Program in Educational Leadership in Higher Education: A mixed methods study. *Research in Higher Education, 48*(1), 93–135.

Jick, T. D. (1979). Mixing qualitative and quantitative methods: Triangulation in action, *Administrative Science Quarterly, 24,* 602–611.

Johnson, G. M. (2010). Internet use and child development: Validation of the ecological techno-subsystem. *Educational Technology & Society, 13*(1), 176–185.

Jones, J. (1999). *The process of structuring a community-based curriculum in a rural school setting: A grounded theory study.* Unpublished doctoral dissertation, University of Nebraska–Lincoln, NB.

Joona, P. A., & Nekby, L. (2012). Intensive coaching of new immigrants: An evaluation based on random program assignment. *The Scandinavian Journal of Economics, 114,* 575–600.

Judge, S., Puckett, K., & Bell, S. M. (2006). Closing the digital divide: Update from the early childhood longitudinal study. *Journal of Educational Research, 100*(1), 52–60.

Kamphoff, C. S. (2010). Bargaining with patriarchy: Former female coaches' experiences and their decision to leave collegiate coaching. *Research Quarterly for Exercise and Sport, 81,* 360–372.

Kandiah, J., & Jones, C. (2002). Nutrition knowledge and food choices of elementary school children. *Early Child Development and Care, 172*(3), 269–273.

Keeney, S., McKenna, H., Fleming, P., & McIlfatrick, S. (2010). Attitudes to cancer and cancer prevention: What do people aged 35–54 years think? *European Journal of Cancer Care, 19,* 769–777.

Kemmis, S. (1994). Action research. In T. Husen & T. N. Postlethwaite (Eds.), *International encyclopedia of education* (2nd ed., pp. 42–49). Oxford, UK, and New York, NY: Pergamon and Elsevier Science.

Kemmis, S., & Wilkinson, M. (1998). Participatory action research and the study of practice. In B. Atweh, S. Kemmis, & P. Weeks (Eds.), *Action research in practice: Partnerships for social justice in education* (pp. 21–36). London, UK: Routledge.

Kerlinger, F. N. (1964). *Foundations of behavioral research.* New York, NY: Holt, Rinehart and Winston.

Kern, P., Wolery, M., & Aldridge, D. (2007). Use of songs to promote independence in morning greeting routines for young children with autism. *Journal of Autism and Developmental Disorders, 37,* 1264–1271.

Kim, R. I., & Goldstein, S. B. (2005). Intercultural attitudes predict favorable study abroad expectations of U.S. college students. *Journal of Studies in International Education, 9*(3), 265–278.

King, K. A., & Vidourek, R. A. (2010). In search of respect: A qualitative study exploring youth perceptions. *The International Journal on School Disaffection, 7*(1), 5–17.

King, S. (2008). Exploring the role of counselor support: Gay, lesbian, bisexual, and questioning adolescents struggling with acceptance and disclosure. *Journal of GLBT Family Studies, 4,* 361–384.

Kirchhoff, A., & Lawrenz, F. (2011). The use of grounded theory to investigate the role of teacher education on STEM teachers' career paths in high-need schools. *Journal of Teacher Education, 62,* 246–259. doi:10.1177/0022487110397840

Knesting, K., & Waldron, N. (2006). Willing to play the game: How at-risk students persist in school. *Psychology in the Schools, 43*(5), 599–611.

Komives, S. R., Owen, J. E., Longerbeam, S. D., Mainella, F. C., & Osteen, L. (2005). Developing a leadership identity: A grounded theory. *Journal of College Student Development, 46*(6), 593–611.

Lalley, J. P., & Miller, R. H. (2006). Effects of pre-teaching and re-teaching on math achievement and academic self-concept of students with low achievement in math. *Education, 126*(4), 747–755.

Landreman, L. M., Rasmussen, C. J., King, P. M., & Jiang, C. X. (2007). A phenomenological study of the development of university educators' critical consciousness. *Journal of College Student Development, 48*(3), 275–296.

Larson, R. W., & Brown, J. R. (2007). Emotional development in adolescence: What can be learned from a high school theater program? *Child Development, 78*(4), 1083–1099.

Lassetter, J. H., Mandleco, B. L., & Roper, S. O. (2007). Family photographs: Expressions of parents raising children with disabilities. *Qualitative Health Research, 17*(4), 456–467.

LeCompte, M. D., Preissle, J., & Tesch, R. (1993). *Ethnography and qualitative design in educational research* (2nd ed.). San Diego, CA: Academic Press.

Leko, M. M., & Brownell, M. T. (2011). Special education preservice teachers' appropriation of pedagogical tools for teaching reading. *Exceptional Children, 77,* 229–251.

Li, G. (2006). Biliteracy and trilingual practices in the home context: Case studies of Chinese-Canadian children. *Journal of Early Childhood Literacy, 6,* 355–381.

Libutti, P. O., & Blandy, S. G. (1995). *Teaching information retrieval and evaluation skills to education students and practitioners: A casebook of applications.* Chicago, IL: Association of College and Research Libraries.

Lieblich, A., Tuval-Mashiach, R., & Zilber, T. (1998). *Narrative research: Reading, analysis, and interpretation.* Thousand Oaks, CA: Sage.

Lindstrom, L., Doren, B., Metheny, J., Johnson, P., & Zane, C. (2007). Transition to employment: Role of the family in career development. *Exceptional Children, 73,* 348–366.

Mak, L., & Marshall, S. K. (2004). Perceived mattering in young adults' romantic relationships. *Journal of Social and Personal Relationships, 24*(4), 469–486.

Mazzola, J. J., Walker, E. J., Shockley, K. M., & Spector, P. E. (2011). Examining stress in graduate assistants: Combining qualitative and quantitative survey methods. *Journal of Mixed Methods Research, 5,* 198–211. doi:10.1177/1558689811402086

McAuley, C., McCurry, N., Knapp, M., Beecham, J., & Sleed, M. (2006). Young families under stress: Assessing maternal and child well-being using a mixed-methods approach. *Child and Family Social Work, 11*(1), 43–54.

McCabe, D. L., Butterfield, K. D., & Treviño, L. K. (2006). Academic dishonesty in graduate business programs: Prevalence, causes, and proposed action. *Academy of Management Learning & Education, 5*(3), 294–305.

McKinney, T. R. F., Plano Clark, V. L., Garrett, A. L., Badiee, M., & Leslie-Pelecky, D. (2012, April). *Professional identity development through a nontraditional program for STEM graduate students: A grounded theory study.* Unpublished paper presented at the American Educational Research Association 2012 Annual Meeting, Vancouver, BC, Canada.

Merriam, S. B. (1998). *Qualitative research and case study applications in education.* San Francisco, CA: Jossey-Bass.

Messinger, A. M. (2011). Invisible victims: Same-sex IPV in the National Violence Against Women Survey. *Journal of Interpersonal Violence, 26*(11), 2228–2243. doi:10.1177/0886260510383023

Miles, M. B., & Huberman, A. M. (1994). *Qualitative data analysis: A sourcebook for new methods* (2nd ed.). Thousand Oaks, CA: Sage.

Miller, D. L., Creswell, J. W., & Olander, L. S. (1998). Writing and retelling multiple ethnographic tales of a soup kitchen for the homeless. *Qualitative Inquiry, 4,* 469–491.

Miller, J. W. (2013). The role of sociability self-concept in the relationship between exposure to and concern about aggression in middle school. *Research in Middle Level Education Online, 36*(7), 1–10.

Mills, G. E. (2007). *Action research: A guide for the teacher researcher* (3rd ed.). Upper Saddle River, NJ: Merrill/Prentice Hall.

Mishna, F. (2004). A qualitative study of bullying from multiple perspectives. *Children & Schools, 26*(4), 234–247.

Morales, A. (2008). *Language brokering in Mexican immigrant families living in the Midwest: A multiple case study* (Unpublished doctoral dissertation). University of Nebraska–Lincoln, Lincoln, NE.

Morse, J. M. (1991). Approaches to qualitative-quantitative methodological triangulation. *Nursing Research, 40,* 120–123.

Morse, J. M., & Niehaus, L. (2009). *Mixed method design: Principles and procedures.* Walnut Grove, CA: Left Coast Press.

Mun, W. K., Hew, K., & Cheung, W. S. (2009). The impact of the use of response pad system on the learning of secondary school physics concepts: A Singapore quasi-experiment study. *British Journal of Educational Technology, 40*(5), 848–860.

Munoz-Plaza, C. E., Morland, K. B., Pierre, J. A., Spark, A., Filomena, S. E., & Noyes, P. (2013). Navigating the urban food environment: Challenges and resilience of community-dwelling older adults. *Journal of Nutrition Education and Behavior, 45*(4), 322–331.

Murphy, J. F., & Tobin, K. (2012). Addressing the problems of homeless adolescents. *Journal of School Leadership, 22*(3), 633–663.

Musher-Eizenman, D. R., Oehlhof, M. W., Young, K. M., Hauser, J. C., Galliger, C., & Sommer, A. (2011). Emerald dragon bites vs veggie beans: Fun food names increase children's consumption of novel healthy foods. *Journal of Early Childhood Research, 9*(3), 191–195. doi:10.1177/1476718X10366729

Myers, C. T., Effgen, S. K., Blanchard, E., Southall, A., Wells, S., & Miller, E. (2011). Factors influencing physical therapists' involvement in preschool transitions. *Physical Therapy, 91*(5), 656–664.

National Art Education Association. (2013). *Research and knowledge resources.* Retrieved from http://www.arteducators.org/research/research

Newman, M. L., Holden, G. W., & Delville, Y. (2011). Coping with the stress of being bullied: Consequences of coping strategies among college students. *Social Psychological and Personality Science, 2*(2), 205–211. doi:10.1177/1948550610386388

Nippold, M. A., Duthie, J. K., & Larsen, J. (2005). Literacy as a leisure activity: Free-time preferences of older children and young adolescents. *Language, Speech, and Hearing Services in Schools, 36,* 93–102.

Njeru, M. K., Blystad, A., Shayo, E. H., Nyamongo, I. K., & Fylkesnes, K. (2011). Practicing provider-initiated HIV testing in high prevalence settings: Consent concerns and misses preventive opportunities. *BMC Health Services Research, 11,* 87. doi:10.1186/1472-6963-11-87

Owen-Smith, A., Sterk, C., McCarty, F., Hankerson-Dyson, D., & DiClemente, R. (2010). Development and evaluation of a complementary and alternative medicine use survey in African-Americans with acquired immune deficiency syndrome. *The Journal of Alternative and Complementary Medicine, 16,* 569–577.

Pace, S. (2004). A grounded theory of the flow experiences of Web users. *International Journal of Human-Computer Studies, 60,* 327–363.

Padilla, R. (2003). Clara: A phenomenology of disability. *American Journal of Occupational Therapy, 57*(4), 413–423.

Patton, M. Q. (2002). *Qualitative research and evaluation methods* (3rd ed.). Thousand Oaks, CA: Sage.

Payne, Y. A. (2008). "Street life" as a site of resiliency: How street life oriented Black men frame opportunity in the United States. *Journal of Black Psychology, 34*(1), 3–31.

Perkins, H. W., Craig, D. W., & Perkins, J. M. (2011). Using social norms to reduce bullying: A research intervention among adolescents in five middle schools. *Group Processes & Intergroup Relations, 14*(5), 703–722. doi:10.1177/1368430210398004

Pipher, M. (2002). *The middle of everywhere: Helping refugees enter the American community.* Orlando, FL: Harcourt.

Plano Clark, V. L. (2005). Cross-disciplinary analysis of the use of mixed methods in physics education research, counseling psychology, and primary care. (Doctoral dissertation, University of Nebraska–Lincoln, 2005). *Dissertation Abstracts International, 66,* 02A.

Plano Clark, V. L., Miller, D. L., Creswell, J. W., McVea, K., McEntarffer, R., Harter, L. M., & Mickelson, W. T. (2002). In conversation: High school students talk to students about tobacco use and prevention strategies. *Qualitative Health Research, 12*(9), 1264–1283.

Plano Clark, V. L., Schumacher, K., West, C., Edrington, J., Dunn, L. B., Harzstark, A., . . . , Miaskowski, C. (2013). Practices for embedding an interpretive qualitative approach within a randomized clinical trial. *Journal of Mixed Methods Research, 7*(3), 219–242.

Poyrazli, S., & Lopez, M. D. (2007). An exploratory study of perceived discrimination and homesickness: A comparison of international students and American students. *The Journal of Psychology, 141*(3), 263–280.

Pryor, C., & Pettinelli, J. D. (2011). A narrative inquiry of international adoption stories. *Journal of Ethnographic & Qualitative Research, 6,* 45–61.

Quan-Haase, A. (2007). University students' local and distant social ties: Using and integrating modes of communication on campus. *Information, Communication & Society, 10,* 671–693. doi:10.1080/13691180701658020

Ramsay, S., Safaii, S., Croschere, T., Branen, L. J., & Wiest, M. (2013). Kindergarteners' entrée intake increases when served a larger entrée portion in school lunch: A quasi-experiment. *Journal of School Health, 83*(4), 1746–1561.

Raspa, M., Bailey, D. B., Olmsted, M. G., Nelson, R., Robinson, N., Simpson, M. E. . . , Houts, R. (2010). Measuring family outcomes in early intervention: Findings from a large-scale assessment. *Exceptional Children, 76*(4), 496–510.

Ravitch, S. M., & Wirth, K. (2007). Developing a pedagogy of opportunity for students and their teachers: Navigations and negotiations in insider action research. *Action Research, 5*(1), 75–91. doi:10.1177/1476750307072878

Richards, L., & Morse, J. M. (2007). *README FIRST for a user's guide to qualitative methods* (2nd ed.). Thousand Oaks, CA: Sage.

Richie, B. S., Fassinger, R. E., Linn, S. G., & Johnson, J. (1997). Persistence, connection, and passion: A qualitative study of the career development of highly achieving African American-Black and White women. *Journal of Counseling Psychology, 44,* 143–148.

Ruff, C. L., & Olson, M. A. (2009). The attitudes of interior design students towards sustainability. *International Journal of Technology and Design Education, 19*(1), 67–77. doi:10.1007/s10798-007-9038-0

Rushton, S. P. (2004). Using narrative inquiry to understand a student-teacher's practical knowledge while teaching in an inner-city school. *The Urban Review, 36*(1), 61–79.

Sanchez, B., Esparza, P., Berardi, L., & Pryce, J. (2011). Mentoring in the context of Latino youth's broader village during their transition from high school. *Youth & Society, 43*(1), 225–252. doi:10.1177/0044118X10363774

Schacter, J., & Jo, B. (2005). Learning when school is not in session: A reading summer day-camp intervention to improve the achievement of exiting first-grade students who are economically disadvantaged. *Journal of Research in Reading, 28*(2), 158–169.

Scheib, J. W. (2003). Role stress in the professional life of the school music teacher: A collective case study. *Journal of Research in Music Education, 51*(2), 124–136.

Schmuck, R. A. (1997). *Practical action research for change.* Arlington Heights, IL: IRI/SkyLight Training and Publishing.

Schnepper, L. C., & McCoy, L. P. (2013). Analysis of misconceptions in high school mathematics. *Networks: An Online Journal for Teacher Research, 15*(1). Retrieved from http://journals.library.wisc.edu/index.php/networks/issue/view/52

Sciarra, D. T., & Ambrosino, K. E. (2011). Post-secondary expectations and educational attainment. *Professional School Counseling, 14*(3), 231–241.

Shadish, W. R., Cook, T. D., & Campbell, D. T. (2002). *Experimental and quasi-experimental designs for generalized causal inference.* Boston, MA: Houghton Mifflin.

Shek, D. T. L. (2007). Perceived parental behavioral control and psychological control in Chinese adolescents in Hong Kong: A replication. *Adolescence, 42*(167), 569–574.

Silverman, M. J., Christenson, G. A., Golden, D., & Chaput-McGovern, J. (2012). Effects of live music on satisfaction of students waiting for treatment in a university health clinic. *Music Therapy Perspectives, 30*(1), 43–48.

Siwatu, K. O. (2011). Preservice teachers' culturally responsive teaching self-efficacy-forming experiences: A mixed methods study. *The Journal of Educational Research, 104*, 360–369. doi:10.1080/0022067.2010.487081

Smith, J. S., Estudillo, A. G., & Kang, H. (2011). Racial differences in eighth grade students' identification with academics. *Education and Urban Society, 43*(1), 73–90. doi:10.1177/0013124510379403

Smith, L. E., Greenberg, J. S., & Seltzer, M. M. (2012). Social support and well-being at mid-life among mothers of adolescents and adults with autism spectrum disorders. *Journal of Autism and Developmental Disorders, 42*, 1818–1826. doi:10.1007/s10803-011-1420-9

Sociological Abstracts, Inc. (1953–). *Sociological abstracts.* San Diego, CA: Author.

Spielberger, C. D. (1973). *Manual for the State-Trait Anxiety Inventory for Children.* Palo Alto, CA: Consulting Psychologists Press.

Spindler, G., & Spindler, L. (1992). Cultural process and ethnography: An anthropological perspective. In M. D. LeCompte, W. L. Millroy, & J. Preissle (Eds.), *The handbook of qualitative research in education* (pp. 53–92). San Diego, CA: Academic Press.

Spradley, J. P. (1980). *Participant observation.* New York, NY: Holt, Rinehart and Winston.

Stake, R. E. (1995). *The art of case study research.* Thousand Oaks, CA: Sage.

Strike, K. A., Anderson, M. S., Curren, R., Geel, T. V., Pritchard, I., & Robertson, E. (2002). *Ethical standards of the American Educational Research Association: Cases and commentary.* Washington, DC: American Educational Research Association.

Stringer, E. T. (1999). *Action research* (2nd ed.). Thousand Oaks, CA: Sage.

Stringer, E. T. (2008). *Action research in education* (2nd ed.). Upper Saddle River, NJ: Merrill/Prentice Hall.

Sun, F., & Long, A. (2008). A theory to guide families and carers of people who are at risk of suicide. *Journal of Clinical Nursing, 17*(14), 1939–1948.

Swidler, S. A. (2000). Notes on a country school tradition: Recitation as an individual strategy. *Journal of Research in Rural Education, 16*(1), 8–21.

Teddlie, C., & Tashakkori, A. (2009). *Foundations of mixed methods research: Integrating quantitative and qualitative approaches in the social and behavioral sciences.* Thousand Oaks, CA: Sage.

Terrill, L., & Gullifer, J. (2010). Growing older: A qualitative inquiry into the textured narratives of older, rural women. *Journal of Health Psychology, 15*(5), 707–715.

Tesch, R. (1990). *Qualitative research: Analysis types and software tools.* Bristol, PA: The Falmer Press.

Thomas, C., & Ryan, M. (2008) Women's perception of the divorce experience: A qualitative study. *Journal of Divorce & Remarriage, 49*(3–4), 210–224. doi:10.1080/10502550802222394

Ting, S. R. (2000). Predicting Asian Americans' academic performance in the first year of college: An approach combining SAT scores and noncognitive variables. *Journal of College Student Development, 41*(4), 442–449.

Tofteng, D., & Husted, M. (2011). Theatre and action research: How drama can empower action research processes in the field of unemployment. *Action Research, 9*(1), 27–41. doi:10.1177/1476750310396953

Topham, G. L., Larson, J. H., & Holman, T. B. (2005). Family-of-origin predictors of hostile conflict in early marriage. *Contemporary Family Therapy, 27*(1), 101–121. doi:10.1007/s10591-004-1973-2

Tozer, R., Atkin, K., & Wenham, A. (2013). Continuity, commitment and context: Adult siblings of people with autism plus learning disability. *Health and Social Care in the Community, 21*(5), 480–488.

Tucker, P., van Zandvoort, M. M., Burke, S. M., & Irwin, J. D. (2011). Physical activity at daycare: Childcare providers' perspectives for improvements. *Journal of Early Child-hood Research, 9*(3), 207–219. doi: 10.1177/1476718X10389144

Unger, M., Faure, M., & Frieg, A. (2006). Strength training in adolescent learners with cerebral palsy: A randomized controlled trial. *Clinical Rehabilitation, 20*, 469–477.

U.S. Department of Education. (2013, June 7). *Race to the Top fund performance.* Retrieved from http://www2.ed.gov/programs/racetothetop/performance.html

Valdez, M. F., Dowrick, P. W., & Maynard, A. E. (2007). Cultural misperceptions and goals for Samoan children's education in Hawaii: Voices from school, home, and community. *The Urban Review, 39*(1), 67–92.

Valois, R. F., Paxton, R. J., Zullig, K. J., & Huebner, E. S. (2006). Life satisfaction and violent behaviors among middle school students. *Journal of Child and Family Studies, 15*(6), 695–707. doi:10.1007/s10826-006-9043-z

Varnam, W. (2011). How to mobilise patients with dementia to a standing position. *Nursing Older People, 23*(8), 31–36.

Ventres, W., Kooienga, S., Vuckovic, N., Marlin, R., Nygren, P., & Stewart, V. (2006). Physicians, patients, and the electronic health record: An ethnographic analysis. *Annals of Family Medicine, 4*(2), 124–131.

Viana, A. G., Trent, L., Tull, M. T., Heiden, L., Damon, J. D., Hight, T. L., & Young, J. (2012). Non-medical use of prescription drugs among Mississippi youth: Constitutional, psychological, and family factors. *Addictive Behaviors, 37*(12), 1382–1388.

Vittersø, J., Akselsen, S., Evjemo, B., Julsrud, T. E., Yttri, B., & Bergvik, S. (2003). Impacts of home-based telework on quality of life for employees and their partners: Quantitative and qualitative results from a European survey. *Journal of Happiness Studies, 4*, 201–233.

Vlasin-Marty, K. (2011). *Food safety for Native American families with young children in Nebraska.* (Unpublished literature review). University of Nebraska–Lincoln, Lincoln, NE.

Walker, C. O., & Greene, B. A. (2009). The relations between student motivational beliefs and cognitive engagement in high school. *The Journal of Educational Research, 102*(6), 463–471.

Wang, C., & Burris, M. (1994). Empowerment through photo novella: Portraits of participation. *Health Education Quarterly, 21*(2), 171–186.

Wang, S. C. (2013). *The experience of being Chinese for three adolescents living in the midwest, U.S.A.: A qualitative multiple case study.* (The University of Nebraska–Lincoln). *ProQuest Dissertations and Theses.* Retrieved from http://search.proquest.com/docview/1026948272

Weber, C. J., & Bizer, G. Y. (2006). The effects of immediate forewarning of test difficulty on test performance. *Journal of General Psychology, 133*(3), 277–285.

Whitney, A. E., Anderson, K., Dawson, C., Kang, S., Rios, E. O., Olcese, N., & Ridgeman, M. (2012). Audience and authority in the professional writing of teacher-authors. *Research in the Teaching of English, 46*(4), 390–419.

Winkle-Wagner, R. (2009). *The unchosen me: Race, gender, and identity among Black women in college.* Baltimore, MD: The Johns Hopkins University Press.

Wittink, M. N., Barg, F. K., & Gallo, J. J. (2006). Unwritten rules of talking to doctors about depression: Integrating qualitative and quantitative methods. *Annals of Family Medicine, 4*(4), 302–309.

Wolcott, H. F. (2008). *Ethnography: A way of seeing* (2nd ed.). Walnut Creek, CA: Alta Mira.

Wylie, L. E., Gibson, C. L., Brank, E. M., Fondacaro, M. R., Smith, S. W., Brown, V. E., & Miller, S. A. (2010). Assessing school and student predictors of weapons reporting. *Youth Violence and Juvenile Justice, 8*(4), 351–372.

Xu, F., Chepyator-Thomson, J., Liu, W., & Schmidlein, R. (2010). Association between social and environmental factors and physical activity opportunities in middle schools. *European Physical Education Review, 16*(2), 183–194. doi:10.1177/1356336X10381308

Yin, R. K. (2009). *Case study research: Design and methods* (4th ed.). Thousand Oaks, CA: Sage.

Young, M. F., Slota, S., Cutter, A. B., Jalette, G., Mullin, G., Lai, B., . . . , Yukhymenko, M. (2012). Our princess is in another castle: A review of trends in serious gaming for education. *Review of Educational Research, 82*(1), 61–89.

Zerillo, C., & Osterman, K. F. (2011). Teacher perceptions of teacher bullying. *Improving Schools, 14*(3), 239–257. doi:10.1177/1365480211419586

Zhang, D., Hsu, H., Katsiyannis, A., Barrett, D. E., & Ju, S. (2011). Adolescents with disabilities in the juvenile justice system: Patterns of recidivism. *Exceptional Children, 77*(3), 283–298.

Name Index

Subject Index